MARKETING CHANNELS

THE PRENTICE HALL SERIES IN MARKETING

PHILIP KOTLER, SERIES EDITOR

FIFTH EDITION

MARKETING CHANNELS

Louis W. Stern

John D. Gray Distinguished Professor of Marketing
Northwestern University

Adel I. El-Ansary

PAPER Foundation Eminent Scholar Chair in Wholesaling
University of North Florida

Anne T. Coughlan

Associate Professor of Marketing
Northwestern University

Prentice Hall, Upper Saddle River, NJ 07458

Library of Congress Cataloging-in-Publication Data

Stern, Louis W.
   Marketing channels / Louis W. Stern, Adel I. El-Ansary. —5th ed.
       p.   cm.
   Includes bibliographical references and index.
   ISBN 0-13-205865-0
   1. Marketing channels.   I. Ansary, Adel I.   II. Title.
HF5415.129.S75   1996
   658.8'4—dc20   95-36321
                                                                          CIP

Acquisitions Editor: David Borkowsky
Assistant Editor: Melissa Steffens
Production Editor: Lois Lombardo
Full Service Liaison: Kathleen Kelly
Marketing Manager: John Chillingworth
Interior Design: Lisa Jones
Cover Design: Lorraine Castellano
Design Director: Patricia H. Wosczyk
Prepress and Manufacturing Buyer: Vincent Scelta
Editorial Assistant: Teresa Festa
Cover Illustration: John Mattos

© 1996, 1992, 1988, 1982, 1977 by Prentice Hall, Inc.
A Simon & Schuster Company
Upper Saddle River, New Jersey 07458

Printed in the United States of America
10   9   8   7   6   5   4   3   2

ISBN 0-13-205865-0

Prentice-Hall International (UK) Limited, *London*
Prentice-Hall of Australia Pty. Limited, *Sydney*
Prentice-Hall Canada, Inc., *Toronto*
Prentice-Hall Hispanoamericana, S.A., *Mexico*
Prentice-Hall of India Private Limited, *New Delhi*
Prentice-Hall of Japan, Inc., *Tokyo*
Simon & Schuster Asia Pte. Ltd., *Singapore*
Editora Prentice-Hall do Brasil, Ltda., *Rio de Janeiro*

CONTENTS ◀◀◀◀◀◀◀◀

3 *Channel Intermediaries: Wholesaling* 107

4 *Logistics of Distribution: Structure and Strategy* 141

PART THREE ▶ CHANNEL DESIGN AND PLANNING

5 *Channel Planning: Designing Channel Systems* 187

6 *Organizational Patterns in Marketing Channels* 223

PART FOUR ▶ CHANNEL MANAGEMENT

7 *Managing Marketing Channels* 281

8 *Marketing Channel Policies and Potential Legal Constraints* 338

9 *Information Systems and Channel Management* 401

10 *Assessing Marketing Channel Performance* 447

PART FIVE ▶ INTERNATIONAL DIMENSIONS

11 *International Marketing Channels* 493

PREFACE

The fifth edition of *Marketing Channels* focuses primarily on how to design, develop, and maintain effective *relationships* among channel members so that sustainable competitive advantages can be achieved for their respective firms, both individually and collectively. Strategic and managerial frames of references are introduced. Emphasis is on how to plan, organize, and control the alliances among the institutions, agencies, and within-company units involved in the process of making certain that products and services are available for consumption by industrial, commercial, and household end-users. The final result of effective marketing channel management is the assurance of end-user satisfaction via the provision of time, place, and possession utilities. Effective channel management is equivalent to total quality management. The focus of the text is on the way in which marketing channels can provide customer service, both for the end-users they serve and the organizations that comprise them.

From a strictly financial perspective, the members of marketing channels (e.g., manufacturers, wholesalers, retailers, and specialized logistics agencies) can achieve high-yield performance primarily through their demand stimulation and delivery activities. But performance requirements at one level of the marketing channel imply execution requirements and expectations at other levels. Retailers, for example, often measure their productivity by employing such criteria as sales per square foot, sales per employee, and sales per transaction. Generation of a high level of sales per square foot may necessitate heavy advertising by manufacturers and the maintenance of high inventory levels by wholesalers. These large promotion and storage burdens may, in turn, reduce the return on investment available to manufacturers and wholesalers. The interface among the various performance requirements, policies, and practices at different levels of marketing channels dictates the need for systemwide compensation, communication, and coordination mechanisms.

Although a great deal of attention in this text is centered on showing how channel member compensation and systemwide coordination can be achieved, we have also taken pains to detail theoretical and analytical frameworks that underlie the channel-management process. We have also included considerable discussion describing the major forces in distribution practice so that a knowledge of "real world" practice can be combined with or compared to the variety of normative structures that can be derived from the theoretical and analytical frameworks.

The text is organized into five parts. *Part One* explores key theoretical concepts associated with the structure and operation of marketing channels. These concepts explain why specialized institutions and agencies have emerged to assist in the task of making goods and services available for industrial, institutional, and household consumption. Among the more critical concepts introduced in Chapter 1 are the notions of "service outputs" and marketing "flows" on which we rely heavily throughout the remainder of the book.

Part Two describes some of the key institutions and agencies making up marketing channels—retailers, wholesalers, and third-party agencies involved in logistical operations, such as common carriers, public and private warehouse facilities, and distribution centers. Part Two outlines the structure, management, and performance requirements of retailing (Chapter 2), wholesaling (Chapter 3), and logistics organizations (Chapter 4) in the channel.

Building on the foundation laid in Parts One and Two, *Part Three* focuses on how management should go about designing, planning, and organizing marketing channels. It consists of two chapters. Chapter 5 lays out a multi-step process for designing end-user driven distribution systems in which the primary emphasis is on the delivery of customer satisfaction. Chapter 6 shows how channels can be organized into a variety of different systems, such as franchises and voluntary groups. It deals with the "make or buy" decision, for example, "hard" vertical integration (via ownership) versus "soft" vertical integration (via relationship management).

Part Four focuses on "ongoing" channel management. It consists of four chapters. Chapter 7 shows how power can be used creatively and positively to manage the marketing channel. It also deals with the conflicts that occur and the conflict management strategies that can be used to keep conflict from destroying potentially effective channel systems. The chapter deals with issues related to channel leadership and the stimulation of channel member effort through appropriate motivation mechanisms. Chapter 8 looks at a large number of channel management policies that can be implemented to encourage specific channel member behavior. It also examines how the policies have been subject to legal scrutiny under the U.S. antitrust laws. It discusses the rationale for the enactment of the policies and indicates the conditions under which they might be viewed negatively by the antitrust enforcement agencies and the federal courts. Chapter 9 examines the means by which channel members acquire and transmit data, information, and knowledge. Special attention is given to the new technologies being used to establish effective channel-wide information and communication systems. Chapter 10 suggests a number of ways in which the performance of individual channel members and channel systems have been or might be assessed.

Part Five looks at channel management in the international arena. Chapter 11 deals with channel structure and management issues in an international setting. It is an application of the previous 10 chapters in a home-host country context. The focus is on the structure, management, and performance issues of home-host country channel relations and the international environmental forces that mediate them.

Because case analysis is frequently used as a scholarly tool in courses dealing with marketing channels, we have included in the *Instructor's Manual* of the fifth edition a comprehensive list of cases of varying lengths and orientations suitable for use with this text. The *Instructor's Manual* has been thoroughly updated. It features syllabi from a wide variety of universities, an outline and an approach for teaching each chapter, teaching notes, and simulation games.

The fifth edition provides an even stronger focus on design and strategic issues than previous editions. It views channel management as the implementation of *management strategies* for high-performance channel relationships. An integrative framework for this is presented in Chapter 1, Marketing Channels: Structure, Functions, and Relationships. The integrative framework provides a wide variety of perspectives and approaches to take in teaching courses on marketing channels. Alternative starting points may be the channel environment, channel strategy, channel performance, or channel management.

Service quality, quality management, relationship marketing, and supplier–reseller partnerships will continue to be key areas of emphasis for both profit and not-for-profit organizations. The channel management frame of reference offers unique opportunities to achieve these goals, thereby leading to sustainable competitive advantage.

Changes from the fourth edition can be detailed as follows. Chapter 1 features a new appendix cataloging over 50 different distribution formats. Chapters 2 (Retailing), 3 (Wholesaling), and 4 (Logistics) have been updated and streamlined. The process of channel design (Chapter 5) has been revised, expanded, and amplified. Chapters 6 and 7 in the fourth edition switched positions in the fifth edition to allow for logical flow of the subject matter. The new Chapter 6 contains an extensive discussion of outsourcing, in addition to other key means for organizing channel resources. Chapter 8 (Legal) has been totally revised and recast as a chapter on Channel Policies. The legal ramifications of channel member decisions regarding these policy issues are examined. Therefore, the focus is on policy decisions rather than merely legal issues. Chapter 9 in the fourth edition (Channel Management by Channel Participants) was eliminated in the fifth edition. Significant materials treated in the chapter have been integrated into previous chapters, particularly Chapter 7 (Channel Management). Chapter 9 (Information Systems and Channel Management)—Chapter 10 in the fourth edition—has been completely rewritten to deal with the impact of information technology on channel flows, structure, management, and performance. Chapter 10 (Performance)—Chapter 11 in the fourth edition—has been revised and updated with added emphasis on activity based costing in the channel. Finally, Chapter 11 (International)—Chapter 12 in the fourth edition—has been updated and revised to reflect the vast changes in the international business environment. Chapter 13 (Services) in the fourth edition has been eliminated in favor of integrating the treatment of marketing channels for services throughout the text; for example, retailing and wholesaling are viewed as major service sectors of the economy. Therefore, the topic is the focus of Chapters 2 and 3. Additionally, service channel examples have been included in almost every chapter.

▶ **ACKNOWLEDGMENTS**

The structure and content of this book have been deeply influenced by many people. Each author appreciates the contributions of a distinct (but sometimes overlapping) set of people, whereas a fourth set of individuals has influenced us all.

Louis Stern is indebted to his wife, Rhona, whose encouragement, humor, support, and affection have been sources of inspiration to him. He is also indebted to all of his colleagues at Northwestern who have, over the years, supplied such enormous intellectual leadership to the marketing field. He is especially grateful for the opportunity he has been given to work with so many outstanding doctoral students, both at Northwestern and at Ohio State, where he previously taught. He would also like to acknowledge the outstanding contribution of Donna Edwards to this text. Her cheerful and extremely competent assistance made the task of completing his work on the text pleasurable and efficient.

Adel El-Ansary would like to acknowledge the encouragement and support of a number of marketing scholars. Many thanks to all, particularly those who have been personally supportive and encouraging over the years. A special debt is owed to Louis W. Stern, William R. Davidson, and the late Bert C. McCammon, Jr. The fifth edition would not have been possible without the capable research assistance of Mary C. Haddock and the word-processing assistance of Leanna Payne. Their dedication, attention to detail, and patience could not have been surpassed. The exciting personal growth and career progress in the doctoral program in economics at the University of Maryland of his son, Waleed, have been inspirational. His capable service, dedication, and creativity as the PAPER Foundation's Research Associate has been instrumental for him as the Chairholder in making significant contributions and addressing challenging tasks.

Anne Coughlan thanks first her husband, Charles B. Jameson, without whose support and help this work could not have been done. This work is also dedicated to C. J. and Catherine Anne, budding marketers in their own right, and to Catherine M. Coughlan and the memory of John M. Coughlan, who have been an inspiration to excellence. Louis W. Stern deserves special thanks for his mentoring over the years. Finally, her colleagues and students in the marketing community deserve recognition for their many insights which have shaped this author's thinking over the years.

Together, we thank Jacqueline M. Tario, master's student at Kellogg, and Ursula Y. Alvarado, marketing doctoral student at Kellogg, for their excellent help on editorial issues and proofreading of this text. We are also especially indebted to the large number of authors whose work we cite throughout the text. Without their efforts, we could not have written this book.

LOUIS W. STERN
Evanston, Illinois

ADEL I. EL-ANSARY
Jacksonville, Florida

ANNE T. COUGHLAN
Evanston, Illinois

MARKETING CHANNELS

MARKETING CHANNELS

◄◄◄◄◄◄◄◄

STRUCTURE, FUNCTIONS, AND RELATIONSHIPS

*I*ndividual consumers and corporate/organizational buyers are aware that literally thousands of goods and services are available through a very large number of diverse channel outlets. What they might not be as well aware of is the fact that the channel structure, or the set of institutions, agencies, and establishments through which the product must move to get to them, can be amazingly complex. Usually, combinations of institutions specializing in manufacturing, wholesaling, retailing, and many other areas join forces in marketing channel arrangements to make possible the delivery of goods to industrial users or customers and to final consumers. For example:

- Eastman Kodak Co.'s Business Imaging Systems Division has created three avenues for marketing microfilm, supplies, and imaging systems and software. These channels are: (1) direct sales representatives, (2) brokers and distributors, and (3) a components marketing organization that markets system components to systems integrators and value-added resellers. More complex systems, such as Kodak Mainframe Software, character recognition systems, and optical disk records management systems, demand long sell cycles. Each customer's specific document handling requirements has to be carefully evaluated to determine what type of system is suitable.[1]

- Benetton Group, Italy's integrated fashion retailer and manufacturer, ships 80 million items each year directly to 7,000 stores in 100 countries with an order cycle time of as little as 7 days. Most items are shipped from a single $50-million automated warehouse employing bar-code technology. Making use of technology and excellent management talent, the company's logistics, manufacturing, and information systems tie together 7,000 stores, 80 company agents, 200 suppliers, 850 subcontractors, major carriers, and an in-house forwarder. The system has helped the company achieve near-perfect customer service levels and no excess stock in-process or in the distribution pipeline.[2]

All these examples show that institutions must depend on each other to cater effectively to end-user demand. Therefore,

> *marketing channels can be viewed as sets of interdependent organizations involved in the process of making a product or service available for consumption or use.*

1 ▶

From the outset, it should be recognized that not only do marketing channels *satisfy* demand by supplying goods and services at the right place, quantity, quality, and price; but they also *stimulate* demand through the promotional activities of the units (e.g., retailers, manufacturers' representatives, sales offices, and wholesalers) constituting them. Therefore, the channel should be viewed as an orchestrated network that creates value for end-users by generating form, possession, time, and place utilities.

Channels of distribution evolve to serve customer needs. For example:

- For companies, the key to making the most of office purchases is finding the supply channel that is best suited to the company's buying habits, order size, delivery needs, and service demands. Office products superstores claim approximately 6% of the $100-billion office supplies industry. Their primary target is small- to medium-size businesses within a 5-mile radius of the store. Superstores buy directly from manufacturers in large quantities and pass on savings to their customers in terms of lower prices. The popularity of direct mail and catalog marketing channels is based primarily on their convenience. Like superstores, these channels have narrow profit margins and avoid intermediaries by dealing directly with the manufacturer. The customer can save money and delivery is quick. Issues business buyers must consider when deciding which channel to use include: (1) shipping time, (2) ordering, (3) technical support, (4) repair service, (5) variety, (6) branded product, and (7) return policy.[3]

Furthermore, channel members' roles and the extent of their cooperation may vary from one context to another.

- Japanese doctors not only prescribe drugs, they also dispense them! The doctors buy their drugs from wholesalers, who typically sell them at a discount from the official prices set by the Japanese government. Doctors are reimbursed by the government for the drugs they prescribe at the official price. This system encourages doctors to prescribe lots of expensive drugs allowing them to pocket the difference between the discount price and the official price. The average Japanese general practitioner earns $327,000 a year, most of which is made by selling drugs, compared with the $213,000 a year earned by the average American doctor.[4]

A major focus of marketing channel management is delivery. It is only through distribution that public and private goods and services can be made available for use or consumption. Producers of such goods and services (including manufacturers of industrial and consumer goods, legislators framing laws, educational administrators conceiving new means for achieving quality education, and insurance companies developing unique health insurance coverage, among many others) are individually capable of generating only form or structural utility for their products and services. They can organize their production capabilities in such a way that the products they have developed can, in fact, be seen, analyzed, debated, and, by a few perhaps, digested. But the actual large-scale delivery of the products to the consuming public demands different types of efforts that create time, place, and possession utilities. For example, consumers cannot obtain a finished product unless the product is transported to where they can gain access to it, stored until they are ready for it, and eventually exchanged for money or other goods or services so that they can acquire it. In fact, the four types of utility (form, time, place, and possession) are inseparable; there can be no "complete" product without incorporating all four into any given object, idea, or service.

As marketers continue to face hostile, unstable, and competitive environments, distribution will play an increasingly important role. Companies are already moving into new distribution channels that match up with market segments more precisely and effectively. For example, marketing channels for personal computers include personal computer superstores, office product superstores, consumer electronic stores, mass merchants, mail-order, telemarketing, company sales forces, and value-added resellers, among others.[5]

Executives will pay more attention in the future to the distribution channels they select to gain a competitive advantage over companies that copy their product designs and undercut their prices. New channels of distribution such as wholesale clubs, factory outlets, electronic shopping channels, franchises of all sorts, direct response operations, and hybrid channels are emerging.[6]

▶ EMERGENCE OF MARKETING CHANNEL STRUCTURES

In order to understand the marketing channel, it is important to grasp the underlying reasons for the emergence of channel structures. Here, emphasis is placed on the economic rationale for the existence of channels, because economic reasons are the foremost determinants of channel structures. Later, it will be possible to introduce other determinants, including key technological, political, and social factors, and to examine how these factors influence the makeup of channel systems.

The emergence and arrangement of the wide variety of distribution-oriented institutions and agencies, typically called *intermediaries* because they stand between production on the one hand and consumption on the other, can be explained in terms of four logically related steps in an economic process:[7]

1. Intermediaries arise in the process of exchange because they can improve the efficiency of the process.
2. Channel intermediaries arise to adjust the discrepancy of assortment through the performance of the sorting processes.
3. Marketing agencies hang together in channel arrangements to provide for the routinization of transactions.
4. Channels facilitate the searching process.

Each of these steps is examined in the following pages.

Efficiency Rationale for Intermediaries

In primitive cultures, most household needs are produced within the household. At an early stage in the development of economic activities, however, exchange replaced production as a means of satisfying individual needs. Exchange is facilitated when there is a surplus in production over current household requirements, and when this surplus cannot be held for future consumption because of the perishable nature of the products or the lack of storage facilities. Thus, if numerous households are able to effect small surpluses of different products, a basis for exchange is developed.

Alderson and Martin formulated the following law of exchange, which specifies the conditions under which an exchange will take place:[8]

> Given that x is an element of the assortment A_1 and y is an element of the assortment A_2, x is exchangeable for y if, and only if, these three conditions hold:
>
> a. x is different from y
> b.   The potency of the assortment A_1 is increased by dropping x and adding y.
> c.   The potency of the assortment A_2 is increased by adding x and dropping y.

These conditions of exchange are more easily met when production becomes specialized and the assortment of goods is broadened. As households find their needs satisfied by an increased quantity and variety of goods, the mechanism of exchange increases in importance.

As the importance of exchange increases, however, so does the difficulty of maintaining mutual interactions among all households. For example, a small village of only five specialized households would require ten transactions to carry out decentralized exchanges (i.e., exchanges at each production point). In order to reduce the complexity of this exchange system and thus facilitate transactions, intermediaries appear in the process. Through the operation of a central market, one dealer can considerably reduce the number of transactions. In the preceding example, only five transactions would be required to carry out a centralized exchange. This concept of decentralized versus centralized exchange is illustrated in Figure 1-1.

Implicit in the preceding example is the notion that a decentralized system of exchange is less efficient than a centralized network that uses intermediaries. The same rationale can be applied to direct selling from manufacturers to retailers relative to selling through wholesalers. For example, given four manufacturers and ten retailers who buy goods from each manufacturer, the number of contact lines amounts to 40. If the manufacturers sold to these retailers through one wholesaler, the number of necessary contacts is reduced to 14.

The number of necessary contacts increases dramatically as more wholesalers are added, however. For example, if the four manufacturers in our example use two wholesalers, the number of contacts rises from 14 to 28, and if four wholesalers are used, the number of contacts will be 56. Thus, employing more and more intermediaries is subject to diminishing returns simply from a *contactual* efficiency perspective.

It should also be noted in this simple illustration that the cost of any two contact lines of transaction—that is, manufacturer–wholesaler, wholesaler–retailer, manufacturer–retailer—is assumed to be the same. Also, it is assumed that whenever more than one wholesaler is employed by a manufacturer, each retailer will avail itself of the services of each of these wholesalers. Obviously, one must account

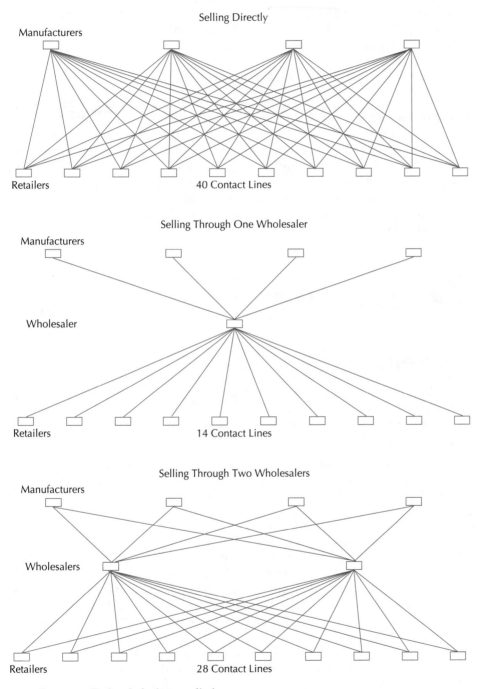

FIGURE 1-1 **Rationale for intermediaries.**

for differences in direct and indirect communication costs, in the effectiveness and efficiency of the institutions involved in the transaction, and in the quality of the contact between the various channel members.

Discrepancy of Assortment and Sorting

In addition to increasing the efficiency of transactions, intermediaries smooth the flow of goods and services by creating possession, place, and time utilities. These utilities enhance the potency of the consumer's assortment. One aspect of this *smoothing* process requires that intermediaries engage in a *sorting* function. This procedure is necessary in order to bridge the *discrepancy* between the assortment of goods and services generated by the producer and the assortment demanded by the consumer. The discrepancy results from the fact that manufacturers typically produce a large quantity of a limited variety of goods, whereas consumers usually desire only a limited quantity of a wide variety of goods.

The sorting function performed by intermediaries includes the following activities:

1. *Sorting out.* This involves breaking down a heterogeneous supply into separate stocks that are relatively homogeneous. (Sorting out is typified by the grading of agricultural products, such as grading eggs according to size and grading beef as either choice or prime.)

2. *Accumulation.* Concerns bringing similar stocks from a number of sources together into a larger homogeneous supply. (Wholesalers accumulate varied goods for retailers, and retailers accumulate goods for their customers.)

3. *Allocation.* Refers to breaking a homogeneous supply down into smaller and smaller lots. (Allocating at the wholesale level is referred to as *breaking bulk.*) Goods received in carloads are sold in case lots. A buyer of case lots in turn sells individual units. The allocation processes generally coincide with geographical dispersal and successive movement of products from origin to end consumer.

4. *Assorting.* This is the building up of an assortment of products for resale in association with each other. (Wholesalers build assortments of goods for retailers, and retailers build assortments for their customers.)[9]

Although sorting out and accumulation predominate in the marketing of agricultural and extractive products, allocation and assorting predominate in the marketing of finished manufactured goods. It should be noted that the discrepancy of assortment induces specialization in the exchange process, and the need for such specialization may impede the vertical integration of marketing agencies. For example, a manufacturer of a limited line of hardware items could open its own retail outlets only if it were willing to accumulate the wide variety of items generally sold through those outlets. In general, hardware wholesalers can perform such services more efficiently than individual manufacturers. Assortment discrepancy also explains why a company such as Bethlehem Steel would tell its small-volume customers not to buy from it directly but rather to obtain from wholesalers the assortments of the wide variety of steel products they require. On the other hand, large-volume buyers who need homogeneous supplies of steel in large lots have been urged to deal directly with Bethlehem's steel mills.[10]

Routinization

Each transaction involves ordering, valuating of, and paying for goods and services. The buyer and seller must agree to the amount, mode, and timing of payment. The cost of distribution can be minimized if the transactions are routinized; otherwise, every transaction is subject to bargaining, with an accompanying loss of efficiency.

Moreover, routinization facilitates the development of the exchange system. It leads to standardization of goods and services whose performance characteristics can be easily compared and assessed. It encourages production of items that are more highly valued. In fact, exchange relationships between buyers and sellers are standardized so that lot size, frequency of delivery and payment, and communication are routinized. Because of routinization, a sequence of marketing agencies can perform more efficiently together in a channel. For example, it can eliminate the cost of placing orders when retail inventory levels reach the reordering point.

> McKesson Corporation, a distributor of pharmaceuticals and personal care products to drugstores, hospitals, and mass marketers, handles up to 5,000 orders an hour at peak periods, and an average of 30,000 per day. Orders are entered electronically. Druggists walk down the aisles with hand-held computers supplied by McKesson that allow them to compile their orders in a format reflecting the layout of their stores. To place an order, a druggist simply plugs the computer into the phone, and the order travels through the McKesson satellite communications network. The orders are processed in anywhere from 12 minutes to 55 minutes by the center's computer. The computers automatically route instructions for completing the order for next-day delivery to whichever of the 45 distribution centers is nearest the druggist. Thus, companies that deal with McKesson are able to achieve high transactional efficiency in their purchasing of pharmaceuticals and personal care products.[11]

Searching

Buyers and sellers are engaged in a double-search process in the marketplace. The process of search involves uncertainty because producers are not certain of consumers' needs, and consumers are not certain that they will be able to find what they want. Marketing channels facilitate the process of searching, as when, for example,

- Wholesale and retail institutions are organized by separate lines of trade, such as drug, hardware, and grocery.

- Products such as over-the-counter drugs are widely available through thousands of drugstores, supermarkets, convenience stores, and even gasoline stations.

- Hundreds of thousands of parts are supplied to automotive repair facilities from local jobbers within hours of the placement of orders.

A marketing or distribution channel comprises a set of interdependent institutions and agencies involved with the task of moving anything of value from its point of conception, extraction, or production to the point of consumption. As an example, some of the institutions and agencies involved in the distribution of food service disposables, that is paper cups, stamped paper plates, and napkins, are portrayed in Figure 1-2. Included in Figure 1-2 are the business firms that are primarily responsible for the flow of title to the merchandise from manufacturer to consumer. Excluded from the figure are the numerous agencies and institutions that *facilitate* the passage of title and the physical movement of the goods, such as common carriers, financial institutions, and advertising agencies. They too are members of the channel for this particular product.

Even though it is incomplete, Figure 1-2 permits at least an initial conceptualization of the various channels of distribution that can be used to deliver a product to customers/end-users. It provides one example of the range of channel alternatives from direct to indirect methods, using various types of middlemen. It also illustrates the options at each channel level of using a retailer's own distribution center, full-function wholesalers, or limited-function wholesalers (cash and carry). Each of these channels may be designed to cater to the needs of a different market, market segment, and/or operational requirement of the wholesalers and retailers involved.

Functions in Marketing Channels

Manufacturers, wholesalers, and retailers as well as other channel members exist in channel arrangements to perform one or more of the following generic functions: carrying of inventory; demand generation, or selling; physical distribution; after-sale service; and extending credit to customers. In getting its goods to end-users, a manufacturer must either assume all these functions or shift some or all of them to channel intermediaries.[12]

The foregoing discussion underscores three important principles in the structure of marketing channels:

1. One can eliminate or substitute institutions in the channel arrangement.
2. The functions these institutions perform, however, cannot be eliminated.
3. When institutions are eliminated, their functions are shifted either forward or backward in the channel and, therefore, are assumed by other members.

To the extent that the same function is performed at more than one level of the marketing channel, the work load for the function is shared by members at all levels. For example, manufacturers, wholesalers, and retailers may all carry inventory. This duplication and redundancy in the channel may increase the distribution cost. However, the increase in cost is justifiable to the extent that it may be necessary in order to provide goods to customers at the right quantity, time, and place. If the increase in cost cannot be justified, then redundancy is wasteful and

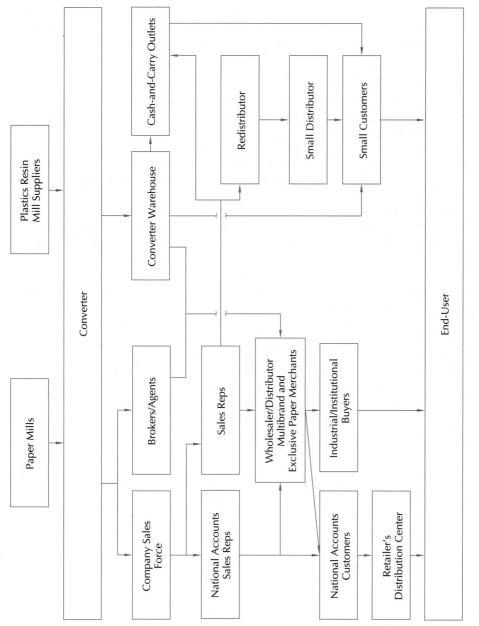

FIGURE 1-2 Channel mapping for a manufacturer of food service disposables.
Source: Center for Research and Education in Wholesaling, University of North Florida, 1994.

inefficient. In fact, much of the emphasis on reengineering and rationalizing value chain architectures during the 1990s has had to do with eliminating redundancies in distribution activities.[13]

Flows in Marketing Channels

In this text, we will refer frequently to *flows* in channels. A *flow* is *a set of functions* performed in sequence by channel members. Therefore, the term *flow* is descriptive of movement. Figure 1-3 depicts eight universal flows or functions. Physical possession, ownership, and promotion are typically forward flows from producer to consumer. Each of these moves "down" the distribution channel—a manufacturer promotes its product to a wholesaler, which in turn promotes it to a retailer, and so on. The negotiation, financing, and risking flows move in both directions, whereas ordering and payment are backward flows.

Negotiations are prevalent throughout the channel. Manufacturers, wholesalers, and retailers negotiate product assortments, prices, and promotions. Some channel members, such as manufacturer representatives and sales representatives, specialize in negotiations. They do not carry title or take physical possession of the goods.

It is important to note that any time inventories are held by one member of the channel system, a financing operation is under way. Thus, when a wholesaler takes title and assumes physical possession of a portion of the output of a manufacturer, the wholesaler is financing the manufacturer. Such a notion is made clear when one examines the carrying costs of inventory. The largest component of carrying cost is the cost of capital tied up when inventories are held in a dormant state. (Other carrying costs are obsolescence, depreciation, pilferage, breakage, storage, insurance, and taxes.) The reason for the significance of capital costs is relatively

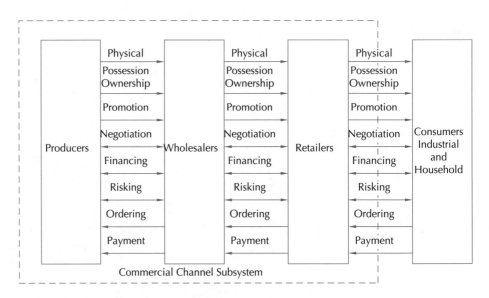

FIGURE 1-3 Marketing flows in channels.

obvious—if money were not tied up in inventory, a firm would be able to invest those funds elsewhere. In effect, capital costs are the opportunity costs of holding inventory. Thus, when one member of a channel has been "freed" from holding inventory—when its inventories have been exchanged for cash—it may reinvest these funds. In the furniture industry, traditional furniture retailers operating on a sold-order basis choose not to participate in the backward financing flow. On the other hand, "warehouse" furniture retailers do participate in this flow directly and thereby receive benefits from manufacturers in the form of lower prices and preferential treatment. Many other examples of the backward flow of financing can be found beyond those associated with the holding of inventory. Thus, when department store buyers commit themselves to purchasing large volumes of a particular fashion good prior to the mass production and shipment of the item, the commitment may be sold to specialized financial institutions called "factors," and the funds used by the garment manufacturer to finance its production process.

The forward flow of financing is even more common. General Motors Acceptance Corporation is a specific institution established by the manufacturer to finance not only ultimate consumers of its automobiles but also inventories held by dealers. In fact, all terms of sale, with the exception of cash on delivery and prepayment, may be viewed as elements of the forward flow of financing.

Channel Member Specialization in Marketing Functions and Participation in Channel Flows

All of the flows or functions in the distribution channel are indispensable—at least one institution or agency within the system must assume responsibility for each of them if the channel is to operate at all. But it is not necessary that every institution participate in the furtherance of all of the flows. In fact, it is for this reason that the channel of distribution is an example of a division of labor on a macro scale. Certain institutions and agencies specialize in one or more of the flows, as indicated in Figure 1-4. The use of these and other intermediaries largely boils down to their superior efficiency in the performance of basic marketing tasks and functions. Marketing intermediaries, through their experience, specialization, contacts, and scale, offer other channel members more than they can usually achieve on their own in terms of their superior efficiency in the performance of basic marketing tasks and functions. The same principles apply to reverse distribution channels, used for recycling, as explained in Appendix 1A.

From a *managerial perspective*, participation by channel members in different flows is akin to their being members of a number of different channels, such as an ownership or title channel, a negotiations channel, a physical distribution channel, a financing channel, and a promotions channel. The task of channel member coordination should be extended to these different channels. Often, new product introduction by manufacturers fails as a result of lack of synchronization of physical and promotional flows or channels. Although national promotion may vigorously proceed on schedule, delays in transportation and lack of distribution warehouse space may impede the availability of the product at retail outlets.

The key to coordination of channel flows is *information sharing* among chan-

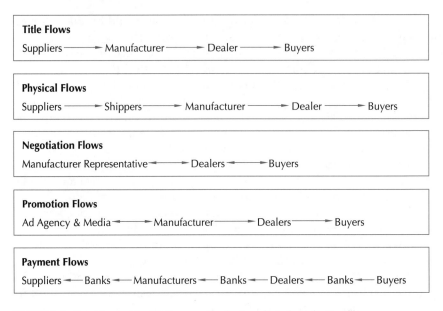

FIGURE 1-4 Channel institutions particular to selected marketing flows.

nel members. Information exchange is inherent in each channel flow. Manufacturers, wholesalers, retailers, banks, and other channel members deploy information and telecommunication systems technology to ensure the exchange of information required to coordinate the channel and enhance customer service. For example,

> Wal-Mart Stores Inc., the U.S.'s fastest-growing retailer, makes extensive use of electronic data interchange (EDI) to communicate with its vendors, which helps speed products through the pipeline. Home Depot Inc. has designed a network that carries EDI transactions and other traffic via its Scientific Atlanta satellite network. To provide for growing bandwidth needs, Toys "R" Us Inc. is upgrading networking capabilities and testing a new Hughes Aircraft Co. satellite that will eventually link its 800 stores. Kmart Corp. has adopted the latest in quick-response technology, that is, UPC bar-code marking and scanning, shipping container marking and reading, and an EDI program involving more than 2,000 vendors. In addition, Kmart is equipping its 2,300 stores with hand-held spread-spectrum RF devices that will speed price checks and automatically trigger reorders and inventory updates.[14]

▶ ANALYZING MARKETING CHANNEL STRUCTURES[15]

Marketing channels evolve over time in response to forces of change, and this evolution process is continuous. Figure 1-5 illustrates some of the facets of this evolution.

As mentioned above, the basic economic rationale for the emergence of channel intermediaries and institutional arrangements can be understood in terms of the need for exchange and exchange efficiency, minimization of assortment discrepancies, routinization, and the facilitation of search procedures. But such a ra-

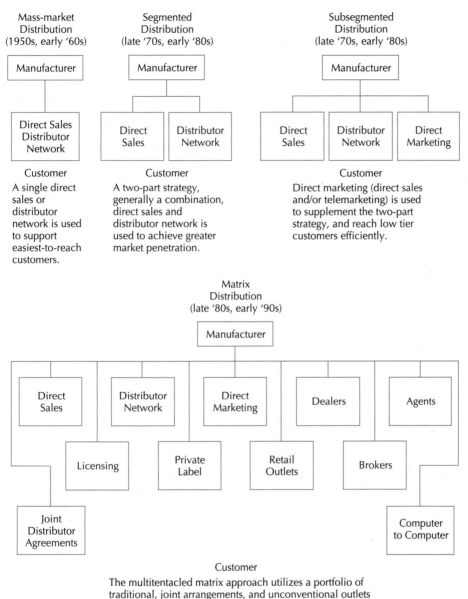

Mass-market Distribution (1950s, early '60s)

Manufacturer

Direct Sales Distributor Network

Customer

A single direct sales or distributor network is used to support easiest-to-reach customers.

Segmented Distribution (late '70s, early '80s)

Manufacturer

Direct Sales | Distributor Network

Customer

A two-part strategy, generally a combination, direct sales and distributor network is used to achieve greater market penetration.

Subsegmented Distribution (late '70s, early '80s)

Manufacturer

Direct Sales | Distributor Network | Direct Marketing

Customer

Direct marketing (direct sales and/or telemarketing) is used to supplement the two-part strategy, and reach low tier customers efficiently.

Matrix Distribution (late '80s, early '90s)

Manufacturer

Direct Sales | Distributor Network | Direct Marketing | Dealers | Agents

Licensing | Private Label | Retail Outlets | Brokers

Joint Distributor Agreements | Computer to Computer

Customer

The multitentacled matrix approach utilizes a portfolio of traditional, joint arrangements, and unconventional outlets to fully support all customer niches.

FIGURE 1-5   Evolving distribution channels.

Source: Reprinted with permission from David Perry, "How You'll Manage Your 1990's Distribution Portfolio," *Business Marketing,* June 1989, p. 54. Copyright, Crain Communications, Inc .

tionale provides little information as to why channels are structured one way or another to satisfy this need. More specifically, how can one account for the variations in channel structure in terms of the number of levels and the extent of specialization of functions or flows?

Channels as a Network of Systems

Perhaps most important to the analysis of channel structure is an understanding that channels consist of *interdependent* institutions and agencies, in other words, that their members are interdependent relative to task performance. A channel can be viewed as a system because of this interdependency—it is a system of *interrelated* and *interdependent* components engaged in producing an output. A distribution channel comprises two major sectors: *commercial* and *end-user*. The commercial sub-system (to which major attention is given in this text) includes a set of vertically aligned marketing institutions and agencies, such as manufacturers, wholesalers, and retailers. Each commercial channel member is dependent on other institutions for achieving its goal(s). A producer (manufacturer, physician, welfare agency) is dependent on others (retailers, hospitals, day-care centers) in getting its product to the end-user and, thereby, in gaining its objectives (profits, improved health care, a reduction in the welfare rolls). For example,

> Chrysler has abandoned unilateral price cuts. It has stopped writing detailed speci-
> fications for many parts. Instead, it relies on suppliers to design and build the right parts
> and to find ways to lower prices. Chrysler and the supplier split the savings, and the
> supplier gets a long-term relationship. "Chrysler and its suppliers are a virtual enter-
> prise," says Chrysler's president. Another Chrysler executive likens it to a Japanese-
> style keiretsu system, but without joint ownership. "At Chrysler, the price doesn't fall
> until the team gets the cost out," says the president of the ITT Automotive Inc. unit of
> ITT Corp., "as opposed to putting a gun to your head and saying, 'Lower your prices.'"[16]

The marketing channel has boundaries, as all systems do. These include ge-
ographic (market area), economic (the capability to handle a certain volume of goods or services), and human (the capability to interact) boundaries. Furthermore, a channel, like other systems, is part of a larger system that provides it with inputs and imposes restrictions on its operation. A channel exists as part of an economy's distribution structure that encompasses other channels. The economy's distribution structure is a subsystem of the national environment, which is a subsystem of the international environments. Both the national and international environments en-compass physical, economic, social, cultural, and political subsystems that influ-ence the development of and impose constraints on the focal channel system. This configuration of systems is portrayed in Figure 1-6. It is important here to recog-nize that marketing channels evolve and function in dynamic environments. A channel structure is determined in part by the environment in which the channel operates. For example,

- The growing emphasis on "green marketing" is leading more channel members not only to conceive of products that are environmentally sound, but also to design and orchestrate reverse marketing channels for recycling products after use or consump-tion.[17]

- Whenever a customer buys an item from a Wal-Mart in the U.S. or a 7-Eleven in Japan, the information goes directly in "real-time," to a manufacturer's plant. The informa-tion is translated into production, inventory replenishment schedules, and even de-

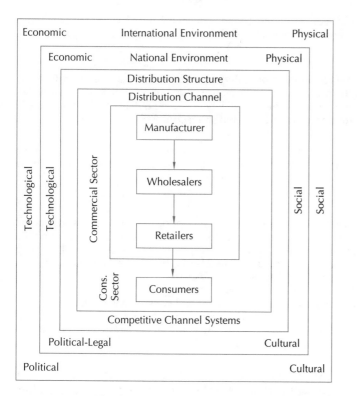

FIGURE 1-6 **The channel as a processing subsystem within the environment.**

livery instructions. Most of the 20% to 30% of the retail price that went toward covering physical distribution cost from the manufacturer to the retailer is largely eliminated in the Wal-Mart system, and 7-Eleven in Japan has eliminated five or six wholesalers from its supply channels.[18]

■ New computer technology applications combined with the capabilities of a vast communication network are changing end-user shopping behavior. Interactive two-way devices, such as *videotext*, allow the end-user to order directly from a company electronically.[19]

■ Consumers are demanding value and convenience as well as a new shopping experience. Emerging technologies such as personal computer (PC) based grocery shopping networks, interactive home TV shopping, screen-based telephones and "electronic malls" enable consumers to enjoy "virtual shopping" without leaving their homes. Some experts predict that in 10 years 28% of consumers will be purchasing more than $47 billion in groceries—particularly low-involvement staples such as soda, detergent, and cleaning supplies—from their homes. To focus on consumers, companies will have to slash nonvalue-added costs and use new processes and information technology to maintain a competitive edge.[20]

■ If you want to shop with comfort in the U.S. these days, just pick up the telephone and talk to Tootie. She will take your order, agree on the method of payment, and tell the warehouse to send off your product. Tootie is not human. She is the recorded voice that answers consumers contacting Home Shopping Network, the main player in the $2-billion business of electronic shopping.[21]

■ The single European Economic Community has caused European manufacturers and retailers to divest themselves of their in-house distribution divisions because they now need greater geographical coverage. They are using outside logistics specialists to provide them with transport and warehousing services.[22]

■ Changing consumer life-styles are bringing about greater demand for a variety of services, including the increased emphasis on leisure time, physical fitness, health maintenance, and/or growth of specialty sporting goods, supermarkets, health spas, health maintenance organizations (HMOs), and 24-hour convenience grocery stores.

■ Time-pressured consumers have rejected the concept of "9 to 5" business hours and are beginning to demand access to information, transactions, and service when it is convenient for them. Many banks have already responded to this change with evening, Saturday, and even Sunday hours, as well as 24-hour telephone banking. Interactive services have been developed that deliver information to consumers and facilitate transactions via telephone line connections to screen phones, wireless connections to personal communicators, and interactive broadband connections to televisions with set-top boxes. There are clearly two engines to the consumer forces driving interest in electronic delivery of financial services—a new consumer definition of convenience and technology's impact on consumer behavior.[23]

The survival and growth of certain channel members and the demise of others is best explained by viewing the channel as an *open system*.[24] Channel members must adapt to a changing environment. As they alter their functions and adjust their organizations and programs to cope with the changing environment, they impact the entire channel organization. Therefore, the evolution of channel systems is an ongoing adaptation of organizations to economic, technological, and sociopolitical forces both within the channel and in the external environment.[25]

Service Outputs as Determinants of Channel Structure

To explain the key elements that determine how channels are structured, Bucklin has developed a rather elaborate theory, the rudiments of which are outlined briefly here.[26] In essence, Bucklin argues that channel members perform various marketing functions to meet expressed demand for service outputs. In order to remain viable in the long run, channel members must perform these functions and participate in channel flows in a manner conducive to the reduction of consumers' search, waiting time, storage, and other costs. Other things being equal (especially price), end-users will prefer to deal with a marketing channel that provides a higher level of service outputs.

Bucklin has specified four generic service outputs: (1) spatial convenience (or market decentralization), (2) lot size, (3) waiting or delivery time, and (4) product variety (or assortment depth and breadth).[27] Spatial convenience provided by market decentralization of wholesale and/or retail outlets increases consumers' satisfaction by reducing transportation requirements and search costs. Community shopping centers and neighborhood supermarkets, convenience stores, vending machines, and gas stations are but a few examples of channel forms designed to satisfy consumers' demand for spatial convenience.

Similarly, the number of units to be purchased at each transaction can obviously affect the industrial or household consumer's welfare. When the marketing channel system allows consumers to buy in small lot sizes, purchases may move directly into the consumption process. If, however, consumers must purchase in larger lots, some disparity between purchasing and consumption patterns will emerge, burdening consumers with product storage and maintenance costs. Consequently, the smaller the lot size allowed by a channel, the higher the channel's service output and, normally, the price to the consumer.

Waiting time, the third service output identified by Bucklin, is defined as the time period that the industrial or household consumer must wait between ordering and receiving goods. Again, the longer the waiting time, the more inconvenient it is for the consumer, who is required to plan his or her consumption far in advance. Usually, when customers are willing to wait, they are compensated in terms of lower prices, as when ordering through catalogs and other direct-response marketing channels.

Finally, the wider the breadth of assortment or the greater the product variety available to the consumer, the higher the output of the marketing channel and the higher the distribution cost, because greater assortment entails carrying more inventory. For example, whereas supermarkets carry, on average, an assortment of 21,000 product line items or stockkeeping units (SKUs),[28] warehouse stores carry a limited assortment of 8,000 SKUs at substantially lower prices.

The main goal underlying all of these service outputs is the delivery of service quality. Service quality is defined as the gap between the consumers' expectations and perceptions; that is, the quality of a service will be rated high when the service delivered exceeds the consumer's expectations, and it will be rated poor when it does not meet them. As illustrated in Figure 1-7, high quality should be designed into the channel service system in response to the customer or end-user's expectations in designing each element of the service.[29]

These service outputs are achieved through the performance of the marketing functions or flows. The decisions on the amount of output to be delivered by channel members are directly influenced by the resource base and capabilities of channel members to perform various marketing functions and by the kind of service outputs desired by end-users. The result of the interaction between channel member resources and end-user requirements is a channel structure or arrangement that is capable of satisfying the needs of both channel members and end-users. Under reasonably competitive conditions and low barriers to entry, the channel structure that evolves over the long run should comprise a group of institutions so well adjusted to the structure's task and environment that no other type of arrangement could create greater returns (e.g., profits or other goals), or more end-user satisfaction per dollar of product cost.[30] This arrangement is called the *normative structure*. The determination of channel structure by service outputs is illustrated in Figure 1-8.

The more service outputs required by end-users, the more likely it is that in-

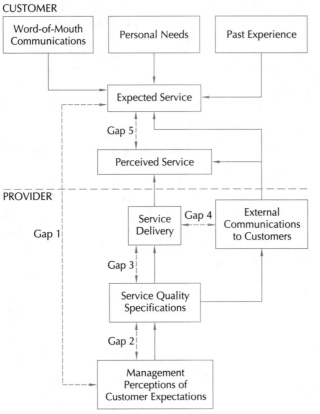

CUSTOMER

FIGURE 1-7 **Conceptual
model of service quality.**
Source: Reprinted with permission of The Free Press, an imprint of Simon & Schuster from
*Delivering Quality Service: Bal-
ancing Customer Perceptions and
Expectations* by Valarie A. Zeithaml, A. Parasuraman, Leonard
L. Berry, p. 46. Copyright © 1990
by The Free Press.

termediaries will be included in the channel structure. Thus, if end-users wish to
purchase in small lots, then there are likely to be numerous intermediaries performing sorting operations between mass producers and the final users. If waiting time is to be reduced, then decentralization of outlets must follow, and, therefore, more intermediaries will be included in the channel structure. The same type
of reasoning can be applied to all of the service outputs. As service outputs increase, however, costs will undoubtedly increase, and these higher costs will tend
to be reflected in higher prices to end-users. End-users are usually faced with a
choice between channel structures that provide few service outputs but relatively
low prices and structures in which both service outputs and prices are high. The
more the end-users participate in the marketing flows (in terms of search, physical possession, financing, and the like), the more they should be compensated for
their efforts. Where channel service outputs are low, end-users are supposedly
compensated for their additional efforts through the lower relative prices provided
by such channel structures. Thus, when construction machinery manufacturers,
such as Caterpillar or J.I. Case, purchase brake parts in carload quantities from
firms like Bendix and are willing to wait several months for delivery from distant
plants, they can expect to pay lower prices than if they were to order the same parts
from a local warehouse distributor who is willing to ship in smaller quantities and

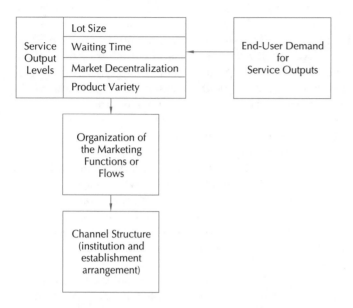

FIGURE 1-8   **The determination of channel structure.**

to deliver the parts much more quickly. The lower the level of service outputs provided, the greater the economy that can be achieved by channel members, and vice versa.

The final structure that emerges is, therefore, a function of the desire of channel members to achieve economies of scale relative to each of the marketing flows and the demand of consumers for various service outputs. An optimal structure is one that minimizes the total costs of the system (both commercial and end-user) by appropriately adjusting the level of the service outputs.[31] Within a channel, members can attempt to shift the degree of their participation in each flow in order to provide the greatest possible service output at the lowest possible cost. But such shifting calls for a tremendous amount of coordination and cooperation. This is one reason the management of channel systems is so critical.[32]

Marketing Cost as a Determinant of Channel Structure

Each marketing flow may be thought to have a differently shaped cost curve, which may include increasing, decreasing, or constant returns. Thus, savings can materialize if the activities or flows subject to increasing returns are performed at a higher output level. A firm with limited resources in a competitive industry will normally delegate these increasing return activities to enterprises that specialize in them. For instance, for its general merchandise categories, a national drugstore chain decided to spin off the inventory function to independent wholesalers because it believed the wholesalers could perform the function more efficiently.[33] Through such delegation (otherwise known as shifting or spinning off the flows), a firm is able, as

Stigler observes, to lower its average and marginal costs and thereby to improve its competitive position.[34]

Moreover, a channel member can also improve its competitive position by assuming only those functions it can perform more efficiently. By shifting other functions to those channels members who can perform them more efficiently, the resulting synergy helps to strengthen the competitiveness of the entire channel.[35] In essence, specialized channel intermediaries provide external economies to firms employing them. Eventually, however, reintegration of the delegated flows may be warranted as a firm's output expands or as technology changes, because the firm may then find itself capable of performing them at an optimum scale.[36]

Such a pattern of vertical disintegration followed by vertical reintegration can be observed in the case of small manufacturers who rely heavily on agent middlemen to represent them in the market, and on specialized storage, transportation, and financing institutions to perform these respective functions in their channels. As these small manufacturers expand, they tend to develop their own sales forces, perform their own storage, transportation, and financing, and thus dispense with the services of agent middlemen and other specialized institutions.

Similar analyses can be applied to wholesalers and retailers. For example, Sears started as a mail-order retailer and expanded horizontally. As its operations grew, Sears integrated backward by operating its own warehousing and other wholesaling facilities. Thus, when a firm's output and its market are limited, it will likely find itself shifting flows onto others in its channel, if it can, in fact, convince others to accept responsibility for these flows.[37] As market size expands, it becomes increasingly economical to integrate vertically, a pattern fully evident among the largest manufacturing and distributive organizations. The more firms vertically integrate, however, the more they prevent themselves from gaining the efficiencies of the open marketplace of services.

It is important to note that there may be considerable problems associated with shifting flows or, as Mallen has put it, "spinning off" functions.[38] It may be exceedingly difficult to separate the joint costs associated with the performance of many marketing flows (e.g., physical possession and ownership). Furthermore, most companies deal with multiple products and services for which costs are shared. There is also a time limitation involved along with many noneconomic considerations. Nevertheless, the concept of shifting flows is a viable one; like so many management decisions, it demands appropriate accounting procedures (e.g., activity-based or distribution cost accounting) to be implemented correctly.

Additional Factors Determining Channel Structure[39]

Added to these economics-oriented explanations of why channels take on certain structural properties are technological, cultural, physical, social, and political factors. For example, the emergence of the supermarket in the structure of food distribution was contingent on the availability of technologies such as the mass media and mass communications, the cash register, packaging and refrigeration, and the automobile. However, the introduction of the supermarket in less-developed countries is impeded by cultural variables, such as high rates of illiteracy, the habit of tasting food products before buying, and the delegation of buying to domestic help. Vending and dollar-change machines provide an example of technological and cultural influences on the distribution of candy, snack foods, beverages, and other items. Thus, in affluent societies with convenience-oriented cultures, consumers are willing to pay the extra cost associated with buying from vending machines. The advent and continued development of sophisticated information systems has enabled manufacturers and intermediaries to assess their distribution costs accurately and redesign their respective channels.

Geography, size of market area, location of production centers, and concentration of population, among other physical factors, also play important roles in determining the structure of channels. Distribution channels tend to be longer (i.e., include more intermediaries) when production is concentrated and population and markets are dispersed. Furthermore, in developing countries one finds that urban areas are served by a wide variety of retail outlets, including department stores, discount stores, and even supermarkets, whereas rural areas may be served solely by a general store.

In addition, local, state, and federal laws can influence channel structure directly and indirectly. There are laws that circumscribe territorial restrictions in distribution, price discrimination, full-line forcing, and unfair sales practices. There are also licensing boards that screen potential entrants to particular channels.

Social and behavioral variables also influence the makeup of a channel. For example, Galbraith advanced the concept of countervailing power as a tentative explanation of channel structure and practices.[40] His theory emphasizes that (1) private economic power is held in check by the countervailing power of those who are subject to it, (2) economic power begets countervailing power, (3) countervailing power is a self-generated force that complements competition as a regulatory force in the economy, and (4) countervailing power can take many forms, the most important of which is threatened or actual vertical integration. Manifestations of the effect of countervailing power on distribution channel structure are provided by the following examples:

- The emergence of the mass retailer and power buyers to countervail the power of large manufacturers.

- The use of private brands by chain retailers to countervail the power of large manufacturers with popular national brands.

- The emergence of voluntary and retailer cooperative chains to countervail the power of the large corporate chains.

- Trade association activities by small retailers (pharmacies, independent service stations, and independent grocery stores) in an attempt to countervail the power of chains and manufacturers.

The main point to be remembered here is that explanations of channel structure in terms of economic variables alone are obviously insufficient, even though such economic models provide an appropriate starting point for understanding why specific structures emerge. The need to go beyond economic variables is made especially clear when one attempts to answer the question of why it is that all channels do not gravitate to or obtain the normative structure specified by Bucklin? The answer comes from examining myriad social, cultural, political, and economic variables. As McCammon points out, uneconomic channels may persist for the following reasons.[41]

1. *Reseller solidarity.* Channel participants organize and function as groups that tend to support traditional trade practices and long-established institutional relationships. Trade association actions, attempts by independent retailers to outlaw chain stores, and department store operators' efforts to block discount store operations attest to the role of reseller solidarity in determining channel structure.

2. *Entrepreneurial values.* Large resellers are growth oriented; they tend to adopt economic criteria for decision-making purposes, and use new, efficient technologies. On the other hand, small resellers have limited expectations, tend to maintain the status quo, view their demand curve as relatively fixed, and resist growth beyond their limited growth expectations.

3. *Organizational rigidity.* Firms respond incrementally to innovations because of organizational rigidities; thus, the process of change takes a long time.

4. *The firm's channel position.* Kriesberg grouped channel intermediaries into insiders, who are members of the dominant channel; strivers, who want to become members of the channel; complementors, who perform functions complementary to functions performed by insiders; and transients, who take advantage of temporary opportunities and are not interested in becoming members.[42] Whereas transients usually disrupt the status quo by engaging in deviant competitive behavior, insiders, strivers, and complementors are more interested in maintaining the status quo. Thus, firms completely outside the channel are most likely to introduce basic and enduring innovations in the channel structure.

5. *Market segmentation.* New institutions do not appeal to all market segments. Traditional institutions seem to have loyal segments to which they appeal. Thus, these institutions are not compelled to change.

Indeed, to have a goal of moving toward a normative channel structure, one must meet the assumptions of low barriers to entry and competitive conditions. In many of the preceding examples, entry is purposely inhibited through group action, product differentiation, industrial norms, and the like. In addition, the concept of a normative channel structure is long-term in nature; in a dynamic environment, such a structure cannot be reached at any one point in time. Change must always take place according to an assessment of future requirements, and thus there will always be a gap between the actual and the ideal. In fact, it is probably best to adopt an evolutionary view of structure, because what exists always seems to be a compromise among past structure, present requirements, and predictions about the future.[43]

It is, perhaps, such an evolutionary view that enables us to explain the existence of over 50 alternative channel formats in the United States' economy today. These formats are briefly explained in Appendix 1B.

▶ CHANNEL MANAGEMENT, CHANNEL RELATIONSHIPS,
AND COMPETITIVE DYNAMICS

Economic battles involving producers versus producers or intermediaries versus intermediaries will not, in the long run, determine the ultimate victors in the marketplace. Rather, the relevant unit of competition is an entire distribution system comprising a network of interrelated institutions and agencies. For example, in the passenger tire industry, Michelin's system is in competition with Goodyear's entire system. The long-term standing of either company will depend in large measure on how well each company manages the relations among the institutions and agencies involved in the distribution task, so as to best satisfy the needs of the end-users of tires. Exhibit 1-1 demonstrates how successful channel management can differentiate a company from competitors.[44]

Exactly the same point applies to other industries as well. For example, there is a trend in the consumer goods markets of domination of the channel by fast-growing retailers like Wal-Mart Stores and Toys "R" Us and hybrid distribution (retail/wholesale) formats. At the same time, mergers among department stores, auto parts stores, and stores representing other lines of merchandise have led to the emergence of megachannels. Fragmented markets are consolidating, and more and more, a smattering of massive, powerful retailers are ruling them.[45]

EXHIBIT 1 - 1 / Knowing What to Manage in the Marketing Channel

What do Frito Lay, Hallmark, Bata Shoe, Caterpillar Tractor, Sony, and Compaq Computer ◀ ◀ ◀ all have in common? If you guessed strong reseller networks, you win the prize! What these companies all share are solid ties to distribution channels that distinguish them from competitors and allow them to exploit their product lines and individual brand advantages. By cleverly managing their chosen channels, these companies have successfully differentiated themselves in their respective markets.

A factor that has contributed to this successful management of the channel is the realization that developing and executing various means of channel support for their reseller networks will achieve ongoing productivity gains from them. No channel strategy, however well it is designed, will pay off unless it is followed by synergistic support.

Now for the million-dollar question—how can a firm distinguish itself with distribution channels that will set it apart from its rivals? The following are strategies that can furnish this kind of competitive advantage.

THE EXCLUSIVITY ROUTE

Exclusivity provides the supplier with tighter "image control," that is, display, sale installation, or repair. It also regulates the number and type of intermediaries, which is a key advantage in managing the network. For example, Honda's Acura Division has used this strategy to create distinctive dealerships for its higher-priced offering; however, the disadvantage

Exhibit 1-1 (continued)

Exhibit 1-1 (continued)

of this channel route is that the exclusive network may not be large enough to service all the developing market opportunities if demand increases. Exclusivity may put the channel in financial jeopardy if insufficient demand exists to sustain a typical dealer's cash flow. Moreover, if some end-users defect to new or different channels to buy the same category of product, this route may also fail. This phenomenon has happened in the personal computer arena—computer customers are buying at "technology supermarkets" like Comp USA.

ENTER THE SECOND BRAND

Another classic differentiation strategy is for a supplier to develop unique second brands for distribution channels with markedly different price positions in a market. For instance, Hallmark markets its Hallmark cards in department stores and its Ambassador cards through discount stores. This strategy allows a company to expand coverage across new channels without hurting the primary brand's image. Unfortunately, if the second brand is not noticeably different from the primary brand, this strategy can backfire. Obviously, people will buy the discount brand believing that they are getting the same thing for less, thus biting into the primary brand sales.

LET'S BE UNIQUE

Another way to differentiate is by using nontraditional channels. Church Shoes in the United Kingdom develops foreign markets by selling its shoes in men's classic apparel stores as opposed to shoe stores. In this way, Church assures that its shoes are identified with a retail setting that denotes quality, which is further reinforced by being the only shoe brand sold in such stores. Although unique channels may limit a brand's coverage, for niche marketers in a market they can represent a way to gain market access and customer attention. Going through distribution channels where competitors are not present can powerfully differentiate a company from rivals and will often avoid head-to-head price wars.

CALL THE EXPERTS

A way to rise above adversaries in an industry is to create and nurture dealers, distributors, or agents who are rated a cut above the rest in regard to customer-service quality. John Deere's farm dealers are a prime example, as they are renowned for being among the best agricultural distributors in the industry. This nurturing requires time, commitment, and follow-up. Developing these relationships within the distribution channel allows for differentiation from competitors because the distribution partners work together cooperatively to ultimately meet customer needs.

Source: Adapted from Allan J. Magrath, "Differentiate Yourself via Distribution," *Sales and Marketing Management*, March 1991, pp. 50–57.

Channel Relationships: From Transactions to Partnerships and Strategic Alliances

In every marketing channel, the members that do business together have some kind of working relationships. The relationship can be harmonious, acrimonious, misunderstood, or mismanaged. As shown in Figure 1-9, harmonious channel rela-

A Harmonious Relationship Requires:

❏ Goal Convergence (the What aspect)
❏ Process Convergence (the How aspect)

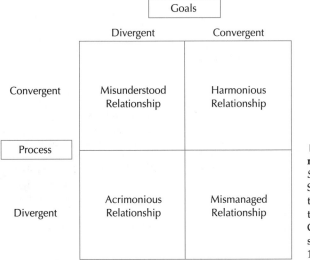

FIGURE 1-9 **Criteria for harmonious relationship marketing.** *Source:* Adapted from Jagdish N. Sheth, "Toward a Theory of Relationship Marketing," Handout at the Relationship Marketing Faculty Consortium, Center for Relationship Marketing, Emory University, 1994.

tionships require similar goals for channel members regarding the various *aspects* of the relationship as well as process convergence, that is, how to achieve effectiveness and efficiency in the process of delivering service outputs required by end-users.[46]

On the extreme ends on the continuum of these relationships, there are ad hoc operationally oriented transactional relationships on one side and ongoing strategic partnering relationships on the other, as shown in Figure 1-10.[47] The dichotomy is helpful in defining the range of relationship types in the channels according to their nature (ad hoc or ongoing), and purpose (strategic or operational). Transactional relationships occur when the customer and supplier focus on the timely exchange of basic products for highly competitive prices. Partnering relationships, or *partnerships,* occur through extensive social, economic, service, and technical ties *over time.* The intent in a strategic partnership is to lower total costs and/or increase value for the channel, thereby achieving mutual benefit.[48] Partnering relationships require communication, cooperation, trust, and commitment among channel members.[49]

Simply put, a channel partnership is an in-depth collaboration between suppliers and their intermediaries or between suppliers and their customers. But what these parties are achieving through partnership could hardly be called simple. Parties must agree on objectives, policies, and procedures for ordering and physically distributing products. They must experiment with, and in some cases, zealously adopt radically new ways of sharing responsibilities for order fulfillment, inventory management, distribution, purchasing, and post-sales service.

Most channel partnerships focus on two key business processes: order-to-de-

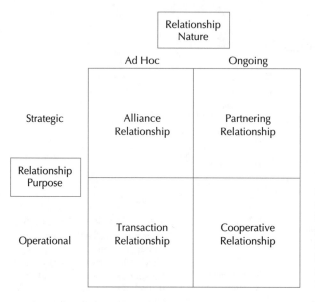

FIGURE 1-10 **Typology of relationship marketing.**
Source: Adapted from Jagdish N. Sheth, "Toward a Theory of Relationship Marketing," Handout at the Relationship Marketing Faculty Consortium, Center for Relationship Marketing, Emory University, 1994.

livery and customer service. The result is major changes in the ways suppliers take orders and deliver goods, and the processes by which their customers purchase, manage inventory, and carry out other back-room functions. Suppliers are taking on activities that their customers historically had held with an iron grip: ordering and paying for product; delivering and warehousing goods; and managing inventory, such as stock on department store shelves and medical goods in hospital supply rooms.[50] In essence, channel partnerships require a paradigm shift from *push to pull* philosophy as illustrated in Figure 1-11.[51]

As explained in Exhibit 1-2, partnerships capitalize on the notion that marketing channels are *vertical value-adding chains* that create *competitive advantage.*

A prime example of a company that has successfully embraced the concept of partnership is the previously mentioned McKesson Corporation. Once a conventional wholesale distributor squeezed by vertically integrated chain stores, McKesson has transformed itself into the center of a large *value-adding partnership (VAP)*—a set of independent companies that work closely together to manage the flow of goods and services along the entire value-added channel—that can more than hold its own against the chains.[52]

McKesson evolved into a VAP because of intense competition by chain drugstores (Walgreen, Osco) that were biting into the business of the independent drugstores McKesson serviced. McKesson realized that if the independents closed their doors, it would soon follow. In order to preserve the company, McKesson's managers began to search for ways to help its customers. In the early stages, the focus was on a rudimentary order-entry system at one of its warehouses and included data collection devices that were wheeled around customer's stores. This significantly reduced the cost of processing orders and restocking. Soon, it was discovered that this system had other applications for increasing efficiency. These

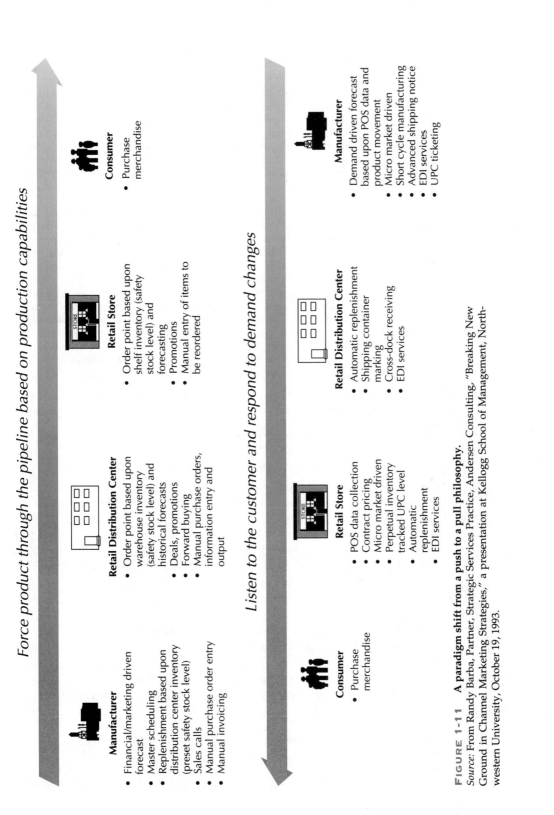

Force product through the pipeline based on production capabilities

Manufacturer
- Financial/marketing driven forecast
- Master scheduling
- Replenishment based upon distribution center inventory (preset safety stock level)
- Sales calls
- Manual purchase order entry
- Manual invoicing

Retail Distribution Center
- Order point based upon warehouse inventory (safety stock level) and historical forecasts
- Deals, promotions
- Forward buying
- Manual purchase orders, information entry and output

Retail Store
- Order point based upon shelf inventory (safety stock level) and forecasting
- Promotions
- Manual entry of items to be reordered

Consumer
- Purchase merchandise

Listen to the customer and respond to demand changes

Consumer
- Purchase merchandise

Retail Store
- POS data collection
- Contract pricing
- Micro market driven
- Perpetual inventory tracked UPC level
- Automatic replenishment
- EDI services

Retail Distribution Center
- Automatic replenishment
- Shipping container marking
- Cross-dock receiving
- EDI services

Manufacturer
- Demand driven forecast based upon POS data and product movement
- Micro market driven
- Short cycle manufacturing
- Advanced shipping notice
- EDI services
- UPC ticketing

FIGURE 1-11 **A paradigm shift from a push to a pull philosophy.**
Source: From Randy Barba, Partner, Strategic Services Practice, Andersen Consulting, "Breaking New Ground in Channel Marketing Strategies," a presentation at Kellogg School of Management, Northwestern University, October 19, 1993.

▶ ▶ ▶

EXHIBIT 1-2 / The Channel Value Chain Advantage

A channel value chain cannot be understood without first taking a look at an individual *firm's value chain.* A value chain breaks a firm down into its strategically relevant activities so we can understand the behavior of costs and the existing and potential sources of differentiation. A company achieves a *competitive advantage* by performing these strategically important activities at a lower cost or better than competitors. Every firm's value chain is made up of nine generic categories of activities that are linked together by shared characteristics: (1) firm infrastructure, (2) human resource management, (3) technology development, (4) procurement, (5) inbound logistics, (6) operations, (7) outbound logistics, (8) marketing and sales, and (9) service.

Value is the amount buyers are willing to pay for what a company provides and is measured by total revenue. Creating value for buyers that exceeds the cost of doing so is the goal of any generic strategy. Value, instead of cost, is used to determine competitive position. The value chain of all activities determines total value for the firm. Although these value activities are the building blocks of competitive advantage, it is not a collection of independent activities, but a *system of interdependent* activities linked together.

A channel value chain is formed through the linkages between the value chains of channel members, called vertical linkages. These linkages provide opportunities for competitive advantage and are similar to firm linkages. The channels have value chains that a firm's product passes through to get to the end-user. Coordinating and jointly optimizing within channels can lower cost or enhance differentiation, and thus create a competitive advantage for the individual firms and channel. Taking advantage of vertical linkages requires information, and modern information systems are creating many new possibilities.

Source: Adapted with the permission of The Free Press, an imprint of Simon & Schuster from *Competitive Advantage: Creating and Sustaining Superior Performance* by Michael E. Porter, pp. 33–53. Copyright © 1985 by Michael E. Porter

---

successful uses of information technology triggered the search for other uses, and the managers soon found numerous ways to help customers and suppliers.

McKesson thus offered the independent drugstores many advantages of computerized systems that no single store could afford by itself. The drugstores were able to give their customers better prices, a more targeted product mix, and improved service, all of which helped them compete with the chains. What makes McKesson so powerful—and what distinguishes it as a VAP—is the understanding that each player in the value-added channel has a stake in the others' success. McKesson managers visualize the entire value-added partnership, not just one part of it, as a single competitive unit.

Partnerships up and down the channel deliver bigger-volume contracts, reduce competition, reduce redundancies in inventories, and provide a predictable market.[53]

An example of a distributor promoting an alliance with its supplier is the Great Lakes Terminal and Transport Company (GLT&T), a distributor of chemicals and plastics.

- GLT&T has agreed to turn over accounts that GLT&T has developed to its suppliers when those accounts exceed the prescribed size for direct sales. GLT&T realizes that manufacturers can serve large accounts more economically, and if GLT&T doesn't transfer them, competing manufacturers will capture the accounts by selling direct at lower prices. By sacrificing its own short-term profits, GLT&T guarantees both its and the manufacturer's market position for the long term. This has strengthened its partnerships with manufacturers who have responded by continuing to give GLT&T a commission for a set transaction period on all sales to these large former accounts, or by paying them a finder's fee. Also, the manufacturers refer small accounts to GLT&T instead of handling them directly.[54]

Strategic alliances and partnerships require certain conditions in order to be effective:

1. Recognition of the interdependence of channel members,
2. Close cooperation between channel members,
3. Careful specification of the roles and functions, that is, joint rights and responsibilities each play in the marketing channel,
4. Coordinated effort focused on a common goal(s), and
5. Trust and communication between channel members.[55]

A trend that is an outgrowth of partnerships is the *seamless channel.* This concept is related to the concept of the seamless organization, which has all departments working together to serve the customer, thereby blurring the organizational lines that separate departments within the organization. The seamless channel blends the borders between channel members by having multiple levels in each organization work together with their counterparts in other channel organizations to deliver quality service to the customer.[56] Partnerships contribute to the seamless channel by giving channel members a sense of being on the same *team.* The adversarial role that is so prevalent is replaced with one built on trust and cooperation. For example, VWR Scientific Corporation, a company that sells glass beakers and other lab equipment, and Du Pont have established a seamless channel. To work together better, Du Pont's computer system has been linked with VWR's, and their close working relationship has made it difficult for the companies to tell where one leaves off and the other one starts.[57]

Competitive Dynamics

Viewing channels as competitive units is significant for all companies, including those that market their products through a number of different channels and those that develop assortments of goods and services by purchasing from a variety of suppliers. The way individual manufacturers coordinate their activities with the various intermediaries with whom they deal, and vice versa, will determine the viability of one type of channel alignment versus other channel alignments made up of different institutions and agencies handling similar or substitutable merchandise.

If, within a given marketing channel, an institution or agency does not see fit to coordinate effectively and efficiently with other members of the same network, but rather pursues its own goals in an independent, self-serving manner, it is possible to predict the eventual demise of the channel alignment. Ideally, then, channel members should attempt to coordinate their objectives, plans, and programs with other members in such a way that the performance of the total distribution system to which they belong is enhanced. Such highly integrated action up and down a marketing channel is rare, but is increasing in frequency exponentially.

Myopic channel members are most concerned about the dealings that take place with those channel members immediately adjacent to them, from whom they buy and to whom they sell.[58] In this sense, such channel intermediaries are not, in fact, functioning as enlisted components of a distribution system, but rather are acting individually as *independent markets,* with each one choosing those products and suppliers that best help him serve the target groups for whom he acts as a purchasing agent. From this perspective, the intermediary's method of operation—the functions it performs, the clients it serves, and the objectives, policies, and programs it adopts—is the result of its own independent decisions.

This notion of each channel intermediary acting as an independent market must be qualified and analyzed with regard to *total channel performance.* Although an "independent" orientation on the part of any channel member may indeed be warranted at times, it is put into effect only at the risk of sacrificing the levels of coordination necessary for overall channel effectiveness, efficiency, growth, and long-run survival. Thus, a high degree of independent, suboptimizing behavior on the part of individual channel participants serves as a detriment to the viability of the total channel network. The goal for actors within any distribution network is, therefore, to cooperate in developing an interorganization system that will minimize suboptimization so that a high degree of channel coordination is attainable. The need for channel management is to coordinate the activities in the channel to ensure that *total quality distribution* is achieved through the channel. Quality customer service is the "product" delivered by the entire channel.[59]

▶ APPROACH OF THE TEXT

The preceding discussion underscores the critical importance of channel member coordination in ensuring channel system viability. The approach of this text is *managerial.* It focuses on *planning, organizing, coordinating, directing,* and *controlling the efforts of channel members.*

The task of channel management is complex and taxing. Most businesses sell a number of products under different labels and operate in a number of different markets. Products and services are marketed through several channels to a wide range of customers. Channel members differ in type, size, location, and many other operating characteristics. This *multimarketing*[60] phenomenon poses difficult channel management issues, which will be dealt with in the remainder of this text.

▶ ORGANIZATION OF THE TEXT

The organization of this text emanates from the framework for understanding channel management shown in Figure 1-12. The framework specifies channel management systems in terms of interrelated sets of structural and managerial variables. The various chapters in the text discuss these sets of variables, as denoted in Fig-

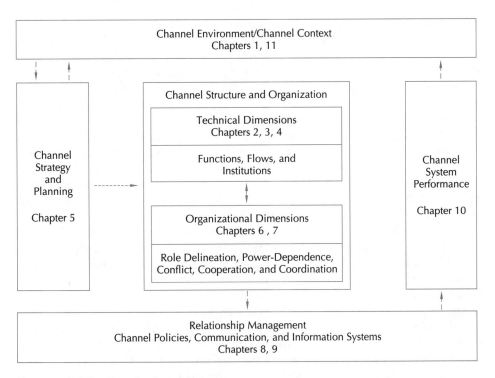

FIGURE 1-12   **Organization of the text.**

ure 1-12. The remainder of this section is devoted to an explanation of the organization of the text as outlined in the framework.

A prerequisite to the effective management of marketing channels is a knowledge of the reasons channels exist, the functions they perform, and the factors that account for the way they are structured. In this first chapter, key theoretical concepts have been examined. These concepts explain why specialized institutions and agencies have emerged to assist in the task of making goods and services available to industrial, institutional, and household consumers. The need for efficient exchange via sorting processes, routinization of marketing activities, and reasonably rapid search procedures compels the existence of a large variety of intermediaries. The way in which these intermediaries are linked together depends on the service outputs demanded by end-users. The higher the output demanded, the greater the number of institutions and agencies that will likely be required to bridge the gap between production and consumption.

Service outputs are generated through the organization of the marketing functions or flows—physical possession, ownership, promotion, negotiation, financing, risking, ordering, and payment. The actual levels of performance of these functions depend, in turn, on the *economics* of distribution. This requires balancing the needs of channel members to achieve profitability and manage risk, on the one hand, and the desires of end-users to receive the highest possible amount of service output at the lowest possible price, on the other hand. In addition to these factors, there are a host of social, political, competitive, and cultural factors impinging on channel members. These factors influence and, in some cases, dictate how a channel will be structured.

All of the concepts introduced in this chapter provide relevant background information that can be used in the management of marketing channels. Without an understanding of each of them and their interaction with one another, any attempts at channel management are likely to be shortsighted and superficial.

Against this backdrop, it is now possible to uncover some of the specific attributes of the intermediaries constituting marketing channels in order to gain a deeper comprehension of their roles within channels and their potential for meeting the needs of the customers they serve. Part Two of this text describes some of the key components of marketing channels—retailers, wholesalers, transportation agencies, public and private warehouse facilities, and distribution centers. These channel intermediaries, classified by the United States Census as "service sectors," specialize in providing value-added services that augment product-service bundles created by the manufacturers. Each of these institutions and agencies has its own structure, performance requirements, and management styles. Because channel members tend to focus on their own goals and performance, these features must be understood before any attempts are made to plan, organize, coordinate, and control the channel as a system. In essence, it is imperative to develop an understanding of the internal management of these component institutions before trying to manage the relationships among them. Therefore, Chapters 2, 3, and 4 deal with the structure, management, and performance requirements of retailing, wholesaling, and physical distribution institutions, respectively.

It should be clearly noted at the outset that manufacturers and end-users are also significant components of marketing channels. However, specific chapters on manufacturer marketing strategy and on industrial or household consumer buying behavior are not included in this text because these topics are extensively covered in almost all basic marketing principles and marketing management texts. In contrast, retailer, wholesaler, and physical distribution agency strategies are subjects that are explained in-depth in this text. Not many readers have had experience and/or training in these areas. Those who do have an adequate background in them may wish to proceed from this chapter directly to Part Three.

Part Three focuses on the management of the marketing channel—on designing, planning, organizing, coordinating, and controlling. Careful selection of channel members and planning of channel arrangements are essential if firms are to survive severe competition in the marketplace. Therefore, Chapter 5 lays out a process for designing marketing channels via a customer-driven, market-focused perspective.

Marketing channels can be organized differently to reach similar or different market segments. Forms of channel organization vary. Channels may be organized as loose coalitions of independently owned manufacturers, wholesalers, retailers, and other institutions. Alternatively, they may be organized as closely aligned marketing systems. In the latter instance, channels may be fully integrated systems, contractual systems, or administered systems. Chapter 6 discusses organizational patterns of marketing channels.

The marketing channel is a complex technical and managerial system. Different forms of channel organization and management necessitate an understanding of channel member behavior. Chapter 7 deals with channel management via the use of power, influence strategies, relationship building, and conflict management, as well as compensation in the channel.

There are a number of policies that channel members can use to administer distribution channels. Chapter 8 catalogues a variety of policies that are available for managing channels and explains the reasons why they might be adopted. However, each and every policy used in managing the marketing channel restrains or redirects the activities of the various members of the channel. The affected parties may react negatively and bring lawsuits challenging the legality of these policies. Therefore, the chapter concurrently lays out when and how such policies might run afoul of the federal antitrust laws.

The implementation of channel planning and organization cannot be effectively achieved without instituting channel coordination through (1) the exercise of leadership, (2) the application of various motivational methods to induce channel members to cooperate, and (3) the development of an appropriate network for communication and exchange of vital information among channel members. Chapter 9 focuses on the deployment of effective channel information systems, and the new technologies used in these systems. Manufacturers, wholesalers, retailers, transportation agencies, and other participants in the marketing channel system need to communicate and share information in order to function effectively. Forecasting sales, controlling and managing inventories, tracking orders and shipments, launching joint promotions, introducing new products, and putting into effect price changes all require information sharing through a carefully planned and designed communication and information system. The chapter deals with issues related to the impact of channel information and communication systems on the performance of channel flows, channel member roles, channel member power, and channel management.

The process of managing a channel system is incomplete without the design and activation of a performance control and audit system. Systematic assessment of channel member and channel system performance, the provision of feedback, and the institution of corrective action mechanisms are necessary to maintain channel control. The final chapter of Part Three, Chapter 10, deals with the assessment of the performance of channel institutions and the channel system from a micro-viewpoint. A number of performance evaluation mechanisms, such as the strategic profit model, distribution cost analysis, activity-based costing, and direct product profit, are examined.

Part Four of the text examines channel management in another context—the international arena. Exploring distribution channels in other countries enriches our managerial analysis. It enables us to examine the impact of different environments and managerial problems on channel system performance. Chapter 11 deals with international marketing channels.

DISCUSSION QUESTIONS

1. What are some approaches to the study of distribution channels besides an inter-organization systems approach?

2. In a low-growth economy, many strategies emphasize demand management rather than demand stimulation. How might this affect a firm's marketing mix, particularly distribution? If there is a continued deemphasis of demand stimulation in the future, will the role of channel management in marketing become more or less important as an influence on overall corporate performance?

3. Peter F. Drucker, a well-known management scholar, has described the distribution function as the "economy's dark continent," implying that this aspect of organizational activity has long been ignored as a potential area for strategic development. Why, do you feel, was there such neglect for so long a period?

4. Consider these examples of marketing channels:

   ■ Avon's distribution system delivering cosmetics direct from manufacturer to consumer through a sales force of 400,000 saleswomen.

   ■ Levitz's warehouse-showroom method of furniture distribution, which stocks large quantities of furniture at each warehouse-showroom at considerable savings, thus enabling Levitz to pass lower prices on to the consumer.

   ■ Sara Lee Corporation's consignment marketing channel for its L'eggs pantyhose, wherein retailers take no title for the goods, make no financial investment, and perform no delivery service or display maintenance, but receive only a certain percentage of the pantyhose sales for their allocation of space to the L'eggs display.

   a. Select one of these channels and speculate who the other channel participants are and to what extent each member participates in the eight universal marketing flows.

   b. How might these flows be shifted, either among the members now in the channel or to different agencies or institutions not presently included? What do you think would be the implications of such shifts?

   c. Within each of these distribution systems, specify what the consumer's role is from a flow-absorption perspective. How, in turn, does this affect the consumer's level of "compensation"?

5. Do you think a channel management approach is useful and applicable to all types of distribution channel systems? Which types of distribution channels would seemingly need it the most? Which would find it the least applicable?

6. Should advertising agencies and financial institutions be considered channel members? Why? Why not?

7. Is it more useful, from a managerial perspective, to think of consumers as members of the channel or as elements of the task environment of the channel? Can consumers be "manipulated" and/or incorporated by channel management?

8. According to Alderson, "the number of intervening marketing agencies tends to go up as distance increases." Distance, in his conception, is measured in terms of "the time and cost involved in communication and transportation." What factors, then, would tend to increase (or decrease) distance?

9. Explain the trade-offs between the number of available product alternatives *and* search and information costs; between spatial convenience *and* seller costs. Apply your answer to channels for health care delivery and for stainless steel.

10. Bucklin and Carman state that "an optimal structure is one which minimizes the total cost (both commercial and consumer) of the system by the appropriate adjustment of . . . level of service outputs." Can you apply this statement to each of the marketing flows?

11. Is it likely that vertical disintegration is typical in growing industries, whereas vertical integration is typical in declining industries? Explain.

12. Why are partnerships beneficial for all members of a channel? Explain.

ENDNOTES

[1]Thomas E. Ferguson, "Customers' Diverse Needs Require Diverse Channels," *Business Marketing*, Vol. 77, March 1992, pp. 64–66.

[2]Thomas A. Foster, "Global Logistics Benetton Style," *Distribution*, Vol. 92, October 1993, pp. 62–66.

[3]Patricia M. Fernberg, "Where to Buy Can Make a Difference," *Modern Office Technology*, Vol. 37, November 1992, pp. 29–33.

[4]"Japan's Drug Industry—Medicinal Madness," *The Economist*, March 27, 1993, p. 73.

[5]Grace Casselman, "Dell Ready to 'Duke It Out' for Direct Sales," *Computing Canada*, Vol. 18, November 9, 1992, p. 26.

[6]William Lazer, Priscilla LaBarbara, James Maclachlan, and Allen Smith, "Marketing 2000 and Beyond," *American Marketing Association*, 1990, pp. 113, 141, 164.

[7]Wroe Alderson, "Factors Governing the Development of Marketing Channels," in Richard M. Clewett (ed.), *Marketing Channels in Manufactured Products* (Homewood, IL: Richard D. Irwin, 1954), pp. 5–22.

[8]Wroe Alderson and Miles W. Martin, "Toward a Formal Theory of Transactions and Transvections," in Bruce E. Mallen (ed.), *The Marketing Channel: A Conceptual Viewpoint*, (New York: John Wiley and Sons, 1967), pp. 50–51.

[9]Other authors have described the sorting processes as "concentration, equalization, and dispersion" and "collecting, sorting, and dispersing." See Rayburn D. Tousley, Eugene Clark, and Fred E. Clark, *Principles of Marketing* (New York: Macmillan Company, 1962), pp. 7 and 8, and Roland S. Vaile, E.T. Grether, and Reavis Cox, *Marketing in the American Economy* (New York: The Ronald Press, 1952), pp. 134–150, respectively.

[10]Robert E. Weigand, "Fit Your Products to Your Markets," *Harvard Business Review* (January–February 1977), p. 102.

[11]Barnaby J. Feder, "McKesson: No. 1 but a Doze on Wall Street," *The New York Times*, March 17, 1991, p. 10.

[12]Frank Cespedes, "Channel Management in General Management," *California Management Review* (Fall 1988), p. 116.

[13]See Michael Hammer and James Champy, *Reengineering the Corporation: A Manifesto for Business Revolution*, 1st ed. (New York: Harper Business, 1993); and Michael E. Porter, *Competitive Advantage: Creating and Sustaining Superior Performance* (New York: Free Press, 1985).

[14]Lucie Juneau, "Retailing and Wholesaling: Luring Consumers with Conspicuous Efficiency," *Computerworld*, Vol. 26, Sept. 14, 1992, pp. 37–41.

[15]For an alternate treatment of the topic of determinants of channel structure see Donald F. Dixon and Ian F. Wilkinson, "Toward A Theory of Channel Structure," *Research in Marketing*, Vol. 8, 1986, pp. 27–70.

[16]Douglas Lavin, "Chrysler's Man of Many Parts Cuts Cost," *Wall Street Journal*, May 14, 1993, p. B1.

[17]See, for example, Jacquelyn A. Ottman, *Green Marketing* (Lincolnwood, IL: NTC Publishing Group, 1992), pp. 73–103.

[18]Peter Drucker, "The Economy's Power Shift," *Wall Street Journal*, September 24, 1992, p. A16.

[19]Arthur Anderson and Company, *The Technology Maze in Wholesale Distribution: Choosing the Right Path*, (Washington, DC: Distribution Research and Education Foundation, 1990), p. 18 and Edith Weiner, "The Fast Approaching Future," *Arthur Anderson Retailing Issues Letter*, Vol. 6, No. 4, July 1994, pp. 1–4.

[20]Tim Triplett, "Smart Store Challenges Executives to Change," *Marketing News*, July 4, 1994, p. 6.

[21]Andrew Fisher, "Speed Is of the Essence," *Financial Times*, August 3, 1993, p. 7.

[22]Paul Abrahams, "The World's the Limit," *Financial Times*, November 6, 1990, p. 1.

[23]Catherine V. Corby, "Consumer Technology and its Effect on Banking," *Bank Marketing*, Vol. 26, March 1994, pp. 24–29.

[24]Louis W. Stern and Torger Reve, "Distribution Channels as Political Economics: A Framework for Comparitive Analysis," *Journal of Marketing*, Vol. 44, (Summer 1980), pp. 52–64.

[25]Michael Morris and M. Joseph Sirgy, "Applications of General Systems Theory Concepts to Marketing Channels," in Robert F. Lusch et al. (eds.), *1985 Educators Conference Proceedings* (Chicago: American Marketing Association, 1985), pp. 336–338.

[26]Louis P. Bucklin, *A Theory of Distribution Channel Structure* (Berkeley, CA: IBER Special Publications, 1966). Much of the paraphrasing of Bucklin's model has been drawn from Michael Etgar, "An Empirical Analysis of the Motivations for the Development of Centrally Coordinated Vertical Marketing Systems: The Case of the Property and Casualty Insurance Industry," unpublished doctoral dissertation, The University of California at Berkeley, 1974, pp. 95–97.

[27]Bucklin, *op cit.*, pp. 7–10; and Louis P. Bucklin, *Competition and Evolution in the Distributive Trades* (Englewood Cliffs, NJ: Prentice-Hall, 1972), pp. 18–31. Clearly, the list of service outputs provided to end-users by a channel can be expanded to include provision of credit, maintenance of product quality, availability of information, stability of supply, availability of personal service and attention, and risk reduction, among others. For exposition purposes, however, the discussion here is limited to the four major service outputs suggested by Bucklin in the monograph and book just cited. For further elaboration of this subject, see Louis P. Bucklin and James M. Carman, "Vertical Market Structure Theory and the Health Care Delivery System," in Jagdish N. Sheth and Peter L. Wright (eds.), *Marketing Analysis for Societal Problems* (Urbana: University of Illinois Bureau of Economic and Business Research, 1974), pp. 7–21; Lee E. Preston and Norman R. Collins, *Studies in a Simulated Market* (Berkeley: University of California Institute of Business and Economic Research, 1966); and Christina Fulop, *Competition for Consumers* (London: Allen and Unwin, 1964), Chapter 2.

[28]Regis McKenna, "Marketing in an Age of Diversity," *Harvard Business Review*, (September–October 1988), pp. 88–95.

[29]Valarie Zeithaml, A. Parasuraman, and Leonard Berry, *Delivering Quality Service: Balancing Customer Perceptions and Expectations* (New York: The Free Press, 1990), pp. 18–20 and 157–158.

[30]Bucklin, *op cit.*, p. 5.

[31]Bucklin and Carman, *op cit.*, p. 12.

[32]For an alternative explanation of the evaluation of channel structure see Ian F. Wilkinson, "Toward a Theory of Structural Change and Evaluation in Marketing Channels," *Journal of Macromarketing*, Vol. 10, No. 2 (Fall 1990), pp. 39–40.

[33]Walter Zinn and Michael Levy, "Speculative Inventory Management: A Total Channel Perspective," *International Journal of Physical Distribution and Materials Management* (May 1988), p. 35.

[34]George J. Stigler, "The Division of Labor Is Limited by the Extent of the Market," *Journal of Political Economy* (June 1951), pp. 185–193.

[35]Ronald Michman, "Managing Structural Changes in Marketing Channels," *The Journal of Business and Industrial Marketing* (Summer–Fall 1990), pp. 6–8.

[36]Control as well as economic considerations are crucial here. In fact, control may override economics in many situations. This factor is discussed in detail in later chapters.

[37]This is not always a foregone conclusion. Very small firms often find it difficult to secure needed services from agents, advertising agencies, and financial institutions, for example, and therefore must integrate these flows, even though it would be more economical to pass them along to someone else.

[38]Bruce E. Mallen, "Functional Spin-off: A Key to Anticipating Change in Distribution Structure," *Journal of Marketing,* Vol. 37 (July 1973), pp. 18–25. Also see William P. Dommermuth and R. Clifton Anderson, "Distribution Systems: Firms, Functions and Efficiencies," *MSU Business Topics,* Vol. 17 (Spring 1969), pp. 51–56.

[39]A comprehensive overview of these factors is presented in Gary L. Frazier, Kirti Sawhney, and Tassu Shervani, "Intensity, Functions, and Integration in Channels of Distribution," in Valarie A. Zeithaml (ed.), *Review of Marketing 1990* (Chicago: American Marketing Association, 1990), pp. 263–298.

[40]John K. Galbraith, *American Capitalism,* rev. ed. (Boston: Houghton Mifflin Co., 1956), pp. 110–114, 117–123.

[41]Bert C. McCammon, Jr., "Alternative Explanations of Institutional Change and Change Evolution," in William G. Moller, Jr., and David L. Wilemon (eds.), *Marketing Channels* (Homewood, IL: Richard D. Irwin, 1971), pp. 136–141.

[42]Louis Kriesberg, "Occupational Controls Among Steel Distributors," in Louis W. Stern (ed.) *Distribution Channels Behavioral Dimensions* (Boston: Houghton Mifflin Co., 1969), pp. 50–60.

[43]For an interesting perspective on the subject see Arun Sharma and Luis V. Dominguez, "Channel Evolution: A Framework for Analysis," *Journal of the Academy of Marketing Science,* Vol. 20, No. 1 (Winter 1992), pp. 1–15; and Janeen Olson and Kent L. Granzin, "Vertical Integration and Economic Development: An Empirical Investigation of Channel Integration," *Journal of Global Marketing,* Vol. 7, No. 3 (1994), pp. 7–39.

[44]For additional examples see Myron Magnet, "The New Golden Rule of Business," *Fortune,* February 21, 1994, pp. 60–64.

[45]Randy Myer, "Suppliers—Manage Your Customers," *Harvard Business Review* (November–December 1989), pp. 160–161.

[46]Jagdish N. Sheth, "Toward a Theory of Relationship Marketing," Handout at the Relationship Marketing Faculty Consortium, Center for Relationship Marketing, Emory University, 1994.

[47]*Ibid.* Also, see Atul Parvityar and Hagdish N. Sheth, "Paradigm Shift in Marketing Theory and Approach, The Emergence of Relationship Marketing," and "Towards a Theory of Alliance Governance," in Jagdish N. Sheth and Atul Parvityar (eds.), *Relationship Marketing: Theory, Methods, and Applications,* Proceedings of the 1994 Research Conference on Relationship Marketing, Center for Relationship Marketing, Emory University, 1994, Sections I-3 and III-1.

[48]James C. Anderson and James A. Narus, "Partnering as a Focused Market Strategy," *California Management Review,* Vol. 33 (Spring 1991), pp. 95–113.

[49]For a comprehensive framework of relationship marketing, see Robert M. Morgan and Shelby D. Hunt, "The Commitment-Trust Theory of Relationship Marketing," *Journal of Marketing,* Vol. 58, No. 3 (July 1994), pp. 20–38.

[50]Michael E. Treacy, Jay M. Michaud, and Fred D. Wiersema, "Channel Partnerships: Cooperating to Compete," *CSC Insights the Journal of Business Reengineering,* Vol. 4, No. 1 (Spring 1992), p. 16. For further elaboration on the definition and concept of partnerships see Robert D. Buzzell and Gwen Getmeyer, *Channel Partnerships: A New Approach to Streamlining Distribution* (Cambridge, MA: Marketing Science Institute, Report Number 94–104, April 1994).

[51]From Randy Barba, Partner, Strategic Services Practice, Anderson Consulting, "Breaking New Ground in Channel Marketing Strategies," a presentation at Kellogg School of Management, Northwestern University, October 19, 1993.

[52]The following discussion about McKesson is based on Russell Johnston and Paul Lawrence, "Beyond Vertical Integration—The Rise of the Value-Adding Partnership," *Harvard Business Review* (July–August 1988), pp. 94–95.

[53]Joseph Weber, "Getting Cozy with Their Customers," *Business Week,* January 8, 1990, p. 86.

[54]Anderson and Narus, *op. cit.,* p. 35.

[55]Adel I. El-Ansary, "Mill Merchant Partnership: Managing Interdependence in Paper Marketing Channels," *Management News* (June 1990), pp. 30–32.

[56]Adel I. El-Ansary, "Salesforce Effectiveness Research: A Top Management Viewpoint," *Management News* (May 1991), pp. 22–25.

[57]Weber, *op. cit.,* p. 86.

[58]Philip McVey, "Are Channels of Distribution What the Textbooks Say?" *Journal of Marketing* (January 1961), pp. 61–65.

[59]Walter, Snullian, and Blumenthal, Public Accountants, *Total Quality Distribution* (Washington, DC: Distribution Research and Education Foundation, 1993).

[60]See Robert Weigand, "Fit Products to Your Markets," *Harvard Business Review* (January–February 1977), pp. 95–105.

APPENDIX

REVERSE DISTRIBUTION CHANNELS
FOR GREEN MARKETING   ◀◀◀◀◀◀◀◀

Reverse distribution is the process of continuously taking back products or packaging materials to avoid further waste disposal in landfills or high energy consumption through the incineration process. In most cases, manufacturers implement reverse distribution because of heightened consumer interest in environmentally friendly products through government legislation. Reverse distribution expands the responsibilities of the channel members because they become responsible for products after they have been sold and after customers have disposed of them. Unintentional benefits for companies with reverse distribution programs include increased control in the distribution function, reduced long-term packaging costs, and corporate image enhancement. The primary obstacle to reverse logistics is economics. Nonreturnable products are cheaper to produce, and virgin materials are priced at levels equal to or lower than recycled materials.[1]

After an initial burst of environmental claims in the late 1980s, major marketers pulled back when environmental groups and state governments claimed that consumers were being misled. But now marketers are going forward by actively marketing green products and coming up with myriad packaging developments, this time with new, more focused strategies. Among other efforts, Procter & Gamble Co. is testing Tide Refill for powder detergents in Florida, and Scott Paper Co. is testing Scotties Recycled, a facial tissue made from 100% recycled paper. Small suppliers are trying to carve out a niche with deep green products (developed especially for the green market), whereas mainstream suppliers are working on improved packaging or coming out with new lines. One area in which green products are finding success is the household cleaner category.[2]

The economies of supply and demand have given a boost to the recycled paper market. More recycled pulp is finding its way into a huge range of products including business and printing papers, newsprint, paperboard, packaging, greeting cards, fast-food bags, and mulch for composting. The primary environmental issue driving recycling today is not saving trees, but rather saving landfills. Between 1978 and 1988 the number of operating landfills in the U.S. declined to about 5,500 from 14,000. Experts predict that number will dip to about 1,800 in the next decade, during which time more than half the states will see all their landfills close. According to a survey of office paper producers, recycled products constituted about 4% of office paper demand, for which consumers paid an average 10% premium in 1992. By 1997, researchers forecast demand for recycled paper at about 7.4% of the office paper market, with a premium charge to buyers of only 1%.[3]

The reverse distribution channels used for recycling differ in several respects from forward logistics flows. Reverse distribution is the movement of goods from a consumer toward a producer in a channel of distribution. The reverse channel begins with the initial collection and storage of recyclable material. Types of channel members include: (1) municipalities, (2) joint ventures, (3) material recovery facilities, (4) brokers, (5) intermediate processors, and (6) end-users. Functions of the reverse logistics channel include: (1) collection, (2) sorting, (3) storage, (4) transport, (5) compacting, shredding, or densification, (6) communication with buyers, (7) processing or filtration, and (8) retromanufacturing. Differing product characteristics, extensive handling, and low-density shipments pose considerable obstacles to establishing an efficient reverse channel for recyclable commodities.[4]

Traditional distribution channels have been used in some recycling efforts. During the immediate post-World War II years and before, distribution of soft drinks, for example, was specifically tied to the use of the returnable bottle. If recycling is to be a feasible solution to waste disposal, some means must be developed to channel these wastes back to firms for further use. Traditional channel concepts must be reversed because, in the case of soft drinks and paper products especially, the consumer is the producer of the waste materials that are to be recycled. Thus, the consumer becomes the first link in the recycling channel of distribution rather than the last. The recycling of waste materials is, therefore, essentially a "reverse-distribution" process.[5]

The contrast between forward and reverse channels is illustrated in Figure 1A-1 and Table 1A-1. The reverse-direction channel returns the reusable waste products from consumer to producer.[6]

Conceptually, reverse distribution is identical to the traditional channel of distribution. The consumer has a product to sell, and in essence, he assumes the same position as a manufacturer selling a new product. The consumer's (seller's) role is to distribute his waste materials to the market that demands his product.

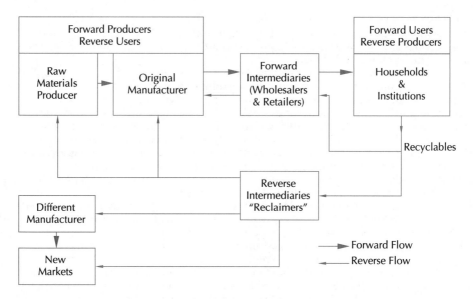

FIGURE 1A-1 **Forward and reverse channels of distribution.**
Source: Reprinted from Joseph Guiltinan and Nonyelu Nwokoye, "Reverse Channels for Recycling: An Analysis of Alternatives and Public Policy Implications," in Ronald C. Curhan (ed.), *1974 Combined Proceedings* (Chicago: American Marketing Association, 1975), p. 341.

However, in most instances, consumers do not consider themselves to be producers of waste materials. Therefore, they are not readily concerned with planning a marketing strategy for their products, which would be reusable wastes. When the producers are unaware of or indifferent to the fact that they are the producers, then the problem becomes acute.[7]

So far, many recycling channels eliminate the middleman, unless that middleman is a voluntary group. The fact that there are generally no established middlemen in these backward channels, between the producer and the consumer of waste products, is unfortunate. It causes the producers (consumers) a number of inconveniences. Foremost is the accumulation of waste materials on their part, without adequate storage facilities, as well as an absence of facilities to transport them.

On the other hand, in the area of trash recycling, private and municipal trash collection systems provide the collection and storage functions. The buyer of the collected wastes may be a power plant, a metals company, a fertilizer company, or the like. This channel is a convenient one for the individual household. Trash collection by basic trash collection agencies, however, may not be the ultimate answer to the recycling problem. Trash needs to be sorted and then routed to storage centers for ultimate transportation to recycling centers, and most municipalities are unwilling to incur the costs associated with these tasks.

If an effective reverse channel of distribution is to become a reality, the ultimate consumer must first be motivated to start the reverse flow. In addition, a greater degree of cooperation has to be achieved among channel members. A barrier to increased cooperation and coordination is the lack of profitability. In the absence of legislation mandating recycling efforts (or taxing noncompliers), improved recycling efforts may depend on a higher order of social responsibility by consumers and middlemen, given the lack of motivation and profits. Several new types of intermediaries are emerging to facilitate recycling processes.

TABLE 1A-1   Forward Versus Reverse Channels: Some Key Distinctions

FORWARD CHANNELS	REVERSE CHANNELS
Products	
High unit value	Low unit value
Highly differentiated	Little or no differentiation
Much product innovation	Little or no innovation
Few producers	Many originators
Markets	
Routinized transactions established	Routinized transactions not established
Many final users	Few final users
Varied customer demands	Standardized demands
Supply often less than or equal to demand	Supply typically greater than demand
Large assortment discrepancy	Small assortment discrepancy
Key functions	
Assorting	Sorting
Allocation	Accumulation
Heavy promotional efforts	Low promotional effort
Speculative inventories	Few speculative inventories
Packaging	Collection

Source: Reprinted from Joseph Guiltinan and Nonyelu Nwokoye, "Reverse Channels for Recycling: An Analysis of Alternatives and Public Policy Implications," in Ronald C. Curhan (ed.), *1974 Combined Proceedings* (Chicago: American Marketing Association, 1975), p. 342.

One of these is the reclamation or recycling center, a modernized "junkyard" placed in a convenient location for the customer, who would be paid an equitable amount for his waste goods. Initial processing of the waste materials, when collected, might be accomplished at these centers.

In addition, central processing warehouses may be developed by existing middlemen in traditional channels, where trash can be stored and where limited processing operations on waste material may be performed. For example, aluminum can producers are equipping beverage distributors with can flatteners, shredders, compactors, and truck trailers to encourage them to accept empty cans for recycling.[8] Transportation costs would likely represent a major barrier to such recycling efforts, however. Other possibilities include such reverse channels as manufacturer-controlled recycling centers, joint venture resource recovery centers, and secondary dealers.[9]

ENDNOTES

[1]Patrick M. Byrne and Alison Deeb, "Logistics Must Meet the 'Green' Challenge," *Transportation & Distribution,* Vol. 34 (February 1993), pp. 33–37.

[2]Jennifer Lawrence, "Green Products Sprouting Again," *Advertising Age,* Vol. 64 (May 10, 1993), p. 12.

[3]Tim Triplett, "Economics Meets Ecology As Recycled Paper Matures," *Marketing News,* Vol. 28 (February 28, 1994), p. 2.

[4]Terrance L. Pohlen and M. Theodore Farris, II, "Reverse Logistics in Plastics Recycling," *International Journal of Physical Distribution & Logistics Management*, Vol. 22, 1992, pp. 35–47.

[5]William G. Zikmund and William J. Stanton, "Recycling Solid Wastes: A Channels-of-Distribution Problem," *Journal of Marketing*, Vol. 35 (July 1971), pp. 34–35.

[6]*Ibid.*, p. 35.

[7]See, for example, Duane L. Davis and Jeff Allen, "The Effects of Economic Incentives on the Reverse Distribution of Aluminum," in Terry L. Childers et al. (eds.), *Marketing Theory Applications* (Chicago: American Marketing Association, 1991), pp. 72–79.

[8]"Recycling Ease Gives Aluminum an Edge over Steel in Beverage-Can Market Battle," *The Wall Street Journal*, January 2, 1980, p. 28.

[9]For a discussion of these latter channels, see Joseph Guiltinan and Nonyelu Nwokoye, "Reverse Channels for Recycling: An Analysis of Alternatives and Public Policy Implications," Ronald C. Curhan (ed.), *1974 Combined Proceedings* (Chicago: American Marketing Association, 1975), pp. 343–344; and Zikmund and Stanton, *op. cit.*, p. 38.

APPENDIX

1B /

ALTERNATE CHANNEL FORMATS: DEFINITIONS AND EXAMPLES

◀◀◀◀◀◀◀◀

Alternate channel formats may be based in any of the three sections of the traditional distribution pipeline—manufacturer, distributor, or customer—but they may also have other bases. The following material summarizes in detail a variety of channel formats and the characteristics on which they rely for strategic advantage, and gives examples of specific companies or types of companies or product categories using that channel format. By comparing each of your markets to this information, you can identify opportunities and vulnerabilities.

MANUFACTURER-BASED CHANNEL FORMATS

1. **Manufacturer Direct.** Product shipped and serviced from manufacturer's warehouse. Sold by company salesforce or agents. Many manufacturer-direct companies also sell through wholesaler-distributors.

    Example: Wide variety of products for customers with few service needs and large orders

2. **Manufacturer-Owned Full Service Wholesaler-Distributor.** Acquired wholesale distribution company serving the parent's and other manufacturers' markets. Typically, these diverse product lines in an industry support synergies between a company's man-

Source: Reprinted from Arthur Andersen and Co., *Facing the Forces of Change 2000* (Washington, D.C.: Distribution Research and Education Foundation, 1992), pp. 163–173.

ufacturing and distribution operations. Due to customer demand, some companies also distribute other manufacturers' products.

Examples: Revlon, Levi Strauss, Kraft Foodservice, GESCO, clothing and apparel products

3.   **Company Store/Manufacturer Outlets.** Retail product outlets in high-density markets; often used to liquidate seconds and excess inventory. They often sell branded consumer products.

Examples: Athletic footware, bakery goods

4.   **License.** Contracting distribution and marketing functions through licensing agreements, usually granting exclusivity for some period of time. Often used for products in the development stage of the life cycle.

Examples: Mattel, Walt Disney, importers

5.   **Consignment/Locker Stock.** Manufacturer ships product to point of consumption but title does not pass until consumed. Risk of obsolescence and ownership is with manufacturer until used. Concerned with high-priced/high-margin items and emergency items.

Examples: Diamonds, fragrances, tool cribs, and machine repair parts

6.   **Broker.** Specialized salesforce contracted by manufacturer; the salesforce carries other comparable product lines and focuses on a narrow customer segment; product is shipped through another format such as those above. Typically used by small manufacturers attempting broad coverage.

Examples: Frozen foods, paper goods, lumber, newer product lines

RETAILER-BASED CHANNEL FORMATS

1.   **Franchise.** Product and merchandising concept is packaged and formatted. Territory rights are sold to franchisees. Various distribution and other services are provided by contract to franchisees for a fee.

Examples: Blockbuster Video, McDonald's

2.   **Dealer Direct.** Franchised retailers carry a limited number of product lines supplied by a limited number of vendors. Often big-ticket items needing high after-sales service support.

Examples: Heavy equipment dealers, auto dealers

3.   **Buying Club.** Buying services requiring membership. Good opportunity for vendors to penetrate certain niche markets or experiment with product variations. They also often provide buyers with a variety of consumer services. Today they are largely consumer-oriented.

Examples: Compact disc/tape clubs, book clubs

4.   **Warehouse Clubs/Wholesale Clubs.** Appeal is to price-conscious shopper. Size is 60,000 square feet or more. Product selection is limited and products are usually sold in bulk sizes in a "no frills" environment.

Examples: Pace, Sam's Club, Price Club, Costco

5.   **Mail Order/Catalog.** Nonstore selling through use of literature sent to potential customers. Does not need "break packs" or pricing. Usually has a central distribution center for receiving and shipping direct to the customer.

Examples: Land's End, Spiegel, Fingerhut

6.   **Food Retailers.** Will buy canned and boxed goods in truckloads to take advantage of pricing and manufacturer rebates. Distribution centers act as consolidators to reduce

the number of trucks received at the store. Pricing is not required as manufacturer bar codes are used. Typically, includes full line of groceries, health and beauty aids, and general merchandise items. Some food retailers have expanded into additional areas, such as prescription and over-the-counter drugs, delicatessens, bakeries, etc.

Examples: Dominick's, Publix, Safeway

7. **Department Stores.** These stores offer a wide variety of merchandise with a moderate depth of selection. The typical product mix includes both soft goods (such as clothing, food, linens) and hard goods (such as appliances, hardware, sporting equipment). Distribution centers act as consolidators of both soft goods and hard goods. Quick response for apparel goods demands direct link with manufacturer. Having stores on a national basis motivates retailers to handle their own distribution.

    Examples: J C Penney, Mervins, R. H. Macy & Co., Dayton Hudson Corp., Federated Stores

8. **Mass Merchandisers.** Similar to department stores, except product selection is broader and prices are usually lower.

    Examples: Wal-Mart, Kmart, Target

9. **Specialty Stores.** Offer merchandise in one line (for example, women's apparel, electronics) with great depth of selection at prices comparable to those of department stores. Due to nature of fashion goods (seasonal) partnership with the manufacturer is essential. Manufacturer will ship in predetermined store assortment and usually will price the goods. Retailer in some cases has joint ownership with the manufacturer.

    Examples: The Limited, The Gap, Kinney Shoes, Musicland, Zale

10. **Specialty Discounters/Category Killers.** Offer merchandise in one line (for example, sporting goods, office supplies, children's merchandise) with great depth of selection at discounted prices. Stores usually range in size from 50,000 to 75,000 square feet. Buys direct in truckloads. Manufacturer will ship direct to the store. Most products do not need to be priced. National chains have created their own distribution centers to act as consolidators.

    Examples: Toys "R" Us, Office Max, Drug Emporium, F & M Distributors

11. **Convenience Store.** A small, higher-margin grocery store that offers a limited selection of staple groceries, nonfoods, and other convenience items; for example, ready-to-heat and ready-to-eat foods. The traditional format includes those stores that started out as strictly convenience stores, but they may also sell gasoline.

    Examples: 7–Eleven; various regional chains

12. **Hypermarket.** A very large food and general merchandise store with at least 100,000 square feet of space. Although these stores typically devote as much as 75% of the selling area to general merchandise, the food-to-general merchandise sales ratio typically is 60/40.

    Examples: Auchan, Super Kmart Centers, Hypermarket USA

SERVICE PROVIDER-BASED CHANNEL FORMATS

1. **Contract Warehousing.** Public warehousing services provided for a fee, typically with guaranteed service levels.

    Examples: Caterpillar Logistics Services, Dry Storage

2. **Sub Processor.** Outsourcing of assembly or sub processing. Usually performed with labor-intensive process or high fixed-asset investment when small orders are needed for customer. These channel players are also beginning to take on traditional wholesale distribution role in some cases.

   Examples: Steel processing; kitting of parts in electronics industry

3. **Cross Docking.** Trucking companies service high-volume inventory needs by warehousing and backhauling product on a routine basis for customer's narrower inventory needs. Driver picks inventory and delivers to customer on picking up customer's shipment.

   Examples: Industrial repair parts and tools, various supply industries

4. **Integration of Truck and Rail (Intermodal).** Joint ventures between trucking and rail companies to ship large orders door-to-door from supplier to customer, with one waybill.

   Examples: Becomes very economical for large orders, or from manufacturer to customer for a manufacturer with a broad product line.

5. **Roller Freight.** Full truckload is sent from manufacturer to high-density customer markets via a transportation company. Product is sold en route, and drivers are directed to customer delivery by satellite communication.

   Examples: Lumber products, large moderately priced items, with "commodity-like" characteristics that require routine orders.

6. **Stack Trains and Road Railers.** Techniques to speed movement and eliminate handling for product to be shipped by multiple formats. For example, importer loads containers directed to specific customers on a truck body in Hong Kong, ships direct, and unloads onto railcars. This can eliminate 2 to 3 days' transit time. Large customer orders using multiple transportation techniques.

   Examples: Importers

7. **Scheduled Trains.** High-speed trains leave daily at prescribed times from high-density areas to high-density destinations. Manufacturer "buys a ticket" and hooks up his railcar, and product is picked up at the other end by the customer.

   Examples: High-density recurring orders to large customers with limited after-sales service needs.

8. **Outsourcing.** Service providers sign a contract to provide total management of a company's activities in an area in which the provider has particular expertise (computer operations, janitorial services, printshop, cafeteria, repair parts, tool crib). The outsourcer then takes over the channel product flow for products associated with outsourced activity (janitorial supplies). Outsourcing has spread to virtually every area of the business (repair part stockroom, legal and accounting department) and may not use merchant wholesaler-distributors. Wide variety of applications and growing.

   Examples: ServiceMaster, ARA, R. R. Donnelly

9. **Direct Mailer.** Direct mail advertising companies expanding services in conjunction with market research data base services in order to direct market narrower line products. Product logistics and support is either performed by manufacturer or outsourced to a third party.

   Examples: Big ticket consumer products, high-margin, low-service-requirement industrial and commercial equipment

10. **Bartering.** Service provider, usually an advertising or media company, signs a barter arrangement with a manufacturer to exchange product for media advertising time or

space for product. Bartered product is then rebartered or redistributed through other channels.

Examples: Consumer and commercial products that have been discontinued or for which demand has slowed considerably

11. **Value-Added Designers/Resellers (VARs).** Designers, engineers, or consultants for a variety of service industries that joint venture or have arrangements with manufacturers of products that are used in their designs. The VARs often get a commission or discount to service the product later and often carry inventory of high-turn items.

Examples: Computer software companies that market hardware for turnkey products; security system designers that joint venture with electronics manufacturers to sell turnkey products

12. **Influencers/Specifiers.** Similar to a VAR, but these firms generally design highly complex, large projects (commercial buildings), do not take title to product, and have a multiple group of suppliers whose products can be specified into the design. Selling effort is focused on both the ultimate customer and the specifier. Distribution of product is handled through other channel formats.

Examples: Architects, designers, consultants

13. **Financial Service Providers.** These formats have historically been initiated by joint venture with financial service companies to finance margin purchases for customers or dealers (such as floor planning). It has been expanded to allow manufacturers to initiate distribution in new markets and assess these markets (with the help of financial provider). High-capital, highly controlled distribution channel for one or two suppliers.

Examples: Branded chemicals, construction equipment

OTHER CHANNEL FORMATS

Door-to-Door Formats. To some extent these are variations on the channel formats previously listed. These formats have existed in the U.S. since pioneer days in situations in which a product has a high personal sales cost and high margins and is sold in relatively small orders (encyclopedias, vacuum cleaners, and so forth). A wide range of variations (for example, the home-party format) attempt to get many small buyers in one location to minimize the sales cost and provide a unique shopping experience. Variations of the format have also spread to the industrial and commercial markets to capitalize on similar market needs (for example, Snap-On Tools uses a variation of the home-party system by driving the product and salesmen to the mechanic's garage and selling to the mechanics on their lunch hour). Each format is different and needs to be analyzed to understand its unique characteristics. A brief summary of the more identifiable formats follows:

1. **Individual On-site.** Very effective for generating new business for high-margin product requiring a high level of interaction with customers.

Examples: Fuller Brush, Electrolux, Encyclopedia Britannica, bottled water, newspapers

2. **Route.** Used for servicing routine repetitive purchases that do not need to be resold on each call. Sometimes price is negotiated once and only changed on an exception basis. This concept was historically more prevalent in consumer lines (for example,

milk deliveries) but has recently spread to a variety of commercial and industrial segments.

Examples: Office deliveries of copier paper and toner

3. **Home Party.** Similar to individual on-site sales, this format takes the product to a group of individuals, as outlined in the introduction above.

Examples: Tupperware, Snap-On Tools

4. **Multi-Level Marketing.** Salesperson not only sells product but recruits other salespeople who become a leveraged salesforce that gives the original salesperson a commission on sales. Channel can be used for "high-sizzle," high-margin, fast-growth opportunities in branded differentiated product.

Examples: Amway, plumbing products, cosmetics, other general merchandise

5. **Service Merchandising/"Rack Jobbing."** Similar to a route but expanded to provide a variety of services with the product. Originally, the rack jobber sold small consumer items to grocery stores, merchandised the product, and owned the inventory, merely paying the retailer a commission for the space. This concept is expanding to the commercial, industrial, and home market in a variety of niches: maintaining a stockroom of office supplies, maintaining repair parts stock, servicing replenishable items in the home such as chemicals, purified water, salt, and so on.

Examples: Specialty items and gadgets or novelties; paperback books, magazines

Buyer-Initiated Formats. These are formats that have been built on the concept of small buyers joining together to buy in large quantities at better prices. This concept has expanded to give these buyers other securities and leverage that they might not be able to obtain on their own (for example, private labeling and advertising design). As with the door-to-door concepts, variations of this concept are proliferating to meet individual buyers' needs.

1. **Co-op.** Companies, usually in the same industry, create an organization in which each member becomes a shareholder. The organization uses the combined strength of the shareholders to get economies of scale in any number of areas of its business, such as purchasing, advertising, or private label manufacturing. This format is generally designed to allow small companies to compete more effectively with large competitors. Although wholesaler-distributors can form or join co-ops, in their use as an alternate channel format co-ops may be direct buyers from nonwholesaler-distributors.

Examples: Topco

2. **Dealer-Owned Co-op.** Similar to the co-op format, except the co-op may perform many of the functions rather than contracting them with third-party suppliers (for example, it may own warehouses). Shareholders/members are generally charged a fee for usage, and all profits in the co-op at year end are refunded to the shareholders on some prorated basis. In many instances, this format has elements of a franchise.

Examples: Distribution America

3. **Buying Group.** Similar to the co-op, except the relationship is usually much less structured. Companies can be members of several buying groups. The loose affiliation format usually does not continually commit the members to performance. This format is being used throughout the economy and has taken on a host of roles. A group can buy through the wholesale distribution channel or direct from manufacturers. Often, wholesaler-distributors are members of buying groups for low-volume items.

Examples: AMC, May Merchandising

Point-of-Consumption Merchandising Formats. This concept has grown from the practice of strategically placing vending machines where the demand is predictable and often discretionary and the cost of selling through a full-time salesperson would be too high. This format has spread into commercial, industrial, and home markets for products and services never before imagined. The increased use of technology and telecommunications has opened this channel to even more products and services.

1. **Vending/Kiosks.** Kiosks have historically been very small retail locations that carry a very narrow product line. Through interactive video, online ordering technology, and artificial intelligence, this format has been significantly enhanced and can operate unattended. It is also being used for point-of-use dispensing of maintenance supplies and tools. "Purchases" are recorded in a log by the computer to control inventory shrinkage and balance inventory levels.

   Examples: Film processing, candy, tobacco, compact discs, and tapes

2. **Pay-Per-Serving Point of Dispensing.** Product is prepared or dispensed by vending machine at the time of purchase. Vending machines for soup and coffee, soft drinks, and candy or food are usual uses of this format, but it is expanding to include such foods as pizza and pasta.

   Examples: Beverages, food

3. **Computer Access Information.** Many of the computer access information formats have not necessarily altered the product flow (products are not available online), but they have significantly altered the service and information flow by uncoupling them from the product. This allows the product to pass through "cheaper channels."

   Examples: Online information services, cable movies, news wire services, shopping services for groceries.

Third-Party Influencer Formats. These formats are designed around the concept that an organization that has a relationship with a large number of people or companies can provide a channel format to these entities for products and services not traditionally associated with the organization (for example, a school selling candy to the community by using the school children as a salesforce). Here again, the concept has broadened across both the commercial and industrial sectors and deepened in terms of the products and services offered.

1. **Charity.** This format typically involves sales of goods and services in which the sponsoring charitable organization receives a commission on the sale. All types of products can be included and can be shipped direct or outsourced. Salesforce may be non-paid volunteers.

   Examples: Market Day, World's Finest Chocolate

2. **Company-Sponsored Program.** Employers contract with companies for products and services for their employees or segments of employees on an as-needed basis. The provider has access to the employee base.

   Examples: Health care and drug services, car maintenance

3. **Premium and Gift Market.** Companies buy products customized with company logos or names for sale or distribution.

   Examples: Pens, plaques, awards, T-shirts, novelties

4. **Product Promotion Mailing with Normal Correspondence.** Promotion of products is done by mailings to customers with letters and perhaps phone call follow-up. Typically involves promotional inserts with credit card and other billings. Logistics and order fulfillment activities may be handled by others.

   Examples: American Express, VISA, MasterCard

5.   **Customer List Cross-Selling.** An unusual format in that the customer list is sold by one company to another. In effect, the marketing function is circumvented. Started in the consumer industry but is migrating to the commercial and industrial segments.

Examples: Catalog companies, credit card companies

Catalog and Technology-Aided Formats. The time-honored catalog marketing channel dates from use by department stores to extend their merchandising ability to the predominantly rural U.S. population of the late 1800s. Catalog use has expanded dramatically to follow the buying habits of consumers and institutions. Although it continues to be a growing threat to the traditional merchant wholesaler-distributor through mail order and linkage to technology, it should be pointed out that catalogs are also a sales tool used by some wholesaler-distributors. Some of the adaptations below illustrate the need to evaluate this format very carefully in all sectors of the market.

1.   **Specialty Catalogs.** Uses catalogs to promote a narrow range of special products or services. Mailings are made to potential and repeat customers. Orders come in by mail or phone.

Examples: Eddie Bauer, Bass Pro Shops, Williams Sonoma

2.   **Business-to-Business Catalogs.** Similar to specialty catalogs except that the product and customer focus is on business.

Examples: Moore Business Forms, Global, CompuAdd, Damart

3.   **Television Home Shopping and Satellite Networks.** Heavily dependent on technology, these offer shopping in the comfort of your home. Also has business application. Orders are placed by phone.

Example: Home Shopping Network

4.   **Interactive Merchandising.** Could embody many of the attributes of 3 above, except that this format allows extensive interactive in-store capabilities, as well as online ordering. It may offer inventory checking or physical modeling capabilities and unusually extensive communication linkages.

Examples: Florsheim, kitchen planning computers in do-it-yourself home centers

5.   **Third-Party Catalog Services.** Catalog selling format in which one or more suppliers provide a combined catalog for a group of customers frequenting a certain place.

Examples: Airline inflight magazines and catalogs, in-room hotel publications

6.   **Trade Shows.** A format used in some segments for direct sales order activities. Suppliers sell from booths at major trade shows or conventions. Also used for retail applications.

Examples: Boats, cars, hardware/software applications

7.   **Database Marketing.** Databases of customer buying habits and demographics are analyzed to enable the company to target customers for future mailings. Also used for retail applications.

Examples: Large grocery/consumer products companies, telephone companies

RETAILING

CRITICAL ELEMENTS
AND STRATEGIC ISSUES

*M*odern retailing is fiercely competitive and innovation oriented. It is populated by an ever-growing variety of institutions and constantly buffeted by a highly fluid environment. The purpose of this chapter is to describe some of the more significant competitive developments that have made retailing so volatile and to illustrate how some of these developments have affected the marketing channels in which retailers participate. An understanding of what is pointed out in this chapter should help channel managers more fully account for "bottom-up" pressures when forming strategies and designing distribution systems.[1]

This chapter is organized as follows: First the distinction between retail sales and wholesale sales is made. Then, the operational characteristics that determine the nature of retailing competition are explained. Next, some of the strategic issues currently present in U.S. retailing are considered. Finally, some international retailing examples are examined.

Retailing Defined

Retailing consists of the activities involved in selling *goods* and *services* to *ultimate consumers* for *personal consumption*. Thus, a retail sale is one in which the buyer is an ultimate consumer, as opposed to a business or institutional purchaser. In contrast to wholesale sales (i.e., purchases for resale or for business, industrial, or institutional use), the buying motive for a retail sale is always personal or family satisfaction stemming from the final consumption of the item being purchased.[2]

Although the distinction between "retail" and "wholesale" sales may seem to be trite, it is really very important, because, as all good marketers know, buying motives are critical in segmenting markets. Companies that sell personal computers to high-school students for use in doing their homework (or, more realistically, for playing computer games) are engaged in making retail sales. Companies that sell personal computers to their parents for use in a family business run out of a home office are engaged in making wholesale sales. CompUSA, Staples, and Office Depot make both retail and wholesale sales; they are indeed schizophrenic. Is it important that these companies understand the differences in serving these different markets, even though they are served out of the same establishments? If you cannot answer this question instantly, you should put this book down and take a nap immediately!

The next chapter focuses on wholesale sales made by wholesalers. Because more and more businesses sell to other businesses out of what look and feel like retail stores, there is considerable discussion of this development in that chapter. Here, though, the focus is on businesses engaged in making retail sales. The discussion includes both store and nonstore (e.g., mail order, telemarketing, and television sales) retailing. But, as has just been pointed out, it is important to realize at the outset that there are considerable overlaps relative to retail and wholesale sales. (Just to see how refreshed you are from your nap, is Home Depot a retailer [engaged in making retail sales], a wholesaler [engaged in making wholesale sales], or both? Now, why does the answer matter?)

Basic Elements of Competition in Retailing

In order to understand how to work effectively with retailers, it is imperative to know what concerns them. Clearly, they are in business to make money, but they tend to make money by running their companies differently than their suppliers. They also tend to watch certain performance indicators more closely than others, given the nature of what they do. In fact, the character of almost all retail institutions is determined by the choices management makes about margin and inventory turnover goals, variety and assortment of merchandise to be carried, location and convenience factors, and customer services to be offered.

MARGIN AND INVENTORY TURNOVER GOALS   The fundamental point of departure between traditional and modern retailing systems might best be conceptualized by contrasting institutions characterized by high margin, low turnover, and numerous personal services with those characterized by low margin, high turnover, and minimum services. Both sets of institutions continue to exist, but in the twentieth century, the spotlight has focused on the revolutionary volume efficiencies flowing out of the latter style of operation. And now, as we enter the twenty-first century, we are beginning to see retailers, like Home Depot, who are able to combine low margin and high turnover with excellent personal service. These retailers, as we shall see later, are able to generate high rates of return on the capital employed in their businesses by continuous improvements in asset management made possible by using sophisticated information systems. Service attracts customers, but it can only be provided if it can be paid for.

Historically, the low-margin/high-turnover model has been oriented toward generating high operational efficiency with the savings generated passed on to the customer. However, many of the savings "passed on to the customer" must be seen as involving a *transfer* of cost (opportunity cost as well as actual "effort" cost) rather than a clear elimination of it. Thus, reductions in service output levels, such as those associated with product selection opportunity, convenience of location, "atmosphere," personal services, financial and delivery accommodations, and the like, accompany the typical retail package offered by the low-margin/high-turnover operation. In essence, then, this operational philosophy is founded on the costs (represented by marketing functions or flows) that certain segments of consumers are willing to absorb in certain classes of purchasing behavior. This terminology (e.g., service outputs, marketing flows) is important, because it is used extensively later in this text when we describe how to go about designing appropriate marketing channels for specific segments of the market. For example, according to McKinsey & Co., the major economic and operating factors driving performance in different types of retail chains are as follows:

Chains	*Economic Drivers*	*Operating Drivers*
Apparel specialty (e.g., The Limited)	High gross margin	Merchandise management; markdown control
	High inventory turns	Merchandise management
Discount (e.g., Wal-Mart)	Low operating expense	Low cost; high sales productivity
	High fixed-asset productivity	Low investment; high sales productivity
Category killer (e.g., Home Depot)	Low operating expense	Low cost; high sales productivity
Department store (e.g., Federated)	High gross margin	Merchandise management
National chains (e.g., Penney's)	High gross margin	Merchandise management

Source: Nancy Karch, Director, McKinsey & Company, presentation at Northwestern University, April 3, 1995.

Of critical importance in determining which path to follow—low margin/high turnover or high margin/low turnover—are management's perceptions of the organization's best chance for achieving its financial target. The appropriate pathway can be highlighted by using the strategic profit model (SPM). The specifics of this model spelled out in detail in Chapter 10. However, a brief description of the SPM is introduced here so that the reader can gain some appreciation of its influence on the margin and turnover dimensions of retail strategy.[3] Basically, the SPM can be laid out as follows:

$$\frac{\text{net profit}}{\text{net sales}} \times \frac{\text{net sales}}{\text{total assets}} = \frac{\text{net profit}}{\text{total assets}} \times \frac{\text{total assets}}{\text{net worth}} = \frac{\text{net profit}}{\text{net worth}}$$

Management can pursue margin management (net profit/net sales), asset turnover (net sales/total assets), *and/or* financial management via financial leverage (total assets/net worth) in order to secure a target return on net worth. (Net sales are gross sales less customer returns and allowances.) If there is tremendous downward pressure on margins, because of competitive forces and economic conditions generally, then a likely path for management to pursue is asset turnover. These sets of conditions have led management to emphasize such criteria as sales per square foot (which reflects space and location productivity), sales per employee (which reflects labor productivity), and sales per transaction (which reflects merchandising program productivity).

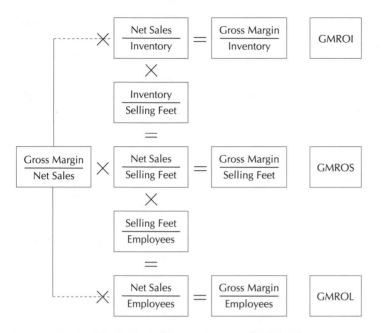

FIGURE 2-1   The Strategic Resource Management Model.
Source: Reproduced from Robert F. Lusch, Patrick Dunne, and Randall Gebhardt, *Retail Marketing*, 2nd Edition (Cincinnati, OH.: South-Western Publishing Co., 1993, p. 41, with the permission of South-Western College Publishing a division of International Thomson Publishing Inc. Copyright © 1993 by South-Western Publishing Co. All rights reserved.

Retailers have turned to an evaluation of three interrelated measures of performance in order to improve their overall profitability. As incorporated in the strategic resource management model (see Figure 2-1), these measures are listed below.

1. *Gross margin return on inventory investment (GMROI).* GMROI combines margin management and inventory management and can be calculated for companies, markets, stores, departments, classes of products, and stockkeeping units (SKUs). GMROI allows the retailer to evaluate inventory on the return on investment it produces and not just on the gross margin percentage. This means that GMROI often considers items with widely varying gross margin percentages as equally profitable, as in the following example.

	gross margin	×	sales to inventory	=	GMROI
A	50%		3		150%
B	30%		5		150%
C	25%		6		150%

2. *Gross margin per full-time equivalent employee (GMROL).* Retailers should *optimize*, not maximize, GMROL. As sales rise per square foot, not all fixed costs (e.g., rent, utilities, and advertising) rise in proportion. In fact, they decline as a percentage of sales as sales increase. Having more salespersons may actually lower average sales per full-time equivalent (FTE) employee and increase profitability.

3. *Gross margin per square foot (GMROS).* Such a measure permits an assessment of how well retailers are using their most unique asset—the shelf or floor space they can allocate to suppliers' products.

A problem with GMROI, however, is that gross margin only accounts for the cost of goods sold and fails to account for differences in variable costs associated with selling different kinds of merchandise. Other measures, such as contribution dollars per square foot of selling space or direct product profit (DPP), as explained in Chapter 10, are more comprehensive, but more difficult to derive. In any case, retailers' use of measures such as GMROI or DPP places pressure on suppliers. They must attend to the gross margins their brands permit retailers to earn, the sales volume (in units) their brands generate, the amount of shelf or floor space consumed by their brands, and the costs incurred in storing, handling, and selling their brands. There is increasing emphasis on systems designed by suppliers to speed up the replenishment of inventory, because faster replenishment rates mean less need for shelf space and less inventory investment, and therefore a reduction in the denominators in the formulas.

VARIETY AND ASSORTMENT   *Variety* describes generically different classes of goods making up the product offering, that is, the *breadth* of product lines. The term *assortment*, on the other hand, refers to the *depth* of product brands or models offered within each generic product category. Discount department stores, like Kmart, Target, and Wal-Mart, have limited assortments of fast-moving, low-priced items across a wide variety of household goods, ready-to-wear, cosmetics, sporting goods, electric appliances, auto accessories, and the like. In contrast, a specialty store dealing only, or primarily, in home audiovisual electronic goods, such as Audio Warehouse, would have a very large and complete line of radios, tape recorders, and high-fidelity equipment, offering the deepest assortment of models, styles, sizes, prices, and so on.

The variety and assortment dimension of retailing operations is clearly a matter that demands the attention of top management, for decisions in this area will color the entire character of the enterprise. Once the basic strategy is established for the organization, however, the task of choosing specific products or brands usually falls to functionaries called *buyers.* Buyers play a central role in retailing; unlike their counterparts in manufacturing concerns, their status within their home organizations is very high. In fact, as discussed later, some retailers generate more profits via negotiations for trade deals and allowances than they do through merchandising efforts. Because buying is such a critical aspect of retailing, it is important to understand the evaluative processes and procedures that take place in merchandise and supplier selection. The appendices to this chapter are geared to that end. Appendix 2A discusses the choice strategies employed by retail buyers; Appendix 2B is a glossary of pricing and buying terms commonly used by retailers; and Appendix 2C briefly describes some of their merchandise planning and control procedures. An example of the vendor attributes required for success by buyers of consumer electronics is provided in Exhibit 2-1.

LOCATION AND CONVENIENCE   In a general sense, products are classified on the basis of consumer purchasing patterns. That is, they are thought of as being convenience, shopping, or specialty goods. Implicit in this understanding is the extent

EXHIBIT 2-1 / Vendor Attributes Required for Success in Marketing Consumer Electronics Through Selected Channels

VENDOR ATTRIBUTES	WAREHOUSE CLUBS	MASS MERCHANDISERS		OFFICE PRODUCT SUPERSTORES	CONSUMER ELECTRONICS RETAILERS	COMPUTER SUPERSTORES
		Self-Service[a]	Salesperson Assisted[b]			
Vendor-driven demand creation	X	X	X	X	X	X
Strong brand equity	X	X	X	X	X	X
World-class logistics	X	X	X	X	X	X
Competitive price performance	X	X	X	X	X	X
High-quality products	X	X	X	X	X	X
"Easy-to-access" service and support	X	X	X	X	X	X
Attractive channel programs		X	X	X	X	X
Excellent merchandising		X	X	X	X	X
Well-targeted product bundle		X	X	X	X	X
Retailer training programs			X	X	X	X
Attractive packaging	X					
Well-balanced product line						X
Channel-specific products	X					

[a]Wal-Mart, Target, Kmart, etc.
[b]Sears, Montgomery Ward, etc.

Source: Adapted from a presentation given at Northwestern University by Adam Hanin, Gemini Consulting, Inc.

of *search-shopping* activity the consumer is willing to undertake. For example, convenience goods should require little effort to obtain, whereas considerable effort may be required to secure highly regarded, relatively scarce specialty goods. Consequently, there are strategic location implications in the product line variety and assortment strategies retailers pursue.

Consumer search-shopping behavior varies between consumer segments as well as between product categories. It also varies over time as demographic and life-style changes occur across market segments. For example, the tendency has been toward less search-shopping activity. The typical consumer visits only one store and rarely more than two. Significantly, such patterns seem to be true even for a variety of shopping goods where comparisons among brands are required. Time saved is becoming as important as money saved. This factor, along with widespread access and exposure to multiple media, is reducing both shopping frequency as well as the necessity of searching for information.

The implications of these observations are profound, because they mean that although location decisions remain critical, the dominant consideration in consumer choice is convenience, usually defined in terms of ease and speed of access. If and when home shopping is truly perfected, it could mean that, for a very significant segment of the population, outlet location will be a non-issue. Assisting consumers in removing stress from the acquisition and consumption process by eliminating tasks (called "streamlining") may overwhelm "location" as a strategic variable in retailers' minds. Indeed, for a number of suppliers of goods and services, retail outlets may become superfluous in a multimedia, interactive world.[4] We return to this topic later in this chapter.

CUSTOMER SERVICE   Virtually all major retail innovations of the twentieth century have relied, to greater or lesser degrees, on manipulating the services variable. The principle is easy to appreciate when we consider such services as in-store sales help. When retailers drop the "friendly" behind-the-counter sales assistant who helps customers locate and compare merchandise and is available for "expert" advice, the whole locate–compare–select process is shifted to the consumer. For suppliers, the change from in-store assistance to self-service on the part of retailers is a major reason for shifting from a "push" strategy to a "pull" strategy.

Retailing is one of the few remaining industries that is highly labor intensive, even though it is becoming less so. Payroll expenses are in the neighborhood of 30% of sales for the higher-priced/higher-service department stores, such as Bloomingdale's. For specialty stores, they are even higher—approximately 35% of sales.[5] Contrast these numbers to Wal-Mart and Home Depot; their operating expenses (which include *all* expenses to operate their companies, not just payroll) are 20% or less. Hence, the savings that can be passed on to the consumer by eliminating certain kinds of in-store assistance and/or improving the productivity of a down-sized work force are usually substantial.

The same is true for delivery functions, but the principle is not immediately apparent for services like customer credit. The fact is, besides the cost of risk and the cost of administering credit plans, the retailer also incurs the cost of holding (in a financial sense) the consumer's purchases for the duration of the credit period. It

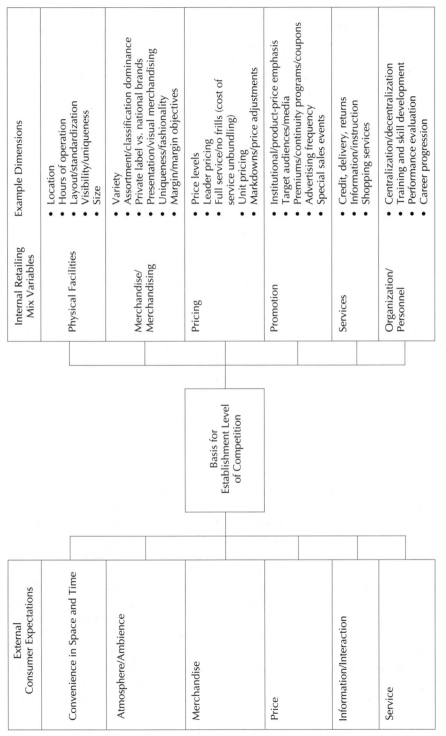

External Consumer Expectations		Internal Retailing Mix Variables	Example Dimensions
Convenience in Space and Time		Physical Facilities	• Location • Hours of operation • Layout/standardization • Visibility/uniqueness • Size
Atmosphere/Ambience		Merchandise/ Merchandising	• Variety • Assortment/classification dominance • Private label vs. national brands • Presentation/visual merchandising • Uniqueness/fashionality • Margin/margin objectives
Merchandise	Basis for Establishment Level of Competition	Pricing	• Price levels • Leader pricing • Full service/no frills (cost of service unbundling) • Unit pricing • Markdowns/price adjustments
Price		Promotion	• Institutional/product-price emphasis • Target audiences/media • Premiums/continuity programs/coupons • Advertising frequency • Special sales events
Information/Interaction		Services	• Credit, delivery, returns • Information/instruction • Shopping services
Service		Organization/ Personnel	• Centralization/decentralization • Training and skill development • Performance evaluation • Career progression

FIGURE 2-2 **Building a Retail Marketing Strategy.**
Source: William R. Davidson, Daniel J. Sweeney, and Ronald W. Stampfl, *Retailing Management*, 5th ed. Copyright ⁼ 1984 by John Wiley & Sons, Inc. Reprinted by permission of John Wiley & Sons, Inc.

takes little imagination to visualize the considerable savings it would mean for operations like Sears to be able to reduce the period for which credit is allowed without charge. Successful operations are built not on transferring "savings" for the sake of savings, however, but on being able to identify the functions that customers are willing to assume and the cost in time, money, effort, and convenience at which taking them on becomes attractive.

Although the basic dimensions of competition in retailing just discussed are key to understanding why retailing establishments run the gamut from small "mom and pop" stores and vending machines to enormous hypermarkets, many others play an important role in determining the character of retailing enterprises. The totality of retailing variables is portrayed in Figure 2-2. These variables permit retailers to map effective strategies for meeting consumer expectations.

▶ STRATEGIC ISSUES IN RETAILING IN THE UNITED STATES

From a marketing channel design and management perspective, suppliers attempting to sell their products to ultimate consumers for personal consumption must understand the major strategic issues concerning retailers. Using the United States as a case example, we focus below on the dominance of so-called "power retailers," the increasing polarity of retailing, the growing influence of retailers over the marketing of packaged goods, the impact of private brands, the importance of convenience, the impact of information technology, the essential nature of positioning to retailers, and the potential of home shopping. Throughout this discussion we point out the lessons suppliers must learn if they are to build successful relationships with retailers.

The Dominance of "Power Retailing"

Power retailing is not restricted to one type of retailing format even though it is a term that is most frequently applied to retailers of general merchandise (soft goods [e.g., apparel, linens] and hard goods [e.g., appliances, hardware] as opposed to food.) It is populated by specialty stores (e.g., The Limited, Nordstrom, Toys"R"Us); discount stores (e.g., Wal-Mart, Target); and electronic superstores (e.g., Circuit City, Sears' Brand Central, Best Buy). Apart from the most significant factor—a sharp definition of their customers and what they want—the attributes that make power retailers so successful are (1) a willingness to take risks via market testing and trend forecasting; (2) ordering early and selling merchandise in high volume, with a consistent emphasis on generating high gross margin returns on inventory investment (GMROI); (3) investing enormous sums in information systems that can deliver to an executive's desk instant sales-trend data from across a large geographic area and multiple locations; (4) a commitment to delivering value so that the price a customer pays is always perceived as fair and commensurate with the promise of the store; and (5) an old-fashioned emphasis on customer service so that shopping is made easier for generally time-impoverished customers.

These retailers generate superior financial performance, high productivity,

TABLE 2-1 **Return on Owners' Investments for Selected Power Retailers, 1993**

STORES	INVESTMENT RETURN (%)
Apparel specialty stores	
The Gap	22.9
The Limited	16.0
Consumer electronic stores	
Circuit City	18.6
Best Buy	13.3
Department stores	
May Co.	21.0
Kohl's	20.6
Nordstrom	12.0
Dillard's	11.6
Discount stores	
Wal-Mart	20.9
Venture	20.6
Family Dollar	19.2
Dollar General	18.6
Home improvement	
Home Depot	16.3
Lowe's	15.5
Miscellaneous stores	
Service Merchandise	29.5
Toys "R" Us	15.3
Williams-Sonoma	11.8
Blockbuster Entertainment	11.5

Source: The First National Bank of Chicago, *1994 Retailing Industry Statistical Review*, (Chicago, IL: The First National Bank of Chicago, 1994), pp. 40, 41, 42, 43, 48, 50.

strong consumer franchises, and sustained competitive advantage. Returns on investment (ROIs) close to or in excess of 15% are common, as shown in Table 2-1.

A number of these retailers concentrate on building dominant or so-called "power" assortments of merchandise so that consumers know, prior to undertaking shopping trips, that they will almost always find what they need at the outlets of the retail chain. Sometimes these assortments are broad and deep (such as those provided by IKEA in furniture and Toys"R"Us in toys); at other times, they are focused, such as those provided by Victoria's Secret, The Gap, or Crate & Barrel. Frequently, the focused assortment programs of power retailers are supported by strong private-label programs, which give added value to their merchandise while making them appear unique.

The assortments of some of the power retailers have so much clout that the stores stocking them have become known as "category killers." Oftentimes, these "killers" are discounters who specialize in one product area, such as toys, electronics, or books, offering wider selections and steeper price cuts. They include such companies as Barnes & Noble and Borders, Inc., two book superstore chains; Streamers, a discount party-supply chain; Sports-Mart, a sporting goods chain;

Circuit City and Tandy's Incredible Universe, two consumer electronics and major appliance discounters; Home Depot, a homecenter chain focused mainly on home improvement products and services; F&M, a health and beauty aids discounter; and, of course, Toys"R"Us. The assortments of the "killers" are so deep and so low-priced relative to those of other, more traditional retailers that consumers are willing to make special trips to purchase individual items there. In fact, consumers forego the low-price, one-stop shopping convenience of Wal-Mart and Target (whose assortments are generally broad but not deep) in favor of the "category killers."[6]

The Increasing Polarity of Retailing

There are two major trends in retailing that have typified the increasing polarity of retail trade (See Figure 2-3). The first trend is the growth of limited line, tightly managed, highly focused specialty store chains, such as The Gap, Body Shop, Eddie Bauer, and Anne Taylor. Many of these chains can be categorized as "power retailers" because they feature deep assortments. They also meet the service needs of customers on a personalized basis, the so-called "high-touch" retailers.

The second trend is the growth of very large stores (in terms of square footage), which oftentimes rely on warehouse technology and self-service to move massive amounts of merchandise at very low margins. Although discount stores such as Kmart, Wal-Mart, Target, and Caldor have traditionally been viewed as "high-tech" retailers, other, more extreme high-turnover/low-margin/massive-volume retailers have come along in the form of home centers (e.g., Home Depot, Handy Andy, and Builders Square [owned by Kmart]) and warehouse clubs (e.g., Price/Costco stores, Sam's Wholesale Clubs [owned by Wal-Mart]), and office supply superstores (Staples, Office Club, and Office Depot).

Although warehouse clubs and office supply superstores were basically established to serve small business customers (thereby making them wholesalers, not

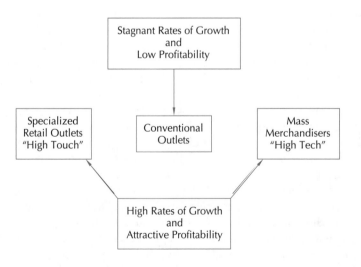

FIGURE 2-3   The polarity of retail trade.

retailers), a significant portion of their trade comes from consumers buying for personal consumption. By carrying only the most popular item in a merchandise category, warehouse clubs strive to achieve high turnover (18 to 20 turns per year) with gross margins as low as 8%–10%. Unlike normal discount retailers, which might carry 80,000 items, a warehouse club's range is usually limited to about 4,000. Their retail and wholesale customers must be so price sensitive that they are willing to sacrifice convenience, brand loyalty, merchandise consistency, and individual packaging for lower prices.

On the "high-touch" side, a number of specialty store chains have been very successful. As Walter K. Levy points out, many specialty store chains have done well because they have been better able or more willing to:

1. Respond to the increasing pluralism of our society and the resulting fragmentation of shoppers by fashion attitude, life-style, and purchase motivation.

2. Assemble and present dominant assortments that encapsulate shopper needs within a narrow niche, whether defined on the basis of classification, end-use, or life-style.

3. Package highly synergistic assortments in a point-of-sale environment that is compelling and also highly sympathetic with the merchandise.

4. Take risks in creating new trading vehicles and own-label merchandise to exploit emerging market niches or those not well developed by conventional retailers.

5. Employ an entrepreneurial approach.[7]

On the high-tech side, the warehouse clubs are facing market saturation and intensified competition. The power retailers mentioned above pose one set of problems, because they have well-informed salespeople to advise on selection and carry competitively priced products. Also, club operators, buoyed by their early success, opened up new outlets at a formidable rate. This led to congestion in certain geographical regions. The result has been tremendous consolidation in the industry—in the 1990s, Price Club merged with Costco to combat Wal-Mart's Sam's Club,[8] and Kmart exited the business. (In the process, Kmart sold 91 of its 113 Pace Division stores to Sam's.) Price/Costco and Sam's now control 90% of the warehouse club industry.

Similarly, electronic superstores, such as Crazy Eddie, Highland, Newmark & Lewis, Silo, and Fretters, have taken their lumps, primarily because they have bumped heads so violently in every major market. (The recession of the early 1990s didn't help, either.) Almost all of these firms have gone bankrupt or merged. The situation was exacerbated by Montgomery Ward's entry with Electric Avenue and Sears' entry with Brand Central into an already over-crowded field in the late 1980s. Best Buy, another major chain, has been particularly aggressive with its self-service, heavy discounting orientation. One major survivor in the bloodbath has been Circuit City, based in Richmond, Virginia, because they appear to have the best distribution system. "Basically, they realize they are selling a commodity, and they have to push that commodity through the system at the lowest possible cost."[9]

Another high-tech winner has been Home Depot, the Atlanta, Georgia-based homecenter operator.

Home Depot's outlets have all the charm of a freight yard and predictably low prices. But they also offer unusually helpful customer service. Although warehouse retailing looks simple, it is not: As discounting cuts into gross profit margins, the merchant must carefully control buying, merchandising, and inventory costs. Throwing in service, which is expensive and hard to systematize, makes the job even tougher. In the do-it-yourself (DIY) segment of the industry . . . Home Depot is the only company that has successfully brought off the union of low prices and high service.[10]

A further example on the high-tech, warehouse-technology side of the pole is IKEA, the Scandinavian retailer that operates one of the world's largest volume furniture chains. IKEA designs and sells solely from its own 200,000-sq. ft. stores a wide range of inexpensive furniture and accessories. Most items come boxed and must be assembled at home. IKEA stores combine furniture showroom and warehouse. With minimal sales staff, customers select furniture in the warehouse and wheel their choices on a heavy cart to a checkout hall. The system hinges on knockdown design, which enables most of the company's 12,000 products to be sold in packages that can fit in a car. Prices are usually 20% to 40% below competitive offerings.[11] IKEA's attractiveness to consumers is so strong that Home Depot (which carries only items for which it can be the dominant supplier) walked away from a profitable $80 million business in unfinished furniture because it could not unseat IKEA as the industry leader.[12]

Another entrant to the high-tech side of the polarity in the U.S. is the supercenter. Supercenters are mammoth 160,000-sq. ft. boxes. They house a full supermarket along with a discount store and are approximately one-third bigger than a regular discount store. All three of the major discount chains—Wal-Mart, Kmart, and Target—are investing in the concept, although both Wal-Mart and Kmart are further along than Target. Regional chains, like Michigan-based Meijer Inc. and Oregon-based Fred Meyer, are also building similar stores. Questions remain, however, about whether consumers will be attracted, in sufficient number, to such massive outlets to shop for both general merchandise and food at the same time. It is also not entirely clear what kind of productivity and distribution gains will be forthcoming by combining the two types of merchandise (e.g., meat and produce with sporting goods). Also, the discounters have had little experience with perishables or prepared foods. (Wal-Mart's purchase of McLane, a food wholesaler, in 1991 was a very important step toward acquiring this expertise.)

Caught in the middle and slammed on either side by specialty stores and by price-oriented, volume-driven outlets are the "all things to all people" department stores, variety stores, "conventional" supermarkets, traditional drugstores, and hardware stores. Only a few department store chains have escaped the crunch exerted by retailers on both sides of them. One is Dillard Department Stores, which has primarily concentrated its efforts in secondary markets where competition isn't as fierce. Through a highly centralized operation, it has developed an elaborate, much-envied management information and control system that provides hourly updates on sales and inventories in each store's departments.

Another firm that hasn't allowed itself to get caught in the middle is May Co. Similar to Dillard, May has built a strong department store company by appealing to mainstream tastes and applying centralized controls. For example, weekly reports from headquarters dictate which items the stores and their ads must emphasize. May's approximately 300 department stores operate mostly as parts of strong regional chains like Hecht's in Washington, Kaufmann's in Pittsburgh, Foley's in Texas, and Filene's in the Northeast. These chains tend to stock popular but moderately priced labels like Liz Claiborne and Chaus in women's apparel, Arrow and Van Heusen in men's shirts, and Estee Lauder in cosmetics. Instead of stressing a chic image and designer goods, the stores push brands that appeal to a loyal middle-class clientele.[13]

Even though there are examples of "winners" who have remained in the "middle," it is very important to note that the winners have also changed dramatically over time. First, they have centralized a lot of management functions and maintained close control over expenses. Second, they have all downsized departments in which they no longer can deliver a differential advantage to their customers. Very few department store chains devote enormous amounts of floor space to toys, sporting goods, or major appliances, for example. Third, because of the more focused nature of their assortments and the way in which they have remodeled their stores, they resemble a series of specialty stores under one roof rather than a "traditional" department store. In fact, many of the stores that are usually put into the "department store" category are, in actuality, departmentalized specialty stores, and a number of them do exceedingly well (e.g., Nordstrom, Lord & Taylor, and Burdine's, to name a few). Not surprisingly, the department store industry continues to consolidate at a rapid rate. For example, the acquisition of R.H. Macy & Co. by Federated Department Stores, Inc. in 1994 brought all of the stores listed below under one corporate "roof."

Macy's (**$6.3 billion**)

111 Macy's and Bullock's department stores
12 I. Magnin specialty stores
65 Aeropostale apparel stores
29 Charter Club apparel stores

Federated (**$7.2 billion**)

35 Abraham & Straus/Jordan Marsh
  stores
16 Bloomingdale's stores
39 Bon Marche stores
44 Burdines stores
50 Lazarus stores
25 Rich's/Goldsmith's stores
21 Stern's stores

As reported in the *Wall Street Journal,*

> . . . the union was viewed by many in the industry as inevitable in a persistently tough environment that has already forced many retailers into bankruptcy. Since the 1980s, department stores have increasingly been forced to consolidate or die because of heavy debt loads as well as shifting shopping patterns and stiff competition from discounters such as Wal-Mart Stores Inc. and specialty retailers such as Gap Inc.[14] Listed among the missing are Korvettes, Ohrbach's, Gimbels, Wieboldt, Goldblatt's, Bonwit Teller, B. Altman, Garfinckels, and Alexander's, among others.

From a marketing-channels perspective, the merger gave the combined company enormous power to squeeze the best deals from suppliers already pressured by the industry's consolidation. This clout allows Federated-Macy to compete even more strongly with May Department Stores, which, until the merger, had been the number one department-store chain with sales of $11 billion in 1993. May is known for its hard-nosed tactics in dealing with suppliers.[15]

Statistics support the overall story of the polarity of retailing. For the top 50 general merchandise retailers, the share of business taken by department stores shrank from 26% in 1982 to 19% in 1992, whereas specialty retail chains grew from 11% to 21% and discounters grew from 27% to 41%. The biggest decline was, however, experienced by variety stores and old line general-merchandise stores, which died in droves during the decade. They dropped to a 19% share from 36% in 1982.[16]

The Increasing Power of Retailers in the Marketing Channels for Packaged Goods

Packaged-goods manufacturers (makers of branded health and beauty aids, and packaged foods and beverages) are, arguably, the smartest marketing people in the world. At one time, the Procter & Gambles, Colgates, Krafts, and Cloroxes dominated retailers; now the retailers tend to dominate them. How could such a thing happen to such intelligent people?

The reasons for this reversal are many and diverse. First, the sales of most items normally sold through grocery, drug, and mass-merchandising chains have not been increasing at rapid rates in the aggregate. This means that if these retailers are to grow, they must take sales away from their competitors rather than waiting for overall demand to expand. Competition has, therefore, evolved into a market share game. This has created enormous pressure on retailers to perform, and given that most chains tend to carry the same products, the type of competition that has consumed them has tended to be price oriented. In other words, better prices (coupled with excellent locations, appealing stores, and reasonable service) have been the major routes to survival and success in this arena. It is little wonder, then, that the chains have increasingly begun to pressure suppliers (sometimes unmercifully) for price concessions, as we shall see in the paragraphs that follow.

Food stores, in particular supermarket chains, still remain the major outlets for packaged goods. Over the past decade, however, warehouse clubs, deep-discount drugstores (e.g., Drug Emporium, F&M Distributors Inc.), and mass merchants (discount stores, primarily) have been growing more rapidly than food stores. Although none of these so-called "alternative formats" to the supermarket can match the supermarket in terms of variety and assortment of grocery items, they have been able to expand at the expense of the supermarket. According to a report by McKinsey & Company, Inc.:

> Most of these (alternative) formats offer a distinctive "value proposition" (i.e., level of consumer benefits and price) that has found a favorable niche with customers. Each of these formats does use value pricing as one component of its value proposition, but other aspects—such as unique item availability, an exciting shopping experience, and strong customer service—also play roles that vary by format.[17]

Given the fact that supermarket profit ratios (net profits-to-sales) are razor thin to begin with (i.e., in the vicinity of 1%), any loss of sales to alternative formats, especially from heavy buyers (such as household heads of large families), could be disastrous. Now that Wal-Mart, Kmart, and Target are investing in supercenters, the lives of food stores are being made even more miserable. Although their power has been diminished by the new entrants, the pressure they feel is being immediately transmitted back up the channel to suppliers. The long-term solution for supermarkets is, however, not going to come via squeezing suppliers, but on meeting the needs of consumers. There is some convincing evidence that the supermarkets of the 1990s are inadequate to serve the evolving needs of consumers in the twenty-first century.[18]

Second, retailers are, as we have pointed out earlier, continuously concerned with improving their productivity. Given the competitive environment, it is virtually impossible for grocery retailers to raise prices, but it is not impossible to find ways to lower costs. They are always trying to achieve economies of scale while simultaneously providing their time-impoverished customers with the convenience of one-stop shopping. Consequently, they have built larger and larger stores, thereby elevating their fixed costs. This has created higher breakeven points, forcing supermarket and mass merchandisers (such as discount stores) to place even greater emphasis on the need to generate enormous sales volumes.

The resulting competition for store traffic has led to consolidation. For example, in 26 out of 50 major markets, the three leading grocery chains in each market control at least 50% of "all commodity volume" (ACV).[19] Because competition in retailing is a highly local phenomenon, these figures indicate that suppliers seeking to sell their wares in these markets don't have a great many alternatives. They must either play ball with the big boys or fade away.

Third, there is more and more pressure on retail buyers as a result of the increased pressures on the companies in which they are employed. At one time, buyers focused primarily on purchasing and maintaining balanced inventories. Now, they are profit centers that are also responsible for capital management, service levels, turnover, retail margins and pricing, quality control, competitiveness and variety, operating costs, shelf space and position, and vendor float and terms.[20] In order to help their companies make money, they look for suppliers to give them lots of price breaks and support, and they become very upset when those price breaks and support aren't forthcoming.[21]

Fourth, the buyers couldn't get nearly as upset as they do if they only had a few products from a few companies from which to choose. But, in addition to the already enormous numbers of products and brands available, thousands upon thousands of new products are being offered to buyers each year. For example, in 1994 alone, 20,076 health, beauty, household, food, and pet products were presented to supermarket buyers for authorization.[22] This quantity is more than the total number of items carried in many supermarkets. And the historical new-product success rate is only 10%, mainly because 70% of the new products are really not new at all, but merely different varieties, formulations, sizes, or packages of existing brands. Add together the facts that (1) shelf space has not increased as rapidly as the number of new products offered to buyers, (2) the number of buying points are declining, and (3) the retail marketplace is consolidating. The result is that the power of retailers over suppliers is growing at a rapid rate. And we're not through telling the story yet.

Fifth, information technology has diffused throughout retailing to such an extent that virtually all of the major retailers can capture item-by-item data, via scanning devices, at their electronic point-of-sale terminals. Many more of the uses and impacts of information technology are addressed in Chapter 9 and a few more later in this chapter. Suffice it to say here that the knowledge gained from this information has permitted retailers to calculate the direct product profitability (DPP) of individual items, track what moves and doesn't move in their stores, engage in forward investment buying, and leverage suppliers. The decade of the 1990s represents the first decade in retailing history in which retailers have more information about particular items than manufacturers.

Although other events have transpired to buttress the influence of retailers, the final one we shall mention here is the proclivity of suppliers to fan the flames. We have already mentioned the rush to introduce lots of new products (many of which are not new at all). In addition, manufacturers have engaged in a never-ending escalation of new product price and promotional allowances as a way of "bribing" their way onto retailers' shelves. These activities merely play into the hands of already powerful buyers. (See Exhibit 2-2 and Table 2-2 for descriptions and objectives of various trade deals.)

▶ **EXHIBIT 2-2 / Description of Trade Deals for Consumer Nondurable Goods**

▶ ▶ ▶

1. *Off invoice.* The purpose of an off-invoice promotion is to discount the product to the dealer for a fixed period of time. It consists of a temporary price cut, and when the time period elapses, the price goes back to its normal level. The specific terms of the discount usually require performance, and the discount lasts for a specified period (e.g., 1 month). Sometimes the trade can buy multiple times and sometimes only once.

2. *Bill-back.* Bill-backs are similar to off-invoice except that the retailer computes the discount per unit for all units bought during the promotional period and then bills the manufacturer for the units sold and any other promotional allowances that are owed after the promotional period is complete. The advantage from the manufacturer's position is the control it gives and guarantees that the retailer performs as the contract indicates before payment is issued. Generally, retailers do not like bill-backs because of the time and effort required.

3. *Free goods.* Usually free goods take the form of extra cases at the same price. For example, buy 3 get 1 free is a free-goods offer.

4. *Cooperative advertising allowances.* Paying for part of the dealers' advertising is called cooperative advertising, which is often abbreviated as co-op advertising. The manufacturer either offers the dealer a fixed dollar amount per unit sold or offers to pay a percentage of the advertising costs. The percentage varies depending on the type of advertising run. If the dealer is prominent in the advertisement, than the manufacturer often pays less, but if the manufacturer is prominent, then he pays more.

5. *Display allowances.* A display allowance is similar to cooperative advertising allowances. The manufacturer wants the retailer to display a given item when a price

promotion is being run. To induce the retailer to do this and to help defray the costs, a display allowance is offered. Display allowances are usually a fixed amount per case, such as 50 cents per case.

6. *Sales drives.* For manufacturers selling through brokers or wholesalers, it is necessary to offer incentives. Sales drives are intended to offer the brokers and wholesalers incentives to push the trade deal to the retailer. For every unit sold during the promotional period, the broker and wholesaler receive a percentage or fixed payment per case sold to the retailer. It works as an additional commission for an independent sales organization or additional margin for a wholesaler.

7. *Terms or inventory financing.* The manufacturer may not require payment for 90 days, thus increasing the profitability to the retailer who does not need to borrow to finance inventories.

8. *Count-recount.* Rather than paying retailers on the number of units ordered, the manufacturer does it on the number of units sold. This is accomplished by determining the number of units on hand at the beginning of the promotional period (count) and then determining the number of units on hand at the end of the period (recount). Then, by tracking orders, the manufacturers know the quantity sold during the promotional period. (This differs from a bill-back because the manufacturer verifies the actual sales in count-recount.)

9. *Slotting allowances.* Manufacturers have been paying retailers funds known as slotting allowances to receive space for new products. When a new product is introduced the manufacturer pays the retailer X dollars for a "slot" for the new product. Slotting allowances offer a fixed payment to the retailer for accepting and testing a new product.

10. *Street money.* Manufacturers have begun to pay retailers lump sums to run promotions. The lump sum, not per case sold, is based on the amount of support (feature advertising, price reduction, and display space) offered by the retailer. The name comes from the manufacturer's need to offer independent retailers a fixed fund to promote the product because the trade deal goes to the wholesaler.

Source: Robert C. Blattberg and Scott A Neslin; *Sales Promotion: Concepts, Methods, and Strategies* (Englewood Cliffs, NJ: Prentice-Hall, Inc., 1990), pp. 318–319.

By the late 1980s, the amount of money spent on trade promotions exceeded the amount of money spent on media advertising.[23] By 1992, 48% of all promotional expenditures was spent on trade promotion versus 29% for media advertising and 23% for consumer promotions.[24] Buyers who received these "deals" grew to love them, nurture them, and eventually, to insist on them as a price of doing business. According to one source, between 1,800 and 2,000 promotional deals are available to buyers at any given time, and between 70% and 90% of all shipments of grocery products to grocers' warehouses are on deal.[25]

The end result of all of these factors and forces is that, for chain buyers, the concept of "value added" has become a euphemism for "let's get as much as we can out of our suppliers." It has been activated by such things as:

- forward buying on deals

- slotting allowances

▶ **TABLE 2-2   Objectives of Trade Deals for Nondurable Goods**

	OBJECTIVES[a]					
Tactics	1	2	3	4	5	6
Off invoice	x	x	x	x	x	
Bill-back	x	x	x	x	x	
Free goods	x		x			
Cooperative advertising	x				x	x
Display allowances	x				x	
Sales drives	x	x				
Slotting allowances		x	x			
Street money	x				x	

[a]Objectives:
1 Retailer merchandising activities.
2 Loading the retailer.
3 Gaining or maintaining distribution.
4 Obtain price reduction.
5 Competitive tool.
6 Retailer "goodwill."

Source: Robert C. Blattberg and Scott A. Neslin, *Sales Promotion: Concepts, Methods, and Strategies* (Englewood Cliffs, NJ: Prentice-Hall, 1990), p. 321.

- failure fees

- payment for participation in newspaper inserts

- deepest case allowances possible

- highest possible payments for displays and even shelf placements

- no-cost new item introductions

- guaranteed returns at full retail

- invoice deductions for late coupon redemption reimbursements

- manufacturer-supplied labor for shelf sets[26]

So as not to engage in overkill (or to induce tears), we will only explain the first three items listed above and leave the rest to the reader's imagination.

FORWARD BUYING ON DEALS   Campbell Soup Co. sometimes sells as much as 40% of its annual chicken noodle soup production to wholesalers and retailers in just 6 weeks. What happens is that wholesalers and retailers (sometimes called "the trade") place unusually large orders when Campbell gives them a 6% to 7% promotional discount. This strategy, known as *forward buying,* plays havoc with Campbell's and other packaged goods manufacturers' costs and marketing plans. When a manufacturer marks down a product by 10%, for example, it has become common practice for the trade to stock up with a 10 to 12 week supply. That means fewer products are purchased at list price after the promotion ends.

A related problem is *diverting*. When manufacturers offer a regional trade promotion on, say, the West Coast, some retailers and wholesalers will buy large volumes and then distribute some cases to stores in the Midwest where the discount isn't available. This practice upsets manufacturers' efforts to tailor marketing efforts to regions or neighborhoods.

SLOTTING ALLOWANCES   Slotting allowances originated in the 1970s as a way to compensate the grocery trade for all the costs of working a new product into their systems: creating a space or "slot" in the warehouse, revising computerized inventory systems, resetting the shelves to make a place in the store, and money to help defray the cost of stocking and restocking the item.[27] Because of the scarcity of shelf space, slotting allowances have grown astronomically. Suppliers paid $300 to $1,500 per new item in 1982; they will likely pay $3,000 to $40,000 before the year 2000.[28] For example, a 50-store chain with a slotting allowance of $100 per store would add $5,000 to the marketing budget of a manufacturer before a single case is shipped out the door. Because those manufacturers with solid track records of successful new-product introductions (such as Procter & Gamble and Kraft) refuse (or aren't being asked) to pay slotting allowances, there is some question as to whether, as indicated in Chapter 8, the allowances are a violation of the Robinson-Patman Act.

FAILURE FEES   Starting in April 1989, J. M. Jones Co., a wholesaling unit of Super Valu Stores Inc., began imposing a fee when it had to pull a flop from its warehouses. If a new product doesn't hit a minimum sales target within 3 months, Jones withdraws it and charges $2,000 for the effort.[29] Although the practice of charging failure fees is not widespread, it is simply another indication of who is in control in the channel of distribution for packaged goods.

Besides experiencing horror, fear, and tremors, what have suppliers done to respond to these developments? The section after next provides some examples. But be forewarned that the battle is far from over. What should the suppliers do? Clearly, they must invest more in research and development in order to differentiate their products. Basically, it will be extremely difficult for them to get out of the box in which they find themselves unless they innovate. With me-too, parity products in mature markets facing a consolidating trade, the future is not likely to be a happy one. And, if anything, the trade will get even more powerful as it becomes more sophisticated in reading all of the numbers coming out of its front-end scanners.

The Broadened Role and Impact of Private Branding

There is some debate as to whether private branding on the part of retailers is increasing or decreasing. Years ago, some retailers—notably Sears, J.C. Penney, Montgomery Ward, and A&P—wedded themselves to private labels as a way of generating loyalty to their stores (rather than to the manufacturers' brands they carried) and of earning extra profits (as private-label merchandise generally affords retailers higher gross margins than comparable branded merchandise). Private labels have always been used to provide consumers with extra value, but they have also usually come in "plain vanilla." In other words, they were money-saving but unexciting alternatives relative to the pizazz of national, heavily advertised brands.

Now, however, a number of retailers are upgrading their private-label programs in order to offer an even-more-direct alternative to what branded suppliers have to offer. A private brand is one that is owned or controlled through contract rights by a retailing company, an affiliated group of retailers, or a buying organization (e.g., Federated-Allied Merchandising Services and Frederick Atkins, Inc.). There are five basic categories of private brands: (1) store-name identification programs (products bear the retailer's store name or logo, e.g., The Gap, Kroger, Ace, NAPA, Benetton); (2) retailer's own brand name identity program (a brand image independent of the store name that is available in only that company's stores, e.g., Forenza [The Limited], Boundary Waters Marketplace [Dayton-Hudson], Kenmore, Craftsman [Sears], True-Value, Tru-Test [Cotter & Co.], Valu-Rite [McKesson]); (3) designer-exclusive programs (merchandise designed and sold under a designer's name in an exclusive arrangement with the retailer, e.g., Halston III [J.C. Penney]); (4) other exclusive licensed name programs (celebrity-endorsed lines or other signature or character label lines developed under exclusive arrangements with the retailer, e.g., Allen Solly [Federated Department Stores], Cheryl Tiegs, McKids [Sears], Jaclyn Smith [Kmart]); and generic programs (goods that are essentially unbranded, e.g., Yellow pack no name [Loblaw], Cost Cutter [Kroger], Valu Time [Topco]).[30]

Increasingly, private brands of large retailing companies are being positioned as the "leading brand" in their assortment. Private brands are a route to gaining exclusivity, thereby permitting their purveyors to avoid direct price competition. Designer and other popular brands of clothes have become so widely distributed that every store in the mall seems to be carrying the same things. In order to distinguish itself from others, Macy's had, at one time, developed more than 50 in-house labels. The Limited's private labels represent 70% of its sales.[31] Indeed, it seems as though a number of highly successful specialty chains have made *themselves* the brand, for example, The Gap, Benetton, Brooks Brothers, and Stefanel.

On the surface, supermarkets and discount stores have a clear incentive for pushing their own offerings: private label goods typically cost consumers 10% to 20% less than other brands, but their profit margins typically run 10%–15% higher. For example, Cott Corporation, the largest supplier of private labelled soft drinks in North America (e.g., Sam's American Choice and Loblaws' President's Choice), has several advantages over Coke and Pepsi resulting in benefits to companies that sign its supply agreements. First, Cott's marketing and advertising expenses pale in comparison to Coke and Pepsi. Second, Cott piggybacks on retailers' centralized warehouse and distribution facilities rather than delivering on an expensive direct-to-store basis as do Coke and Pepsi. And third, the cost to bottlers of Cott concentrate is significantly less than that for Coke and Pepsi.[32] Sainsbury Classic Cola, which is bottled by Cott, accounts for over 60% of the cola sold by Britain's largest food retailer.

Although there has been a great deal of media attention given to the use of private brands by supermarkets, the reality is that, in 1993, they accounted for only 14.8% of total dollar supermarket sales. Furthermore, the percentage hasn't changed much over a relatively long period of time. (In comparison, approximately 20% of apparel purchases are private-label clothes.) For specific product classes, however, there are large deviations from the mean. According to Hoch and Banerji, private labels tend to do well in grocery categories where they offer quality comparable to national brands. (Surprisingly, high quality is much more important than lower price.) They also perform better in large dollar-volume categories offering high margins (e.g., paper goods, bleach). They do much worse in categories in which there are multiple national manufacturers investing lots of money in national advertising.[33]

The use of private branding has resulted in even greater power for the retailer in the channel of distribution. It has changed the character of manufacturer–retailer relationships in that there is more (1) retailer initiative or responsibility for fashion direction, trend setting, innovation, etc.; (2) retailer responsibility for marketing to consumers, as opposed to an orientation as a distributing agent for suppliers; and (3) strategic concern on the part of many suppliers on marketing to important retailers as opposed to direct concern with the consumer market.[34] Salmon and Cmar suggest that manufacturers of branded goods facing such trends ought to be sure that the fashion, features, quality, retail price, and overall appeal of their own brands represent at least fair value for the consumer compared with private labels, and, if this value is in doubt, they should be prepared to accept some immediate profit sacrifice for restoration of a favorable value comparison.[35] However, from a legal perspective, the situation is mixed. In 1994, a federal appeals court ruled that private labels can mimic national brand packaging without violating trademark law; in 1995, the Supreme Court ruled that companies may get trademarks for colors associated with their products, thereby shielding the products from imitation.[36]

On the other hand, private label is not a bed of roses for retailers. For apparel, in particular, developing and marketing a distinctive private label can be difficult, costly, and risky, especially if a store does not have the prestige of a Neiman-Marcus or a Saks Fifth Avenue. But the problem goes beyond the prestige factor. Even for upscale merchants, many private labels are uninspired in design, mainly because retailers generally have little talent in that part of the marketing process. Nevertheless, many of the larger apparel chains are putting their own labels on their best clothes.[37]

In addition, a private-label program can go too far. Private-label programs often must rely on a strong national-brand program in order for the value comparison to come alive to consumers.[38] When store brands soared to 35% of A&P's sales mix in the 1960s, shoppers, perceiving a lack of choice, defected to competitors. In the late 1980s, Sears began to add more brand-name goods so that it could begin to appeal to a broader base of customers for whom brands other than Sears' Kenmore, Craftsman, and DieHard were appealing.

Suppliers' Strategic Responses to the Growing Power of the Retail Sector

Taken together, the sections on power retailers, polarity issues, the packaged-goods situation, and private branding contain information sufficient to induce considerable heartburn on the part of suppliers. There can be little question that there is a shift in power to the retail level in virtually all lines of trade (e.g., food, apparel, electronics, etc.). Although much of the remainder of this text focuses on how managers can work successfully with their channels of distribution, it might be useful to provide some current examples of concrete steps that suppliers are taking to confront the situation facing them.

Perhaps the boldest, riskiest, and most highly publicized strategy adopted by any supplier was Procter & Gamble's 1992 decision to adopt "value pricing." As Edwin L. Artzt, Chairman and CEO of P&G explained at the time, value pricing means that "we're taking a portion of our trade dollars, along with savings from increasing system efficiency, to fund reduced list prices. This provides more consistent, reliable pricing day-in and day-out, with smaller deal-to-deal swings."[39] What this meant was that P&G wiped out much of the trade promotion allowances and discounting on 40% of its product line, including cake mixes, liquid laundry detergents, dishwashing liquids, fabric softener sheets, toilet tissue, and automatic dishwasher detergents. Instead, P&G reduced its list prices by 12 to 24% on nearly all of its U.S. brands and adopted a policy of "every day low (wholesale) prices." Artzt explained P&G's rationale for the move as follows:

> Over the past decade, as markets have matured, many manufacturers, including P&G, have resorted to short-term, deep-discount promotional deals to attract buyers.... Price cuts of 30–40% off the regular shelf price for short periods of time are not unusual. In this environment, a brand's loyal users—who buy the brand day in and day out and who account for the majority of purchases—are penalized as they regularly pay a higher price for their favorite brands.... These wide swings between deal and shelf pricing can create consumer confusion and doubt about a brand's true price and value.
>
> These swings also create variability and massive inefficiency in the manufacturing and distribution system. To meet heavy, short-term demand, manufacturers must build raw material inventory, design peaks and valleys into their production schedules, and build up finished inventory. In addition, the proliferation of deals creates potential pricing errors and rework. This is an inefficient way to do business ... Cash gets tied up, there are warehousing costs, excessive shipping rates, and handling costs.[40]

A number of retailers and wholesalers used to living off the money available from trade allowances were unhappy with P&G's decision. Rite-Aid drugstores, A&P, and Safeway, for example, pruned their variety of P&G sizes or eliminated marginal brands, such as Prell and Gleem. Super Valu, the largest wholesaler in the U.S., added surcharges to some P&G products and pared back orders, to compensate for the profits it says it lost under the new pricing system. And Certified Grocers, a Midwestern wholesaler, dropped about 50 of the 300 P&G varieties it stocked.[41] Nevertheless, P&G's strategy seems to be working, because most of its brands are holding their own—they are still number 1 or 2 in their categories.[42]

However, it should be pointed out that this kind of strategy may only work if a supplier has enough clout (e.g., the brands and stature) to back it up. In this sense, P&G may be a special case.

Another move that shook the marketing world was the April 2, 1993, announcement by Philip Morris Companies, Inc. that it was lowering the price of its Marlboro premium brand cigarette to fend off competition from rapidly growing lower-priced discount cigarettes. Marlboro raised its prices 9.6% a year for a decade and saw market share drop from 26.3% in 1989 to 22.2% in 1993. Private-label products grew to over 30% of the market.[43] What has transpired since Marlboro cut prices is that some manufacturers have followed suit by lowering prices on brands in product categories that are particularly vulnerable to private-brand competition.

Although the appeal to consumers of private-label brands can be, to some extent, traced to belt-tightening during the recessionary period in the early 1990s, it can also be traced to consumers' ability to be more discriminating about getting genuine value at all price levels. For example, car buyers did not desert Mercedes-Benz earlier in this decade for ordinary family cars but for marques such as Toyota's Lexus, which were comparably engineered and equipped. Other charge cards now offer more cheaply services once unique to American Express. The quality and service differences between many premium brands and private brands are simply not great enough to warrant significant price gaps.

This fact has caused a number of manufacturers to increase their spending on promotional support and advertising for products on which private labels are gaining share—Pillsbury (refrigerated dough), Coca-Cola (colas), Kellogg and General Mills (corn flakes and raisin bran).[44] Other strategies being used are (1) working with retailers to demonstrate that while private brands may have higher margins, they are not necessarily bigger profit contributors, especially if the national brand is store-delivered and the private brand is warehoused (e.g., soft drinks); (2) product innovation; (3) seeking efficiencies in promotion and operations by focusing on best-selling products and not necessarily an entire line; (4) cutting back on consumer couponing; and (5) streamlining logistics systems, making it easier for retailers to order and receive merchandise. And some suppliers have developed so-called "fighting brands"—P&G (Joy dishwashing detergent; Era liquid laundry detergent; Camay beauty soap), Miller Brewing (Miller High Life), and Kodak (Funtime, a new low-price film aimed at private brands).[45]

Some suppliers market different products and brands in different channels in order to avoid placing all their "eggs" in one basket (thereby becoming too dependent on, say, discount stores) and to serve the needs of different consumer segments. For example, Salton-Maxim sells its Salton brand in the discount chains. The Salton line includes products in the lower price range like $10 jewelry cleaners, curling wands, and brushes. Its Maxim line is made up primarily of elaborate tools for food preparation, such as its $250 bread maker. Those products are sold in department and specialty stores because they require detailed instruction.[46]

To some extent, the outlet store phenomenon, most prevalent in general merchandise categories like apparel, is a reaction to the power of retailers, even though retailers themselves are opening outlets as well (e.g., Nordstrom, Macy's, and Saks). Decades ago, manufacturers opened outlet stores near their factories and used them to unload "seconds" or imperfect goods, as well as merchandise that was over-produced or had been sent back unsold by retailers. But now, most of the merchandise in their outlet stores is flawless, deep in size and selection, and manufactured expressly for the outlet market. Sales in 1993 were $9.9 billion, about 2% of total retail sales. There are over 11,000 outlet stores nationwide.[47] Besides permitting manufacturers to utilize excess production capacity, the outlets are very profitable when compared to selling to retailers.

The trend has angered retailers who don't want their suppliers competing against them even if the merchandise varies. A few groups, like the National Sporting Goods Association and the National Shoe Association, have urged members to reduce or eliminate purchases from manufacturers establishing outlet stores. To appease the retailers, developers locate outlet malls outside major cities, in towns too small to maintain a strong retail industry. In addition, some apparel manufacturers keep their outlets stocked with clothes that are at least a season behind, giving their retailers a more up-to-date offering.

A final example of what suppliers are doing in reaction to the growth of retailer power (although certainly not the last that could be given) is the decision by many packaged goods manufacturers to sell to and support alternative format stores (warehouse clubs, mass merchandisers, and deep-discount drug chains). Although the growth of these alternate formats over the past decade has been tremendously appealing to these suppliers, the truth is that suppliers have been badly bruised by the slotting allowances, forward buying, and other practices engaged in by grocery stores. It might be argued that the suppliers are going from the frying pan into the fire, but, at this point at least, the punishment sustained at the hands of the alternate formats (e.g., making up special packs, setting up warehousing systems that permit shipment direct to stores) is less than the punishment sustained from the grocers.

The Increasing Importance of Convenience

Convenience is measured by the time required to make a purchase, including getting to and from the store, getting in and out of the store, and, where applicable, getting delivery of what you came to get. In survey after survey, consumers have indicated that speed and convenience are more important to them than price and that in order to assure themselves of achieving speed and convenience, they frequently prefer to wait on themselves.[48] In fact, many consumers are so convinced that self-service is the height of good service that they are willing to pay extra for the privilege (e.g., to use automatic teller machines or tap their own computers for desired databases). Consumers are often far more comfortable wrestling with electronic aides (e.g., touch-screen kiosks) than they are wrestling with inattentive, surly, and/or hard-to-find salespeople.[49]

On the other hand, when companies can really provide first-rate service—bold, fast, unexpected, innovative, and customized—they can achieve a remarkable differential advantage.[50] Outstanding retailing examples are Lexus in automobiles, Nordstrom in apparel, Home Depot in home improvement products, and Taco Bell in fast food.

Even in the absence of technological assistance, the drive to make life simpler (spurred by dual-income families or time-poor, increasingly wealthy singles) has spawned all sorts of convenience marketers, from child-care centers to maid services. The almost frantic growth of the convenience-store sector, fueled by the entry of petroleum marketers like Arco (with its AM/PM Stores); the continuing experiments with home shopping, home banking, and videotext services; the diversification of vending machine operators into food, clothing, and videotapes; and the increased share of the retailing market being taken by direct response marketing (e.g., telephone selling and direct mail advertising) are all testimony to the quest for convenience on the part of consumers. And, on top of all this, consumers are unwilling to trade quality for convenience, which means that delivering customer satisfaction at a profit—the main goal of marketers—is becoming more difficult to achieve.

The Growing Impact of Information Technology

Although information technology (IT) is one of the keys to enhancing convenience, it is also critical in improving in-store and delivery service, preventing out-of-stocks, and permitting retailers to configure their stores and develop assortments that are most pleasing to the consumers they are trying to satisfy. Because of the importance of information systems to the management of marketing channels, we devote an entire chapter (Chapter 9) to a discussion of them. Here, we shall touch briefly on some of the more notable examples of how IT is helping retailing become more productive and more responsive to consumer needs. According to Thomas Stewart,

> The most valuable links on the (value) chain tend to belong to people who own knowledge—particularly about customers . . . He who controls information in many cases controls the business.[51]

One of the major reasons for Wal-Mart's success has been its investment in state-of-the-art IT. The Wal-Mart electronic system consists of (1) front-end scanners that track store sales by stockkeeping unit (SKU) and monitor the supply on store shelves, (2) the beaming of store orders via satellite to a computer at headquarters in Bentonville, Arkansas, (3) the scheduling of shipments to Wal-Mart's distribution centers by vendors to satisfy Wal-Mart's needs, (4) the movement (via conveyors) of merchandise from the distribution centers into one of Wal-Mart's trucks, (5) the shelf placement of the merchandise within 36 hours of a store's order, and (6) communication via satellite about vendor discounts on merchandise.[52]

Perhaps Wal-Mart's most sophisticated distribution arrangement is with Procter & Gamble. Using disposable diapers as an example, P&G receives daily data by satellite on Wal-Mart's Pampers' sales and forecasts and ships orders automatically. As a result, Wal-Mart can maintain smaller inventories and, at the same time, reduce the number of times it runs out of Pampers.[53] Because of the speed of this system, Wal-Mart pays P&G for the Pampers *after* the merchandise passes over the scanners as the consumer goes through the checkout lane.

Dillard Department Stores, like Wal-Mart, has had a near-fanatical focus on IT. The most valuable feature of Dillard's system is its ability to get goods onto the selling floor faster than almost any other department store chain. The program is called Quick Response, and it means that basic items (e.g., men's dress shirts or ladies' lingerie) can be electronically reordered from the vendor every week, based on the previous week's sales, without human intervention. Goods that usually take a month to reorder and get into stores take only 12 days with Quick Response.[54]

J.C. Penney, the fourth-largest U.S. retailer, has installed video networks in 1,100 stores. When, for example, the company hears about fast-selling apparel items in West Germany, it has a picture transmitted to South Korea where a copy of the item is made up in a few days. Pictures of the item are beamed to the video screens in the company's stores. Orders for the items are then relayed back to South Korea.[55] The network helps cut weeks and perhaps even months off of the buying cycle for fashion goods.

Critical to all retailers is speedy, virtually automatic replenishment. As explained by Buzzell and Ortmeyer:

> Replenishment of basic merchandise begins with the electronic capture of sales information at the point-of-sale using UPC [Universal Product Code]-coded price tickets and scanning technology, which allow for instantaneous updating of inventory records. Periodically, the amount of inventory on hand of each stockkeeping unit (SKU) is compared with the amount specified in a "model stock" that is developed jointly by the supplier and the retailer for each individual store. The model stock for an item is usually based on its recent sales history, modified to take into account anticipated promotional activities and market trends. . . . The model stock quantity for an SKU is set at a level sufficient to cover expected demand, 95 percent of the time, between placement of an order and its arrival at the store.[56]

The drive to achieve continuous replenishment, quick response, or just-in-time deliveries (where shipments are timed to replace products just as they are sold off the shelf) is pervasive throughout retailing. A main goal is to reduce inventory carrying costs and the likelihood of stocking warehouses full of obsolete, out-of-date, or stale merchandise. But there is a down-side risk to such systems: stock-outs. Retailers are beginning to realize that these systems sometimes don't give them enough time to take advantage of surprise hits. This risk is a special problem for goods like toys, which are greatly subject to fad buying, especially during the relatively short Christmas season. Just-in-time helped create a near panic in 1993 as parents scrambled to find Power Rangers and other toys in short supply.[57]

Perhaps the most significant impact of the 1990 purchase of 75% of Southland Corp. (the parent of the 7-Eleven convenience store chain in the U.S.) by Ito-Yokado, a Japanese retail group and the parent of 7-Eleven Japan, will eventually be the technological improvements that the Japanese firm will transfer to the U.S. The key to success for 7-Eleven Japan is a $200 million information system that monitors inventory and tracks customer preferences. Clerks even key in the gender and approximate age of each customer to monitor buying patterns. Orders are transmitted instantly via satellite to distribution centers and manufacturers. Sales of specific products can be plotted against the hours of the day, days of the week, or whatever.[58] As a result, 7-Eleven Japan stocks some of its stores as often as three times a day; an order can be at a store within 8 hours of having been placed. This allows the stores to keep inventory small and ensure that the products are fresh. Anything that doesn't move is immediately discontinued; of the 3,000 items each franchisee carries, 70% are replaced annually. Indeed, its computerized system has permitted it to practice "micromarketing" (as discussed in the next section of this chapter) for over a decade.

A prerequisite for achieving the major benefits IT has to offer is the building of effective interorganizational links between retailers and their suppliers.[59] Although these links involve data, they go far beyond technology. Indeed, they require marketing channel partnerships, as pointed out in Chapter 1. For example, in the face of the severe pressures it faces, the grocery industry has committed itself to achieving total supply chain savings of $30 billion through something called "Efficient Consumer Response" or ECR.

> ECR is a grocery-industry strategy in which distributors and suppliers are working closely together to bring better value to the grocery consumer. By jointly focusing on the efficiency of the total grocery supply system, rather than the efficiency of individual components, they are reducing total system costs, inventories, and physical assets while improving the consumer's choice of high quality, fresh grocery products. The ultimate goal of ECR is a responsive, consumer-driven system in which distributors and suppliers work together as business allies to maximize consumer satisfaction and minimize cost.[60]

According to Buzzell and Ortmeyer, specific requirements for successful partnerships based on IT include:

- Adequate technologies, especially those needed for bar-coding, scanning, and electronic data interchange (EDI).

- Support by top management in both retailer and supplier firms.

- Adjustment in performance measures and reward systems for retail buyers and supplier salespeople.

- Agreement on objectives for a partnership and periodic review of actual results. Relevant measures include inventory turnover, shipment accuracy, order lead times, incidence of out-of-stock conditions, and the extent of markdowns in retail selling prices, among others.[61]

The Essential Nature of Positioning

The old joke in retailing circles used to be:

> *Question:*   What are the three most important factors making for success in retailing?
> *Answer:*   Location, location, location.

Although no one doubts that location is critical, nowadays we have to add three additional factors in order to complete the picture: positioning, positioning, positioning. Think of The Gap, The Limited, Tiffany's, Pier 1, the stores on Rodeo Drive in Beverley Hills, Publix Supermarkets and Burdine's Department Stores in Florida, Toys"R"Us, Stop 'N Go Convenience Stores, Waldenbooks, Benetton's 012, Egghead Inc., Tianguis Supermarkets in Southern California, Laura Ashley, Foot Locker, Gucci, and F.A.O. Schwartz. Although not all of these names are going to be familiar to all readers, we bet that you can immediately describe those stores with which you are familiar—and your description will not be vague (e.g., as if you were trying to tell someone about Carson Pirie Scott or The Broadway Stores or Woolworth.)

The reason why you will be efficient and accurate in your storytelling is that the companies running these stores have bent over backwards to make a clear statement to their consumers about what they are all about. They appeal to particular age, life-style, or interest groups. They have been configured and operated so as to deliver what they promise (even if the promise is very narrow). They do not confuse consumers by trying to be many things to everybody under one roof. And they are very, very conscious of the neighborhoods in which they market. In other words, they practice "micro" rather than "macro" or "mass" marketing.

This emphasis on positioning is obviously a manifestation of the polarity of trade phenomenon mentioned earlier. It is very similar to what packaged goods manufacturers have been practicing for years—target marketing. After all, a retailing concept can be equated to a product concept, but in retailing, the entire outlet makes a statement. Product assortment, ambience, pricing, sales clerks, location, and a host of retailing-related attributes go into the articulation of that statement.

Few retailing pundits would take exception to the statement that, with 15 separate divisions, The Limited, Inc. has been the quintessential example of this approach. By amassing a collection of specialty-apparel store concepts, each with different styles and price ranges, The Limited, Inc. has the impact of a department store in many malls. The positioning of its stores is laid out in Table 2-3. The Limited sells mainly sportswear to the "thirty-something" woman who wants fashion but isn't trendy and is concerned about price; Express is younger and more trendy in its orientation; Victoria's Secret sells what might be called flirtatious lingerie; Lane Bryant and Lerner Woman are dedicated to larger-sizes; Lerner is budget-priced; Henri Bendel is high-class, chic, and pricey; Abercombie & Fitch retails rugged sportwear for young men and women; Limited Too targets mothers seeking fashionable clothes for their young daughters; Structure provides European fashion at moderate prices for younger men; and Bath & Bodyworks focuses on women's toiletries, such as fragrances and soaps. Brylane is a catalogue operation. Victoria's Secret and Structure also have catalogue operations.

A few additional examples (among many that could be mentioned) of crisp positioning (sometimes called, even by retailers, "targeting") are:

- *Egghead, Inc.,* a Bothell, Washington-based software retailing chain. Egghead stores are typically located in shopping centers, often near a computer store. Like a bookstore,

TABLE 2-3   The Positioning of The Limited, Inc.'s Offerings

SIZES		PRICE POINTS			
	Budget	Popular		Better	Designer
		under 30	over 30	under 30	over 30
14 and under	Lerner	Express Structure Victoria's Secret	Limited Victoria's Secret	Abercrombie & Fitch	Henri Bendel
16 and over			Lane Bryant Lerner Woman Brylane		

hundreds of software titles are separated by category, such as entertainment, and by type of computer the programs will run on. Customers are allowed to try out the merchandise and can seek help from salespeople who must learn new programs every week.[62]

- *Pier 1 Imports Inc.,* a Fort Worth, Texas-based specialty home-furnishing chain. Its stores are piled to the rafters with pricey wicker settees, French stemware, and decorative Italian tables that appeal to the stores' customers—college-educated women between the ages of 25 and 44 who earn more than $35,000 a year.[63]

- *Tiffany,* the jewelry store chain. When Avon Products owned Tiffany from 1979 to 1984, the direct-selling cosmetics manufacturer broadened Tiffany's base of customers by adding low-priced products and trinkets. It was said at the time that "those in the know don't go to Tiffany for jewels anymore. It's for tourists." Since a management group bought Tiffany from Avon, the chain has made a remarkable comeback. The focus has been placed on highly paid working women who want striking pieces to wear at the office. To meet these needs, the stores now carry "medium-priced" gold jewelry accented with diamonds, costing $1,000 to $15,000. (Cartier, a major competitor, sells similar merchandise for $3,000 to $25,000.)[64]

What is becoming increasingly important to retailers in their efforts to position themselves to serve specific target markets is their ability to tailor each store to the neighborhoods in which the stores are located. Benetton S.p.A., the Italian clothing company, is a master at making each one of its stores conform to the demographic and life-style makeup of its locale. Another example is Burdines, Florida's largest department store chain, which understands that the Gulf Coast has attracted thousands of price-sensitive retirees who lead quiet lives, that the folks in the Panhandle are more like those in rural Alabama than Miami, that Central Florida has a Midwestern atmosphere, and that flashy Southeast Florida prides itself on having the latest fashions.[65] Another is Tianguis, a Southern California chain launched by Vons Cos. in 1987, whose stores are located in Hispanic neighborhoods. Tianguis has designed and managed its stores knowing that most Hispanics view shopping as an eagerly awaited social event and want to spend hours browsing and chatting. Hispanics want to eat while they shop and listen to music that reminds them of home.[66]

A final example is National Convenience Stores Inc.'s Stop 'N Go stores, which have been focused to target mainstream, upscale, and Hispanic neighborhoods. Stores in upper-income neighborhoods carry high-priced wines, publications such as *Vanity Fair,* gourmet pasta sauces, oat bran cereals, and Weight Watchers and Pritikin products. Stores in Hispanic areas stock an assortment of Spanish-language magazines, Mexican cooking items and candies. Stores in the company's core middle-class (mainstream) market carry more frozen and quick-to-prepare foods and a greater selection of bottled water.[67]

This kind of neighborhood-by-neighborhood positioning means that retailers must involve themselves in "micromarketing." Micromarketing entails (1) having data on each store's existing and potential customer base; (2) building assortments for each store based on a knowledge of the customer base's needs; (3) using targeted media to reach the customer base; (4) sponsoring events to reach local and ethnic markets; and (5) reaching customers while they are in the store, because they make most buying decisions while they're shopping.[68]

A necessary condition for practicing effective micromarketing is the building of a relevant customer database. One company, Arbeit & Company, Ltd. of New York, has worked out a segmentation approach and a consumer decision model that has been applied to retailers' neighborhood-by-neighborhood micromarketing opportunities. Arbeit calls the application "Guerilla Marketing." The methodology involves:

1. *Qualitative analysis.* Focus groups composed of a retailer's existing and potential customers are conducted.

2. *Quantitative analysis:*
    (a) Trading area definition. Shoppers' license plates are counted in the parking lots of the retailer's stores and competitors' stores. These data are processed and then fed through a national geodemographic model to define trading areas by census tract, and to determine the demographics of those tracts. The relative shopping use by consumers from each tract for each store in the trading area is also measured.
    (b) Values and life-styles. SRI's values and life-styles study of consumer "psychographics" is combined with the geodemographic model cluster definitions to provide a consumer VALS profile of each tract and, therefore, of each store's customers. A Simmons Storyfinder Analysis of diary panel data is employed to develop predictive product mixes for each segment.
    (c) Scanner data. The retailer's own scanner data are analyzed by store, by category, by product, and by brand to gain an understanding of the differences in product movement for each store.

From all of these data, clusters of consumers can be identified whose demographic, psychographic, and behavioral differences appear to explain differences in a store's product movement and its performance against the competition. The retailer's scanner data are then linked to the consumer segments. Understanding the differences in cluster composition among the individual store trading areas helps to explain differences in the performance of various departments, or even items within the departments.[69]

Recognizing the importance of targeting for neighborhoods, Wal-Mart is using its information infrastructure to customize merchandise for individual outlets. Forty regional buyers make sure that Portland, Oregon gets a different color palette in sheets and towels than Portland, Maine does. The company currently keeps track of 6,000 consumer purchasing variables—including such things as the times they buy. "The plan is to customize each linear foot of shelf space in each department in each store with goods in the right quantity at precisely the right time, and to advertise to a segment of one."[70]

The Potential of Home Shopping

The only way it is possible to advertise to a "segment of one" is with a database that provides information about the characteristics of individual consumers. Once databases are fully developed and widely available, however, it is possible to go far beyond simply communicating with individuals. Rather, the whole marketing process—from product customization through to the final sale—can be accomplished one consumer at a time. The major social and business concerns will have to do with privacy and economics, not with feasibility from a technological perspective. Recall the initial discussion of convenience early in the chapter, and you may come to the same question we raised there—will location matter if companies are able to provide consumers almost everything they desire as they sit at home?

Although home shopping is currently a relatively minor factor in the world of retailing, its potential is huge, perhaps colossal. In developed markets, home shopping accounts for only between 3 and 6% of all retail sales, mainly fueled by mail order and telemarketing.[71] But virtually all observers have higher expectations for electronic retailing, particularly in the increasingly multimedia environment. With cable television and telephone companies investing billions of dollars to provide homes with two-way communications, interactive shopping is inevitable. Consumers will be able to tell their television sets to show them things they want to buy and order them at the touch of a button. And, if the economics of home delivery can be made to work, interactivity might, for example, tilt the balance of power between packaged goods manufacturers and retailers in a new direction, because through it, the manufacturers would have an alternative route, straight to the consumer.[72]

Pictures painted of the electronic interactive era are simply fascinating.

In the early days of this interactive era, a typical home shopping channel will probably allow consumers to enter an electronic shopping mall featuring a number of stores selling different kinds of merchandise. Viewers will select the store they want to enter; choose the department that interests them; go to the items they want to view; then, after calling up any product information they require, press a button to transmit an order.

Very soon, the system will move on to a more sophisticated level by building up personal profiles of users through their buying habits. For example, they will quickly learn viewers' measurements, so enabling it to order clothing in the correct size. It will also pick up their favorite colors and their tastes in fashion, music, or food, so that it can offer increasingly tempting products while learning not to waste their time with unwanted goods. It will have a pretty accurate idea of what they can afford, too.

Beyond this, it does not require a great leap of imagination to see the day when virtual reality enters the world of electronic retailing. At a simple level, consumers will be able to try on clothes at home by watching computer-generated images of themselves (or someone else) wearing them. Later, instead of watching a television screen, people will probably be able to don a virtual reality helmet and gloves, then transport themselves into the stores of their choice. They will roam the virtual aisles, examining virtual goods and quizzing virtual sales assistants for more information if required.[73]

Already in place and working toward the interactive world is the Home Shopping Network and QVC.[74] Also available is on-line computer shopping, a phenomenon revisited later in Chapter 9. Prodigy offers products from 125 merchants. On Compuserve, choices range from a Brooks Brothers suit to contact lenses, life insurance, or a honey-baked ham. America On-line allows subscribers to offer their homes for sale. The Internet Shopping Network has an "electronics superstore," offering more than 15,000 computers, software, and related products. Scores of other services, such as ScanFone, GEnie, and Peapod, offer different varieties of home shopping.

Although the full promise of home shopping is still years away, the question that must be in everyone's mind is "What's the future of store retailing?" Another question is "Will retailing, as we know it, be necessary, and if necessary, how will it change to accommodate the world of interactive media?" And yet another question is "What will be the marketing role of consumer goods manufacturers in this new world?" In trying to answer these questions (which we are going to leave to the reader), we want to give you a massive hint that will start you on your way: There is no such thing as a homogeneous marketplace. Even if there are segments of one, those segments will be very different in terms of their needs, expectations, and desires. It is, therefore, always likely to be the case that there will have to be "different strokes for different folks," an insight that managers planning marketing channels must always keep in mind. For example, a large portion of the billions of dollars that U.S. retail banks are investing in technology is being focused on delivery channels, that is, finding better ways of getting to their customers, especially at home or at work. Yet, as a senior vice president in Chase Manhattan's retail bank puts it: "It's not about one channel or one product being better than another. It's enabling your customers to access you through multiple channels and multiple products."[75]

▶ STRATEGIC ISSUES IN INTERNATIONAL RETAILING

In this section, we show you, very briefly, how some of the developments in U.S. retailing are found elsewhere. It is not our intention to cover all continents and countries, but rather to provide examples of the pervasiveness of some of the phenomena previously discussed. More insights are available later in this text in the chapter dealing with international marketing channels. Of the 20 largest retailers in the world in 1993, only 7 were based in the United States, as shown in Table 2-4.

TABLE 2-4   The Largest 20 Retailers in the World in 1993

NAME	HOME COUNTRY	1993 SALES ($ BILLIONS)
Wal-Mart	United States	68.0
Metro Int.	Germany	48.4
Kmart	United States	34.6
Sears, Roebuck	United States	29.6
Tengelmann	Germany	29.5
Rewe Zentrale	Germany	27.2
Ito-Yokado	Japan	26.0
Daiei	Japan	22.6
Kroger	United States	22.4
Carrefour	France	21.7
Leclerc, Centres	France	21.1
Aldi	Germany	20.9
Intermarche	France	20.7
J.C. Penney	United States	19.6
Dayton Hudson	United States	19.2
American Stores	United States	18.8
Edeka Zentrale	Germany	17.9
Promodes	France	16.0
J. Sainsbury	United Kingdom	15.9
Jusco	Japan	15.8

Source: "Retailing Survey," *The Economist*, March 4, 1995, p. 4.

Examples from North America (Canada and Mexico)

CANADA   In the late 1980s, Canadians streamed to border cities, such as Buffalo, Detroit, and Seattle, to take advantage of low prices, wide variety, and friendly service—all of which were lacking at home.[76] Since the U.S.–Canada Free Trade Agreement took effect in 1989, warehouse clubs, category killers, power retailers, and discount stores from the U.S. have been charging after the Canadian market. Wal-Mart has converted 122 Canadian Woolco stores that it bought in March 1994. Home Depot launched Home Depot Canada after buying 75% of Aikenhead's 8-store home improvement chain in February 1994. The Gap grew to 64 stores in 1994. And Price/Costco has opened more than 40 stores in Canada since 1985.

In general, U.S. retailers are ahead of most Canadian retailers in buying practices, distribution, and the use of computer technology.[77] Exceptions are the 425-store Canadian Tire hard goods chain and Loblaw, the nation's largest supermarket chain. In fact, it was the president of Loblaw, David Nichol, who was responsible for the development of North America's most popular upscale private label, President's Choice.

MEXICO   Mexican retailing is undergoing a revolution spurred by competition, the opening of the economy to imports, and the North American Free Trade Agreement (NAFTA). Small corner stores are losing sales to supermarkets. In turn, small supermarkets are being swallowed up by a handful of large Mexican chains. And the large chains are forming alliances with giant U.S. retailers. Wal-Mart's partner is

Cifra, Mexico's largest retailer. Gigante, Mexico's second largest retailer, has formed a joint venture with Fleming, a major grocery wholesaler. Liverpool, Mexico's upscale retail chain, has a joint venture with Kmart. And, in October 1994, Dillard Department Stores and Wal-Mart formed a venture with Cifra to open Dillard stores in Mexico. The U.S. retailers have gained access to an emerging, consumer-starved market of 85 million people. The Mexicans, in turn, have gained immediate access to U.S. technology, distribution, and buying power.[78]

The entry of foreign retailers has not been hassle-free, however. Mexico's bureaucracy, the Secretariat for Trade & Industrial Promotion, has plagued the foreigners with mountains of paperwork, ever-changing regulations, customs delays, and tariffs of up to 300% on low-priced Chinese imports.[79] Government inspectors made surprise visits to Wal-Mart's 200,000-sq.ft. supercenter in Mexico City and discovered thousands of products improperly labeled or lacking instructions in Spanish. Once, in 1994, the store was ordered shut for 72 hours. In addition, distribution systems are very different in Mexico, where thousands of suppliers ship directly to stores rather than to retailer warehouses. According to the director of administration for Wal-Mart de Mexico, "The key to (the Mexican) market is distribution. The retailer who solves that will dominate this market."[80]

An Example from South America

BRAZIL Since the introduction of the *Plan Real* (named after a new currency) in July 1994, Brazil's monthly inflation rate has fallen from 45% to under 2%. The impact on the sale of consumer goods, and thus on retailing, has been monumental. Sales volume and the use of credit and debit cards have increased geometrically. In contrast with the past, most of the demand is coming from lower-middle and working-class people. For example, sales at discount and bargain stores, like Lojas Americanas and Magazine Luiza, are booming.[81]

Prior to *Plan Real*, retailers' profits came from taking advantage of the rampant inflation; they paid their suppliers long after they collected cash from their customers. Foreign competitors are seeing increasd opportunity in Brazil as a result of the turn of events. France's Carrefour and Holland's Makro are already well-established while Wal-Mart is opening a number of warehouse clubs in a joint venture with Lojas Americans.

Examples from Europe

WESTERN EUROPE Although it is probably unfair to generalize across the whole of Western European retailing because there are always exceptions to be found, it is a good bet that there is a gap between where retailing is in the U.S. and where it is in Europe. On average, European retailing is less technologically advanced, less sophisticated, less price competitive, and less productive. For example, with regard to productivity (output per hour of work), a 1992 report by the McKinsey Global Institute found that general merchandise retailers in the U.S. are 4% more productive than German retailers, 18% more so than British, and 31% more than French.[82] To a significant extent, the gap is caused by the fact that many Western European countries discourage competition among suppliers and inhibit retailers from having flexibility in the type of stores they operate and their hours of operation. There still exists a protectionist mentality relative to small, neighborhood shops. Indeed, local habits and cultures, planning restrictions, and infrastructure all affect the success or failure of a retailing format and can easily derail efforts of new entrants. For instance, Greece has idiosyncratic shopping hours; Italy has stringent planning restrictions (building permits are granted by regional committees dominated by small retailers); Denmark has a well-entrenched cooperative movement whose shops account for 35 to 40% of retail sales; France, Belgium, Germany, and Portugal have occasionally halted authorizations for new supermarkets larger than 12,000 sq. ft.; Britain and the Netherlands have created so-called Green Belts outside towns and cities that are off-limits to superstores; and Austria has made it very difficult to get a permit for a store over 8,000 sq. ft.

For decades, Europeans have endured high prices, short shopping hours, and limited selection, whereas high-cost producers, inefficient retailers, and shop workers' unions have enjoyed all kinds of legislative protection.[83] But times are changing. First, downtown and corner stores are being threatened with extinction as suburban superstores selling "everything under one roof," from food and cosmetics to clothing and electronics, become more popular. But these so-called "soft discount" superstores, like Dutch-owned Makro Warehouse Club in the U.K., are, in turn, being threatened by "hard discount" stores, particularly in food retailing. Hard discounters, such as Germany's Aldi and Lidl & Schwarz and Denmark's Netto, rent small, run-down sites on street corners and fill them with a limited range of fast-moving goods, many of which are sold straight out of their boxes. This "no frills" approach keeps operating costs low and allows them to undercut supermarket prices by 25–40%. Hard discounters have gained a significant share of the food market in Germany, Belgium, Denmark, and France, and are presently attacking the U.K. And these "no frills" small-store operations may shortly be threatened by an invasion of category killers, warehouse clubs, and other assorted mass merchandising/hard discounting retailers from the U.S.[84]

But Western European retailers, seeing the potential U.S. invasion, are not simply rolling over and playing dead. For example, Britain's supermarket chains have been commendably quick to defend their market share by cutting prices. They have begun to form alliances, especially in food retailing, in order to develop countervailing power relative to consumer goods manufacturers and to gain efficiencies in technology and product development. The Institute of Grocery Distribution, a U.K. industry-research group, has identified four types of alliances that have developed over the past decade:

- The buying group, where members cooperate in purchasing. An example is Eurogroup, made up of Belgium's GIB, Switzerland's Co-op Schweiz, Germany's Rewe, and Vendex of the Netherlands.

- The development-based alliance, an agreement between retailers to cooperate on a specific project. An example is the agreement for Tengelmann of Germany to take a stake in Superal of Italy, giving Tengelmann a toehold in the Italian market, and Superal the benefit of Tengelmann's management experience.

- The skills-based alliance, where retailers share knowledge and expertise. Belgium's GIB group, for example, and the U.K.'s Sainsbury's cooperated in developing the Homebase home-improvement chain, using GIB's experience in the home-improvement business and Sainsbury's U.K. presence.

- The multifunctional group, which combines elements of the other three types. The best known are the European Retail Alliance (ERA), made up of the U.K.'s Argyll, Ahold of the Netherlands, and France's Casino, and Associated Marketing Services, which includes the ERA members plus retailers from Germany, Switzerland, Sweden, Finland, and Spain. In 1994 Sainsbury's, Italy's Esselunga, Belgium's Delhaize, and France's Docks de France formalized a partnership called SEDD "with the objective of developing opportunities in the European market in distribution, marketing, trading, and information technology."[85]

As yet, however, there is little evidence that any of these alliances have been very successful in meeting their objectives or in blunting the threats to their markets.

One area where Western European retailers, particularly food retailers in the U.K., have been world leaders is in the development of effective private-brand programs. As a percent of grocery sales, private labels account for 30% in the U.K., about 23% in Germany and Switzerland, and around 20% in France, Sweden, Belgium, Denmark, and the Netherlands.[86] British supermarkets view the private-label business as a means to increase their margins, differentiate between products, and enhance the power of their own brands. In the process, they have not just captured sales from manufacturer brands, but have asserted growing strategic control over the development, quality standards, and marketing of the products they sell. The two preeminent retailers of private brands are J. Sainsbury and Marks & Spencer. In fact, Marks & Spencer has had enormous success in building a 100% private-label business (primarily under the St Michael brand), first in clothing and later in food. Both Sainbury's and Marks & Spencer are considered among the finest retailers in the world.

EASTERN AND CENTRAL EUROPE   When communism collapsed, the state-owned distribution systems and retail stores were found to be in about the same shape as the rest of the economies in which they were housed—in a word, awful! In Russia and other former Soviet republics, to replace or supplement what existed, tens of thousands of kiosks have opened up on city sidewalks. Moscow alone has over 15,000 stalls, which sell everything from U.S.-made Snickers candy bars to Israeli orange juice to Chinese running shoes and parkas.[87] The entrepeneurs who run the kiosks make a decent living, by Eastern and Central Europe standards, but must confront a heavy dose of both bureaucracy and organized crime in order to survive (financially and literally).[88] And, although the famed GUM department store across from Red Square still exists, it has become a monument to capitalism where clerks actually smile (from time to time) and mark-ups are closely watched. Still, in comparison with, say, Britain and Germany, Russia has relatively little retailing space. Although roughly 95% of its shops are privately owned, the task of transforming them into something resembling Western shops has only just begun. Most Russian retailers have stuck to the old system of forcing a customer to stand in line to choose a product, stand in another line to pay for it, and stand in a third line to physically collect it.

When Kmart bought a chain of stores in the former Czechoslovakia, it basically bought an anachronism. The inventory was ancient, even by Kmart "blue-light special" standards. Markdowns were a mystery. Lighting was dim. Customer service was a frown and a growl. In such a situation, you go back to fundamentals: a new computer system, management streamlining, an initial stab at centralized buying, and uniform prices.[89] Never mind power retailing; the main concern is whether you'll get a dial tone when you pick up a phone!!!

When IKEA entered Warsaw, it started from scratch. It built its own building rather than acquiring one. Because incomes are so low in Eastern Europe, compared with the West, building and occupancy costs had to be kept as low as possible so that prices could be set at a level commensurate with the low incomes. That meant fewer toilets, no air conditioning, spartan flooring, and only rudimentary electrical systems permitting the simplest of lighting for furniture displays. To assure itself of supply, it was forced to take financial stakes in several suppliers, something it never does in the West. Pricing is mainly guesswork, because estimating rivals' cost of goods is close to impossible. But demand is so strong that IKEA can't advertise or use direct mail, because, if it did, it would be swamped with more customers than it could handle, even though those customers can only afford to buy a single spoon or cup at a time rather than a set of silverware or dishes.[90]

Examples from Asia

SOUTHEAST ASIA   The economies of Singapore, Thailand, Taiwan, Indonesia, and Malaysia are just about to hit one of those "magic moments" that retailers dream about—points in time when a large part of the population crosses an income threshold beyond which people buy entirely new categories of goods. For example, in 1987 only 3% of the Taiwanese population bought groceries in a "modern" shop, such as a supermarket; by 1993, the figure had risen to 50%.[91] Amazingly, two of the five largest shopping malls in the world are in Bangkok. It is little wonder, then, that foreign retailers are targeting Southeast Asia.

An excellent illustration of what can happen is the development of Orchard Road, the center of Singapore's prime retailing district. It now houses Toys"R"Us, Galeries Lafayette from France, Marks & Spencer from Britain, and Takashimaya and Isetan from Japan. But there are threats to Orchard Road's long-term dominance because of an accelerating shift in retail trade to the suburbs.

However, the growth of supermarkets and general merchandise stores, although extremely high, has been hampered by Singapore's primitive and costly distribution methods, which involve irregular deliveries of individual products in small quantities by different suppliers.[92] This is a problem for the whole of Southeast Asia and Japan as well, as we shall see. Some foreign entrants want to overturn the local distribution system by bypassing local intermediaries.

In addition to distribution problems, Southeast Asian retailing is usually snared in red tape. For example, Indonesia prohibits direct foreign investment in retailing, so joint ventures are the only ways in. In fact, throughout the region, it is best to find a local partner. In Thailand, Makro has joined with the powerful Chareon Pokphand conglomerate as has 7-Eleven, which has over 300 stores in the country. In Singapore, Toys"R"Us built its success on a partnership with Metro, a local firm, and Kmart chose the same partner for its joint venture. Not surprisingly, the most prominent retail entrants are Japanese retailers; the Japanese are the world's foremost experts on joint venturing and forging strategic alliances.

JAPAN   According to the study on service productivity by McKinsey Global Institute mentioned earlier, U.S. general merchandise retailers are 56% more productive than Japanese retailers.[93] The inefficiencies in the Japanese distribution system developed for social and political reasons. Since World War II, a top priority of Japanese economic policy has been to nurture the network of small neighborhood shops. (Japan has 13 retailers for every 1,000 inhabitants, compared with 6 per 1,000 in the U.S. and Europe.) A web of secondary and tertiary wholesalers evolved to supply them, often on a daily basis. The wholesalers, in turn, were linked through larger distributors to manufacturers or to Japan's giant trading companies.

In order to protect the system from competition, manufacturers would set a complex array of "suggested" wholesale and retail prices for thousands of products. According to a spokesperson for Ajinomoto, a major Japanese food processing company:

> In a typical case, we would set a price for the primary wholesaler, another one for the secondary wholesaler with a 5 percent markup, and then another one for a restaurant or the retailer, adding another 15 percent to the price. All this was subject to rebates for volume deliveries or length of service, to say nothing of wholesaler fees for using their own vans to collect goods from our factories. The system got so complicated that we could hardly blame foreigners for saying the market was opaque and impenetrable to outsiders.[94]

One of every five Japanese workers is employed in distribution. To protect those jobs, the government has gone to great lengths. Retail regulations make it extremely difficult for developers of large stores to displace existing "mom and pop" shops. Other laws restrict the size of buildings that retailers can erect or dictate store layouts and even construction materials. Furthermore, tradition and culture work against change.[95]

Much has been written about the retailing revolution taking place in Japan, the efforts of the U.S. government to lower barriers to entry, and the success of Toys"R"Us in penetrating the Japanese market.[96] Even Ajinomoto has abandoned "multiple price fixing," setting a single price for the first wholesaler and leaving the rest to the market. Private labels are more prevalent,[97] and discounting is on the rise.[98] Most big electronics manufacturers have stopped lending money to smaller retailers and don't even refer to them as private networks any longer. Instead, they are just called "local shops," no different in essence from any other retailers selling the same manufacturer's product.[99]

If all of this is happening, then why did we bore you with that bit of history at the outset? If Japanese distribution is rapidly mirroring the U.S., then why worry about all of those ancient patterns? The answer is "Don't kid yourself!" Although Japan is changing, its structure of retailing is where the U.S. was 30 years ago. It is not going to take 30 years for Japan to cover the same ground, but it's going to take time, nonetheless. And, for now, success in Japan is often linked to a company's ability to use the traditional system to its advantage.

Consider the case of Warner-Lambert's Schick brand of razor blades, which has 70% of Japan's market for wet shave products despite competition from two Japanese brands. The key for Warner-Lambert has been its tie-in with Hattori Seiko, its Japanese distributor, through which it began selling Schick blades in Japan in 1960. Hattori Seiko handles all importation, warehousing, and distribution. It also handled selling until 1993 when Warner-Lambert set up its own sales force. The tie-in proved invaluable for Schick in dealing with the complex distribution system with its layers of wholesalers, because, in Japan, it is still difficult to get products on to shelves by directly approaching the retailer.[100]

The Emergence of Global Retailing

One phenomenon that cuts across virtually the entire world is international expansion by retailers. Wal-Mart has, as already mentioned, moved into Canada and Mexico. It has formed a joint venture in Hong Kong from which it will expand into China. It has also announced plans to move into Argentina and Brazil. France's Promodes and Carrefour, Germany's Aldi and Tengelmann, Belgium's Delhaize, Netherlands' Ahold, and Britain's J. Sainsbury have significant sales (e.g., as much as 70% of their total revenue, in the case of Delhaize) outside their home countries. Other retailers that can be considered even more global in outreach are Italy's Benetton, Sweden's IKEA, Toys "R" Us, Marks & Spencer, and McDonald's. Japanese groups such as Sogo, Takashimaya, and Yaohan have spread across Singapore, Hong Kong, and Thailand, and are now coming to the West.[101] It used to be a rule of retailing that those companies which succeeded beyond their home countries' borders matched their assortments and images with the particular nations they entered. Currently they seem to be succeeding, because they sell a wider range of products with superior quality at better prices than their local competitors.

The major reasons for the increased international activity are: (1) saturation of domestic markets; (2) falling barriers to entry into markets worldwide; (3) suppliers' ability to service retailers globally; (4) increased foreign travel by consumers; and (5) the spread of cross-border mass media such as satellite television.[102] Coopers & Lybrand have identified 10 target markets for retailers, divided into the "tough three," the "torrid three," and the "formidable four."

- The "tough three": Italy, South Korea, and Japan (strong economies with large middle classes, but where local restrictions have limited the degree of concentration of retailing and entry by foreign groups).

- The "torrid three": Mexico, Turkey, and Argentina (rapid but volatile economic growth with an undeveloped retail sector).

- The "formidable four": Brazil, China, Russia, and India (greatest political and economic risks with a poor retail infrastructure, but rapidly growing middle classes hungry for consumer goods).[103]

▶ SUMMARY AND CONCLUSIONS

Retailing involves the direct sale of goods and services to ultimate consumers for personal consumption. The primary strategies available to retailers revolve around four operational elements. The first is concerned with margins and inventory turnover rates. During the twentieth century, a heavy emphasis has been placed on low-margin, high-turnover, minimum-service operations. Such operations have traded off between the services they perform for consumers and the prices they charge. Consumers have been increasingly willing to participate more heavily in the marketing flows.

The second element is concerned with variety and assortments, whereby retailing institutions design and evolve product-mix strategies to suit changing shopping patterns. The third element focuses on location and convenience. Decreased search-shopping patterns are making the location decision, particularly site selection, even more important. Although the emphasis is on convenience, there is a difficult tradeoff between one-stop shopping convenience and spatial convenience for many lines of retail trade. Paradoxically, however, location may eventually diminish in importance if the promise of interactive multimedia is achieved. The fourth element is customer service. Large retailers are becoming increasingly sophisticated at dividing their markets into segments with high, moderate, and low service requirements and have developed different means (through acquisition or internal growth) to serve each segment.

Competition in retailing has become awesome. Retailing is dominated by power retailers, some of whom are, in reality, "category killers." The retailing organizations making up these groups tend to be highly sophisticated, technology-oriented, centrally driven, and extremely well-focused on operations. In actuality, the basic "product" they all market are their systems of operation, and their systems of operation are their means of differentiating themselves. The "category killers" have such deep assortments and such strong pricing that they decimate their competition.

Retailing is also continuing to polarize itself into high-tech, warehouse-type operations and high-touch, specialty-type operations. There are some excellent examples of retailers who have managed to stay in the middle, but they are the exception rather than the rule. They are also consolidating at a rapid rate, for example, the Federated-Macy merger. Furthermore, defining a position and executing strategies designed to articulate that position clearly and crisply for consumers seems to be as important in retailing as it is in the world of consumer goods manufacturing.

Even though manufacturers make considerable efforts to differentiate their brands in the marketplace so that consumers will desire to buy them and retailers will want to carry them, it appears that the power in marketing channels is increasingly shifting toward retailers. In fact, regardless of their place on the pole (e.g., high-tech or high-touch), retailers are playing gatekeeper roles. They are using private branding, consumer demand for convenience, superior information, and an attention to neighborhoods (i.e., micromarketing) to establish and buttress their positions in marketing channels.

The most speculative aspect of retailing, however, is trying to estimate the eventual impact of home shopping. If it achieves its full potential, there is no question that it will absorb a significant share of the dollars available to existing retailers. But just how significant that share will be is, at present, a great subject for conversation at cocktail parties and on blind dates.

It seems as if U.S. retailing has a lead over the rest of the world in terms of its sophistication, both technologically and from a marketing/merchandising perspective. There are, however, exceptions to this statement. (Few retailers are as solid as Marks & Spencer or as clever as 7-Eleven Japan, for example.) What seems likely, though, is that U.S.-style discounting will begin to move across the globe. If it continues to do so, there will be a better deal for consumers everywhere. The biggest problem is the desire of governments to protect retail competitors from retailing competion.

DISCUSSION QUESTIONS

1. Does Home Depot make retail sales? wholesale sales? both? What difference does categorizing its sales make? If it does make both kinds of sales, is Home Depot mainly a retailer or a wholesaler? Again, what difference does it make?

2. Classify the sales, into retail or wholesale or both, of the outlets with the following names over their doors:

Circuit City	Walgreen
Office Max	Athlete's Foot
Marshall Field	Computerland

3. The poet Paul Valery once remarked, "Once destiny was an honest game of cards which followed certain conventions, with a limited number of cards and values. Now the player realizes in amazement that the hand of his future contains cards never seen before and that the rules of the game are modified by each play." Relate Valery's statement to the problems facing high-level retail executives today.

4. Professor Bert McCammon, following Schumpeter, once described the revolution in retailing as a process of "creative destruction," because of the many new institutions that have appeared in this industry over the years. If institutional life cycles have shortened to approximately 10 years or less, what types of institutional forms do you predict will arise by the year 2000 to "creatively destroy" the institutions that are emerging as powers in retail trade today (e.g., warehouse clubs and supercenters)?

5. Consider these environmental factors in answering the following questions:

   a. Assume that you are a high-level retail executive for a major chain of supermarkets. Given your assumptions about the future, what strategies would you initiate to adapt your organization to the impending environment?

    b. If you were a manufacturer of household consumer durables, what action would you take relative to future retail distribution outlets for your products?

6. In your opinion, what kind of competition exists in retailing—perfect, monopolistically competitive (atomistic), oligopolistic, or monopolistic? Explain in full, using a variety of lines of retail trade to illustrate.

7. Why is an understanding of the retail buying process important from an *interorganizational* perspective? If, through market research, a manufacturer determined that a retail buyer was using a linear-choice model in making a merchandise selection, what general promotional tactics might the manufacturer employ to help ensure his/her product's selection? How would his/her tactics differ if the retail buyer were instead using:

    a. a conjunctive model

    b. a lexicographic model

    c. a disjunctive model

On an a priori basis, what situational factors might prompt the retail buyer to use one choice model instead of another? (*Hint:* Consider, for example, such situational factors as *perceived risk attached to the buyer's decision* and *amount of time available to make the decision.*) An answer to this question requires a reading of Appendix 2A.

8. What is meant by merchandising variety and assortment? What are the dimensions of assortment? What purposes does the merchandising budget serve? (See Appendix 2C.)

9. As the retailing environment becomes more turbulent, which of the following policy decision areas—location, merchandise selection, or inventory control—do you believe becomes more important, as well as more difficult for the retailer? Offer at least *three* compelling reasons in support of your position.

10. In the face of various stages of interactive home shopping hinted at in the discussion of home shopping, what will be the role of store retailing during each stage? Will store retailing eventually disappear? Why or why not? Do you think that home shopping will ever account for 50% or more of retail sales?

11. For each international example given in the chapter, point out which strategic issue in U.S. retailing seems to be at play, for example, the dominance of power retailing, the increasing polarity of retailing, and so on.

ENDNOTES

[1]For a more comprehensive and in-depth discussion of retailing structure, competition, and management than space allows here, the reader is urged to consult Michael Levy and Barton A. Weitz, *Retailing Management*, 2nd ed. (Chicago: Richard D. Irwin, Inc., 1995) or J. Barry Mason and Morris L. Mayer, *Modern Retailing: Theory and Practice*, 5th edition (Homewood, IL: BPI/Irwin, 1990).

[2]William R. Davidson, Daniel J. Sweeney, and Ronald W. Stampfl, *Retailing Management*, 5th ed. (New York: John Wiley & Sons, 1984), p. 14.

[3]For a detailed discussion of financial strategies adopted by retailers, including the strategic profit model (SPM), see Levy and Weitz, *op. cit.*, pp. 157–183.

[4]For an excellent discussion of this issue, see Stratford Sherman, "Will the Information Superhighway be the Death of Retailing?" *Fortune*, April 18, 1994, pp. 98–110.

[5]Data on payroll expenses compiled from the National Retail Federation, *Financial and Operating Results of Retail Stores in 1992* (Washington, DC: National Retail Federation, 1993), pp. 46–56, 124–134.

[6]Joseph Pereira, "Discount Department Stores Struggle Against Rivals that Strike Aisle by Aisle," *Wall Street Journal,* June 19, 1990, p. B1. See, also, "Pile 'em High and Go Bust," *The Economist,* July 7, 1990, p. 70 and Cyndee Miller, "Retailers Do What They Must to Ring Up Sales," *Marketing News,* Vol. 29, May 22, 1995, pp. 1, 10, and 11.

[7]Walter K. Levy, "Department Stores, The Next Generation: Form and Rationale," *Arthur Anderson & Co. Retailing Issues Letter,* Vol. 1, No. 1 (1987), p. 1.

[8]The merger unraveled in 1994 due to cultural differences between the managements of the two companies. See Bob Ortega, "Price/Costco's Spinoff Reflects a Difficult Marriage, *Wall Street Journal,* July 19, 1994, p. B4.

[9]Terry Bivens, "Best Bets 1989," *Dealerscope Merchandising,* January 1989, p. 14.

[10]Bill Saporito, "The Fix is in at Home Depot," *Fortune,* February 29, 1988, p. 73. Also see "Will Home Depot be 'The Wal-Mart of the 90s'," *Business Week,* March 19, 1990, pp. 124–126; Susan Cameniti, "The New Champs of Retailing," *Fortune,* September 24, 1990, pp. 85–100; and Michael J. McCarthy, "Home Depot's Do-It-Yourself Powerhouse," *Wall Street Journal,* July 17, 1990, p. B1.

[11]See "Stephen D. Moore, "IKEA Bucks Home-Furnishings Trends," *Wall Street Journal,* February 23, 1990, p. B3C; and Bill Saporito, "IKEA's Got 'Em Lining Up," *Fortune,* March 11, 1991, p. 72.

[12]Claudia H. Deutsch, "All About Home Improvement," *The New York Times,* Section F, June 2, 1991, p. 5.

[13]"If May Stores are Plain Janes, Who Needs Flash?" *Business Week,* January 22, 1990, p. 32; Francine Schwadel, "As Retailing's Chic and Indebted Stumble, Bland May Co. Thrives," *Wall Street Journal,* January 19, 1990, p. A1.

[14]Patrick M. Reilly and Laura Jereski, "Macy, Federated Reach Accord in Merger Talks," *Wall Street Journal,* July 15, 1994, p. A3.

[15]Gregory Patterson and Christina Duff, "Retail Sector Mulls Effects of Federated-Macy Merger," *Wall Street Journal,* July 15, 1994, p. B4.

[16]Data from presentation of Nancy Karch, Director, McKinsey & Company, at Northwestern University in April 1994.

[17]McKinsey & Company, Inc., *Evaluating the Impact of Alternative Store Formats, Final Report* (Chicago: McKinsey & Company, Inc., May 1992), p. 2.

[18]For an excellent discussion of this issue, see Bill Saporito, "What's For Dinner?" *Fortune,* May 15, 1995, pp. 50–64.

[19]*1992/1993 Profiles of Nielsen SCANTRACK Marketing,* A.C. Nielsen Company, December 1993.

[20]Christopher W. Hoyt, "Key Account Manager Fills Hot Seat in Food Business," *Marketing News,* November 6, 1987, p. 22.

[21]The pressure on suppliers seems universal. See Christina Duff, "Nation's Retailers Ask Vendors to Help Share Expenses," *Wall Street Journal,* August 4, 1993, p. B3.

[22]"How to Turn Junk Mail into a Goldmine—or Perhaps Not," *The Economist,* April 1, 1995, p. 51.

[23]Robert Schmitz, "Who Owns the Customer?" in Randolph E. Bucklin and Diane H. Schmalensee (eds.), *Viewpoints on the Changing Consumer Goods Distribution Scene* (Cambridge, MA: Marketing Science Institute, 1987), p. 19.

[24]Deloitte & Touche, *Grocery Manufacturers' Sales Force Management Survey* (Wilton, CT: Deloitte & Touche, 1992), p.6.

[25]"Money as an Uncontrolled Substance," *Supermarket Business,* April 1988, p. 21.

[26]Christopher W. Hoyt, *op. cit.,* p. 22.

[27]Joann Muller, "Rent Goes Up on Grocery Shelf," *Chicago Tribune,* Section 7, April 16, 1989, p. 14D.

[28]*Ibid.*

[29]Elliott Zwiebach, "Super Valu Division Imposes Failure Fee," *Supermarket News,* May 8, 1989, p. 1.

[30]Daniel J. Sweeney, *Product Development and Branding* (Dublin, OH: Management Horizons, 1987).

[31]Walter J. Salmon and Karen A. Cmar, "Private Labels are Back in Fashion," *Harvard Business Review,* May–June 1987, p. 99.

[32]Bernard Simon, "Upstart Cott Shakes Cola Kings," *The Financial Times,* June 15, 1994, p. 18.

[33]Raj Sethuraman, "The Effect of Marketplace Factors on Private Label Penetration in Grocery Products," University of Iowa Working Paper, December 1991; Stephen J. Hoch and Shumeet Banerji, "When Do Private Labels Succeed?" *Sloan Management Review,* Summer 1993, pp. 57–67.

[34]Daniel J. Sweeney, *op. cit.*

[35]Walter J. Salmon and Karen A. Cmar, *op. cit.,* p. 105.

[36]Junda Woo, "Vaseline Ruling Deals Setback to Big Brands," *Wall Street Journal,* October 7, 1994, p.B10; *Conopco Inc. v. May Department Stores Co.,* Court of Appeals for the Federal Circuit, 92-1412; Paul M. Barrett, "High Court Sees Color as a Basis for Trademarks," *Wall Street Journal,* March 29, 1995, p. A6.

[37]Tri Agins, "Big Stores Put Own Labels on Best Clothes," *Wall Street Journal,* September 26, 1994, p. B1.

[38]For example, Perrigo Company supplies no less than 857 knockoffs of major health and beauty aid brands to chains like Wal-Mart, Kmart, and Rite Aid. See Gabriella Stern, "Perrigo's Knockoffs of Name-Brand Drugs Turn into Big Sellers," *Wall Street Journal,* July 15, 1993, p. A1.

[39]Edwin L. Artzt, "Redefining Quality," a speech delivered at the Quality Forum VIII in New York City on October 1, 1992, p.3.

[40]*Ibid.,* pp. 2, 3.

[41]Valerie Reitman, "Eliminated Discounts on P&G Goods Annoy Many Who Sell Them," *Wall Street Journal,* August 11, 1992, p. A1.

[42]"Ed Artzt's Elbow Grease has P&G Shining," *Business Week,* October 10, 1994, p. 84.

[43]"Brands on the Run," *Business Week,* April 19, 1993, p. 27.

[44]Gabriella Stern, "Brand Names Are Getting Steamed Up to Peel Off their Private-Label Rivals," *Wall Street Journal,* April 21 1993, p. B1.

[45]"Attack of the Fighting Brands," *Business Week,* May 2, 1994, p. 125.

[46]Nancy Ryan, "Houseware Makers Catch Discount Bug," *Chicago Tribune,* Section 7, January 12, 1992, p. 3.

[47]Christina Duff, "Brighter Lights, Fewer Bargains: Outlets Go Upscale," *Wall Street Journal,* April 11, 1994, p.B1.

[48]Claudia H. Deutsch, "The Powerful Push for Self-Service," *New York Times,* Section 3, April 9, 1989, p. 1.

[49]Neil Buckley, "Reality Catches Up with Vision," *The Financial Times,* July 22, 1994, p. 10.

[50]See Ronald Henkoff, "Service is Everybody's Business," *Fortune,* June 27, 1994, p. 48.

[51]Thomas A. Stewart, "The Information Wars: What You Don't Know Will Hurt You," *Fortune,* June 12, 1995, p. 119.

[52]John Huey, "Wal-Mart, Will It Take over the World?" *Fortune,* January 30, 1989, p. 54.

[53]"Stalking the New Consumer," *Business Week,* August 28, 1989, p. 62. See also Brian Dumaine, "P&G Rewrites the Marketing Rules," *Fortune,* November 6, 1989, p.42.

[54]Susan Caminiti, "A Quiet Superstar Rises in Retailing," *Fortune,* October 23, 1989, pp. 167, 169.

[55]"Tough on the Streets," *The Economist,* February 24, 1990, p. 70.

[56]Robert Buzzell and Gwen Ortmeyer, "Channel Partnership: A New Approach to Streamling Distribution," Marketing Science Institute Report No. 94-104, Cambridge, MA, April 1994, pp. 15–16.

[57]Joseph Pereira, "Toy Industry Finds It's Harder and Harder to Pick the Winners," *Wall Street Journal,* December 21, 1993, p. A1.

[58]"Listening to Shoppers' Voices," *Business Week/Reinvent America,* 1992, p. 69.

[59]For substantiation, see "The Power of Interorganizational Systems," *Indications: Perspectives on the Management of Information Technology,* Volume 11 (Cambridge, MA: CSC Index, 1994).

[60]Kurt Salmon Associates, Inc., *Efficient Consumer Response: Enhancing Consumer Value in the Grocery Industry* (Washington DC: Food Marketing Institute, 1993), p. 1.

[61]Buzzell and Ortmeyer, *op. cit.,* pp. 21–22.

[62]Hank Gilman, "Learning a New Pitch: Software Retailers Adopt Mainstream Marketing Techniques," *Wall Street Journal,* September 30, 1987, p. 39.

[63]Michael Totty, "Pier 1's Counterculture Days Are Gone," *Wall Street Journal,* April 27, 1988, p. 6.

[64]Faye Rice, "Tiffany Tries the Cartier Formula," *Fortune,* November 20, 1989, p. 141–148.

[65]Jeffrey A. Trachtenberg, "Burdines Bets It Knows Florida Best," *Wall Street Journal,* December 18, 1989, p. B1.

[66]Alfredo Corchado, "Hispanic Supermarkets Are Blossoming," *Wall Street Journal,* January 23, 1989, p. B1.

[67]Kevin Helliker, "Stop 'N Go's Van Horn Wants to Reinvent the Convenience Store," *Wall Street Journal,* February 1991, p. A1, and Karen Blumenthal, "All Stop 'N Go Stores Plan to Rearrange Merchandise to Cater Better to Localities," *Wall Street Journal,* October 26, 1989, p. B4.

[68]Adapted from "Stalking the New Consumer," *Business Week,* August 28, 1989, p. 54.

[69]Ken Partch and Stephen P. Arbeit, "Sorting Out Today's Consumers as Specific Market Targets," *Supermarket Business,* June 1988, pp. 21–24.

[70]Bill Saporito, "And the Winner is Still . . . Wal-Mart," *Fortune,* May 2, 1994, p. 64.

[71]Neil Buckley, "Last Post for the Big Books," *Financial Times,* August 17, 1993, p. 13.

[72]See "Interactive Bazaar Opens," *The Economist,* August 20, 1994, pp. 49–51.

[73]Richard Tompkins, "Shop-till-you-drop at the Touch of a Button," *Financial Times,* June 9, 1994, p. 11. See also Stratford Sherman, "Will the Information Superhighway be the Death of Retailing?" *Fortune,* April 18, 1994, pp. 98–110. ª 1994 Time Inc. All rights reserved.

[74]See "Retailing Will Never Be the Same," *Business Week,* July 26, 1993, pp. 54–60.

[75]Richard Waters, "Branching Out," *The Financial Times,* October 14, 1994, p. 12. For reasons why the promise of interactive television and database (segment of one) marketing is still off in the future, see "How the People of Rochester Saw the Future and Yawned," *The Economist,* February 25, 1995, pp. 63–64 and "How to Turn Junk Mail into a Goldmine—or Perhaps Not," *The Economist,* April 1, 1995, pp. 51–52.

[76]"Barbarians at the Checkout," *The Economist,* September 17, 1994, p. 75.

[77]"Invasion of the Retail Snatchers," *Business Week,* May 9, 1994, p. 72.

[78]Damian Fraser, "Retailing Revolution South of the Border," *The Financial Times,* January 19, 1993, p. 21.

[79]"NAFTA: A Green Light for Red Tape," *Business Week,* July 25, 1994, p. 48.

[80]Bob Ortega, "Wal-Mart Is Slowed by Problems of Price and Culture in Mexico," *Wall Street Journal,* July 29, 1994, p. A1.

[81]"The Carnival Begins," *The Economist,* pp. 66–68.

[82]David Wessel, "U.S. Excels in Service Productivity Poll," *Wall Street Journal,* October 13, 1992 p. A2. An exception seems to be the British supermarket chain Tesco which has implemented highly sophisticated information and logistics systems comparable to the best among U.S. supermarket chains. See "Tesco's New Tricks," *The Economist,* April 15, 1995, pp. 61–62.

[83]"Shop Till You Drop Hits Europe," *Business Week,* November 29, 1993, p. 58.

[84]See Kevin Helliker, "U.S. Discount Retailers are Targeting Europe and Its Fat Margins," *Wall Street Journal,* September 20, 1993, p. A1.

[85]"Links in the Food Chain," *EuroBusiness,* May 1994, p. 15. See also, Neil Buckley, "Baked Beans Across Europe," adapted from *The Financial Times,* April 14, 1994.

[86]Guy de Jonquieres, "New Challenge for Big Brands," *The Financial Times,* June 15, 1993, p. 30. One study has shown that British supermarkets' greater use of private labels is the main explanation for their superior profitability when compared with French hypermarket chains. See Judy Corstjens, Marcel Corstjens, and Rajiv Lal, "Retail Competition in the Fast-Moving Consumer Goods Industry: The Case of France and the UK," INSEAD Working Paper, March 1995 and "Bon Marché or Super Marketing," *The Economist,* April 29, 1995, p. 74.

[87]"Where Russia's Elite Can Shop Till They Drop," *Business Week,* December 13, 1993, p. 14.

[88]For a detailed example of Russian gangsterism at work, see Adi Ignatius, "GM Dealer Hits Rough Road in Russia," *Wall Street Journal,* June 28, 1994, p. A15.

[89]Neil King, Jr., "Kmart's Czech Invasion Lurches Along ," *Wall Street Journal,* June 8, 1993, p. A11.

[90]Stephen D. Moore, "Sweden's IKEA Forges Into Eastern Europe," *Wall Street Journal,* June 28, 1993, p. B54.

[91]"Teach Me Shopping," *The Economist,* December 18, 1993, p. 64.

[92]Guy de Jonquieres, "Shoppers Spoilt for Choice," *The Financial Times*, Special Section, April 18, 1994, p. VI.

[93]David Wessel, *op. cit.*, p. A2.

[94]Charles Smith, "Opening Times," *Far Eastern Economic Review*, May 5, 1994, pp. 63–64.

[95]Emily Thornton, "Revolution in Japanese Retailing," *Fortune*, February 7, 1994, p. 144.

[96]For starters, see Emily Thornton, *op. cit.*, Charles Smith, *op. cit.*, "A Bargain Basement Called Japan," *Business Week*, June 27, 1994, p. 42; William Dawkins, "Revolution in Toyland," *The Financial Times*, April 8, 1994, p. 9.

[97]Yumiko Ono, "The Rising Sun Shines on Private Labels," *Wall Street Journal*, April 26, 1993 p. B1.

[98]See for example, Hiroshi Fukunaga and Kyoko Chinone, "Taking on the System," *Tokyo Business*, May 1994, pp. 4–14; Yukimo Ono, "As Discounting Rises in Japan, People Learn to Hunt for Bargains," *Wall Street Journal*, December 31, 1993, p. A1.

[99]Charles Smith, *op. cit.*, p. 63.

[100]Michiyo Nakamoto, "Use the System, Win Shelf Space," *The Financial Times*, February 16, 1994, p. 11.

[101]Neil Buckley, "Retailers' Global Shopping Spree," *The Financial Times*, October 12, 1994, p. 17. For an outstanding discussion of developments in global retailing, see "Retailing Survey," *The Economist*, March 4, 1995, pp. 1–18. See, also, Carla Rapoport and Justin Martin. "Retailers Go Global," *Fortune*, February 20, 1995, pp. 102–108.

[102]*Ibid.*

[103]*Ibid.*

APPENDIX

EVALUATIVE PROCEDURES (CHOICE STRATEGIES) USED BY RETAIL BUYERS ◀◀◀◀◀◀◀◀◀

The evaluative procedures employed by retail buyers can be classified as particular types of decision rules or **choice strategies**.[1] The actual choice strategy that retail buyers use is a direct result of the type of decision problem they face when making their merchandise selection.[2] Because buyers must generally select merchandise from among a number of competing brands, all of which can be described in terms of their various attributes, the situation confronting the buyer can be accurately described as a **multiple-attribute decision problem**.[3] In general, evaluating individual brands and their respective sources of supply involves rating alternative sources along some or all of the following 10 product attributes or performance parameters:[4]

- Demonstrated consumer demand (or projected demand, if a new product)

- Projected gross margin

- Expected volume

- Merchandise suitability

- Prices and terms

- Service level offered

- Manufacturer reputation

- Quality of the brand

- Promotional assistance

- Vendor's distribution policy (national, regional, or local; exclusive, selective or intensive)

The choice strategy, then, is the method by which the retail buyer evaluates each multiattribute brand alternative and discriminates it from the others in order to arrive at a merchandise selection.

There are many choice strategies that a buyer might adopt.[5] To illustrate the application of multiattribute decision models, consider the situation of a retail buyer choosing among potential suppliers of wristwatches. The buyer employing a *linear additive* choice strategy would first assign subjective weights to each of the ten product attributes according to the importance he/she places on each. For example, in the case of wristwatches, a manufacturer's reputation and demonstrated consumer demand might be considered more important by some retailers than a factor like promotional assistance. Second, the buyer would judge each alternative according to the extent to which it seemingly possessed each of the attributes. One brand, for example, might be perceived as being of higher quality than the other brands under consideration. After assessing each alternative relative to each attribute, the retail buyer would then combine each of these unidimensional judgments according to a simple linear rule. This rule would dictate the selection, through a process similar to the one depicted in Table 2A-1, of the supply source offering the highest global utility index. In the wristwatch example, the buyer would choose brand 4 because of its superior overall evaluation.

On the other hand, the retail buyer might use a **conjunctive** choice strategy in making a selection. The results in this case could be different from those arrived at through application of the linear strategy.[6] Using a conjunctive model, the buyer would establish minimum cutoff values for each attribute and then compare competing brands against these values. If any of the brands were rated below the cutoff value on any of the attributes, it would be rejected as a choice possibility. For example, in Table 2A-1, if the retail buyer established a minimum cutoff value of 0.5 for each of the ten dimensions, brand 1 would be selected as the best choice, because it is the only brand that meets or surpasses the established cutoff on each attribute.

Another approach that the retail buyer might use is a **lexicographic** choice strategy. Here, the buyer first orders the different attributes according to importance. Then the buyer compares all the alternative sources of supply on the single most important dimension. If one brand offers a noticeably better outcome on that dimension, it is selected. If, however, a number of alternative brands qualify, so that the buyer still cannot discriminate among the various available choices, he then drops down to the second most important attribute and repeats the procedure. This one-dimension-at-a-time process is followed until a choice is identified. In the wristwatch example depicted in Table 2A-1, brand 2 would now be selected, because it is perceived as surpassing all the other alternatives on the most important dimension—demonstrated consumer demand.

TABLE 2A-1 **Hypothetical Application of a Linear Additive Choice Strategy for Choosing Among Alternative Brands of Wristwatches**

ATTRIBUTE CONSIDERED	IMPORTANCE OF THE ATTRIBUTES TO THE RETAIL BUYER (A)	JUDGMENTS ABOUT INDIVIDUAL BRANDS OF WRISTWATCHES ACROSS ALL ATTRIBUTES			
		Brand 1 (B_1)	Brand 2 (B_2)	Brand 3 (B_3)	Brand 4 (B_4)
Demonstrated consumer demand (or projected demand, if a new product)	0.9	0.5	0.9	0.4	0.8
Projected gross margin	0.8	0.6	0.6	0.4	0.6
Expected volume	0.7	0.6	0.7	0.3	0.7
Merchandise suitability	0.6	0.5	0.4	0.4	0.4
Prices and terms	0.5	0.5	0.4	0.6	0.5
Service level offered	0.5	0.5	0.3	0.4	0.5
Manufacturer reputation	0.6	0.5	0.6	0.3	0.8
Quality of the brand	0.7	0.6	0.5	0.3	0.8
Promotional assistance	0.3	0.5	0.4	0.5	0.5
Vendor's distribution policy	0.4	0.5	0.3	0.4	0.7
Global utility index for each alternative $U = \sum_{i=1}^{n} A_i B_{ij}$		3.22	3.32	2.33	3.90

where

U= overall judged utility of brand alternative
A_i= numerical weight assigned to the ith dimension
B_{ij}= a numerical value for the jth brand alternative on the ith dimension

There are other choice strategies available to the retail buyer. These, as well as those already mentioned, are summarized in Exhibit 2A-1. Not presented are the hybrid or modified versions that some of these strategies may take on.[7] For example, because it is possible for several alternatives to exceed all established cutoff values when a conjunctive strategy is used, a further discrimination procedure may be necessary to identify a final choice for the retail buyer. One such mode of discrimination is to combine the conjunctive strategy with a first-choice rule, whereby the brand chosen is the first one that meets all standards. Another mode of discrimination would be a multistage use of strategies, whereby the retail buyer might use a conjunctive scheme to narrow the number of brand alternatives and then apply linear strategy in making the final choice.

As mentioned, the choice strategy the retail buyer uses in judging brand alternatives has significant implications for the planning of marketing efforts on the part of suppliers seeking to serve the buyer. For example, if the buyer is using a lexicographic strategy, a supplier would do best to focus promotional efforts on what the buyer perceives as the product's most important attribute, because the supplier's brand will be chosen if it surpasses all other alternatives on the dimension. However, such an approach may not prove effective if the buyer is instead employing a conjunctive decision rule. Convincing the buyer that a supplier's brand is outstanding in one dimension will not be sufficient if the brand falls below standards set for the other dimensions considered. When a linear additive choice strategy is used, marketing efforts could be directed by a supplier toward increasing his brand's rating on

▶**E**XHIBIT **2A-1** / **Possible Choice Strategies a Retail Buyer May Employ When Selecting Sources of Supply**

▶ ▶ ▶

CHOICE STRATEGY MODEL	SPECIFIC STRATEGIES	STRATEGY DESCRIPTION
Linear	Linear additive	Weights are assigned to each attribute according to its perceived importance. Each supplier/brand alternative then receives a rating on each dimension. These are combined linearly to form an overall judgment for each supplier/brand alternative that can be compared in making the final selection.
	Linear averaging	Same as a linear additive, except that the evaluative weights must sum to one to indicate a dependency among the dimensions.[a]
Lexicographic	Regular lexicography	All supplier/brand alternatives are compared on the single most important dimension. If one surpasses all others on that dimension, it is selected. If not, the process continues along the other dimensions until the supplier(s)/brand(s) is (are) selected.
	Lexicographic semiorder	Same as regular lexicography, except that, even when a supplier/brand alternative surpasses other alternatives on the single most important dimension, if the difference is not a significant one, the comparison continues along the other dimensions until the supplier(s)/brand(s) is (are) selected.
Multiple cutoff	Conjunctive	All suppliers/brands are compared against some minimum cutoff on each dimension. Those supplier/brand alternatives *below* the cutoff on any dimension are rejected.
	Disjunctive	Same as conjunctive, except that any supplier/brand alternative *above* the cutoff on any single dimension is accepted.
	Elimination by aspects	Minimum cutoffs are established for each attribute. Supplier/brand alternatives are eliminated that fail to surpass the cutoff on the most discriminating dimension, then the second most discriminating, etc., until all dimensions are exhausted or the supplier(s)/brand(s) is (are) selected. The most discriminating dimension is the one that will eliminate the most alternatives from further consideration.
	Sequential elimination	Minimum cutoffs are established for each dimension. Supplier/brand alternatives are eliminated that fail to surpass the cutoff on the most important dimension, then the second most important, etc., until all dimensions are exhausted or the supplier(s)/brand(s) is (are) selected.

[a]For example, the weights, or A_i's in the utility index of Table 2A-1, would have to sum to one in order to indicate the *relative* importance of the dimensions, if it were to be an averaging model.

Source: Lynn W. Phillips, "Evaluation Process Models: An Overview," an unpublished doctoral seminar paper, Northwestern University, 1975.

any dimension, because in light of the additive nature of the choice process the increase would positively affect the overall evaluation of the brand.

ENDNOTES

[1]Development of the choice strategy concept is found in Peter Wright, "Consumer Choice Strategies: Simplifying vs. Optimizing," *Journal of Marketing Research,* Vol. 7 (February 1975), pp. 60–67.

[2]The authors wish to acknowledge the significant contribution of Lynn W. Phillips to the development of the following discussion.

[3]For an overview of this type of decision problem see Kenneth R. MacCrimmon, "An Overview of Multiple Objective Decision Making," in J.L. Cochrane and M. Zeleny (eds.), *Multiple Criteria Decision Making* (Columbia, SC: University of South Carolina Press, 1973), pp. 18–44.

[4]This list is not necessarily in order of importance. Furthermore, the number of attributes considered by the buyer obviously varies from situation to situation. Doyle and Weinber, for example, in a study of supermarket buyers' decisions, found that buyers examined only 8 dimensions, whereas Montgomery, in a similar study, reported that 18 factors were taken into consideration. See Peter Doyle and Charles B. Weinberg, "Effective New Product Decisions for Supermarkets," *Operations Research Quarterly,* Vol. 24 (March 1973), pp. 45–54; and David B. Montgomery, "New Product Distribution: An Analysis of Supermarket Buyer Decision," *Journal of Marketing Research,* Vol. 12 (November 1975), pp. 255–264.

[5]All choice strategies may be carried out overtly, such as by pencil and paper calculation, or cognitively. In fact, most investigations of choice strategy paradigms involve an examination of how well they approximate actual cognitive processes. Although retail buyers could use either approach, their evaluations of potential suppliers often are done quickly and judgmentally because of their workload. See, for example, Doyle and Weinberg, *op. cit.,* p. 51. One possible strategy is the *linear additive* method of evaluation. For a review of this choice model, see William Wilkie and Edgar A. Pessemier, "Issues in Marketing's Use of Multi-Attribute Attitude Models," *Journal of Marketing Research,* Vol. 10 (November 1973), pp. 428–442. Empirical evidence indicating that retail buyers may cognitively use a linear additive method of evaluation has been marshaled by Roger M. Heller, Michael J. Kearney, and Bruce J. Mehaffey in "Modeling Supermarket Product Selection," *Journal of Marketing Research,* Vol. 10 (February 1973), pp. 34–37.

[6]Both Wright and Russ offer extended discussions of the nonlinear models presented here. See Peter Wright, "The Simplifying Consumer: Perspectives on Information Processing Strategies," a paper presented at the American Marketing Association Doctoral Consortium, East Lansing, Michigan, 1973; and Frederick Russ, "Consumer Evaluation of Alternative Product Models," *Combined Proceedings of the 1971 Spring and Fall Conferences* (Chicago: American Marketing Association, 1972), pp. 664–668.

[7]See Hillel Einhorn, "The Use of Nonlinear, Noncompensatory Models in Decision Making," *Psychological Bulletin,* Vol. 73 (1970), pp. 221–230.

APPENDIX

A Glossary Of Pricing and Buying Terms Commonly Used By Retailers

◀◀◀◀◀◀◀◀◀

Original Retail: The first price at which the merchandise is offered for sale.

Sales Retail: The final selling price.

Merchandise Cost: The billed cost of merchandise less any applicable trade or quantity discounts plus inbound transportation costs, if paid by the buyer. Cash discounts are not deducted to arrive at merchandise cost. Usually, they are either deducted from "aggregate cost of goods sold" at the end of an accounting period or added to net operating profits. If cash discounts are added to net operating profit, the amount added is treated as financial income with no effect on gross margins.

Markup: The difference between merchandise cost and the retail price.

Initial Markup or Mark-on: The difference between merchandise cost and the original retail value.

Maintained Markup or Margin: The difference between the *gross* cost of goods sold and net sales.

Gross Margin of Profit: The dollar difference between the *total* cost of goods and net sales.

Gross Margin Return on Inventory (GMROI): Gross margin divided by average inventory (at cost). GMROI is used most appropriately in measuring the performance of products within a single merchandise category. The measure permits the buyer to look at products with different gross margin percentages and different rates of inventory turnover and make a relatively quick evaluation as to which are the best performers. The components of GMROI are:

$$
\underbrace{\frac{\text{gross margin}}{\text{net sales}}}_{\text{(Gross Margin Percentage)}} \times \underbrace{\frac{\text{net sales}}{\substack{\text{average inventory} \\ \text{(at cost)}}}}_{\text{(Sales-to-Inventory Ratio)}} = \underbrace{\frac{\text{gross margin}}{\substack{\text{average inventory} \\ \text{(at cost)}}}}_{\text{(GMROI)}}
$$

Total Cost: Total cost of goods sold—gross cost of goods sold + workroom costs – cash discounts.

Markdown: A reduction in the original or previous retail price of merchandise. The *markdown percentage* is the ratio of the dollar markdown during a period to the net sales for the same period.

Off-Retail: Designates specific reductions off the original retail price. Retailers can express markup in terms of retail price or cost. Large retailers and progressive small retailers express markups in terms of retail for several reasons. First, other operating ratios are expressed in terms of percentage net sales. Second, net sales figures are available more often than cost figures. Finally, most trade statistics are expressed in terms of sales.

Markup on retail can be converted to cost base by using the following formula:

$$
\text{markup \% on cost} = \frac{\text{markup \% on retail}}{100\% - \text{markup \% on retail}}
$$

On the other hand,

$$
\text{markup \% on retail} = \frac{\text{markup \% on cost}}{100\% + \text{markup \% on cost}}
$$

F.O.B.: The seller places the merchandise "free on board" the carrier at the point of shipment or other predesignated place. The buyer assumes title to the merchandise and pays all freight charges from this point.

Delivered Sale: The seller pays all freight charges to the buyer's destination and retains title to the goods until they are received by the buyer.

Freight Allowances: F.O.B. terms can be used with freight allowances to transfer the title to the buyer at the point of shipping, whereas the seller absorbs the transportation cost. The seller ships F.O.B. and the buyer deducts freight costs from his invoice payment.

Trade Discount: Vendors usually quote a list price and offer a trade discount to provide the purchaser a reasonable margin to cover his operating expenses and provide for net profit margin. Trade discounts are sometimes labeled *functional discounts*. They are usually quoted in a series of percentages, such as list price less 33%, 15%, 5%, for different channel intermediaries. Therefore, if a list price of $100 is assumed, the discount applies as follows for the different channel members:

List price	$100.00		
Less 33%		33.00	retailer
		$67.00	
Less 15%		10.05	wholesaler
		56.95	
Less 5%		2.85	manufacturer's representative
		$54.10	

Quantity Discounts: Vendors offer two types of quantity discounts: noncumulative and cumulative. Although noncumulative discounts are offered on volume of each order, cumulative discounts are offered on total volume for a specified period. Quantity discounts are offered to encourage volume buying. Legally, they should not exceed production and distribution cost savings to the seller because of volume buying.

Seasonal Discounts: Discounts offered to buyers of seasonal products who place their order before the season's buying period. This enables the manufacturer to use his equipment more efficiently by spreading production throughout the year.

Cash Discount: Vendors selling on credit offer a cash discount for payment within a specified period. The cash discount is usually expressed in the following format :"2/10, net 30." This means that the seller extends credit for 30 days. If payment is made within 10 days, a 2% discount is offered to the buyer. The 2% interest rate for 10 days is equivalent to a 36% effective interest rate per year. Therefore, passing up cash discounts can be very costly. Some middlemen who operate on slim margins simply cannot realize a profit on a merchandise shipment unless they take advantage of the cash discount. Channel intermediaries usually maintain a line of credit at low interest rates to pay their bills within the cash discount period.

Cash Datings: Cash datings include C.O.D. (cash on delivery), C.W.O. (cash with order), R.O.G. (receipt of goods), S.D.-B.L. (sight draft - bill of lading). S.D.-B.L. means that a sight draft is attached to the bill of lading and must be honored before the buyer takes possession of the shipment.

Future Datings: Future datings include

1. ordinary dating, such as "2/10, net 30."
2. end-of-month dating, such as "2/10, net 30, E.O.M.," where the cash discount and the net credit periods begin on the first day of the following month rather than on the invoice date.
3. proximo dating, such as "2%, 10th proximo, net 60," which specifies a date in the following month on which payment must be made in order to take the cash discount.

4.   extra dating, such as "2/10 - 30 days extra," which means that the buyer has 70 days from the invoice date to pay his bill and benefit from the discount.

5.   advance or season dating, such as "2/10, net 30 as of May 1," which means that the discount and net periods are calculated from May 1. Sometimes extra dating is accompanied with an anticipation allowance. For example, if the buyer is quoted "2/10, 60 days extra," he pays in 10 days, or 60 days ahead, an additional discount is made available to him.

APPENDIX

MERCHANDISE PLANNING
AND CONTROL

◀◀◀◀◀◀◀◀◀

Merchandise planning and control start with decisions about merchandise variety and assortment. Variety decisions involve determining the different kinds of goods to be carried or services offered. For example, a department store carries a wide variety of merchandise ranging from men's clothing and women's fashions to sports equipment and appliances. On the other hand, assortment decisions involve determination of the range of choice (e.g., brands, styles or models, colors, sizes, prices) offered to the customer within a variety classification. The more carefully and wisely decisions on variety and assortment are made, the more likely the retailer is to achieve a satisfactory rate of *stockturn*.

The rate of stockturn (stock turnover) is the number of times during a given period in which the average amount of stock on hand is sold. It is most commonly determined by dividing the average inventory at cost into the cost of the merchandise sold.[1] To achieve a high rate of stockturn, retailers frequently attempt to limit their investment in inventory, which, in turn, reduces storage space as well as such expenses as interest, taxes, and insurance on merchandise. "Fresher" merchandise will be on hand, thereby generating more sales. Thus, a rapid stockturn can lead to greater returns on invested capital.[2]

Although the retailing firms with the highest rates of turnover tend to realize the greatest profit-to-sales ratios,[3] significant problems may be encountered by adopting high-turnover goals. For example, higher sales volume can be generated through lower margins, which in turn reduce profitability; lower inventory levels may result in lost sales due to out-of-stock conditions; purchasing in small quantities may result in additional ordering (clerical) costs and the loss of quantity discounts; and greater expense may be involved in receiving, checking, and marking merchandise. Merchandise budget planning provides the means by which the appropriate balance can be achieved between retail stock and sales volume.

MERCHANDISE BUDGETING

The merchandise budget plan is a forecast of specified merchandise-related activities for a definite period. Although the usual period is one season of 6 months, in practice it is often broken down into monthly or even shorter periods. Merchandise budgeting requires the retail decision maker to make forecasts and plans relative to five basic variables: sales, stock levels, reductions, purchases, and gross margin and operating profit.[4] Each of these variables will be addressed briefly.

Planned Sales and Stock Levels

The *first step* in budget determination is the preparation of the *sales forecast* for the season and for each month in the season for which the budget is being prepared. The *second step* involves the determination of the *beginning-of-the-month* (B.O.M.) *inventory* (stock on hand), which necessitates specification of a desired rate of stockturn for each month of the season. If, for example, the desired stock-sales ratio for the month of June is 4 and forecasted (planned) sales during June are $10,000, then the planned B.O.M. stock would be $40,000.[5] It is also important, for budgeting purposes, to calculate stock available at the end of the month (E.O.M. stock). This figure is identical to the B.O.M. stock for the following month. Thus, in our example, May's E.O.M. stock is $40,000 (or June's B.O.M. stock).

Planned Reductions

This *third step* in budget preparation involves accounting for markdowns, shortages, and employee discounts. Reduction planning is critical because any amount of reductions has exactly the same effect on the value of stock as an equal amount of sales. Markdowns vary from month to month, depending on special and sales events. In addition, shortages are becoming an increasing problem to retailers. Shortages result from shoplifting, employee pilferage, miscounting, and pricing and checkout mistakes. Generally, merchandise managers can rely on past data in forecasting both shortages and employee discounts.

Planned Purchases

When figures for sales, opening (B.O.M.) and closing (E.O.M.) stocks, and reductions have been forecast, the *fourth step,* the *planning of purchases* in dollars, becomes merely a mechanical mathematical operation. Thus, planned purchases are equal to planned stock at the end of the month (E.O.M.) + planned sales + planned reductions – stock at the beginning of the month (B.O.M.). Suppose, for example, that the planned E.O.M. stock for June was $67,500[6] and that reductions for June were forecast to be $2,500. Then,

Planned E.O.M. stock (June 30)	$67,500
Planned sales (June 1–June 30)	10,000
Planned reductions	2,500
Total	$80,000
Less	
Planned B.O.M. stock (June 1)	40,000
Planned purchases	$40,000

The planned-purchases figure is, however, based on *retail prices.* To determine the financial resources needed to acquire the merchandise, it is necessary to determine planned purchases at *cost.* The difference between planned purchases at retail and at cost represents the initial markup goal for the merchandise in question. This goal is established by determining the amount of operating expenses necessary to achieve the forecasted sales volume, as well as the profits desired from the specific operation, and combining this information with the data on reductions. Thus,

$$\text{initial markup goal} = \frac{\text{expenses} + \text{profit} + \text{reductions}}{\text{net sales} + \text{reductions}}$$

A term frequently used in retailing is *open-to-buy*. It refers to the amount, in terms of retail prices or at cost, that a buyer can receive into stock during a certain period on the basis of the plans formulated.[7] Thus, planned purchases and open-to-buy may be synonymous where forecasts coincide with actual results. However, adjustments in inventories, fluctuations in sales volume, unplanned markdowns, and goods ordered but not received all serve to complicate the determination of the amount that a buyer may spend.[8]

Planned Gross Margin and Operating Profit

The *gross margin* is the initial markup adjusted for price changes, stock shortages, and other reductions. The difference between gross margin and expenses required to generate sales will yield either a contribution to profit or a *net operating profit* (before taxes), depending, of course, on the sophistication of a retailer's accounting system and the narrowness of his merchandise budgeting.

ENDNOTES

[1]It is also computed by dividing average inventory at retail into the net sales figure or by dividing average inventory in physical units into sales in physical units.

[2]Delbert J. Duncan, Stanley C. Hollander, and Ronald Savitt, *Modern Retailing Management*, 10th ed. (Homewood, IL: Richard D. Irwin, 1983), p. 266.

[3]*Ibid.*, pp. 266–267.

[4]All of these variables have been treated more completely elsewhere, should the reader desire more detail. See Duncan, Hollander, and Savitt, *op. cit.* See, also, Michael Levy and Barton A. Weitz, *Retailing Management*, 2nd ed. (Chicago: Richard D. Irwin, Inc., 1995), pp. 303–324.

[5]There are numerous variations used to determine B.O.M. stock. See Duncan, Hollander, and Savitt, *op. cit.*, p. 229.

[6]Derived from a desired stock-sales ratio for July of 4.5 and projected sales for July of $15,000. Remember, June's E.O.M. is the same as July's B.O.M.

[7]Duncan, Hollander, and Savitt, *op. cit.*, p. 234.

[8]*Ibid.*

3/ CHANNEL INTERMEDIARIES ◄◄◄◄◄◄

WHOLESALING

*B*ecause few people visit wholesale warehouses or are exposed to purchasing transactions other than retailing, the wholesale distribution industry may go virtually unnoticed by the general public. However, the wholesale industry is a very large and diverse sector of the U.S. economy. Wholesaling accounts for approximately 10% of the national economic output, involves about 280,000 firms that sell through over 495,000 establishments, employs approximately 5.8 million people, and sells an estimated $3.2 trillion in raw materials and manufactured products.[1]

The focus of this chapter is on the functions of intermediaries between producers and organizational buyers, that is, channel members engaged in wholesaling. First, we define wholesaling and explain the rationale for the emergence of modern wholesalers. Second, we examine the structure of the wholesaling sector and the forces of change it is facing. Third, we discuss the selection and use of wholesalers by manufacturers, retailers, and business and industrial users. Finally, we discuss the paths of renewal of the wholesalers' strategies, structure, and management practices in order to better serve their suppliers and customers.

► WHOLESALING DEFINED

> Wholesaling is concerned with the activities of those persons or establishments which sell to retailers and other merchants, and/or to industrial, institutional, and commercial users, but who do not sell in significant amounts to ultimate consumers.

Of course, accepting this definition as the gospel truth means that every sale made by every organization to anyone but an ultimate consumer is a "wholesale transaction." This includes every sale by a manufacturing firm (with the exception of the small amount of sales made through factory outlets to household consumers) as well as sales made by such diverse organizations as hotels, insurance companies, and accounting firms when they deal with "industrial, institutional, and commercial" users in booking rooms, arranging pension plans, or preparing annual reports. In actuality, almost all organizations (except those dealing exclusively with ultimate consumers) are engaged in wholesaling in one form or another, and those specific transactions are classified as wholesale transactions.

The U.S. Bureau of the Census categorizes wholesale trade in three ways: (1) manufacturers' sales branches, who sell direct; (2) agents and brokers, who sell manufacturers' goods but do not take title to them; and (3) merchant wholesalers, who take title and usually possession of goods for resale.[2] In 1992 the last census of wholesale trade, merchant wholesalers accounted for 57.2% of the goods sold in the wholesale channel compared with 32% for manufacturers' sales branches and offices and 10.8 percent for agents, brokers, and commission merchants.[3] Of the $3.2 trillion of goods that moved through wholesale trade in the United States in 1993, $1.9 trillion moved through merchant wholesalers. Merchant wholesalers accounted for nearly 90% of all wholesaling firms and constituted the dominant wholesale distribution channel for each of the major product lines carried by wholesalers with the exception of motor vehicles and auto parts.[4]

The common perception is that goods go from a manufacturer, to a wholesaler-distributor, and then to a retail store where they are purchased by consumers. In reality, the way goods move to market is more complicated. Products can go through the hands of several manufacturers and distributors and never even end up at a retail store. The end-user of these products may be a business, not a consumer. Copper, for instance, can go through a series of transactions between several manufacturers and wholesalers before it is finally purchased by the end-user as a component of another product. It can be sold from a metals producer to a metals wholesaler-distributor to a wire manufacturer to a wire wholesaler-distributor. The copper wire can next go to a motor manufacturer who sells its motors to an industrial distributor. The motor, with copper components, is then sold to a forklift manufacturer who sells it to a materials handling distributor, where it is purchased finally by a woodworking shop. This example of an extended distribution channel holds true for components of consumer items sold in retail stores as well.

The wholesaler's functions are shaped by the task of coordinating production and consumption, or of matching mixed demands for assortments at various levels within distribution.[5] Thus, wholesalers aid in bridging the gap between periods and places in which goods are produced and those in which they are consumed or used.

As explained in Chapter 1, the sorting process performed by channel intermediaries, such as wholesalers, is the key to their economic viability. It frequently happens that the quantities in which goods are produced or the characteristics with which they are endowed by nature do not match either the quantities in which they are demanded, or the characteristics desired by those who ultimately use or consume them. Wholesalers, together with retailers, essentially solve the discrepancy between the assortments of goods and services required by industrial and household consumers and the assortments available directly from individual pro-

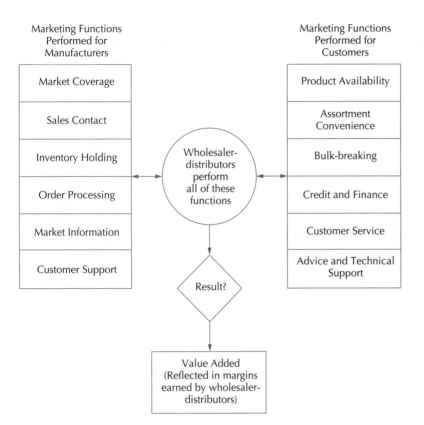

FIGURE 3-1   Value added by wholesaler-distributors through the performance of marketing functions.
Source: Reprinted from Bert Rosenbloom. *Marketing Functions and the Wholesaler-Distributor* (Washington, D.C.: Distribution Research and Education Foundation, 1987), p. 26.

ducers. In other words, manufacturers usually produce a large quantity of a limited number of products, whereas consumers purchase only a small quantity of many diverse products. Middlemen reduce this discrepancy of the assortment size and enable consumers to avoid dealing directly with individual manufacturers to satisfy their needs.

Wholesalers may participate in the performance of any or all of the marketing flows, that is, ownership, physical possession, promotion, financing, risk-taking, negotiating, ordering, and payment described in Chapter 1. Wholesalers' existence, however, is justified by the "value-adding" functions they perform, as illustrated in Figure 3-1. Their economic justification is based on what it is that they can do for their clientele, whether their clients are retailers, institutions (e.g., hospitals, schools, restaurants), manufacturers, or another type of business enterprise. For example, in the case of industrial goods needed in the assembly of a given product (e.g., chips for computers), it may be cost effective for the purchasing organization to place the burden of handling, owning, storing, delivering, and ordering the goods on a wholesaler rather than having to order in very large lots directly from the manufacturer, especially if the goods have to be held for a considerable length of time before they are used in the production process.

▶ THE WHOLESALING SECTOR

Wholesaling may be characterized as a sector of the economy in which the degree of specialization has constantly increased in response to changes in customer demand for service outputs. In fact, as depicted in Exhibit 3-1, the number of different types of wholesaling institutions is almost overwhelming. Such a variety offers buyers and sellers many choices within the channels of distribution, as dictated by such considerations as size, market segmentation, financial strength, services offered, and chosen method of operation. It also makes a high degree of marketing flow or functional movement possible, whereby any of the functions performed at the wholesale level of distribution may be shifted from one type of agency to another.

EXHIBIT 3-1 / Types of Operation, Wholesale Trade

▶ ▶ ▶

- **Merchant Wholesaler**
  Wholesale merchants or jobbers
  Industrial distributors
  Voluntary group wholesalers
  Importers
  Exporters
  Cash-and-carry wholesalers
  Retailer cooperative warehouses
  Terminal and country grain elevators
  Farm products assemblers
  Wholesale cooperative associations
  Petroleum bulk plants and terminals

- **Manufacturers' Sales Branches and Offices**
  Sales branches (with stocks)
  Sales offices (without stocks)

- **Agents, Brokers, and Commission Merchants**
  Auction companies
  Import agents
  Export agents
  Selling agents

Merchandise brokers
Commission merchants
Manufacturers' agents

Source: U.S. Department of Commerce, Bureau of the Census, 1987 Census of Wholesale Trade, Subject Series, Report No. WC87-5-1 (Washington, DC: U.S. Government Printing Office, 1990), Appendix A, pp. A-10, A11.

From a channel-analysis perspective, it is important to understand what specific roles wholesaling institutions and agencies assume, so that appropriate changes can be made when a channel is designed or adjusted. Assuming a manufacturer's or a retailer's perspective for the moment, what is it that one could reasonably expect to receive from a wholesaler in the way of services performed? Clearly, the more services performed, the higher the wholesaler's compensation will have to be from the channel as a whole. Appendix 3-A provides a detailed listing of the flows (participated in by the variety of wholesaling enterprises). Table 3-1 provides a summary of the appendix.

An examination of Table 3-1 indicates that full-function merchant wholesalers participate in all the flows, whereas brokers and manufacturers' agents participate in only a few of them. Therefore, if manufacturers were to "employ" full-function merchant wholesalers, the functional discount granted to these wholesalers would have to be considerably more than the commission paid to manufacturers' agents or brokers. But when manufacturers do not use full-function wholesalers, they do not "save" the discount, because they must perform all of the services the wholesalers would have provided. This is why the discount is called "functional." It is granted to wholesalers to compensate them for the cost incurred in the performance of these functions.

The structure of wholesaling in the United States is undergoing shifts in terms of the number of wholesalers. Arthur Andersen predicts that by the year 2000, there will be 15% fewer wholesale distributors due to mergers, acquisitions, and business failures. Large wholesalers are expected to hold a 43% to 52% share by the year 2000.[6] For example, Supervalu Inc., the largest U.S. food wholesaler, is planning to gain an even greater market share. It plans on increasing sales volume by buying weaker wholesalers and picking up customers from wholesalers that shut down.[7] The trend of consolidations and mergers in the manufacturing and retailing sectors is also taking place in the wholesaling sector. Consolidation occurs for different reasons, depending on the size of the players. Economies of scale motivate large players, whereas the desire to gain market share and financial instability drives consolidations for small- and medium-size distributorships.[8] This trend of mergers and acquisitions has led to a drastic reduction in the number of wholesalers in a number of industries, especially in food and pharmaceutical distribution. For example, in 1992, there were 77 drug wholesalers with 253 distribution centers, compared to the 1980s' complement of 139 wholesalers with 347 distribution centers.[9]

TABLE 3-1 Summary of Wholesalers' Participation in the Marketing Flows

	PHYSICAL POSSESSION	OWNER-SHIP	PROMOTION	NEGOTIATION	FINANCING	RISK	ORDERING	PAYMENT
A. Merchant wholesalers								
1. Full-function or service wholesalers	High	High	High	High	High	High	High	High
2. Limited-function wholesalers								
a. Drop shipper (desk jobber)	None	High	Low	High	High	High	High	High
b. Cash-carry wholesalers	High	High	Low	High	None	Low	High	High
c. Wagon (truck) jobbing	Low	Low	Low	High	Low	Low	High	High
d. Rack jobbers (service merchandise)	High	High	High	High	High	High	High	High
e. Converters	Low	High	Low	High	High	High	High	High
f. Wholesaler-sponsored (voluntary) chains	High	High	High	High	High	High	High	High
B. Retailer-sponsored cooperatives	High	High	High	High	High	High	High	High
C. Functional middlemen (agents and brokers)								
1. Brokers	None	None	High	Low	None	None	High	Low
2. Manufacturers' agents	None	None	High	None	None	None	High	Low
3. Selling agents	None	None	High	High	None	None	High	Low
4. Commission merchants	High	None	High	High	High	High	High	High

Competitive Dynamics

Dramatic challenges in the distribution industry demand that manufacturers and retailers reassess the wholesaler's role in the marketing channel. During the late 1980s and in the 1990s, the wholesaling industry continues to be confronted by emerging alternate distribution channels, growth in direct-buying programs, and a rising tide of imports that often bypass domestic wholesalers on the way to retail shelves.

The most important alternative channels of wholesale distribution are direct manufacturer-to-retail arrangements, such as those used by many retail chain stores, warehouse clubs, discount stores, and home-center stores. Other alternative channels include mail order and catalog sales. The size of the current and potential market for wholesalers is diminished by the volume of products distributed through the alternative channels. In fact, according to industry specialists, about one-fourth of all merchandise usually handled by merchant wholesalers, agents, or manufacturer's branch offices is now being distributed through alternative channels, and traditional wholesalers have lost millions of dollars in sales. Merchant wholesalers' share of the total wholesale market dropped from 58.3% in 1987 to 57.2% in 1992.[10]

As customer market segments fragment, alternate channel formats emerge to serve them. Figure 3-2 shows alternate channel formats that compete with traditional wholesalers in various market segments classified according to the customers' volume and service needs. Changes in the channel are pressuring manufacturers to reexamine what they expect from wholesalers and use another channel format (i.e., warehouse clubs, category killers), if it provides the services they need at an acceptable price.[11]

Perhaps the most significant threat to wholesalers has emanated from the powerful large-volume dominant-buyer[12] type of merchandisers, such as warehouse or price clubs (Sam's Club, Price Club, Costco, and PJ's Wholesale Club), supercenters, and category killers (such as Office Depot, Staples, Office Max, Toys "R" Us, and Home Depot).

Wholesale or warehouse clubs represent a growing share of wholesaling in the United States. As mentioned in Chapter 2, they typically cater to small businesses making wholesale purchases as well as consumers who purchase the products for their own personal use and who have paid a modest membership fee. Gross margins are exceptionally low on the limited number of SKUs offered in each merchandised category. The assortment changes according to the "best buys" in the various categories and most commodity items are generally only available in large quantities or in multiple packs of ordinary quantities. The clubs tend to be large (over 100,000 square feet), are located on secondary sites, and have the ambiance of a warehouse. There is virtually no customer service. Media advertising is generally limited to an announcement of an impending opening; thereafter marketing consists mainly of programs for membership solicitation and activation.[13]

Adding insult to injury, slow economic growth has led all channel members to seek out ways to reduce costs. One of the most efficient ways is to purchase from fewer suppliers, increase the amount of business with each remaining supplier, and receive the economies of scale and purchasing clout that come with being a volume

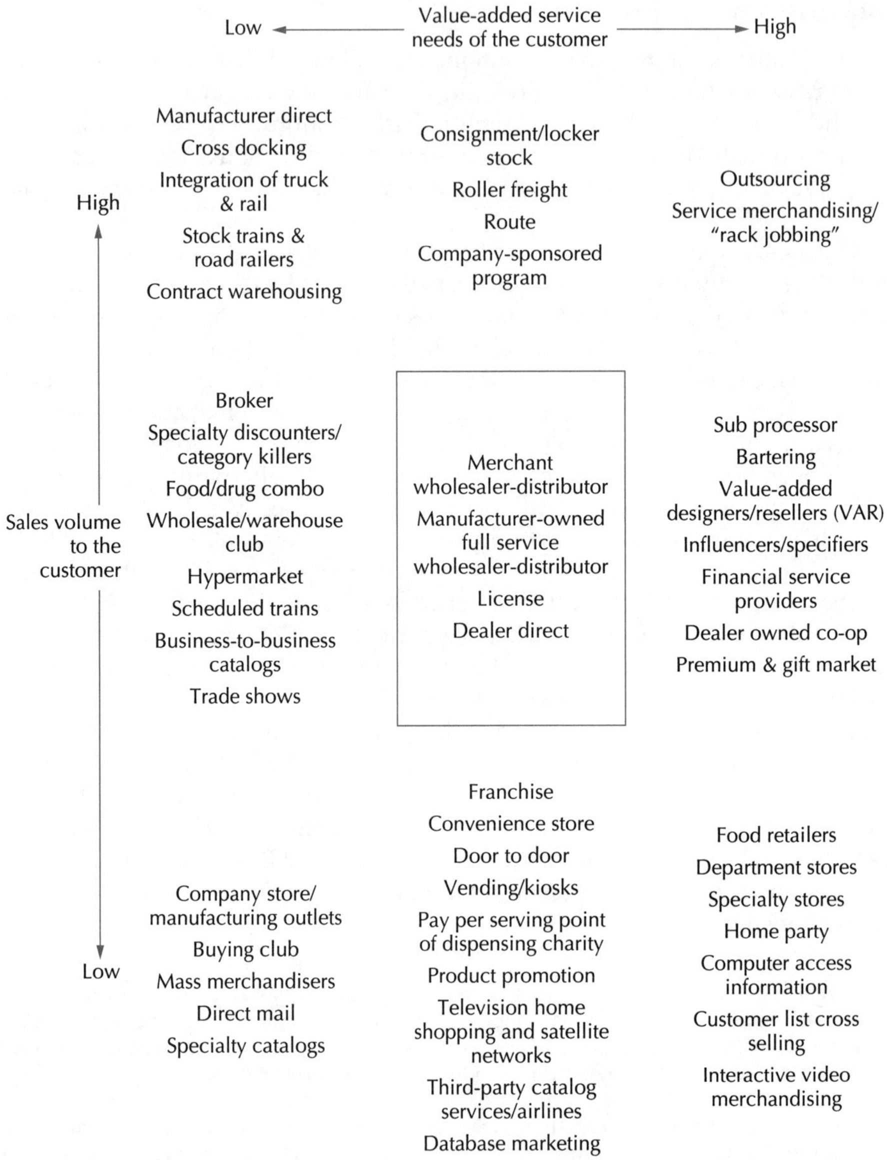

Low ◄─────── Value-added service needs of the customer ───────► High

High

Sales volume to the customer

Low

Manufacturer direct
Cross docking
Integration of truck & rail
Stock trains & road railers
Contract warehousing

Consignment/locker stock
Roller freight
Route
Company-sponsored program

Outsourcing
Service merchandising/ "rack jobbing"

Broker
Specialty discounters/ category killers
Food/drug combo
Wholesale/warehouse club
Hypermarket
Scheduled trains
Business-to-business catalogs
Trade shows

Merchant wholesaler-distributor
Manufacturer-owned full service wholesaler-distributor
License
Dealer direct

Sub processor
Bartering
Value-added designers/resellers (VAR)
Influencers/specifiers
Financial service providers
Dealer owned co-op
Premium & gift market

Company store/ manufacturing outlets
Buying club
Mass merchandisers
Direct mail
Specialty catalogs

Franchise
Convenience store
Door to door
Vending/kiosks
Pay per serving point of dispensing charity
Product promotion
Television home shopping and satellite networks
Third-party catalog services/airlines
Database marketing

Food retailers
Department stores
Specialty stores
Home party
Computer access information
Customer list cross selling
Interactive video merchandising

FIGURE 3-2   Alternate channels
Source: Reprinted from Arthur Andersen and Company. *Facing the Forces of Change 2000: The New Realities in Wholesale Distribution* (Washington, D.C.: The Distribution Research and Education Foundation, 1992), p. 172.

customer. Wholesalers who are fortunate enough to be chosen as a "primary" supplier have a chance of increasing market share, whereas other wholesalers face the possibility of going out of business.[14] The key to the wholesalers' gaining the position of a primary supplier is to develop a better understanding of why their suppliers and customers select them as preferred distribution partners.

▶ SELECTING AND USING WHOLESALERS

It is an old axiom of marketing that it is possible to eliminate wholesalers (or any middlemen, for that matter) but impossible to eliminate their functions. The major question facing manufacturers is whether they can perform the functions more efficiently and effectively than a wholesaler by integrating vertically (that is, by establishing their own sales branches and warehouse facilities). This question is a cause of considerable controversy in formulating marketing-channel strategy.[15] The controversy and related issues are addressed in detail in Chapters 5 and 6.

The reality is that the cost of marketing through wholesalers is not going to be vastly different from the funds a firm would have to expend on its own to provide the same services. If this is so, then what accounts for the large amount of direct selling that goes on? Why is vertical integration of wholesaling functions so popular, especially among large manufacturing and retailing firms?

The answer lies not only in **efficiency** considerations but also in **effectiveness** considerations. The fact that a given type of wholesaling firm participates in a number of marketing flows gives some idea about the potential for a division of labor in the channel. But the crucial question from a management perspective is to what extent (i.e., how heavily) and with what level of quality does the firm participate? To answer this question, we must examine what services wholesalers can provide, and juxtapose this potential against an assessment of the true orientation of many wholesalers.

Wholesalers' Services to Suppliers

Ideally, wholesalers have a great deal of potential as channel partners for suppliers. From an operational perspective, suppliers of both industrial and consumer goods may rely on wholesalers for several key reasons:

1. Wholesalers have continuity in and intimacy with local markets. Being close to customers, they are in a position to take the initial steps in the sale of any products— identifying prospective users and determining the extent of their needs.
2. Wholesalers have inventory available in each locale and thereby relieve suppliers of small-order business, which the latter can seldom conduct on a profitable basis. Also, wholesalers tend to have an acute understanding of the costs of holding and handling inventory in which they have made major investments.
3. Within their territories, wholesalers can provide suppliers with a sales force that is in touch with the needs of customers and prospects. Also, because wholesalers represent a significant number of customers, prospects, and suppliers, they can often cover a given territory at a lower cost than manufacturers' own sales representatives.
4. Wholesalers perform financial services for suppliers by providing volume cash markets through which they can recover capital that would otherwise be invested in inventories.

The economic role of wholesalers is to transfer marketing costs from the manufacturers into their own business. This is achieved through the performance of critical marketing functions by the wholesalers on behalf of the manufacturers they represent.

From the viewpoint of the manufacturer, the performance of the functions shown in Exhibit 3-2 by wholesalers must be evaluated in determining the type of wholesaling establishment to use. Such evaluation must always be conditioned by the nature of the ultimate market for the goods in question. Therefore, manufacturers must equally examine how well each wholesaler performs functions viewed as critical by their retail business customers and industrial users, as shown in Exhibit 3-3.

EXHIBIT **3-2 / Marketing Functions Performed by Wholesaler-Distributors for Manufacturers**

▶ ▶ ▶ **MARKET COVERAGE FUNCTION**

Markets for the products of most manufacturers consist of many customers spread over large geographic areas. To have good market coverage so that their products are readily available to customers when needed, manufacturers can call on wholesaler-distributors to secure the necessary market coverage at reasonable cost.

SALES CONTACT FUNCTION

The cost to manufacturers of maintaining outside sales forces is quite high. If manufacturers' products are sold to a large number of customers spread out over a large geographic area, the cost to manufacturers of covering all customers with their own sales force can be prohibitive. By using wholesaler-distributors to cover all or a substantial portion of their customers, manufacturers may be able to reduce significantly the costs of outside sales contacts because their sales forces would be calling on a relatively small number of wholesaler-distributors rather than the much larger number of customers

INVENTORY HOLDING FUNCTION

Wholesaler-distributors take title to and usually stock the products of the manufacturers whom they represent. By so doing, they can reduce the manufacturers' financial burden and reduce some of the manufacturers' risk associated with holding large inventories. Moreover, by providing a ready outlet for manufacturers' products, wholesaler-distributors can help manufacturers to better plan their production schedules.

ORDER PROCESSING FUNCTION

Many customers buy in very small quantities. Yet manufacturers both large and small receive a number of small orders from thousands of customers. By carrying the products of many manufacturers, wholesaler-distributors' order-processing costs can be absorbed by the sale of a broader array of products than that of the typical manufacturer.

MARKET INFORMATION FUNCTION

Wholesaler-distributors are usually quite close to their customers geographically and in many cases have continual contact through frequent sales calls on their customers. Hence, they are in a good position to learn about customer product and service requirements. Such information if passed on to manufacturers can be valuable for product planning, pricing, and the development of competitive marketing strategy.

CUSTOMER SUPPORT FUNCTION

Besides buying products, customers need many types of service support. Products may need to be exchanged or returned, set up and adjustment may be required, as well as repairs and technical assistance. For manufacturers to provide all such service directly to large numbers of accounts can be very costly and ineffective. Instead, wholesaler-distributors can be used by manufacturers to assist them in providing these services to customers.

Source: Reprinted from Bert Rosenbloom, *Marketing Functions and the Wholesaler-Distributor: Achieving Excellence in Distribution* (Washington, D.C.: Distribution Research and Education Foundation, 1987), p. 73.

▶ EXHIBIT **3-3** / Functions Performed by Wholesaler-Distributors for Customers

PRODUCT AVAILABILITY FUNCTION   ◀ ◀ ◀

Probably the most basic marketing function offered by wholesaler-distributors to their customers is providing for the ready availability of products. Sometimes this even includes fabricating operations, assembly, and set up of products. Because of the closeness of wholesaler-distributors to their customers and/or their sensitivity to their customers' needs, they can provide a level of product availability that many manufacturers would be hard put to match.

ASSORTMENT CONVENIENCE FUNCTION

Closely related to the previous function is the wholesaler-distributors' ability to bring together from a variety of manufacturers an assortment of products that can greatly simplify their customers' ordering tasks. So customers, instead of having to order from dozens or even hundreds of manufacturers, can turn to one or a few general line or specialty wholesaler-distributors who can provide them with all or most of the products they need.

BULK-BREAKING FUNCTION

Quite often customers do not need large quantities, or even if they do, at times they may need only small quantities of products in a given order. Many manufacturers find it costly

Exhibit 3-3 (continued)

Exhibit 3-3 (continued)

to sell directly to small-order customers and so they establish minimum order requirements to discourage small orders. By buying from manufacturers in large quantities and breaking these bulk orders down into the smaller quantities desired by customers, wholesaler-distributors provide customers with the ability to buy only in the quantities they need.

CREDIT AND FINANCE FUNCTION

Wholesaler-distributors provide their customer with financial assistance in two ways. First, by extending open account credit on products sold, their customers have time to use products in their businesses before having to pay for them. Second, by stocking and providing ready availability for many of the items needed by their customers, wholesaler-distributors significantly reduce the financial inventory burden their customers would bear if they had to stock all of the products themselves.

CUSTOMER SERVICE FUNCTION

Customers often require many types of services such as delivery, repairs, warranty work, and so on. By making these services available to their customers, wholesaler-distributors can save their customers considerable effort and expense.

ADVICE AND TECHNICAL SUPPORT FUNCTION

Many products, even those that are not considered technical, may still require a certain amount of technical advice and assistance for proper use, as well as advice on how they should be sold. Wholesaler-distributors, often through the use of trained outside sales forces, are able to provide this kind of technical and business assistance to customers.

Source: Reprinted from Bert Rosenbloom, *Marketing Functions and the Wholesaler-Distributor: Achieving Excellence in Distribution* (Washington, D.C.: Distribution Research and Education Foundation, 1987), p. 74.

Wholesalers' Services to Retailers

Manufacturers want retailers to promote and sell their brands from their product lines. On the other hand, wholesalers have a strong vested interest in building up their retail customers as merchants of assortments of multiple brands in multiple product lines. Hence, it is quite likely that an individual wholesaler will be able to supply a large part of the retailer's requirements for merchandise, particularly in the case of smaller retail establishments. It is in the wholesaler's interest to spend considerable effort and resources on training, stimulating, and helping retailers become better merchandisers. High-performance wholesalers are very knowledgeable in retail merchandise management. The benefits to the retailer derived from using traditional wholesalers may be described as follows:

1. Wholesalers can give their retail customers a great deal of direct selling aid in the form of price concessions of featured items, point-of-sale promotional materials, and coop-

erative advertising, most of which are frequently generated by suppliers for wholesalers to pass along to retailers.

2. Wholesalers often can provide assistance in planning store layout, building design, and material specifications.

3. Wholesalers can offer retailers guidance and counsel in public relations, housekeeping and accounting methods, information systems, administrative procedures, and the like, such as in the case of a wholesaler-sponsored type of chain.

In the toy industry, for instance, many retailers, including Toys "R" Us, prefer to make a significant proportion of their total annual toy purchases from wholesalers rather than from manufacturers for the following reasons:

1. Reorders are frequently filled more quickly.

2. Wholesalers guarantee the sale (any items not sold can be returned for full credit).

3. Defective products are replaced promptly.

4. The wholesaler extends long-term credit.

5. The percentage of markup by working through a wholesaler is more than offset by decreased inventory carrying costs and improved service levels.

Obviously, the foremost advantages for many retailers in relying on wholesalers is that the latter buy in large quantities, break bulk to suit the convenience of their customers, and realize savings both in cost and transportation. These savings are frequently very favorable when compared with the costs of obtaining merchandise directly from suppliers in large lots from distant points. Thus, by using wholesalers, independent retailers can avoid diluting the energies of their often overtaxed executive staffs. Furthermore, wholesalers give retailers access to a large group of products from small manufacturers that might not otherwise be available to them.

Even for large establishments, reliance on wholesalers allows conversion of dead-weight storage space, formerly devoted to merchandise storage, into profit-making selling or customer service space. For example, although supermarket and discount chains can buy at the same price as rack jobbers or service merchandisers, the latter's hold on the market comes from knowing precisely what to buy and minimizing the handling and inventory costs of a variety of nonfood products, such as health and beauty aids, tapes and records, paperback books, magazines, hardware, and sporting goods. Even for more mainstream grocery items, managers of large chains operating in widely scattered areas have found it beneficial to get many of their supplies from wholesalers.

Retailers have been particularly active in revolutionizing physical distribution practices. They have taken advantage of large-volume purchasing, warehousing, and delivery operations by forming mass-merchandising chain organizations. To a large extent, as the chains grew and prospered, wholesalers were quickly relegated to meeting the needs of small businesses. Because there are still tens of thousands of small manufacturers and retailers in existence, many wholesalers of consumer goods have continued to serve an economic purpose, but to a shrinking portion of the market.

On the other hand, those wholesalers who saw the handwriting on the wall and tried to secure the marketing and physical distribution advantages of large-scale retail chain operations, while permitting local ownership of individual retail units have succeeded handsomely. They formed voluntary (wholesaler-sponsored) chains, franchised systems, and administered systems in order to gain efficiencies in purchasing, advertising, warehousing, accounting, inventory control, and virtually every other business function. They also permitted themselves to become part of retailer-owned cooperatives, for example, Ace Hardware and True-Value.

Beyond those consumer goods wholesalers who have formed vertical marketing systems, there are those who have been successful without changing their corporate organization. Some have restricted their activities to a limited range of products and have sought market niches that do not require high sales volume to be competitive. In groceries, drugs, hardware, periodicals, and jewelry, specialty wholesalers have been able to develop a substantial volume of business. For example, in the grocery trade, such firms supply frozen foods, dairy products, fancy or gourmet foods, bread and baked goods, and beverages. Another good example is service merchandisers. They have been particularly effective because they focus on supplying value-added services such as merchandising, computer support, in-store support, and distribution support services.[16] The more successful specialty wholesalers have been able to serve both large suppliers and large buyers, thus reducing the wholesalers' traditional dependence on small-scale retailers as their main customers.

On the other hand, there have also been a number of general- or full-line consumer goods wholesalers who have achieved viability. Their route to success has been to improve their management and marketing practices, particularly by creatively using advanced information-processing technology. Excellent examples are wholesalers who sell pharmaceuticals, over-the-counter drugs, and toiletries to small, independently owned drugstores. Leading wholesalers have adopted innovative electronic data-processing procedures that have brought efficiencies to pharmacists' handling of inventories. For example, a clerk in a drugstore can alert a hand-held computer to a product's identity by simply waving a small wand across a code on a shelf label. Then the clerk can feed the computer an order for that particular item, and the machine relays it over telephone lines directly to the wholesaler's warehouses. Electronic systems have helped drugstores not only eliminate errors and reduce clerical expenses, but they also keep inventories down because wholesalers can deliver within 24 hours. The wholesalers also sell customized shelf labels and stickers for each product, priced to the druggist's specifications. They can pack items in the order in which the merchandise will be placed on the shelves. The wholesalers also provide retailers with management information reports, which measure sales and markups for groups of products in each store. Naturally, the wholesaler is compensated for performing these value-added services.

The wholesalers have set up computerized accounts receivable programs that enable pharmacists to offer charge accounts to preferred customers—something most small businesses cannot handle without investing in processing equipment of their own. The pharmacists can also check a patient's drug allergies or provide customers with records of drug purchases for submission with their tax returns.[17]

Wholesalers' Services to Business and Industrial Users

Business and industrial users form a particular market segment comprised of manufacturers of large components that purchase small subcomponents from wholesalers, and of businesses and organizations that purchase maintenance, repair, or operating (MRO) supplies from wholesaler-distributors. Although wholesalers offer many of the advantages mentioned for retailers to industrial and business users, some additional factors are briefly discussed here.

Manufacturers of many types of industrial goods tend to be more engineering-oriented than marketing-oriented. They prefer to allocate resources to research and production rather than to distribution, which they know has historically delivered a much lower return on investment. Given this orientation, it is not surprising that manufacturers frequently turn "troublesome" marketing problems over to distribution specialists. This is one of the reasons that industrial distribution, in contrast with consumer goods distribution, has been a particularly viable sector of wholesaling over the years.

Industrial distributors sell primarily to manufacturers. Industrial distributors stock the products they sell, have at least one outside salesperson as well as an inside telephone and/or counter salesperson, and perform a broad variety of marketing channel functions. The products stocked include: maintenance, repair, and operating supplies (MRO items); original equipment manufacturer supplies (OEM), such as fasteners, power transmission components, fluid power equipment, and small rubber parts, which become part of the manufacturer's finished product; equipment used in the operation of a business, such as hand tools, power tools, and conveyors; and machinery used to transform raw materials and semi-finished goods into finished products. Industrial distributors are usually small (under $5 million),[18] but the median size is increasing as the number of distributors declines and the market expands.

The distributor's importance in the marketing channel for industrial goods is increasing for a variety of reasons: the manufacturers' desire to shift more physical distribution responsibilities to distributors as a result of deflationary cost pressures; the tendency for products (e.g., bearings) to become commodities, which permits distributors to have more control over the relationship with the customer because of the diminishing importance of brand names; and the increased value that distributors are adding to products by performing special services, such as assembly and submanufacturing.

Many types of wholesalers provide unique forms of technical assistance that are relatively costly to duplicate elsewhere, except in situations in which a buyer can purchase in very large quantities.

For example, wholesalers of machine tool and accessories often have specialists on their staffs who are available to help customers with problems pertaining to the selection and use of tools and parts. It is not unusual to find such technically trained persons as metallurgists, chemists, draftsmen, and mechanical and civil engineers employed by wholesalers for this purpose. And in data processing, wholesalers called value-added resellers (VARs) have emerged. The VARs package computer software with computing equipment to solve specific problems for specific industries (e.g., inventory control for auto parts dealers). Even managerial assistance is being increasingly provided to business users by wholesalers. For example, one electronics distributor analyzes the stockkeeping methods of one of its industrial customers and recommends revised delivery schedules, prearranged items, packs suitable for assembly line use, and standardized item identification. The customer was able to reduce the possession costs of its stock by 15% of its value.[19]

Recognition of the ultimate cost concept by both wholesalers and their customers has led to a phenomenon called systems selling.

> *Systems selling* is a broad, inclusive term that may be used to describe any form of cooperative contracting relationship between industrial distributors or other wholesalers and their customers for the ordering and distribution of low-value, repetitively used items for maintenance, repair, or operating (MRO) purposes, or for use in manufacturing original equipment.[20]

Wholesalers offer such purchasing systems in order to alleviate the high cost and paperwork facing firms which seek to acquire a wide variety of items, ranging from power tools and welding supplies to lamps, electronic equipment, and hardware. The major means employed by wholesalers' system-selling arrangements to solve these problems include (1) shifting the bulk of customer's on-premises MRO inventory back to the stocking wholesaler, (2) providing for automatic and semiautomatic ordering of these items on an as-needed basis, and (3) providing one-day delivery of the ordered items.[21]

The short lead times on deliveries made available through wholesalers are especially important to industrial users. Flexibility in production scheduling can generally be achieved if production planners know that speedy local deliveries can be forthcoming. Just-in-time inventory scheduling is requiring industrial distributors to work more closely with manufacturing customers in planning inventory needs. The introduction of just-in-time is requiring distributors to hold larger inventories, thus pressuring their profit margins. However, just-in-time represents a great opportunity for many distributors who are capable of capitalizing on it.

> Only 600 yards from the main gate of PPG Industries' sprawling chemical manufacturing complex in Lake Charles, La., sits an industrial office park that is unlike any other in the country. This five-acre park, known as Vendor City, contains nine separate, independent distributorships responsible for delivering a specific family of MRO products to PPG. These distributors are true partners with PPG in every sense of the word. Each distributorship is linked by computer with the chemical company. There are no invoices, distributors are paid on the 15th of every month, products are delivered daily on a just-in-time basis and there is little adversarial relationship between buyers and distributors. Sound too good to be true? Not at Vendor City where nine distributors fill orders at a rate of 98% and where PPG has such confidence in its distributors they maintain no safety stock in certain products.[22]

From the supplier's perspective, industrial distributors have become more capable in fulfilling their major responsibility in the channel. The wholesalers' job in the past has been primarily to contact present and potential customers, ensure product availability, and provide the necessary support services, such as delivery, credit, and technical advice. In this respect, suppliers may have discouraged the kind of integration of wholesaling functions so prevalent in consumer goods channels. In fact, it is much easier for the industrial goods manufacturer to go "direct" than it is for the consumer goods manufacturer. In consumer goods the major problem facing wholesalers is the backward vertical integration of retailers into wholesaling. In industrial goods, the problem is one of manufacturers integrating forward. Although such integration is occurring in the industrial-distribution sector, the problem for wholesalers appears to be more acute relative to consumer goods.

Industrial distributors have maintained and even increased their importance in the marketing channel by forming distributor chains. Entrepreneurs have either acquired or established multiple outlets. As a result, they have been able to secure significant economies of scale by establishing one highly sophisticated inventory, purchasing, and distribution system. The formation of distribution chains is critical for serving national accounts in the hospitality, health care, and fast-food industries. Some of the advantages that distributor chains have over small, privately owned, single-warehouse firms are as follows:

1. Inventory power—Chain inventories are not only deeper and cheaper but also broader and more diversified.

2. Large, linked warehouses—Improved warehouse efficiency by adding highly sophisticated computerized systems, purchasing in quantity, and stocking larger inventories, which result in lower warehousing costs per unit.

3. Quantity discounts—Chain wholesalers can purchase in larger quantities at bulk prices and pass the savings on to customers.

4. Multiple-brand coverage—Chain wholesalers typically have a broader customer base, making it more attractive for various manufacturers to offer their brands to the distributor, resulting in a greater variety of brands represented by the chain.

5. Private labeling—This movement is particularly strong for product lines such as bearings, electrical motors and equipment, and MRO supplies because it offers lower prices to the customer.

Wholesale distribution chains incorporate many of the attributes that are important to industrial customers in choosing a source of supply. They are able to keep delivery promises, offer a better discount structure, maintain an efficient phone-order system, provide stock breadth and depth, offer technical services, enact appropriate sales procedures (e.g., regular sales calls), maintain a strong assortment of brand names, offer quick delivery time, and provide quality assurance. Indeed, because of their capabilities, wholesalers have created serious policy questions for manufacturers seeking to employ both independent and chain distributors in their channels. Some of these questions are as follows:

1. Can we afford to offer exclusives to independents? To chains? If we offer them to independents, is there any way to protect existing exclusives and still sell to chains?

2. How do we sell to chains? Do we need separate sales forces, one for chains and one for independents?

3. Is our volume to chains large enough to permit us to withdraw our branch warehousing support to independents?

4. Should we help independents to pool?

5. How large a reduction in price are we willing to grant chains for assuming the entire warehousing burden?

6. Do we want to provide private labels?

7. What kind of discount structure should we employ?

Business users and retailers alike must be concerned with the overall or ultimate cost of the goods they purchase, handle, and store—not merely with the price at which such goods are obtained. When all factors are considered, it can often be found that the ultimate cost of dealing with wholesalers is less than the ultimate cost of dealing directly with manufacturers, even though the quantity discounts made available by the latter are not generally available when wholesalers are used as suppliers. This ultimate cost concept can justify the use of wholesalers in situations where they might not otherwise appear to be economical.

Demands by customers for rapid delivery are expected to increase. A study of future trends in wholesaling reports that "the durable goods wholesalers' customers are expected to place a greater value on the frequency and speed of delivery, principally because of the increased focus on just-in-time inventory requirements and the manufacturers' increased attention to productivity."[23]

Industrial distributors are being scrutinized by suppliers and customers, alike. Procurement departments are wondering, "What real value do distributors provide me? What are the services provided by the distributors worth?" Many are insisting on pricing terms of activity-based costing (ABC), that is, the customer pays for the product plus each value-added service that is provided, based on a dollar value of the function performed.[24]

As the drive to reduce costs and streamline merchandising processes in the channel continues, more agreements and stocking plans will develop in which distributors are stitched together into networks that cut across product lines on a cross-functional basis to provide products at a lower cost and improved service level. The next decade is likely to see a restructuring in the distribution industry that can best be described as an interactive shift. An interactive shift can be defined as a change in emphasis from merely selling product to filling customer needs with an optimal mix of products and services that best fit the customers' requirements. Many of today's large distributors are likely to evolve into super distributors, representing a number of manufacturers across many product lines. [25] Examples of tomorrow's super distributors include:[26]

- Avnet, Great Neck, New York. A $3-billion distributor of electronics.

- W.W. Grainger, Skokie, Illinois. A $2.4-billion distributor of general line industrial products.

- Graybar Electric, St. Louis, Missouri. A $1.89-billion distributor of electrical products.

- Arrow Electronics, Melville, New York. A $1.5-billion distributor of electronics.

- Consolidated Electric, Westlake Village, California. A $1.2-billion distributor of electrical products.

- Motion Industries, Birmingham, Alabama. A $1-billion distributor of bearings and fluid power.

Super distributors will have a number of advantages over smaller distributors, such as being independent of the manufacturers by having considerable channel control, exercising quality control, possessing marketing expertise superior to the manufacturer's, and possessing the financial resources to implement extensive information system networks.[27]

▶ THE PATHS OF RENEWAL IN WHOLESALE DISTRIBUTION[28]

Despite the challenges they face from demanding customers and tough competitors, many wholesalers have revitalized their businesses and are emerging as savier, more competitive channel members. The key strategies adopted by wholesalers are summarized below.

Focus Strategy

Many wholesalers have reevaluated their basic strategic missions. Some have decided to spin off or divest marginal or peripheral operations that did not complement the company's objectives and focus on product assortments and market segments where they have competitive advantage.

- *Supervalu* decided to concentrate on food operations and spun off its ShopKo general merchandise store division. Subsequently, Supervalu acquired Wetterau to become the largest food wholesaler in the United States.

- In the wholesale drug industry, *Owens & Minor* elected to concentrate on the distribution of medical and surgical supplies and sold its pharmaceutical distribution operations to Bergen Brunswig. In turn, Bergen Brunswig sold its home-entertainment subsidiary, Commtron, and strengthened its drug distribution operations through the acquisition of Durr-Fillauer Medical.

- In Canada, *Univa* (formerly *Provigo*) is refocusing its core businesses on food distribution and has sold or is planning to divest assets invested in general merchandise distribution, drug wholesaling, and sporting and leisure goods distribution.

Marketing Support Philosophy

Today many wholesalers define their companies as being in the "marketing support business" rather than merely in the distribution business. They recognize their primary purpose is to help both suppliers and customers develop effective marketing programs. The marketing support-oriented wholesaler is willing to support any task, activity, or function for either suppliers or customers that will result in more effective and efficient marketing for the entire channel.

Wholesalers in some lines of trade, such as grocery wholesaling, hardware wholesaling, and the automotive parts after-market, have well-established merchandising programs that reflect this philosophy.

- Grocery wholesalers such as *Fleming* and *Supervalu* are pioneers in developing comprehensive merchandising programs for affiliated retailers. These programs range from private labels to store planning and development, from electronic information services to advertising.

- In the hardware industry, *Ace* and *Cotter*, both retailer-owned hardware wholesalers, have extensive customer-service programs. In addition, Ace has developed the "Ace 2000" program, a partnership among dealers, vendors, and Ace that enables the entire Ace team to achieve high-performance retailing results.

- Automotive parts jobbers, particularly *Genuine Parts* in the United States, and *UAP* and *Acklands* in Canada, offer a complete array of products and services to affiliated customers. Genuine Parts can tailor an inventory package for everyone of its 6,000 NAPA stores, enabling each to compete more effectively in specific markets and niches.

Wholesalers are coming up with ingenious ways to increase their importance to their customers and suppliers, and remain an essential link in the channel. A number of wholesaler-distributors are doing this by forming strategic alliances and partnerships with either their suppliers or customers to provide specialized services required of them, and to reduce redundancies in the channel.

Customers and suppliers who are serious about forming enduring partnerships are investing heavily in software necessary for paperless transactions and technology that will change their operations to accommodate more efficient inventory management. The affordability of technology has dramatically increased the number of alliances formed since the early 1990s.[29]

- A successful alliance was completed when *W.W. Grainger, Inc.* and *Kennametal, Inc.* agreed to market MRO supplies and meticulating tools and accessories through each others' media, for example, catalogs. This provided Grainger with a new customer base for its MRO supplies, and granted immediate access for Kennametal to customers who were loyal to Grainger and needed a supplier for meticulating tools. The alliance opened a complementary customer base for each party.[30]

- *FoxMeyer*, a drug wholesaler, has entered into strategic alliances to take over warehousing and distribution functions for several drug store chains, thus allowing these customers to focus on retail operations.

Exploring International Markets

As the U.S. and Canadian economies continue to integrate, an increasing number of U.S. wholesalers are seeking growth opportunities in Canada, and Canadian companies are conversely investing in U.S. distribution companies. More than one-third of the U.S. large, publicly held wholesalers have operations in Canada, and nearly half of Canadian wholesalers have U.S. operations.[31] In addition, many of the 280,000 U.S. wholesalers are expanding their operations overseas through joint ventures and marketing alliances.

The National Association of Wholesaler-Distributors predicts that by the year 2000, wholesalers will generate 18% of their revenues outside the U.S. Because wholesalers fundamentally are locally oriented, many hire foreign nationals to run their businesses in international markets. Drug wholesaler McKesson Corp. relies almost entirely on locals to manage its operation in Canada because they are more familiar with the regulations on the distribution of pharmaceuticals in Canada. Even some wholesalers expecting strong sales at home are eager to expand overseas. For example, in 1993, McLane Co., a $4.8 billion Wal-Mart Stores, Inc. unit, started supplying convenience stores such as 7-Eleven in the UK with candy and food.[32]

Durable-goods wholesalers, particularly those in the industrial, chemical, electronics, and computer fields, are most likely to have significant foreign operations, although many nondurable-goods industries, including paper, drugs, and food, also are making sizable commitments to NAFTA and other international markets. Rather than risk seeking distributors in foreign markets on their own, manufacturers can turn to their North American wholesalers' foreign operation for instant representation. Available data suggest that this trend will accelerate over the decade ahead not only in Canada and Mexico, but also in Western Europe and the free-market economies in Eastern Europe and Eastern Asia.

- More than half of *Sigma-Aldrich's* chemical sales come from customers outside the United States. The company strengthened its foreign presence by acquiring Fluka Chemie AG, a Swiss corporation, in 1989 and by opening overseas sales offices.

- In addition to narrowing its operating focus to paper and office products distribution, *Alco-Standard* is aggressively pursuing a global acquisition strategy. The company has made several large acquisitions in Canada and in Germany and is seeking additional expansion in the United Kingdom.

- *Ace Hardware*, a dealer-owned hardware wholesaler, has been aggressive in recruiting affiliates in other countries. In 1991 Ace began supplying a 321-store chain in South Africa and now serves more than 500 locations in 38 countries. In many cases, wholesalers and manufacturers are joining forces to enter or expand their marketing efforts in foreign markets.

- *Univar*, a chemical wholesaler, acquired four chemical distribution operations in Scandinavia, the United Kingdom, Switzerland, and Italy in the early 1990s. Univar funded its investment in this European subsidiary through the sale of newly issued stock to Dow Chemical Co. Dow also agreed to provide additional capital to continue Univar's expansion in Europe.

- With the U.S. food market becoming more saturated, domestic companies are beginning to look to NAFTA and other international markets for growth. For example, *Fleming* has a joint supermarket project in Mexico. A number of other wholesalers such as *Supervalu*, have taken more ambitious actions or are exploring the possibilities.[33]

Deployment of Technology

Technology encompasses everything from bar-coding and scanning devices to fully automated warehouses, from electronic data interchange links to communications satellites and video text equipment. Technology can cut costs, increase productivity, enhance information management, and improve customer service and marketing. Detailed discussion of these topics is presented in Chapters 4 and 9 of the text.

Advances in information-systems technology are significantly enhancing the wholesaler's ability to serve customers more effectively and efficiently. For example, a large, 500-bed hospital spends $30 to $40 in overhead each time it places an order. Suppliers spend $24 to $28 simply to process an order. Electronic data interchange, or EDI, an electronic protocol already widely used by manufacturers and retailers to control inventories and carry out transactions, has been adopted by wholesalers to consolidate orders from a number of suppliers and expedite the flow of information and goods and to reduce costs. For example,

- Eastman Kodak Co., Rochester, NY, a supplier of imaging products; Boise Cascade Corp., Boise, ID, a marketer of office products; and Bergen Brunswig Corp., Orange, CA, a pharmaceutical distributor, are initial sponsors of generic interchangeable EDI standards for all vendors. The project runs on desktop computers with software marketed by TSI International Software Ltd., Wilton, CT, a closely held supplier of EDI software. The software automates purchasing functions. Later versions are expected to include electronic invoices, a catalog that will enable hospitals to compare prices of competing goods on-line, and electronic payment, eliminating the need to cut and deposit checks.[34]

The use of technology and effective information-management systems is potentially the greatest force of change in all distribution channels. Direct-link capabilities between manufacturers and retailers provide constant information flows that bypasses intermediaries. At the same time, wholesalers with effective technological and information systems can be indispensable to suppliers and customers unable or unwilling to make their own investments in that area.

- *Bergen Brunswig*, a drug wholesaler, currently receives 99% of its orders through electronic order-entry systems and sends 95% of purchase requests to suppliers electronically. Bergen Brunswig credits its distribution technologies with contributing to sales increases, cutting inventory requirements, and reducing labor costs and operating expenses.

- *Arrow Electronics'* inventory management system tracks every item in stock. Three of the company's distribution centers are advanced automated warehouses, one of which is a robotics facility. In addition, 3,500 on-line terminals worldwide can access and check inventory and product status.

- *Avnet,* an electronics distributor, has an EDI system connecting it to suppliers and customers. The system provides information, such as supplier lead times, inventory levels, and order status, for sophisticated inventory analysis. It can forecast inventory needs and send purchase orders to suppliers; later, it sends point-of-sale and inventory data back to suppliers along with electronic invoices. Using this technology, Avnet has been able to maximize efficiency, and reduce administrative, clerical, and materials handling personnel.

Distribution technologies improve communications and, thereby, enhance customer service, which benefits everyone in the channel. Regardless of the line of trade, nearly all wholesalers recognize the importance of using state-of-the-art information and computer technology to assist in developing closer working relations with manufacturers, retailers, and other customers. Effective management of the vast amounts of information this technology generates also is critical to enhancing a company's marketing capabilities.

- *Viking* is a direct marketer of office products, and sells to small- and medium-sized businesses via the 50 different catalogs it produces each year. In addition to using computers to assist in catalog creation, Viking maintains a sophisticated customer database that tracks recency, frequency, amounts of purchase, and specific items ordered. Armed with this computer-generated information, Viking can adjust the frequency and type of catalog mailing to specific groups of customers to improve response rates and profitability.

- *Richfood,* a regional food distributor, has installed a computerized on-line purchasing system that allows buyers to track inventory, place orders, and analyze seasonal buying trends and promotions. Richfood's customers also can obtain product cost data, promotional pricing information, and gross profit data on any product available.

- *Software Spectrum,* a distributor of business software, has developed a number of proprietary systems. With its on-line ordering system, a sales representative can determine the inventory status of products being ordered while reviewing the customer's buying profile. One proprietary database contains answers to all questions the company received in the past about various products. Another system contains information on how and where to locate hard-to-find software packages.

Commitment to Total Quality Distribution

Many wholesalers have begun exploring the advantages of total quality management (TQM) programs. Historically, wholesalers have measured tangible outcomes—such as sales, cases sold, tons handled, or profits generated—to assess the profitability of company operations. At the same time, they measured productivity by comparing outcomes achieved to the resources required, such as sales to inventory or sales per employee. TQM is a move toward managing processes to improve outcomes as perceived by customers, and many wholesalers are making strong commitments to such programs.[35]

As a logical extension of their increasing concern with total customer satisfaction, many wholesalers are performing quality assessments of their suppliers' products. And, as they absorb more of the quality assurance function in the channel, the wholesaler's traditional role is expanding significantly.

- *VWR*, a distributor of laboratory equipment and supplies, defines total quality performance as "understanding who the customer is, what the requirements are, and meeting those requirements, error-free, on time, every time." Furthermore, company goals are to exceed those requirements. Employees attend seminars designed to encourage them to "think, work, and live" the TQM philosophy. Some results of the program are measured objectively in terms of order fill rate, on-time shipments, and error-free work.

- *Pioneer-Standard*, an electronics distributor, has established a company-wide culture with the goal of doing "the right things right the first time." Through its quality-management program, Pioneer-Standard aims to increase customer satisfaction, improve efficiency, and reduce cycle times through horizontally oriented, cross-functional employee teams.

- *Vallen*, an industrial health and safety products distributor, has developed the Supplier Tracking and Measuring Process (STAMP) program allowing the company to evaluate the quality of its suppliers. Vallen credits the program for improving on-time delivery and inventory turnover rates as well as attracting several new regional and national customers. *W.W. Grainger*, a broad-line industrial distributor of MRO items, has developed similar vendor rating systems.

- *Lawson*, an industrial distributor, carries safety ratings on its products, sets specifications for its manufacturing vendors, and chooses products that have higher safety ratings.

Although the above paths for renewal are credited to large publicly held wholesalers, some of their smaller- and medium-sized counterparts have created their own paths for renewal.[36]

- A full-service construction materials wholesaler has found that a profitable marketing niche is a group of small builders of high-quality houses. Many of the small builders felt that larger suppliers were neglecting them in favor of large construction companies. The wholesaler has provided its sales force with extensive training in the needs of small, upscale home builders, who gladly pay a higher price to have their specialized needs met. The sales force can arrange for expedited shipments, flexible terms of sale, and can consolidate orders from different customers to minimize freight bills to small contractors.

- A regional paint and related-products wholesaler uses the strategy of furnishing a product line that is much broader than those of manufacturers' sales branches and other general hardware wholesalers. This strategy is successful because numerous paint retailers are finding that their customers are looking for a wider variety of color and composition than they did in the past. The retailers find it to be very convenient to purchase from one paint wholesaler that carries everything it needs, and the retailer is more likely to qualify for discount pricing as well. The proliferation of demand for a variety of paints has allowed the wholesaler to gain entry into more paint, hardware, and general merchandise retail outlets at the expense of its competitors. Many of the latter are now broadening their paint product lines but will find it difficult to penetrate the entrenched position of the pioneering wholesaler.

- A regional auto parts wholesaler has found prosperity by covering geographic areas that most producers do not want to serve directly: mainly thinly populated areas of the mountain West. Through a combination of efficient routing and telemarketing, the wholesaler can economically and effectively cover the area. Competitors have largely stayed out of this region, apparently because the wholesaler has preempted the market. This company owns a market niche that is populated by satisfied customers who are unlikely to change suppliers.

- A hardware wholesaler follows the strategy of providing more service to its customers than do manufacturers' sales branches and other wholesalers. By providing liberal credit, transportation, storage, consulting, buying, and packaging services to customers, it has established a devoted customer base that is willing to pay for the abundance of value-added services. In some cases, the company will sell on consignment and guarantee specified sales levels. The wholesaler's sales reps serve as troubleshooters for customers and are ordered to immediately investigate customer complaints and problems. These actions provide customers with a sense of true commitment on the part of the wholesaler. An 800 number is available to customers who are unable to reach the wholesalers' sales force immediately.

We can safely conclude that size does not guarantee competitive advantage in wholesaling. Improvements in technology and delivery systems now mean that small companies can serve a national customer base; economies of scale enjoyed by large companies do not necessarily offset the other costs and risks involved in growing. Conversely, large companies are able to compete in very small market niches via technology and strategic decision-making techniques. It is imperative for wholesalers to understand the characteristics that give their company a strategic advantage. The wholesaler must work closely with each customer individually, responding to individual strategic concerns by offering a specific set of services that respond to those particular concerns. The sales force must be trained to find out what percentage of the customer's business the distributor has, who has the remaining business, and why the customer does not give more business to the wholesaler.[37] This will give the wholesaler the information necessary to serve the customer as a "market segment of one."

▶ **SUMMARY AND CONCLUSIONS**

The significance of the wholesalers' roles in channels of distribution is defined by the efficiency of their sorting function, whereby they help match the heterogeneous output of suppliers on the one hand with the diverse needs of retailers and industrial and business users on the other. Many suppliers use wholesalers to reach small customers because they prefer to turn troublesome, supposedly lower-return distribution activities over to specialists. The benefits available to suppliers (manufacturers, growers, etc.) from wholesalers are continuity in, and intimacy with local markets, local availability of stocks, coverage of small-order business, lower costs because wholesalers can spread overhead over many suppliers' products, and relief from the burden of holding inventory.

A study of trends in wholesale distribution sponsored by the Distribution Research and Education Foundation and conducted by Arthur Andersen outlines "eleven new realities" that wholesalers face in the 1990s.[38] Our conclusion draws heavily on these realities and their implications for wholesalers.

Wholesalers are the sales forces and marketing agents of the manufacturers they represent. Increased competition means that wholesaler-distributors must lower sales costs and at the same time increase sales force productivity. The sales force must be deployed to focus on better penetrating existing customer bases and gaining new customers. By increasing sales training, using sophisticated technology, and establishing a strong inside sales/support staff, the productivity of the sales force can increase dramatically.

Wholesalers are the buying agents or purchasing departments of their customers. The wholesaler must assure quality and maximum productivity in all of the basic functions of their businesses, while simultaneously creating new value-added services that reduce customers' costs and improve productivity. The three most important performance characteristics that channel partners expect from wholesalers are reliability, timeliness, and accuracy. Wholesalers can meet these demands if they focus on achieving optimal results by doing the job more efficiently and doing the right things the right way the first time.

Often wholesalers' perceived interests are directly involved with the well-being of retailers and other customers/end-users; therefore, it is logical to assume that wholesalers would develop approaches to assure the survival of retailers. Many wholesalers do, in fact, offer retailers direct selling aid, expert assistance in all respects of retail operations, local and speedy delivery, relief from inventory burdens, quick adjustments, credit extension, and, in some cases, guaranteed sales. Business users can receive many of the same benefits, which may be especially important when it comes to production scheduling and technical assistance.

Wholesalers must perform services for channel partners that will streamline the entire process for all channel members and reduce redundancy in the channel. They should focus on six basic services to suppliers and customers to ensure their success: lower cost for value received, improve efficiency, improve quality, simplify the channel, improve information between channel members, and demonstrate the value of value-added services. By excelling at these services, wholesalers can maintain a faithful clientele that expects perfection from their suppliers.

Nontraditional channel formats are taking market share away from wholesaler-distributors; distributors can no longer be certain who their competitors are. Changes in the channel are pressuring manufacturers and customers to reexamine what they expect from wholesalers and to use another channel format (i.e., warehouse clubs, category killers) if it provides the services they need at an acceptable price. It is imperative that wholesalers keep abreast of market changes and pay particular attention to other industries that may enter the market.[39]

The slow economic growth of the late 1980s and early 1990s has led all channel members to seek out ways to reduce costs. One of the most efficient ways is to purchase from fewer suppliers, increase the amount of business with each remaining supplier, and receive the economies of scale and purchasing clout that come with being a volume customer. Wholesalers who are fortunate enough to be chosen as a "primary" supplier have a chance of increasing market share, whereas other wholesalers who watch their market share decline face the possibility of going out of business.

Strategic alliances between wholesalers and other channel members are forming primarily for two reasons. First, manufacturers and customers are demanding that wholesalers assist in reducing costs within the channel and perform a variety of customer-specific value-added services. Usually this requires a substantial investment of time and money, requires the good will of both parties, and is intended to result in a lasting relationship. Second, the wholesalers are interested in preserving their livelihood and take proactive measures to increase other members' reliance on the wholesalers' expertise to ensure their survival.

Although these strategic alliances and partnerships are designed to help establish wholesalers as viable channel members, the onus is on the wholesalers themselves to pursue managerial strategies to ensure a vibrant role for themselves in the marketing channels for goods and services. These and other issues pertaining to incorporating wholesalers and other channel members into an overall channel design, planning, and management scheme are discussed in detail in Chapters 5 and 6 of this text.

DISCUSSION QUESTIONS

1. Distinguish between a wholesale and a retail sale (e.g., sales at wholesale versus sales at retail).

2. Consider the following statement: "A wholesaling operation can be eliminated as an entity, but someone must perform the wholesaling tasks and absorb the costs sustained by the wholesaler if it is assumed that those tasks are necessary." Take a position on this statement, pro or con, and offer support for your reasoning.

3. Why do manufacturers appear to have a "keener desire to participate more actively in the wholesaling process," as evidenced by the existence of manufacturer sales branches and sales offices?

4. Debate the pros and cons of forward vertical integration of wholesaling functions by manufacturers and by retailers. Support your discussions with examples from any of the commodity lines.

5. Prescribe what a wholesaler needs to do over the next 10 years to remain viable. Should the wholesaler stand pat or make changes? If the latter, what changes? (Pick specific industries, such as steel, groceries, hardware, drugs, electronics.)

6. Inventories and account receivables represent 65% to 85% of the total assets of a wholesaler. Would you say that inventory control is a more or less important policy decision for wholesalers than it is for retailers? How might inventory management and control problems and approaches differ between wholesalers and retailers?

7. Wholesaling is often thought of as a less glamorous intermediary venture when compared with other channel intermediary operations, such as retailing. In your opinion, which of these two would be the more difficult to manage—a wholesaling or a retailing operation? Which would seem to have the best chance, on the average, of achieving a high ROI (return on investment) today? Which would you say has had to face more challenges to its survival in the last 50 years?

ENDNOTES

[1]U.S. Department of Commerce, *1992 Census of Wholesale Trade,* Geographic Area Series, United States (Washington, DC: U.S. Government Printing Office, 1995), p. US-2.

[2]The U.S. Department of Commerce divides wholesale trade into durable and nondurable goods and further splits these categories into 18 Standard Industrial Classification (SIC) product groupings. These groupings are further broken down into specific classifications according to common characteristics referred to as "commodity lines." Commodity line refers to the goods and services that the wholesaler supplies to its customers, for example, agricultural machinery equipment, motor vehicles, photo equipment and supplies, packaged frozen foods, and printing and writing paper.

[3]*1992 Census of Wholesale Trade, op. cit.*

[4]U.S. Industrial Outlook, *Wholesaling,* (Washington, DC: U.S. Department of Commerce, 1994), p. 38-1

[5]Wroe Alderson, "Factors Governing the Development of Marketing Channels," in William G. Moller, Jr., and David L. Wilemon (eds.), *Marketing Channels: A Systems Viewpoint* (Homewood, IL: Richard D. Irwin, 1971), p. 20.

[6]Christine Forbes, "Acquisition Drive Industry Change," *Industrial Distribution,* Vol. 82, No. 3, March 1993, pp. 22–24.

[7]W. Westerfield, "Warehouse Clubs Hypermarkets! Supercenters!" Speech at the National Retail Federation's Financial Executive Conference, San Francisco, June 24–26, 1992, and Kathleen Morris, "Beyond Jurassic Park," *Financial World,* Vol. 162, No. 13 (June 22, 1993), pp. 28–30; and Douglas J. Tigert, et al. "Warehouse Membership Clubs in North America: Are They Retailers of Wholesalers? And Who is at Risk?" *Babson College Retailing Research Reports,* Report No. 6, April 1992.

[8]Christine Forbes, *op. cit.*

[9]Iris Rosendal, "Merger Moves Still Strong in Drug Wholesaling," *Drug Topics,* Vol. 136, No. 21 (November 9, 1992), pp. 101–105; and "The Middlemen Stay on the March: Wholesalers and Distributors Should See Plenty of Growth Along with Some Consolidation," *Business Week,* January 9, 1995, p. 87.

[10]U.S. Industrial Outlook, *op. cit.*

[11]Arthur Andersen and Company, *Facing the Forces of Change 2000: The New Realities in Wholesale Distribution* (Washington, DC: Distribution Research and Education Foundation, 1992), pp. 153–161. Also, see "Why Sam's Wants Businesses to Join the Club," *Business Week,* June 27, 1994, p. 48.

[12]For detailed discussion of dominant buyers and their practices see Bert Rosenbloom and Diane Mollenkopf, "Dominant Buyers: Are They Changing the Wholesaler's Role in Marketing Channels?" *Journal of Marketing Channels,* Vol. 3, No. 1 (1993), p. 74. For empirical evidence of the competitive impact of warehouse clubs, warehouse home centers, and office supply superstores on the traditional wholesaler see Robert F. Lusch and Deborah Zizzo, *Competing for Customers: How Wholesaler-Distributors Can Meet the Power Retailer Challenges* (Washington, DC: Distribution Research and Education Foundation, 1995).

[13]Wholesale Club Industry, Harvard Business School, Case 5-594-035, November 9, 1993, and Teaching Note 5-594-043, October 8, 1993.

[14]*Facing the Forces of Change 2000, op. cit.*

[15]"Cut the Middleman? Never—Distributors and Wholesalers are Learning How to Make Themselves Indispensable," *Business Week,* January 10, 1994, p. 96.

[16]Takeuchi, Hirotaka, *A Note on Wholesale Institutions,* 9-581-011. Boston, Harvard Business School, 1980; p. 12.

[17] See Raymond Corey, "The Role of Information and Communications Technology in Industrial Distribution," in Robert D. Buzzell (ed.), *Marketing in an Electronic Age* (Boston: Harvard Business School Press, 1985), pp. 29–51. For more information about EDI systems, see Louis W. Stern and Patrick J. Kaufman, "Electronic Data Interchange in Selected Consumer Goods Industries: An Interorganizational Perspective," in Buzzell (ed), *op. cit.,* pp. 52–73.

[18]According to Steve Hearn of the Industrial Distribution Association (IDA), the sales volume of 70% of the membership of IDA is $5 million or less. About 21% have volumes ranging from over $5 million to $15 million. The remaining 9% have volumes of over $50 million. Industrial Distribution Association, Atlanta, GA, November 29, 1994.

[19]Burt C. McCammon, Jr. et al., *Wholesaling in Transition: An Executive Chart Book* (Norman, OK: Distribution Research Program), University of Oklahoma, 1989, p. 21.

[20]William J. Hannaford, *Systems Selling: A Marketing Guide for Wholesaler-Distributors,* 3rd ed. (Washington, DC: Distribution Research and Education Foundation, 1983), p. 144.

[21]*Ibid.*

[22]Jack Keough, and Christine Forbes, "Welcome to Vendor City," *Industrial Distribution,* Vol. 80 , No. 7 (May 15, 1991), p. 32.

[23]Arthur Andersen and Company, *Facing the Forces of Change: Beyond Future Trends in Wholesale Distribution* (Washington, DC: Distribution Research and Education Foundation, 1987), p. 35.

[24]Morgan, James P., "Is This the Age of the Super Distributor?" *Modern Distribution Management,* Vol. 24, No. 7 (April 10, 1994), pp. 6–7.

[25]*Ibid.,* p. 7.

[26]*Ibid.,* p. 5.

[27]*Ibid.,* p. 7.

[28]This section in its entirety is excerpted from Robert F. Lusch, Deborah Zizzo, James M. Kenderdine, "Strategic Renewal in Distribution," *Marketing Management,* Vol. 2, No. 2 (1993), pp. 20–29 published by and reprinted with the permission of the American Marketing Association, except as noted in subsequent footnotes. For a detailed discussion of the strategic options adopted by wholesalers see also Deborah Zizzo et al. *The Changing Economics of Wholesaling: A North American Chartbook* (Norman, OK: University of Oklahoma, Distribution Research Program, 1993).

[29]Bruce Merrifield, Jr., " 'Infotech' Applications for Distribution Channels," *Modern Distribution Management,* Vol. 24, No. 18 (September 25, 1994), p. 5.

[30]"Grainger/Kennametal: The Latest Alliance," *Modern Distribution Management,* Vol. 24, No. 21 (November 10, 1994), p. 3.

[31]Deborah Zizzo, James Kenderdine, and Robert Lusch. *The Changing Economics of Wholesaling: A North American Chartbook* (Norman, OK: University of Oklahoma, Distribution Research Program, 1993), p. A-5.

[32]Joseph Weber, "1993 Industry Outlook: Wholesaling—On a Fast Boat to Anywhere," *Business Week,* January 11, 1993, p. 94.

[33]Steve Weinstein, "Spanning the Globe," *Progressive Grocer,* Vol. 71 (October 1992), pp. 65–70.

[34]Ron Winslow, "Four Hospital Suppliers Will Launch Common Electronic Ordering System," *The Wall Street Journal,* April 12, 1994, p. 38.

[35]For detailed discussion of the topic see Walpert, Smullian, and Blumenthal, Public Accountants, *Total Quality Distribution* (Washington, DC: Distribution Research and Education Foundation, 1993).

[36]Robin T. Peterson, "Wholesalers Far from Being Eliminated," *Marketing News,* (October 10, 1994), p. 19.

[37]For more details about sales force effectiveness in wholesale distribution see Adel I. El-Ansary et al. *Winning Customers, Building Accounts. Some Do It Better* (Great Neck, NY: PAPER Foundation, 1994).

[38]*Facing the Forces of Change, op.cit.,* pp. 84–90.

[39]*Ibid.,* pp. 91–97.

APPENDIX

PARTICIPATION IN THE MARKETING FLOWS BY DIFFERENT TYPES OF WHOLESALERS

◀◀◀◀◀◀◀

Wholesaling agencies, their functions, and the marketing flows are described in this appendix. (Note: All of the agencies described are pure types; in real life we often find agencies that are composites of several of these types.)

A. *Merchant wholesalers.* Merchants whose principal business is buying goods in job lots and reselling them for a profit to customers who (1) resell the goods again to someone else, or (2) consume the goods in the course of operating a profit-making enterprise. A merchant wholesaler's compensation is a *profit* made *on the sale of the goods.*
    1. *Full-function or service wholesalers.* The "traditional" wholesalers who perform all or most of the marketing functions normally associated with wholesaling. Participate directly in all or most of the flows of marketing. Particularly useful in broad retail lines, such as groceries and drugs.
        a. *Physical possession flow.*
           (1) Take possession of goods.
           (2) Maintain storage facilities.
           (3) Maintain stocks of goods sufficient in both variety and quantity to supply customers on regular basis.
           (4) Deliver goods to customer.

Source: Department of Marketing, Wharton School, University of Pennsylvania.

b. *Ownership flow.* Take legal title (ownership) from supplier, pass it on to customer when sale is made.

c. *Promotion.* May participate in manufacturer's advertising allowances; may print catalogs for trade; may advertise to trade; maintain sales force.

d. *Negotiation.* Make contact and negotiate over prices, quality, quantity, terms of sale, and so on, with *both* supplier and customer.

e. *Financing.* Extend credit to customers (thereby financing the customer's inventory). Help to finance manufacturer to extent that wholesaler relieves manufacturer of burden of carrying large stocks of finished goods.

f. *Risking.* By taking ownership, assume all risks of failure to sell goods and of changes in the prices of the goods. Risk assumption may be offset by manufacturer's willingness to accept returns and/or guarantee price.

g. *Ordering.* In effect, flow of ordering moves from retailer to manufacturer. In reality, anticipate needs of retailers and order from manufacturer in advance of actual sale to retailer (see "Risking").

h. *Payment.* Accept payment for goods from customers; pass payment minus expenses and profit to supplier. May pay supplier *before* collecting from customer (another form of risk).

2. *Limited-function wholesalers.* Wholesalers who do not perform some of the marketing functions, either eliminating them entirely or passing them on to someone else. Some limited-function wholesalers *participate* in all of the marketing flows, but their *degree* of participation in any one flow may be considerably less than that of the service wholesaler.

a. *Drop shipper (desk jobber).* A wholesale merchant who passes on the order of his customer with instructions to the manufacturer to ship directly to a location specified by the customer. Maintains no warehouse or inventory, *does not take physical possession* of the goods. Much contact with his customers by telephone, hence may have no sales force and may be much less active in promotional flow. Particularly useful in bulky goods and where merchandise typically moves in carlot quantities. (Sometimes called a *carlot wholesaler.*)

b. *Cash-carry wholesalers.*

   (1) *Financing.* Do not finance customers because of no-credit policy.

   (2) *Physical possession flow.* Same position in this flow as the service wholesaler, except that customer assumes burden of delivery.

   (3) *Promotion.* Operation, by its nature, is a cost-cutting one. Dealing often in small orders with small retailers, therefore less likely to have an outside sales force.

c. *Wagon jobbing (truck jobbing).*

   (1) *Wagon jobbers* (self-employed merchants).

      (a) Little capital, often extend no credit to customers.

      (b) May own goods, but often get them on consignment from supplier.

      (c) Often maintain no warehouse, buy on hand-to-mouth basis.

   (2) *Driver-sales agents* (not really wholesalers). Take goods on consignment or salary rather than profit.

   (3) Used with perishables and semiperishables; sometimes with auto parts, cigars and cigarettes, candy, sundries.

d. *Rack jobbers.* Important in variety and specialty lines, especially in supermarkets. Maintain racks stocked with merchandise at the retailer's location.

   (1) *Ownership and risk.* Heavy assumption of risk because the *jobber keeps title* and the *retailer is billed only for goods sold from the rack.*

   (2) *Finance.* Assume the sole financial burden for the goods, finance customer's inventory by maintaining ownership. Retailer's only investment is in the space allotted to the rack.

   (3) *Promotion.* Deal widely in highly advertised, branded, well-known goods. Have to do little promotion of the goods, which are "self-selling" through display. (*Note:* Use of the well-known brands partially offsets the risks of ownership.)

3. *Other types of wholesale operations, often of a special-purpose nature.*
   a. *Converters.*
      (1) *Ownership.* Purchase cloth from textile mills; process, dye, or print it on contract basis for garment manufacturers.
      (2) *Physical possession.* Cloth frequently finished in outside plants; converter may never touch it.
      (3) *Finance.* May take entire output of textile mill; may extend heavy credit to garment manufacturers.
      (4) *Risking.* Ownership risk assumed by converter heavy because of fluid changes in popularity of patterns and colors; risk also strong when financing small garment manufacturers (high bankruptcy rate).
      (5) *Ordering.* Highly anticipatory of needs of garment makers.
   b. *Franchise wholesalers.* Retailers affiliate with existing wholesaler, who gives them right (franchise) to use certain name or storefront design. Most *voluntary chains* operate under franchises from wholesalers.
      (1) *Promotion.* May furnish advertising material for affiliates; may aid retailers in display and point-of-sale promotion.
      (2) Often operate on a *cost-plus* basis.
      (3) Often use *preprinted order forms;* outside sales force may give service more of an advisory nature to retailers.
      (4) May furnish accounting service for retailers.
      (5) Participation in marketing flows very similar to that of service wholesalers except that *more services* are often provided to affiliates.

B. *Retailer-sponsored cooperatives.* Independent *retailers* form an association, which buys or builds wholesale warehouse facilities that they own cooperatively. The *wholesale* operation is thus not a profit-making institution, but exists only as an arm of the associated retailers. *As a unit,* however, it participates in many of the marketing flows.
   1. *Ownership.* As a legal entity, the cooperative takes title to the merchandise. Legal responsibilities will depend on the form of organization.
   2. *Physical possession.* Cooperative performs all acts of possession, and physical handling of goods.
   3. *Promotion.* Cooperative advertising is executed by the staff of the organization for the membership. Sales force for *selling* purposes often eliminated; outside staff members may render aid to member stores in display, point-of-sale promotion, and so on.
   4. *Negotiation.* The cooperative negotiates (on behalf of its membership) with suppliers. Cooperative organization usually set up so that members are supplied on *cost-plus* basis (landed or invoice cost plus estimated allowable expenses).
   5. *Financing.* May carry members' accounts on credit basis, but does not really finance members because it is the *member's* capital that finances the cooperative.
   6. *Risking.* The cooperative, as a unit, may lose money on inventories, but the risk (and profits or losses) are shared by the membership.
   7. *Ordering.* The cooperative is, in effect, passing on the orders of the membership to suppliers. Often uses *preprinted order forms.*
   8. *Flow of payment.* Normal membership, through organization to suppliers.

C. *Other agencies involved in wholesaling. Functional middlemen,* specializing in performance of one or more specific marketing tasks, especially those concerned with *negotiation.* As a rule, participate in only a *few* of the flows. *Not merchants:* their compensation is in the form of a commission or fee for a service rendered, *not* a profit on the sale of goods.
   1. *Brokers.* Agents who specialize in buying or selling goods for a principal. Usually have neither title to, nor possession of, the merchandise.
      a. *Ownership and physical possession.* Through making a sale, they *facilitate*

changes in ownership and possession. They do not participate directly in these flows.

b. *Promotion.* May advertise in trade journals, have sales agents to call on trade. Broker himself may be a salesman.

c. *Negotiation.* Negotiate with customers on price, quantity, quality, terms of sale, and so on, within limitations of authority granted by principal. Results of negotiation *binding* on principal so long as broker does not exceed authority given him.

d. *Financing.* Brokers seldom give or receive credit. Financial arrangements between principal and customer.

e. *Risking.* Brokers never own goods, take no risk on them, do not figure in the flow of risk *on the goods.* (Naturally, they take their own risks in choosing whom to represent, etc.)

f. *Ordering.* Customer orders from principal, through broker.

g. *Payment.* Payment for goods usually goes from their customers to the suppliers. They *may* (but not always) collect from customer and deduct their commission.

h. With free-lance brokers, each sale is a separate and distinct transaction; may frequently change principals whom they represent.

2. *Manufacturers' agents.* Sell part of the output of manufacturers on an extended contract basis.
   a. Difference from brokers.
      (1) Represent limited number of principals, whom they represent regularly,
      (2) Usually represent several noncompeting lines from different manufacturers.
      (3) Territory definite and limited.
      (4) Prices, terms of sale, and so on, set by principal.
   b. Involvement in marketing flows similar to broker, except:
      (1) May be more active in promotional aspects of selling (e.g., having outside sales representatives) than broker.
      (2) Will often sell in smaller lots than broker.

3. *Selling (or sales) agents.*
   a. Normally handle entire output of the principal (thus, in effect, become sales force of manufacturer).
   b. Usually given more complete authority over prices, terms of sale, territory, and so on.
   c. May use manufacturers' agents or brokers in places where they maintain no office.
   d. May have quite an extensive sales force and promotional program.

4. *Commission merchants* (sometimes called *factors*). Receive goods on consignment for sale on a commission basis.
   a. Maintain a warehouse, involved in physical handling of goods, thus participate in the flow of *physical possession.*
   b. *Ownership.* Receive goods on consignment basis, have no title.
   c. *Promotion.* May maintain full sales force, print catalogs, have sales offices in various cities, advertise in trade magazines.
   d. *Negotiation.* Have full power to negotiate price, terms of sale, and so on, with customer.
   e. *Financing.* May extend credit to customers, often assuming the risk of making collections as *del credere* agent.
      (1) *Factoring.* Finance their principals, often by *discounting accounts receivable* from buyers.

f. *Risking.* May assume risk of collecting accounts in factoring; may be responsible for payment to principal prior to collection of discounted account receivable.

g. *Ordering.* May order entire output of manufacturer on consignment in anticipation of orders from customers.

h. *Payment.* May collect from customers, forward payment to principal after deduction of expenses and commission.

LOGISTICS of DISTRIBUTION

◀◀◀◀◀◀

STRUCTURE AND STRATEGY

*I*n all marketing channels the product must be moved in the right quantity at the right time to a specific place in order to be delivered most efficiently to the end-user. *Logistics* or *supply-chain management* are the terms widely used for the management of the flow of goods and services and related information from the point of origin to the point of consumption.[1]

A supply chain is the network of suppliers and customers in which any business operates. In a time of shortening product life cycles, complex corporate joint ventures, and stiffening requirements for customer service, it is necessary to consider the complete scope of supply-chain management, from the supplier of raw materials, through factories and warehouses, to the demand from the end-user/customer for a finished product.[2] The differences between the traditional and supply-chain management approaches to materials and physical distribution management in the channel are presented in Table 4-1. The concept of supply-chain management is adopted by companies locally and globally to achieve superior customer service and even competitive advantage for nations. For example:

- Committed to global supply-chain management as a customer service strategy, Becton Dickinson & Co. has invested $45 million in two adjacent distribution centers located in Temse, Belgium, which will centralize the medical supplies and equipment company's European distribution system. The Belgian site was selected for several reasons: (1) the port facilities at Antwerp, Belgium, (2) tax grants and financial incentives, and (3) the existence of a strong base of information technology capability. The latter reason was particularly important as a key element of Becton Dickinson's strategy involves electronic data interchange (EDI) transfers between various European sales offices and the Belgium facility. The facilities have accomplished specific customer-service goals, such as greater product availability, fewer split deliveries, increased full-order fulfillment, more-frequent on-time deliveries, and improved service on late request and emergency deliveries.[3]

- The Dutch clearly dominate distribution and value-added logistics (VAL). According to an Ernst & Young report, the Netherlands is Europe's preferred location for distribution-related companies. Using the distribution resources of vehicles, airplanes, and ships in the name of immediate market responsiveness defines VAL. Dutch officials boast of the country's competitive telecommunications system, multilingual work force, politically neutral global stance, and reliance on international business. The Dutch view VAL in terms of customer response. Excellent service distinguishes Dutch companies involved in distribution.[4]

▶**TABLE 4-1 Traditional and Supply Chain Management Approaches Compared**

ELEMENT	APPROACH	
	Traditional	Supply Chain
Inventory management approach:	Independent efforts	Joint reduction in channel inventories
Total cost approach:	Minimize firm costs	Channel-wide cost efficiencies
Time horizon:	Short-term	Long-term
Amount of information sharing and monitoring:	Limited to needs of current transaction	As required for planning and monitoring processes
Amount of coordination of multiple levels in the channel:	Single contact for the transaction between channel pairs	Multiple contacts between levels in firms and levels of channel
Joint planning:	Transaction-based	Ongoing
Compatibility of corporate philosophies:	Not relevant	Compatible at least for key relationships
Breadth of supplier base:	Large to increase competition and spread risk	Small to increase coordination
Channel leadership:	Not needed	Needed for coordination focus
Amount of sharing of risks and rewards:	Each on its own	Risks and rewards shared over the long-term
Speed of operations, information and inventory flows:	"Warehouse" orientation (storage, safety stock) interrupted by barriers to flows; Localized to channel pairs	"Distribution Center" orientation (inventory velocity) interconnecting flows; JIT, Quick Response across the channel

Source: Martha C. Cooper and Lisa M. Ellram, "Characteristics of Supply Chain Management and Implications for Purchasing and Logistics Strategy," *The International Journal of Logistics Management*, Vol. 4, No. 2 (1993), p. 16.

Logistics management encompasses two distinct but integrated cycles, that is, materials management and physical distribution management.

THE MATERIALS MANAGEMENT CYCLE   Goods and services flow to the firm through a process of material acquisition (or purchasing) and must be managed as incoming material with an effective system that includes inbound transportation and inventory management. This process is called the *materials management cycle* in most firms. Transportation and purchasing strategies, warehousing designs and operation, and inventory control methods are tailored in this cycle to the cost-effective introduction of these material resources into the firm. Methods used include materials requirements planning (MRP), just-in-time (JIT) systems, and co-maker purchasing. As channel members continue to improve service, they evolved MRP and JIT into MRP I and II and JIT I and II. These methods will be explained later in this chapter.

The emphasis on inbound materials management cycle is clearly on the efficient acquisition, delivery, control, and application of raw materials, finished or semifinished goods, and services used in the internal operations of the firm. This materials management flow, which involves an interface with vendors and suppliers, is tied directly to internal firm operations. Scheduling, control, information flow, coordination, and smooth interface with both vendors and the transportation systems are paramount to ensure profitability. Demand projections for raw materials and supplies are often based on a projected production schedule or other internal usage plan. Given discipline in internal planning, these demand projections provide an opportunity for a highly integrated materials-management process. We will examine current approaches to integrated materials management later in this chapter.

THE PHYSICAL DISTRIBUTION CYCLE   *Physical distribution* is a term more appropriately applied to the outgoing product flow from the firm to customers through some defined network of transportation links and storage or distribution nodes called a *distribution network.* This network may tie the firm to an individual consumer or to other firms that may either use the products produced in another stage of manufacturing, conversion, or service generation, or serve as wholesalers or retailers in the distribution of the products to another set of customers. Thus, the physical distribution cycle as viewed from the producer of the product is often likely to represent the materials management cycle to the buyer of the product, and it is often repeated several times in a given marketing channel.

Perhaps the key to the methods used to manage transportation, storage, and inventory control in the physical distribution cycle of a firm is the nature of the materials-management process of the buyer. Where products or services are being distributed in a physical distribution network subject to stochastic customer demand, inventories are often decoupled both from production and from related inventories and managed under traditional reorder point systems. Some forward-looking firms have implemented so-called distribution requirements planning (DRP) DRP I, DRP II, quick response (QR), or efficient consumer response (ECR) systems for these inventories. However, where products or services are distributed in a physical distribution network subject to deterministic demand (for example, fixed long-term orders), production, transportation, and inventory control decisions can often be tied directly to the buyer's materials-management process.

Viewed together, the materials management cycle and the physical distribution cycle form the overall logistics cycle for the firm. Thus, the term *logistics management* encompasses the total flow of materials from acquisition of raw materials to the delivery of the finished product to the ultimate consumer and the counter-flow of information that controls and records the material movement. Because of the common use of the term *physical distribution* to refer to all logistics activities in the channel, we use that term and *logistics* interchangeably in this chapter. Figure 4-1 illustrates the components of the logistics system and Figure 4-2 presents an operational view of the system. The components and flows of the logistics system, as shown in Figure 4-3, are discussed in detail throughout this chapter. The discussion focuses on strategic decision making relating to system design and tactical decisions relating to system operation.

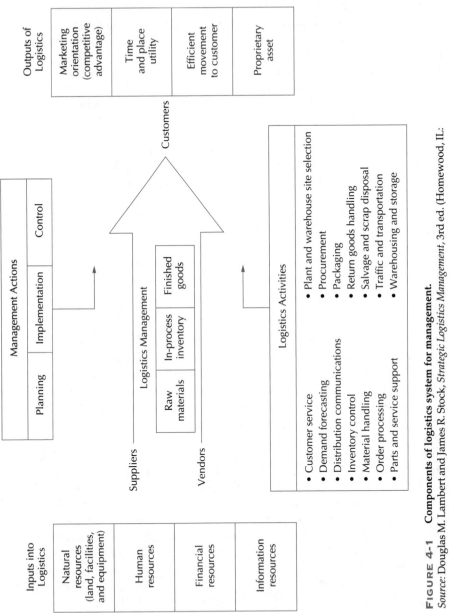

FIGURE 4-1 Components of logistics system for management.
Source: Douglas M. Lambert and James R. Stock, *Strategic Logistics Management*, 3rd ed. (Homewood, IL: Richard D. Irwin, 1993), p. 5.

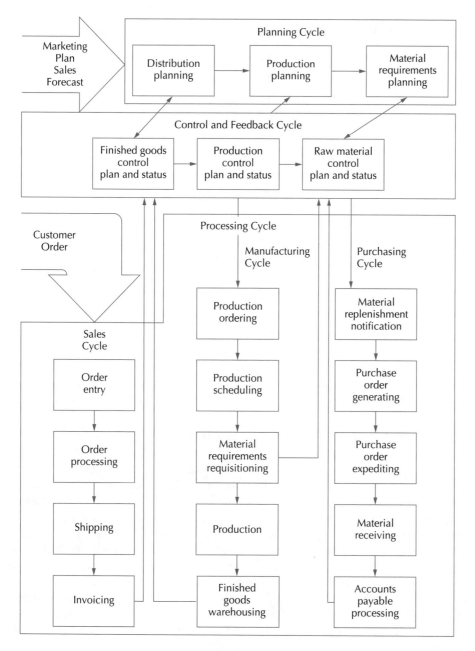

FIGURE 4-2 Operational elements of a physical distribution system.
Source: Harrison J. Appleby, "Organizing the Logistics Function to Optimize Benefits," in *Proceedings of the Sixteenth Annual Conference of the National Council of Physical Distribution Management,* October 16–18, 1978, p. 184.

FLOW OF INFORMATION	FUNCTION	FLOW OF MATERIAL
	Forecasting	
	Order processing	
	Finished product transport, warehouse to customer	
	Finished product inventory control	
	Distribution center warehousing	
	Transportation from plant to distribution center	
	Packaging	
	Production planning	
	Plant storage	
	Production material control	
	Raw material storage	
	Raw material transportation	
	Raw material inventory control	
	Procurement	

FIGURE 4-3   **Flows within the logistics pipeline.**
Source: Reprinted by permission from p.7 of *Logistics Strategy: Cases and Concepts* by Joy D. Shapiro and James L. Heskett; Copyright © 1985 by West Publishing Company. All rights reserved.

▶ THE SIGNIFICANCE OF PHYSICAL DISTRIBUTION

Physical distribution functions are costly. One survey reported physical distribution costs ranging from a low of 4.02% of sales for firms shipping pharmaceuticals to a high of 13.06% of sales for firms shipping hospital and medical goods. The total distribution cost of an "average" U.S. firm was 8.01% of sales.[5] Although physical distribution costs may vary for different companies and industries, the importance of this aspect of marketing channels in the entire economy is intensified by the fact that the physical distribution of goods from point of origin to ultimate consumers costs $600 billion a year, or 11% of Gross National Product (GNP).[6] Perhaps the best way to illustrate the role logistics plays in the U.S. economy is to compare logistical expenditures with other societal activities. Business logistics costs ten times as much as advertising and twice as much as national defense, and is equal to the cost of medical care.[7]

Not only has physical distribution taken on increased economic significance, it has also taken on increased management significance, for several reasons. First, many managers have realized that improving the efficiency of individual logistics operations such as production, warehousing, or transportation is useless if the efficiency of the individual function throws the total system out of balance. Second, the logistics system has become an important competitive tool and is the area where the struggle to control distribution takes place.[8] Third, many of the technological developments over the last 20 years have been system oriented and as such, force consideration of the logistics system as a whole. Finally, logistics is no longer just a part of the business where cost can be minimized, but is seen instead as an important strategic consideration.

> Logistics have become central to product strategy because, it is increasingly clear, products are not just things-with-features. They are things-with-features *bundled with services*. Companies do not create value for customers and sustainable advantages for themselves merely by offering varieties of tangible goods. Rather, they offer goods in distinct ways, presuming that consumers value convenience, reliability, and support. They are in an implicit and complex *relationship* with customers. The challenge is to manage the whole of it.[9]

► IMPLICATIONS FOR PHYSICAL DISTRIBUTION MANAGEMENT

The physical distribution function offers great potential for profit improvement. The fact is, in many industries, distribution costs can be as much as 30 to 40% of total cost, can exceed 25% of each sales dollar at the manufacturing level, and the assets required by distribution can account for more than 30% of corporate assets.[10] With an integrated physical distribution system, *visible costs*, such as transportation, warehousing, and inventory management can be reduced. Therefore, one of the concerns of physical distribution management is to keep these visible costs down. In addition to controlling visible distribution costs, the physical distribution manager must also be concerned with *hidden costs*. These are the profit opportunities lost due to failure to ship the product on time and the cost of lost sales, canceled orders, and customer dissatisfaction associated with stockouts.

In theory, management cost control is very straightforward. In practice it is often very difficult to identify hidden costs, pinpoint controllable costs, and assign organizational responsibility for control of these costs. Also, the interdependence of customer service levels and these costs makes the job of controlling costs even more difficult.[11] Improving the service level provided by the physical distribution system increases costs; conversely, a cost reduction may lower the level of customer service. The total cost concept or physical distribution concept, as it is called here, provides guidelines for achieving the critical balance between costs and the level of service provided by the system.

► THE PHYSICAL DISTRIBUTION CONCEPT: A TOTAL SYSTEM PERSPECTIVE

The *physical distribution* (PD) concept emerged from a renowned study completed 40 years ago.[12] This concept can be described as a *cost-service* orientation, backed by an integrated physical distribution network, that is aimed at *minimizing* the total costs of distribution at a *given level of customer service*. The four main components of the PD concept are (1) a total cost perspective, (2) the understanding of relevant trade-offs among costs, (3) the notion of zero suboptimization, and (4) the total system perspective or supply chain management. Each is discussed briefly here.

The Total Cost Perspective

The key to the total cost approach is to consider *simultaneously* the cost of all physical distribution elements, visible and hidden, when trying to achieve specified levels of customer service. Because all physical distribution activities are interdependent, a change in one will affect the others. Management should strive to minimize the *total* costs of physical distribution rather than attempt to minimize the cost of each element.[13]

Cost Trade-offs

The cost trade-offs concept, which goes hand in hand with the total cost approach, recognizes that the cost patterns of the different activities of the firm sometimes display characteristics that put them in economic conflict with one another.[14] This can be shown in Figure 4-4. Notice that as the number of warehouses increases, the transportation costs decline and the inventory and order processing costs increase. Even though certain costs may increase while others are purposely reduced, the desired result, under the PD concept, is that total distribution cost will decline.

Zero Suboptimization

When one distribution function is optimized, the result will likely be an impairment of the *performance* of other distribution functions. For example,

- Lowering warehousing costs by reducing inventory levels might also reduce customer service or inhibit corporate purchasing agents from making advantageous purchases.

- Reducing inventories might involve reducing assortment and thus reducing the system's ability to fill orders on time.

- Increasing the speed of delivery might increase customer service but could also involve higher transportation costs and thus a higher total cost.

- Setting a high level of customer service might involve an increase in inventory and in inventory-carrying costs.

- Attaining a goal of lower transportation costs might result in increased inventories and a reduced level of customer service.

Distribution network goals should be set with the realization that the achievement of goals in one area of distribution may affect the attainment of goals in other distribution areas.

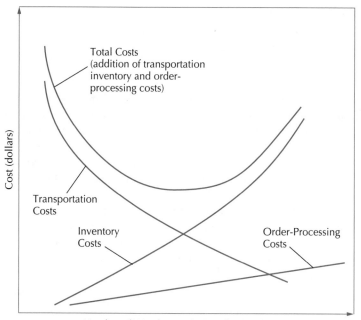

FIGURE 4-4   Basic cost trade-offs in determining the number of ware-houses in a distribution system.
Source: Ronald Ballou, *Business Logistics Management*, 3rd ed. (Upper Saddle River, NJ: Prentice-Hall, Inc., 1992), p. 41. Reprinted by permission of Prentice-Hall, Upper Saddle River, NJ.

When physical distribution functions are coordinated and integrated, the focus of system management should be to minimize suboptimization or, ideally, reach zero suboptimization, that is, eliminate suboptimization. At the same time, logistics is just one subsystem of the firm and should not be optimized at the expense of another function of the business. Also, each firm is a member of a channel, and firm optimization should not be done at the cost of channel efficiency.

The Total System Perspective

This concept is an extension of the PD concept and is the key to managing the physical distribution function. It extends the PD concept to cover trading off the cost of performing different functions throughout the entire marketing channel. For example, price-ticketing of goods is normally performed at the retail level. The process is time-consuming and labor intensive. Some large retailers have resorted to direct negotiations with suppliers of goods to shift the price-ticketing operation to the assembly line at the supplier's production facilities. Retailers provide up-to-date price lists to their suppliers, and the goods are received preticketed at the retailer's premises. Naturally, manufacturers have increased their prices to retailers to compensate for the prolonged production process resulting from the assumption of the price-ticketing function. Usually retailers are ready for these increases, because they are more than offset by the reduction of their own cost. The result is a reduction in the total distribution cost in the channel system.

Channel Integration

The total systems perspective of the 1960s evolved into channel integration strategies in the 1990s. Channel integration, not to be confused with vertical integration requiring ownership, involves establishing channel partnerships and strategic alliances. Their purpose is to streamline physical and information channel flows by reengineering the distribution process. Channel reengineering is achieved through the deployment of a broad range of information and telecommunication technologies as discussed in detail in Chapter 1.

Channel integration shifts the point of logistics management from simply total cost reduction to a return on investment focus. By emphasizing return on investment for logistics decisions, management is forced to consider the full impact of the logistics system on the balance sheet and income statement. It is necessary to derive a detailed evaluation of the impact of the logistics system on the following items to make sure the logistics system is making the greatest possible contribution to corporate goals:

■ *Revenues.* Positioning stocks of goods in locations and facilities where they can be delivered reliably and swiftly to a customer will generally lead to higher sales revenues. This is especially true if a company is thereby able to serve the market better than its competitors can.

■ *Expenses.* All cost-incurring activities and their interdependence must be assessed within the "total cost" approach. Critical here are transportation, warehousing, and inventory. Together they frequently represent up to 90% of total logistics costs.

■ *Capital Investment.* The search for improved customer service or lower logistics costs or both may require additional capital investment. An assessment should be made of those areas in which investing seems most beneficial: in plant and manufacturing equipment, or in a proliferation of inventories at strategic locations across the country.[15]

Kmart, Kodak, and Lee Apparel adopted the channel integration approach to coordinate the flow of product from the warehouse to the store floor known as channel integration. This process depends on retailers sharing information on sales at the store level with suppliers. This exchange of information enables suppliers to manufacture at the level of actual demand for a product and ship only the product needed. Channel integration allows both the supplier and the retailer to carry the barest minimum of inventory in their warehouses. With the possibility of revolutionizing the way U.S. retailers and suppliers do business, channel integration could become the most important logistics concept of the later half of the 1990s. Both retailers and manufacturers benefit from channel integration by reducing inventory levels and lowering handling and transportation costs.[16]

In order to achieve channel integration, management must design and implement a logistics system that coordinates the components of the entire system, so

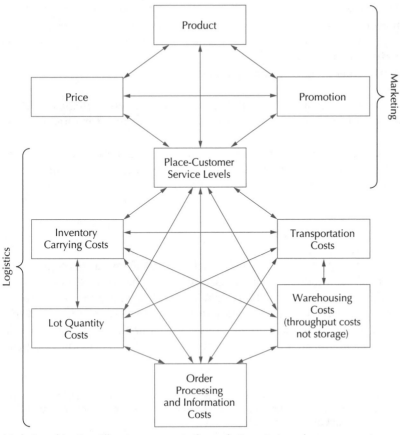

Marketing objective: Allocate resources to the marketing mix in such a manner as to maximize the long-run profitability of the firm.

Logistics objective: Minimize total costs given the customer service objective.

Where total costs equal transportation costs + warehousing costs + order processing and information costs + lot quantity costs + inventory carrying costs.

FIGURE 4-5   Cost trade-offs required in marketing and logistics.
Source: Adapted from Douglas M. Lambert, *The Development of an Inventory Costing Methodology: A Study of the Cost Associated with Holding Inventory* (Chicago: National Council of Physical Distribution Management, 1976), p. 7, as reported in Douglas M. Lambert and James R. Stock, *Strategic Logistics Management,* 3rd ed. (Homewood, IL: Richard D. Irwin, 1993), p. 42.

as to minimize its total cost at a given level of customer service, as shown in Figure 4-5. The core component of the system is customer service standards, shown in the center of the diagram. Below it are the five basic PD system components; above it are support system components.

This chapter concentrates on the six core and basic components:

1.   The development of customer service standards.
2.   The selection of transportation modes.

3. The determination of the optimal number and location of warehousing facilities.

4. The setting of inventory management and control procedures.

5. The determination of production scheduling involving the quantity and kind of finished products to produce.

6. The design of order processing and information systems.

We emphasize these six areas because they represent the most strategic as well as the most cost-significant components of physical distribution for most channel members.

Once system design is accomplished, attention to logistics system management, or the effective melding of all decision areas into a meaningful whole, is required. We discuss this in the final section of the chapter.

▶ CUSTOMER SERVICE STANDARDS

It must be continually emphasized that channel strategy formulation begins with a determination of customer needs and requirements, that is, customer service standards. Customer service standards are detailed breakdowns of service level outputs discussed in Chapter 1. The key elements of *customer service*, identified in a study sponsored by the National Council of Logistics Management, are shown in Figure 4-6. Those elements are grouped into pretransaction, transaction, and posttransaction categories.

- *Pretransaction* elements, though not directly involved with physical distribution, provide the opportunity to establish a climate for good customer service. As such they have a sizable impact on product sales.

- *Transaction* elements are those activities that are directly associated with the delivery of the product to the customer. Thus, the customer is directly affected by the level of service provided here.

- *Posttransaction* elements are those activities that support the product after it has been sold; protect customers from defective products; provide for the return of packages; and handle complaints, claims, and returns. Those services can have a significant impact on the purchase decision.[17]

The first step in developing customer service standards is to determine which of the elements in Figure 4-6 are most important to the customers. This information can be obtained through questionnaires or customer service surveys.[18] The service standards *must* be set according to customer needs, not according to what management thinks these needs are. Any discrepancies between actual and desired performance should be reported to the appropriate level of management on a regular basis. Naturally, the importance of each of these elements will vary from industry to industry and even from company to company within an industry. In addition, the distribution manager's level of control over each element varies.[19] The challenge is to give customers *what* they want just in time. However, discovering

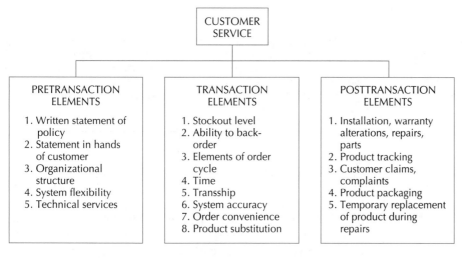

FIGURE 4-6   Elements of customer service.
Source: Ronald H. Ballou, *Business Logistics Management,* 3rd ed. (Upper Saddle River, NJ: Prentice-Hall, Inc., 1992), p. 81. Reprinted by permission of Prentice-Hall, Inc., Upper Saddle River, NJ.

exactly what customers want is not always easy. Finding out what to deliver means keeping an eye on several sets of customers as illustrated in the Coors beer example in Exhibit 4-1.

The following four steps must be taken after the important elements of customer service are determined:

1. Quantitative standards of performance for each service element must be set.
2. Actual performance for each service element must be measured.
3. Variance between actual services provided and the set standard must be analyzed.
4. Corrective action must be taken as needed to reduce the variance between actual performance and the set standard.

EXHIBIT 4-1 / Delivering What Customers Want

Coors' commitment to freshness has garnered it an enviable word-of-mouth reputation. ◀ ◀ ◀
Coors' beer is dated for a shelf life that is two-thirds that of its major competitors (for instance, 90 days for cans and bottles compared to competitors' 120 days or more). That means less time to sell before the product becomes a loss.

When Coors decided to distribute beyond its 14-state Rocky Mountain area, logistics became a key concern. "We had to bring logistics functions together to keep quality high," said Coors' vice president of logistics.

Coors was trying to satisfy three sets of customers: final consumers who wanted freshness and product variety; 650 distributors, who wanted quick and accurate response to their orders; and retailers, who wanted last-minute flexibility.

For instance, if a grocery chain promoting a six-pack sells three times more than it ex-

Exhibit 4-1 (continued)

Exhibit 4-1 (continued)

pected, it may want to triple next week's order. This can be a challenge for distributors, who place orders three weeks in advance via Coorslink, the on-line beer ordering system.

But Coors' integrated system was designed to accept such changes, even during the critical final three weeks of production and packaging. The companies that want to be successful need to follow Coors' example and respond flexibly to customer demand.

Source: E. J. Graff, "Just-Right Delivery," *Enterprise* (Summer 1990), pp. 28–29.

Finally, a strategy for improving customer service performance must be determined. This strategy must be in line with the long-range profit and return on investment objectives of the company.

Competitive intelligence is a necessity for strategic logistics planning to determine how logistics can be used to differentiate a firm in the marketplace and provide a distinct competitive advantage.[20] Within the present environment, customer service is becoming an increasingly important competitive factor.[21] The level of technology that a channel member is willing to invest in has a direct impact on customer service performance. Without accurate and timely information, effective customer service cannot be achieved.

In a study by Douglas Lambert and Thomas Harrington, three underlying logistics constructs were reported to be common to the industries in the study: information system capability, availability, and lead time. The study concluded that investing in a new logistics information system would lead to improved performance in all three areas. Therefore, the first channel member in an industry to implement a real-time, interactive logistics information system will have a competitive advantage.[22]

In summary, a major way a channel member can achieve outstanding customer service is to *integrate logistics* by:

- *Using a networked information system.* Companies move the product faster and stay better informed.

- *Managing by exception.* Integrated systems alert managers when something goes wrong.

- *Thinking from supplier to customer.* Everyone in the distribution chain cooperates to cut handling and costs and to improve forecast accuracy.

- *Seeing all jobs as customer service.* Immediate access to information encourages individuals to do whatever it takes to deliver what the customer wants.

- *Empowering the employees and flattening hierarchies.* The job gets done most efficiently when peers confer directly.

- *Changing the management structure.* New structures highlight a smooth product flow rather than functional area distinctions.

- *Planning for change.* Long-term planning must include ways to adapt quickly to change.[23]

▶ TRANSPORTATION DECISIONS

The problems of inadequate transportation service and uncertain transit times can cause a company to hold several days' more inventory than physical distribution plans call for. This problem, in turn, adds to the cost of carrying inventory and reduces the number of times that capital invested in inventory can be turned over during the year, not to mention the undesirable effects of poor customer service and missed product promotions. Consequently, the selection of appropriate transportation modes and the maintenance of a concerted effort by physical distribution management to ensure efficient and reliable transportation are prerequisites for accomplishing distribution objectives. In this section, we describe various transportation modes and the functions they can perform for various channel members in facilitating the movement of products.

In the United States, there are a variety of options available to a firm that must move its goods from one point to another. The five basic modes of transportation are rail, truck, water, air, and pipeline. In addition, a variety of combinations are available, including rail-motor (piggyback), motor–water (fishyback), motor–air, and rail–water. These combinations can provide services normally not provided by a single mode. For example, sea–air transport is an intermodal option for a shipment that is time-sensitive, but not so sensitive that it requires the high-cost outlay of an all-air transport mode. Relatively speaking, sea-air transport is cheap and fast. Pioneered in the 1960s by United Airlines, it works best in today's global logistics environment where just-in-time inventory management is commonplace. Sea–air transport can be offered only by those port regions that have: (1) a short, easy cargo commute between the docks and the airport, (2) superb customs clearance and on-ground transport procedures, (3) committed port authorities, and (4) the willingness of regional transportation providers to prioritize sea–air shipments. Seattle is the largest sea–air transit hub, accounting for about 40% of the total U.S. sea–air market and about 23% of worldwide volumes. Miami is now offering itself as a hub for shipments moving from the Pacific Rim and Europe into Central and South America.[24] Freight movement, whether by a single mode or by a combination, is facilitated by a variety of transportation agencies, including freight forwarders, shippers' associations, parcel post, and air express.

In making transportation mode selection decisions, logistics managers in the marketing channel must consider cost, dependability, and possibility of loss and damage associated with the modes available to them. Table 4-2 ranks the cost and performance characteristics of each of the five basic modes of transportation according to these criteria. A detailed discussion of transportation structure and modes in the United States is presented in the annual edition of the *U.S. Industrial Outlook*.[25]

TABLE 4-2 **Relative Rankings of Cost and Operating Performance Characteristics by Transportation Mode**[a]

| | | | PERFORMANCE CHARACTERISTICS | | |
| | | | Delivery Time Variability | | |
Mode Transportation	Cost[b] 1 = Highest	Average Delivery Time[c] 1 = Fastest	Absolute 1 = Least	Percentage[d] 1 = Least	Loss and Damage 1 = Least
Rail	3	3	4	3	5
Truck	2	2	3	2	4
Water	5	5	5	4	2
Pipe	4	4	2	1	1
Air	1	1	1	5	3

[a]Service is assumed to be available.
[b]Cost per ton-mile.
[c]Door-to-door speed.
[d]Ratio of absolute variation in delivery time to average delivery time.

Source: Ronald Ballou, *Business Logistics Management,* 3rd ed. (Upper Saddle River, NJ: Prentice-Hall, Inc., 1992), p. 185. Reprinted by permission of Prentice-Hall, Inc., Upper Saddle River, NJ.

▶ **WAREHOUSING DECISIONS**

There are two basic types of warehouse facilities available to channel members—private (company-owned) facilities and public facilities, in which space is leased by retailers, wholesalers, or manufacturers. In general, private warehouses offer greater flexibility in design to meet special storage and handling needs, greater control over the warehouse facility and its operations, more effective information feedback, and lower cost per unit since it does not have to recover advertising and selling costs.

In contrast, public warehouse facilities require no fixed investment by the firm; offer location flexibility and the ability to increase warehouse space to cover peak requirements; and can offer lower cost under certain circumstances, as when it is necessary to store seasonal inventories. Often public warehouse personnel will provide many other services in order to compete with their private warehouse counterparts.

Distribution centers are established primarily for the movement rather than the storage of goods. As one distribution executive observed regarding his company's distribution center,[26]

> Our goal is to not store anything if we can help it. What we wanted to design is a distribution center that distributes.

Thus, the rationale underlying the development of distribution centers is to maintain the company's product in a constant and efficient flow from the moment it leaves production until the day it arrives at its destination.

Many large corporations now operate distribution centers as an integral part of their physical distribution systems.[27] Rich's Department Stores has a $17-million distribution center based on the flow-through concept. Nearly 90% of the merchandise that arrives at the center's receiving docks flows through the building to the shipping area without ever being placed in storage. In fact, it typically takes a total of just 20 minutes for an incoming carton to be unloaded, bar-coded, transported, sorted, and then loaded into an outbound trailer.[28]

A survey conducted by *Transportation and Distribution* in 1990 revealed a distinct trend that shows companies are reducing the number of distribution centers they have. Specifically, businesses are finding that they do not need hundreds of distribution centers spread across the country because a few, in strategic locations providing necessary service at a reasonable cost, are enough to stay competitive.[29] Moreover, information technology has helped fuel the trend toward eliminating some distribution centers. Improvements in information management and better inventory control have decreased the need for warehouses in the channel; the less information you have, the greater the need for more warehouses. The big investments in an information technology infrastructure, that is, point-of-sale communications and inventory management, are paying off (see Chapter 9). Bar-coding and electronic data interchange (EDI) have made it possible for vendors to ship directly to stores, bypassing the holding bins at warehouses.

- Kmart estimates that 45% of all nonapparel items are shipped directly from the vendor to the store as a result of the use of hand-held computers. A store manager goes down an aisle and scans it with a hand-held and then plugs it into a computer that sends the information to headquarters. A purchase order is then sent to the vendor who ships the product to the store.

- Levi Strauss & Company's vice president of EDI services says that bar-coding allows stores to receive merchandise directly from a vendor and allows the retailer the flexibility to alter orders easily in response to buying trends, to avoid overstocking because they can order more frequently, and to make sure their shelves are stocked.[30]

Whether a channel member chooses to use public or private warehousing operations in his physical distribution system, the questions of how many warehouses to establish and where they should be located must be answered. The determination of the number and location of warehouses is directly dependent on the customer service level set by the firm and the purpose the warehouses are intended to serve.

A channel member with high customer service requirements will often establish a series of warehouses. A warehouse will often be located close to the manufacturing plant if the material it stores needs to be processed. In contrast, if the warehouse is to be used for maintaining finished goods, it will most likely be located near the consumer market. When all variables are considered, warehouses must be positioned so that they provide the desired level of service at the least distribution cost. The least-cost solution is unique for each organization because of differences in customer service standards, inventory-carrying costs, transportation costs, and other physical distribution costs, but the total cost of the logistical network can be generalized as illustrated earlier in Figure 4-4.

Transportation costs decline, inventory and warehousing costs increase at an increasing rate, and order processing costs increase at a constant rate as the number of warehouses in the system increases. Thus, once cost trade-offs have been accounted for, the lowest total cost of the overall logistical system is seen in Figure 4-4 to be the point at which the two cost curves coincide.

The location of warehouse facilities will also have a significant impact on the competitive thrust of an organization and, concomitantly, of an entire marketing channel. Just as the number of warehouses established directly affects the ability of the organization and channel to serve its customers and at the same time keep logistical costs in line, so too does the location of warehouses.

Storage in transit—the time that goods remain in transportation facilities during delivery—reduces the need for and cost of warehousing. For example,[31]

> The United Processors Company harvests and processes a variety of fruits and vegetables in southern and western farming regions of the country. For certain of these products, such as strawberries and watermelons, there tends to be strong demand in the East and Midwest just ahead of the local growing season. Because United must harvest earlier than the northern climates allow, supply builds before demand peaks. Inventories normally build in the growing areas before truck shipments are made to the demand areas. By switching to rail service and the longer delivery times associated with it, the company can, in many cases, ship immediately after harvesting and have the products arrive in the marketplace just as strong demand develops. The railroad serves the warehousing function. The result is a substantial reduction in warehousing costs and transportation costs, too!

Therefore, transportation equipment can be viewed as moving warehouses and be used accordingly.

Third-Party Logistics—An Alternative Distribution Channel

Even though approximately 90% of American businesses still perform logistics functions themselves, long-term alliances with specialized logistics companies are increasing. The same trend is taking hold in Europe.[32] These third-party providers can be segmented into three groups: (1) diversified, which handle a variety of products and can be either asset-based companies moving into logistics or established freight forwarders, (2) product specific, which have expertise within an industry, and (3) customized, which assume total control of a client's supply chain.

Third-party, independent companies that specialize in the development and application of new and innovative methods of packaging, handling, shipping, controlling, and distributing freight can contribute greatly to logistics technology and help it to keep pace in a high-tech world. For example,

▪ Norvanco International (Kent, Washington) demonstrates the value of this approach in Asia. On April 1, 1992, Norvanco announced the opening of a new kind of freight processing facility at Singapore. The facility, a three-story, 300,000-square foot freight processing plant, is the consummation of a joint venture formed by Norvanco with Integrated Agency Pte. Ltd. of Singapore. It is operated under the name Main Distribution Services Pte. Ltd. The new freight service center brings advanced technology to the planning, preparation, loading, dispatch, control, and delivery of containerized freight. The facility is equipped with state-of-the-art unitizing equipment, stretch film wrappers, and lift trucks equipped with push/pull attachments. Norvanco's new freight processing facility could be the prototype for similar facilities throughout the world by the turn of the century.[33]

- In 1991 Becton Dickinson & Co., a medical supplies and equipment firm, and Preston Trucking Co., Inc., a regional LTL (less-than-truckload) carrier, developed a partnership with the objective of eliminating steps from the logistics process, cutting costs, and improving service and quality. With commitment from the highest levels of management the partnership began with 26 meetings of managers from both companies in which a 65-item list of shared goals and objectives was developed. The improved performance delivered by the partnership earned Becton Dickinson the 1993 LTL Shipper of the Year Award and saved the company $100,000 in the first year. The partnership relies on innovation by both companies to manage the supply chain on an integrated basis so that high-quality goods and services can be supplied to customers throughout the chain. Project teams convert identified business needs into technical and commercial objectives, develop technology, implement project action plans, and measure results.[34]

There are several reasons why channel members are using third-party systems: (1) to liquidate their warehouse and distribution functions to protect their assets and bring value to shareholders, (2) to achieve more latitude to focus on their core businesses, (3) to eliminate staffing and internal system development costs, (4) to reduce the initial start-up distribution organizing and staffing costs that exhaust initial capital investment, (5) to control costs and improve service on a worldwide basis, and in many cases (6) to add market value to products through resident expertise.[35]

Third parties can add value to the distribution channel by offering speed and consistency for just-in-time operations without having to move existing manufacturing and/or warehousing facilities to be close to the buyer.

- Catalina Information Resources, a joint venture between Information Resources Inc. and Catalina Marketing Corp., is building toward a national network that can provide such services as identifying potential out-of-stocks in grocery stores, check prices, make merchandising and promotion more efficient, and improve order processing. The network is part of the ECR (efficient consumer response) initiative in the packaged-goods industry to improve customer service and eliminate costs in the system for both manufacturers and retailers.[36]

- Lynn Fritz's deployment of technology in customer service has transformed the once small San Francisco customs brokerage house founded by his father in 1933 into a rapidly growing public global logistics company. With a fully automated purchase-order-to-final-delivery system (known as FLEX) now in place, $141.6 million Fritz Cos. is enjoying a surge in sales from a variety of its blue-chip customers like Sears, Target, N.A. Philips, Mack Truck, Lexmark, and Wal-Mart. So impressed was Office Depot that it turned over its full line of logistics needs, from freight forwarding to warehousing, to Fritz Cos. Some Fritz customers prefer not to use the entire FLEX system, choosing instead to buy a la carte from Fritz's menu of services. For example, Ace Hardware Corp. relies on Fritz for nearly all its logistics needs, excluding ocean transport. More than a dozen Fritz customers meet each quarter, at their own expense, for a 3-

day conference during which they share information and strategies for reducing their global logistics expenditures.[37]

A service-effective and cost-effective third-party logistics system can be a critical element for Europe to make the successful transition to a new economic era. In the area of logistics, environmental standards vary enormously among the European countries—from packaging standards and truck sizes and weights to vehicle emissions and vehicle bans/noise pollution controls. Companies that contract for logistics services can gain a presence in Europe without bearing the cost of establishing a complete Pan-European network. As a result of deregulation the European Community will not only achieve reduction in transportation costs but also the overall reduction in logistics process costs.[38]

A successful contract logistics program requires cross-functional management commitment to logistics as a process involving purchasing, operations, and physical distribution, and it must interact with sales and marketing. Issues that management should weigh in the selection of a logistics supplier include: (1) compatibility in approach, attitude, and culture; (2) focus on quality; (3) experience in a particular industry; (4) financial strength; (5) proven performance record; (6) flexibility; and (7) customer preferences.

▶ INVENTORY MANAGEMENT AND CONTROL ISSUES

In this section we discuss the control of inventories held in a distribution channel to meet anticipated customer demand. These inventories may be held at the point of production or positioned in wholesale or retail distribution centers that serve, together with outbound transportation, to define the physical distribution strategy of the firm. In a later section we will address the management of inventories held to support production or the firm's internal operations in the materials management cycle.

If it were not for the presence of and need for inventories, there would be no purpose served in discussing warehousing decisions. In fact, although the decisions involving ownership, type, and location of warehouses are obviously important, solutions to problems associated with inventory management and control are crucial to the viability of all commercial channel members, irrespective of the warehousing decisions made. There are significant differences in the average number of days of inventory in stock between companies with the best and the worst logistics practices. Those companies at the high end of the scale pay a significant penalty, which escalates during times of high interest. In addition, they operate at a decided competitive disadvantage. This observation is particularly salient when you consider that inventory represents the largest single investment in assets for most manufacturers, wholesalers, and retailers. For example, the inventory investment of manufacturers can represent 30% of their total investment in assets. For wholesalers and retailers, inventory can represent more than 50% of assets. This tendency to maintain such a large inventory is frequently observed in today's highly competitive markets, where companies are trying to satisfy the needs of diverse market segments. In addition, today's consumer is accustomed to and demands high levels of product availability. In order to meet these demands, firms have reacted by maintaining high levels of inventory.

However, the Tax Reform Act of 1986 requires companies with sales of more than $10 million to record inventory-related expenses like purchasing, handling, and warehousing and add them to the cost of inventory. These capitalized expenses cannot be deducted until the inventory is sold; the less a channel member has in deductions, the more it pays in taxes.[39] Therefore, lower inventory will be more desirable.

In general, inventory control theory deals with the determination of optimal procedures for procuring stocks of commodities to meet future demand.[40] The decision concerning when and how much to reorder is a matter of balancing a number of conflicting cost functions. The objective is to minimize total inventory costs subject to demand and service constraints. The primary cost functions that must be balanced are those associated with holding inventory, ordering inventory, and risking stockouts. The fundamental purpose of any inventory control system is to tell a firm (1) how much to reorder, (2) when to reorder, and (3) how to control stockouts at the lowest cost. The following discussion focuses on these three key problem areas and on related issues, including the amount of safety stock that should be kept on hand and the need for and impact of sales forecasting on inventory management.

How Much to Reorder and When to Reorder[41]

The traditional approach to managing distribution inventories, where customer demand is stochastic (random) and cannot be forecast with complete accuracy, is the classic reorder point inventory model. The reorder point approach uses forecast demand and forecast resupply lead time to develop inventory levels that minimize the total variable costs of investment in inventory subject to a specified maximum rate of stockouts or lost sales. To meet these objectives, this family of models develops three separate inventory levels, each intended to serve a separate purpose:

ORDER LEVEL   This is the level of inventory intended to satisfy expected demand between reorders. It is equivalent to the order quantity and is determined through standard economic order quantity (EOQ) computations, which balance the cost to order the item against the cost to hold the item, thereby arriving at the lowest total variable cost. When reorder is required in a reorder point system, the order level or order quantity determines how much material the firm will order.

LEAD-TIME LEVEL   This is the level of inventory required to meet expected customer demand during expected resupply lead time. In a world of complete certainty (or perfect forecasting), the lead-time level would be used to alert the firm to reorder and would serve as the reorder point of the system.

SAFETY LEVEL   This is the level of inventory that is held to meet unexpected variation in either customer demand or in resupply lead time during the reorder cycle. Often called *buffer stocks* or *hedge stocks*, safety level inventory allows the firm to manage the percentage of stockouts it is willing to experience. In combination with the lead-time level, the safety level determines the reorder point in most reorder point systems, and it is the reorder point that triggers the replenishment action in the system. Clearly, the existence of safety stocks in an inventory system reflects a recognition that customer demand for distribution inventories is often difficult to predict with a high degree of accuracy. Exhibit 4-2 illustrates how one company has streamlined the inventory reordering process.

Nevertheless, cost pressures in today's logistics environment are forcing firms to develop innovative alternatives to the classic reorder point approach. One of these alternatives, which is becoming increasingly popular in managing distribution inventories, is distribution requirements planning.

EXHIBIT **4-2 / Centralizing the Inventory Reordering Process**

▶ ▶ ▶

The question of when and how much to reorder has been answered by Koenig Corporation, an art supply store. The company has developed a computerized cash register system that rings up and records each sale of its 8,000 to 40,000 coded products in each of its 120 outlets. Each night a mainframe computer at Koenig's headquarters automatically telephones each cash register and calls up a list of every item sold.

Once a week, the headquarters computer tallies the product sales for each store, subtracts the total from the known inventory in each outlet, and matches the difference against a minimum and maximum inventory level. Within a day of the weekly tally, replenishment stocks are on the way to the outlet, thereby relieving managers of time-consuming routine reordering and the need to set aside valuable store space for reserve supplies. The company estimates that the centralized inventory system cuts the cost of goods at each outlet to 50 cents for every $1 sale after markdowns and discounts. The industry's average cost of goods is 10 cents more.

Source: Selwyn Feinstein, "Koenig Finds Customers Where None Existed Before, Art Supply Shops Surmount Hurdle of Belonging to Slow-Growth Industry," *The Wall Street Journal*, December 29, 1989, p. B2. Reprinted by permission of *The Wall Street Journal*, 1989 Dow Jones & Company, Inc. All Rights Reserved Worldwide.

Distribution Requirements Planning Systems[42]

Distribution requirements planning (DRP) systems are intended to link the production process (or a wholesale level of inventory) to other inventory levels positioned further down in the distribution channel. Hence, DRP methods generally apply to several layers of inventory in a given distribution channel but would not typically be used to develop inventory requirements for the lowest retail level, which supports the ultimate customer directly. Thus, the presumption in a DRP system is that the inventories being managed are intended to resupply other inventories. Given this important assumption, DRP systems take advantage of the fact that lower-level inventories have established demand forecasts, lead times, and order quantities in order to plan for future requirements. Pioneered by Abbott Laboratories, DRP systems do more than simply develop inventory requirements. They allow for the planning, scheduling, and allocating of other key logistics resources as well, including the transportation and personnel needed to fulfill customer requirements.

The central feature of DRP systems is their ability to reforecast inventory requirements continually as the inventory position of lower-level inventories in the distribution channel changes. Thus, DRP systems require that echelons of inventory be linked electronically and that higher-level inventory managers have visibility of demand, inventory assets, and planned reorder points for all lower-level inventory customers. Given this visibility and the timely update of these parameters, an upper-level inventory manager can plan for inventories needed at a specific point to meet a specific customer reorder. Planning for inventory requirements in a time-phased manner means that the need to actually stock material in inventory at the upper level is minimized. For example, a production facility supporting a lower-level inventory is able, through DRP systems, to schedule production in lot sizes equal to the EOQ of the lower-level inventory manager and to schedule this production to meet the anticipated reorder timing inherent in the reorder point system being used at the higher level. Transportation scheduling and personnel assignments are derived from the DRP system to move any finished goods inventory to the end-user/customers.

Forecasting[45]

Whether the long-used methods of inventory control or a new innovative method such as DRP is used, an accurate sales forecast of future demand is a critical variable in achieving effective inventory management. In fact, the short-term sales forecast is the heart of any system designed to manage inventory. For any channel member, the type of forecasting method to be used depends on the type of demand pattern his customers exhibit.

In general, customer demand patterns can be categorized as (1) regular and highly predictable, (2) irregular but mathematically consistent, and (3) irregular and unpredictable. Regular and highly predictable demand does not require a sophisticated sales forecast system. Type 2 demand (irregular but mathematically consistent) requires statistical forecasting, whereas type 3 demand requires the greatest degree of sophistication in designing an inventory control system.

For most types of customer demand patterns, a short-term forecast is the most effective and most consistent way of obtaining future sales projections. It assumes that the historical sales patterns of a product can be used to predict its future sales, and therefore relies on such historical data-based forecasting methods as moving averages, weighted moving averages, regression, and exponential smoothing.

Exponential smoothing, the most popular of these techniques, uses the past forecast of demand together with the most recent actual demand observation to determine the forecast of demand for the coming period. The system assumes that the past forecast represents the best estimate of demand prior to the current period and that this forecast, updated appropriately with information from the current period, will provide an accurate forecast for the coming period. In applying the exponential smoothing methodology, smoothing weights must be selected. The issue in making this determination is one of sensitivity. The manager must determine how much weight to place on the most recent observed demand value relative to the previous demand for the item. This is analytically equivalent to choosing the base period to be used in any moving average technique. Typically, alternative smoothing weight combinations should be analyzed to determine the combination that provides a balance of stability, accuracy, and sensitivity in demand forecasts. Exponential smoothing methods are quite common in mechanized inventory control systems and are particularly effective in estimating demand for type 1 and 2 patterns. Although the application of such historical data-based techniques is less reliable for type 3 demand patterns, this problem can be alleviated somewhat by considerably reducing the forecasting interval—say, to one week—which enhances the reliability of the data and, hence, improves prediction.

Lack of a sales forecast, inaccurate sales forecasting, and/or lack of sales forecast information sharing among retailers, wholesalers, and manufacturers can create inventory problems throughout the marketing channel. A sudden increase in sales volume at the retail level creates a ripple effect back through the channel because of time lags in order processing and in the flow of goods. This may result in stockouts with their attendant lost sales and customer ill will.

Controlling Stockouts

Many companies believe that, if they had accurate sales forecasts, manufacturing problems would be eliminated. Companies that are truly world-class have selected flexibility and responsiveness as strategic weapons for mitigating inaccurate sales forecasts. One popular weapon is the computer, specifically MRP II (manufacturing resource planning) software. However, even the smallest company can ruin itself by trying to track the detailed movement of dozens or even hundreds of orders throughout its plant. The alternative is considering doing more with less. Companies can: (1) decrease leadtime to respond to customer needs, (2) examine ways to completely eliminate transactions from having to be reported, and (3) avoid complex systems when simple manual procedures will suffice.[44]

If sales forecasting were perfectly accurate, stockouts would never occur. If, however, it is known in advance that each forecast will have some error in it (as it almost surely will), then action must be taken to ensure that this error does not seriously weaken customer service.

Ideally, a firm would never have a stockout, but maintaining a 100% service level is usually prohibitively costly. The firm must balance the cost of maintaining the desired level of service with the cost associated with a stockout.

The visible cost of a stockout is the direct loss of revenue to the supplier and possibly to the store. In addition, if a store frequently encounters stockouts, its customer service is weakened, and it may begin to lose its power to attract patrons. Therefore, it is important to predict the likely forecasting error. The term used for this prediction is the *standard error of the estimate* (S.E.). The standard error is employed to determine how much extra safety stock is needed to cushion against customer demand larger than the sales forecast.[45] As indicated, every channel member must determine through research the customer service level best suited to it by balancing the cost of holding additional safety stock versus the costs of stockouts.

Production Control and Materials Requirement Planning (MRP)

In most organizations, production control, purchasing, and raw materials handling fall under the materials management function. A few contemporary organizations include these activities as an integral part of a larger logistics organization. Naturally, there is a great deal of interface among physical distribution, materials management, manufacturing, and marketing, as shown in Figure 4-7.[46]

Often the operating objectives set by management for each of those areas will not coincide. This may lead to a lack of coordination among PD activities as a whole, which in turn could lead to lower customer service levels and/or total physical distribution costs that are higher than necessary. Thus, to maintain the necessary level of customer service, *production control* must be seen as an integral element of the physical distribution network. The role of production in the physical distribution process is twofold. The production activity determines how much and what kinds of finished products are produced, which in turn influences when and how the products are distributed to the firm's customers. Also, the company's need for raw materials, subassemblies, and parts is directly affected by production.

A new concept is emerging for manufacturing to aid production scheduling and materials requirements planning by electronically linking the plant floor and such support functions as design and purchasing into a dynamically responsive environment. Cross-scheduling of just-in-time delivery of inventory is already happening in some industries, most notably pharmaceuticals. Electronic commerce is made possible by technologies such as electronic data interchange, product-data exchange specification, and computer-aided acquisition and logistics support. During the 1990s, some small manufacturers have set up local computer networks to form collective, virtual enterprises with more clout. Roughly 75 of these manufacturing networks, which are often funded by state or local development agencies, operate in a dozen or more states.[47]

Organizations that adopt the spirit of the physical distribution concept integrate raw materials requirement planning, purchasing, receiving, handling, inventory control, warehousing, and sometimes production scheduling under a single manager. This single manager is in charge of the planning, organizing, motivating, and controlling of all those activities and personnel principally concerned with the flow of materials into an organization. Typically, the materials manager is responsible for the following basic activities:

1. Forecasting materials requirements.
2. Developing the materials requirement plan.
3. Sourcing and obtaining materials.
4. Introducing materials into the organization.
5. Monitoring the status of materials as a current asset.

Materials requirements planning is critical to the success of a materials management system. "MRP is a computer-based production and inventory-control system that attempts to minimize inventories, yet maintain adequate materials for the

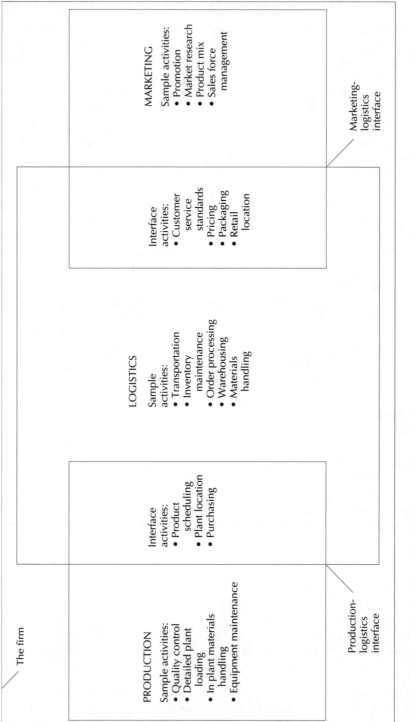

FIGURE 4-7 The logistics interfaces with marketing and production.
Source: Ronald Ballou, *Business Logistics Management*, 3rd ed. (Upper Saddle River, NJ: Prentice-Hall, Inc., 1992), p. 24. Reprinted by permission of Prentice-Hall, Inc., Upper Saddle River, NJ.

production process."[48] Once MRP is completed, the materials manager may proceed with *sourcing decisions* and other tasks of materials management.

MRP systems provide the link between vendors and the internal production processes of the firm. The success of MRP is based on several critical factors:

- The material requirements of the firm must be based on a known production schedule that exhibits a high degree of stability over a given MRP planning horizon. Production discipline is a very important prerequisite to making MRP work effectively.

- Individual material requirements for parts, subcomponents, raw materials, and so on, must be quantified relative to the planned production levels for the finished product. These relationships are typically established through a bill-of-materials file.

- Supplier lead times must be within the production planning horizon and must be reasonably accurate.

Given these factors, an MRP system allows the firm to support internal operations effectively while minimizing the investment in incoming and work-in-process inventories. A stable, disciplined master production schedule provides a deterministic demand base on which to build material requirements. Thus, orders in an MRP system are placed in a discrete pattern at the latest point possible to arrive in time to support production. With stable lead times and dependable suppliers, safety stocks are eliminated or at least minimized.

In summary, the functions materials managers are responsible for are purchasing and procurement, production control, inbound traffic and transportation, warehousing and storage, management of components of the firm's information system, inventory planning and control, and salvage and scrap disposal. The activities performed in materials management are very similar to those performed in the distribution of finished goods. The materials manager is concerned with inventory control, warehousing and storage, order processing, transportation, and almost all other distribution activities. The major differences between materials management and finished goods distribution are that the items handled in materials management are all raw materials, parts, and subassemblies rather than finished goods, and the recipient of the product is the production or manufacturing group as opposed to the final consumer.

What started in the mid-1960s as materials requirements planning quickly grew into closed-loop MRP, with the integration of master scheduling, capacity planning, shop flow control, and purchasing. Manufacturing resource planning (MRP II) was born in the 1970s, when cost data and selling price capabilities were added. The essence of MRP II is its integration. Computer-integrated manufacturing reinforces and extends the drive toward integrating the entire materials requirements planning throughout the channel. Just-in-time, total quality management, and other programs also recognize the interdependence of all parts of the organization. MRP II does not work effectively until the barriers caused by the lack of integration and lack of communication between different groups have been eliminated. Successful integration relies on strong leadership and a firm commitment from the highest levels of the organization. Moreover, users must be taught how, when, and under what conditions the tools should be used, and strong incentives should be in place to protect the database.

The 1980s brought two major improvements. The first was the expansion of production planning into sales and operations planning. Just-in-time (JIT) had a major impact on MRP II as well. JIT and MRP II work better together than alone. The evolution continues into the 1990s. Supply chain management is one example.[49]

Just-in-Time Logistics Systems

Faced with increasing cost pressures, the opportunity costs of inflated inventories, and growing operational problems, many U.S. firms are embracing an innovative approach to logistics management called *just-in-time* (JIT). The JIT philosophy is quite simple: material resources should flow through the logistics system so that they arrive at the point of intended use "just in time." In theory the system provides for the right materials in the right quantities at the right time, and does so without the need for inventories. Finished goods are produced and delivered just in time to be sold, subassemblies just in time to be assembled into finished goods, fabricated parts just in time to go into subassemblies, and materials just in time to be transformed into fabricated parts. The JIT concept calls for all materials to be active as work-in-process (WIP); there is never a pause to collect carrying charges. It is a hand-to-mouth operation in which the ratio of production and delivery quantities approaches one.

The JIT exchange relationship requires the integration of the engineering, purchasing, production, material management, and marketing systems of the supplier and buyer to promote the efficient flow of parts and materials. Thus, JIT systems focus on material movement and recognize the importance of maximizing the productivity with which material assets are applied in a logistics system. The basic goal of the JIT exchange relationship is to eliminate waste from all areas of the production and delivery systems of the channel. Waste can be defined as anything over the minimum amount of equipment, materials, parts, and labor that is absolutely necessary to produce or resell.[50] Further, today's JIT systems take full advantage of the technology available to manage information and to coordinate material flows effectively.

In reality, JIT systems are much more than inventory control systems, in that the implementation of JIT will substantially affect purchasing, transportation, warehousing, production, quality control, and data processing within a firm. In each of these functional areas, JIT processing requires a level of discipline and coordination that is beyond the capability of many organizations. This requirement must be recognized if JIT is to be implemented successfully. For example, consider the following requirements for the smooth implementation of JIT.

PURCHASING   Purchasing must locate and cultivate a limited number of highly reliable suppliers and establish workable, mutually beneficial long-term contractual relationships with them. Suppliers must be particularly strong in lead-time dependability and quality. Moreover, suppliers must have access to the production and inventory planning data of the buyers in order to plan adequately for their own production. On-line electronic data interchange is a necessity, and suppliers must be committed over a realistic time horizon to providing continuing material support to the buyers.

TRANSPORTATION   Transportation is a critical element in any JIT system where it is called on to perform at a level of efficiency and dependability much greater than that required in traditional logistics systems, where buffers of inventory essentially decouple the transportation system from the operations of the firm. Delivery schedules and turnaround times for transportation assets are often highly disciplined in JIT systems. Shipment sizes tend to be small and shipment frequencies greater in JIT systems, and the ability to effectively monitor and control the transportation process becomes extremely important.

WAREHOUSING   JIT systems, by their design, focus on material movement and not on material storage. Automated storage systems, therefore, are far less important than the ability to move material quickly and efficiently to the point of use within the organization. Central storage facilities are often eliminated in favor of very limited staging capabilities adjacent to the point of use.

INVENTORY CONTROL   The inventory control function (including the management of incoming inventories of raw materials, semifinished goods, and components; the management of work-in-process inventories; and the management of finished goods or distribution inventories) is a central element in a JIT system. As safety stocks are eliminated and order quantities tied to a specific and time-phased intended use are implemented, room for error in the inventory system is significantly reduced. Traditional approaches, which assume the existence of inventories of materials in storage, give way to MRP and DRP, which assume inventory in motion. Production lot sizes are reduced and WIP inventories decline. Ideally, the JIT concept results in a smooth material flow from the basic raw material source, through various stages of conversion, to some ultimate level of inventory that directly supports a customer who cannot, by the nature of the customer demand, be linked directly to the flow.

PRODUCTION   JIT systems rely on small production lots, short production runs, and rapid setup times in flexible manufacturing systems to stabilize the flow of materials and products through the manufacturing process. In the best case, production at each stage is geared directly to support input requirements at the following stage and WIP buffers are eliminated.

QUALITY CONTROL   As stationary inventories are minimized throughout the logistics system, the importance of quality grows proportionally. Because each unit of inventory is moving to some intended use, there are no allowances in the system for defective units either in incoming deliveries or in the WIP pipeline. Quality problems force an interruption of the flow and are often very expensive to the firm in a JIT environment. The improvements in quality reduce the number of labor hours needed to remake or repair defects and reduce material waste. The JIT process by its very design forces quality problems to the surface and dictates timely resolution of them.

JIT works best in repetitive manufacturing situations involving at least some of the following criteria: (1) there are significant levels of inventory to begin with; (2) demand and production can be forecast accurately; and (3) suppliers are located nearby, manufacture quality parts, and are willing to cooperate.[51] Today, examples of major firms across a variety of industries that have given top priority to the establishment and maintenance of JIT exchanges include: Boeing, Ford, Harley-Davidson, Hewlett-Packard, IBM, and Xerox. The following example illustrates the benefits of JIT:[52]

> NCR Ithaca, a transaction document printer manufacturer, implemented JIT in 1987, and as a result, inventory is down from 120 days on hand to just 21 days. Work in process decreased from 45 days to 3, floor space for manufacturing was reduced from 45,000 sq. ft. to 19,000 sq. ft. for the same level of production, manufacturing cycle time for forecasted orders has decreased from 60 days to 6, $500,000 of nonvalue added jobs were no longer needed in the Quality Assurance department, and parts shortages fell drastically due to stepped-up quality efforts and partnership relationships with suppliers.

In summary, JIT systems are intended to stress the functional linkages in the logistics flow, to force operating inefficiencies to the surface, and to reduce the costs of the logistics process. Adopting and implementing JIT requires continuous progress toward the ultimate goals of one-at-a-time delivery, perfectly synchronized and continuous product flows, perfect quality of incoming parts and materials that are simple and standardized in their design, and short production runs.[53] Typically, JIT systems have proved successful when the concept is implemented by each participant in a given distribution channel. In this way, the benefits of the JIT approach are shared throughout the channel.[54]

JIT II   Successful applications of JIT led to the development of JIT II. JIT II is a creative new partnership between customers and suppliers that has evolved at various U.S. companies, such as Honeywell, Bose, and AT&T. Bose, a producer of audio electronics, conceived just-in-time II (JIT II). Whereas the original JIT eliminated inventory and brought the customer and supplier on a closer operational basis, JIT II had more benefits, including the elimination of the buyer and salesman from the customer–supplier relationship. Having a vendor's representative at the Bose location was not the major advantage; rather, it was that the vendor's representative was empowered to use Bose's system. Bose also applied the JIT II precepts to its transportation area, whereby material in transit can be planned just like inventory in the warehouse.[55]

JIT II brings the vendor into the plant to sit in the purchasing office of the customer on a full-time daily basis, replacing the buyer and the salesperson. As an empowered facilitator, this in-plant worker can help develop greater rapport between the supplier and customer company employees. The practice is customer-focused, cost-effective, team-based, and quality-driven. Having vendor representatives working with Bose engineers on designs has substantially improved design quality and productivity.[56]

Stockless inventory is the JIT application in the wholesaling-retailing sector of the channel and in-service industries. For example, in hospitals, stockless programs shift the storeroom and most of the central distribution operation from the hospital to the distributor. The distributor delivers supplies at "each" level, sorted by user department, to the hospital receiving dock, where they are transported directly to the departments. In effect, the hospital "outsources" its logistics function to a supplier who can do it more efficiently.

A study by the Health Care Industry Distributors Association (HIDA) showed that implementing stockless programs can provide hospitals with significant annual savings—8 to 14% of total purchases (e.g., medical/surgical, forms, film, etc.) for a 200 to 350 bed hospital—even after taking into account the typical supplier's service fee.[57]

According to the study, stockless programs offer the following benefits for hospitals of all types:

- Inventory and related carrying cost reduction (both official and unofficial).

- Employee reduction—both direct (receiving and central supply) and indirect (clinical, nursing, payables, administration).

- Space requirements reduction including warehouse elimination.

- Revenue enhancement.

- Transaction processing cost reduction.

- Lower product costs.

- Better service levels to user departments.

Clearly, suppliers' costs increase as they take on the added responsibilities and increased service levels required by stockless programs. The hospital pays for the increased service out of its total delivered cost savings. This payment may be made in the form of a separate service fee to the distributor or may be incorporated into the price of the product.

The fees for the services will vary depending on the products and breadth of services included in the program through the negotiation process. To date, most distributors have charged stockless service fees ranging from 3 to 8% of normal product purchase price, and have been profitable once a certain level of activity has been achieved.

Even with the service fee considered, hospitals can benefit substantially from stockless inventories. Furthermore, these benefits affect the entire supply pipeline—costs are eliminated, not just shifted from one player to another. A number of factors drive the favorable economics:

- Labor rates are 10–15% less at the distributor.

- Costs per square foot are generally significantly higher for a hospital than for a distributor.

- Distributors have better systems to support inventory control and higher fill rates.

- Distributors are able to leverage their operations over a much larger customer base.

One common element across the stockless spectrum is the concept of sharing information in the supply pipeline. This implies a heavy dose of technology to accomplish the exchange of data efficiently. Those considering buying or selling stockless programs should not underestimate the critical role of systems, and the impact stockless has on the systems function. In addition, distributors providing stockless services have to invest in people, time, capital, and technology.[58]

Determining the type of inventory management system to use in a hospital depends on one's technical abilities, the culture of the institution, and the capabilities of the vendor. For example, Mount Sinai Hospital Medical Center (Chicago) has chosen a variety of inventory management systems to meet specific requirements and is in the process of implementing those systems. These include: (1) just-in-time inventory; (2) stockless systems for office supplies and forms; (3) outsourcing for selected supply, processing, and distribution supplies and functions; (4) facilities management for the print shop-copy center; (5) enhanced delivery systems from the vendors; and (6) recycling corrugated paper.[59]

▶ ORDER PROCESSING AND RELATED INFORMATION SYSTEM FLOWS

A customer order is the message that sets the physical distribution process in motion. The customer order cycle indicates the total time consumed by order preparation and transmittal, order receipt, order entry, order processing, warehouse picking and packing, order transportation, and delivery and unloading at the customer's dock. Therefore, the length of the customer's order cycle is determined not only by the speed of the physical movement of the goods but also by the speed and efficiency of the information and communication flows in the marketing channel. The experience of major corporations such as Eli Lilly, American Cyanamid, and E. R. Squibb and Sons demonstrates that faster order cycles achieved through the institution of an on-line computer-to-computer ordering system result in reduced order lead time, reduced ordering errors, reduced inventory, and fewer stockouts. Chapter 9 of this text is devoted to channel communications and information systems, including computer-to-computer ordering systems, as well as to other aspects of electronic data interchange in marketing channels.

For scores of companies across the U.S., information technology has proved invaluable in their efforts to upgrade the quality of logistics operations. It has given logistics managers the ability to handle and process the information necessary to manage their distribution activities better than ever. The information technology in use in today's warehouses and transportation departments includes bar-code systems, electronic data interchange, computer systems and software, radio-frequency devices, image-processing systems, and satellite communications. As a result, the application of technology has upped the ante in the quality game, improving on-time performance, lowering error rates, and even reducing damage levels. It has brought about reductions in cycle time, the lag time between order placement and final delivery of the product to the customer. It has also resulted in more accurate picking and shipping of product to fill orders. The biggest impact of these technological developments on logistics quality is that they have brought suppliers closer to their customers.[60]

There is a number of commercially available software packages[61] for integrated logistics management including:

- Ordering Processing

- Inventory Control

- Inventory Planning and Forecasting

- Distribution Requirements Planning

- Materials Requirements Planning

- Purchasing

- Transportation Analysis

- Traffic Routing and Scheduling

- Physical Distribution System Modeling

- Warehousing Management

- Stock Locations

- Labor Utilization and Analysis

Sorted into hierarchical categories these functional areas yield four systems:[62]

- Transaction Systems: Distribution order-processing systems encompass order status, allocation of customer orders, backorder processing, invoicing and preparation of shipping documents. Purchasing systems prepare documents, facilitate receiving, and manage expediting.

- Short-term Scheduling Systems: Inventory control systems maintain accurate current status, trends in demand, stock status and adjustments through techniques such as cycle counting. Routing and scheduling sequences vehicle stops for delivery and paths that a vehicle will take.

- Flow Planning: Inventory planning and forecasting, distribution requirements planning and materials requirements planning determine inventory replenishment, inventory timing and quantity for a given level of service, and the timing of production with material lead time considerations.

▪ Network Design/Optimization: Determination and optimization of infrastructure based on use of capacity, facilities location, and effectiveness of flow planning.

Commercially available software for integrated logistics do not address all four hierarchical categories with the exception of one or two software packages.[63]

Information technology (IT) can play an important role in the new competitive environment facing many companies by allowing organizations to interact with each other. The relationship between IT and interfirm coordination became evident in the consumer packaged-goods industry, with the introduction and use of electronic checkout scanners. IT creates many opportunities for restructuring interfirm relationships, thus improving total channel efficiency through increased coordination. However, IT-based improvements in coordination may not equally benefit all parties. Changes in channel relationships that increase coordination may, at the same time, affect each party's bargaining power.[64]

Telecommunications technology has significant impacts on most aspects of operations in both manufacturing and service industries. Inventory management benefits the most from technology applications. Telecommunications technology impacts speed and accuracy of channel information and physical flows involving: (1) pricing, (2) procurement, (3) inbound logistics, (4) sales/marketing, (5) outbound logistics, and (6) storing and distributing inventory. Telecommunications enhances the JIT-required relationships between firms and suppliers. It provides the media and means of linking geographically separated firms and suppliers, allowing them to communicate on a continuing basis. Time-based competition requires a seamless integration of all business units in the firm. Telecommunications systems can fill this requirement.[65]

Efficient Consumer Response Systems

Efficient Consumer Response (ECR) has become the code word for how the consumer packaged-goods channel will operate in the future. ECR is the continuous replenishment of inventories throughout the channel in response to end-customer demand. ECR involves collaboration between consumer-goods manufacturers and retailers to enhance merchandising effectiveness, inventory- and material-flow efficiency, and the channel's administrative efficiency, as illustrated in Figure 4-8. ECR is expected to eliminate billions of dollars of waste annually from the consumer packaged-goods channel. ECR involves initiatives in three core areas: (1) merchandising/marketing, (2) logistics and product flow, and (3) administration and technology.[66]

The entire grocery distribution supply chain is reengineering using Efficient Consumer Response from plant to store shelf in order to eliminate inefficiencies and excessive costs. ECR deals with optimal product assortment, promotion, and product introduction. It is a holistic approach that addresses the entire value chain of a manufacturer/retailer relationship. It forces the traditional logistics, sales, and marketing functions into a new alignment for optimum efficiency and consumer value.

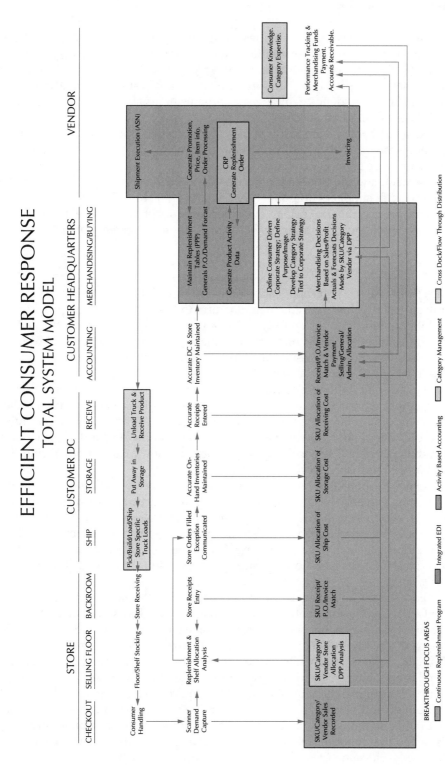

FIGURE 4-8   Efficient consumer response.

Source: Reprinted with permission from "A User's Guide to Efficient Consumer Response," *Grocery Marketing,* August 1993, p. 14.

ECR encompasses six major activities within an organization: (1) integrated electronic data interchange, (2) continuous replenishment, (3) computer-assisted ordering, (4) flow-through distribution, (5) activity-based costing, and (6) category management. The principles supporting ECR are applicable to virtually every industry and offer guidance to all logistics organizations about the nature of future capabilities required for success.[67]

Retailers benefit from ECR via increased sales per store, higher productivity of selling space, and the need for less back room area. Wholesalers can also continue to upgrade services to retailers such as inventory management, replenishment management, and assortment planning—freeing them to focus on building relationships with shoppers. Manufacturers will benefit from ECR via lower manufacturing and distribution costs and more effective use of promotional funds, as well as from knowing where product is in the pipeline at any given moment.[68]

Quick Response Systems

Quick Response (QR), the application of just-in-time (JIT) concepts throughout the entire supply pipeline, from the manufacturer to the final consumer, provides the capability to reorder merchandise as it is sold. The data-collection and recording capabilities of bar-code technology and the ability to communicate those data throughout the supply pipeline via electronic data interchange are the tools needed to build a Quick Response system.[69]

For example, with its electronic data interchange, Wal-Mart goes well beyond conventional transactions to explore such aspects as forecasting, planning data, model stock information, replenishment, point of sale, and shipping information. Since 1977, the chain has been electronically transmitting demand information to its trading partners. The once-proprietary format is now a rapidly advancing, 90% standardized, full quick-response system.[70]

Quick Response's most significant effects have been to take work out of the distribution process. The QR technologies—vendor-marked universal product code (UPC) labeling, electronic data interchange transactions such as the Advanced Ship Notice, and barcoded carton labeling—have all contributed to extracting work out of distribution-center (DC) processing. The net effect of reduced work and improved technologies has shown some significant results in retail distribution networks.[71]

For example, the Haggar Apparel Co. has some 100 major merchants, who represent about 26,000 store "entities," on its Haggar Order Transmission (HOT) Quick Response System. Smaller specialty retailers have become involved in the system. Some are already connected by a PC/software package from Envoy Corp. (Nashville, Tennessee) that allows them to scan their inventory and produce orders in a relatively inexpensive way. Envoy puts the smaller merchant in the same position as a major merchant by allowing it to acquire the right merchandise quickly and keep inventories down. Haggar is working in every segment of the business to reduce cycle times and minimize the amount of inventory a retailer must carry. It is hoped that modular manufacturing will help the manufacturer of suit separates apply the same Quick Response on short runs for stock-outs and fashion goods. The technique was tested for a year in one of Haggar's smaller plants and has been transferred to a much larger plant.[72]

Thomson Consumer Electronics (Paris, France) distributes electronic products directly to retailers. Its customers are also attempting to reduce inventory levels through quick response and vendor-managed inventory. In retailing, QR is the ability to respond to point-of-sale (POS) information and reduce inventory. Instead of carrying 4 to 6 weeks' inventory, stores now carry 1 to 2 weeks' worth. Thomson's vendor-managed inventory system means the retailer provides POS information but does not issue purchase orders. Thomson, as the supplier, uses the information to anticipate need, generate purchase orders, and supply the merchandise. It notifies the retailer electronically with an advance ship notice so its customers can anticipate delivery. Transport firms are selected on cost, quality of service, performance, transit times, and electronic data interchange capability.[73]

The final piece of retail's Quick Response puzzle—the piece that will leverage retailers' technology and advance their return on investment—is known as floor-ready merchandise (FRM). Establishing industry-wide guidelines for FRM has become a top priority, and department store retailers, anxious to reap the rewards of their technology investments, are leading the charge. Essentially, retailers want to be able to move merchandise shipments through their distribution centers (DC) within one hour without having to open more than a handful of cartons to check for accuracy. That will require the combined use of UPC bar codes, carton labels, the preticketing and prehanging of goods, and other technical protocols.[74]

▶ PHYSICAL DISTRIBUTION STRATEGY REVISION[75]

The question most often asked by management is when to revise the firm's physical distribution strategy. Existing strategies can become outdated even if they are continually undergoing improvement. Substantial changes in the following factors may indicate a need for strategy revision.

1. *Demand.* Geographic dispersion and level of demand greatly determine the configuration of distribution networks. Firms may project disproportionate growth or decline in one region of the country compared with a general growth or decline overall. Although the adjustment to general growth or decline may require only expansion or contraction at current facilities, shifting demand patterns may require that new warehouses be located in rapidly growing markets, whereas facilities in slow-growth areas experience little or no expansion.

2. *Customer Service.* This usually includes inventory availability, speed of delivery, and order-filling speed and accuracy. The costs of transportation, warehousing, inventory carrying, and order processing rise disproportionately as service levels are increased. Therefore, distribution costs will be sensitive to the level of customer service provided, especially if it is already high. Replanning usually is needed when service levels are changed due to competitive forces, policy revisions, or arbitrary service goals different from those on which the distribution strategy originally was based. Conversely, minor changes in service levels—when they already are low—probably will not trigger the need for replanning.

3. *Product Characteristics.* Distribution costs are sensitive to product weight, volume, value, and risk. In the channel, these characteristics can be altered through package design or finished state of the product during shipment and storage. For example, shipping a product in a knocked-down form can considerably affect the weight-bulk ratio of the product and the associated transportation and storage rates. But if altering a product characteristic substantially changes one cost element of distribution without affecting others, a new cost balance point for the distribution system is created, and replanning would be needed.

4. *Distribution Costs.* The amount of money a firm spends on distribution often determines how often its strategy should be replanned. All other factors being equal, a firm producing high-valued goods, such as machine tools and computers, with total distribution costs of 10% of sales or less may give little attention to distribution strategy. On the other hand, companies producing packaged industrial chemicals or food products may have distribution costs as high as 30% of sales. When costs are that high, even small changes in interest rates and fuel prices can make distribution strategy reformulation worthwhile.

5. *Pricing Policy.* Some suppliers transfer the responsibility and cost of transportation to the buyer, thus taking decisions on important distribution cost elements out of their own hands. Many industrial products firms do this through pricing policies such as free-on-board (F.O.B.) factory, prepaid transportation charges, and invoice add-ons. Because these firms do not pay for transportation, there is little incentive to include it as an economic force in setting distribution strategy. Should the price policy be changed to a delivered arrangement, the supplying firm would directly incur the transportation charges. This can result in the addition of warehouses and inventory to the distribution system. Shifting the terms of the price policy, especially shipment routing and quantities and responsibility for the transportation decision, can signal a need for strategy reformulation.

If changes have occurred in one or more of these five areas, substantial cost-reduction opportunities are available. Firms usually start by replanning inventory policy, location, freight consolidation and scheduling, and customer service.[76]

Benchmarking/Best Practices

In addition to logistics system revisions initiated as a result of factor shifts noted above, an increasing number of companies continuously revise their logistics system as a result of benchmarking. Benchmarking is the process of comparing and measuring an organization's business process against business leaders to determine best practices, that is, the best way to perform a process.[77] Benchmarking involves a number of steps.[78]

1. Determine what to benchmark.
2. Understand your own process.
3. Obtain, understand, and analyze best practices.
4. Analyze current and future performance gaps.
5. Adapt and incorporate best practices.

Figure 4-9 illustrates process definition and performance measures for the distribution process. Benchmarked companies do not necessarily have to be in the same industry or commodity line. For example, a concrete mix manufacturer bench-

FIGURE 4-9 Distribution process definition and performance measures.

Source: Reprinted with permission from Arthur Andersen, *Best Practices/Benchmarking: Executive Overview*, presented at the National Faculty Consortium in Wholesale-Distribution, August 9–10, 1994, San Francisco, CA.

	Process Performance Measures			GBP Numbers & Processes	Data Points required to calculate the measures at left
	Cost	**Quality**	**Time**		
5.2 Warehousing	Stocking cost per unit (PH)	Percent of inventory compliance (cycle counting) (KH)	Stocking time per unit (OI)	5.2.5 Package and store product	A Total company sales B Warehouse payroll C Warehouse equipment and systems expense D Damage/spoilage expense E Total distribution expense F Number of warehouse supervisors G Number of warehouse employees H Number of units sold I Number of units on hand J Number of units damaged/spoiled K Number of units unaccounted for L Number of picking errors M Warehousing space cubic feet N Unit volume cubic feet O Periodic measures of process-specific cycle time P Process-specific labor, systems, and equipment costs
Glossary avg-average dstb-distribution exp-expense	Holding cost per unit (PH)	Percent of holding damaged or spoiled (JI)	Avg holding time per unit (OI)		
	Damage/spoilage expense as a percentage of sales (DA)	Warehouse space utilization percentage (MN)		5.2.6 Stage product for delivery	
	Picking cost per unit (PI)	Percent of picking errors (LH)	Picking time per unit (OH)		
	Warehousing payroll cost per employee (BG)	Number of supervisors per stocking employee (FG)			
	Warehousing expense as a percentage of total dstb exp (BCE)			5.4.2 Manage Inventories	
5.3 Shipping	Shipping cost per order (ACF)	Percent of damaged shipments (GF)	Percent of on-time deliveries (IF)		A Shipping payroll expense B Total distribution expense C Shipping equipment and systems expense D Number of shipping supervisors E Number of shipping employees F Number of orders damaged H Number of orders incomplete I Number of late shipments J Period measure of process-specific cycle time
	Shipping expense as percentage of total dstrb exp (ACB)	Percent of incomplete shipments (HF)	Avg shipping elapsed time (I)	5.3.2 Deliver products to customers	
	Shipping payroll cost per employee (AE)	Number of employees per supervisor (ED)			

marked against Domino's Pizza because fast delivery is dictated by product characteristics in both industries! Each minute delay in the delivery of concrete mix to a construction site costs the contractor on the average $50 to $60. By self-imposing a stiff penalty for any orders that reached a construction job late, the concrete mix manufacturer has increased its punctuality and developed a faithful customer base that values the on-time delivery.

▶ SUMMARY AND CONCLUSIONS

Logistics management is a critical factor in the effective and efficient marketing of all products. However, the costs of activities associated with the flow of physical possession are surprisingly high—so high, in fact, that efforts must be expended to reduce them if distributive firms are to reach their profit goals, particularly when sales are increasing at very slow rates. Underlying effective and efficient physical distribution management is the physical distribution concept. This concept takes a cost-service orientation that is aimed at minimizing the costs of distribution at any given level of customer service. The tenets of the concept can be achieved only through a coordinated systemwide physical distribution network.

Developing an integrated logistics management system should begin with the determination of customer-service standards. Arriving at an appropriate customer-service standard involves determining the important elements of customer service from the customer's viewpoint. This information can be obtained through questionnaires or surveys. Once this is done, quantitative standards of performance must be set for each service element, actual performance for each service element should be measured and compared with the standards that have been set, and corrective action must be taken as needed if there is variance between the actual performance and the standard. Once customer-service standards are developed, management can undertake a selection of the transportation, warehousing, inventory, and production policies that will assure their proper implementation.

Problems in transporting merchandise can create difficulties in maintaining proper inventory levels and can impair customer service. Therefore, selection of suitable transportation modes is an integral part of developing a sound integrated logistics management system. Rail, highway, water, air, and pipeline networks each have advantages for different shippers and receivers. Combinations of the various modes are being used. Aided by various transportation agencies, such as freight forwarders, the transportation system presents channel members with a myriad of reasonably efficient transport choices. Many channel members are also relying increasingly on third-party logistics to reduce costs, focus on core businesses, improve service, and capitalize on resident expertise.

The two basic categories of warehouses available to channel members are private facilities, which are either owned or leased by the firm, and public facilities, in which space is rented by the firm. The choice between the two often involves trade-offs between managerial control on the one hand and capital investment on the other. Use of public warehouses appears to be growing rapidly, because the public warehousing industry is becoming more sophisticated in the scope and performance of a wide variety of distributive services. For firms having private warehouses, the development of distribution centers has emerged as a major service factor in physical distribution management. Determining the number and location of warehouses is a problem the manager faces, irrespective of the private-versus-public decision. A total cost approach is required, because the solution demands trade-offs among all physical distribution costs, especially those costs associated with warehouse operation, transportation, inventory, and lost sales resulting from slow service.

Inventory management and control will always play a vital role in the operation of firms directly involved in distribution; their significance is even more salient in periods of shortages, slow economic growth, and high interest rates. Inventory control encompasses decisions over how much and when to order as well as how much inventory to keep in stock. The objective of inventory control is to minimize total inventory cost subject to demand and service constraints. New approaches to inventory control include just-in-time, MRP, DRP, QR, and ECR systems. These systems allow channel members to produce and deliver materials just in time to be transformed into fabricated parts, fabricated parts just in time to go into subassemblies, subassemblies just in time to be assembled into finished goods, and finished goods just in time to be sold. They are hand-to-mouth modes of operation in which the ratio of production and delivery quantities approaches one.

Critical to decisions on when and how much to order is an accurate sales forecast. The forecasting model used depends on whether customer demand can be categorized as regular and highly predictable, irregular but mathematically consistent, or irregular and unpredictable. Exponential smoothing models are frequently used by manufacturers and wholesalers, because the demand facing them is generally not highly volatile. Retailers, though, often face fluctuating or, at least, highly seasonal demand. Therefore, adaptive forecasting and sharing of point-of-sale scanner data with suppliers are needed to cope with the latter's inventory problems. Furthermore, because sales forecasts are subject to error, controls must be established so that these errors do not lead to a reduction in customer service standards. To deal with these problems retailers and other channel members are adopting QR and ECR systems.

Production control is an important element of the logistics system. It is just one function performed by the materials manager. When and how finished products are distributed to the customer are affected by how much and what kinds of products a firm produces. These are production decisions that indirectly influence the level of customer service.

Logistics system management is a complex task involving the integration of all system components. It is critical to the continued success of a firm that the distribution strategy not become outdated. Thus, the question most often asked by management is when to revise the firm's strategy. Substantial changes in demand, customer service, product characteristics, distribution costs, or pricing policy can indicate a need for strategy revision.

DISCUSSION QUESTIONS

1. What is systems analysis? Why is it viewed as a useful approach to managing physical distribution activities?

2. The physical distribution manager has been called "a manager of trade-offs." Explain what this means.

3. Customer service in the channel can be defined as an activity, a performance measure, or a corporate philosophy. Explain in reference to pretransaction, transaction, and posttransaction elements of customer service.

4. MRP, DRP, JIT, QR, and ECR are inventory control and flow management systems. How do you account for the multiplicity of these systems in the channel of distribution? Are they conceptually and operationally different? What are these similarities and differences?

5. What is the major advantage of using JIT inventory control? What are its assumptions, and how do they compare with the EOQ assumptions in terms of applicability to retailers?

6. Compare and contrast private ownership of storage space with rented storage space, with reference to:

   a. the services that can be obtained with each;

   b. the cost of storage;

   c. the degree of administrative control;

   d. the flexibility to meet future uncertainties.

7. Order cycle variability impacts inventory levels at the wholesale and retail levels. Explain the impact of this variability on overall logistics system performance. Are there any tools at the disposal of logistics managers to ameliorate the impact of such variability?

8. Assume that you are employed by a retailing firm. What are the trade-offs involved in obtaining delivery of a given item in three to four days from a wholesaler versus delivery in three to four weeks from the manufacturer?

9. Automation of order-processing systems represents an attractive opportunity for improving customer service. Explain how information systems and telecommunication technology can be deployed to automate order processing.

ENDNOTES

[1] For an examination of the relationship between logistics organization in the information system see Philip Schary and James Coakley "Logistics Organization and the Information System," *The Journal of International Logistics Management*, Vol. 2, no. 2 (1991), pp. 22–29.

[2] Tom Davis, "Effective Supply Chain Management," *Sloan Management Review*, Vol. 34, no. 4 (1993), pp. 35–46.

[3] E. J. Muller, "Key Links in the Supply Chain," *Distribution*, Vol. 92, no. 10 (1993), pp. 52–56.

[4] Warren Strugatch, "High Times in Holland," *World Trade*, Vol. 6, no. 5 (1993), pp. 72–76.

[5] Herbert W. Davis, "Physical Distribution Costs: Performance in Selected Industries, 1987," *Papers, Annual Meeting of the Council of Logistics Management*, 1987, p. 373.

[6]Douglas M. Lambert and James R. Stock, *Strategic Logistics Management*, 3rd ed. (Homewood, IL: Richard D. Irwin, 1993), pp. 5–6.

[7]Robert V. Delaney, "CLIs 'State of Logistics' Annual Report," Press Conference Remaster and the National Press Club, Washington, DC, June 2, 1991, p. 4.

[8]For examples see Ronald Henkoff, "Delivering the Goods," *Fortune*, November 28, 1994, pp. 64–66, 70, 74–75.

[9]James B. Fuller, James O'Conor, and Richard Rawlinson, "Tailored Logistics: The Next Advantage," *Harvard Business Review* (May–June 1993), pp. 87–88.

[10]See for example, Tim R. V. Davis, "The Distribution Revolution," *Planning Review* (March–April 1994), pp. 46–49.

[11]John F. Magee, William A. Copacino, and Donald B. Rosenfield, *Modern Logistics Management* (New York: John Wiley and Sons, 1985), pp. 8–9.

[12]Howard T. Lewis, James W. Culliton, and Jack D. Steele, *The Role of Air Freight in Physical Distribution* (Boston: Division of Research, Harvard University Graduate School of Business Administration, 1956). See also John F. Magee, "The Logistics of Distribution," *Harvard Business Review*, Vol. 38 (July–August 1960), pp. 89–101.

[13]Lambert and Stock, *op. cit.*, p. 45. See also Paul D. Larson and Robert F. Lusch, "Functional Integration in Marketing Channels: A Determinant of Product Quality and Total Cost," *Journal of Marketing Channels*, Vol. 2, no. 1 (1992), pp. 1–28.

[14]Ronald H. Ballou, *Business Logistics Management*, 3rd ed. (Englewood Cliffs, NJ: Prentice-Hall, Inc., 1992), pp. 40–43.

[15]Don Firth, Jim Apple, Ron Denham, Jeff Hall, Paul Inglis, and Al Saipe, *Profitable Logistics Management* (New York: McGraw-Hill Ryerson Limited, 1988), pp. 24–26.

[16]James Aaron Cooke, "Supply-Chain Management '90s Style," *Traffic Management*, Vol. 31, no. 5 (May 1992), pp. 57–59.

[17]Ballou, *op.cit.*, p. 81.

[18]For an example of a customer service survey, see Lambert and Stock, *op. cit.*, pp. 151–158.

[19]For a menu for establishing customer needs, see Joseph B. Fuller, James O'Conor, and Richard Rawlinson, "Tailored Logistics: The Next Advantage," *Harvard Business Review* (May–June 1993), p. 92.

[20]See for example, Joseph B. Fuller, James O'Conor, and Richard Rawlinson, "Tailored Logistics: The Next Advantage," *Harvard Business Review* (May–June 1993), pp. 87–98.

[21]Douglas Lambert and Arun Sharma, "A Customer-Based Competitive Analysis for Logistics Decisions," *International Journal of Physical Distribution and Logistics Management*, Vol. 20, no. 1 (1990), p. 17.

[22]Douglas Lambert and Thomas Harrington, "Establishing Customer Service Strategies Within the Marketing Mix: More Empirical Evidence," *Journal of Business Logistics*, Vol. 10, no. 2 (1989), p. 58.

[23]E. J. Graff, "Just-Right Delivery," *Enterprise* (Summer 1990), pp. 27–28.

[24]Donna Delia-Loyle, "Sea-Air: Cheap and Fast," *Global Trade*, Vol. 112, no. 2 (Feb. 1992), pp. 16–18.

[25]See for example, U.S. Department of Commerce, *U.S. Industrial Outlook 1994* (Washington, DC: U.S. Government Printing Office, January 1994), pp. 40-1–40.15.

[26]Les Gould, "The Flow-through Concept: We Don't Store It—We Ship It," *Modern Materials Handling*, June 1990, p. 65.

[27]Bruce Caldwell and Rich Layne, "Retailers Centralize to Stay Alive," *Information Week* (January 30, 1989), p. 13.

[28]Gould, *op. cit.*

[29]Les Artman and David Clancy, "Distribution Follows Consumer Movement," *Transportation and Distribution* (June 1990), pp. 18–20.

[30]Caldwell and Layne, *op. cit.*

[31]Ballou, *op. cit.*, p. 252.

[32]"Relentless Drive to Reduce Cost," *Financial Times* (September 21, 1994), Financial Times Survey, Logistics, p. I.

[33]C. W. Ebeling, "Freight Processing Centers: Logistics' Missing Link," *Transportation & Distribution*, Vol. 33, no. 8, August 1992, pp. 52, 54.

[34]Jim Thomas, "1 + 1 = Innovation," *Distribution*, Vol. 92, no. 9 (Sept. 1993), pp. 44–48.

[35]Martin Keller, "Changing Channels," *Express Magazine* (Winter 1990), p. 2.

[36]Howard Schlossberg, "Info Network Promotes Better Manufacturer-Retailer Logistics," *Marketing News*, Vol. 28, no. 1 (Jan. 3, 1994), p. 26.

[37]Hal Plotkin, "Profiting from Logistics," *International Business*, Vol. 6, no. 8 (Aug. 1993), pp. 31–32.

[38]Patrick Byrne, "A New Road Map for Contract Logistics," *Transportation & Distribution*, Vol. 34, no. 4 (April 1993), pp. 58–62.

[39]Steven Galante and Sanford Jacobs, "New Inventory-Expense Rules Increase Costs at Many Firms," *The Wall Street Journal*, June 29, 1987, p. 29.

[40]This discussion of optimal procedures for procuring stocks draws on Richard J. Schonberger, "Why the Japanese Produce Just in Time," *Industry Week*, November 29, 1982, and Vivian Brownstein, "The War on Inventories Is Real This Time," *Fortune*, June 11, 1984.

[41]For detailed treatment of the topic see Everett E. Adam, Jr. and Ronald J. Ebert, *Production and Operations Management*, 5th ed. (Englewood Cliffs, NJ: Prentice-Hall, 1992), pp. 450–520.

[42]For detailed discussion of DRP see Adam and Ebert, *Ibid.*, pp. 521–559 and Ronald H. Ballou, *op. cit.*, pp. 541–545.

[43]For an excellent discussion of the topic and its applications in logistics management, see Marshall L. Fisher, Janice H. Hammond, Walter R. Obermeyer, and Ananth Raman, "Making Supply Meet Demand in an Uncertain World," *Harvard Business Review* (May–June 1994), pp. 83–93.

[44]Denis C. Picard, "The Myth of the Accurate Forecast," *Industry Week*, Vol. 243, no. 2 (Jan. 17, 1994), p. 36.

[45]For a detailed technical discussion of this and other related inventory management concepts, see Douglas M. Lambert and James R. Stock, *Strategic Logistics Management, op. cit.*, Chapter 10, pp. 398–442.

[46]For a detailed discussion of operations marketing, logistics interface see Lloyd M. Rinehart, M. Bixby Cooper, and George D. Wagenheim, "Furthering Integration of Marketing and Logistics through Customer Service in the Channel," *Journal of the Academy of Marketing Science*, Vol. 17, no. 1 (Winter 1989), pp. 63–71; and John T. Mentzer, Roger Gomes, and Robert E. Krapfel, Jr., "Physical Distribution Service: A Fundamental Marketing Concept?" *Journal of The Academy of Marketing Science*, Vol. 17, no. 1 (Winter 1989), pp. 53–62.

[47]Otis Port, "The Responsive Factory," *Business Week* (Oct. 22, 1993), pp. 48–53.

[48]Lambert and Stock, *op. cit.*, pp. 472–475.

[49]Walter E. Goddard, "MRP II: The Evolution Continues," *Modern Materials Handling*, Vol. 49, no. 4 (April 1994), p. 40.

[50]Gary Frazier, Robert Spekman, and Charles O'Neal, "Just-in-Time Exchange Relationships in Industrial Markets," *Journal of Marketing* (October 1988), p. 53.

[51]Craig R. Waters, "Why Everybody's Talking About 'JUST-IN-TIME,' " *Inc.* (March 1984), pp. 78–80.

[52]John Sheridan, "An Edict for Excellence," *Industry Week* (August 21, 1989), p. 38.

[53]Frazier, Spekman, and O'Neal, *op. cit.*, pp. 53–54.

[54]Thomas J. Billesbach and Roger Hayen, "Long-Term Impact of Just-in-Time on Inventory Performance Measures," *Production and Inventory Management Journal*, Vol. 35, no. 1 (1994), pp. 62–67.

[55]Sherwin Greenblatt, "Continuous Improvement in Supply Chain Management," *Chief Executive*, No. 86 (June 1993), pp. 40–43.

[56]Martin M. Stein, "The Ultimate Customer-Supplier Relationship at Bose, Honeywell, and AT&T," *National Productivity Review*, Vol. 12, no. 4 (Autumn 1993), pp. 543–548.

[57]"Stockless Materials Management: How it Fits into the Healthcare Cost Puzzle," Healthcare Industry Distributors Association (HIDA), 1990.

[58]*Ibid.*

[59]William H. Saphir, "Implementing a New Inventory Management System," *Hospital Material Management Quarterly*, Vol. 15, no. 3 (Feb. 1994), pp. 42–45.

[60]James Aaron Cook, "Technology Ups the Ante in the Quality Game," *Traffic Management*, Vol. 33, no. 4 (Apr. 1994), pp. 64–68.

[61]For a comprehensive listing see *The Software Encyclopedia*, Vol. 2, System Compatibility/Applications Index, R. R. Bowker and *The Software Catalog—Microcomputers* Part II (1994), Elsevier.

[62]Alan J. Stenger, Steven C. Dunn, and Richard R. Young, "Commercially Available Software for Integrated Logistics Management," *International Journal of Logistics Management*, Vol. 4, no. 2 (1993), p. 66.

[63]*Ibid.*

[64]Eric K. Clemons and Michael C. Row, "Information, Power, and Control of the Distribution Channel," *Chief Executive*, no. 85 (May 1993), pp. 64–67.

[65]Godwin J. Udo, "The Impact of Telecommunications on Inventory Management," *Production & Inventory Management Journal*, Vol. 34, no. 2 (Second Quarter 1993), pp. 32–37.

[66]William C. Copacino, "Efficient Consumer Response," *Traffic Management*, Vol. 32, no. 7 (July 1993), pp. 28–29.

[67]David G. deRoulet, "ECR: Better Information Cuts Costs," *Transportation & Distribution*, Vol. 34, no. 10 (Oct. 1993), p. 63.

[68]Warren G. Thayer, "Harding Offers Blueprint for Forming ECR Program," *Frozen Food Age*, Vol. 42, no. 9 (Apr. 1994), pp. 3, 24+.

[69]Mitchell E. MacDonald, "The Fast Track to Customer Service," *Traffic Management*, Vol. 30, no. 4 (Apr. 1991), pp. 54–56.

[70]Renee Covino Rouland, "Wal-Mart's Advances in EDI," *Discount Merchandiser*, Vol. 30, no. 9 (Sept. 1990), pp. 32–33.

[71]Gary Robins, "Less Work, More Speed," *Stores*, Vol. 76, no. 3 (Mar. 1994), pp. 24–26.

[72]"Haggar Makes the Modular Move in Slacks Production," *Bobbin*, Vol. 33, no. 10 (June 1992), p. 80.

[73]"Thomson Consumer Electronics," *Transportation & Distribution*, Vol. 34, no. 9 (Sept. 1993), p. 42.

[74]Susan Reda, "Floor-Ready Merchandise," *Stores*, Vol. 76, no. 4 (Apr. 1994), pp. 41–44.

[75]For a detailed discussion of strategic logistics planning see, Alan Rushton and Richard Saw, "A Methodology for Logistics Strategy Planning," *The International Journal for Logistics Management*, Vol. 3, no. 1 (1992), pp. 46–62; M. J. Ploos Van Amstel and M. F. G. M. Verstegen, "Development of a Total Logistics Concept: A Method for Improving Logistics Performance," *The International Journal of Logistics Management*, Vol. 2, no. 2 (1991), pp. 63–73; and Kevin A. O'Laughlin and William C. Copacino, "Strategic Logistics Planning Process," in Chapter 4, Logistics Strategy, in William C. Copacino and James F. Robeson, *The Logistics Handbook*, 1994, pp. 71–75.

[76]Ronald H. Ballou, *Business Logistics Management*, 3rd ed. (Englewood Cliffs, NJ: Prentice-Hall, 1992), pp. 38–40.

[77]For detailed discussion of benchmarking and best practices see Ronald Fink, "Group Therapy—Not a Fad or a Quick Fix, But a Way of Managing Change: That's Benchmarking," *Financial World* (September 29, 1993), pp. 42–62.

[78]Arthur Andersen, *Best Practices/Benchmarking: Executive Overview*, presented at the National Faculty Consortium in Wholesale-Distribution, August 9–10, 1994, San Francisco, CA.

5/ CHANNEL PLANNING

DESIGNING CHANNEL SYSTEMS

Creative, well-executed marketing channel strategies provide some of the more potent means by which companies can enhance their ability to compete domestically and internationally. For example, the Hospital Supply Division of Baxter Healthcare has combined elements of vertical integration of supply, outsourcing, and sophisticated electronic linkages with its customers to dominate its markets. Packard Bell Electronics became the United States' number one personal-computer maker in unit sales by focusing all of its efforts, energies, and resources on partnering with discount stores and electronics chains. Caterpillar has built such a formidable dealer system for heavy construction equipment that it represents Cat's primary advantage vis-à-vis its archrival, Komatsu.[1] Steelcase and Herman Miller have set such high standards for distribution performance in delivering complex office furniture installations complete and on time that their competitors have had to struggle simply to stay in sight. And Federal Express set the small package delivery industry on its ear with radically new, efficient, and customer-oriented approaches.

For a large number of companies, the emphasis during the decade of the 1990s has been on implementing total quality management (TQM) philosophies and procedures and achieving quantum improvements in customer service via process reengineering. This commitment has brought a nearly universal realization that critical assessments and revisions of marketing channels were long overdue. Evidence is found in the Efficient Consumer Response (ECR), quick response, and just-in-time movements discussed in previous chapters. The focus on quality, customer service, and reengineering is generic, cutting across all industries and geographies. It has been impelled and sharpened by the growing power and polarity of retailing and wholesaling, the widespread use of and improvement in information technology, the need to eliminate redundancies in distribution, the emphasis on value creation in response to demands of buyers, and a host of other factors.

In this chapter, a marketing channel planning approach is laid out that permits both for-profit and not-for-profit organizations to reorient their distribution systems so that they are more responsive to customer needs. The approach provides answers to the following questions:

1. What kinds of services have to be provided to end-users by marketing channels in order to assure end-user satisfaction, regardless of the specific channels employed?

2. What kinds of marketing and/or logistical activities or functions will have to be performed to generate those services?

3. Which types of institutions or agencies are in the best positions to perform the activities, taking into account their effectiveness and their efficiency at doing so? Is it more desirable for potential channel members (e.g., manufacturers, wholesalers, and retailers) to divide distribution labor with one another or is vertical integration likely to be more successful in accomplishing the objectives established by the focal organization?

An underlying goal of the process is to deliver superior customer value. It focuses on two major value disciplines—operational excellence and customer intimacy.[2] Operational excellence means providing customers with reliable products or services at competitive prices and delivered with minimal difficulty or inconvenience. Customer intimacy means segmenting and targeting markets precisely and then tailoring offerings to match exactly the demands of those niches.[3] Delivering superior customer value is the key to generating customer loyalty, and customer loyalty leads to repeat sales, referrals, lower costs of doing business, and higher profits (i.e., a decrease in the customer defection rate by 5% can increase profits by 25% to 95%).[4]

The approach focuses on the design of what have been called "customer-driven distribution systems."[5] The examples (although disguised) and insights used throughout this chapter in illustrating the approach have been drawn from a decade of studies for major corporations in a variety of highly diverse industries.[6] The 14-step process required in implementing this approach is outlined in Figure 5-1 (affectionately referred to as "Starship Enterprise").

▶ A BLUEPRINT FOR DESIGNING MARKETING CHANNELS

The implementor of the process laid out in Figure 5-1 should be forewarned—the fourteen steps are not simple or quick. Furthermore, none of the steps should be skipped in the interest of expediency, even though the process may be accelerated by performing some of them concurrently rather than sequentially. (For example, Steps 1 through 4 can be conducted at the same time as Steps 7 through 11.) Being complete is mandatory, because of all the marketing decisions an organization can make, decisions regarding distribution are the most long term in nature. A company can change its prices, its advertising, hire or fire a market research agency, revamp its sales promotion program, and modify its product line in the short run. Once management sets up its distribution channels, though, there seems to be great reluctance to modify them. But change, although frequently difficult and frustrating, is indeed possible. IBM violated all its cultural norms by marketing its personal computers through retailers and dealers like Sears and Computerland and through its own IBM Product Centers. (It sold its Product Centers to NYNEX in yet another shift in its channels strategy.) The J.I. Case Division of Tenneco moved swiftly following its acquisition of International Harvester's farm equipment business and reduced the number of dealers in the combined enterprise by nearly 800. But such

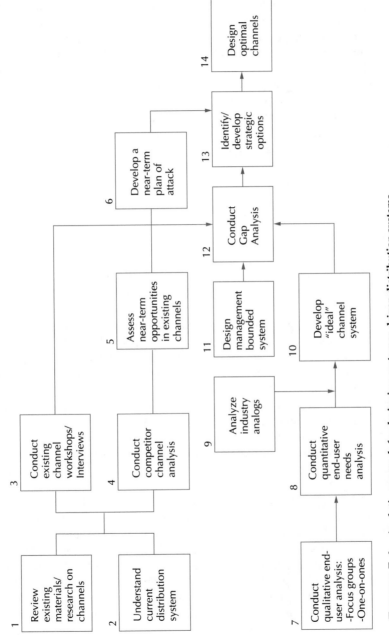

FIGURE 5-1   Analytic approach for designing customer-driven distribution systems.
Source: Gemini Consulting, Inc. and Louis W. Stern.

pruning can be very painful and can stimulate costly lawsuits. The bottom line is that channel change should be approached very carefully and deliberately.[7] The channel-design process cannot begin, however, without having a product/market strategy in place. Channels are conduits to the marketplace for products and services. Without a clear idea of the product or service (e.g., compact automobile, heavy-duty mix-master, brown socks, homeowner's insurance) to be offered for sale, channel design is a meaningless exercise. In addition, the market for which the product or service is to be targeted must also be clearly delineated (e.g., first-time car buyers, restaurants, adult males, apartment dwellers). Furthermore, all of the hard work required to reengineer channels will go to waste unless the product or service being offered for sale has real value in it for at least one segment of the delineated market. If the end-users for whom the product or service is intended don't perceive it as having competitive price/performance, positive image, and/or substantial quality characteristics, distribution—no matter how well thought through—won't save it.

Steps 1 through 4. Complete Understanding of Existing Conditions and Challenges

Although seemingly mundane, these four steps are critical to an organization's ability to make changes later, if changes are warranted. They involve interviewing key management personnel, salespersons, and channel members to gain an understanding of what channel issues and opportunities face the organization. A goal of these four steps is to generate an accurate description of what the current distribution channel looks like, the market coverage it provides, the value-added activities it performs, and the present and future challenges it faces. Existing research materials and secondary sources are invaluable in piecing together a reasonable picture of the distribution systems employed by the company and the members of its industry, but they must be supplemented and validated in discussions with people on the "firing line" (Steps 1 and 3). Although it might seem that such searches and discussions are unnecessary for scoping out a company's channels (after all, everyone within the company should be intimately familiar with how the company goes to market), an assumption of perfect knowledge is inappropriate, at best, and foolhardy, at worst.

At this stage of the process, it is necessary to isolate (1) the company's operative paths to the marketplace, (2) the logistic and sales functions being performed within each path, (3) the way in which labor (i.e., the marketing flows) is divided between the company and external organizations, and (4) the economics of the system (costs, discounts, gross and net margins, and the like). The review of current sales and distribution processes should uncover what is working and what is not.

Step 2 as well as Step 1 require attention to significant macroeconomic, technological, or behavioral trends that will likely have an impact on channel strategy over time. Much research has been conducted over the past two decades looking at how environmental factors affect the structure of marketing channels.[8] Basically, this research indicates that the more variable, diverse, turbulent, and uncertain a channel's environment is, the more control is required over the behavior of channel members in order to cope with all of the contingencies facing the channel. But there is also a need for flexibility in adapting to the rapidly changing marketplace, and this need is at odds with the need for control. Therefore, there is a constant strain in channels faced with complex and dynamic environments. This strain generates much channel conflict, as discussed in Chapter 7.

In order to assess how external conditions might inhibit the decision space of firms, it is necessary to look intensively at each of the following factors:

- industry concentration

- macroeconomic indicators

- the present and projected state of technology

- the extent of regulation/deregulation and trends

- entry barriers

- competitors' behavior

- the strength of end-user loyalties

- the geographical dispersion of end-users

- the stage in the product life cycle

- the extent of turbulence and diversity in the marketplace[9]

In the industry that sells paper to printers and publishers, for example, there has been significant consolidation of key end-user markets, increased power of indirect marketing channels (i.e., paper merchants), industry capacity additions, heavy investment in fixed costs, rising costs of raw materials, growth of geographically dispersed end-user segments, and arrival at the maturity stage of the product life cycle for most products in the industry.

All of these factors impact the degrees of freedom management has in designing channels. They impact the number and type of industry scenarios and, as a result, the assortment of alternative channels that should be considered. With regard to the product life cycle, for instance, Lele argues that the best channels for a product change over time.[10] In the introductory stage, the most appropriate channels are those that add substantial value. In the growth stage, channels must be able to handle greater sales volume, but they won't have to provide all the services offered by the channels in the introductory stage. In the maturity stage, channels do not emphasize value-added service, because end-users focus on low price. And in the decline stage, channels such as direct mail that add even less value become dominant.[11] It should be noted, however, that Lele's suggestions are meaningful in the aggregate. Different end-user segments will focus on different things, regardless of stage in the product life cycle.

In Steps 3 and 4, a great deal of effort should be allocated to finding out what competitors are doing with their marketing channels. In order to gather the intelligence, primary data may have to be collected through workshops, focus groups, or one-on-one interviews with individuals knowledgable about current channel developments. Special attention should be given to learning how specific competitors are able to maintain margin and expense pressures on the industry. It is important to examine the marketing strategies they employ in stimulating demand and the marketing programs they use to support their channels. For example, Figure 5-2 provides an example of the extent of support that Compaq, Hewlett Packard, and IBM gave to their resellers in 1994. The information was developed for one of their competitors in the computer industry (hereafter referred to as Company X) from primary and secondary sources. Data from the study also indicated that, relative to personal computers and perhaps even to servers, Compaq posed the major threat to Company X at that time. Therefore, during Step 4, information on Compaq's strategies was developed, such as that shown in Figures 5-3 and 5-4. This information gave Company X a picture of what it was up against if it hoped to challenge Compaq. Although many of these insights came from benchmarking studies, secondary sources provided a significant number as well, which goes to show that there is a lot of competitive intelligence readily available in the public library.

Steps 5 and 6: Generating Quick "Hits"

It is possible that as a result of the insights gained during Steps 1 through 4, immediate changes in specific channel strategies, tactics, and policies may be warranted. For example, promotional programs could be improved right away on the basis of feedback from channel members or from competitor analysis. (For example, Company X made some quick adjustments once it saw Figure 5-2.) If something is blatantly wrong or presents a clear and obvious opportunity, it is foolish to wait for the remainder of the 14 steps to be completed to make a change.

Making changes at this stage of the process is not risk-free, however, because a policy could be established now that is difficult to alter later in the face of more complete information. It would probably be best, during Steps 5 and 6, to focus on short-term issues rather than to set in motion major changes with long-term implications. An example of the latter would be to have suggested to Company X at this stage in the process that it revamp its salesforce to make it look more like Compaq's (see Figure 5-4). Such a recommendation, if desirable, should wait until the entire 14-step process is completed.

Steps 7 through 10: Designing the "Ideal" Channel System

During these steps in the process, a totally fresh approach to channel strategy is adopted. It requires that a firm forget about the fact that it already has a distribution system in place. The best way to design a system is to start with a blank sheet of paper, leaving past history behind. Management must suspend conventional wisdom for the time being and not bind its imagination by adhering to the existing model. Such a suggestion is very similar to the philosophy that Michael Hammer

Marketing Program Availability and Costs to Resellers:

Legend:
- ● Available free
- ◗ Available for fee/coop
- ◖ Not Readily Available
- ○ Not Available

Program	Compaq	HP	IBM	Best-in-Class Program from Competitor
Coop funding:				
• Dealer/VAR	1%–7%	2%–3%	1%–2%	IBM—Testing aggressive co-op/MDF support to hold AS/400 in the channels
• Retailer	Negotiated	NA	2%–10%	
Lead referral:				
• Prospect database	○	○	◖	IBM—On-line access to IBM prospects/D&B database through Partner Serv
• Direct mail leads	●	●	●	HP—Organizes direct mailings followed by telemarketing
• Telemarketer leads	●	●	●	HP—Organizes teleconferences with up to 200 customers and follows-up
• End-user inquiries	●	◗	◗	Compaq—On-line info about end-users through "Reseller Locator Hotline"
Event Marketing:				
• Trade shows	◖	●	◗	HP—Co-sponsors booths for Premier Solution Partners at no cost to reseller
• Industry events	○	◗	○	IBM—Organizes industry shows in which resellers present to customers
Sales Material:				
• Brochures/product info.	●	●	◖	Compaq—$150 free material each quarter
• Shelf displays	●	○	○	Compaq—Providers computer "hoods" to resellers to boost sales
• Custom artwork	●	●	●	IBM—Access ad agency to proof and place ads
Reseller Sales Support:				
• Missionary/joint sales	●	●	◖	HP—Reps make more joint sales calls with resellers than the typical vendor
• Sales training	◖	●	◗	Compaq—Require sales training for resellers
• Press releases/articles		●	●	IBM—Creates custom newsletters/press releases

FIGURE 5-2 Reseller support provided by major competitors in the computer industry (disguised).
Source: Gemini Consulting, Inc. and Louis W. Stern.

As PC prices dropped 66% between 1991 and 1993, Compaq reduced costs by 75%:

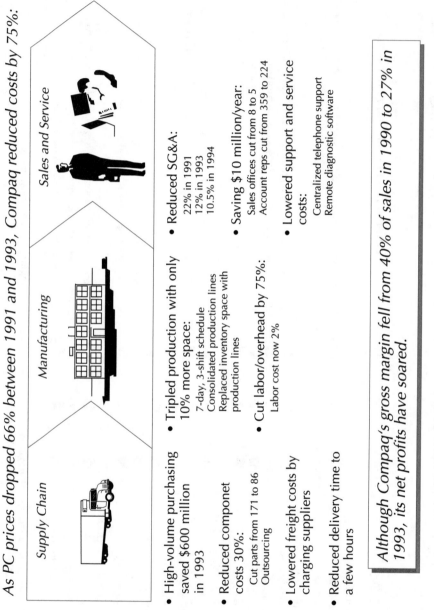

| Supply Chain | Manufacturing | Sales and Service |

- High-volume purchasing saved $600 million in 1993

- Reduced componet costs 30%:
  Cut parts from 171 to 86
  Outsourcing

- Lowered freight costs by charging suppliers

- Reduced delivery time to a few hours

- Tripled production with only 10% more space:
  7-day, 3-shift schedule
  Consolidated production lines
  Replaced inventory space with production lines

- Cut labor/overhead by 75%:
  Labor cost now 2%

- Reduced SG&A:
  22% in 1991
  12% in 1993
  10.5% in 1994

- Saving $10 million/year:
  Sales offices cut from 8 to 5
  Account reps cut from 359 to 224

- Lowered support and service costs:
  Centralized telephone support
  Remote diagnostic software

Although Compaq's gross margin fell from 40% of sales in 1990 to 27% in 1993, its net profits have soared.

FIGURE 5-3   Compaq's aggressive efforts to cut costs and increase quality along the value chain.

Source: Gemini Consulting, Inc. and Louis W. Stern.

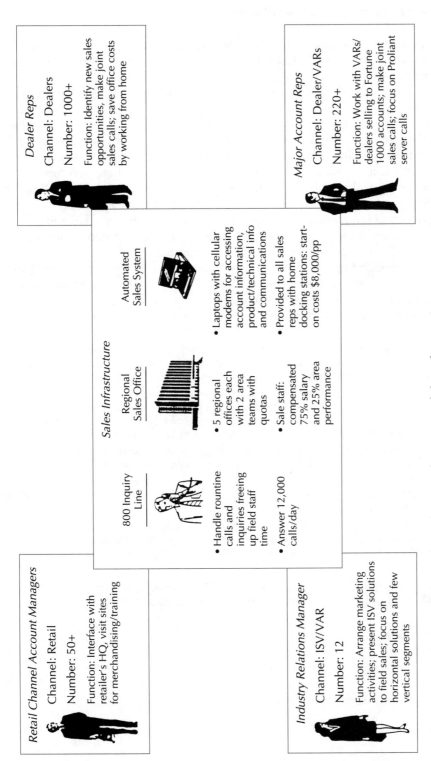

Retail Channel Account Managers

Channel: Retail

Number: 50+

Function: Interface with retailer's HQ, visit sites for merchandising/training

Dealer Reps

Channel: Dealers

Number: 1000+

Function: Identify new sales opportunities, make joint sales calls; save office costs by working from home

Sales Infrastructure

800 Inquiry Line

- Handle rountine calls and inquiries freeing up field staff time
- Answer 12,000 calls/day

Regional Sales Office

- 5 regional offices each with 2 area teams with quotas
- Sale staff: compensated 75% salary and 25% area performance

Automated Sales System

- Laptops with cellular modems for accessing account information, product/technical info and communications
- Provided to all sales reps with home docking stations: start-on costs $8,000/pp

Industry Relations Manager

Channel: ISV/VAR

Number: 12

Function: Arrange marketing activities; present ISV solutions to field sales; focus on horizontal solutions and few vertical segments

Major Account Reps

Channel: Dealer/VARs

Number: 220+

Function: Work with VARs/dealers selling to Fortune 1000 accounts; make joint sales calls; focus on Proliant server calls

FIGURE 5-4 **Compaq's sales force is focused on several customer and channel segments.**

Source: Gemini Consulting, Inc. and Louis W. Stern.

espoused when, in coining the term "business reengineering," he counseled "don't automate—obliterate!"[12] Business reengineering means starting all over, starting from scratch.[13]

During Steps 7 and 8, all attention is focused on learning what it is that end-users want in the way of *service outputs*, regardless of the outlets from which they are to obtain the firm's products or services. Four generic types of service outputs are lot size (in addition to dollar value of a potential purchase, does an end-user want to buy in units of one or in multiple units?), market decentralization (does an end-user want around-the-corner convenience, information, and technical assistance, or is he/she willing to deal across great distances, say via an "800" number?), delivery or waiting time (does the end-user want immediate delivery or is he/she more concerned about delivery assurance?), and product variety and assortment (does the end-user prefer one-stop shopping [for many different products under one "roof"] or is depth of assortment more important?).[14]

Although the list above is, indeed, generic across all channels and products, it is not necessarily comprehensive. For example, in addition to the four generic service outputs, Rangan, Menezes, and Maier[15] identified five additional service outputs in their study of the marketing of industrial goods.

1. *Product information.* Customers seek more information on certain kinds of products, particularly products that are new and/or technically complex and those that have a rapidly changing technological component.

2. *Product customization.* Some products inherently need technical "adjustment"; they require customization to fit the customer's production requirements (e.g., special steel for a maker of surgical instruments). Commonly, however, even a standard product must fulfill specific customer requirements on factors such as size or grade.

3. *Product quality assurance.* A customer might place emphasis on product integrity and reliability because of the consequences the product has for the customer's own operations.

4. *After-sales service.* Customers need services such as installation, repair, maintenance, and warranty

5. *Logistics.* Transporting, storing, and supplying products to the end-user involve levels of complexity. For example, transshipping and transporting hazardous chemicals may require special investments that are likely to increase handling costs.

More specifically, in one industry—personal computers—the following (in alphabetical order) were found to be important among business customers:

- availability

- brand/product selection/variety

- delivery (speed, reliability)

- flexibility

- information

- internal politics

- payment terms/payment process

- price

- product demonstration

- relationship with current supplier

- reputation

- responsiveness

- service

- stability

- support

- warehousing

The problem with lists like this, however, is that they are too general. There is no such thing as a truly homogeneous market where *all* end-users emphasize the *same* service outputs in identical ways. Attention must, therefore, focus on what different segments desire or on how the market might be broken up into segments desiring common service outputs. Not only do segments prefer different dimensions, but preferences for different levels of each dimension also vary among segments. For some end-users, "convenience" means a 5-minute walk from home; for others, a 15-minute automobile ride is accessible enough.

Steps 7 and 8 in the channel-design process calls for thorough research to find out (1) what it is that end-users want from the buying process, beyond a first-rate product, and (2) how these preferences can be used to group end-users into discrete segments. To generate a list of service outputs that could encompass an entire product/market (e.g., personal computers for use by businesses), it is usually necessary to conduct focus groups and one-on-one interviews (Step 7), unless one is lucky enough to find data sources that already contain comprehensive and meaningful lists.[16]

Once it is known what all end-users seem to value, examination of the segmentation issue can proceed in two different ways. The market can be divided into a priori segments (such as those often used in product or advertising decisions) and then analyzed in order to see whether those segments share common purchasing preferences. Or research can be conducted in order to define segments that seem best to match end-users with purchasing patterns. From a purely theoretical perspective, it is much better to follow the latter path than the former, because how end-users prefer to shop for products and services will not necessarily correlate highly with their preferences for product features, their media habits, their life styles, or whatever other common segmentation schemes management usually employs. For example, when marketing products and services to commercial markets, firms generally use a segmentation scheme based on convenience—they divide their markets into small (say, 1 to 50 employees), medium (say, 50 to 500 employees), and large (say, over 500 employees) companies. It is not immediately clear why the service outputs desired by large companies should necessarily be different from those desired by medium and small companies, except, perhaps, along the lot-size dimension. It would be far better to let the data determine the answer rather than to impose an arbitrary segmentation scheme or one based on convenience or conventional wisdom. Theoretically, the segmentation process should produce groups of buyers who are (a) maximally similar *within* a group; (b) maximally different *between* groups, and it should also be true that (c) the segments so defined differ on dimensions that *matter* for building a distribution system.

In either case, what one must look for is the linkage between purchasing patterns and relevant segments. This matching keeps the focus where it belongs—on segments rather than on markets made up of potential or existing buyers with heterogeneous needs. For example, if one is selling office equipment to the small business market, self-employed accountants are likely to be found in a different segment from engineers in, say, start-up scientific research firms.

Significant insights are also gained by asking end-users to assess their satisfaction and comfort level with different channel options. In addition, for *new* products, channels can be designed by focusing on individuals or organizations that are so-called "lead users." As defined by Von Hippel, lead users of a novel or enhanced product, process, or service display two characteristics with respect to it:

1. Lead users face needs that will be general in a marketplace, but they face them months or years before the bulk of that marketplace encounters them, *and*
2. Lead users are positioned to benefit significantly by obtaining a solution to those needs.[17]

Step 8 requires survey research to permit the quantitative analysis of end-user needs. The starting point is the list of service outputs generated in Step 7. But when conducting the necessary research, it is not enough to simply ask respondents which of the service outputs they prefer. Given "free choice," individuals are always going to opt for everything. Respondents must be forced to trade-off attributes (e.g., locational convenience vs. low price vs. extensive product variety vs. expert sales assistance) so that, eventually, it will be possible to compare the importance of the attributes across segments. A number of marketing research techniques are available to assist this step of the process, among them conjoint analysis, hybrid modelling, and constant-sum scales.[18]

Several examples of this type of analysis, using constant-sum scales, can illustrate this approach. Table 5-1 shows the disguised results relative to telecommunications equipment and services being sold to the business (as opposed to the residential) marketplace. The service outputs (ongoing relationship/personal calls, wide range of products/service, etc.) are listed down the left hand side of the table. The

TABLE 5-1   **Service Output Segments for Telecommunications Equipment and Services (Disguised Data): Relative Importance on 100-Point Scale by Service Output**

	SEGMENTS				
SERVICE OUTPUTS	Brand Variety/ Demonstration	Support Intensive	Relationship	Price Sensitive	Product Variety/ Advice
Ongoing relationship/ personal calls	13	8	31	6	11
Wide range of products/advice	13	9	12	7	29
Support/maintenance/ reliability	23	58	29	33	32
Brand variety	14	8	8	7	6
Low price	20	8	10	38	12
Product demonstration	17	9	10	9	10
Total	100.0	100.0	100.0	100.0	100.0
Percentage of revenue in this cluster	21	26	25	15	13

Source: Gemini Consulting, Inc. and Louis W. Stern.

columns represent the segments (brand variety/demonstration, support intensive, etc.) that emerge from a cluster analysis. The names assigned to the segments were derived from the strength of the preferences for specific service outputs. For example, the support intensive segment assigned 58 out of 100 points to the service output "support/ maintenance/reliability." Finally, the percentage of revenue accounted for by each segment is given at the bottom of each column, indicating that all segments represent a substantial opportunity in this multibillion dollar marketplace.

Several interesting insights can be generated from Table 5-1. First, marketing channels serving the various segments must be able to deliver more of some service outputs than others. This means that it is unlikely that any one channel will be able to satisfy the needs of all segments. Second, all segments value support highly; therefore, support capability must be designed into every channel and/or any channel selected to market telecommunications equipment and services had better be able to provide support to its customers. Third, because of the importance attached to "support," separate attention is required, highlighting its delivery from the kinds of outputs that are normally generated by "sales channels."

Once segments are isolated, demographic profiles can be developed for each in order to determine whether the end-users comprising them come from the same industry, are approximately the same size, are located in particular regions of the country, etc. If there are commonalities, then marketing to the segments will be much easier than if the segments represent a random cross-section of the population. For example, the "support intensive" segment is heavily (but not completely) represented by large firms selling financial services.

▶TABLE 5-2 **Service Output Segments for Office Supplies (Disguised Data): Relative Importance on a 100-point Scale by Service Outputs**

SERVICE OUTPUTS	SEGMENTS (SELECTED EXAMPLES ONLY)		
	Price	Advice/ Relationship	Service Preferring
Advice/Relationship	9.0	42.0	10.0
Variety	5.0	8.0	6.0
See/Touch	3.0	4.0	2.0
Returns	8.0	9.0	9.0
Quality	12.0	10.0	9.0
Well-known	2.0	4.0	2.0
Price	48.0	9.0	18.0
Sales Calls	2.0	6.0	4.0
Service	11.0	8.0	40.0
Total	100.0	100.0	100.0
Percentage of Sample	11.0	20.0	13.0

Source: Gemini Consulting, Inc. and Louis W. Stern.

Table 5-2 shows an analysis similar to the one shown in Table 5-1, only here the focal product was printing supplies and the market targeted was small business.

Depending on the methodology employed, it is possible to expand the number of service outputs included in a study and still achieve valid results. For example, in a new car distribution study conducted for a major automobile company, Louis W. Stern and Paul E. Green were, using hybrid conjoint analysis, able to include 17 service outputs with multiple levels for each output (e.g., "convenience" is an output; 15-minute drive from home vs. 30-minute drive from home vs. 45-minute drive from home are levels.) The study permitted 806 million different combinations and permutations of the attributes and levels. However, two sets of the combinations and permutations were, by far, the most "popular," accounting for 95% coverage of the new car marketplace.

Step 8 is not merely a snapshot-in-time of existing customer needs. It focuses on service outputs rather than on specific channel mechanisms that presently exist. For example, the research involves asking end-users about benefits ("convenient access to money without waiting in line") rather than about specific channels ("ATMs"). This fact lengthens the half-life of this kind of research and also allows for more creative design of ideal channels in later steps. In the same survey instrument, however, end-users are also asked to evaluate the ability of existing channels to deliver the service outputs they desire as well as their degree of comfort with a number of alternative channels and the likelihood that they would actually buy and be serviced by these channel alternatives. These data are used later in the process (Step 12).

Step 9. Analyze Industry Analogs

Step 8 focuses on the clusters of "shopping" attributes or service outputs that define a segment. Suppose, for example, that the following attributes cluster together relative to the purchase of a consumer durable (e.g., television set, dishwasher, refrigerator, or automobile): very low price, self-service, somewhat broad but shallow assortments of merchandise, limited after-sale service, relatively spartan atmosphere, multiple brands available. Clearly, the set of consumers attracted to such an outlet is willing to trade-off the amenities of up-scale service and close-in convenience for very low prices. Indeed, those characteristics seem more to typify a discount store operation than an upscale department store. For industrial goods such as maintenance, operating, and repair items, one cluster of shopping characteristics might contain moderate (reasonable, but not lowest) price, emergency delivery service, extended credit terms, availability of multiple brands and very broad assortments, locally maintained inventories, ordering simplicity (e.g., via computer terminal), and occasional advice on new items and uses. This set seems more to typify an industrial/full-function distributor than a manufacturer's distribution center. Here, customers appear to want lots of service and availability and are willing to sacrifice some price benefits to get them.

Each cluster of service outputs should, if possible, be labeled using the names of existing institutional analogs in order to provide an anchor point for Step 10. For example, the retailing analogs relative to the sale of new cars that emerged from the previously mentioned automobile study are shown in Exhibit 5-1. It is, however, important to keep one's eyes open for hybrids and to note carefully the deviations in the clusters from any institution or agency presently available in distribution. And, as in Exhibit 5-1, the labeling should not be hamstrung by industry experience. For instance, if the chemical industry has no analogy to a discount store or a rack jobber, but that is what the service outputs desired by a significant segment of end-users describe, then the appropriate label should be affixed to the clusters, regardless of industry history. It helps the creative channel-design process to think across industries as well as across consumer and industrial channel types. There is no reason to assume that consumer channel types could not be adapted to business-to-business marketing and vice versa. For example, think of CompUSA Superstores selling computers and software, Staples Superstores selling office supplies, and financial "supermarkets" (Merrill Lynch) selling stocks, bonds, certificates of deposit, mortgages, and trust services.

Because this process is more social science than rocket science, approximations will provide wonderful, within-the-ballpark insights. For example, in another proprietary study for a company marketing a consumer electronics durable, three major consumer segments were isolated: price shoppers, price and training/repair buyers, and support/relationship seekers. Based on analysis of the service output data for these segments, the "ideal" outlets shown in Figure 5-5 were isolated.

Step 9 demands a great deal of creativity. In looking at the clusters that come out of Step 8, the ability to visualize an outlet is critical. As mentioned above, la-

Exhibit 5-1 / Retail Store Analogs for New Car Sales

▶ ▶ ▶

Department Store: Many brands, all models merchandised by product category, upscale decor, inventory on site, many services, reasonably convenient.

General Merchandise Store: Single brand, all models, extensive inventory on site, limited services, nonfocal product merchandise available, reasonably convenient.

High-Priced Specialty Store: Most major luxury brands of the focal product, upscale decor, separate service facility, no inventory—special orders only, reasonably convenient.

Supermarket: Most major brands, fast-selling models, purchase from inventory, limited services, separate service facility, reasonably convenient, good prices.

Convenience Store: Selected fast-selling brands and models, purchase from inventory, very limited services, no after-sales support, very convenient, high prices.

Warehouse Store: Most major brands, fast-selling models, bare decor, purchase from inventory, limited services, no after-sale support, not convenient, very good prices.

Catalog Showroom: Most major brands, fast-selling models, special orders only, limited services, no after-sale support, reasonably convenient, good prices.

Discount House: Most major brands, inexpensive economy models, purchase from inventory, bare decor, very limited services, no after-sale support, reasonably convenient, good prices.

Existing Retailer: Single brand, all models, inventory on site, many services, convenient.

Emerging Retailer: Many brands, all models, inventory on-site, many services, not convenient.

beling the clusters is important, because the labels serve as reference points, anchoring the outlets to existing institutional types but not necessarily describing the existing types in any exact way. If it is possible to "hook" the outlets to real-world analogs, it will be possible to learn from experience (rather than reinventing the wheel) by eventually questioning experts familiar with setting up similar systems and obtaining their advice. For those clusters that do not fit well-known categories, new names may have to be coined that permit positioning the clusters along the extremely wide continuum of industrial or consumer goods outlets.

It is also extremely important that, in collecting data in Steps 7 and 8, as many service outputs as possible be admitted to the analysis, because if end-users are not given the opportunity to assess the value of an attribute, that attribute will not appear later in the analysis. In other words, in order for a shopping characteristic to influence the labeling of a cluster of characteristics in Step 9, it must have the opportunity for showing up in Step 8. Myopia during Steps 7 and 8 of this process could undermine the whole exercise.

Beyond institutional analogs, it is also important in Step 9 that benchmarking studies be undertaken to uncover insights from companies that are known to do distribution well, no matter what industry they are in. Some excellent benchmarking candidates, among many that could be mentioned, are Hewlett-Packard (printers), Publix Markets (groceries), Toro (power lawnmowers), Parker Hannifin (hoses and fittings), Saturn (new cars), McKesson (health and beauty aids and pharmaceuticals), W.W. Grainger (fans, motors, and other industrial supplies), General Electric and Whirlpool (major appliances), and Allen Bradley (programmable con-

Segment	Price Shoppers	Price and Training/Repair Buyers	Support/Relationship Seekers
Percent of Respondents	33%	28%	39%
Key Channel Characteristics	• Low Price • Low support	• Low price • Training • Rapid repair • Brand variety	• Advice/relationship • Product information • Rapid repair • Training
Channel Missions/ Requirements	• Provide low-priced purchase fulfillment to self-reliant buyers • Other services, if offered, priced separately	• Provide lowest generally available price in market • Describe product features, as necessary, to potential buyers • Close "push" sales of most profitable items • Provide access to training and repair	• Provide product information and advice • Provide full range aftersale training and support • Form personal relationships with buyers/engage in consultative selling • Offer broad range of products and brands
"Ideal Outlet"	• Inbound telemarketing • Discount outlet	• Low price retailer backed up with strong training/repair	• High support, relationship-oriented retailer

FIGURE 5-5 **"Ideal outlets" for service output segments for a consumer electronics durable (disguised data).**
Source: Gemini Consulting, Inc. and Louis W. Stern.

trollers). Two of the major lessons to come from benchmarking are: (1) excellence is not an industry-specific attribute and (2) excellence can be cloned. For example, the primary consumer wants/needs around which Saturn built its distribution system, as shown in Exhibit 5-2, are clearly transferable to a wide variety of product classes beyond automobiles. The analysis of analogs is particularly important in the design of channels for new products where it provides a number of likely future scenarios.

Step 10. Designing the "Ideal" Distribution System

Up to this point, a great deal of attention has been focused on clustering market-driven service outputs and imagining these as outlet types that satisfy end-users. Throughout Steps 7, 8, and 9, the customer is king, emperor, baron, and potentate wrapped into one. In Step 10, it is still important to hold onto this perspective. However, now the customer-driven process will be subjected to the first of many reality checks.

▎**E**XHIBIT **5-2** / **Primary Consumer Wants/Needs for Service Outputs Driving the Design of Saturn's Distribution System**

▶ ▶ ▶   **Shopping Wants/Needs**

High-quality information
- comprehensive, including competitors
- accurate/credible/objective
- current
- easy to understand/compare

Comfortable/convenient access to information
- lack of pressure, nonthreatening

Evaluation assistance

Buying Wants/Needs

Fair price
Fair negotiation process
- free of pressure
- easy to understand, all costs clear
- free of deception, dishonesty

Convenience
Honest, courteous treatment
Inventory availability

Service Wants/Needs

Quality of workmanship
- done right the first time
- use quality parts
- guarantee quality of work

Convenience
Timeliness
Honest, courteous treatment
Diagnose and recommend needed repairs accurately and honestly
Fair price

Source: Presentation at Northwestern University by Saturn executives in May 1992.

At this juncture, it is essential to assess whether it is feasible to combine the statistically derived attributes into outlets as done in Step 9. As suggested above, this often requires collecting opinions of individuals intimately familiar with outlets similar to those isolated. In this feasibility check, negative reactions should not be taken as final judgments. A presumption should be made, however, against any outlet that experts believe combines attributes in ways that would be impossible to realize or foolhardy to attempt.

Next, it is necessary to enumerate the kinds of effort required to assure that the service outputs can be delivered to relevant segments by the set of feasible outlets. Outlets do not work in isolation; they are the end-points of distribution systems. The entire distribution system works together to assure that the desired output is achieved. And if the effort is likely to be infinite, no matter what kind of help is recruited, it is better to give up on that system during this step in the process.

The energy sources fueling the delivery of service outputs to end-users are distribution activities called marketing "flows" or sets of functions performed by channel members. Although the list can be changed to fit the circumstances of any given industry, eight generic marketing flows are listed below. Each flow has associated costs. These costs must be incurred if the service outputs desired by end-users are ever to issue forth.

Marketing Flow	Costs Represented
Physical possession	Storage and delivery
Ownership	Inventory carrying costs
Promotion	Personal selling, advertising, sales promotion, publicity, public relations costs
Negotiation	Time and legal costs
Risking	Price guarantees, warranties, insurance, installation, repair, and after-sale service costs
Financing	Credit terms, terms and conditions of sale
Ordering	Order-processing costs
Payment	Collections, bad debt costs

Suppose, for example, that a segment of end-users requires rapid delivery. That is, people in this segment desire instant ("off-the-shelf") possession of what they want to buy. In terms of the marketing flows, this means that the "ideal" distribution system (comprised of an "ideal" outlet and back-up support) must somehow provide for local storage; otherwise, the product will not be available fast enough. Saying this does not imply anything about the flow of ownership, because title does not have to transfer instantaneously, only physical possession. Therefore, merchandise can often be consigned to local stocks (as in the case of Hanes' L'eggs Hosiery or Continental's Wonder Bread) in order to make certain that enough of it is on hand to satisfy the needs of consumers for immediate delivery.

The critical feature of Step 10, therefore, is to determine what it will take, in the way of marketing flows or activities (and their associated costs), to deliver the service outputs. This is no easy task! Some distribution cost accounting methods, such as activity-based costing, are enumerated in Chapter 10, but by and large, such cost allocations are mainly an art form, demanding a tremendous amount of inventive thinking, an ability to concentrate on direct and traceable costs, and several aspirin tablets. It is important, however, to try and answer the following questions when structuring the ideal system:

■ What nonvalued functions (e.g., excessive sales calls) can be eliminated without damaging customer or channel satisfaction?

- Are there likely to be any redundant activities? Which could be eliminated to result in the lowest cost for the entire system?

- Is there a way to eliminate, redefine, or combine certain tasks in order to minimize the steps in a sale or reduce its cycle time?

- Is there the potential to automate certain activities that, although increasing fixed costs, will actually reduce the unit cost of getting products to market?

- Are there opportunities to modify information systems to reduce the costs of prospecting, order entry, or quote generation activities?[19]

It should also be noted here that sometimes the distinction between service outputs and marketing flows is fuzzy. For example, recall the earlier list of service outputs for industrial products developed by Rangan and his colleagues.[20] There, logistics (transporting, storing, and supplying products) was a service output; here, it is a marketing flow. Does it matter very much what label is applied? Not really! What does matter, however, is determining what it is that end-users require and what activities must be performed to fulfill end-users' expectations. The nomenclature should not get in the way of the analysis. What is important is that Steps 7 and 8 provide a list of service output needs that is as complete as possible in order to design the appropriate channel mechanisms across all channel dimensions.

The design of the ideal distribution system requires the application of the principle of postponement-speculation developed by Louis P. Bucklin.[21] Simply put, the postponement-speculation principle proposes that there is a strategic drive to both "postpone" and "speculate" on the part of organizations and individuals. For manufacturing firms, postponing often means delaying production until orders are received, thereby avoiding differentiation of, say, raw material (e.g., iron ore) into finished goods (e.g., carbon steel). This minimizes the manufacturers' risk of selling what is produced as well as eliminating the cost associated with holding relatively expensive inventory. But if customers want to receive goods instantly, manufacturers who engage in postponement cannot meet their needs.

An example of this dilemma is provided by Dell Computer. Originally, Dell relied on postponement as a marketing strategy. Dell contended that its assemble-to-order, direct-response (primarily mail and telephone) business was more certain to meet customer needs. The strategy avoided the large costs and inflexibility of building parts in-house that could be easily bought. Instead of building up inventories of finished personal computers, its plants only finished machines once a customer specified which features were needed. However, as it became increasingly simple for competitors to sell easy-to-customize or preconfigured personal computers at similar prices through places such as BestBuy and CompUSA, Dell began to open retail channels, which forced it to speculate.[22] But the margins it was able to earn selling through retail channels were so slim that it wasn't able to make adequate profits doing so. It returned to its "roots" as a direct-response, make-to-order (postponement) company, thereby sacrificing the considerable sales volume that was potentially available to it through the more speculatively oriented retail channels.

Customers who postpone their purchases to the latest point in time and then expect rapid delivery cause manufacturers to speculate. In other words, goods must be produced in anticipation of orders. Although speculation is risky and creates costs associated with holding finished goods inventory, it also permits economies of scale in production, something that postponing doesn't do. Consumers also speculate when they are offered particularly good deals (e.g., bananas go on sale). But when they speculate, they also tie up their capital in household inventory and run the risk of obsolescence (e.g., half the bananas go rotten before they're eaten). The postponement–speculation principle forges a link between service outputs (e.g., required speed of delivery) and marketing flows (e.g., the costs associated with ownership, physical possession, risking, and financing).

The primary benefit of the postponement–speculation principle is that it can be used to determine whether a channel should be designed with a speculative (or intermediate) inventory built into it. Consider the following. Suppose that the costs of moving products directly from a manufacturer to a customer are as shown in Graph 1 in Exhibit 5-3. Note that as the delivery time required by the customer gets shorter, the average cost of moving the goods on a direct basis becomes increasingly higher. Very short delivery times are prohibitively expensive. Now suppose that a speculative or intermediate inventory is established somewhere between the manufacturer and the customer and that the costs associated with moving goods to the customer from the intermediate inventory are as shown in Graph 2 in Exhibit 5-3. Very short delivery times are now feasible, even though expensive, although relatively rapid delivery can be accomplished at reasonable cost, especially when compared to direct shipments. Graph 3 puts both schedules together; E is the delivery time at which the average cost of direct and indirect shipments is the same. C–E–B represents the least cost curve with respect to delivery time.

The picture is, however, incomplete unless we take into consideration the customer's cost of holding inventory. (Remember the bananas!) The concern here is with building an efficient distribution system, not simply with minimizing the manufacturer's costs. The cost to the customer is shown in Graph 4—costs increase as delivery time increases, because the customer is forced to hold more and more safety stock.

Now that we know the seller's and buyer's costs, it is possible to make a decision (using cost as the criterion) as to whether to ship on a direct basis (postpone) or to establish an intermediate inventory (speculate). Graph 5 provides the answer. H–I–K–M is the total cost curve for the distribution system. It sums the seller's costs and the buyer's costs. Because the seller will only consider decisions with the lowest costs, the relevant schedule for the seller's cost is C–E–B. Adding F–G to C–E–B gives H–I–K–M. The breakeven point between direct and indirect shipments causes the discontinuity at K. The lowest point on the total cost curve (H–I–K–M) is at point I. Therefore, the decision is to establish an intermediate inventory, that is, an indirect channel. In other words, channel design, using the postponement–speculation principle, is determined by the location of the low point on the total cost curve.

The same type of analysis could be applied to the costs (i.e., marketing flows) associated with providing other service outputs, for example, availability, lot size, product variety, and information. The major drawback of the analysis is that it fo-

EXHIBIT 5-3 / Using the Postponement-Speculation Principle to Design Channels

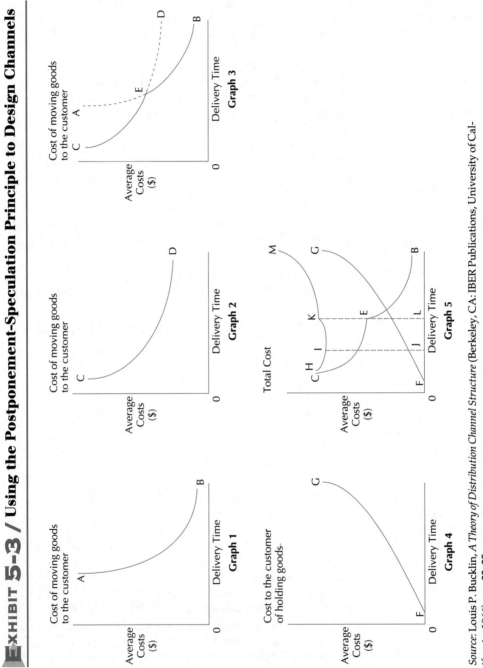

Source: Louis P. Bucklin, *A Theory of Distribution Channel Structure* (Berkeley, CA: IBER Publications, University of California, 1966), pp. 22–25.

cuses only on the efficiency of providing service outputs. It says nothing about effectiveness, adaptability, or quality, which are some of the other major criteria that must be considered when making distribution decisions.

At this point in the 14-step process, it should be reasonably (although somewhat imperfectly) clear to the analyst what it will take, in terms of energy, effort, and money, to satisfy the shopping requirements of end-users, segment by segment. It is here that questions about "make or buy" get raised for the first time. Although the "make or buy" decision is examined, in detail, in Chapter 6, suffice it to say here that "make" (performing all marketing flows oneself via vertical integration) should basically be treated as a fall-back position. Why? Because, as suggested by Quinn and Hilmer, if managers wish to leverage their companies' skills and resources, they should combine two strategic approaches:

- Concentrate the firm's own resources on a set of "core competencies" where it can achieve definable preeminence and provide unique value for customers.

- Strategically outsource other activities—including many traditionally considered integral to any company—for which the firm has neither a critical strategic need nor special capabilities.[23]

What this means is that, because not *all* marketing flows are likely to be within the set of core competencies of *any* organization, companies should almost always want to "outsource" at least some activities (i.e., divide marketing channel labor with others, such as wholesalers, retailers, agents, common carriers, and the like) rather than incur the full (and, generally, fixed) costs of distribution on their own. Although improvements in information technology are permitting firms to reengineer their distribution systems so that they have more direct influence over what transpires throughout them, it makes little sense to own all or even parts of the system if the funds can be used more productively elsewhere. Indeed, it is very difficult to find *any* company that is fully vertically integrated with regard to each of the eight flows listed above. (We return to this subject in the next chapter when we discuss a variety of ways in which channels can be organized short of, and including, vertical integration.)

This lesson has, only recently, dawned on automobile manufacturers who are increasingly turning to independent suppliers to provide such critical components as instrument panels, seats, and electronics. Automakers are seeking suppliers capable of not just making a part but also designing, engineering, and integrating it with surrounding parts, and delivering it globally. The retreat from vertical integration has permitted cost containment, improved flexibility, and quicker access to new technologies. General Motors, Ford, and Chrysler "have been selling off parts making operations that can be run more cheaply and better by outsiders with greater expertise, fewer distractions, and lower labor costs."[24]

Another excellent example of "outsourcing," among the literally hundreds that could be provided, is Microsoft's 1994 decision to concentrate on software development while seeking business partners to service and support large customers. (Service and support includes maintenance, systems integration, consultancy, and training.) It chose Britain's ICL to service its products and customers across Europe.[25] The company has also changed its European distribution methods as part of its strategy to retreat from activities other than software development and manufacture. As explained by the president of Microsoft Europe, "Microsoft is a software company, not a distributor, and if we are to continue to be successful, we must focus on this."[26] As a result, it has become increasingly reliant on wholesalers such as Merisel and Frontline to manage the distribution of its products.

If, however, performing distribution activities is a core competence of an organization, outsourcing is inappropriate. In addition, there are other circumstances in which "making" may be better than "buying." If it is immediately apparent that there is next-to-no-chance that the required service outputs can be delivered to end-users by relying on "third-parties" or "outsiders," then vertical integration is mandated. The "make versus buy" decision could also be based on an assessment of the total costs to an entire distribution system of delivering specific service outputs. In other words, a vertically integrated channel may be more cost effective than alternative channels. Furthermore, when it becomes extremely difficult to influence the actions of "outsiders," even though they perform effectively and efficiently, vertical integration may be warranted as a hedge against power. We return to all of these arguments, and more, in Chapter 6.

Whatever is decided at this stage—to make or to buy, the marketing channels that result from this step of the process are supposedly "ideal" from the perspective of end-users. They are truly customer-driven distribution systems. Figure 5-6 provides a snapshot of what the "ideal" sales channels might look like for telecommunications equipment and services. The shaded areas of the segments represent small companies whose needs are the same as large-company members of the same segment. The complexity of Figure 5-6 indicates once again that when faced with a heterogeneous marketplace, companies will be required to use multiple channels in order to serve the needs of multiple segments.

It is also possible to combine different channels so as to obtain a mutually supportive yet highly efficient approach to the market. For example, in its direct-response system, Dell uses advertising, direct mail, and telemarketing to identify buyers; mail order and an "800" number to handle orders; public warehouses and United Parcel Service (UPS) to handle delivery; and Xerox field service and an "800" number to provide postsale and technical support. "Hybrid" or "modular" channels, like Dell's, are becoming increasingly popular means for the division of distribution labor.[27]

Step 11. Investigating Management and Other Constraints

Eventually, when this 14-step process is finished, management is going to be called on to make a decision about what the marketing channels for the firm ought to look like. Basically, though, up to this point, the number of realities faced have been relatively few. Some appear in Step 10 when the "ideal" marketing channel is designed. A number of others show up in Steps 1 through 4, when the existing sys-

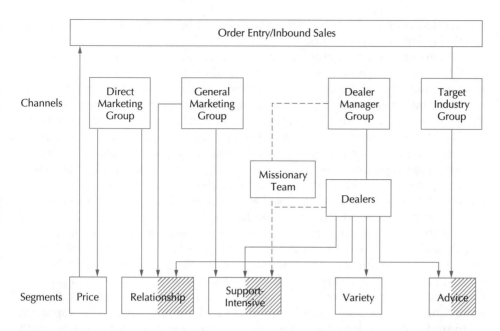

FIGURE 5-6   "Ideal" channel system for corporate office equipment and services (disguised).
Source: Gemini Consulting, Inc. and Louis W. Stern.

tem is examined and where environmental factors surrounding the channel decision are uncovered. But it is in Step 11 that accounting is explicitly made for the biases, objectives, constraints, and threats imposed by internal and external forces.

Via in-depth interviews with the executives who determine channel policy, an assessment is made of the risk profile of the focal organization's management. Are they risk-takers or risk averse? Also, internal politics, organization structure (e.g., which group "owns" channels within the firm: sales, marketing, or operations?), and culture are important to understand, if the eventual results and recommendations are going to be endorsed and implemented. For example, just how strong are the forces of conventional wisdom and inertia? Can the power of evidence and logic really win out? Is there anyone in the company, including the chief executive officer, who has the power and/or the authority to institute channel change? Surprisingly, and unfortunately, there appear to be enormous barriers to action in this area of management strategy.

Step 11 actually permits management to "bound" the "ideal" distribution channel. Now, management can impose guidelines dealing with efficiency (e.g., expense-to-revenue issues), effectiveness (e.g., market share and return-on-investment issues), and adaptability (e.g., issues related to the fluidity of capital invested, the ability to market new products, and the ability to adjust to new technologies in sales and marketing). A cross-section of the company's marketing and sales executives is asked to lay out what the specific present and future objectives are or should be with regard to any distribution channel the company might choose to employ. Importantly, managers should be encouraged to include their concerns about what distribution is or is not doing; the survey should be open-ended, and no limits should be imposed on answers.

At the same time, executives should be asked about the constraints that they would impose on channel-system design. Are there any unalterable sacred cows? In most industries, there are historical rigidities, and some of the rigidities get translated into laws. For example, in the automobile industry, the dealer system has existed, basically unaltered, for over 60 years, in part because of peculiarities in the legal structure of automobile distribution (e.g., franchise laws, dealer-day-in-court laws) and in part because industry folklore and values have sanctified the dealer system. Other rigidities come from deep-seated prejudices. In the high-tech medical equipment industry, there are sales executives in one major company who would suffer major emotional trauma if anyone so much as suggested that they sell their equipment through distributors or dealers, for instance.

In Step 11, all rational and irrational objectives and constraints should be explicitly laid out. A series of concerns are likely to originate from the difficulty of changing distribution channels once they are in place. As Rangan and his colleagues point out, "such change could cause disruptive conflicts and lead to a dysfunctional exercise of power."[28] They also agree that it is essential to "consider contextual, firm-specific constraints," but that, as we have advocated, "it is important . . . to start with the unconstrained solution first in order to know the loss imposed by the constraint."[29]

Once generated, the list of management objectives and constraints should be translated into a structured survey instrument and sent to all executives within the company having a stake in distribution matters.[30] The executives should be forced into a trade-off analysis similar to that performed for outlet design so that, when the data are analyzed, the relative importance of the objectives and constraints can be determined.

Eventually, in Step 13, management will be called on to support its beliefs and set aside its prejudices. These objectives and constraints will be critical in determining the distribution system that will finally be implemented. However, at this stage of the process, these prejudices remain unchallenged. They will serve to "bound" the possible "solution set" by dictating, for example, that the company remain loyal to certain types of channel intermediaries, earn a hurdle rate of return, or limit legal exposure. Clearly, then, these factors can force a reconfiguration of the theoretically ideal system, making it over into a system that reflects not consumer demands but management's biases. These factors will also aid in the design of a "change management" program aimed at enabling the implementation of a new distribution system. Companies frequently underestimate the difficulty of implementing the new system and do not engage in enough formal planning around execution issues.

In addition to management constraints, constraints and opportunities presented by the macroenvironment and by competitors should be brought forward from Steps 1 through 4. For example, it is possible that technology is changing so rapidly, that some existing channels will shortly be made obsolete. Think of the potential effect of interactive electronic media. It is also possible that some competitors have such an entrenched position in certain channels that they have effectively foreclosed new entrants and/or have forestalled all other competitors. All of these kinds of data should be explicitly introduced to the process during Step 11. Some of them may have already impacted Steps 5 and 6, resulting in a few "quick hits."

Step 12. Delineating the Options: Gap Analysis

At the end of Step 11, potentially three *different* distribution systems can be isolated: (1) an "ideal" (customer-driven) system, (2) the existing system, and (3) a management-"bounded" system (i.e., the "ideal" system reconfigured by management's objectives and constraints). In Step 12, the three systems are compared, and a "gap" analysis is performed.

As an illustration, three possible outcomes could emerge from the comparison, as depicted in Figure 5-7. In the first situation ("Fit"), the existing, management-

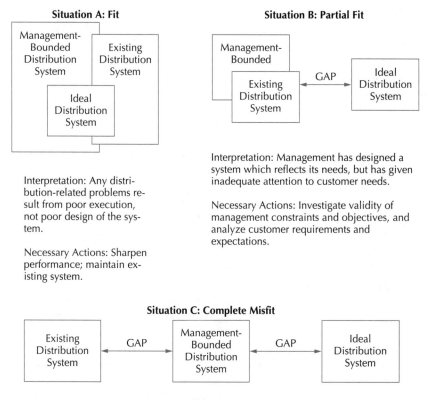

FIGURE 5-7   **What the gap analysis reveals.**
Source: Gemini Consulting, Inc. and Louis W. Stern.

bounded, and ideal systems closely resemble each other. If this is the case, then management knows that the existing system is, from a design perspective, "on the mark" because it has the potential to deliver what end-users want. If, however, end-users often complain about the existing system, management knows that the system's problems lie not with its structure but with the way the system has been managed. Execution is the culprit, not basic design. For example, many automobile buyers would undoubtedly like to shop for cars in a specialty store environment where they could examine lots of different models; receive sales and, if needed, financial assistance; drive relatively short distances to get to an outlet; obtain after-sales service; and obtain new cars at reasonable prices, in line with the service outputs they desire. Basically, what has just been described are the attributes (on paper, at least) of most new car dealerships. If this is the case, then why do so many consumers of new cars leave dealers' showrooms or service areas dissatisfied? The answer is simple—it's not the design of the system that may be at fault; it's the management of it. (Channel management is the subject of Chapter 7.) In the second situation ("Partial Fit"), the existing and management-bounded systems are similar to each other but substantially different from the "ideal." This outcome would suggest that the objectives/constraints adopted by management are causing the gap. Such a finding calls for a careful investigation of the validity of the objectives/constraints, which is accomplished during Step 13.

In the third situation ("Complete Misfit"), all three systems are substantially different. Assuming that the management-bounded system is positioned *between* the existing and the "ideal," some improvements in creating end-user satisfaction should be possible without relaxing the objectives/constraints. However, relaxation of certain management constraints would likely provide even greater end-user benefits.

The "ideal" system is the yardstick against which all other systems are measured. It is a system or set of systems that, if actually constructed and properly managed, would satisfy end-users. It is synonomous with total quality management. Therefore, if the management-bounded system is not similar to the "ideal," the message is unyielding: management is willing to sacrifice end-user satisfaction (quality) in order to further other objectives or abide by specific constraints. Although such a deviation may be warranted, management should permit such a compromise only with full understanding of the risk. The possible consequence of this decision is that, if some alternative system is developed by a competitor that does, in fact, mirror the "ideal," the company's market stature could suffer significantly.

Central to conducting a meaningful gap analysis is an assessment of the existing distribution system. Even if no structural changes are recommended as a result of the 14-step process, the insights gained relative to the existing system may, by themselves, add tremendous value. The description of the existing system generated in Steps 1, 2, and 3 along with the data developed in Step 8 regarding end-user needs form the basis of the evaluation. An appraisal of existing marketing channels requires determining the effectiveness of the existing system in meeting the service output requirements of customers.

An example of how to look at the performance of existing channels in providing service outputs is available from the study of telecommunications equipment

TABLE 5-3   **Telecommunications Equipment and Services**

How well do each of these characteristics describe the following providers (on a scale of 1 through 9, where "1" means "doesn't describe at all," and "9" means "describes perfectly")?

CHARACTERISTICS	EQUIPMENT COMPANY REP	SERVICE CO. REP	RETAIL STORE
Establish ongoing relationship; call on me in person	4.0	5.1	2.7
Provide after-sale support, maintenance; Provide reliable products/services	6.3	5.5	3.7
Offer products/services from different companies	2.0	3.1	5.0
Offer lowest price level available	3.2	4.6	4.9
Provide demonstrations of products/services in use	4.1	2.8	5.0
Standard Errors	*0.1*	*0.1*	*0.1*

Source: Gemini Consulting, Inc. and Louis W. Stern.

and services referred to previously. Three of the numerous existing channels employed by this industry involve the use of equipment company representatives, service company representatives, and retail stores. A sample of existing and potential users were asked how well each of the channel "providers" perform with regard to delivering desired service outputs. The disguised results are shown in Table 5-3.

Several facts jump out from the data in this table. First, the channels differ significantly in the value they provide to end-users. Equipment company reps are best at establishing ongoing relationships and retail stores are worst, whereas retail stores are best at offering products/services from different companies and service company reps are worst. Second, the highest possible rating is a "9," and the highest actual rating is a "6.3" (earned by equipment company reps for their ability to provide after-sale support and maintenance). Most of the scores are below "5." This means (to put it very mildly) that there is a major opportunity to serve end-users better in this industry.

Another less bleak but highly informative example comes from the study of printing supplies. Again, the data have been disguised. From the results in Table 5-4, it is clear that existing outlets in the form of local dealers or office supply stores do a better job at providing many of the service outputs required by end-users. They are not perceived to be as strong as other existing channels in the pricing, sales call, and general reputation/ recognition areas, however.

It is very important to note that both Tables 5-3 and 5-4 deal with aggregate end-user data. Therefore, to obtain an accurate assessment of the existing system, the data must be broken down into relevant end-user segments. For example, in the printing supply study, once the appropriate segmentation scheme was overlaid on the data, it became obvious that the price-sensitive segment (which represented a significant number of end-users) was very dissatisfied with local dealers. The level of dissatisfaction within this large segment paved the way for Office Depot, Office Max, and Staples to enter the market successfully and to take significant share away from local dealers.

TABLE 5-4 Evaluating Five Existing Channels for Printing Supplies (Disguised Data)

	DIRECT MAIL CATALOGUES	REPRESENTATIVES OF A MANUFACTURER	WAREHOUSE WHOLESALER	LOCAL DEALER	SALESPEOPLE WHO CONTACT YOU OVER THE PHONE
1. Has knowledgeable sales people	3.4	5.2	2.8	7.3	3.6
2. Offers a wide variety of products	6.5	2.6	5.1	7.0	3.6
3. Lets you see and touch the products you buy	1.7	3.9	4.6	7.3	1.9
4. Accepts product returns without hassle	5.0	4.6	4.4	7.8	3.3
5. Carries high-quality products	6.2	6.6	5.2	7.8	4.1
6. Is part of a well-known recognized company	6.3	6.7	4.6	5.7	3.4
7. Has generally low price levels	6.5	4.1	6.0	5.6	3.9
8. Will make personal sales calls to you at your office	1.6	6.1	1.8	5.4	3.0
9. Offers a full range of services	6.4	5.8	3.1	7.1	4.2

Source: Gemini Consulting, Inc. and Louis W. Stern.

Step 13: Identify/Develop Strategic Options

This step begins with a check on the validity of management's prejudices. Here, the objectives and constraints must be presented to individuals outside the company and to selected individuals within in order to assess management's preferences and perceptions. For example, a common method of protecting the status quo is to claim, as a constraint, that laws restrict behavior and that change would fly in the face of the law. (The Robinson–Patman Act is probably the foremost excuse heard in corporate corridors for not making needed changes in discount structures.)

This tendency has been one of the reasons why the automobile industry has clung steadfastly to the dealer franchise system. Porsche executives were nearly physically attacked when they announced a new distribution scheme to their North American dealers in the early 1980s. A united front by the dealers and the threat of very costly litigation caused Porsche to make a hasty retreat.[31] Automobile companies everywhere are now convinced that what happened to Porsche could happen to them. One of the purposes of Step 13 is to investigate such claims, for example, to estimate how many lawsuits could be expected and what the cost of those lawsuits might be, measured against the benefits of changing the system. Next, management is asked to confront the gap between its position and the ideal position. To underline the significance of this event in the channel-design process, an off-site session should be planned. At this meeting, descriptions of the "ideal" distribution system should be presented, and the results of Steps 12 shared. (In reality, senior management should be exposed to the mounting logic at key steps along the way. Otherwise, the chances of "buy-in" are virtually nil if management enters this step of the process with negative attitudes.) Top management should review the objectives and constraints that were used to "bound" the "ideal" and then shown the effect of these factors on the ideal, that is, how the objectives and constraints resulted in different "answers" than what end-users really desire. Next, any data challenging the validity of these factors should be made available. Finally, the macroenvironmental and competitive opportunities and constraints should be laid out.

All of this information will serve as background for what should prove to be a very provocative discussion. Management may find that achieving the ideal requires a major restructuring of its system. Such was the case for a personal care products company. Attaining the ideal called for the elimination of one level in its existing distribution system—its brokers. It was a big step even to contemplate, considering that the brokers had played a key role in providing access to the retail trade when the company's brand lacked visibility or strong consumer demand. Over the years, however, the brand had emerged as the best seller in its category and had established a strong consumer franchise. The brokers' function, which had been so important in the early years, no longer added value to the distribution process. They had become an unnecessary, and expensive, redundancy. Yet, management still felt a strong sense of loyalty and indebtedness to the brokers. A growing price sensitivity on the part of consumers, coupled with the inefficiencies of the broker system, placed the manufacturer in a vulnerable position. Management had to come face-to-face with the trade-off between its loyalty to brokers and the expectations of end-users.

Step 14: Reaching the Optimal Distribution System/Preparing for Implementation

The final step in the process is to pass the "ideal" distribution system (from Step 10) by the set of objectives/constraints still retained or endorsed by management at the completion of Step 13. (Executives will always hold onto some of their strongly held beliefs. But they need to form a consensus about them as well as the major environmental and competitive forces facing their companies.) The resulting distribution system should be the subject of intensive implementation planning, because what comes out at this juncture represents the "optimal" or most favorable marketing channel for the firm, taking into account everything that has been learned via the process. The "optimal" system may not be "ideal," but it will meet, to the best of its ability, management's standards for quality (i.e., delivering end-user satisfaction), efficiency, effectiveness, and adaptability. If it is not congruent with the "ideal," the "optimal" system will still leave the company vulnerable to competitors who actually design a customer-driven distribution system. Chances are high, though, that the "optimal" will be much more market-driven than the existing system.

In order to assure implementation of the optimal system, it is recommended that:

1. "Buy-in" be achieved across the organization. Participation and voice in the 14-step process must be given to all relevant functions and levels.

2. An energetic champion be found to manage the change process. The champion must have power, credibility, political skills, and, most important, tenacity.

3. It is made clear, as soon as possible in the process, who or which group in the organization is responsible for channels. Task forces comprised of key individuals from various interest groups help buy-in if they are involved with the process from the outset.

4. The approach truly be customer-driven, because then the results are very difficult to argue against, unless someone prefers to be seen as opposed to delivering customer satisfaction. Nevertheless, patience and persistence are required, because movement toward the optimal system will not be immediate, given the tradition-bounded ideas that generally surround channel decisions.

5. Make certain that, no matter what the proposed system looks like, there is a mechanism built into the design that permits the organization to stay in touch with the end-users of its products or services.[32]

6. The business units and senior management must jointly develop a business case (specifying opportunity costs, potential benefits, and implementation resources required by the choice of distribution system). Also, management must commit, upfront, the time and resources that will be needed at critical junctures during implementation.

7. An effective plan needs to be developed that will guide the individuals responsible for implementation. The plan should deal with mobilization (specifying the activities, milestones, and key interdependencies required to carry out the effort), the tactics required to launch it, and measurement (the indicators of success or failure as well as contingency factors).

8. A change management process, including "war rooms" as well as communication and training vehicles, needs to be produced, announced, and activated.

9. At least one senior executive must serve as reviewer, participant, coach, facilitator (e.g., removing barriers), and motivator.

▶ **SUMMARY AND CONCLUSIONS**

Channel design is a critical element of marketing strategy. A 14-step blueprint is proposed that forces individuals involved with the design process to keep their eyes on the most important people in the entire channel system—end-users.

The process starts with a full unfolding of the distribution system currently being used by the focal organization for the product or service isolated for analysis. Steps 1, 2, 3, and 4 involve an examination of the institutions and agencies engaged in distribution activities relative to the product or service, the costs incurred in running the system, and the challenges being confronted by the system. Analysis of the macroenvironment and competition is required during these steps. Steps 5 and 6 (which include "quick hits") are directly related to Steps 1 through 4, because it is highly likely that immediate changes in the existing distribution can be made as a result of the data collected during the first several stages of the process.

Steps 7 through 10 require "wiping the slate clean," similar to what has been suggested for business reengineering. Rather than starting with preconceived notions about what channels should look like or which channels are presently being used, the focus is on end-user demands for service outputs. And, because no market for any product or service is homogeneous, attention must be given to the desires of relevant segments of the market. Step 10 culminates in the design of an "ideal" distibution system.

It is not until Step 11 that management biases are allowed to enter the process. But now they are, in fact, encouraged to surface. In addition, both macroenvironmental and competitive constraints come strongly into the picture at this stage. The result is a "management-bounded" distribution system—the "ideal" constrained by reality and, frequently, executive fear and fantasy.

Step 12 compares the ideal system to the "management-bounded" and the existing systems. If gaps appear among the three, plans must be laid to close them. Those plans are formulated in Step 13. In Step 14, the ideal system is once again bounded by whatever constraints remain, and an "optimal" distribution system emerges.

The blueprint is time-consuming, costly, and frustrating. At several points, it forces a doubling back over ground already covered. It is confrontational and very demanding. Given all these "pleasant" attributes, why is it necessary?

The process is necessary because distribution still remains the dark side of marketing. It is necessary because rarely do firms invest as much in learning how end-users like to obtain goods and services as they do in learning what the goods and services ought to look like. And, aside from offering a highly valued product, no other element of marketing is as important to a firm in achieving a differential advantage.

The magnitude and complexity of the task involved in following the blueprint depends largely on the extent of the modifications needed in the existing system and the nature of the changes required. It is wrong to assume that the process will always identify large gaps. For example, in one case, the existing system looked, when it was sketched out on a piece of paper, horribly complex, but it met all of the criteria of an ideal system. The recommendation: "Don't mess with it! Leave it alone! Don't touch a thing!"

It is important to understand that there are problems and pitfalls in undertaking such a process. A few are: (1) end-users are often blinded by their own experience (which means that elements of creativity must be built into the entire exercise); (2) costing out new distribution systems demands informed guesswork; (3) management can display a pit-bull hold on established distribution systems; and (4) the economic, political, and social impediments to channel change often make strong individuals very weak in the knees.

DISCUSSION QUESTIONS

1. Explain how the shopping characteristics for the following consumer and industrial goods affect the channels for them:

Consumer Goods	Industrial Goods
Bread	Typewriter ribbons
Breakfast cereal	Uranium (for nuclear power plants)
Women's hats	Cement
Refrigerators	Data-processing equipment

2. Based on the information given in the exhibits in the text about competitors' marketing programs and about Compaq's strategy, what "quick hits" might you recommend to Company X? (Assume that Company X's market share is less than any of the competitors mentioned.)

3. Which of the two automobile outlet types (e.g., department store, specialty store, etc.) do you think accounted for 95% of the market coverage in the study mentioned in the text? Why? Do you think the answer varies by market segment? How?

4. Why is it that "small, medium, and large" is not as strong a segmentation scheme for service outputs as it might be for product attributes? Use a business-to-business product/market in your answer, for example, steel, semi-conductors, fax machines sold to sheet metal fabricators, computer companies, and insurance agents, respectively.

5. How might the postponement–speculation framework apply to other service outputs than delivery time? Give an example.

6. What do you think might be some of the major obstacles to implementing an ideal distribution system? Use a for-profit (e.g., Xerox and copiers; Snapple and fruit drinks) and a not-for-profit example (e.g., CARE and the distribution of food to impoverished nations).

7. Suggest channel strategies for office supplies, based on the exhibit in the text. What does the exhibit tell you?

ENDNOTES

[1]See Robert L. Rose, "Komatsu Throttles Back on Construction Equipments," *Wall Street Journal* (May 13, 1992), p. B4.

[2]Michael Treacy and Fred Wiersema, "Customer Intimacy and Other Value Disciplines," *Harvard Business Review*, Vol. 71 (January–February 1993), pp. 84–93.

[3]*Ibid.*, p. 84.

[4]Rahul Jacob, "Why Some Customers are More Equal Than Others," *Fortune*, September 19, 1994, p. 216.

[5]The approach was first outlined in Louis W. Stern and Frederick D. Sturdivant, "Customer-Driven Distribution Systems," *Harvard Business Review*, Vol. 65 (July–August 1987), pp. 34–41.

[6]Special thanks in assisting in the development, improvement, and implementation of this framework are due Frederick D. Sturdivant, Gary A. Getz, Gabriel E. Bresler, Gail J. Breslow, Pierre Loewe, Dar Wiatr, Wendy MacKinnon, and Mark D. Johnson, all of whom are or were associated with Gemini Consulting, Inc.

[7]See Louis W. Stern, Frederick D. Sturdivant, Gary A. Getz, "Accomplishing Marketing Channel Change: Paths and Pitfalls," *European Management Journal*, Vol. 11 (March 1993), pp. 1–8.

[8]See, for example, Ravi S. Achrol, Torger Reve, and Louis W. Stern, "The Environment of Marketing Channel Dyads: A Framework for Comparative Analysis," *Journal of Marketing*, Vol. 47 (Fall 1983), pp. 55–67; Ravi S. Achrol and Louis W. Stern, "Environmental Determinants of Decision-Making Uncertainty in Marketing Channels," *Journal of Marketing Research*, Vol. 25 (February 1988), pp. 36–50; Michael Etgar, "Channel Environment and Channel Leadership," *Journal of Marketing Research*, Vol. 15 (February 1977), pp. 69–76; F. Robert Dwyer and Sejo Oh, "Output Sector Munificence Effects on the Internal Political Economy of Marketing Channels," *Journal of Marketing Research*, Vol. 24 (November 1987), pp. 347–358; and F. Robert Dwyer and M. Ann Welsh, "Environmental Relationships of the Internal Political Economy of Marketing Channels," *Journal of Marketing Research*, Vol. 22 (November 1985), pp. 397–414.

[9]See Ravi S. Achrol and Louis W. Stern, "Environmental Determinants of Decision-Making Uncertainty in Marketing Channels," *Journal of Marketing Research*, Vol. 25 (February 1988), pp. 36–50.

[10]Milind Lele, "Matching Your Channels to Your Product's Life Cycle," *Business Marketing*, December 1986, pp. 61–69.

[11]*Ibid.*, p. 64.

[12]Michael Hammer, "Reengineering Work: Don't Automate, Obliterate!" *Harvard Business Review*, Vol. 68 (July–August 1990), pp. 104–112.

[13]Michael Hammer and James Champy, *Reengineering the Corporation: A Manifesto for Business Revolution* (New York: HarperCollins Publishers Inc., 1993).

[14]Louis P. Bucklin, *Productivity in Marketing* (Chicago: American Marketing Association, 1978), pp. 90-94. Also see Louis P. Bucklin, *A Theory of Distribution Channel Structure* (Berkeley, CA: IBER Publications, 1966).

[15]V. Kasturi Rangan, Melvyn A.J. Menezes, and E.P. Maier, "Channel Selection for New Industrial Products: A Framework, Method, and Application," *Journal of Marketing*, Vol. 56 (July 1992), pp. 72–73.

[16]For example, such data actually do already exist in the computer industry. They are collected by such firms as IntelliQuest, Incorporated and International Data Group.

[17]Eric Von Hippel, *The Sources of Innovation* (New York: Oxford University Press, 1988), p. 107. For an application, see Rangan, Menezes, and Maier, *op. cit.*, pp. 69–82.

[18]See Paul E. Green, "Hybrid Models for Conjoint Analysis: An Expository Review," *Journal of Marketing Research*, Vol. 21 (May 1984), pp. 155–169. See also, Gilbert A. Churchill, Jr., *Marketing Research*, 4th ed. (Chicago: The Dryden Press, 1987), pp. 364–376.

[19]Adapted from Gary Gebhardt, "Achieving Maximum Marketing Efficiency," *Frank Lynn Associates, Inc. Client Communique*, Vol. 4 (January 1992), p. 3.

[20]Rangan, Menezes, and Maier, *op. cit.*, pp. 69–82.

[21]Louis P. Bucklin, "Postponement, Speculation and the Structure of Distribution Channels," in Bruce E. Mallen (ed.), *The Marketing Channel: A Conceptual Viewpoint* (New York: John Wiley & Sons, Inc., 1967), pp. 67–74.

[22]"The Education of Michael Dell," *Business Week*, March 22, 1993, p. 86.

[23]James Brian Quinn and Frederick G. Hilmer, "Strategic Outsourcing," *Sloan Management Review*, Summer 1994 p. 43. See also C.K. Prahalad and Gary Hamel, "The Core Competence of the Corporation," *Harvard Business Review*, Vol. 68 (May–June 1990), pp. 79–91.

[24]Alex Taylor III, "The Auto Industry Meets the New Economy," *Fortune*, September 5, (1994), p. 53.

[25]Alan Cane, "Microsoft Signs Up ICL for Servicing," *The Financial Times*, August 8, 1994, p. 15.

[26]Alan Cane, "Microsoft Alters Distribution Chain for Europe," *The Financial Times*, November 12, 1993, p. 20.

[27]See Rowland T. Moriarty and Ursula Moran, "Managing Hybrid Marketing Systems," *Harvard Business Review*, Vol. 68 (November–December 1990), pp. 146–155, and Sue Heintz, "The Build-it-yourself Phenomenon: A Modular Approach to Channel Design," *Frank Lynn & Associates, Inc. Client Communique*, Vol. 3 (January 1991), pp. 2, 3.

[28]Rangan, Menezes, and Maier, *op. cit.*, p. 74.

[29]*Ibid.*

[30]Relative to the channel-design process for new industrial products, Rangan, Menezes, and Maier, *op. cit.*, pp. 74–75, have suggested a useful and efficient methodology for combining the judgmental projections of experienced sales managers, and product development engineers.

[31]See David B. Tinnin, "Porsche's Civil War with Its Dealers," *Fortune* (April 16, 1984), pp. 63–68.

[32]Points 1 through 5 can also be found in Stern, Sturdivant, and Getz, *op. cit.*, p. 7.

6 / ORGANIZATIONAL ◄◄◄◄◄ PATTERNS *in* MARKETING CHANNELS

*T*o understand the dynamics, complexity, and challenge in constructing and organizing marketing channels that meet end-user needs for service outputs, it is instructive to take a brief look at an industry in which change is happening at the speed of light—entertainment. It is important to note that the entertainment business is a service industry, because, for the most part, the theories and frameworks examined throughout this text apply to intangibles as well as to physical products.

Until very recently, seven major studios dominated film and television production in the U.S., whereas a handful of networks delivered the programming to mass audiences. Now, the number of distribution channels is exploding, and the historic relationship between producers and distributors is eroding.

Several trends are intensifying competition: (1) government regulations that barred broadcast networks from owning TV programs have been phased out; (2) the rules that prohibit telephone and cable companies from invading one another's turf are being eliminated; and (3) emerging digital technology has vastly expanded the carrying capacity of cable and telephone networks.[1] A frenzied search for high-impact programming is being undertaken by every company in the business of distributing movies, videotapes, and/or TV shows. And the producers are looking to lock in or create high-impact distribution channels. Some of the searches have resulted in vertical alliances whereas others have involved vertical integration. For example:

- Six regional Bell operating companies (RBOCs) have allied with Walt Disney Co. (Southwestern Bell, Ameritech, BellSouth) or Hollywood agent Michael Ovitz (Bell Atlantic, Pacific Telesis, Nynex) to buy or invest in programs that existing studios produce. The RBOCs plan to distribute the shows over their telephone networks. (The specific configuration of those ventures is uncertain, because in August 1995, Mr. Ovitz was appointed president of Walt Disney Co.)

- In 1995, Walt Disney Co. executed a stunning $19 billion takeover of Capital Cities/ABC Inc. Prior to the takeover, Capital Cities/ABC had started a television studio in partnership with an entertainment company owned by Jeffrey Katzenberg, David Geffen, and Steven Spielberg, believing that the so-called Hollywood "Dream Team" would be a powerful force for creative programming concepts.

- Warner Bros. Inc. and Paramount Pictures, major TV producers, are spending millions on new TV networks to compete with NBC, ABC, CBS, and Fox. They both hope to create captive, brand-name distribution outlets for programs they produce and sell.

■ Viacom Inc., originally a cable television company, paid $10 billion to acquire Paramount Communications Inc. (In fact, Viacom sold its cable systems in order to concentrate on making television programs and movies, rather than on trying to build a larger distribution system.) Turner Broadcasting System spent $1 billion to buy and combine two movie-production companies, New Line Cinema Corp. and Castle Rock Entertainment.

■ Blockbuster Entertainment, the largest U.S. video rental company, has a controlling interest in two production companies, Spelling Entertainment and Republic Entertainment. In addition to film production, Blockbuster has gained control, via its investment, over the film and program libraries of the two companies. Spelling owns the former program library of NBC, and Republic owns the ABC's library.

■ Sony purchased Columbia Pictures in 1989 for $3.4 billion. Matsushita purchased MCA, the owner of Universal Studios, for $6.1 billion in 1990.

Clearly, access to both programming and distribution is imperative for success in the entertainment industry, but the question that must continually be raised is how should the various marketing channels be organized in order to assure future success for the companies comprising them. If vertical integration is adopted, then the fixed costs associated with running the enterprise are immense. That is why Turner Broadcasting is not investing in studio lots; instead, it is renting them for the production companies it owns. Others are buying only minority stakes in studios. Indeed, it has been predicted that: " . . . minority investors and owners of 'virtual' studios will proliferate along with the number of distribution channels. 'Distribution is so much easier to have today that the old barriers to creating a studio just don't exist any longer.' "[2]

Being able to compete without buying a studio outright has encouraged foreign companies such as PolyGram to enter the business. Rather than buy a studio, PolyGram has allied itself with filmmakers, like Jodie Foster, and has laid plans to produce 20 films a year.[3]

Even though the "make versus buy" issue is unresolved, it is certain that, instead of three major and one smaller network, there will be many networks. Television stations will be choosing from among several program suppliers. Coverage levels and scheduling patterns will be variable, depending more on local tastes than on advertiser preferences. In all this, viewers (end-users) benefit in terms of service outputs received. Producers and networks will vie to provide the most popular programming. Greater competition is likely to mean an increase in quality as well as choice.

To a large extent, the manner in which channels should be organized is resolved by addressing this "make versus buy" issue. In other words, under what conditions is vertical integration ("making" the channel oneself via internal growth or acquisition) a sensible strategy and under what conditions does relying on independently owned and operated institutions and agencies ("buying" the services of third parties) make more sense? Because it is the position of this text that all channels should somehow be purposively organized, we refer to the "make" decision as involving "hard" integration and the "buy" decision as involving "soft" integration or integration by socialization rather than by ownership. Therefore, we first examine the reasons favoring "hard" vertical integration, remembering from Chapter 5 that, in distribution, "hard" vertical integration should be seen as a "fall back" rather than an initial step. Next, we examine the reasons for outsourcing rather than owning. Then, we turn to a variety of ways in which marketing channels can be organized via "soft" integration, including various forms of administered systems and franchising. Finally, we discuss the need for hybrid channels and plural systems.

▶ "HARD" VERTICAL INTEGRATION

Rationale for "Hard" Vertical Integration

Anderson and Weitz suggest that vertical integration is a logical strategy to pursue when:

1. There are few "outsiders" available that can perform specific activities satisfactorily.
2. It would take a very long time and be very costly to switch to new channel partners if the existing channel partners fail to perform.
3. A company's terms, procedures, and products are unique, and lots of training would be required to bring an "outsider" up to speed.
4. The buying decision is complex and highly involved.
5. Close coordination is essential for the performance of a marketing activity.
6. Buyers form strong loyalties with salespeople, not companies.
7. Economies of scale are present in the performance of marketing activities or flows.
8. The environment is highly uncertain.
9. It is extremely difficult to monitor the performance of "outsiders."
10. It is very easy for channel members to "free ride" on the efforts of others.
11. Transactions are sizable *and* frequent.[4]

Anderson and Coughlan have extended this list by proposing that vertical integration should also be pursued when (1) a product is in the early stages of its life cycle, (2) service levels required by buyers are high, and (3) a product is closely related to the company's core business.[5] (The reader is encouraged to think how each of the points listed above apply to the entertainment industry example.) By and large, a great deal of the reasoning underlying many of the points made by Anderson, Weitz, and Coughlan on "hard" vertical integration has been derived from a theory called "transaction cost analysis" (TCA) developed by economist Oliver E. Williamson.[6] The theory addresses when the costs of transacting business "across a market" (with "outsiders" or "third-parties" or independently owned institutions and agencies) are too high relative to those of bringing the transaction in-house via "hard" vertical integration. Profit maximizing firms will choose to undertake internally only those activities that they find cheaper to administer themselves than to purchase in the market.

According to TCA, transacting through the market should be viewed as the default option. But, prior to a relationship being established, transaction costs "across a market" become excessively high when it is very difficult to (1) locate appropriate partners and information regarding the abilities of those who are found; (2) draft an agreement that will cover the host of contingencies that will arise during the relationship; (3) negotiate an equitable arrangement; and (4) build adequate safeguards into the agreement so that critical interests can be protected. After establishing a relationship, transaction costs also escalate when it is very difficult to (1) monitor and enforce an agreement; (2) adjust the agreement; (3) maintain and ensure the relationship; and (4) assure its continued efficacy.

Three factors tend to intensify these problems. The first is the fact that every individual and organization is subject to bounded rationality, that is, it is impossible to make truly rational decisions because we can't assimilate enough information and develop appropriate decision rules for every contingency that might occur in our lives. The second is the fact that many of us are highly opportunistic, which (as defined by Williamson) means that we are willing to deceive our partners in order to achieve our own interests. And the third is that, in order to build successful relationships, it is necessary to make transaction-specific investments, that is, put nonsalvagable assets at risk in order to assure that the relationship will work. These are sunk costs that make the party doing the investing highly vulnerable and subject, as Williamson puts it, to be "held up" (as in a robbery). All of these factors, when combined with the prerelationship and postrelationship costs, can bring about "market failure" and, thus, drive an organization to "hard" vertical integration. Considerable empirical support has been generated for parts or all of the tenets of TCA in marketing channel contexts.[7]

A number of the items on the lists developed by Anderson and her colleagues, Weitz and Coughlan, relate to economies of scale issues. In fact, companies often desire control over their marketing channels so as to assure the delivery of service outputs and/or to expropriate profits. This leads them to prefer vertical integration, but such arrangements are not feasible unless associated fixed costs can be spread over a large volume of business. Furthermore, as the volume of business increases, firms are able to specialize in the performance of marketing-distribution functions and reap the benefits of scalar economies.[8]

Perhaps the most important reason for engaging in or maintaining vertical integration is to protect and further a firm's or an organization's core competencies. As alluded to in Chapter 5, core competencies are the fundamentals of what a company can do better than anyone else, thereby giving it a strategic competitive advantage.[9] As an axiom, no organization should ever outsource its core competence. But the crucial question in the "make" versus "buy" decision is whether the organization can achieve a maintainable competitive edge by performing an activity internally—cheaper, better, quicker, or with some unique capability—on a continuous basis. Quinn and Hilmer warn:

> Many companies unfortunately assume that because they have performed an activity internally, or because it seems integral to their business, the activity should be insourced. However, on closer investigation and with careful benchmarking, its inter-

nal capabilities may turn out to be significantly below those of best-in-world suppliers.[10]

"Hard" vertical integration is found when any one of the eight marketing flows is assumed by one organization across any two levels of distribution. If a manufacturer owns distribution centers from which products are shipped to retailers, then the manufacturer has vertically integrated the storage function (part of the physical possession flow) down through the wholesale level. However, if common carriers (as opposed to its own truck fleet) are employed to transport the products to the distribution centers and then on to the retailers, the delivery function is not vertically integrated. If a retail grocery chain owns its own warehouse, then the chain has vertically integrated backward in the same way in which the manufacturer has integrated forward. Furthermore, any company that makes *any* sale directly to channel intermediaries or end-users via a company-employed salesperson, a telephone operator, or the mail is engaged in forward integration. Understanding the extent of vertical integration demands a flow-by-flow analysis.

By virtue of "owning" a marketing activity, a firm increases the probability that it will gain absolute *control* over how the activity is performed across several levels of distribution. Control permits a firm to assure itself that the service outputs demanded by its customers will be appropriately delivered. Otherwise, the firm will have to negotiate across open markets with other firms in order to arrive at terms of trade (e.g., prices, warranties, freight allowances, etc.) that will accomplish what it needs to accomplish from a service output perspective. In other words, it will have to face the consequences of elevated transaction costs and, possibly, market failure (as Williamson terms it).

For example, the four leading liquor marketers—Allied Lyons, Grand Metropolitan, Guinness of the United Kingdom, and Seagram of Canada—have exerted increasing control over their distribution channels by forming, through acquisition and joint ventures, tightly managed networks that now cover all the world's major markets. Without strength in distribution, no brand with international pretensions can hope to make much headway, especially as sales are shifting away from on-premise (bars and pubs) consumption to supermarkets operated by powerful retailers.

> . . . the multinationals have reaped additional downstream profits from their brands by cutting out payments to agents (i.e., distributors); and they have been able to exercise much tighter control of both marketing and pricing strategy.
>
> Guinness' United Distillers, for instance, found after the takeover of DCL (Distillers Company Ltd.) that its brands were being handled by 244 agents in Europe, all doing their own thing and sometimes in fierce competition with each other. (Via vertical integration), control of prices and margins gave the company the ability to decide what proportion of the margin should be put behind the brands and how it should be spent. By setting its own prices, it could also combat more effectively the problem of "paralleling"—cut-price competition from unofficial suppliers.
>
> Remy Martin, the French cognac, champagne, and liqueurs group, decided to create its own distribution network in the mid-1970s when it was still purely a cognac producer. According to the chairman of the group's distribution company, "We had great difficulty in getting some of our agents to follow our marketing strategies. They

wanted to go for volume, sell at a discount, and did not give a fig for the brand's image." As Remy started acquiring distributors in national markets, it found other benefits. "Without our own distribution system, we would never have been able to expand into champagne and other drinks. The real cost of acquiring new brands is reduced if you can put them through an existing distribution system."[11]

At the same time, vertical integration can produce, in a number of situations, distribution synergies and scale economies. In fact, in the liquor industry example above, Remy Martin's rationale in support of "making" over "buying" relates to both economies of scale *and* control. When Sony bought Columbia Pictures and when Matsushita bought MCA, prospective scale economies provided some of the major reasons for the acquisitions. As explained by the president of Matsushita, the purpose of the MCA acquisition was to take advantage of the converging trends of video hardware and software. Videocassette sales are Hollywood's single biggest source of revenue, and Matsushita is the world's largest manufacturer of VCRs. In 1995, Matsushita sold 80% of MCA to Seagram Co., the liquor giant. Nevertheless, MCA remains central to the Japanese company's original strategy of combining software and hardware, using a producer of entertainment to help it sell its own equipment. Both Sony's and Matsushita's main aim is to make sure that they are at the forefront of a new generation of video hardware, especially high definition television (HDTV). Almost every existing television receiver in the world may be replaced over the long term by HDTV. The two companies will be able to produce HDTV videotapes of the huge film libraries they have bought and use them to show off the technology. Sony's acquisition of Columbia was also motivated by its desire to promote its 8mm videotape standard and the prospect of converting Hollywood studios from film to video technology. Sony is the world market leader in professional video equipment.[12]

Three brief examples provide insights into some of the major motives for vertical integration in distribution:

1. *Service.* Several British insurance companies, including Direct Line (which is owned by Royal Bank of Scotland), have started a trend in Europe toward the development of direct-sales subsidiaries. The underlying idea is that by dealing directly with clients over the telephone, instead of through agents and brokers, insurance companies can offer quicker and cheaper service. By offering prices that were as much as 35% lower than traditional U.K. insurers, Direct Line has grown in eight years to become Britain's largest automobile insurer. Direct marketing requires substantial investment from the beginning, notably in data processing equipment and advertising. Because of this, it confers first-mover advantages and also erects entry barriers to less well-capitalized companies.[13]

2. *Profit, Marketing Research.* Some apparel makers, such as Anne Klein, Liz Claiborne, Ralph Lauren, Calvin Klein, and Adrienne Vittadini, have opened retail outlets, and/or have opened boutiques within department stores, and/or send employees to work on the selling floors of large stores. Other manufacturers are beginning to produce and place their own magazine ads, because they are fed up with sharing the cost of department store advertising.[14] The reasons given by the apparel makers for opening their own retail stores are: (a) department stores only carry a relatively small sample of the

makers' collections; (b) they can gain bigger profit margins via controlling distribution and markdown activity; (c) retailers are increasingly using aggressive tactics to extract more money from vendors; (d) they can provide a better ambience with a broader selection of merchandise, better displays, and more attentive service; (e) they can use their own stores to test styles, colors, and prices; (f) they can be closer to the customer; and (g), as discussed in Chapter 2, a number of department stores are in trouble, due to a variety of factors.[15]

3. *Control, Marketing Research.* Unlike most of its competitors who distribute primarily through supermarket warehouses and independent distributors, Dreyer's Grand Ice Cream controls all of its distribution through a network of 350 company-owned delivery trucks. Direct access to the supermarket shelf provides immediate benefits in getting, maintaining, and managing optimum placement at retail. Additionally, Dreyer's is able to use a wealth of proprietary data it generates at store level through hand-held computers, which allows the company to micro-market its products. In California, where the company got its start, Dreyer's dominates the ice cream category with a 25 to 30% share. Nationally, Dreyer's/Edy's share is about 9%, making it the number 2 brand in the industry.[16]

Problems with "Hard" Vertical Integration

Some of the costs, along with the benefits, of vertical integration in distribution are listed in Exhibit 6-1. Phillips puts the arguments against vertical integration neatly:

> Shifting a transaction from the market to the firm does not . . . ensure greater efficiency. A decision to integrate vertically into the wholesale or retail stage of an industry necessarily entails expanding the size and complexity of the enterprise. As firms grow larger and more complex, various inefficiencies can emerge. Diseconomies of scale may be associated with the internalization of marketing tasks, resulting in management's inability to control efficiently such aspects of distribution operations as inventory costs and salesforce expenditures. Also, because the vertically integrated unit has a captive source of supply instead of having to compete for business, incentives to perform efficiently may be dulled. In turn, managers and employees of the integrated units may pursue goals incongruent with corporate objectives, such as . . . investment in unproductive overhead. . . . The cumulative result of these and other inefficiencies is termed *control loss*—that is, the failure of a vertically integrated firm to achieve goal pursuit and cost behavior on the part of employees consistent with profit-maximization objectives.[17]

There is, to the best of our knowledge, no firm that is *totally* vertically integrated. On the contrary, it frequently makes more sense to divide labor in distribution than it does to make fixed investments in activities outside of a firm's core competencies. For this reason and others, the next section of this chapter deals with outsourcing as contrasted with insourcing, which has been the subject of this section.

Among the numerous difficulties associated with making "hard" vertical integration work, one of the most significant is the need to overcome mobility barriers. (Warning: mobility barrier is not another name for entry barrier.) When a firm tries to move from one strategic core business (e.g., manufacturing mainframe com-

EXHIBIT 6-1 / Benefits and Costs of Vertical Integration

BENEFITS

Porter[a]	Williamson[b]	Buzzell[c]	Bhasin and Stern[d]

1. Secure economies of:
  a. combined operations
  b. internal control and coordination
  c. information
  d. avoiding the market
  e. stable relationships
2. Tap into technology (esp. via tapered integration)
3. Ensure supply and/or demand
4. Offset bargaining
5. Enhance ability to differentiate (value added)
6. Elevate entry and mobility barriers
7. Enter a higher-return business
8. Defend against foreclosure
	1. Facilitate adaptive sequential decision making (economize on bounded rationality)
	2. Attenuate opportunism
	3. Promote convergent expectations (reduce uncertainty)
	4. Overcome conditions of information impactedness
	5. Obtain a more satisfying atmosphere
		1. Reduce transaction costs
		2. Ensure supply
		3. Improve coordination
		4. Enhance technological capabilities
		5. Elevate entry barriers
			1. Secure supply
			2. Rationalize inventory levels
			3. Use managerial slack
			4. Secure operating economies via:
			  a. technological interdependencies
			  b. eliminating risk premiums
			  c. reduced transaction costs
			  d. economies of scale
			  e. reducing the risk buffer
			  f. stable relationships
			  g. obtaining capital resources
			5. Gain material information
			6. Achieve product differentiation
			7. Achieve price differentiation
			8. Adaptability
			9. Coordinate demand and supply
			10. Erect entry barriers
			11. Achieve diversification

puters, retailing women's ready-to-wear clothing) to another strategic core business (e.g., selling personal computers through retail product centers, designing ready-to-wear private label clothing), the gap between the two businesses may be too wide to leap. For example, in 1991, Intelligent Electronics Inc., one of the largest wholesalers of name-brand personal computers, paid $195 million for the 57-store retail chain BizMart. It sold BizMart in March 1993. An article in the *Wall Street Journal* catalogued the mobility barrier facing Richard Sanford, the founder and chairman of Intelligent Electronics:

> (Sanford) was over his head at BizMart. While accustomed to (computer) dealers who drove hard bargains, he badly miscalculated the tightfistedness of retail customers. Mr. Sanford went from managing two warehouses and a headquarters to opening 50 BizMart stores in addition to expanding those he bought. And nothing he learned in the mundane business of wholesaling prepared him for the task of making shoppers enthusiastic to visit his stores.[18]

Another major pitfall is that vertical integration frequently puts a company into competition with its suppliers or its channel partners. Thus, when IBM decided,

		COSTS		
Porter[a]	**Williamson**[b]	**Buzzell**[c]	**Bhasin and Stern**[d]
1. Cost of overcoming mobility barriers	1. Biases favoring the maintenance or extension of internal operations	1. Capital requirement	1. Diseconomies of: a. imbalanced stages of integrated operations b. management c. lower returns d. transactional distortions
2. Increased operating leverage	2. Communication distortion	2. Unbalanced throughput	2. Increased operating leverage
3. Reduced flexibility to change partners	3. Internal opportunism	3. Reduced flexibility	3. Barriers to mobility
4. Higher overall exit barriers	4. Bounded rationality (spans of control)	4. Loss of specialization	
5. Capital investment requirements	5. Bureaucratic insularity		
6. Foreclosure of access to supplier of consumer research or know-how	6. Loss of moral involvement		
7. Maintaining balance	7. Dulled incentives		
8. Dulled incentives			
9. Differing managerial requirements			

Sources:
[a]Michael E. Porter, *Competitive Strategy* (New York: The Free Press, 1980).
[b]Oliver E. Williamson, *Markets and Hierarchies: Analysis and Antitrust Implications* (New York: The Free Press, 1975) Oliver E. Williamson, *The Economic Institutions of Capitalism* (New York: The Free Press, 1985).
[c]Robert D. Buzzell, "Is Vertical Integration Profitable?" *Harvard Business Review*, Vol. 61 (January–February 1983) pp. 92–102.
[d]Ajay Bhasin and Louis W. Stern, "Vertical Integration: Considerations of Efficiency, Risk, and Strategy," in M. G Harvey and R. F. Lusch (eds.), *Marketing Channels: Domestic and International Perspectives* (Norman OK: University o Oklahoma Printing Services, 1982).

in 1993, to clone Intel Corporation's microprocessors, it complicated one of high technology's most tangled relationships. Intel is one of IBM's major suppliers, and the two companies collaborate on microchip research. As explained by an IBM executive: "Our relationships include customer, supplier, partner, competitor. We have managed all those relationships very successfully."[19] One hopes that the executive is correct, but don't bet on it!

"Hard" vertical integration is a means for governing exchange in a marketing channel. In effect, the operation of the channel is determined by the legitimate power of its owner. (The use of power and influence strategies is addressed in Chapter 7.) Heide points out that the management of such structures, as well as the other authority-based or unilateral channel structures discussed later in this chapter, requires that the following stages of the relationship be detailed:

1. *Initiation.* This involves extensive screening, training, and socialization.
2. *Maintenance.* This involves thorough role specification, the development of binding contingency plans, specifying explicit mechanisms for change, the adoption of moni-

toring and measurement systems tied to output and behavior, and the delineation of means of enforcement.

3. *Termination.* This involves specifying the length of the relationship and explicit mechanisms for termination.[20]

There are available a number of less expensive, viable alternatives to vertical financial ownership. In fact, a number of economists strongly believe that vertical contracting (e.g., "soft" integration) is, on balance and in general, superior to "hard" integration.[21] In an analysis of the profitability of vertical integration, Buzzell issues the following warnings, among others:

1. *Beware heightened investment.* Rising investment requirements offset the higher profit margins associated with intensified vertical integration. If integration can somehow be achieved without the penalty of a proportionately higher investment base, then increasing vertical integrations should be extremely beneficial.
2. *Consider alternatives to ownership.* Long-term contracts and long-term relationships with suppliers or distributors can produce benefits comparable to vertical integration.
3. *Carefully analyze scale requirements.* A significant risk in many vertical integration strategies is that a production or distribution stage has too small a scope to be run competitively against independent suppliers or customers.[22]

Harrigan's research has shown that if channel members can use their power creatively, they can administer their channels and achieve performance levels equal to or better than those in channels that are more formally integrated via ownership.[23]

▶ OUTSOURCING

It should be recalled from earlier in this chapter and from the discussion in Chapter 5 that "hard" vertical integration ought to be considered a "fall back" strategy. In other words, managers should "make" rather than "buy" only after they have convinced themselves, through rigorous analysis, that ownership is necessary. Although extreme, Prahalad and Hamel as well as Quinn and Hilmer even suggest that, except for those activities that can be defined as their core competencies, firms should strategically outsource all other activities—including many traditionally considered integral.[24]

The rationale for outsourcing is really the reverse of the rationale for insourcing ("hard" vertical integration). The advantages of outsourcing are that it permits firms to:

1. convert fixed costs to variable costs
2. balance work force requirements
3. reduce capital investment requirements
4. reduce costs (via partners' economies of scale and lower wage structures)
5. accelerate new product development

6.   gain access to invention and innovation from partners

7.   focus on high-value-added activities[25]

It is, however, best to remember a lesson learned from Japanese firms—their primary motive for outsourcing is to improve quality and efficiency; cuts in labor and other overhead costs are a secondary consideration.[26]

Perhaps the best way to demonstrate the pervasiveness and diversity of outsourcing is by selected examples—it ranges from outsourcing components, products, and services to facilities management to modular networks to virtual corporations as well as all sorts of variations in between.

Basic Outsourcing Examples: Automobile Parts and Logistics Services

1.   **Autoparts.** Traditionally, outsourcing in the U.S. automobile industry meant sending detailed specifications for a particular part around the world in search of the low-cost producer. Now, U.S. car manufacturers, following the example set by Japanese manufacturers, are seeking so-called Tier-1 suppliers capable of not just making a part but also designing it, engineering it, integrating it with surrounding parts, and delivering it globally. Even though U.S. automakers are still more wedded to "making" rather than "buying" compared to their Japanese counterparts (Toyota makes only about 25% of its own parts vs. 47% at General Motors), they are retreating from vertical integration. This trend "provides a windfall of opportunities to bring costs down, improve flexibility, and get quick access to new technologies. Chrysler is the industry's low-cost producer and makes the highest profit per vehicle, partly because of its new-age relationship with suppliers."[27]

2.   **Logistics Services.** As discussed in Chapter 4, more and more companies are using contract distribution services from firms such as Federal Express, DHL, and TNT rather than investing their funds in fixed facilities.[28] FedEx Business Logistics offers users a detailed menu of international logistics services with a set price for each service. Clients can rent pallet space by the week in a bonded storage area and call off goods to be picked and dispatched to or from anywhere in the world. FedEx has, for example, assumed joint responsibility for Laura Ashley's supply chain, helping to ensure the most efficient delivery of goods from the retailer's international network of suppliers to its 500 stores in 28 countries. DHL has an integrated international system for direct, door-to-door, guaranteed delivery. TNT, an Australian company, has set up TNT Fulfillment USA to meet the needs of U.S. companies interested in developing markets in Europe. Services available include the provision of mailing lists, direct mail, customer service/order entry, collection and consolidation, freight distribution to Europe by sea or air, customs clearance, bonded warehousing, full picking, packing, labeling, preassembly billing, debt collection, and after-sales activities.[29] Employing a third-party logistics company removes the need to operate a vehicle fleet, to acquire and maintain warehouse space, and to manage the intricacies of world-wide distribution.

Facilities Management Example: Data-Processing Services

In information services, facilities management most often refers to the practice of turning over a company's data-processing operations to a third-party vendor. In its fullest application, the client company actually sells its hardware and software to the outsource vendor, which often also hires many of the client's data-processing employees. The major suppliers of these programs are EDS, IBM, Andersen Consulting, Digital Equipment, and CSC. (In the medical supplies industry, the stockless purchasing programs run by Baxter Healthcare, Owens & Minor, and other distributors operate similarly relative to the hospitals' materials management departments.)

When applied fully, facilities management can free up clients' capital. It can also provide a means for companies to stay on the cutting edge of technology. The arrangement that seemed to start the trend toward outsourcing of computer services occurred in 1989 when Eastman Kodak Co. shifted 40% of its management information staff and a large portion of its data-processing operations to IBM. However, Kodak never gave up control of the strategic technology functions it considers key to its business. The company still maintains a sizable in-house staff of information systems workers for applications development and other crucial tasks, including the monitoring of data-processing applications within individual business units.[30]

Modular Network Examples: Apparel and Toys

Modular networks are hubs surounded by networks of suppliers. The manufacturing, distribution, and service units are modular—they can be added or taken away with considerable ease and speed. Using the modular model, companies can achieve rapid growth with small amounts of capital and a managerial core. Miles and Snow refer to these forms of outsourcing as "stable networks," which include a set of component firms, each tied closely to a core firm by contractual arrangements, but each maintaining its competitive fitness by serving firms outside the network.[31] Apparel companies have been the modular pioneers.

> Nike and Reebok have prospered by concentrating on their strengths: designing and marketing high-tech, fashionable footwear for sports and fitness. Nike owns one small factory that makes some sneaker parts. Reebok owns no plants. The two rivals contract virtually all footwear production to suppliers in Taiwan, South Korea, and other Asian countries. Sparse fixed assets translate into bountiful profitability.[32]

Another example of a modular corporation is Lewis Galoob Toys Inc. Approximately 100 employees run the entire operation. Independent inventors and entertainment companies think up most of Galoob's products, while outside specialists do most of the design and engineering. Galoob outsources manufacturing and packaging to contractors in Hong Kong, and they, in turn, pass on the most labor-intensive work to factories in China. When the toys land in the U.S., they are distributed by commissioned manufacturers' representatives. Galoob doesn't even collect its accounts; it sells its receivables to Commercial Credit Corp., a factoring company that also sets Galoob's credit policy.[33]

Virtual Corporations

Although more futuristic than current, a "virtual" corporation is a transitory network of firms organized around a specific market opportunity, lasting only for the length of that opportunity. Miles and Snow refer to this as a "dynamic network" in which independent firms are linked together for the one-time or short-term production of a particular good or service.[34] In a virtual corporation, companies can share costs, skills, and access to global markets, with each partner focusing on its core competencies. Prerequisites for the realization and success of such organizations are (1) information networks that will permit far-flung companies to link-up and work together from inception to completion, (2) informality and flexibility, (3) trust among the partners, and (4) no concerns over the absence of traditional boundaries between companies.[35] It is also essential that there are numerous firms (or units of firms) operating at each of the points along the value chain, ready to be pulled together for a given project and then disassembled to become part of another temporary alignment.[36] According to *Business Week:*

> The virtual corporation is a temporary network of independent companies—suppliers, customers, even erstwhile rivals—linked by information technology to share skills, costs, and access to one another's markets. It will have neither central office nor organization chart. It will have no hierarchy, no vertical integration."[37]

It is possible that the entertainment "Dream Team" of Katzenberg, Spielberg, and Geffen is in the process of forming the largest virtual corporation in the industry's history. After all, the process of producing and distributing an individual motion picture frequently requires the formation of a virtual corporation comprised of studios, actors, producers, distributors, exhibitors, cameramen, and a host of other independent agents. And there are even indications that advanced digital technology will permit the formation of the virtual studio, eliminating much of the costs associated with the traditional process.[38]

Problems with Outsourcing

Perhaps the major drawback of outsourcing is the reason that drives firms to vertically integrate—the costs of transacting business across a market (i.e., the potential for "market failure"). For example, outsourcing often involves the hazards associated with forming an alliance with a potential competitor. As Bettis, Bradley, and Hamel warn:

> The more the supplier's intentions seem potentially to involve the acquisition of your technology and/or market knowledge, and the closer the proximity of outsourcing to your core competences, the higher the risks. It should be noted that a supplier bent on using the relationship primarily to learn is likely to offer a financially attractive deal and go to great lengths to be accommodating. In other words, the most dangerous suppliers can often appear to be the most attractive on the surface during the early phases of the relationship.[39]

In addition, to have outsourcing work correctly, sensitive information on such subjects as pricing, profit margins, and market strategies must be shared from the outset.[40]

Major problems arise when management has expectations for facilities management that are simply unrealistic. For instance, some companies hope that they are going to obtain much better service for much lower costs. They then spend a lot of money and end up receiving much less than they thought they would. For example, one study concluded that the operating cost of an effectively managed in-house operation was unlikely to differ much from one contracted out.[41] Many companies continue to run some activities in-house as an insurance policy and a benchmark with which to compare their contractors' performance. Also, facilities management, especially for data processing, frequently involves long-term (e.g., 10 years) contracts. This can lead to trouble if the buyer and supplier turn out to be incompatible. The contracts can also create incompatibilities; contractors may expect inflation-linked cost increases even when their partners' sales are declining.[42] Worse yet, some companies find that many computer-service companies often know very little about how their industries work or about their individual corporate cultures.[43]

Relative to logistics services, a 1994 study of United Kingdom companies indicated that 40% were dissatisfied with the way their affairs were handled and felt there were insufficient controls. Outsourcers often fail to appreciate that they must still work closely with their logistics suppliers, sharing management information and even integrating staffs. It is recommended that the scope of the contract, the services to be provided, and performance standards to be used should be defined in detail at the outset.[44]

A danger in modular networks observed by Miles and Snow is that a given supplier or distributor may be overused, leading to an unhealthy dependence on the core firm. For example, as a subcontractor is drawn closer to the core company, it can become overspecialized and unable to compete in markets outside the network. Worse yet, it may lose the innovative edge it gained from working for several, equally demanding customers. Also, they warn that high expectations for cooperation can limit the creativity of partners.[45] They believe that virtual corporations (i.e., dynamic networks) "run the risk of quality variation across firms, of needed expertise being temporarily unavailable, and of possible exploitation of proprietary knowledge or technology."[46] One of the obvious problems with the virtual corporation is the loss of control over some operations and, concomitantly, the need for a high level of trust within the network.

▶ "SOFT" VERTICAL INTEGRATION

What should be abundantly clear by now is that leaving things to chance is not a recommended strategy for marketing channels. As the title to this chapter indicates, "organization" is the name of the game. Given all of the concerns about "hard" vertical integration and the fact that outsourcing without organization also brings potential problems, the key question is: Is it possible to gain the benefits of "hard" vertical integration without all of the costs? The answer is "yes," and the route is quasi-integration via the creative use of appropriate influence and conflict management strategies to achieve trust, commitment, cooperation, and coordination. All of these management techniques are addressed in Chapter 7. Here, we discuss the structural side of the question—the organizational forms that promote sociological integration as opposed to financial integration. These include a number of so-called nonmarket governance forms, such as administered vertical marketing systems and contractual vertical marketing systems, like franchising.

By and large, there are still a large number of channels throughout the world in which very few attempts are made to organize resources in a purposeful fashion. These channels are piecemeal coalitions of independently owned and managed institutions, each of which is only concerned with its own short-run financial performance. Coordination among channel members is achieved primarily through bargaining and negotiation over virtually every transaction. The operating units within such channels are frequently unable to achieve systemic economies. Furthermore, there is usually a low index of member loyalty and relatively easy entry to the channels. The networks, then, tend to be relatively unstable. Firms at each level only concern themselves with the distribution of a product to the next adjacent level. These channels are governed basically by the impersonal operation of prices and the related modes of market mechanisms. There is no planning, incentives are short-term and tied to output, and the primary means of enforcement are provided by the legal system, competition, or offsetting investments.[47]

Within these channels, there are a large number of decision makers who tend to be preoccupied with cost, volume, and investment relationships at a *single* stage of the marketing process. Decisions are often tradition-oriented, and decision makers are frequently emotionally committed to established patterns of operation and interaction. From an interoganization management perspective, such channels have no inclusive goals. The locus of decision making and authority is exclusively at the unit or individual channel member level. There is no formally structured division of labor, and commitment is only to one's own organization. In fact, there is little or no prescribed systemwide orientation of the members.[48] The members are almost totally self-oriented as they pursue their goals.

Several significant modes of channel organization have emerged as ways to eliminate or penalize the suboptimization that frequently exists in these freeform, loosely connected channels and thus to improve channel effectiveness and efficiency. Each safeguards against market failure by limiting behavior. The goal is to assure that the service output requirements of end-users are satisfied or exceeded and that transaction costs—defined very broadly to include the costs associated with allocation of marketing activities and the establishment of the terms of trade among channel members—are held to reasonable levels.

Administered Vertical Marketing Systems

Administered vertical marketing systems are one step removed, in an analytical sense, from the transactions-oriented, freeform (market- and price-driven) channels mentioned previously. In an administered system, coordination of marketing activities is achieved through programs developed by one or a limited number of firms rather than by open market forces. In such systems, administrative strategies combined with the exercise of power are relied on to obtain systemic economies. Successfully administered systems are freeform channels in which the principles of effective interorganization management detailed in Chapter 7 have been correctly applied.

In administered systems, units can exist with disparate goals, but a mechanism exists for informal collaboration on inclusive goals. Decision making takes place by virtue of the effective interaction of channel members in the absence of a formal inclusive structure; however, the locus of authority remains with the individual channel members. Each channel member operates on its own but is willing to agree to an ad hoc division of labor. In contrast to freeform channels, there is at least a minimum amount of systemwide orientation among the members of the channel.[49]

Perhaps the origin of administered vertical marketing systems started with the programmed merchandising agreement. Under this arrangement, manufacturers formulate specialized merchandising plans for each type of outlet they serve. Manufacturing organizations currently engaged in programmed merchandising activities include Baumritter (on its Ethan Allen furniture line in nonfranchised outlets), Sealy (on its Posturepedic line of mattresses), Villager (on its dress and sportswear lines), Scott (on its lawn-care products), Hanes (on its L'eggs pantyhose), and General Electric (on major appliances).[50] General Electric's Direct Connect Program is outlined in Exhibit 6-2.

▶ EXHIBIT 6-2 / General Electric's Direct Connect Program

▶ ▶ ▶   Products Covered: Major Appliances
Channel Targeted: Independent Dealers

BENEFITS OFFERED DEALERS

1. The best price regardless of size of order (with only a difference in freight charges).

2. Access to an order-processing system available 24 hours a day, every day.

3. Next-day delivery when processed by a cut-off time, and notification via the system when a model is not immediately available. (Core models are kept in GE inventory to ensure that 90% of orders can be filled within one or two days of order.)

4. Priority in the delivery trucks over non-Direct Connect customers.

5. Retail financing with 90 days of no interest (through GE Capital Corporation).

6. Fifteen percent discounts for changing out display units.

7. Consumer referrals at the GE "Answer Center."

8. On-line inquiry on products (availability, price, model description) and their own sales history, plus a messaging system broadcasting new promotions, products, etc.

DEALER OBLIGATIONS

1.   Commit to selling nine major GE product categories (while stocking in inventory only the carry-out products, microwaves and air conditioners).
2.   Ensure GE products would represent 50% of sales (with open books open for review).
3.   Pay through electronics funds transfer on the 25th of the month after purchase.
4.   Purchase a hardware/software package from GE.

Source: CSC Index, Inc., *Channel Partnerships: An Investigation* (Cambridge, MA: CSC Index, 1991), p. 33.

Marketing channels can be fully administered (i.e., all aspects of the system can be "programmed") or they may be partially administered (i.e., only a few of the marketing flows are purposively managed.) In either case, the channel qualifies as an administered system. Here are some prominent examples:

■   Newell Co., a major marketer of hardware and housewares, fills the needs of the national mass merchandisers to whom it sells so overwhelmingly that it has become indispensable. Newell does this by selling a unified, tailored program—an orchestrated display of paintbrushes and rollers of all kinds and prices or an attractive 20-foot counter display of cookware or drapery hardware, laid out by computer-aided design to play up the highest-margin items. Newell customizes products, packaging, displays, and promotions. The company uses sophisticated information systems to assist retailers in keeping inventories to a minimum while at the same time keeping shelves and hangers always filled with the right merchandise. (Retailers typically lose 30% of possible sales by being out of stock on the items Newell sells.)[51]

■   Grocery wholesalers, such as Fleming Companies and Super Valu, provide independent retail grocers with a variety of services, such as shelf management programs, retail accounting programs, and pricing assistance. They help their retailers to plan, buy, and maintain scanning equipment. They have private-label programs, store-development programs, and store-location and construction programs. Their sales service representatives counsel retailers on promotion and advertising, merchandise display, store layout, space management, and the like.

■   Owens & Minor, Stuarts, Baxter, Koley's, and other distributors of hospital supplies provide stockless services for hospitals in addition to just-in-time delivery. Stockless distribution is a highly disciplined system that delivers in single units to nursing stations and other points-of-use in the hospital on a daily basis, while just-in-time delivers more frequently to general stores or central supply, considerably reducing the amount of inventory on hand.[52] The range of logistics programming available in the industry is shown in Figure 6-1.

■   Wrigley has become a "front-end merchandising expert." Its strategy includes the following tenets: (1) ensure that checkout merchandising continues to flourish; (2) be an objective source of data on all confectionery products merchandised at the checkout, even though they compete with Wrigley for space; (3) stress return on inventory investment as the fairest and most objective way to compare the performance of items merchandised at the checkout; (4) provide superior display fixtures for retailers to bet-

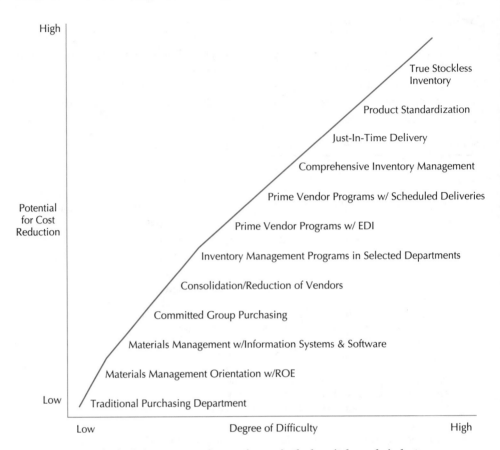

FIGURE 6-1 **The logistics programming continuum in the hospital supply industry.**
Source: David Cassak, "Baxter and the Trend Toward Stockless Distribution—Part II," *In Vivo,* June 1990, p. 20.

ter merchandise their checkout area; and (5) do continuing research at the retail store level in order to constantly increase knowledge of the area. As a result of this and other marketing programs, Wrigley has gained considerable influence over checkout merchandising in virtually every major food, drug, convenience, and mass merchandiser chain in the U.S.[53]

The list could go on and on, to include such activities as VF Corporation's computerized "market-response systems" that monitor what shoppers buy, allowing VF to rapidly restock stores with its Lee and Wrangler jeans and its Vanity Fair women's undergarments; AlliedSignal's long-term purchasing arrangements with its suppliers of pipes, valves, and fittings; Genuine Parts' organization of the NAPA auto parts system; General Electric Credit Corporation's financing plans for wholesalers and retailers; McDonald's purchasing arrangements with its suppliers and distributors (forged primarily on the basis of "gentlemen's agreements," not by contracts); Fisher-Price's shelf management planograms for discount stores; O. M. Scott's merchandising programs for the sale of lawn-care products; Milliken's customized computer graphics system for interior designers to use in inventing their own carpet patterns; and Gallo's joint selling programs with wine distributors.

One of the reasons why administering channels and programmed merchandising have become so popular is that suppliers have finally learned that channels are systems (i.e., sets of interrelated and interdependent institutions and agencies producing an output). As observed by *The Economist*: "This fashion for vertical coordination is inspired by the realization that, far from being the prerogative of a particular company, creating value is the responsibility of an entire chain of firms."[54]

This systemwide or value-chain orientation has, to a significant extent, been forced on suppliers as they have watched "downstream" channel members (e.g., retailers, wholesalers, value-added resellers, etc.) become more powerful and/or more cost effective at performing distribution tasks other than their own vertically integrated units (e.g., salesforces, distribution centers, and product centers). For example, success in marketing personal computers is now totally dependent on gaining support from channels not owned by the computer companies (e.g., computer superstores, value-added resellers (VARS), wholesalers, computer dealers, mass merchants, etc.). This has provided a rude awakening for some firms in the industry. Also, in a number of other industries, industrial distributors, such as Avnet, W.W. Grainger, Graybar Electric, Arrow Electronics, Ryerson, and Van Waters & Rogers, have become so powerful that they are administering the channel. Some of the reasons why they can do so are:

1.   They have the financial strength to act independently rather than as extensions of manufacturers' salesforces.
2.   They are oftentimes more capable than the manufacturers they represent in launching marketing campaigns, coordinating advertising, exercising quality control over product quality, managing inventories and logistics, and controlling costs.
3.   They have outstanding information systems and, as a result, control critical data about the marketplace.
4.   Given their financial capabilities and geographical spread, they have little difficulty in presenting multiplant buyers with cost effective packages of goods and services.[55]

But the rudest awakening has come in channels selling packaged goods and grocery products, as explained in Chapter 2.

One of the major aspects of the Efficient Consumer Response (ECR) efforts within the channels of distribution for grocery products is the emphasis on something called "category management." The "efficient" part of ECR focuses mainly on cost-saving or cost-cutting activities, whereas the "consumer response" part refers to responding to the consumer with a product mix that increases revenue in order to grow profits and improve return on assets. The latter is the job of category management. As described by Management Horizons, a consulting division of Price Waterhouse, category management is

> a process of managing items within a product category as a strategic business unit, with the price, merchandising strategy, promotional efforts and overall product mix of the items within the category determined based on specific goals, the competitive environment, and consumer behavior. For a category management-driven retailer, the

retail store is viewed as a *portfolio of businesses*. The goal is to optimize each business as a part of the whole store. For manufacturers, category management is a process of assisting key accounts with the formulation of category goals, objectives, and strategies. These are then aligned with the manufacturer's own marketing activities and programs so as to increase the total category's profits for both."[56]

The objective of a manufacturer working with a category management-driven retailer is "to become the lead supplier for one or more categories" or the "category captain."[57] Outstanding practitioners of category management are H.E.B. Grocery Company, Shaws, Schnuck's, and Wal-Mart, among retailers, and Kraft/General Foods (KGF), Procter & Gamble, Quaker Oats, Johnson & Johnson/McNeil Consumer Products, Hallmark/Ambassador Cards, and Wrigley, among manufacturers. For example, KGF practices what it calls "micromerchandising." Basically, KGF combines comprehensive data profiles of stores and their customers to make pinpointed recommendations on every aspect of selling product through the supermarket. Under KGF's system, distribution, shelving, and promotion programs match each store's volume demands and address the most important consumer groups for each product, defined by affinity and interest as well as by household size and income. KGF classifies each store in a trading area by type—everyday low price, margin, price leader, neighborhood, upscale. It then determines the composition of each store by six basic classes of shoppers, defined by shopping patterns, demographics, life-styles, and attitudes. Next, KGF analyzes each store's positioning. It uses these data to set stores' objectives on volume, sales, and profit, and to establish the merchandising plans for optimal product mix and placement in a wide range of categories. Finally, it assumes the responsibility for testing, refining, and measuring the merchandising system it creates.[58]

In developing an administered system, one must usually couple expertise with financial incentives. The channel members to be influenced must first be convinced that the "administrator" (1) is trustworthy and (2) knows more about how to seize the opportunity than they do. They must then be given incentives to do what the administrator would like. The channel compensation system outlined in Chapter 7 as an example of the equitable use of reward power is one type of channel incentive system that can be used. To assure that channels for industrial goods are properly administered, attention must be given to the presale, transactional, and postsale support activities listed in Exhibit 6-3.

▶ **EXHIBIT 6-3 / Support Activities Required in Administered Vertical Marketing Systems for Industrial Goods**

▶ ▶ ▶   **Presale Support**

- Product advertising designed to educate end-users about the benefits of a technology

- More generic company communications designed to build strong brand awareness

- Promotional activities, including trade shows and technical seminars

- Product literature and catalogs

- Needs assessments to help the customer determine the correct application or system configuration

- Product demonstrations or application testing

- Appropriate pricing and information for economic cost/benefit analyses

- Information on where and how to buy the product

Transactional Support

- Off-the-shelf product availability

- Quick pricing decisions in "last-look" bid situations

- On-the-spot resource commitments for delivery, installation, training, etc.

- Leasing and other special financing arrangements for small and large capital equipment

Postsale Support

- Warranty service

- Initial and ongoing customer training

- Technical support (i.e., engineering, 800-number hotlines, documentation, etc.)

- Installation

- Spare parts kits and ongoing maintenance

- Product upgrades and updates

- Account management, reinforcement, and maintenance activities

Source: Frank Lynn & Associates, Inc., *Marketplace Chemistry* (Chicago: Frank Lynn & Associates, Inc., 1986), pp. 10, 11.

Many of the efforts, such as category management, made by firms to administer channel relationships in a less adversarial, more partnership-oriented way (in contrast to freeform channels) have been facilitated by widespread and impactful use of information technology (IT) throughout the channel.[59] The role of IT has grown to such importance in distribution that we have devoted an entire chapter of this text (Chapter 9) to a description of some of the more significant developments. The oftentimes transaction-specific nature of the investment in IT by each channel member (for example, the need to conform to idiosyncratic communication standards) means that both suppliers and distributors must be willing to make "credible commitments." These commitments give channel members an incentive to maintain and build relationships with one another.[60] Because of the attention given to IT in Chapter 9, only one brief example is given here of its use in administered vertical marketing systems.

> Lithonia Lighting, the world's largest manufacturer of lighting equipment, sells its products through channels comprised of contractors, distributors, and sales agents. Computers link each part of Lithonia's channel network, from specifiers to agents to Lithonia's own factories. Computer-aided design and artificial-intelligence systems help specifiers design a lighting layout to suit any project. Automated, flexible manufacturing systems (linked into the overall computer network) mean that Lithonia can swiftly modify its product lines; feedback from customers and agents helps design new products. Product catalogues can be tailored to show specific ranges and prices for individual customers. Contractors, distributors, and agents check the availability of products and order them from Lithonia on-line. The progress of each order can be tracked throughout the system. Even Lithonia's delivery trucks (are) linked into the computer network so that customers . . . know exactly when their order will arrive.[61]

Contractual Vertical Marketing Systems

Often organizations desire to formalize the division of marketing "labor" within their channels so that they can assure themselves that the responsibility for performing specific distribution tasks is clearly placed. In these situations, vertical coordination is frequently accomplished through the use of contractual agreements. Whereas virtually every transaction among businesses and between businesses and individuals is covered by some form of contract, either explicit or implied, the function of the contracts in these vertical marketing systems should, theoretically at least, be to specify, in writing, the roles and obligations to be assumed by each party to the contract.[62] We say "should" and "theoretically," because, unfortunately, the contracts are generally written by lawyers who wish to use them as punitive documents if something goes wrong rather than as vehicles for achieving "soft" vertical integration.

Contractual integration takes a variety of forms, as shown in Exhibit 6-4. However, we concentrate attention here mainly on three principal types: wholesaler-sponsored voluntary groups, retailer-sponsored cooperative groups, and franchise systems.

From an interorganization management perspective, contractual vertical marketing systems can be viewed as networks in which the channel members have disparate goals but where there exists some formal organization for inclusive goals. Decision making is generally made at the top of the inclusive structure but is subject to the ratification of the members. The locus of authority in such networks resides primarily (but not exclusively) with the individual members. The latter op-

EXHIBIT 6-4 / Principal Types of Contractual Vertical Marketing Systems

Contractual Systems Involving Forward Integration   ◄ ◄ ◄

- Wholesaler-sponsored voluntary groups

- Wholesaler-sponsored programmed groups

- Supplier franchise programs for individual brands and specific departments

- Supplier franchise program covering all phases of the licensee's operation

- Nonprofit shipping associations

- Leased department arrangements

- Producer marketing cooperatives

Contractual Systems Involving Backward Integration

- Retailer-sponsored cooperative groups

- Retailer/wholesaler-sponsored buying groups

- Retailer-sponsored promotional groups

- Nonprofit shipping associations

- Retailer/wholesaler resident buying offices

- Industrial, wholesale, and retail procurement contracts

- Producer buying cooperatives

erate independently, but will generally agree to a division of labor that may in turn affect the basic structure of the channel. In such networks, norms of moderate commitment to the channel system exist, and there is at least a moderate amount of systemwide orientation among the members.[63]

Clearly, along each of these dimensions, contractual systems are more tightly knit than administered systems. To a significant extent, channel members are willing to trade some degree of autonomy to gain scale economies and market impact.

By setting up a contractual vertical marketing system, the organizer hopes to gain all of the benefits of "hard" vertical integration without sustaining all of its costs. Most importantly, the organizer hopes to secure the potential efficiencies, creativeness, and energies of entrepreneurs and independent companies available only by dealing across markets. But, in order to achieve this, it must safeguard against market failure via the use of the contract and other control mechanisms.

VOLUNTARY AND COOPERATIVE GROUPS   A wholesaler, by banding together a number of independently owned retailers in a voluntary group, can provide goods and support services far more economically than these same retailers could secure solely as individuals. Perhaps the most well-known wholesaler-sponsored voluntary is the Independent Grocers Alliance (IGA). In the hardware field, Pro, Liberty, and Sentry are examples of wholesalers who provide retail establishments with services similar to those found in the IGA system. Other examples of voluntary groups are found in the automobile accessory market (Western Auto, which is owned by Sears) and in the notions and general merchandise market (Ben Franklin). The principal services provided by a number of major hardware voluntaries are listed in Exhibit 6-5.

EXHIBIT **6-5** / **Principal Services Provided by Major Hardware Wholesaler-Sponsored Voluntary Groups and Wholesaler Buying Groups**

▶ ▶ ▶
        Store identification
        Telephone ordering
        Microfiche of prices and compatible parts numbers
        Catalog service
        Private-label merchandise
        Merchandising aid
        Basic stock lists
        Direct-drop ship programs
        Pool orders
        Consumer advertising
        Co-op advertising programs
        Advertising planning, aid
        Preprinted order forms
        Data-processing programs
        Inventory control systems
        Accounting services
        Management consultation services
        Employee training
        Dealer meetings
        Volume rebates/dividends
        Store planning, layout
        Financing
        Insurance programs
        Field supervisors/salesmen
        Dealer shows

Automatic Service, Super Valu, Fleming, Canadian Tire, North American Food Service, and McKesson are other leading proponents of the voluntary group concept. Automatic Service sponsors a voluntary group program for vending machine operators. Super Valu and Fleming are leading voluntary group wholesalers in the food field. (They also have administered systems as well, as described previously. In addition, Super Valu operates about 250 company-owned stores, including Cub Food, Shop 'n Save, Laneco/Twin Value, and Save-A-Lot outlets.) Canadian Tire is a large voluntary group wholesaler that supplies affiliated stores with a variety of lines, including automotive parts and accessories, hardware, housewares, small appliances, and sporting goods. A typical Canadian Tire outlet contains approximately 25,000 square feet of space and carries over 20,000 items in inventory. North American Food Service is the largest independent food-service distributor in the U.S. It has a highly organized network of affiliates, each of which is a major distributor in its market. McKesson's greatest strength is the nearly 3,300 independent drugstores that operate as part of its voluntary chain under the Valu-Rite name, which provides purchasing power, sales promotions, and ancillary services from car leasing to insurance.

The retailer-owned cooperative is also a voluntary association, but the impetus for the group comes from the retailers rather than from a wholesaler. The retailers organize and democratically operate their own wholesale company, which then performs services for member retailers. In addition to stock dividends (if the cooperative makes money), the members receive rebates at the end of the year based on their cumulative purchases from the cooperative. Historically, retailer-owned cooperatives have been important in the marketing of foods (e.g., Topco Associates, Associated Grocers, and Certified Grocers). For example, Topco Associates is owned cooperatively by a group of supermarket chains and grocery wholesalers located in various markets throughout the country. Topco's central function is to serve its 25 owner-member companies in the purchasing, product development, quality control, packaging, and promotion of a wide variety of private-label (controlled-brand) food and nonfood products. Its $3.5 billion in sales in 1994 included such private labels as Top Frost, Top Crest, Top Care and Food Club, among others. Its owner-members represent more than 10% of U.S. supermarket sales, and include such firms as Meijer, Inc. in Grand Rapids, Michigan; Schnuck Markets in St. Louis, Missouri; and Smith's Food & Drug Center, in Salt Lake City, Utah. Retailer-sponsored and owned cooperatives have also become prominent in the hardware business. Thumbnail sketches of the two largest, Cotter and Ace, are given in Exhibit 6-6. In the 1990s, retailer-sponsored cooperatives grew popular among fast-food franchises. For example, a cooperative named Restaurant Services Inc. now handles $1.5 billion in annual food, packaging, and equipment purchases for more than 6,000 Burger King franchisees.

Except for ownership differences, wholesaler-sponsored and retailer-owned contractual systems operate in much the same ways. Members join with the understanding that they will purchase a substantial portion of their merchandise from the group and will standardize retail advertising, identification, and operating procedures as necessary to conform with those of the group to obtain economies and

▶ ▶ ▶

EXHIBIT **6-6** / **Thumbnail Sketches of the Two Largest Retailer-Sponsored Cooperatives in the Hardware Industry**

COTTER & COMPANY, CHICAGO

Cotter & Company is the world's largest 100% Member-owned wholesaler of hardware and related products. Cotter has 15 distribution centers that serve as the axis of a sprawling operation that includes its own manufacturing facilities, a finance company, a real estate agency, and a wholesale subsidiary operating on a cash-and-carry basis. With more than 6,000 Member-retailers, Cotter has put its famous True Value sign up over an estimated one out of every five hardware stores in the country. Its sales are over $2.4 billion. Cotter prides itself on keeping its distribution costs low and on its national advertising program. To join, a retailer must operate a hardware store or know of an investment opportunity in a market without a True Value member, purchase 10 shares of Class A voting stock at $100 each, and agree to minimum purchase requirements on a yearly basis. Cotter has full lines of private-label products in hand tools (Master Mechanic), paint (Tru-Test), plumbing (Master Plumber), electrical (Master Electrician), and outdoor power equipment (Lawn Chief). Cotter manufactures lawn-mowers, paint, lawn and garden wheel goods, and electric heaters in its own factories.

ACE HARDWARE CORPORATION, OAK BROOK, IL

Ace has grown into the second largest dealer-owned distributor in the hardware industry, covering all 50 states and over 50 foreign countries. It delivers goods to over 5,200 retailers. Ace has 14 distribution centers. Sales exceed $2.3 billion. With roughly 42,000 SKUs available out of warehouse, Ace probably offers the broadest product selection of any dealer-owned hardware distributor. Like other dealer-owned distributors, Ace is governed by a board of directors consisting of Ace retailers elected regionally. Ace members order via electronic order entry. Ace offers semiannual dealer shows, ongoing dealer education programs, and regular weekly delivery of merchandise. Warehoused items are available to members at distributor cost plus zero to 10%. (A few promotional items are available at 0%.) Seasonal and promotional items are available at cost plus 6%. Ace dealers can also buy from manufacturers on a drop-ship basis at handling charges ranging between 0 and 2%. Ace offers its dealers purchase analysis reports, preprinted price tickets, bin tags, and other services designed to enable dealers to control costs. Ace requires dealers to invest $5,000 in corporate stock plus a $400 franchise fee.

Source: Information obtained directly, via telephone, from Cotter & Company and Ace Hardware Corporation during January 1995.

better impact. Members usually contribute to a common advertising fund and operate stores under a common name.

Nationally, the share of grocery store sales enjoyed by voluntary and cooperative chains combined is equal to that held by corporate chains, such as Safeway, Kroger, and Winn-Dixie. One of the reasons for their staying power is the "clarity of total offer" made possible by the implementation of systemwide programs. Once customers see the store sign, they understand the outlet's marketing orientation, including the product, service, and atmosphere.[64]

In theory, wholesaler-sponsored voluntary groups should be more effective competitors than retailer-owned cooperatives, primarily because of the difference in channel organization between the two. In the former, a wholesaler can provide strong leadership, because it represents the locus of power within the system. In a retailer-sponsored cooperative, power is diffused throughout the membership, and therefore role specification and resource allocation are more difficult to accomplish. In the voluntary groups, the retail members have relinquished some of their autonomy by making themselves highly dependent on specific wholesalers for expertise. (As will be seen in Chapter 7, the more one party depends on another, the more the latter will be able to influence the former.) In retailer-owned cooperatives, individual members tend to retain more autonomy and thus may tend to depend much less strongly on the supply unit for assistance and direction. In reality, however, some retailer-owned cooperatives have been more successful than voluntary groups. For example, although about 65 hardware wholesalers have organized or participate in major hardware voluntaries, dealer-owned coops account for nearly 48% of wholesale sales. In fact, according to Dwyer and Oh, dealer cooperatives in the hardware industry reflect a higher degree of formalization than voluntaries.[65] To a large degree, this is explained by the fact that the retailers make greater transaction-specific investments in the form of moderate stock ownership, vested supplier-based store identity, and end-of-the-year rebates on purchases that combine to erect significant exit barriers.[66] Dwyer and Oh also observe that:

> Even in the absence of a prominent leadership position, a (dealer) coop can achieve channel coordination, a unified image, and system survival, even growth, through reasoned codes of conduct approved and maintained by the membership. In essence, . . . the system is administered by effective procedures that appeal to the membership. . . . [D]ealers buy into the cooperative's code of conduct and system of member rights.[67]

Before we turn to perhaps the most popular form of contractual vertical marketing system—franchising—we should note that one other type of cooperative has played a major role in distribution in the United States—the farm cooperative. Although the subject of the emergence and growth of farm cooperatives could fill an entire textbook, suffice it to say here that organizations such as Farmland Industries, Associated Milk Producers, Agway, Sunkist, Ocean Spray, and Land O'Lakes have become extremely powerful forces on behalf of their memberships in organizing both the farm equipment and supply market as well as the markets into which farmers sell their produce. Although some farm coops have vertically integrated both backward and forward within their marketing channels, they are primarily wholesalers of goods and services, and they administer the channels that they control with the approval of the farmers who own them.

Another type of cooperative—the consumer cooperative—has also had an impact on distribution. The most famous is Switzerland's Migros, which is organized as a federation of 12 cooperative societies. As many as three-quarters of Switzerland's two million households are owners of the cooperative or so-called "co-operators" (i.e., members of one of the 12 societies). In the U.S., an example is Recreational Equipment, Inc. (REI), a marketer of climbing equipment, with over 900,000 active member-owners.

In Italy, the entire cooperative movement represents one of the biggest businesses in the country. The largest, Lega delle Cooperative (known as the League), is comprised of 11,000 cooperatives employing 200,000 people and doing everything from gutting fish to performing plays. However, many of the League's cooperatives are having difficult times, such as those in retailing and construction, as modern forces challenge their traditional ways of operating.[68]

FRANCHISE SYSTEMS   Franchise systems constitute a major component of the distribution structure of the United States. In 1991 sales of goods and services by all franchising companies totaled nearly $760 billion. Approximately 40% of all U.S. retail sales flow through franchisees or company-owned units in franchise chains. There are roughly half a million establishments in franchise-related businesses.[69] Franchise arrangements take many forms, as shown in Exhibit 6-7. The number and sales of franchised outlets by business category for 1991 are presented in Table 6-1.

EXHIBIT 6-7 / Types of Franchise Systems

Type	Explanation
Territorial franchise	The franchise granted encompasses several counties or states. The holder of the franchise assumes the responsibility for setting up and training individual franchises within his territory and obtains an "override" on all sales in his territory.
Operating franchise	The individual independent franchisee who runs his own franchise. He deals either directly with the parent organization or with the territorial franchise holder.
Mobile franchise	A franchise that dispenses its product from a moving vehicle, which is either owned by the franchisee or leased from the franchisor. Examples include Country Store on Wheels and Snap-On Tools.
Distributorship	The franchisee takes title to various goods and further distributes them to subfranchisees. The distributor has exclusive coverage of a wide geographical area and acts as a supply house for the franchisees who carry the product.
Co-ownership	The franchisor and franchisee share the investment and profits. Examples include Denny's Restaurants.
Co-management	The franchisor controls the major part of the investment. The partner-manager shares profits proportionately. Examples include TraveLodge and Holiday Inn in the hotel and motel business.
Leasing	The franchisor leases the land, buildings, and equipment to franchisees. Leasing is used in conjunction with other provisions.
Licensing	The franchisor licenses the franchisee to use his trademarks and business techniques. The franchisor either supplies the product or provides franchisees with a list of approved suppliers.
Manufacturing	The franchisor grants a franchise to manufacture its product through the use of specified materials and techniques. The franchise distributes the product, using the franchisor's techniques. This method enables a national manufacturer to distribute regionally when distribution costs from central manufacturing facilities are prohibitive. An example of this type is Sealy.

Service   The franchisor describes patterns by which a franchisee supplies a
                 professional service, as exemplified by employment agencies.

Source: Based on Gerald Pintel and Jay Diamond, *Retailing,* 4th ed. (Upper Saddle River, NJ: Prentice-
Hall, 1987), pp. 73–76.

▼ABLE 6-1 **Number and Sales of Franchised Outlets by Type of Franchised System,
                 1991**

	NUMBER OF ESTABLISHMENTS (THOUSANDS)	PERCENTAGE OF TOTAL	SALES (BILLIONS)	PERCENTAGE OF TOTAL
Manufacturer-Retailer	133.5	24.6%	$497.7	65.7%
Automobile and truck dealers	26.6	4.9	354.5	46.8
Gasoline service stations	107.0	19.7	143.2	18.9
Manufacturer-Wholesaler	0.8	.1	28.0	3.7
Soft-drink bottlers	0.8	.1	28.0	3.7
Wholesaler-Retailer	99.2	18.3	46.9	6.2
Automotive products and services	42.2	7.8	15.5	2.1
Retailing (nonfood)	57.0	10.5	31.4	4.1
Business aids and services[a]	69.5	12.8	20.8	2.7
Construction, home improvement maintenance and cleaning services	30.6	5.6	7.1	.9
Convenience grocery stores	17.3	3.1	15.0	2.0
Educational products and services	13.9	2.6	2.3	.3
Restaurants (all types)	103.3	19.0	85.5	11.3
Food retailing (other than restaurants and convenience stores)	25.4	4.6	12.2	1.6
Hotels, motels and campgrounds	11.4	2.1	26.0	3.4
Laundry and dry cleaning services	3.5	.6	0.5	
Recreation, entertainment, and travel	11.6	2.1	4.8	.6
Auto, truck rental services	11.1	2.0	8.0	1.1
Equipment Rental Services	2.9	.5	0.8	.1
Miscellaneous	8.6	1.6	2.6	.3
Total, All Franchising	542.5	100.0%	$757.8	100.0%

[a]Includes employment, tax services, tax preparation accounting, credit, collection, real estate, and printing and copying services, among others.

Source: U.S. Bureau of the Census, *Statistical Abstract of the United States: 1994,* 114th edition (Washington, DC: U.S.
Government Printing Office, 1994), p. 790.

Perhaps one of the most confusing problems in understanding contractual vertical marketing systems is the term *franchise* itself. *Franchising* generally refers to a specific way of getting into business and ensuring a revenue stream once outlets are established. It involves such things as royalty payments, fees, and initial charges that *franchisees* pay to *franchisors*. There are, however, many franchise arrangements that do not involve such cumbersome transactions. In these cases, frequently called "product franchising," a supplier (a manufacturer or a wholesaler, usually) *franchises* (authorizes) retailers or dealers to be part of its system of selective or exclusive distribution. Payment to the organizer of the system is mainly though the gross margins received on the sale of merchandise to the "authorized franchise outlets," although fees for specific services may also be charged. For example, Saturn charges its authorized dealers (called "franchisees" in its offering circular and "retailers" by its salesforce) fees for (1) the initial market survey, (2) facility design and remodeling, (3) training, (4) joint advertising and merchandising, and (5) change of ownership.[70]

Microage stores are authorized franchise outlets for IBM personal computers; in contrast the local McDonald's restaurant is most likely a franchisee of McDonald's Corporation.[71] In both cases the retailers are independent businessmen, and in both cases a contract exists that specifies roles. But the systems are very different in terms of the financial and managerial arrangements that bind the parties. In the former instance, the relationship between Microage and IBM is forged with respect to specific products trademarked by IBM that it sells outright to Microage. In the latter case, McDonald's relationship with its franchisees involves royalties and an entire business format that McDonald's instructs its franchisees to use. Nearly 50% of franchise system sales are made by automobile and truck dealers (see Table 6-1); yet these types of franchises possess only a few of the characteristics of a full-fledged, business-format franchisor/franchisee program. White and Bates argue that auto and truck dealers "are really highly elaborate forms of authorized dealerships and should be excluded when developing a true understanding of the franchising phenomenon."[72]

As pointed out in detail in Chapter 8, all sorts of legislation affects distribution channel strategy. The franchising area has been subject to a great deal of scrutiny over time. Later in this section we mention franchise disclosure rules. The Federal Trade Commission's trade-regulation rule on franchising and business-opportunity ventures, for example, is designed to protect relatively unsophisticated and inexperienced investors by requiring franchisors to disclose to prospective franchise *purchasers* information needed to make informed *investment* decisions. Note that the words *purchasers* and *investment* are emphasized here, because the FTC's rule is basically aimed at franchisor/franchisee relationships, not at authorized franchise dealers. This is why it was logical for the FTC to issue the following statement about wholesaler-sponsored voluntary chains (such as IGA) that "franchise" retail outlets:

> Grocery chains organized by wholesale grocers who supply independent retailers have been exempted from the Federal Trade Commission's franchise rule. . . . The exemption means the presale disclosure requirements of the franchise rule do not apply

when a wholesale grocer offers grocery retailers the chance to join the wholesaler's chain. . . . Unlike franchisors, wholesale grocers offer a chain affiliation on a voluntary basis with or without the other optional services they provide, have no economic incentive to engage in unfair or deceptive practices, and no prior record of such practices.[73]

It is because of this confusion that the remainder of this section is divided into two parts, the first dealing with authorized franchise systems and the other with franchisee/franchisor systems.

AUTHORIZED FRANCHISE SYSTEMS   To maintain some semblance of control over the marketing of their products, suppliers will *authorize* wholesale or retail outlets. Simply put, this means that they are trying to limit the distribution of their products to those outlets that meet some minimum criteria they have established regarding the outlet's degree of participation in one or more of the marketing flows. In these situations, a franchisor authorizes distributors (wholesalers or retailers or both) to sell a product or product line using its trade name for promotional purposes. The focus in product franchising is on what is sold.[74] Examples are authorized tire, auto, computer, major appliance, television, and household furniture dealers whose suppliers have established strong brand names. Such authorization can also be granted at the wholesale level—for example, to soft drink bottlers and to distributors or dealers by manufacturers of electrical and electronics equipment (Square D, Allen Bradley, General Electric), office furniture (Steelcase), machine tools (DoAll), and semiconductors (Texas Instruments, Motorola). Cotter authorizes True Value hardware stores, as we saw in Exhibit 6-6, and Wetterau (a major grocery wholesaler owned by Super Valu) authorizes IGA, Foodland, and Red & White stores in the markets it serves.

Goodyear Tire & Rubber Company distributes its Goodyear-brand automotive replacement tires through independent authorized franchise dealers, company-owned outlets, franchised dealers, and selected mass merchants (e.g., Sears). Approximately 50% of its sales come from the independent dealers for whom Goodyear provides a variety of services, including the following:

Expertise and training on issues such as financing, architecture, wholesaling, operations, and merchandising.

Certified Auto Service, which allows dealers to attend training classes and become certified in auto services.

The Goodyear Business Management System, a computer system to help dealers with inventory and accounting.

National and regional advertising to support dealer sales.

Research on market trends, such as information on the popularity of each tire, by size, in a given market.

Assistance in outlet location, either in selling company-owned outlets to independent dealers or in avoiding locations for company-owned outlets that would compete with dealers.[75]

When they are first admitted to the Goodyear distribution system, however, dealers are franchised in a unique way. For three years, Goodyear provides the new entrant with training in operations, finance, and other aspects of the business. As explained by a Goodyear executive:

> Goodyear's franchises are designed somewhat differently from those of other companies who have become franchisors. Rather than trying to earn money from franchising per se, Goodyear simply wants to use the channel to move tires, and its fee structures are set up to facilitate this objective. Goodyear requires no franchise fee and has only two requirements of the prospective franchisee: (1) an unincumbered $50,000 for working capital and (2) a good track record in business (it does not want these outlets to fail). As for continuing fees, there is only a small fee on sales, to cover the cost to Goodyear of the data processing, accounting, and counseling services for the franchisees.[76]

After three years, the dealers then become "normal" independent dealers. The number of so-called franchised dealers is kept small, that is, less than 10% of the total dealer base. (Additional examples of authorized franchise systems are given in Exhibit 6-8.)

▶ EXHIBIT 6-8 / Examples of Authorized Franchise Systems

▶ ▶ ▶ **AT&T NETWORK SYSTEMS**

AT&T Network Systems National Sales Division, headquartered in Morristown, New Jersey, has established a nationwide network of authorized AT&T distributors. AT&T distributors have AT&T products in inventory, backed by the technical expertise and services capable of meeting the demands of virtually all industries. The distributors provide value-added services, 24-hour ordering, and credit terms tailored to their customers. The distributor network offers "one-stop shopping" for AT&T copper and fiber optic cable and apparatus, transmission equipment, office voice and data equipment, and consumer products. Many distributors offer such services as material management, just-in-time inventory, cutting cables to length, repackaging, respooling, bus and tag services, connectorizing, stripping, palletizing, and restamping.

HEWLETT-PACKARD

Hewlett-Packard (H-P) uses authorized value-added resellers (VARs) to sell to specific vertical markets, such as medical practices, education, aerospace, and law firms. VARs are evaluated on their credit rating, vertical market focus, quality of sales force, marketing programs, technical expertise, and overall value added. All VARs sign the same one-year contract with a six-month grace period, giving them 18 months to meet their quotas. H-P offers VARs various leases and installment contracts. It also offers direct customer financing for H-P products sold through the VAR channel. H-P assigns a value-added sales representative to each VAR account as a local contact. VARs' software solutions are promoted to the H-P direct salesforce via newsletters, success stories, catalogs, application notes, and training seminars. Joint seminars, trade show loaner systems, mailings, and direct marketing activities promote reseller solutions to end-users. The H-P Executive Training Series offers training for VAR company employees in marketing, business, product, and sales skills.

Suppliers can also include, as part of their authorized franchise network, outlets that are already part of an ongoing "independent" franchisor/franchisee relationship. Thus, Entre is the name of a franchisee/franchisor system of computer stores. IBM has authorized Entre to sell its personal computers. Therefore, IBM has a dual channel management problem: it must work closely with each Entre store to make certain that the appropriate service outputs are being delivered to end-users *and* it must work with the franchisor, who plays a critical role in the performance of the franchisees via the various programs the franchisor administers and the incentives it establishes. To make certain it can control its own destiny, however, IBM has developed contracts specifying role relationships with the *individual* stores in franchising systems such as Entre's and Microage's. It has also retained the right *not* to authorize individual stores within a franchising system if the stores do not meet its criteria for admission to its authorized dealer network.

Like an administered vertical marketing system, establishing an authorized franchise system is another means available to suppliers for guaranteeing, in the absence of financial ownership, that channel members will provide the appropriate type and level of service outputs to end-users. A major way in which organizers of authorized franchise systems have achieved this end is to specify or impose restrictions on how channels members can operate. These policies or restraints deal with market and customer coverage, products, prices, and promotion and are addressed in detail in Chapter 8. It should always be remembered however, that even if it were desirable, it is impossible to write contracts governing the behavior of channel members covering all contingencies. Channel management is, of necessity, imperfect and open-ended. There are, in fact, no guarantees, even with "hard" vertical integration.

FRANCHISOR/FRANCHISEE SYSTEMS   A franchisor/franchisee system is defined here as an entire business format in which one firm (the franchisor) licenses a number of outlets (franchisees) to market a product or service and engage in a business developed by the franchisor using the latter's trade names, trademarks, service marks, know-how, and methods of doing business. In contrast to product franchising, the focus is on how the business is run.[77] The franchisor's primary compensation comes in the form of royalties and/or fees. While circumscribed by law, as pointed out in Chapter 8, the franchisor may also sell the products, sell or lease the equipment, and/or sell or lease the premises necessary to the operation. For example, McDonald's insists that all of its units purchase from approved suppliers, provides building and design specifications, provides or helps locate financing for its franchisees, and issues quality standards that each unit must abide by in order to hold its franchise.

Franchisor/franchisee systems are present in almost all business fields, as indicated in Exhibit 6-9. It can be readily seen that the franchise system covers a wide variety of goods and services—accounting services, auto accessories, auto rentals, campgrounds, computer services, dry cleaning, employment agencies, fast foods, convenience food markets, and vending machine operations, among others. Like entrepreneurs, franchisees invest their money and own their businesses, but they don't have to develop a new product, create a new company, or test the market. In

▶**E**XHIBIT **6-9** / **Business Classification of Franchise Organizations, with Representative Examples**

▶ ▶ ▶

Accounting and Tax
Services
  H&R Block, Inc.
Advertising Services
  Money Mailer Inc.
Amusement and Recreation
  Kampgrounds of
  America
Athletic Facilities/Sporting
Goods
  The Athlete's Foot
Auto/Truck Trailer Rentals
  Budget Rent-a-Car
Automotive Products and
Services
  AAMCO Transmissions,
  Inc.
Bath Closet
  California Closet
  Company
Beauty Products and
Services
  The Body Shop
  International PLC
Beverages
  Gloria Jeans Coffee Bean
Book Stores
  The Little Professor Book
  Center
Building and Remodeling
Products and Services
  Ever Dry Waterproofing
Business Aids and Services
  HQ Business Center
Candy/Popcorn/Snack
Shops
  Karmelkorn Shoppes
Car Washes
  Mermaid Car Wash
Carpet Upholstery
  Duraclean
Carry-outs/Drive-in
Restaurants
  Chequers

Childcare
  Goddard Early Learning
  Center
Children's Products and
Services
  Gymboree
Cleaning Supplies and
Services
  Servicemaster
Clothing Stores
  Fashion, Ltd.
Computer/Electronics
Sales and Services
  Radio Shack
Convenience Stores
  7-Eleven
Decorative Products
  Ben Franklin Variety and
  Crafts
Donut/Bakery/Cookie
Shops
  Dunkin' Donuts
Educational Products and
Services
  Sylvan Learning Corp.
Employment/Personnel
Services
  Time Temporaries
Entertainment
  Arthur Murray Dance
  Studio
Fast-Food
  McDonald's Corporation
Financial Services
  Check-X-Change
Florists
  Florida Tropical
Formalwear Rental
  Gingiss Formalware
Hair Salons and Services
  Supercuts
Health Aids and Services
  United Surgical Centers
Health and Fitness
  General Nutrition

Home Furnishing Stores
  Ethan Allen
Home Improvement and
Hardware Stores
  Coast to Coast Stores, Inc.
Hotels/Motels
  Holiday Inn Hotels
Ice Cream/Yogurt Shops
  Baskin-Robin's Ice Cream
  and Yogurt
Laundry and Dry Cleaning
  Duds'N Suds
Lawn and Garden Supplies
and Services
  Servicemaster Lawncare
Maid and Personal Services
  The Maids International
Optical Services
  Pearle Vision, Inc.
Pet Sales and Supplies
  Docktor Pet Center
Pizza Shops
  Domino's Pizza
Printing Photocopying
Services
  Pip Printing International
Real Estate
  Century 21 Real Estate
  Corporation
Restaurants
  Big Boy Restaurants
Shipping Packaging
  Mail Boxes Etc. U.S.A.
Sign Products and Services
  Mr. Sign
Transportation Services
  Valet Park International
Travel
  Carlson Travel Network
Video/Audio Services
  Blockbuster Video
Weight Control
  Jenny Craig Weight Loss
  Centers

Source: Susan Boyles Martin, *Worldwide Franchise Directory* (Detroit, MI: Gale Research Inc., 1991).

return, the franchisees give up some independence and pay franchisors anywhere from 1.5 to 12% of gross sales, as well as sometimes hefty initial fixed franchise fees.

Most of the growth in franchising in recent years has come from business format franchising (vs. product franchising) in which the franchisor rules nearly every aspect of the enterprise, from an outlet's appearance to worker training.[78] However, holding a franchise or operating under a franchise name apparently has no connection at all with chances of entrepreneurial survival.[79]

Rationale for Franchising. Franchise systems represent an extreme safeguard against market failure, short of outright ownership. That is, through the stipulations in the contracts they sign, the parties purposely subvert and circumscribe the marketplace existing between them so as to manage transaction costs. Schedules are set, precautions are instituted, programs are constructed, and commitments are made so that the end-user can receive the beneficial outcome of the (hopefully) synergistic efforts of the franchisor and franchisee.

Franchise systems facilitate the flow of critical market information between franchisors and franchisees so that consumer preferences, complaints, and purchasing intentions can more quickly be reflected in marketing and production planning. Routinizing information flows is also important when it is necessary to monitor compensation claims, such as those for warranty work. Uniform accounting and reporting procedures and greater access to information permit effective monitoring of the entire franchise system.[80]

The franchise system also provides needed investment incentives by making substantial sales, service, and management assistance readily available to potential franchisees; by harmonizing interdependent investment decision making through realignments of business risks; and by reducing opportunities for the exploitation of invested capital by free-rider franchisees. For smaller companies, a major reason for establishing a franchise system is to finance a faster rate of growth.

> ... the growing company does not have to buy or lease new outlets or finance inventory. It also gains from bulk buying of products, services, and advertising, and has lower head office overheads; it needs no distribution system and has no sales force to manage.[81]

Even for large companies, franchising is often a cost effective means to grow. Marks and Spencer, the U.K.-based retailer, has been rapidly expanding its network of franchises in small markets (e.g., Bahamas, Norway, Israel, and Singapore) with almost no capital investment on its part.[82]

Finally, and perhaps most importantly, a key benefit from franchising is the creation of proper incentives. As explained by Paul H. Rubin,

> ... if the outlet is run by someone who gets all of the profits, as does an owner, then there is a proper incentive for efficient operation. A franchise is exactly such an en-

deavor: The manager of the outlet is the owner and has residual rights in all the profits, so that there is an incentive for efficient operation. This improvement in incentives for efficient management is the ultimate gain from franchising.[83]

Managers who are not owners but rather employees have a reduced incentive to supervise an outlet efficiently because they do not receive the profits associated with maintaining labor productivity. In the language of economists, these managers tend to "shirk"; therefore, monitoring of their behavior by headquarters is extremely important. Such extensive monitoring is, theoretically at least, not required in a franchise system because of the appropriate alignment of incentives. This reasoning may account for why approximately 90% of McDonald's U.S. outlets are run by franchisees, up from 70% 15 years ago. (The percentage is, however, lower abroad, especially in developing nations.)

The appeal of franchising is so high that some companies are converting existing administered or vertically integrated systems to franchised (contractual) systems. For example, Snap-on Tools Corp. sold its tools through independent dealers and sales representatives since shortly after the firm's founding in 1920. However, on January 1, 1992, the company began signing on all new dealers as franchisees and gave existing dealers the option to convert if they wished. Motivated in part by the fact that some dealers had accused Snap-on of bad faith and misrepresentation in assigning sales territories, the company explained that:

> Under the franchise system, there is a much more detailed disclosure of the rights and obligations of both the company and dealers . . . . Essentially, the dealer's operation will remain the same. But we'll be able to have a little more control. Now, we're at arm's length. Each dealer is an independent businessman. With a franchise operation, the company can make sure that our proven sales methods are followed. In today's world, a dealer can do what he wants. Under a franchise, he has to follow our rules. We will set certain standards that they will have to abide by. Our main concern is to assure his success."[84]

Likewise, Eastern Lobby Shops (a newsstand operator), Ipco Corp. (an optical-products retailer), General Nutrition Inc. (a vitamin retailer), and Movie Superstore Inc. (a video outlet operator) are examples of companies that also converted to franchises, but, in contrast to Snap-on, they converted from wholly owned (vertically integrated) outlets. Some of the reasons given for the changes were:

> "No one will take care of customers like an owner-operator will."

> "Many of the units sold were underperformers in that they really weren't meeting their potential. Now they are. Instead of having employees managing the stores, you have partners running them."

> "It's more difficult for a company to run operations that are average or below average, while a franchisee is there every day. He's going to make it work."

> "By franchising and collecting a royalty, your investment is less. Of course, your returns are lower, too, but you've shifted the risk of running the business to the franchisee."[85]

According to a study by The Naisbitt Group commissioned by the International Franchise Association, sales by business-format franchises will likely reach $1.3 trillion in the year 2010.[86] The startling growth of franchising will take place as a result of five emerging trends:

■ The transition from a manufacturing-based to a service economy. Franchising has long been at the forefront of the service sector.

■ Consumer preference for convenience and consistent quality—two of the principal strengths of franchising.

■ A rise in consumer demand for specialty items.

■ The increasing numbers of women and minorities in franchising. This trend will usher into the franchising arena new markets, new products, and a largely untapped management pool.

■ Franchising abroad. Franchising is quickly becoming an export business.

The rationale for franchising has extended to postcommunist Europe. For many foreign companies, franchising has been the only way to side-step the run-down, state-controlled distribution systems, which had no incentive to deliver products on time, if at all. With its own network and its own shops, a franchisor can be sure that its products actually get onto shelves. Also, franchisees who have been trained by franchisors in Western sales and service practices have an edge over local competitors. Quality and price can be controlled more effectively. And, as it does everywhere, franchising lowers the investment risk in uncertain markets. It can often bring brand recognition, and thus sales, at a far lower cost than direct investment or joint ventures. Hungary, Poland, the former Czechoslovakia, and what once was East Germany have been particularly fertile territories for franchisor cultivation in this respect.[87]

As David Warsh points out, even the Mafia is organized as a series of franchises, created by entrepreneurs, sharing a brand name and operating as a cartel to discipline errant members and protect investment in the network.

> Its members even cooperate in the development of a highly recognizable trademark—all the mannerisms associated with the "wise guy," from the snazzy clothes to the slow, hip-swinging walk that Sicilians denote by the verb *annacare* to the deliberately oblique talk captured so perfectly by Marlon Brando in *The Godfather*.[88]

Modes of Operation. All franchisees are expected to provide a continuing market for a franchisor's product or service. The product or service offering is, in theory, differentiated from those offered by conventional outlets by its *consistent* quantity and quality and its strong promotion. Through its market- and image-building promotional strategy, which is instituted at an early stage of a franchise system's development, a franchisor hopes to gain automatic and immediate acceptance from prospective franchisees and the public.

Franchisors provide both *initial* and *continuous* services to their franchisees. *Initial services* include:

- Market survey and site selection

- Facility design and layout

- Lease negotiation advice

- Financing advice

- Operating manuals

- Management training programs

- Franchisee employee training

Although the *amount* of involvement with franchisees is usually high, a franchisor's provision of an initial service indicates nothing about the *depth* of its involvement. For example, over 95% of all franchised outlets are built from the ground up. That is, similar and ongoing businesses did not previously exist on the current franchisee's location. However, the degree of involvement a franchisor exercises in site location and development varies widely. On the one hand, McDonald's does all site analysis and most land acquisition and development; on the other hand, Budget Rent-A-Car merely assigns a territory and allows the franchisee to build where he/she pleases, subject to franchisor review and advice. Also, franchisee employee training varies in length based on the complexity of the operation and the degree to which the franchisor uses this service to enhance the stability of a franchise. For instance, training by Hilton Hotels is a major selling point of its franchise program. In fact, Hilton provides such a host of training services that it never fully escapes the personnel difficulties inherent in company-owned, service-related outlets. As an example of the comprehensiveness of some initial services, information from Southland Corporation, the franchisor of 7-Eleven Convenience Food Stores, is reproduced in Appendix 6A.

Continuous services include:

- Field supervision

- Merchandising and promotional materials

- Management and employee retraining

- Quality inspection

- National advertising

- Centralized planning

- Market data and guidance

- Auditing and record keeping

- Management reports

- Group insurance plans

Almost all franchisors have a continuous program of field services. Field representatives visit the franchise outlet to aid the franchisee in everyday operation, check the quality of product and service, and monitor performance.

All franchisees are usually required to report monthly or semimonthly on key elements of their operations—weekly sales, local advertising, employee turnover, profits, and other financial and marketing information. This regular reporting is intended to facilitate the various financial, operating, and marketing control procedures.

As might be expected, the reaction of franchisees to field services and operating controls is not always positive. Franchisees are independent businesspersons, even though they have signed contractual agreements with franchisors. When conflict over supervision exists within their systems, franchisors have tended to rely on their field representatives to act as channel diplomats. However, these representatives not only are responsible for field service and liaison with franchisees but also must recruit additional franchisees. Complaints are often heard that the franchisor is providing too little attention to franchisees' management problems, especially when the field representatives have too many conflicting responsibilities.

Another source of conflict is the fact that many franchisors own a number of their outlets, and some of these outlets compete with those owned by franchisees. For example, in 1994, General Nutrition Cos., the largest vitamin retailer in the U.S., had approximately 700 franchisee and 1,300 company-owned stores. Franchisees complained that the company favored company-owned stores by supplying products to them more often, while making franchisees wait. They also asserted that company-owned stores engaged in price wars, thereby squeezing franchise margins.[89]

There are, however, a number of reasons why franchisors may own a portion of their outlets.[90] First, ownership of certain outlets may be necessary because of bankruptcy of the franchisee (the franchisors may be the only available source of funds for ownership in these cases). Second, franchisor-owned and -operated units serve as models for the rest of the system and can be used for research, training, and experimentation purposes. Third, such units may accelerate network growth, especially during the initial development period. Fourth, wholly owned units may be profitable. They will also permit the franchisor firsthand insight into day-to-day operating problems. Fifth, owned outlets may facilitate establishing a ceiling on prices. They may also assure a minimum level of demand for suppliers. Finally, court decisions and legislation restricting how franchisors deal with franchisees may force franchisors to own more and more of their outlets if they wish to maintain strong control over the operations of the system as a whole.

In addition to disagreements over supervision and company-owned outlets, there are lots of conflicts between franchisors and franchisees over contract restrictions on competition after termination, inaccurate revenue projections, and fulfillment of obligations regarding managerial and promotional support.[91] Disagreements also involve territorial, remodeling, and size-of-royalty issues. For example, Taco Bell more than quintupled its so-called "points of access" from 4,500 in 1992 to nearly 25,000 in 1994 by selling its food products at kiosks and movable carts in malls, corner gasoline stations, supermarkets, and in school-lunch programs as well as via its traditional restaurants. It hopes to have in excess of 200,000 distribution points by 2001. Baskin-Robbins has spread to airports, colleges, convenience stores, and spaces in other franchisors' outlets.[92] All of this activity is creating enormous friction between franchisors and existing franchisees. The founders of Subway sandwich shops and TCBY Enterprises (yogurt shops) have been sued for opening new outlets so close to existing ones that the existing owners claimed they could not make a living.[93] McDonald's has been known to negotiate compensation agreements for some owners faced with encroachment from a new store or to minimize the potential for conflict by offering them the new franchise.[94] Unlike most chains, however, McDonald's grants its franchises for a specific address or location rather than for a territory; there is nothing in its contracts to prevent the company from following Taco Bell's lead.

Kentucky Fried Chicken, Holiday Inn, and International Dairy Queen have faced major problems over getting their franchisees to invest in remodeling and upgrading activities.[95] And, at one time, ComputerLand franchisees threatened to stop paying royalties and leave the network if ComputerLand's royalty structure and key management were not changed.

> Price erosion had driven the gross margins of ComputerLand dealers to the 25 percent range, down from the 40 percent levels. . . . Concurrently, rising costs drove profits from ten percent down to break-even. These reductions did not stop ComputerLand from requiring franchisees to pay nine percent royalties on all sales. As a result, franchisees were no longer making money and were losing their competitive edge to one-tier, company-owned chains.[96]

Underlying all of these sources of contention is the fact that franchisor–franchisee economic goals are basically incompatible. Franchisors earn their money from franchisees' top line (gross sales volume), whereas franchisees earn their money from the bottom line (net profits). Nevertheless, as franchisees become more and more sophisticated and achieve countervailing power, they have made it more and more difficult for franchisors to overwhelm them.[97]

Sources of Franchisor Revenue. Sources of franchisor revenue include:

1. *Initial Franchise Fees.* Many franchisors charge an initial fee to new franchisees. The fee ranges from $1,000 to $150,000, with the mode falling between $10,000 and $25,000. The fee is charged to cover the franchisor's expenses for site location, training, setting

of operating controls, and other initial services as well as developmental costs in building the system. Initial fees tend to rise as a franchise becomes more successful.

2. *Royalty Fees.* Franchisors charge a royalty fee or commission. The fee is usually based on the gross value of a franchisee's sales volume. Five percent of gross sales is the most common royalty agreement in franchising. Some franchisors require a minimum payment of $150 to $200 per month. In certain cases the royalty rate decreases as sales volume increases, whereas in others the royalty fee is a flat rate regardless of the sales volume. Some franchisors collect a royalty on a unit-of-sale basis. For example, motel franchisors charge a fee per room; soft ice cream franchisors charge a fee for each gallon of mix sold to the franchisee; car wash equipment franchisors charge a fee per car washed.

3. *Advertising Fees.* To achieve name recognition for their franchises, franchisors must advertise, and the funds for doing so are collected from the franchisees in the form of advertising fees. McDonald's spends over one-half billion dollars on advertising a year, and most of this is funded by charging franchisees 4% of gross annual sales. Table 6-2 gives a profile of the some of the various financial requirements for a franchise, including advertising fees for individual units.

4. *Sales of Products.* Some franchisors function as wholesalers in that they supply franchisees with raw materials and finished products. Other franchisors manufacture their products; for example, a significant amount of Coca-Cola's revenue is derived from the sale of its soft drink syrups to its franchised bottlers. In some cases, the franchise company sells the equipment needed by the franchisee.

5. *Rental and Lease Fees.* The franchise company often leases the building, equipment, and fixtures used in its outlets. Some franchise contracts involve an escalator clause that requires the franchisee to increase his/her lease payment as sales volume increases.

6. *License Fees.* The franchisee sometimes is required to pay for the use and display of the franchisor's trademark. The license fee is used more in conjunction with industrial franchises, where a local manufacturer is licensed to use a particular patent or process.

7. *Management Fees.* In a few cases, franchisees are charged fees for consulting services received from the franchisor, such as management reports and training.

Clearly, arrangements vary across systems. For example, the 7-Eleven chain includes more than 3,000 franchised units in the U.S., where Southland Corp., the franchisor, is the largest operator of convenience stores. Franchisees operate 7-Eleven stores constructed by Southland; the company serves as landlord and also as accountant. In return, it receives sometimes as much as 58% of each store's gross profit. This is more than most other franchisors receive, but few others promise or provide as many services, as shown in Appendix 6A. 7-Eleven's initial franchise fees are also comparatively low—one reason the chain often appeals to potential franchisees with little cash.[98]

Applicants for McDonald's franchises must pass a two-year screening process, which includes working in a store and training, before gaining final approval. Then, they must give McDonald's $45,000 and sign a 20-year contract that guarantees the company a royalty of 4% of sales, another 8.5% for rent, and 4% for advertising.[99]

Despite the fee and royalty structures in franchisee/franchisor systems, many new franchisors grossly underestimate the amount of money it takes to build a network.

They believe the franchise fee will be a windfall. They also rely on royalty income too early in the game. The franchise fee, they soon learn, is needed to cover the costs

TABLE 6-2 **Profile of the Franchise Offering**

TOTAL INITIAL INVESTMENT FOR FRANCHISEE

	Lowest 25%	Median	Lowest 75%	High	Average
Individual	$35,000	$98,000	$150,000	$4,200,000	$148,848[a]

[a]Excludes 3 cases with extremely high responses

FRANCHISE FEE

	Lowest 25%	Median	Lowest 75%	High	Average
Individual	$12,900	$20,000	$25,000	$100,000[b]	$21,202[b]

[b]Excludes 1 case with extremely high response

ROYALTIES FOR INDIVIDUAL UNIT

Percentage of Gross Sales	Percentage of Respondents
0.0–2.0	3.3
2.1–4.0	25.1
4.1–6.0	47.9
6.1–8.0	13.7
Above 8.0	10.0

ADVERTISING FEES FOR INDIVIDUAL UNIT

Percentage of Gross Sales	Percentage of Respondents
0.0–2.0	75.0
2.1–4.0	17.5
4.1–6.0	6.5
6.1–8.0	1.0
Above 8.0	0.0

Source: Helen La Van and Patrick J. Boroian, *Franchise Marketing & Sales Survey 1990–1991* (Chicago: DePaul University and Francorp, 1990), p. 12.

of backup systems for franchisees—particularly marketing materials and advisory services. And in general royalties do not cover the franchisor's operating and selling expenses until a large network of units with good sales has been built up.[100]

For example, site selection generally costs $1,000 to $3,000 for a local or regional franchisor whose personnel don't have to travel long distances. Lease negotiation and assistance with construction contracts may run a few thousand dollars more. Management training for franchisees and their key people can run from $500 to $10,000 per franchisee depending on the amount of instruction involved and the sophistication of the training facility. Salaries and travel costs for two people to provide hands-on help for two weeks during the opening of a new unit will run roughly $4,000. According to Robert T. Justis, director of Louisiana State University's International Franchise Center, "most franchisors are going to accumulate losses of $250,000 to $600,000 in the first two years."[101]

Examples of start-up costs on the part of *franchisees* are shown in Table 6-3. Unfortunately, a number of ex-executives from major corporations who decided to purchase franchises have found that the size of the investment and the entrepreneurial skills required to be a successful franchisee were well beyond their initial expectations.[102]

Controversies Surrounding Franchising. Business-format franchising seems to have generated a great deal of attention not simply because of the success of such companies as McDonald's but because there seems to be a history of shady operators running around selling franchises to naive individuals.[103] Also, franchise agreements (the "contract" in contractual vertical marketing systems) are frequently one-sided in favor of the franchisor. The Federal Trade Commission and a number of states have taken a hand in regulating franchising, in addition to relying on the antitrust laws (see Chapter 8) that govern channel relationships. The controversies have generated so much heat that a staff report by the Small Business Committee of the U.S. House of Representatives has proposed developing federal standards of good cause to govern franchise terminations, renewals, and transfers. It also has called for guidelines defining when part of a franchisee's investment should be refunded if a franchise agreement ends.[104]

The FTC enforces a trade regulation rule entitled "Disclosure Requirement and Prohibitions Concerning Franchising and Business Opportunity Ventures." The rule requires franchisors to furnish disclosure documents to prospective franchisees, including financial statements of franchisors; the names and addresses of at least 10 franchisees nearest to the proposed location; litigation and bankruptcy disclosures by the franchisor and key executives; and details about the franchise relationship (including any financing assistance, expansion plans in the area, information about franchisees that have been terminated, and conditions under which the relationship can be ended). To meet the FTC's definition of a franchise, three conditions must be satisfied; a company must:

1. distribute goods or services identified by a trademark;
2. offer significant assistance and exercise control over the franchisees' operations; and
3. require a franchise fee or payment of $500 or more in the first six months of operation.

What drives franchisors crazy, though, is the fact that state franchise laws take precedence over federal regulations, except in rare instances where the federal rules are the stricter of the two. Fifteen states require franchisors to register disclosure statements with them, and because the requirements about disclosure often

▶ **TABLE 6-3** **Examples of Franchisee Start-Up Costs[a] by Business Classification of Franchises**

	LOWER UNIT COST	MODERATE UNIT COST	HIGHER UNIT COST
Amusement and Recreation			
Kampgrounds of America	$343,000		$1,345,000
Athletic Facilities/Sporting Goods			
The Athlete's Foot	139,500		284,500
Automotive Products and Services			
Meineke Discount Muffler Shops, Inc.	94,622		119,368
Car Washes			
Mermaid Car Washes	1,735,000		1,845,000
Carry Outs/Drive-in Restaurants			
Checkers	253,000		344,000
Childcare			
Goddard Early Learning Center		$166,000	
Computer/Electronics Sales and Services			
ComputerLand Corporation	162,300		312,500
Decorative Products and Services			
Ben Franklin Variety and Crafts	652,000		776,000
Fast Food			
Popeyes Famous Fried Chicken & Biscuits	164,200		203,000
Formalware Rental			
Gingiss Formalwear	63,200	98,700	179,200
Hair Salons and Services			
Supercuts	93,400		204,700
Home Improvement and Hardware Stores			
Coast to Coast Stores, Inc.	210,500		597,500
Hotels/Motels			
Holiday Inn Hotels	14,103,200		31,609,200
Ice Cream/Yogurt Shops			
I Can't Believe It's Yogurt	124,000		182,500
Laundry and Dry Cleaning			
Duds'N Suds	177,500		
Optical Services			
Sterling Optical	275,000		
Pet Sales and Supplies			
Docktor Pet Center	139,800		197,500
Pizza Shops			
Godfather's Pizza (full service)	136,500		291,000
Printing/Photocopying Services			
Pip Printing International		167,900	
Restaurants			
Pepe's Mexican Restaurants	140,000		265,000
Shipping/Packaging/Mailing Services			
Mail Boxes Etc. U.S.A.	43,035		76,280

[a]Costs generally include initial franchise fee, site improvement major equipment purchase, opening inventory, grand opening advertising, and miscellaneous costs.
Source: Susan Boyles Martin, *Worldwide Franchise Directory*, (Detroit, MI: Gale Research Inc., 1991).

vary from state to state, the task of opening up "shop" on a nationwide basis is slightly to the left of massive.[105]

▶ COMBINATIONS OF "HARD" AND "SOFT" VERTICAL INTEGRATION

From the discussion in Chapter 5 about channel-design issues, one fact should have become abundantly clear—because there is no such phenomenon as a perfectly homogeneous market for any good or service (i.e., all markets can be segmented), it is extremely unlikely that one unique channel of distribution or single pathway to the marketplace is going to satisfy the service output needs of all existing and potential customer segments. This is why personal computers are sold via value-added resellers, direct mail, computer superstores, direct salesforces, office products dealers, and a host of other channels. It is also why refrigerators, power tools, insurance, clothing, and virtually everything else are sold through multiple channels. Because of this, organizations that are thoughtful and insightful in designing their marketing channels have constructed systems comprised of combinations of both "hard" and "soft" vertical integration. These combinations are often structured somewhat differently. In some cases, they are so-called "hybrid channels" and, in others, they are "plural systems." They are both aimed at accommodating, in cost effective ways, the heterogeneity in the marketplace.

Hybrid Channels

Reinforcing the general theme of this book, Rowland Moriarty has observed that a major challenge to management is to decide what "bridges" should be built between the company and its customers, for example, direct sales, national account manager, distributors, industrial stores, field service organizations, direct mail, and/or telemarketing.[106] Historically, many companies "bridged" to customers via one channel: a direct sales force. As Moriarty points out, however, "with direct sales-force costs escalating over the past 10 years to an average $300 per hour of face time, many firms, for example, have added telemarketing—averaging $17 per hour—either as a new channel, or as some type of channel support mechanism."[107]

The strategic blending of multimethod and multichannel approaches that encompass both direct and indirect bridges to the customer is what Moriarty terms "hybrid marketing systems." Specific selling tasks (e.g., lead generation, qualifying leads, presale contact, closing sales, account management, and postsales and service) can, for example, be assumed by different selling and service mechanisms depending upon which is most cost effective in performing them. Direct mail might be best for lead generation, telemarketing for qualifying sales, national account management for presales contact and closing sales to large accounts, and so forth. The same type of thinking can be applied to logistics, financing, and credit and collections activities. In any case, the type of mechanism to be used may vary depending on the specific task to perform, even though the customer is the same across the various tasks. This is what is meant by "hybrid marketing."

Plural Systems

The different ways of categorizing channels outlined in this chapter are, as discussed previously, modes of organizing transactions or governance structures.[108] As explored by Heide, governance encompasses initiation, termination, and ongoing relationship maintenance between channel members.[109] It includes elements of establishing and structuring channel relationships as well as aspects of monitoring and enforcement.

The ways of governing or organizing channels can be combined in numerous variations, such as when franchisors own some of their own units ("hard" vertical integration) and franchise others ("soft" vertical integration). The use of different channels for the same product by one company is called "dual distribution." Each channel will likely be subject to different modes of coordination. A direct salesforce may, for example, be mainly coordinated by authority; authorized franchise dealers by authority and trust; outsourcing more by trust than authority; and freeform, arms-length relationships by price mechanisms.

Bradach and Eccles suggest that these three mechanisms—authority, trust, and price—can be combined in numerous ways, thereby producing coexisting transactional forms.[110] Different forms provide different service outputs and, thereby, can assist firms in meeting the needs of heterogeneous markets. An example of some of the additional payoffs to maintaining plural systems was provided earlier when discussing why franchisors own some of their outlets. They gain the benefits of "hard" and "soft" integration (along with the costs). Both Goodyear and Super Valu manage plural systems, as indicated earlier in this chapter.

A major problem with maintaining plural systems is the fact that conflict is likely to occur, especially if the different channels compete for the same customers. The emergence and management of conflict in marketing channels are topics covered in detail in Chapter 7.

Finally, it is important to understand that the three coordinating mechanisms (price, authority, and trust) are often used simultaneously *within* a channel as well as *across* channels. As Heide points out:

> *Within a given relationship*, processes from different governance forms can be combined in different fashions. For example, franchisors frequently combine extensive socialization efforts (relying on trust) with explicit . . . monitoring (relying on authority). Thus, many actual channel relationships can be viewed most appropriately as (mixed) organizational forms."[111]

Prescriptives for the effective use of authority, trust, and price in managing marketing channel relationships is the main topic of the next chapter of this text.

▶ **SUMMARY AND CONCLUSIONS**

In organizing marketing channels to deliver the service outputs desired by end-users, a major concern is whether it is better to "make" or to "buy" distribution activities. Relying on market efficiencies is always preferred. Unfortunately, markets sometimes fail because the transaction costs associated with dealing across them elevate to such an extent that vertical integration by ownership (so-called "hard" vertical integration) becomes a more efficient and effective way of getting the job done.

In systems using "hard" vertical integration, channel members assume financial ownership with regard to one or more of the marketing flows over at least two separate levels (e.g., manufacturing and wholesaling) of distribution. The key tradeoffs in instituting "hard" vertical integration are the investment required plus the flexibility lost, on the one hand, versus the control secured over marketing activities of channel members plus the operating economies gained, on the other. The general rule of thumb developed by modern management strategists is that a firm should own (or insource) those core activities that provide it with its differential advantage in the marketplace. It should outsource all other activities.

Outsourcing has taken a variety of forms, however, from contracting with suppliers or distributors for specific services, components, and products to facilities management to modular networks to virtual corporations. However, similar to freeform channel arrangements that are not purposively organized, outsourcing is subject to market failure unless adequate safeguards are installed. This is one of the main reasons why more and more organizations are turning to the use of administered and contractual vertical marketing systems.

Vertical marketing systems have emerged as significant forms of channel organization. They represent, for the most part, sophisticated attempts by management to achieve the benefits of "hard" vertical integration without some of its costs. Administered vertical marketing systems are those in which marketing activities are coordinated through the use of programs developed by one or a limited number of firms. Administrative strategies are dependent for their success on the effective use of influence strategies in the development of cooperation, trust, and commitment, subjects addressed in the next chapter.

Contractual vertical marketing systems are those in which independent firms at different channel levels integrate their programs on a contractual basis to achieve systemic economies and increased market impact. They include, among other forms of organization, wholesaler-sponsored voluntary groups, retailer-owned cooperative groups, and franchise systems. By virtue of the use of legitimate power in their formulation, contractual systems tend to be more tightly knit than administered systems.

From a managerial perspective, vertical marketing systems appear to offer a series of advantages. They employ a systemic approach and are committed to scientific decision making while engendering channel member loyalty and network stability. Tasks are routinized, and economies of standardization are likely. Because a locus of power is available and used in a positive manner, it is possible to gain at least some control over the cost and quality of the functions performed by various channel members. Furthermore, inherent within systems management is the notion that the channel, taken as a whole, is the relevant unit of competition. Only by adopting a systems perspective and by building effective linkages and relationships throughout the entire channel can organizations achieve the impact in the marketplace they seek.

DISCUSSION QUESTIONS

1. Using the information on the entertainment industry given at the beginning of this chapter, what types of channel organizing strategies do you think would be best from the perspective of any individual actor in the system, for example, individual actors for entertainment, television networks, movie studios, cable companies, producers, viewers, etc.?

2. According to Bucklin, the issue of channel performance focuses on the major conflict that exists between two major dimensions of channel performance. On the one hand, consumers and users are concerned primarily with lowering the costs of the goods and services sold and therefore with reducing the costs of distribution. On the other hand, consumers want to benefit from and receive some marketing services in conjunction with the good or service they purchase. However, provision of these services increases the cost of distribution.

   Compare and contrast "hard" and "soft" vertical integration relative to the performance dimensions mentioned by Bucklin. Which would tend to be superior overall?

3. It has been argued that the price mechanism is the formal means through which vertical coordination is achieved in freeform, unorganized channels. What does this mean, and what are its consequences for channel performance, both from a macro and a micro perspective?

4. What are the advantages of administered systems versus contractual systems? What are the disadvantages of administered systems that might be overcome through the formation of contractual systems?

5. A number of concessions are available to suppliers who are seeking to gain reseller support of their marketing programs. Define and explain the use of three items under each of the headings below, that is, three under Price Concessions A, three under Price Concessions B, three under Financial Assistance A, etc.

Price Concessions

A. Discount Structure:
   Trade (functional) discounts
   Quantity discounts
   Cash discounts
   Anticipation discounts
   Free goods
   Prepaid flight
   Seasonal discounts
   Mixed carload privilege
   Drop shipping privilege
   Trade deals

B. Discount Substitutes:
   Display materials
   Premarked merchandise
   Inventory control programs
   Sales promotion literature
   Training programs
   Shelf-stocking programs
   Management consulting
     services
   Sales "spiffs"
   Technical assistance

Financial Assistance

A. Conventional Lending
   Arrangements:
   Term loans
   Inventory floor plans
   Notes payable financing
   Installment financing of
     fixtures and equipment
   Lease and note guarantee
     programs

B. Extended Dating:
   E.O.M. (end-of-month) dating
   Seasonal dating
   R.O.G. (receipt-of-goods) dating
   "Extra" dating
   Post dating

Protective Provisions

A. Price Protection:
    Premarked merchandise
    "Franchise" pricing
    Agency agreements

B. Territorial Protection:
    Selective distribution
    Exclusive distribution

C. Inventory Protection:
    Consignment selling
    Memorandum selling
    Liberal returns allowance
    Rebate programs
    Reorder programs
    Guaranteed support of sale
        events
    Fast delivery

6. Which of the various concessions listed in question 5 are likely to be useful in marketing through supermarkets? Through department stores? Through catalog showrooms? Through warehouse showrooms? Through industrial (full-function) distributors?

7. Which type of cooperative—wholesaler-sponsored, retailer-owned, or consumer-owned—would you expect to be most successful? Why have consumer cooperatives never enjoyed widespread popularity in the United States?

8. Write a plan for starting your own franchising operation. What would be the essential ingredients of the plan? What specific points would you include in the contractual arrangement you establish with your franchisees?

9. Assume you are the manufacturer of a broad line of moderately priced furniture. When would you seriously consider owning your own retail outlets? What factors would you take into account in making your decision?

10. What is the difference between a "hybrid marketing system" and a "plural system"? Which would be more difficult to manage? Why?

ENDNOTES

[1]"Hollywood Shuffle," *Business Week*, December 12, 1994, p. 37.

[2]*Ibid.* p. 38.

[3]Laura Landro, "Studio Tours, " *Wall Street Journal*, Special Section, September 9, 1994, p. R4.

[4]Erin Anderson and Barton A. Weitz, "Make-or-Buy Decisions: Vertical Integration and Marketing Productivity," *Sloan Management Review*, Spring 1986, pp. 3–19. Reprint No. 2531.

[5]Erin Anderson and Anne T. Coughlan, "International Market Entry and Expansion via Independent or Integrated Channels of Distribution," *Journal of Marketing*, Vol. 51 (January 1987), p. 74.

[6]Oliver E. Williamson, *The Economic Institutions of Capitalism*, (New York: The Free Press, 1985); Oliver E. Williamson, "Transaction-Cost Economics: The Governance of Contractual Relations," *Journal of Law and Economics*, Vol. 22 (October 1979), pp. 233–262; and Oliver E. Williamson, *Markets and Hierarchies: Analysis and Antitrust Implications* (New York: The Free Press, 1975). For a comprehensive treatment of the topics covered in this chapter written by economists relying, to a large extent, on Williamson's work, see Roger D. Blair and David L. Kaserman, *Law and Economics of Vertical Integration and Control* (New York: Academic Press, 1983) and Martin K. Perry, "Vertical Integration: Determinants and Effects," in R. Schmalensee and R. D. Willig (eds.), *Handbook of Industrial Organization* (Amsterdam: Elsevier Science Publishers B.V., 1989), pp.183–255.

[7]See, for example, Saul Klein, Gary L. Frazier, and Victor J. Roth, "A Transaction Cost Analysis Model of Channel Integration in International Markets," *Journal of Marketing Research*, Vol. 27 (May 1990), pp. 196–208; George John and Barton A. Weitz, "Forward Integration into Distribution: An Empirical Test of Transaction Cost Analysis," *Journal of Law, Economics, and Organization*, Vol. 4 (Fall 1988), pp. 337–355; Erin Anderson, "The Salesperson as Outside Agent or Employee: A Transaction Cost Analysis," *Marketing Science*, Vol. 4 (Summer 1985), pp. 234–254; George John, "An Empirical Investigation of Some Antecedents of Opportunism in a Marketing Channel," *Journal of Marketing Research*, Vol. 21 (August 1984), pp. 278–289; and Lynn W. Phillips, "Explaining Control Losses in Corporate Marketing Channels: An Organization Analysis," *Journal of Marketing Research*, Vol. 19 (November 1982), pp. 525–549.

[8]See Klein, Frazier, and Roth, *op. cit.*, p. 204.

[9]The concept of core competencies is explained by C. K. Prahalad and Gary Hamel, "The Core Competence of the Corporation," *Harvard Business Review*, May–June 1990, pp. 79–91. See also, James Brian Quinn and Frederick G. Hilmer, "Strategic Outsourcing," *Sloan Management Review*, Summer 1994, pp. 45–55.

[10]*Ibid.*, p. 48.

[11]Philip Rawstorne, "How Firmer Control Boosts the Margins," adapted from the *Financial Times*, November 29, 1990, p. 30. See also, "The Liquor Baron's Morning After," *The Economist*, December 24, 1994–January 6, 1995, p. 81.

[12]Ian Rodger, "Matsushita, the Cautious Imitator," *Financial Times*, November 27, 1990, p. 23. See also, Laura Landro and Eben Shapiro, "Seagram Will Trade DuPont for MCA Inc.; Does It Make Sense?" *Wall Street Journal*, April 7, 1995, p. A1.

[13]Charles Fleming, "European Insurers Dial Up Customers," *Wall Street Journal*, April 4, 1994, p. A9B; and Richard Lapper, "Direct Selling of Insurance Gets Continental Break," *Financial Times*, June 6, 1994, p. 23.

[14]Teri Agins, "Apparel Makers Increasingly Market Their Clothes Directly to Consumers," *Wall Street Journal*, February 2, 1990, p. A5B.

[15]Teri Agins, "Clothing Makers Don Retailers' Garb," *Wall Street Journal*, July 13, 1989, p. B1; "Can Ms. Fashion Bounce Back?" *Business Week*, January 16, 1989, pp. 64–70.

[16]Jean-Michel Valette, "Branded Consumer Growth Company—A Revolution in What and How We Buy," Hambrecht & Quist Inc. Institutional Research, March 17, 1993, p. 25.

[17]Lynn W. Phillips, "Explaining Control Losses in Corporate Marketing Channels: An Organizational Analysis," *Journal of Marketing Research*, Vol. 19 (November 1982), pp. 525–526.

[18]Leslie Scism, "Intelligent Electronics, Wiser Now, Returns to Profit," *Wall Street Journal*, July 15, 1993, p. B4.

[19]Michael W. Miller, "IBM Plans to Clone Intel Microprocessors in Bid to Recapture Bulk of PC Business," *Wall Street Journal*, August 24, 1993, p. A3.

[20]Jan B. Heide, "Interorganizational Governance in Marketing Channels," *Journal of Marketing*, Vol. 58 (January 1994), p. 75.

[21]For overviews of this position along with relevant citations, see Joseph T. Mahoney, "Choice of Organizational Form: Vertical Financial Ownership Versus Other Methods of Vertical Integration," *Strategic Management Journal*, Vol. 13 (1992), pp. 559–584 and John Stuckey and David White, "When and When Not to Vertically Integrate," *Sloan Management Review*, (Spring 1993), pp. 71–83.

[22]Robert D. Buzzell, "Is Vertical Integration Profitable?" *Harvard Business Review*, Vol. 61 (January–February 1983), pp. 96, 100.

[23]Kathryn Rudie Harrigan, "A Framework for Looking at Vertical Integration," *Journal of Business Strategy*, Vol. 3 (Winter 1983), p. 34.

[24]Prahalad and Hamel, *op cit.*, pp. 79–91; Quinn and Hilmer, *op. cit.*, pp. 45–55.

[25]James A. Welch and P. Ranganath Nayak, "Strategic Sourcing: A Progressive Approach to the Make-or-Buy Decision," *Academy of Management Executive*, Vol. 6 (1992), p. 23.

[26]"The Ins and Outs of Outing," *The Economist*, August 31, 1991, p. 56.

[27]Alex Taylor III, "The Auto Industry Meets the New Economy," *Fortune*, September 5, 1994, p. 53. For additional examples, see Neal Templin and Jeff Cole, "Manufacturers Use Suppliers to Help Them Develop New Products," *Wall Street Journal*, December 19, 1994, p. A1.

[28]Phillip Hastings, "The Flexibility Factor," *Financial Times*, Section III, July 24, 1991, p. III.

[29]*Ibid.*

[30]Michael J. McDermott, "Who Let the Strangers in Your Files?" *Profiles*, October 1992, pp. 34–40. See also, J. Mark May, *Facilities Management* (Chicago, IL: The Richmark Group, 1991).

[31]Raymond E. Miles and Charles C. Snow, "Causes of Failure in Network Organizations," *California Management Review*, Summer 1992, p. 63.

[32]Shawn Tully, "The Modular Corporation," *Fortune*, February 8, 1993, p. 107. For insights into the operation and management of business networks, see James C. Anderson, Hakan Hakansson, and Jan Johanson, "Dyadic Business Relationships Within a Business Network Context," *Journal of Marketing*, Vol. 58 (October 1994), pp. 1–15.

[33]The authors are grateful to Professor Charles C. Snow for supplying the Galoob example.

[34]Miles and Snow, *op. cit.*, p. 66.

[35]"The Virtual Corporation," *Business Week*, February 8, 1993, pp. 98–99.

[36]Miles and Snow, *op. cit.*, pp. 66–67.

[37]*Ibid.*, p. 99.

[38]See "Computers Come to Tinseltown," *The Economist*, December 24, 1994–January 6, 1995, pp. 87–89. For an outstanding discussion of how the concept of virtual corporations is applied in the making of motion pictures, see Joel Kotkin, "Why Every Business Will Be Like Show Business," *Inc.*, March 1995, pp. 64–78.

[39]Richard A. Bettis, Stephen P. Bradley, and Gary Hamel, "Outsourcing and Industrial Decline," *Academy of Management Executive*, Vol. 6 (1992), p. 15.

[40]Templin and Cole, *op. cit.*, p. A6.

[41]Philip Hastings, "Contracting Out: Debate Is Renewed," *The Financial Times*, October 5, 1993, p. 30; see also McDermott, *op. cit.*, p. 36.

[42]Philip Hastings, "Mixed Pattern of Change," *The Financial Times*, Section III, September 3, 1992, p. II.

[43]Louise Lee, "Hiring Outside Firms to Run Computers Isn't Always a Bargain," *Wall Street Journal*, May 18, 1995, p. A1.

[44]Charles Batchelor, "Relentless Drive to Reduce Costs," *Financial Times*, Logistics Survey, September 21, 1994, p. I.

[45]Miles and Snow, *op.cit.*, p. 64.

[46]Charles C. Snow, Raymond E. Miles, and Henry J. Coleman Jr., "Managing 21st Century Network Organizations," *Organizational Dynamics*, Vol. 20 (Winter 1992), p. 11.

[47]Heide, *op. cit.*, p. 75.

[48]The basis for this perspective can be found in Roland L. Warren, "The Interorganizational Field as a Focus for Investigation," in M. B. Brinkerhoff and P. R. Kunz (eds.), *Complex Organizations and Their Environments* (Dubuque, IA: Wm. C. Brown Co., 1972), p. 316.

[49]Adapted from Roland L. Warren, "The Interorganizational Field as a Focus for Investigation," in M. B. Brinkeroff and P. R. Kunz (eds.), *Complex Organizations and Their Environments* (Dubuque, IA: Wm. C. Brown Co., 1972), p. 316.

[50]For additional examples, see Stephanie Strom, "More Suppliers Helping Stores Push the Goods," *New York Times*, Section C, January 20, 1992, p. 1.

[51]Myron Magnet, "Meet the New Revolutionaries," *Fortune*, February 24, 1992, pp. 98, 100.

[52]For an excellent discussion of the channel issues surrounding the implementation of such systems, see David Cassak, "Baxter and the Trend Toward Stockless Distribution," *In Vivo*, May 1990, pp. 15–19 and June 1990, pp. 16–21.

[53]Presentation by Ronald O. Cox, Group Vice President of Sales and Marketing, Wm. Wrigley Jr. Company, at J. L. Kellogg Graduate School of Management, Northwestern University, May 11, 1995.

[54]Tying the Knot," *The Economist*, May 14, 1994, p. 73.

[55]James P. Morgan, "Is This the Age of Super Distributor," *Purchasing*, February 17, 1994, p. 43.

[56]Management Horizons, a Consulting Division of Price Waterhouse LLP, Columbus, OH, 1994.

[57]*Ibid.*

[58]Fred Pfaff, "Micro-Merchandising with KGF," *Food & Beverage Marketing*, June 1991.

[59]See, for example, Barnaby J. Feder, "Moving the Pampers Faster Cuts Everyone's Cost," *New York Times*, Section F, July 14, 1991, p. 5.

[60]Erin Anderson and Barton Weitz, "Credible Commitments in Channel Relationships," a presentation to a conference of the Marketing Science Institute in Boston, MA on November 1, 1990.

[61]"Lighting the Way," *The Economist*, October 6, 1990, p. 77.

[62]For an excellent example, see Aeroquip's Premier Distributor Agreement reproduced in Appendix 8A.

[63]Warren, *op. cit.*, p. 316.

[64]For an excellent description of Super Valu's operation, see Bill Saporito, "Super Valu Does Two Things Well," *Fortune* (April 18, 1983), pp. 114–118.

[65]F. Robert Dwyer and Sejo Oh, "A Transaction Cost Perspective on Vertical Contractual Structure and Interchannel Competitive Strategies," *Journal of Marketing*, Vol. 52 (April 1988), p. 31.

[66]*Ibid.*, p. 24.

[67]*Ibid.*, p. 31.

[68]"Certainly Not in the Same League," *The Economist*, April 29, 1995, p. 76.

[69]U.S. Bureau of the Census, *Statistical Abstract of the United States: 1994*, 114th edition (Washington, DC: U.S. Government Printing Office, 1994), p. 790.

[70]Saturn Distribution Corporation, *Franchise Offering Circular for Prospective Franchisees* (Troy MI: Saturn Distribution Corporation, March 31, 1989).

[71]It is "most likely" but not "certain," because McDonald's owns about 10% of its U.S. outlets; the remainder are franchised.

[72]Phillip D. White and Albert D. Bates, "Franchising Will Remain Retailing Fixture, but Its Salad Days Have Long Since Gone," *Marketing News* (February 17, 1984), p. 14.

[73]"Franchise Rule Exemption for Wholesale Grocers Announced by Federal Trade Commission," *FTC News Note*, Vol. 25–83 (March 18, 1983), p. 3.

[74]Bruce J. Walker, "Franchising in the 1990s," *Arthur Andersen Retailing Issues Letter*, Vol. 3 (January 1991), p. 1.

[75]*Goodyear: The Aquatred Launch,* Harvard Business School, Case No. 9-594-106, Rev. December 2, 1993, p. 11.

[76]William T. Ross, "Managing Marketing Channel Relationships," *Marketing Science Institute Working Paper Series,* Report No. 85-105 (Cambridge, MA: Marketing Science Institute, 1985), p. 8.

[77]Walker, *op. cit.*, p. 1.

[78]See "Why Franchising Is Taking Off," *Fortune*, February 12, 1990, p. 124.

[79]See Andrew E. Serwer, "Trouble in Franchise Nation," *Fortune,* March 6, 1995, p. 120 and Jeffrey A. Tannenbaum, "Retail Franchises Appear Riskier Than Other Start-Ups," *Wall Street Journal,* February 28, 1995, p. B2.

[80]For an outstanding example of routinization of information flows, see Craig Zarley, "Captains of Video," *PC Week* (September 10, 1985), pp. 53–56, which describes National Video's franchise linking PC network.

[81]Richard Gourlay, "Bring on the Clones," *The Financial Times*, April 12, 1994, p. 10.

[82]John Thornhill, "A European Spark for Marks," *The Financial Times*, July 13, 1992, p. 8.

[83]Paul H. Rubin, *Managing Business Transactions* (New York: The Free Press, 1990), p. 137.

[84]Bob Wiedrich, "Snap-on Tooling Up for New Approach," *Chicago Tribune*, Section 7, December 9, 1990, p. 3.

[85]Michael Selz, "More Concerns Are Franchising Existing Outlets," *Wall Street Journal*, December 17, 1990, p. B1.

[86]Meg Whittemore, "Franchising's Future: More Than $1.3 Trillion Sold," *Daily Market Digest*, April 28, 1986, p. 22.

[87]See "McGoulash to Go," *The Economist*, April 6, 1991, pp. 70-71; Charles Batchelor, "Expanding Prospects," *The Financial Times*, September 29, 1992, p. 12.

[88]David Warsh, "Where There Is No Trust, Mafia Franchises Pop Up," *Chicago Tribune,* Section 4, May 8, 1995, p. 2.

[89]"Is General Nutrition Headed for Civil War?," *Business Week*, November 21, 1994, pp. 58–59.

[90]For a comprehensive discussion of this new issue, see Rajiv P. Dant, Patrick J. Kaufmann, and Audhesh K. Paswan, "Ownership Redirection in Franchised Channels," *Journal of Public Policy & Marketing*, Vol. 11 (Spring 1992), pp. 33–44.

[91]For a comprehensive list and thorough discussion of key conflict issues and resolution mechanisms, see James M. Carman and Thomas A. Klein, "Power, Property, and Performance in Franchising," *Research in Marketing*, Vol. 8, (1986), pp. 71–130. See also, Andrew E. Sewer, "Trouble in Franchising," *Fortune*, March 6, 1995, pp. 115–129 and Jeffrey A. Tan-

nenbaum, "To Pacify Irate Franchisees, Franchisers Extend Services," *Wall Street Journal*, February 24, 1995, p. B1.

[92]Jeffrey A. Tannenbaum, "Food Franchisers Expand by Pursuing Customers Into Every Nook and Cranny," *Wall Street Journal*, October 26, 1994, p. B1.

[93]See Barbara Marsh, "Sandwich-Shop Chain Surges, but to Run One Can Take Heroic Effort," *Wall Street Journal*, September 16, 1992, p. A1; "Flaring Tempers at the Frozen-Yogurt King," *Business Week*, September 10, 1990, pp. 88–90. For examples in the lodging industry, see Jonathan Dahl, "While Traveling, You Frequently Are a Guest of a Two-Man Team," *Wall Street Journal*, November 28, 1994, p. A1; Kevin Helliker, "How a Motel Chain Lost Its Moorings After 1980s Buy-Out," *Wall Street Journal*, May 26, 1992, p. A1. See also, Patrick J. Kaufmann and Kasturi Rangan, "A Model for Managing System Conflict During Franchise Expansion," *Journal of Retailing*, Vol. 66 (Summer 1990), pp. 155–173.

[94]Barnaby J. Feder, "McDonald's Finds There's Still Plenty of Room to Grow," *New York Times*, Business Section, January 9, 1994, p. 5.

[95]See Jeffrey A. Tannenbaum and Barbara Marsh, "Firms Try to Tighten Grip on Franchisees," *Wall Street Journal*, January 15, 1990, p. B1; Barbara Marsh, "When Franchisees Go Their Own Way," *Wall Street Journal*, July 6, 1989, p. B1; and Nikki Tait, "Bass Finds Running Hotels Is No Holiday," *The Financial Times*, May 12, 1992, p. 21.

[96]Ken Waters, "Managing Close Channel Relationships: The ComputerLand Story," *Frank Lynn & Associates Client Communique*, Vol. 2 (April 1990), p. 2. See also "How a Quick Fix Backfired at ComputerLand," *Business Week*, October 10, 1988, pp. 114–116.

[97]See Buck Brown, "Believing They Can Do Better, Franchisees Are Seizing the Reins of Their Companies," *Wall Street Journal*, November 29, 1988, p. B1; Buck Brown, "New Owners of Franchises Belie Mom-and-Pop Image," *Wall Street Journal*, August 29, 1988, p. 13; Michael J. McCarthy, "When Franchisees Become Rebellious," *Wall Street Journal*, September 13, 1989, p. B1; Hal Kreiger et al., "Franchising Creates Conflicts and Is No Guarantee of Success," *Marketing News*, February 19, 1990, p. 6; Donald D. Boroian and Patrick J. Boroian, *The Franchise Advantage* (Chicago: Prism Creative Group, Ltd., 1987), pp. 203–209.

[98]Jeffrey A. Tannenbaum, "Franchisee Lawsuit Seeks $1 Billion From Southland," *Wall Street Journal*, April 8, 1994, p. B2.

[99]Andrew E. Serwer, "McDonald's Conquers the World," *Fortune*, October 17, 1994, p. 112.

[100]See Faye Rice, "How to Succeed at Cloning a Small Business," *Fortune*, October 28, 1985, p. 61.

[101]See Sanford L. Jacobs, "Branching Out," *Wall Street Journal*, February 24, 1989, p. R22. See also, Robert Justis and Richard Judd, *Franchising* (Cincinnati, OH: SouthWestern Publishing Co., 1989); Boroian and Boroian, *op. cit.*, for detailed advice to prospective franchisors and franchisees.

[102]Michael Selz, "Many Ex-Executives Turn to Franchising, Often Find Frustrations," *Wall Street Journal*, October 14, 1992, p. A1.

[103]Jeffrey A. Tannenbaum, "FTC Says Franchisers Fed Clients a Line and Failed to Deliver," *Wall Street Journal*, May 16, 1994, p. A1.

[104]Jean Saddler, "Franchise Pacts Can End in Suits Over Contracts," *Wall Street Journal*, January 15, 1991, p. B1; Dean M. Sagar, *Franchising in the U.S. Economy: Prospects and Problems*, Committee on Small Business, U.S. House of Representatives, 101st Congress, 2nd Session (Washington, DC: U.S. Government Printing Office, 1990), pp. 74–76.

[105]For example, see Richard Gibson, "McDonald's Is Challenging Iowa's New Franchise Law," *Wall Street Journal*, May 14, 1992, B2; Richard Gibson," Judge Overturns Much of Iowa Law That Increased Power of Franchises," *Wall Street Journal*, May 17, 1993, p. B2; and Jeffrey A. Tannenbaum,"New Rulings Cloak Franchisees with Sturdier Armor," *Wall Street Journal*, December 30, 1993, p. B2.

[106]Rowland Moriarty, "Going to Market in the 1990s," Senior Management Interchange *Meeting Summary* (Cambridge, MA: Index Group, Inc., 1990), p. 2. See also, Rowland T. Moriarty and Ursula Moran, "Managing Hybrid Marketing Systems," *Harvard Business Review*, November–December 1990, pp. 147–155; and Frank P. Cespedes and E. Raymond Corey, "Managing Multiple Channels," *Business Horizons*, July–August 1990, pp. 67–77.

[107]Moriarity, *Ibid.*

[108]Oliver E. Williamson and William G. Ouchi, "The Markets and Hierarchies Program of Research: Origins, Implications, Prospects," in A. H. Van de Ven and W. F. Joyce (eds.), *Perspectives on Organization Design and Behavior* (New York: John Wiley & Sons, 1981), 347–370.

[109]Heide, *op. cit.*, p. 72.

[110]Jeffrey L. Bradach and Robert Eccles, "Price Authority, and Trust: Ideal Types to Plural Forms," *Annual Review of Sociology*, Vol. 15 (1989), pp. 97–118.

[111]Heide, *op cit.*, p. 81. Emphasis and parenthesis added. Heide uses the term "hybrid" instead of "mixed." We have used the latter to avoid confusion with Moriarty's term "hybrid marketing systems."

APPENDIX

/ THE 7-ELEVEN® STORE FRANCHISE   ◀◀◀◀◀◀◀◀

7-ELEVEN . . . A WAY OF LIFE

7-ELEVEN is, to busy people of all ages, the friendly convenience store. It's the convenient place to stop for a loaf of bread, quart of milk, package of cigarettes, groceries, beverages, picnic supplies, candy, "Deli Central" foods, or everyone's favorite ice drink . . . Slurpee. 7-ELEVEN Stores are small, compact, easily accessible, and open for business 24 hours a day, 7 days a week. Their convenient locations, fast service, and friendly image have combined to make 7-ELEVEN shopping a familiar part of the American life-style.

7-ELEVEN is a division of The Southland Corporation and the premier name in the convenience retailing industry. It is also the world's largest operator and franchisor of convenience stores. Approximately 5,600 7-ELEVEN Stores are located in the United States and, in some areas, stores are available for franchise to qualified applicants.

7-ELEVEN offers a business system for a ready-to-operate store. It includes training, counselling, bookkeeping, merchandising assistance, and some financing. This brochure, which briefly introduces the 7-ELEVEN System, is your invitation to discuss in detail how you and your family can become a part of 7-ELEVEN.

Source: The Southland Corporation, *The 7-ELEVEN Franchise,* informational article. Reprinted with the permission of The Southland Corporation.

REAL ESTATE

7-ELEVEN's real estate representatives research and select sites based on population, traffic flow, convenience to homes, and competition. After 7-ELEVEN buys or leases a site, the completed 7-ELEVEN store is leased to the franchisee.

EQUIPMENT

All equipment in the store, including heating and air conditioning, vaults, shelving, cash registers, and refrigerated cases, are included in the lease to the franchisee, who is responsible for certain repairs and maintenance.

MERCHANDISE

7-ELEVEN arranges for the initial inventory of merchandise in the store. Thereafter, the franchisee orders and stocks all the merchandise. 7-ELEVEN provides continuing merchandising services which include recommending vendors, merchandise and selling prices, producing bulletins and providing general advice and assistance. The recommendations are based on the Company's many years of experience in convenience store merchandising. 7-ELEVEN also recommends vendors based on a combination of price, service, quality, and market acceptance. A franchisee is free to purchase merchandise from any vendor and to establish the retail prices. The franchisee receives credit for all discounts and allowances on merchandise purchased.

ADVERTISING

Advertising plays a significant role in assisting a franchisee in building sales and profits. For many years, 7-ELEVEN advertising has received widespread recognition:

> "AMERICA LIKES THE FREEDOM"
> "IT'S ABOUT TIME"
> "IF IT'S NOT AROUND THE HOUSE,
> IT'S JUST AROUND THE CORNER"
> "OH THANK HEAVEN FOR 7-ELEVEN"

A franchisee is, of course, free to place additional advertising as it relates to the operation of the Store.

TRAINING

Prior to final acceptance by 7-ELEVEN franchise applicants are required to successfully complete the 7-ELEVEN Store Operations Training Program, including actual in-store experience in a Training Store, which is an operating 7-ELEVEN Store. The Training Store experience is followed by one week of classroom training in our Dallas, Texas, Training Center, where the prospective franchisee learns a variety of management skills, techniques, and procedures essential to successful operation of a 7-ELEVEN store. The cost of training is included in the initial Franchisee Fee.

EMPLOYEES

Although some franchised 7-ELEVEN Stores are family operated, it is usually necessary for the franchisee to employ additional part-time and full-time help. The franchisee is responsible for the hiring and training of employees and for all payroll expenses, including employee taxes. Based on the franchisee's authorization and employee's time cards, 7-ELEVEN prepares the payroll checks for the franchisee's employees.

BOOKKEEPING

7-ELEVEN keeps bookkeeping records on the franchisee's operation of the 7-ELEVEN Store. A franchisee makes daily cash deposits of sales receipts. From these, 7-ELEVEN pays for all operating expenses and merchandising purchases approved by the franchisee in connection with operations of the store.

INVESTMENT

The investment requirements for a 7-ELEVEN Store franchise include the cost of inventory, the cash register fund, and the estimated cost of all business licenses, permits, and bonds. The exact amount varies depending on the location of the store and the inventory requirements. On December 31, 1994, the average total investment in the inventory for a 7-ELEVEN Store was $37,000, the average cash register fund began at about $150, and the approximate cost for licenses and permits was $500. 7-ELEVEN will finance a portion of the investment for qualified applicants.

FRANCHISE FEE

The initial franchise fee for a 7-ELEVEN Store franchise will vary by Store. While the franchise fee in some lower sales volume Stores may be as low as $10,000, the franchise fee may exceed $130,000 in the highest sales volume Stores. For Stores with at least 12 full months of sales history, the initial franchise fee will either be a fixed amount or an amount equal to a pre-determined percentage of the Store's total gross profit (excluding gasoline profits) for the preceding 12 months. The fees for two Stores in the same neighborhood may vary greatly due to the sales trends of the individual Stores.

The initial franchise fee for a new Store or Store with less than 12 full months sales history is calculated by using a designated group of Stores within 7-ELEVEN's operating division of Stores in which the Store is or is to be located.

A FRANCHISEE CAN MOST AFFECT PROFITS BY

- General management aptitude

- Ability to hire and train competent employees

- Control of employee and customer pilferage

- Creative salesmanship

- Sincere customer relations

- Ability to create a friendly store atmosphere

- Maintenance of a clean and orderly store

PROFITS

A local 7-ELEVEN representative will discuss the financial history of the store being considered.

The GROSS PROFIT of the store is shared by the franchisee and 7-ELEVEN. Under the gross profit split system, the financial return to both Southland and the franchisee is tied to the profitability of the Store. The percentage of GROSS PROFIT paid by the franchisee to 7-ELEVEN is a continuing charge for the license of the service mark and system, lease of the facility, and continuing services.

From the franchisee's share of the GROSS PROFIT, the franchisee pays all other operating expenses, such as

Payroll	Cash Variation	Equipment Repair
Store Supplies	Extra Advertising for the Store	General Maintenance
Telephone	Employees' Group	Janitorial Service
Laundry	Insurance	Interest Expense
Payroll Taxes	Security Expense	Taxes and License
Bad Checks	Bad Merchandise	Miscellaneous Expense
	Inventory Variation	

The amount remaining, if any, after payment of the operating expenses is the franchisee's net income.

MANAGING
MARKETING
CHANNELS

◄◄◄◄◄◄◄

We have previously discussed how to design an efficient distribution channel that meets target consumers' demands for service outputs. We call that channel the optimal customer-driven channel. However, the job of a channel manager is not done when that optimal channel is designed; the manager now has to make that channel *work!* There is no guarantee that the optimally designed channel will actually operate successfully. Realistic, cost-effective implementation and first-rate execution are accomplished only with purposive coordination, motivation, and direction. Without such conscious concentration and effort, channels rarely gravitate toward excellent performance, regardless of the way in which they have been structured.

To understand what is necessary to manage marketing channels correctly, one must consider what a channel really is. As discussed in Chapter 1, a marketing channel can be viewed as a *superorganization* comprised of interdependent institutions and agencies involved in the task of making products and services available for consumption by end-users. This notion may seem unnatural, as many channels contain companies that pride themselves on their autonomy and independence. Such companies are not likely to admit that they are part of a larger whole—that despite their independence, they are also interdependent, and need to recognize that interdependence in order to focus on the superordinate goals of the channel. Indeed, the popularity today of channel terms and forms such as "strategic alliances," "channel commitment," "channel trust," or "relational contracting" suggests the realization inside at least some channels of a sense of *joint* engagement in the pursuit of a *single* goal: the satisfaction of the target customer's desire for service outputs.

A superorganization has two interesting characteristics: (1) it exhibits "subadditivity of costs,"[1] and (2) the orientations and objectives of its separate members naturally and frequently diverge. By "subadditivity of costs," we mean that the cost of delivering a given set of service outputs to a target group of customers is lower in total when two organizations combine their activities than when they do them separately. For example, there might be redundancy in inventory-holding throughout a distribution channel, and if the inventory-holding function is consolidated in the hands of one channel member, the total cost of running the channel falls. Conversely, we can say that subadditivity of costs implies that for a given total channel cost outlay, a superorganization can produce a greater level of service outputs than can a set of separate, noncoordinated organizations. Subadditivity of costs thus results from a combination of (1) the differentiation of functions among the various members of the superorganization, combined with (2) members' interdependency with respect to task performance. In short, there are gains from trade and specialization in forming a superorganization in the distribution channel. Although it still must be decided how to split the channel profit pie, recognition that the size of the total pie is larger in a superorganization is a necessary precursor to cooperative channel activity.

Channels as superorganizations are also generally characterized by the natural tendency for their members' objectives and attitudes to diverge. This would not be a problem were the success of the distribution effort not dependent integrally on the joint efforts of all its members. The natural complexity of a superorganization, combined with this tendency toward different orientations and attitudes, necessitates some set of controls to make it function smoothly and generate the maximum possible performance levels. Members of an *effective* superorganization thus tend to (1) communicate with each other easily, (2) cooperate with each other in the pursuit of collective channel goals, and either (3a) have a clearly defined superior-subordinate or authority system in place, or (3b) have inducements in place in the channel that encourage appropriate behaviors among its members. Thus, it is incumbent on the channel members both to understand the potential for inconsistent behaviors inside the channel, and to purposefully act to minimize those inconsistent behaviors through the use of controls, incentives, contracts, agreements, and communication inside the channel.

These controls should be used in pursuit of a customer-driven channel, that is, one that profitably serves target customers with the service outputs they demand. The channel will not be effective unless it is fundamentally customer-driven. Customer service is a continuous process in the channel, and effective service requires that the channel look seamless from the customer's standpoint. A number of different decisions must be made that affect the delivery of service outputs. Different channel members have power over different issues. The channel thus needs a coordinating force to guarantee that all of these decisions lead to the most profitable, most customer-driven outcome.

Managing the optimal customer-driven channel thus builds on our channel-planning process and organizational patterns decisions from Chapters 5 and 6, as is outlined in Figure 7-1. Stage 1 of this process comprises the channel-planning activities discussed in Chapter 5, whereas Stage 2 of the process concerns the choice of organizational patterns covered in Chapter 6. Stage 3 focuses on channel management issues, the concern of this chapter. The first step of Stage 3 involves harnessing the resources necessary to make the optimal channel design of Stages 1 and 2 a market reality. The second step is to identify both potential and actual ways in which these resources may *not* be applied—that is, sources of channel conflict that can inhibit channel performance. The third step is the design and implementation of ongoing conflict management techniques to minimize poor performance in the channel. Of course, all of these steps are taken in the context of key channel policy issues and legal constraints (the topic of Chapter 8).

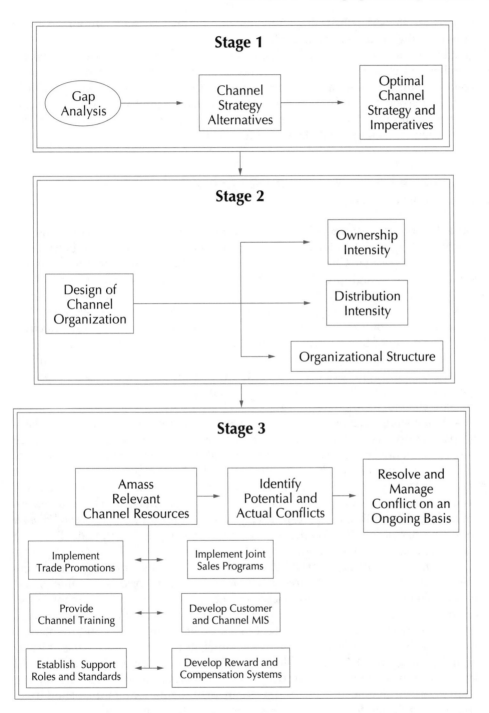

FIGURE 7-1   The marketing channel management process.

These steps may be followed by just one channel member, whom we might designate the "channel captain," but the chances for channel coordination are greater if the steps are undertaken jointly or collectively by more than one channel member, in a channel structure where power is more equally shared or balanced. Following this process for channel management helps to give a strong product a competitive boost in the marketplace: a coordinated channel to deliver the optimal service outputs to its target markets. In the following discussion, we amplify on each of the channel management elements identified in Figure 7-1.

▶ MARSHALLING RESOURCES FOR PRODUCTIVE CHANNEL MANAGEMENT

Once the optimal customer-driven distribution system has been designed, as discussed in Chapter 5, and the organizational pattern of the channel has been determined, as discussed in Chapter 6, channel members have a blueprint for action that should produce a high-profit, high-satisfaction distribution system. Clearly, satisfying target customers' demands for service outputs requires that channel members use costly resources (e.g., warehouses, toll-free telephone lines, salesforce time and effort, electronic data interchange linkages, and so on) to maximize effectiveness. The name of the game in maximizing channel productivity (given an effective design) is *marshalling the resources to make the design work.* If the right incentives to contribute the appropriate resources to the distribution effort, both in type and amount, are absent, all the channel planning and design in the world will not help increase channel profitability.

Marshalling relevant channel resources means first choosing the right channel partners to execute the channel strategy. The choice and resulting performance of specific channel partners are, of course, the ultimate determinants of the success or failure of a marketing channel. All of the planning suggested up to this point means absolutely nothing if the right parties cannot be found to execute it. Lists of criteria for the choice of specific channel partners by suppliers and by retailers are found in Exhibits 7-1 and 7-2, respectively. These criteria or attributes can be used in the multiattribute decision models discussed in Chapter 2, Appendix 2A as an aid to making the correct choices.

Marshalling the appropriate channel resources means knowing what levers are available to induce productive behavior. In a perfect world, all channel members would have consistent world views and aims, and channel management would be an automatic process. But in our imperfect world, there are many reasons why channel "partners" may not always act in a partnerlike manner. Thus, to increase the productivity and effectiveness of the channel, its members need to use any and all mechanisms available to produce a coordinated outcome. There are several levers that can be brought to bear to organize channel activity productively, among them the use of channel power, the development of channel commitment and trust, and contract design techniques. A discussion of each of these follows.

EXHIBIT 7-1 / Criteria for Choosing Channel Partners: The Supplier's Viewpoint

1. Financial strength of prospective channel partner
   a. Revenue, profit, and loss
   b. Balance sheet
2. Sales strength
   a. Number of sales agents
   b. Sales and technical competence
3. Product lines
   a. Competitive products
   b. Compatible products
   c. Complementary products
4. Reputation
   a. Leadership
   b. Well established
   c. Community standing
   d. Background of key executives
   e. Level of expertise
5. Market coverage
   a. Geographic coverage: outlets per market area
   b. Industry coverage
   c. Call frequency or intensity of coverage
6. Sales performance
   a. Performance of related lines
   b. General sales performance
   c. Growth prospects
   d. Ability to penetrate accounts
   e. Success in reaching target markets/individuals
   f. After-sales follow-up
7. Managment strength
   a. Planning
   b. Employee relations
   c. Marketing orientation
   d. Strategic direction

8. Advertising and sales promotion programs
9. Training programs
   a. Self-administered
   b. Willingness to allow suppliers to participate
10. Sales compensation programs
11. Plant, equipment, and facilities
    a. Transportation/delivery methods and record
    b. Inventory
       (1) kind and size
       (2) inventory minimums: safety stocks
       (3) service levels
    c. Warehousing
       (1) supplied in field
       (2) ability to handle shipments efficiently
12. Ordering and payment procedures
13. Installation and repair services
    a. After-sales follow-up
    b. Warranty work
14. Quality of demonstrator programs
15. Willingness to commit resources to individual lines/brands
16. Willingness to cooperate in joint programs
17. Willingness to share data
    a. Customers
    b. Sales force
    c. Inventory
    d. Delivery
18. Willingness to accept a quota

▶ ▶ ▶ **E**XHIBIT **7-2** / **Factors Retailers Use in Choosing Suppliers**

1. Accepts damaged merchandise returns
2. Has quick and easy ordering procedures
3. Accepts unsold merchandise returns
4. Provides prompt delivery
5. Maintains adequate supply
6. Handles complaints promptly
7. Is known as being honest
8. Has good reputation
9. Carries large product breadth
10. Provides small lot delivery
11. Offers frequent promotional allowances
12. Requires no minimum order size
13. Makes new products available

14. Has understanding sales representatives
15. Provides adequate margins on suggested list prices
16. Offers quantity discounts
17. Extends credit beyond 30 days
18. Employs well-trained sales representatives
19. Offers adequate overall promotional support
20. Offers cooperative advertising
21. Provides store displays
22. Has low sales representative turnover
23. Offers promotional advice for specific products

Source: Adapted from James R. Brown and Prem C. Purwar, "A Cross-Channel Comparison of Retail Supplier Selection Factors," in Richard P. Bagozzi et al. (eds.) *Marketing in the 80's: Changes and Challenges* (Chicago: American Marketing Association, 1980), pp. 217–220, published by the American Marketing Association.

Channel Power

We start from a presumption that channel members are unlikely to coordinate their activities spontaneously. This is because the actions of one channel member do not typically benefit another channel member. Unguided channel activity, with each channel member independently seeking its own self-interest, is therefore apt to lead to suboptimal performance. Only through the exertion of *channel power* can the actions of disparate channel members be coordinated. *Power is the ability of one channel member to get another channel member to do what it otherwise would not have done.* Power is usually required to motivate and direct the efforts of any collection of non-identical organizations or individuals.

Whenever the term "power" is brought up in polite company, almost everyone associates it with strong-arm tactics, political clout, or gunboat diplomacy. Such a view is altogether too myopic. Power is actually obtained through the possession and control of *resources* that are *valued* by another party. These resources are the assets, attributes, and conditions within a relationship that generate and represent each channel member's dependence, indebtedness, or allegiance to another. Power is, of course, a two-way street; each and every channel member has *some* valued resources at its command. Thus, the use of these resources in influencing others may not bring instantaneous results in the form of changed behavior patterns inside the channel. More rigorously, we can say that channel member A's power over channel member B is the net increase in the probability of B's enacting a behavior after A has made an intervention, compared with the probability of B's enacting the behavior in the absence of A's intervention.[2] Several implications of this formal definition should be noted:

1. In stating a power relationship, it is not sufficient to say, "A is powerful"; rather, A must be powerful over someone else (e.g., B). Think of Sears relative to Tinkertoy versus Sears relative to Goodyear.

2. The definition makes no distinction as to the means of getting B to do what he or she would not otherwise have done. The range of available means—rewards, coercion, expertise, reference, and legitimacy—are discussed later in this section.

3. The definition does not require each application of power by A to result in overt reactions by B in order to be considered successful. Power attempts may only increase the probability of desired overt action by B. Additional efforts may be required to achieve the actual movement of B.[3]

This formal statement of power can be put into marketing language as follows:

> The power of a channel member is its ability to control the decision variables in the marketing strategy of another member in a given channel at a different level of distribution. For this control to qualify as power, it should be different from the influenced member's original level of control over its own marketing strategy.[4]

In addition, power can be viewed in terms of the extent to which one channel member depends on another. The more highly dependent B is on A, the more power A has over B. For example, a small neighborhood druggist may be much more dependent on its wholesaler than the wholesaler is on the druggist. According to Emerson, the dependence of B on A is (1) directly proportional to B's motivational investment in goals mediated by or controlled by A and (2) inversely proportional to the availability of those goals to B outside of the A–B relation.[5] That is, the more A can directly affect B's goal attainment and the fewer the number of alternatives open to B to obtain what he or she needs in order to function properly, the greater the power A has over B.

When the dependencies of channel members are not equal, those who are the *most* dependent have the least amount of power *relative* to the others.[6] The ability of channel member A to get channel member B to do what he/she otherwise would not have done is based on the dependence of B on A for desired outcomes that cannot be obtained from other sources.[7] In other words, dependency and sources of power are inseparable.[8] To the extent that channel member A controls the resources that channel member B desires and cannot obtain elsewhere, or to the extent that A copes with or reduces uncertainties that are critical to B, then B is said to be dependent on A, and A is said to have power over B.[9]

A dramatic example of the significance of dependency relationships in marketing channels is provided by just-in-time production/delivery methods. As discussed in Chapter 4, just-in-time is an exacting discipline. Parts and materials should arrive at the factory just as they are needed in the manufacturing process. This lets the manufacturer eliminate inventories and the costs of carrying them.

Too often the dream turns into a nightmare for suppliers. They must ensure not only that materials get there at the right moment, but also, in some cases, that different parts, sizes, and colors arrive in precisely the right sequence for the assembly line. Even more taxing, suppliers have to deliver materials of uniformly high quality; with just-in-time, there is no backup inventory to reach into if a newly arrived part is defective. . . .

Just-in-time suppliers need a lot of handholding from their customers. Suppliers must have plenty of advance notice of what and how much to make, and the customers must stick to the schedules. A few smart companies are even bringing suppliers in on the early stages of designing new products. This helps ensure that the supplier can fulfill the contract at a profit, and that the customer gets the quality needed. And when customers help suppliers get on a just-in-time footing with *their* suppliers, inventories dissolve throughout the [marketing channel], along with the carrying costs. If inventory just gets pushed down onto someone else in the [channel], the cost of carrying it eventually gets pushed back onto the customer.[10]

A number of consumer goods manufacturers have sometimes felt that some large retailers force down prices and use the manufacturers' brand names to lure consumers into the store only to switch them to cheaper, private label, or no-name brands. To reduce their dependence on such retailers and gain control over their products' distribution, these manufacturers have devised new programs to protect small, loyal dealers and are taking new precautions when selling to the large chains.[11] In other words, they are managing their dependency relationships and beginning to place increased emphasis on those in which retailers are more dependent on them rather than the reverse.

In sum, (a) channel members do not incline naturally toward coordinated behavior; (b) the lack of natural inclination in this direction can and does cause suboptimal channel outcomes; and (c) channel power is necessary to alter actions by channel members to induce a more coordinated outcome. The valued resources that channel members stockpile are known as their "bases" of power. These include rewards, coercion, expertness, reference, and legitimacy.[12] We discuss the sources and uses of each in turn below.

REWARD POWER   Reward power is based on the belief by B that A has the ability to grant rewards to B. The effective use of reward power rests on A's possession of some resource that B values and believes he or she can obtain by conforming to A's request. Specific rewards that may be used by individual channel members include the granting of wider margins, the allocation of various promotional allowances or other compensation elements, functional discount schemes, and the assignment of exclusive territories. (Rationales for the use of these and other policies are discussed in detail in Chapter 8, along with legalities constraining when and how they may be used.) For example, in the early 1990s, large travel agencies in the United States were able to command "override" payments from airlines for selling certain quotas of tickets. Total commissions to travel agents could reach as much as 15% on domestic tickets and even 25% on international tickets. How could travel agents command these payments? Because the airlines knew that large travel agents controlled the travel arrangements of the Fortune 500 companies, and the airlines highly valued the business travelers represented in this segment. Thus, the travel agents had control over a reward that was very valuable to the airlines. To get a feeling for the amounts of money involved, U.S. airlines paid travel agents $5.3 billion in total in 1992, whereas those same U.S. airlines in the aggregate reported losses of $2 billion![13]

An example of a functional discount scheme is given in Appendix 7-1, which outlines the preliminary functional discount schedule proposed to its distributors by Aeroquip Corporation, a manufacturer of industrial hoses and fittings. It shows how different levels of distributors earn greater or smaller discounts by performing more or fewer channel flows and functions.

One of the most common uses of reward power in channels is the setting of sales force compensation.[14] Research has shown that monetary compensation is a key element of reward power in coordinating channel activities.[15] Because salespeople do not naturally share their employers' objective functions, it is up to sales management to come up with creative solutions to the problem of the natural divergence between the salesperson's and the firm's interests. The judicious use of reward power through careful compensation design pays off by making the salesperson want to behave in ways that advance the company's profit or other goals. For example, companies routinely offer higher commission payments to salespeople for selling to new customers on the belief that it is harder to land a new account than to sell to a current customer. Without the offer of this reward to the salesperson, fewer new customers would be signed on than the company wants. Just as inside an employee salesforce, reward power is used throughout the channel to allocate the total channel profit pie. For example, *functional discounts* are a commonly used mechanism whereby manufacturers offer percentage discounts to distributors for the performance of specific channel functions and flows. These functional discounts are an effective way for the manufacturer to use the reward power at its disposal to direct and alter the behavior of channel members. Functional discounts are offered for such activities as early payment, inventory maintenance, or merchandising.

One of the key questions facing a channel manager seeking to set appropriate rewards in the channel system, however, is what the right level of reward is for any given activity. That is, what is the right split of channel benefits or profits? The answer lies in what we call the *equity principle:*

> *Compensation in the distribution channel should be given on the basis of the degree of each channel member's participation in the marketing flows and each channel member's contribution to the generation of relevant service outputs in the channel system.*

Simply put, channel members should be compensated for what they do. On a deeper level, this means understanding both what *costs* each channel member has borne in performing marketing flows and functions, and what *value* has been added to the channel system as a result.

The consulting firm Frank Lynn & Associates espouses the equity principle in the form of "value-based compensation":

> We believe that value-based compensation is the model that will replace traditional discount structures in the next few years. . . . The manufacturer determines the spe-

cific marketing costs that it wants to transfer to the channel, sets an economic value on those costs and pays the channel for incurring these costs. These marketing costs could include the standard marketing costs that are included in the present channel discount structures, or they could reflect incremental marketing costs that are of particular value to the manufacturer. . . . In instances where the manufacturer takes on marketing costs that are presently being performed by the channel, the channel's compensation for these marketing functions would be reduced. . . . Making value-based compensation systems work will require both parties to know a great deal more about their marketing and sales costs than they know today. . . . [But] the beauty of value-based compensation structures is to more closely link the business objectives of the manufacturer with the business objectives of the channel through a compensation system that more directly reflects the value that the channel brings to this marketing relationship.[16]

Although the equity principle may sound obvious, it is rarely put to use. Here, we'll show how it can be implemented. The steps to be followed can be summarized as follows:

1. Define service outputs demanded by target market.
2. Isolate the marketing flows or activities that are required to generate these outputs.
3. Cost out each of the flows.
4. Structure an incentive system that will induce each channel member to add value to the products sold in the channel system in ways that best serve the target customers' needs for service outputs.

To illustrate the procedure, let's assume that we are a manufacturer of farm equipment and that we have already determined the service outputs desired by farmers when they "shop" for tractors, combines, etc. Let's also assume that we've isolated, for attack, a particular segment of farmers (e.g., tomato) to whom we are trying to market a specific model of tractor (which, we have already determined, is a valuable product in their eyes). Further, let's assume that we know which marketing activities will have to be performed and at what level in order to deliver the desired service outputs to this segment for this product. And finally, let's assume (for a very short while), that we are *not* going to divide labor in marketing the tractor, that is, we are going to take full responsibility for delivering the service outputs ourselves via vertical integration.

First, we should estimate what we will have to spend on each one of the marketing flows in order to assure that the tomato farmers whom we are targeting are satisfied in dealing with us. However, such estimates require using activity-based[17] or distribution cost accounting (see Chapter 10). Such cost accounting is oftentimes a Herculean task, and many companies simply do not have detailed enough data or cannot generate reasonable enough estimates to enable the process to go forward quickly. So, in the absence of "hard" objective cost data, we will instead try to figure out what percentage of our total available marketing/distribution budget we would have to allocate to the marketing flows to get the job done.

The total budget equals 100%. The percentages (or weights, if you will) that we will assign to each of the marketing flows will be based on our assessment of what has to be done to deliver the service outputs, what it is likely to cost (relative to other tasks that have to be accomplished), and how important the flow is relative to the overall marketing strategy of the firm. For example, hypothetically, it may cost our tractor firm more money to establish local storage facilities to provide farmers with rapid delivery of our tractor model than to train and deploy a sales force to sell the tractors; yet the presence of the sales force may be more essential to our long-term success than the presence of local storage. The algorithm that we use to assign weights should reflect effort, cost, and importance, jointly.

Suppose what we come up with, after thinking through what we need to do, looks as follows:

MARKETING FLOW	WEIGHT (%)
Physical Possession	20
Ownership	5
Promotion	30
Negotiation	2
Financing	18
Risking	15
Ordering	6
Payment	4
Total:	**100**

Next, we say to ourselves, "Wouldn't it be wonderful if we could divide labor with someone rather than doing all this work and incurring all these costs on our own?" So, in answer to our desire, we start looking around for potential partners, and we begin to consider the possibility of aligning ourselves with farm-equipment dealers. But if we were to "employ" these dealers, what should we pay them for helping us and what amount should we keep for ourselves? (The answer is: compensation in the channel should be given on the basis of the degree of participation in the marketing flows, remember?)

In figuring out the exact compensation, we need to work up a matrix, like the one here:

MARKETING FLOW	WEIGHT (%)	MANUFACTURER	DEALERS	END-USERS (TOMATO FARMERS)
Physical Possession	20			
Ownership	5			
Promotion	30			
Negotiation	2			
Financing	18			
Risking	15			
Ordering	6			
Payment	4			
Total:	**100**			

Next, we have to ask ourselves what would be the most appropriate division of labor with regard to each of the flows, based on what the end-user wants and who is in the best position to deliver it. We also must keep in mind that a channel is a partnership, which means that each party is going to have to support the other in order to make sure the job gets done. So, relative to physical possession, for example, we realize that dealers will bear the brunt of most of the local storage and delivery costs, but that we, as the manufacturer, are going to have to have back-up stocks located in distribution centers as well as some stocks near our plants as the tractors roll off the production line. For promotion, the dealers will have the most salespeople ("feet on the street"), but we will have to maintain a missionary sales force and a dealer management team, as well as engage in extensive advertising. This type of reasoning goes forward with each and every flow, and eventually results in data that look something like this:

MARKETING FLOW	WEIGHT (%)	MANUFACTURER (%)	DEALERS (%)	END-USERS (TOMATO FARMERS) (%)
Physical Possession	20	20	80	100[a]
Ownership	5	30	70	100
Promotion	30	25	75	100
Negotiation	2	10	90	100
Financing	18	60	40	100
Risking	15	50	50	100
Ordering	6	30	70	100
Payment	4	15	85	100
Total:	**100**			

[a]The "end-user" column always adds up to 100%, because the sum total of the effort of the manufacturer and the dealer is 100%. (It is possible to add additional parties to this analysis, and even to assess the end-user's efforts with respect to the flows, but we are keeping the illustration simple so that it can be easily understood.)

The next step is to multiply the weights times the cell values in the manufacturer and in the dealer columns and then sum each column. Thus, for the manufacturer column, the sum is **.339** or $[(.20 \times .20) + (.05 \times .30) + (.30 \times .25) + (.02 \times .10) + (.18 \times .60) + (.15 \times .50) + (.06 \times .30) + (04 \times .15)]$, and for the dealer, the sum is **.661** or $[(.20 \times .80) + (.05 \times .70) + (.30 \times .75) + (.02 \times .90) + (.18 \times .40) + (.15 \times .50) + (.06 \times .70) + (.04 \times .85)]$. This means that, based on an ideal concept of what they both ought to be doing in the channel of distribution, the manufacturer should receive 33.9% of the money available for distribution, and the dealers should receive 66.1% (notice that the sum of their compensation equals 100%).

Now, the next obvious question is "what money?" The answer is, in theory, found in the following way. First, one must figure out what the actual final prices end-users of the manufacturer's tractors have been paying or estimate the likely prices they will pay (list prices are usually not helpful, because they tend to be fictional.) Then, the actual number of units sold at the final prices charged must be determined or else a realistic forecast must be made of likely sales at likely prices. These pieces of information will give either actual or projected revenue (sales) at *"retail."* From this number must be subtracted cost of goods sold at the *manufacturer's* level (i.e., the cost of the tractors as they enter the distribution system) in order to derive the sum of money available for distribution. Some accountants would argue that, to cost of goods sold, the manufacturer should add a number to reflect a rate of return to manufacturing or to R&D. It should be remembered, however, that anything added to cost of goods sold at the manufacturing level shrinks the pot of money available for distribution.

For example, suppose the best-guess final price of the tractor model was projected to average $60,000 during the upcoming model year. Suppose, also, that the manufacturer projected sales to be 1000 units during the year. Total forecasted revenue generated by the model would be $60,000,000. Assume that the manufacturer's cost of goods sold is $36,000 (or 60%) per tractor or a projected $36,000,000. This means that $24,000,000 would be available to pay for the marketing flows.

As we have determined above, the manufacturer should get 33.9% of available money, and the dealers should get 66.1%, based on their contributions to the marketing flows. Thus, the manufacturer should receive $8,136,000, and the dealers, collectively, should receive $15,864,000. Therefore, the dealers need a margin of 26.4% on their sales of $60,000,000 to end-users, whereas the manufacturer requires a margin of 18.4% on its sales to the dealers ($60,000,000 less [$60,000,000 · .264]).

This same analysis can be performed for the manufacturer's existing marketing channel, and the "ideal" margins can be compared to the "existing" margins. Frequently, when examining an "existing" channel system, the "existing" margins do not truly reflect the contribution of individual channel members, regardless of what the "ideal" might be. Therefore, the entire excursion into the compensation issue can open up a great many questions. For example, in 1988, Lotus Development Corp., the Cambridge, Massachusetts-based software company, eliminated volume rebates to most of its dealers and instituted rebates based on how much support—in the form of sales efforts, seminars, and training—the dealers provide end-users.[18] Only by performing an analysis similar to that suggested previously can such rebates be arrived at rationally and reasonably.

In reality, there are so many things that influence the level of margins in distribution channels that the exercise suggested above may seem overly simplistic. After all, competitive forces, the amount of power held by channel members, the state of supply and demand, stage in the product life cycle, and a host of other factors play critical roles in determining who gets what. The value of the analysis laid out above comes from the fact that (1) it follows the equity principle and (2) it provides "stakes in the ground." If rewards in the channel deviate from what has been theoretically derived, it is essential that the firm find out why. If the rewards to a given channel member are exorbitant relative to the value it is adding to channel performance, then the equity principle has been violated, and it is time to consider changing the compensation system or, if that is impossible, changing the structure of the channel itself.

COERCIVE POWER   Coercive power stems from B's expectation of punishment by A if B fails to conform to A's influence attempt. Coercion involves any negative sanction or punishment of which a firm is perceived to be capable. Examples are reductions in margins, the withdrawal of rewards previously granted (e.g., an exclusive territorial right), and the slowing down of shipments. In fact, coercive power can be viewed as the "flip side" of reward power. It should be noted, however, that the threat and use of negative sanctions can often be viewed as "pathological" and may be less functional over the long run than other power bases that may produce more positive side effects.[19] Therefore, coercion should be employed only when all other avenues to evoke change have been traveled.

General Motors received extraordinarily low satisfaction ratings from its suppliers in 1993 because of accusations that GM acted coercively against the suppliers in trying to squeeze cost out of its supply channel. GM's former head of North American purchasing, Jose Ignacio Lopez de Arriortua, often disregarded long-term contracts that had been signed with suppliers, demanding that they be renegotiated at much more beneficial terms to GM. He is alleged also to have leaked proprietary information to competitive suppliers in attempts to get lower-cost parts, and to have exaggerated how low some bids were in order to get rivals to bid lower still. In a survey of 110 automotive suppliers done by ELM International Inc., a research firm, GM ranked last among a dozen North American companies in professionalism, cooperation, and communication. Some suppliers were so convinced that the change at GM was permanent that they took their best engineers off of GM products and on to work for Ford and Chrysler. The long-term result could have been that GM products of the future would have been of poorer quality than its rivals'. After Lopez was recruited away to join Volkswagen in Europe, the management of GM maintained its backing of the cost-cutting program, but engaged in an uphill battle to win back the trust it lost with the use of so many coercive actions.[20] Thus, although coercion may work in the short run, this power source can backfire once one's channel partners have somewhere else to turn.

Coercion can even be illegal in distribution channels. At one time, lawsuits charged Honda Motor Company with corruption in the allocation of cars to dealerships. Dealers, it was argued, were required to make "gifts" to people in the company to guarantee shipments of hard-to-get automobiles. Those who did not make payments got less than their fair share of cars for sale, the suits argued. Honda could extract these payments because, at the time, the Honda automobiles were in such high demand that dealers were in any case making large profits over sticker price on the cars, and there was thus enough money in the system to finance the payments.[21]

This does not mean, however, that there are never any situations where coercive power might be productively employed. For example, so-called gray marketers (unauthorized outlets) sell IBM personal computers for 20% or more below list price. Gray marketers buy the machines from authorized dealers, corporations, universities, and other large purchasers, who get them at discounts of 30% to more than 40%, depending on volume. The large buyers can resell the computers profitably for less than what a small buyer would pay IBM. In many cases, they can make money simply by ordering huge quantities to earn the biggest discount and then selling the excess at cost.[22] Even more damaging has been widespread copying of compact discs and computer software in markets such as the People's Republic of China by unauthorized dealers, who sell the bootleg products at a deep discount.

The troublesome thing about these practices is that the unauthorized gray or black market dealers do not provide advice and service, and sometimes they make unauthorized alterations in the equipment or products. Most important, these dealers undermine the efforts of legitimate dealers. The former get a free ride from the latter's attempts to cultivate and educate potential customers. IBM has exercised its coercive power by cutting off or threatening to cut off suppliers to unauthorized dealers. Because gray markets are virtually impossible to police and eliminate, IBM's coercive actions are largely symbolic. Even so, they reinforce in the minds of its legitimate dealers the company' interest in building a channel system that will deliver the appropriate service outputs to end-users. In support of this goal, it is willing to flex its muscles.

From a channel-management perspective, it would appear that the use of reward power should generally produce better results in helping forge long-term working relationships than would the use of coercive power. After all, the prospect of receiving a reward is a lot more pleasant than the prospect of receiving a punishment. Rewards can be suspect, however, because they are so closely related to coercive measures. First, withdrawing a reward is perceived as a coercive act. Second, rewards are subject to diminishing returns. To keep rewards salient, it is necessary to increase their size over time. Third, both coercive and reward power demand that the influence agent monitor the actions of the party whose behavior is supposed to change, so that the appropriate rewards or punishments can be administered in case of compliance or noncompliance. In other words, reward power has many of the attributes of coercive power, and therefore it is a double-edged base of power. Rather than focusing on reward and coercion, one should pay more attention to the remaining three power bases, even though there may be no feasible way to avoid using the first two.

EXPERT POWER   Expert power is based on B's perception that A has special knowledge. Examples of channel members assuming expert roles are widespread; indeed, such expertness is at the heart of the notion of division of labor, specialization, and comparative advantage in channel function organization. For example, as discussed earlier in this text, it has become very common for small retailers to rely heavily on their wholesale suppliers for expert advice. In the drug, grocery, automotive parts, and hardware trades, merchant wholesalers, such as McKesson, Super Valu, Genuine Parts, and Cotter, generally provide retailers with sales promotion counsel and aids, sales training for store employees, information about other retailers' promotions, advice on getting special displays, advice on store layout and arrangement, information on sources of items not stocked by the wholesaler, and managerial counseling.[23] Such services may also be provided by manufacturers in the form of management training for marketing intermediaries.

In the market for CD-ROM (compact disk—read only memory) multimedia disks, there are three major types of players: small-firm developers that are creative but lack marketing resources; publishers who specialize in marketing; and large distribution firms that have come into the CD-ROM industry from other media markets. The developers must rely on the marketing insights of publishers and distribution firms, because it is almost impossible to penetrate the software distribution channel without expertise and cash. One developer and publisher estimates that specialized marketing knowledge is so valuable that developers who are able to publish a CD-ROM title themselves can make profits of up to 2 1/2 times as much as those who must use a distribution partner.[24]

Efforts to amass expert power in distribution sometimes emerge out of joint efforts made by channel members. For example, Wal-Mart has entered into agreements with Procter & Gamble where P&G, not Wal-Mart, is responsible for inventory for a specific number of store racks of Pampers disposable diapers. P&G gets space in Wal-Mart's warehouse, but Wal-Mart does not pay for the Pampers until they are sold. To enable this arrangement to work, Wal-Mart tells P&G how fast and at what price it is selling Pampers, a disclosure viewed as impossible a few years ago.[25]

The durability of expert power presents a problem in channel management, however. If expert advice, once given, provides the recipient with the ability to operate without such assistance in the future, then the expertise has been transferred, and the power of the original expert in the relationship is reduced considerably. A firm that wishes to retain expert power in its relationships with other firms in a given channel over the long run has three options. First, it can dole out its expertise in small portions, always retaining enough vital data so that other channel members will remain dependent on it. But this would mean it would have to keep other channel members in the dark about some critical aspect of channel performance. Such a strategy would be self-defeating, because it is important that all channel members work up to their capacities if the channel as a whole is to function successfully. Second, the firm can continually invest in learning, and thereby always have new and important information to offer its channel partners. This means the firm would have to try to accumulate knowledge about market trends, threats, and opportunities that other channel members would find difficult to generate on their own. The cost of this option is not trivial, but the benefits, in terms of achieving channel goals, are likely to be high.

A third option is to encourage channel partners to invest in transaction-specific expertise that would be so specialized that they could not easily transfer it to other products or services.[26] In other words, the specific nature of the expertise, along with the costs involved in acquiring it, would impede exit from the channel. In cases where expertise can be readily transferred to "outsiders," marketers have sometimes taken rather drastic action to protect it. For example, the McDonald's franchise contract specifies that McDonald's may take over a restaurant without advance notice if a franchisee discloses confidential McDonald's documents. The contract also forbids franchisees from investing in another restaurant business.[27]

Crucial to the retention of expert power is the ability of a channel member to position itself well in the flow of communication and information within a channel system. For example, manufacturers may be highly dependent on other channel members for information on consumer demand. Retailers and industrial distributors occupy preferred positions in this respect because of their close contacts with consumers of the manufacturers' products. By gathering, interpreting, and transmitting valuable market information, a channel member can absorb uncertainty for other channel members. Through this process of *uncertainty absorption*,[28] the latter become more dependent on the former for inferences about market developments. For example, several decades ago General Foods (now called Kraft Foods) conducted a massive study of materials handling in distribution warehouses and then made its results and recommendations available to wholesalers through a group of specialists carefully trained to help implement the recommendations. The company also undertook a major study of retail space profitability and then offered supermarket owners the opportunity to learn a new approach to space-productivity accounting called *direct product profit*. The approach, which is outlined in Chapter 10, has since received widespread attention by mass merchandisers.

The use of expert power is a sticky wicket. First, to be able to exercise expert power, a channel member must be trusted. Otherwise, the expert advice is perceived as merely an attempt at manipulation. Second, experts are usually accorded very high status; therefore, they are difficult people with whom to identify. Third, independent-minded, entrepreneurially oriented businesspeople don't like to be told what to do. They believe that they are the experts. For example, in a survey of value-added computer resellers' (VARs) opinions of their vendors taken by International Data Corporation, Framingham, Massachusetts, it was found that

> in addition to wanting freedom from their vendor, VARs exhibit an independent streak in the factors they rate as **least** important. For example, VARs place little value on issues relating to general business assistance. They rate business training, sales training, and vendor help with a business plan near the bottom of their priority lists. VARs also see software help from a vendor as relatively unnecessary.[29]

REFERENT/IDENTIFICATION POWER   According to French and Raven, identification power and referent power are linked in a cause-and-effect sense.

> The referent power of A over B has its basis in the identification of B with A. By identification, we mean a feeling of oneness of B to A, or a desire for such an identity. . . . If A is an attractive group, B will have a feeling of membership or a desire to join. If B is already closely associated with A, he will want to maintain this relationship.[30]

Consider, for example, an individual who is simultaneously offered a Mercedes Benz dealership and a Hyundai dealership. If he or she discovers, through careful analysis, that both dealerships will yield him or her the same rate of return on his or her investment and that the management of both companies will give him or her comparable support in promotion, training service people, finding a location, and the like, the individual might choose the Mercedes Benz dealership because of the greater desire to be *identified* as a Mercedes dealer. In turn, the Mercedes organization would be able to exercise referent power over its new dealership.

The existence of referent power within many channels is undeniable, especially in situations where wholesalers or retailers pride themselves on carrying certain brands (e.g., Harley-Davidson motorcycles, Ralph Lauren clothing, Estee Lauder perfumes) and where manufacturers pride themselves on having their brands carried in certain outlets (e.g., Neiman-Marcus, Nordstrom, and Saks Fifth Avenue). For example, one of the ways in which Estee Lauder has achieved its referent power is by sticking to the company's basic formula: sell in upscale department stores and avoid new brands that only steal sales from existing ones.[31] One of the reasons Lauder is able to dominate the cosmetics counter in department stores is that the company refused to follow such competitors as Revlon or L'Oreal into the drug stores. Lauder didn't want to dilute its prestige image. On the other hand, as Levi's jeans, OshKosh's overalls, and Apple's personal computers broadened their distribution, they risked weakening their long-established referent power.[32]

One sign of a company's referent power is the willingness of its customers and dealers to give it the benefit of the doubt when it makes a mistake. Great Plains Software, a maker of high-end accounting software programs, benefited from its significant investments in knowing its customers and providing them superior service when launching an upgrade of its software package in 1993. The company has such solid customer relations that it convinced an astounding 42% of its Version 6 customers to upgrade to Version 7 of the software. But Version 7 turned out to have "bugs" in it. Concern for its sterling reputation led the company to spend $250,000 to mail new disks to every Version 7 buyer. The chief executive officer (CEO), Doug Bergum, also wrote to all 2,700 Great Plains dealers to admit to not testing Version 7 properly and to offer cash compensation to any dealer whose business suffered as a result. But instead of being inundated with dealer claims, more dealers responded to praise Bergum's handling of the situation than to ask for compensation! Total compensation to dealers amounted to only $25,000, which was less than 0.5% of Version 7's revenues. A trade magazine praised Bergum's behavior as a model of how such situations should be handled.[33] Thus, because of his brand equity with his dealers and customers, Bergum was able to turn a potential business disaster into a reaffirmation of his commitment to the marketplace.

In the world of business-to-business marketing channels, referent power is frequently achieved by focusing a manufacturer's salespeople on competing for the "mindshare" of distributors' sales forces. According to the Richmark Group, a Chicago-based consulting firm, a proven technique for managing mindshare is to develop a mutually beneficial business relationship with the distributors' sales forces. The goal is to develop the distributors' reps into a part-time extension of the manufacturer's direct selling capability. Richmark has observed that calling on and selling to the owner managers of most distributorships has minimal impact in building referent power with sales forces, because the former usually have little direct influence on the latter's day-to-day activities.

One company that has achieved referent power with VARs has been Hewlett-Packard. For example, according to a marketing manager for Ask Computer Systems Inc., Mountain View, California, HP's largest VAR:

> Hewlett-Packard is a very open, honest, trustworthy group of people. They are consistently people you would want to do business with.[34]

Clearly, just as is true with expert power, trust is a major prerequisite to building referent power. Trust is the belief that a party's word or promise is reliable, and the party will fulfill its obligations in an exchange relationship.[35] A firm is likely to trust its channel partner when it believes the partner to be both honest (i.e., stands by its word) and benevolent (i.e., interested in the firm's welfare).[36] Anderson and Weitz found substantial empirical support for the following proposition:

A channel member's trust in a manufacturer increases when:

a. the better the manufacturer's reputation is in its dealings with channel members;
b. the more the manufacturer offers in the way of sales support;
c. the more congruent are the manufacturer's and channel member's goals;
d. the greater the cultural similarity is between the manufacturer and channel member;
e. the relationship is long-standing;
f. the higher the communication level is in the relationship;
g. the more balanced the power is in the relationship.[37]

Building trust involves a willingness to put oneself at risk. This means that early in a relationship, it will be difficult to find high levels of trust, because there would have been little opportunity to see another party engage in risk-taking behavior.[38] In marketing channels, it is likely that coordination on marketing activities that involve some risk-taking on the part of all parties must precede (rather than succeed) the development of trust.[39]

LEGITIMATE POWER   Legitimate power stems from values internalized by B that give B a feeling that A "should" or "has a right to" exert influence and that B has an obligation to accept it. The appearance of legitimate power is most obvious in intraorganizational relations. That is, when a supervisor gives a directive to a subordinate, the latter feels that the former has a right to direct her/him in a certain manner and therefore will generally conform to the superior's desires. Such legitimized power is synonymous with authority.

Within a nonintegrated marketing channel, there is no formal hierarchy of authority. However, individual firms may perceive that such a hierarchy exists, or norms of behavior may define roles and effectively confer legitimate power on certain channel members. For example, the largest firm could be considered the leader by other channel members. If this is the case, then legitimate power may be available to that firm. It is also likely that retailers and industrial distributors will believe that they have a right to tell their suppliers what to do simply because they are positioned next to markets and their suppliers aren't. However, the scope of legitimate power may be limited; that is, the number of marketing flows over which a firm may be thought to have a right to exert influence may be quite small (e.g., wholesalers may have legitimate power relative to physical possession, and retailers relative to the flow of local promotion and pricing).

Obviously, the law allows firms to maintain agreements, such as franchises and other contracts, that confer legitimate power. In addition, patent and trademark laws give owners a certain amount of freedom and justification in supervising the distribution of their products. Another example of this type of legitimate power is the protection afforded a manufacturer and its dealers when the former adopts an exclusive distribution policy.

COMBINING THE POWER BASES   The preceding discussion of power bases has treated each separately. In reality, however, the power bases are used in combination. This can create certain synergistic effects; for example, legitimacy may enhance expertise and vice versa, identification may increase with the use of appropriate rewards, and coercion may sometimes be necessary to reinforce legitimacy. Expert, referent, or legitimate power may also be accompanied by reward power that contributes to a channel member's willingness to change its behavior. Thus, Toys "R" Us allowed McDonald's to open McDonald's restaurants inside of Toys "R" Us stores in Japan because of McDonald's legitimate power (through an equity stake McDonald's held in the Japanese Toys "R" Us operations), expertise power (McDonald's knew how to do business in Japan and where to locate stores), but also because of McDonald's reward power (Toys "R" Us expected to make more money by doing this than through some other process). On the other hand, there may be conflict between certain bases. For example, the use of coercion by a channel member may destroy any referent power that member might have been able to accumulate. It may have a similar effect on expert power, for which trust is a prerequisite.

In addition, there are economic, social, and political costs associated with the use of the various power bases, and these must be taken into account prior to the implementation of programs in which they are incorporated. Influence attempts are also constrained by norms that exist within channel systems. These norms, which are, in fact, "rules" of the competitive "game," aid in defining appropriate industrial behavior and can be even more restrictive than public laws in certain situations. For example, during periods of short supply in the steel industry, many buyers are willing to pay above-"normal" prices for steel. This alternative is less expensive than shutting down production. Because of short supply, steel distributors in the established marketing channels can command higher prices; however, they frequently refrain from doing so, because they feel that their customers expect a certain level of restraint from them, even though some of their customers go outside the established channel structure and purchase higher-priced steel from gray market sources. The established distributors also refrain from using coercive power, such as boycotts, against their customers who buy from these sources, because the norms of market behavior among them do not sanction such actions.

In sum, power exists in many forms, and is useful in guiding the behavior of channel members in ways and directions they otherwise would not have chosen. It can thus be used to coordinate the actions of diverse channel members in the pursuit of the overall channel's goals, or in pursuit of a single powerful channel member's goals.

DEVELOPING CHANNEL POWER   Channel power is an important descriptive characteristic of a channel member at a point in time—something that describes that channel member's current sources of leverage in the distribution system. But as the above examples imply, it should be remembered that channel members can also invest in power sources to increase their ability to affect channel behaviors and outcomes.

Companies routinely make investments in new technologies for marketing. For example, Anixter Brothers, an electrical wire and cable distributor, was one of the first in its industry to invest in an information technology system to manage its inventory in the early 1980s. This computerized system endowed *expert power* on

Anixter, because it could offer its downstream customers (e.g., building contractors) quicker and more reliable deliveries and could track where its inventories were in any of the warehouses it operated at any time. It even was able to offer an inventory management service to its customers, where the customer might purchase all its wire and cable needs through Anixter, but then Anixter would hold the inventory until it was needed at the building site. Pilferage and waste, as well as on-site inventory holding costs, were minimized through this service; Anixter was able to offer it at a lower cost than would be required for a contractor to perform the services itself. Thus, investing in information technology can confer expert power on a channel member and change the balance of power in the entire channel system.

The recent rush of pharmaceutical firms to enter into alliances with, or to acquire, pharmaceutical distributors is an example of investment in expert, reward, and legitimate power. Merck's acquisition of Medco, a new type of distributor in the Pharmacy Benefit Management (PBM) business, in 1993 for $6.6 billion is a good example. Medco claims to handle the prescriptions of 38 million people in the United States under assorted managed care arrangements. The expert power of distributors like Medco arises from the database they maintain connecting prescriptions to doctors, patients, payors, and managed care companies; their ability to discount heavily; their contracts to fill prescriptions under many company health plans; and their maintenance of formularies, which are lists of recommended drugs to which doctors are steered when prescribing for patients. Not only has Merck made this type of investment in expert power in the pharmaceutical distribution channel; so have SmithKline Beecham (which bought Diversified Pharmaceutical Services) and McKesson (whose subsidiary PCS is also in the PBM business). Estimates are that more than half of all Americans buy ethical drugs through such companies.[40]

Investments to increase *referent power* are also common. Whenever a company like McDonald's runs an image advertising campaign at the corporate level, it is investing in the brand equity of the McDonald's name. This brand equity confers referent power on McDonald's, because it makes the brand name more attractive to potential and current franchisees. In turn, the franchisees are more likely to do what McDonald's would like them to do, because they identify with the powerful brand name that McDonald's has built.

Channel members can invest in *legitimate power* also. For example, they can engage in lobbying efforts with governmental bodies. As mentioned in Chapter 2, Japan's Large-Scale Retail Store Law protected "mom-and-pop" Japanese retailers from the encroachments of retailers who wanted to build larger stores: the law provided that any store of greater than 5,000 square meters required the approval of the other merchants in the area where the new store was to be built! This effectively prevented the establishment of large retailers in established retailing areas. However, recent negotiations between the U.S. and Japanese governments have relaxed the terms of the Large-Scale Retail Store Law, and retailers like Toys "R" Us have opened large stores in Japan as a result. It is debatable whether Toys "R" Us would have ever gotten approval to open a large toy store in Japan without the extra efforts by the U.S. government, adding to its legitimate power in the Japanese channel structure.

Thus, it is important to remember that the power positions held by channel members at a given point in time are not just given and exogenous. They can change through the members' purposeful efforts. This implies that channel members should seek opportunities to invest wisely in developing bases of power, and also that they should be aware of other channel members' equal incentives to make such investments.

Channel Commitment and Trust

How are commitment and trust generated in a channel relationship, and what are the effects of doing so?[41] Trust between channel members can be increased through shared values, through increasing the value of channel outcomes, and through communication, and can be decreased if one or both parties exhibit opportunistic behavior. Relationship commitment tends to be higher the greater are the shared values of the partners, the relationship benefits to both parties, and the costs of terminating the relationship. Further, trust itself is found to affect commitment positively.

The benefits of developing trust and relationship commitment, in turn, are many. Trust tends to decrease the uncertainty perceived by channel members, and increases cooperation and "functional conflict" (that is, constructive differences, rather than pathological conflicts). Relationship commitment also increases cooperation, satisfaction, and acquiescence in a channel relationship, and decreases each channel partner's propensity to leave the relationship.

Channel managers can distinguish among multiple types of channel commitment. *Affective commitment* (maintaining a relationship because one wants to) produces more positive results than *moral commitment* (maintaining the relationship because one feels one should do so), whereas *calculative commitment* (maintaining the relationship because one has to) has a strong negative impact on a channel member's desire to invest in and stay in the channel relationship.

This modern focus on channel commitment and trust is a function of the realization that some distribution channel structures are neither arms'-length market-based relationships, nor are they vertically integrated organizations, but are something in between. They may be "administered systems," "strategic alliances," "contractual systems," "long-term relationships," or "working partnerships." Our approach to channel management must be able to explain and analyze such structures. The relational contracting literature focuses on such exchange relations. "Free-form, arms'-length" exchange refers to any transaction that is governed by the rules of the marketplace; it is essentially a purely economic relation. In contrast, Heide notes that a relational exchange

> accounts explicitly for the historical and social context in which transactions take place and views enforcement of obligations as following from the mutuality of interest that exists between a set of parties. . . . [In] relational exchange, . . . individuals' utility functions are subsumed by the global utility of the system. . . . Concern for the long-run benefit of the system serves as a restraint on individual tendencies to pursue their self-interest in an opportunistic fashion.[42]

TABLE 7-1 Dimensions and Forms of Interfirm Relationships

	RELATIONSHIP FORM		
DIMENSION	**Free-Form**[a]	**Authority-Based**[b]	**Partner-Based**[c]
1. **Relationship Initiation**	No particular initiation process	Selective entry; skill training	Selective entry; value training
2. **Relationship Maintenance**			
2.1. Role Specification	Individual roles applied to individual transactions	Individual roles applied to entire relationship	Overlapping roles; joint activities and team responsibilities
2.2. Nature of Planning	Nonexistent; or limited to individual transactions	Proactive/unilateral; binding contingency plans	Proactive/joint; plans subject to change
2.3. Nature of Adjustments	Nonexistent; or giving rise to exit or immediate compensation	*Ex ante*/explicit mechanism for change	Bilateral/predominantly negotiated changes through mutual adjustment
2.4. Monitoring Procedures	External/reactive; measurement of output	External/reactive; measurement of output and behavior	Internal/proactive; based on self-control
2.5. Incentive System	Short-term; tied to output	Short- and long-term; tied to output and behavior	Long-term; tied to display of system-relevant attitudes
2.6. Means of Enforcement	External to the relationship; legal system/competition/offsetting investments	Internal to the relationship; legitimate authority	Internal to the relationship; mutuality of interest
3. **Relationship Termination**	Completion of discrete transaction	Fixed relationship length, or explicit mechanisms for termination	Open-ended relationship

[a]Heide refers to this as "market governance."
[b]Heide refers to this as "unilateral/hierarchical nonmarket governance."
[c]Heide refers to this as "bilateral nonmarket governance."

Source: Adapted from Jan B. Heide, "Interorganizational Governance in Marketing Channels," *Journal of Marketing,* Vol. 58 (January 1994), p. 75.

Heide uses these concepts to differentiate among "free-form," "authority-based," and "partner-based" interfirm relationships. Partner-based relationships are most similar to the notion of relational exchange, whereas authority-based relationships involve "an authority structure that provides one exchange partner with the ability to develop rules, give instructions, and in effect impose decisions on the other."[43] Table 7-1 summarizes the differences among the three types of interfirm relationships. Notice that a key difference between free-form relationships and the other two forms lies in the "relationship initiation" stage: nonmarket governance involves a selective entry process in which some potential channel partners might be excluded, whereas market governance imposes no particular initiation process on the participants.

Thus, there is an important focus in a bilateral governance system on designing the relationship from day one to maximize mutuality of interests and coordination of actions. The goal is to make it worth one's while to act in a manner constructive to the relationship. Indeed, in such a channel structure, the whole concept of Williamsonian "opportunism," as discussed in Chapter 6, loses some of its sting: the notion of self-seeking becomes completely compatible with that of seeking the welfare of the system as a whole.[44]

Clearly, then, creating a channel relationship that exhibits trust and commitment is important because it can have a significant effect on the productivity and longevity of the relationship as a whole. These issues need to be dealt with when the distribution channel arrangement is first being created. But even the best-designed relationships can malfunction at some point during the relationship, requiring constant care and nurturing to maintain coordination in the channel.

Contractual Mechanisms

Hostages, the bargaining solution, credible commitments, self-enforcing agreements: the language describing some of today's contractual arrangements to coordinate channel behavior is very colorful. It reflects the emergence and increasing importance of channel forms that are not quite arms'-length market contracting, and not quite vertical integration, but involve considerable commitment between channel members.

The unifying theme in these arrangements is that *there are gains from specialization if channel members can only figure out a way to reliably cooperate with each other.* This is the heart of what is known as the bargaining solution. To understand the concept, consider a basic market-governed, arms'-length channel "relationship" (if such a commercial interaction can be called a "relationship"). The parties involved may be considering making a stronger commitment to each other, involving specialization by one party in some channel functions (e.g., the distributor may specialize in physical possession and ownership of inventory) and by the other party in other channel functions (e.g., the manufacturer may specialize in promotion). Specialization in the channel will reduce redundancy in the performance of these flows and hence reduce overall channel costs. As a result, *even if no changes are made that influence market demand,* the size of the channel profit pie will increase. There are gains from specialization, and these gains can be split between the channel members according to whatever bargain they strike with each other. The fact that there is more overall profit to distribute between the two parties means that, no matter what the current split of channel profits, *both channel members can be made better off without either being made worse off.* So, there is always some bargain that can be struck that should make the channel members happy to specialize their channel flow performance and coordinate more closely.

Of course, this point of view may be a little too optimistic. Consider the example of Bayou Gasket & Hose, located in Vendor City, an industrial park in Lake Charles, Louisiana. Vendor City was built by one of Bayou's biggest customers, PPG Industries, just 600 yards away from PPG's facility. Bayou signed a 10-year lease on its space in Vendor City in the hopes of increasing its business with PPG. Further, Bayou has integrated its information system with that of PPG, and also practices just-in-time delivery to PPG.[45] These alliance-specific investments by Bayou Gasket & Hose are clearly very risky; suppose its business with PPG does not increase? PPG might not be seriously hurt by such a turn of events, but it could be catastrophic for Bayou, since it has chosen to locate its supply facility close to PPG, not close to the rest of the market for its products. Indeed, the surprising story is that Bayou Gasket & Hose chose to set up shop in Vendor City at all!

The key issue facing the company was precisely this: how could it benefit from the bargaining solution in the face of the threat of opportunistic behavior by PPG? Their solution involved the *mutual posting of bonds,* or to put it another way, *mutual hostage taking.* Both PPG and its suppliers (fully nine suppliers have leased space in Vendor City) made significant investments that, once made, had little salvage value outside the specific relationship. PPG, for its part, promised its suppliers a 10-year lease with guarantees in case PPG should want to move the supplier out of the distribution space in the new facility before the lease term was up. The distributors, for their part, bore the cost of moving their distribution facilities to the PPG warehouse, a location with little apparent outside market value. Each of these investments is like a "hostage" that is held by the other party in the distribution channel. Reneging on the distribution agreement would entail significant costs to the deviating channel member, because of the exchange of hostages that took place.

Further, note that in the PPG case, the posting of these bonds or exchange of these hostages was a *credible commitment* by both parties. That is, it is not obvious how one would "wriggle out" of having made that commitment a priori. After all, PPG did build a new facility—the very existence of the building is something that cannot be reversed, once accomplished. Hence, it is a credible commitment. In general, any physical capital commitment is likely to be a credible commitment as long as it cannot be "unmade" or "un-invested-in." The supplier's decision to relocate to the PPG facility is also a credible commitment, because once the relocation costs have been incurred, they cannot be undone. Nor is the choice to leave Vendor City without its own incremental fixed costs. Thus, the combination of (a) mutual exchange of hostages and (b) the credibility of these commitments makes it feasible for PPG and its suppliers to turn what originally was a situation of mutual concern and mistrust into one of enthusiastic partnership with a long-term horizon.

▶ IDENTIFYING POTENTIAL AND ACTUAL CHANNEL CONFLICTS

Despite a channel manager's best efforts to design a channel structure that is both efficient and effective, in many situations the channel simply does not work as planned. First, it is impossible to foresee all contingencies when planning a channel structure, because, as transaction cost analysis reminds us, humans tend to be boundedly rational: they find it hard to cope with all the available information about the market, consumers, and the environment. Second, even if one *could* cope with all the available market information at the time the channel is originally designed, the climate in which the channel operates is dynamic and stochastic. When the competitive, environmental, consumer, or internal circumstances change unexpectedly, a previously well-working channel can fall into disarray, and channel members need to be ready to respond to meet new market challenges.

When a channel is misdesigned or when new market conditions make an old channel design unworkable, the result can be dissatisfaction, arguments, and decreased effort levels throughout the channel. Unguided channel activity, with each channel member independently seeking its own self-interest, generally leads to *channel conflict* (because channel members are unlikely to coordinate their activities spontaneously). To be equipped to deal with these possibilities, we need to know what channel conflict is, what types of conflict can arise in channels, and whether and under what circumstances channel conflict can be constructive. This section deals with these issues.

Types of Conflict

The roots of channel conflict lie in the inherent interdependence of channel members on each other. Channel members tend to specialize in certain functions: manufacturers might specialize in production and national promotions, whereas retailers might specialize in merchandising, distribution, and local promotions. This specialization induces interdependence. Channel members are "pushed" into these interdependencies because of their need for resources—not only money, but also specialized skills, access to particular kinds of markets, and the like. Thus, functional interdependence requires a minimum level of coordination in order to accomplish the channel task.

However, organizations strain to maximize their autonomy; therefore, the establishment of interdependencies creates conflicts of interest. In channels comprising independently owned institutions and agencies, this strain toward autonomy will be juxtaposed with the desire to coordinate; a mixture of motives will be present. The greater the interdependence, the greater the opportunity for interference with goal attainment, and hence the greater the potential for conflict among organizations. We can formalize these notions with the following definition of channel conflict:

> *Channel conflict* is a situation in which one channel member perceives another channel member(s) to be engaged in behavior that prevents or impedes it from achieving its goals. The amount of conflict is, to a large extent, a function of goal incompatibility, domain dissensus, and differing perceptions of reality.[46]

The frequency and intensity of disagreements between channel members can be combined and classified into three levels of conflict, as Magrath and Hardy point out. Figure 7-2 shows these levels.

> The *intensity of conflicts* can range from minor flare-ups that are easily forgotten to major disagreements marked by terminations, lawsuits, or other types of counter-sanctioning. *Conflict frequency* can range from sporadic disputes and occasional disagreements to protracted, bitter relations. *Conflict importance* . . . provides a third dimension. The combined intensity, frequency, and importance provide a general measure of conflict level that we have arbitrarily classified as low, medium, or high conflict.[47]

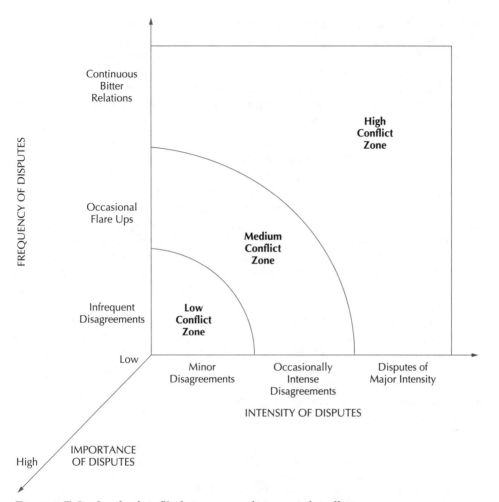

FIGURE 7-2 **Levels of conflict between manufacturers and resellers.**
Source: Allen J. Magrath and Kenneth G. Hardy, "A Strategic Framework for Diagnosing Manufacturer-Reseller Conflict," *Marketing Science Institute Report* No. 88-101 (Cambridge, MA: Marketing Science Institute, 1988), p. 3.

Channel management problems can be identified at two different points in time in a channel relationship: before the relationship starts (the *ex ante* time frame) or at some time during the ongoing channel relationship (the *ex post* time frame). Clearly, channel partners will seek to identify as many potential sources of conflict as possible before the relationship ever starts and design mechanisms to forestall the occurrence of those conflicts. Nevertheless, once the relationship starts, unforeseen events may generate conflicts that were not forecast earlier, and these conflicts must be identified and dealt with as they arise. For example, one franchise business, Postal Instant Press, Inc., enjoyed happy relationships with its franchisees in the early 1980s. But PIP's founder, Bill LeVine, who had provided high-quality assistance and support to his franchisees, stepped down from running the business in 1985. In 1993, 30 current and former franchisees sued PIP, arguing that the franchisor breached its contracts by cutting franchisee services. Such conflict could not have been foreseen at the time the franchisees first entered into business with PIP.[48] Thus, at both stages of the channel relationship, *ex ante* and *ex post*, identification and management of conflict is crucial to channel coordination. We therefore turn next to a discussion of the three major sources of conflict: goal divergence, domain dissensus, and differing perceptions of reality.

GOAL DIVERGENCE   Each channel member has a set of goals and objectives that are often very different from those of other channel members. These divergences cause channel conflict, because they induce behavior by one channel member that is inconsistent with the achievement of another channel member's goals. To see the importance of goal conflict in inhibiting channel coordination, consider what transaction cost analysis would be without goal divergence. As explained in Chapter 6, one of the central tenets of transaction cost analysis is "opportunism," or "self-interest seeking with guile."[49] This type of behavior would be a nonproblem if all channel members started out with coincident goals. With coincident goals among all channel members, self-interest seeking, with or without guile, would produce exactly the coordinated outcome!

Goal conflict also looms large in the *agency theoretic* approach to channel management problems. Agency theory is concerned with the relationship between a *principal* and his or her *agent.* Two parties are said to have an *agency relationship* whenever the principal hires, or depends on, the agent to perform a duty or set of duties on behalf of the principal. Although such relationships clearly exist between a company and its law firm or between a corporate board and the CEO of the firm, agency relationships pervade the marketing, and particularly the channels, context as well:

> Agency relationships are pervasive in marketing because the essence of marketing is exchange, and "the agency relationship is . . . a significant component of almost all [exchange] transactions" (Arrow 1985). This is particularly true because most goods and services are distributed through intermediaries—such as wholesalers, retailers, or franchisees—who act as agents (in an agency theory sense) of the manufacturer or franchisor. . . . The ultimate customer also can be viewed as engaging in an agency relationship as he or she attempts to gain accurate product information and desired product benefits from a supplier who may be viewed as his or her agent.[50]

A so-called *agency problem* exists when the agent cannot be guaranteed to act completely in the principal's best interest (a) because the agent has different objectives, orientations, and attitudes than the principal (i.e., has divergent goals from those of the principal), and (b) when the principal cannot fully monitor the agent's performance to see whether the agent is doing what is required of him. Note that both conditions (a) and (b) above must hold for there to be an agency problem. Suppose condition (b) does not hold, that is, the principal really can completely infer the agent's effort level from his output level, but there is goal conflict. Then the principal can construct a contract with the agent, specifying a payment based on the agent's output, that induces the agent to exert the "right" amount of effort (because there is a perfect one-to-one relationship between effort and output). Such a contract is called a *forcing contract.* Conversely, if the agent's effort is not perfectly observable by the principal, but goal conflict is absent, then there is no agency problem: the agent naturally wants to do what the principal asks of him. Thus, the two conditions must be jointly present to produce an agency problem.

Goal conflict is extremely common, one example being in the dealer channel for personal computers. Compaq, for instance, has sought to expand its reach beyond its traditional dealer channel into newer channels such as mail-order sales and superstores. In periods of short supply and heavy demand, it has rationed supplies of computers to its traditional dealers in an effort to serve all of its channels fairly and to reach consumers with different service output demands. But the goal of the traditional dealers does not include supplying other channels with Compaq computers. (Indeed, that serves only to increase intrachannel competition as far as they are concerned.) The dealers have expressed their dissatisfaction with Compaq by steering their customers to competitors' brands rather than lose the customer to a rival retailer.[51]

Given the centrality of goal conflict in agency relationships, designing a contract that solves or minimizes the agency problem becomes critical:

> The focus of [agency] theory is on determining the most efficient contract to govern a particular relationship given the characteristics of the parties involved and the fact that environmental uncertainty and the costs of obtaining information make it impossible for the principal to monitor the agent completely.[52]

Figure 7-3 shows the many influences on the optimal contract between a principal and its agent. This contract might specify functions and flows to be performed by each channel member, the payouts to each channel member contingent on achieving specified outcomes, and the structure of ownership arrangements inside the channel. The solution to the agency problem thus revolves around creating contractual solutions that make the agent behave *as if* it had the same goals as the principal—that is, as if goal conflict were absent.

DOMAIN DISSENSUS Conflict in marketing channels can also be caused by differences in domain definitions among channel members. A channel domain comprises four critical elements:

1. *Population to be served.* For example, are all large accounts supposed to be handled by the direct sales force and all small accounts by distributors or dealers?
2. *Territory to be covered.* For example, what is distributor A's area of primary responsibility, and are there any overlaps with distributors B or C?
3. *Functions or duties to be performed.* What exactly is the role of each channel member regarding each of the eight marketing flows?
4. *Technology to be employed in marketing.* For example, how are prospects to be approached? What level of training is required for the sales force? What should be the role of telemarketing? Are computer linkups required for order placement? Should the sales process employ hard-sell or soft-sell techniques?

Real-world domain conflict of all four types can be observed in many different marketing channels. Below are some examples of each.

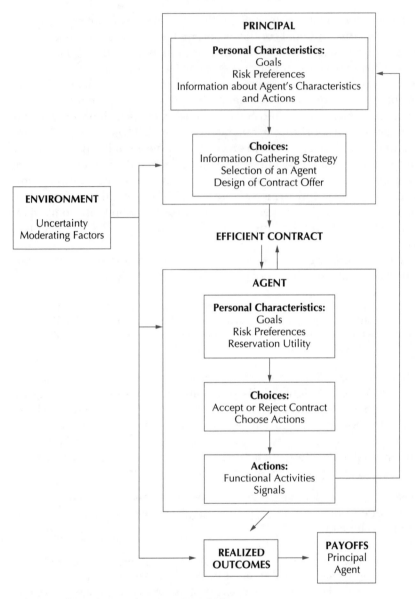

FIGURE 7-3 **Agency theory contract design process.**
Source: Mark Bergen, Shantanu Dutta, and Orville C. Walker, Jr., "Agency Relationships in Marketing: A Review of the Implications and Applications of Agency and Related Theories," *Journal of Marketing,* Vol. 56 no. 3, (July 1992), p. 3.

Population Issues. Perhaps one of the most heated issues in marketing channels has to do with who owns which accounts. It is very difficult, for example, for direct sales forces to share accounts with "outsiders," and vice versa. Anytime a supplier opens up multiple channels (which is the rule, not the exception), there is always the likelihood that a customer will deal with one channel on one occasion and another channel on a different occasion or that the customer will play the channels off against each other. The initial seller will nearly always claim that latecomers are taking a "free ride" off the efforts it took to get the door open in the first place. This competition on the "horizontal" level of distribution (e.g., among distributors) almost always breeds "vertical" conflict (e.g., between the distributors and their supplier).

For example, Goodyear Tire & Rubber Co. has expanded its channels from a traditional exclusive dealer network to include Sears, Roebuck and Discount Tire Co. (a Phoenix-based tire retailer). Although this change increases the market reach of Goodyear's tires, it comes at the expense of its exclusive dealers' goodwill. The dealers, who carry only Goodyear tires, complain that the products' brand equity is diluted by being sold next to other brands in these new retailers' outlets. Goodyear now pursues a strategy of "selling tires wherever people buy them."[53] However, in response to the dealers' complaints (and in some cases, lawsuits), it has given the dealers exclusive rights to sell specific brands of Goodyear tires.

There is an important difference between competition and conflict. Pure, wholesome, healthy competition is goal- or object-centered behavior. It is indirect and impersonal. The goal or object is held by a third party. Most swimming events, with the exception of water polo, are examples of "competition," as are events such as the high jump, hurdles, and the 100-meter dash. Golf qualifies, unless one competitor kicks his rival's ball into the rough or steps on it deliberately while walking up the fairway. Conflict, on the other hand, is opponent-centered behavior. It is very direct and highly personal. The goal or object is held by the opponent, because unless the opponent is somehow interfered with, he or she will take home the trophy. Boxing, football, soccer, basketball, and even tennis (white shorts and all!) are basically examples of "conflict" sports.[54]

In distribution, there is nothing wrong with pure, wholesome, healthy competition among channels, even if they are pursuing the same customer. In fact, the customer ought to be very pleased that he or she has a choice. IBM has consciously multiplied the channels through which it offers its products to the market: not only through the traditional "Blue Suited" sales force, but also through 20,000-plus "business partners" and its original equipment manufacturer (OEM) program. The business partners' program accounted for 1992 sales of $2.5 billion, and the OEM program for $1.25 billion. Business partners are aimed at selling to small and medium-sized accounts, which formerly belonged to the employee sales force. This shift has created some tension, but management emphasizes the "competitive" rather than "conflictual" nature of the situation, and reaffirms that competition will continue.[55]

A customer will be confused, though, if all of the "competitors" look identical. At that point, he or she will begin to play one channel off against another. But if there are significant points of difference—if each channel delivers different service outputs—then the customer can determine which channel can best serve his or her needs, and given the opportunity to make his or her own choice, the probability is that satisfaction with the selection will be high. However, when channels are identical in terms of what they can deliver, they begin to engage in opponent-centered behavior in order to get the sale, disparaging one another in front of the customer. The end result is that the lack of channel management on the supplier's part has set up a situation in which chaos begins to reign, and the customer becomes frustrated. "Horizontal" competition becomes "horizontal" conflict, which, in turn, breeds "vertical" conflict.

The moral of the story is that there is nothing wrong with channel competition as long as the channels put in place are distinctive, that is, capable of delivering different service outputs. On the other hand, horizontal channel conflict can create enormous problems, causing transaction costs to increase significantly.

Territory Issues. Turf problems associated with the assignment of territories or primary areas of responsibility are legion. The underlying issue revolves around the extent of intrabrand (that is, within-brand) competition a channel member faces (a topic addressed in detail in Chapter 8). The question is whether channel members are going to be able to generate adequate sales at reasonable profit levels on the manufacturers' brands they have agreed to carry. Company sales forces have the same sort of squabbles as well.

The issue has been given the most publicity in franchise situations. As Kaufmann and Rangan point out,[56]

> Because the franchisor's optimal number and configuration of stores in a market will generally reflect a significantly more intensive distribution strategy than would be optimal for the franchisees, market development is a source of constant tension. Conflict over the degree of market penetration can impose severe governance costs on the franchise system: (1) because of the formal and informal processes that may be required to resolve intrasystem disputes and (2) because of the effort involved in maintaining franchisee morale. One national franchisor reported . . . that 40 percent of its development group's time was devoted to resolving conflicts arising from new store introductions.

The only way to head off such disputes is to conduct rigorous and reasonable trading area analyses that show, conclusively, that existing channel members will be able to thrive even if intrabrand competition is increased. Because nothing in the social sciences can ever rival physics for accuracy, however, we can be sure that territorial issues will continue to cause conflict in distribution channels long into the future.

Division of Labor Issues. The level of marketing support provided by suppliers and the degree of value added provided by other members of the channel relative to the compensation they are given for doing what they do are sources of considerable frustration in distribution. Apparently many channels could benefit from an application of the Equity Principle discussed above, with its associated tools for measuring the value contributed by each channel member to overall channel performance. In the contact-lens industry, for example, many users of disposable lenses (which must be replaced once or twice a month) now prefer to buy the lenses through mail-order channels, because the price can be as little as half that found in optometrists' offices. But some lens manufacturers, such as Johnson & Johnson, Bausch & Lomb, and Ciba-Geigy's United States unit, refuse to sell their lenses through mail-order suppliers. These manufacturers claim that a mail-order channel cannot provide the necessary consumer services relative to fit and vision. They believe these services are critical, and argue that the only channel member who can perform them is an optometrist.[57]

The division of labor issue also comes up in relations between manufacturers and retailers. General-merchandise retailers, facing slimmer and slimmer gross margins, try to move channel functions and their costs up the channel to their suppliers. Kmart asks its toy retailers to sell their products on consignment. Kmart does not pay for the goods when they arrive at the retailer's distribution center; rather, they wait until they appear in the retail stores. Federated Department Stores asks some apparel suppliers to provide higher-quality hangers for clothes so that Federated does not have to spend time and money changing hangers once they take possession of the merchandise. Federated management argues that cost can be cut out of the total channel system by eliminating the extra hanging step at the retail level. And Sharper Image, the specialty-goods retailer and catalog operation, asks for "guaranteed sale" rights from some suppliers, whereby the supplier must take back unsold goods. This effectively shifts product risk back to the supplier level from the retail level.[58]

Technology Issues. The word "technology" should not be restricted in its application to situations involving hardware and software. It is really a much broader term. There is a technology of production that involves inputs, transformations, and outputs. There is also a technology of marketing. The problem is that the various members of distribution channels often approach marketing very differently. Retailers and wholesalers are focused on operations, especially those involving logistics and human resources. Manufacturers tend to be more strategic in their orientation to marketing, but sometimes have little appreciation for the operational nuances that plague their downstream counterparts. The vast gulf that frequently exists between strategy and tactics or implementation creates large conflicts in marketing channels.

For example, makers of consumer electronics products argue with their retailers about the appropriate sales and returns "technology" to use with consumers. Currently, many retailers offer "no questions asked" return policies, and some (such as Kmart) give a full refund no matter how long it has been since the date of purchase. Retail personnel are often not trained enough to be able to tell whether a returned product is indeed faulty, as some consumers maintain, or correctly working, and they simply return the unit to the manufacturer for a refund. Manufacturers even refer to the "Super Bowl Problem" in the television department, where a consumer buys a large-screen TV the Friday before the Super Bowl is telecast and then returns it the following Monday; and the "Wedding Problem," where the father of the bride buys a camcorder on Friday to record his daughter's wedding on Saturday, returning the unit on Monday. A report issued in 1994 by the manufacturers' group, the Electronic Industries Association, recommends that retailers improve their mechanisms for determining why a product was returned and improve retail sales personnel training as first steps to control this channel problem.[59]

DIFFERING PERCEPTIONS OF REALITY   Differing perceptions of reality are also important sources of conflict, because they indicate that there will be differing bases of action in response to the same situation. Additionally, one channel member may misperceive what another channel member has done in the way of marketing channel functions and flows, creating another instance of perception-of-reality conflict. Further, if channel members are inhibited by uncertainty and an inability to process all available information, there is a significant possibility that they will differ in how they perceive "reality," because in fact "reality" can mean different things to different channel members under these circumstances. Finally, a lack of communication can exacerbate the perception of reality conflict. Morgan and Hunt note that "timely communication ... fosters trust by assisting in resolving disputes and aligning perceptions and expectations."[60] Thus, they hypothesize that improvements in communication between channel members decrease the probability of perception-of-reality conflicts, and conversely, lack of communication can lead to such conflicts.

The fact that differing perceptions of reality can cause significant channel conflict is evident in the Compaq example above. Compaq dealers believed they were not getting enough computers and that they were being hurt by the company's expansion into multiple channel outlets, such as mail-order outlets and superstore vendors. But Compaq management stated that the company made record shipments in mid-1993, at levels that were continually increasing. Although both sides might have agreed on the actual numbers of computers being sent, the dealers were focusing on how the pie was sliced, whereas Compaq itself focused on the total size of the pie.[61]

Pathological Conflict versus Constructive Conflict

Without *any* conflict, channel members will tend to become passive and noninnovative. Eventually, the system of which they are a part will lose its viability. Conflict motivates channel members to adapt, grow, and seize new opportunities. Conflict should impel better channel performance, especially if (1) moderate levels of conflict are not considered too costly by channel members, (2) divergent views produce better ideas, and (3) aggression is not irrational or destructive.[62] Anderson and Narus echo this view, arguing that "functional conflict" is a consequence of trust in a channel relationship:

> When partner firms use disagreements as a means of "clearing the air" of potentially harmful tensions and ill-will, conflict can have functional and productive consequences. By making conflict functional, partner firms maintain cordial relations and tend to give each other the "benefit of the doubt" in conflict episodes. ... We believe that firms that have developed strong trust in a relationship are more likely to work out their disagreements amicably and, in fact, accept some level of conflict as being "just another part of doing business."[63]

However, because conflict is opponent-centered behavior, it can degenerate into actions calculated to destroy, injure, or thwart another party in an interdependent relationship. What one must seek to avoid is *pathological conflict*—moves that are malignant for the parties involved and for the entire system itself.[64] For example, John has found that coercive or overly bureaucratic channel management practices can induce "self-interest seeking with guile," Williamson's definition for opportunistic behavior in a channel.[65]

When conflict management mechanisms are either nonexistent or inadequate, a pathological situation can result like that experienced by Nissan Motor, the Japanese automaker, in 1990 in the United Kingdom. At the end of that year, the company suddenly terminated its distribution agreement with Nissan UK (NUK), its privately owned British importer/distributor for the previous 21 years. Nissan claimed that the owner of NUK, Octav Botnar, was unpredictable, whimsical, and volatile. It said that NUK had failed to pick up cars at the time stipulated, that it had delayed payments, and that its provision of forward sales plans to allow Nissan to plan production had been haphazard for at least six to seven years. NUK accused Nissan of acting unfairly against the British consumer by pricing one of its new cars (called the Primera) too high compared with the prices charged to Nissan's wholly owned distributors in Germany, the Netherlands, and Belgium. The pathological conflict ended up in the law courts, where NUK lost the battle to retain its franchise. By the end of 1991, Nissan had gone through the difficult and costly process of establishing an entirely new U.K. import and distribution operation and had replaced nearly 400 dealers who among them had sold 138,000 Nissan cars and commercial vehicles in 1990, giving Nissan the leading market share among Japanese cars sold in the United Kingdom.[66]

We close this section with the reminder that the parties inaugurating a channel relationship should assess the *potential* for conflict. A great deal of time should be spent focusing on trying to design the channel's structure and "game plan" to minimize the chance of conflict occurrence once the relationship begins. Both *ex ante* and *ex post* conflict identification must be done to guarantee at every stage of the relationship that conflict remains at the constructive, not the pathological, level.

▶ CONFLICT-MANAGEMENT TECHNIQUES

Once we accept that conflict is likely to arise in normal channel relations, it becomes necessary to consider how such conflict will be managed or controlled. If conflict is not addressed in the channel, it is unlikely that coordinated channel outcomes can result. The specific conflict-management strategy employed will depend not only on the cause of the conflict but also on the weight of power of the channel member seeking to manage the conflict.[67] Therefore, the effective use of power is required not only in specifying roles within the channel but also in dealing with the conflicts that inevitably arise among channel members.

Dant and Schul use a typology of conflict resolution processes first developed by March and Simon.[68] "Information-intensive" conflict-resolution strategies involve significant information exchanges between channel members, and hence entail the possibility for significant downside informational losses. Conversely, "information-protecting" conflict-resolution strategies carry low exposure because information sharing is kept to a minimum. Below, we identify and give examples of the two types of conflict-resolution strategies, and discuss when one or the other is more likely to be used.

Types of Conflict Resolution Strategies

INFORMATION-INTENSIVE STRATEGIES   Information-intensive strategies for resolving conflict involve the open exchange of information in the conflict-resolution process. Exchanging information can imply a loss of control. Trust and cooperation are therefore likely (but not necessary) conditions for the successful application of information-intensive conflict-resolution processes.

The importance of information sharing is highlighted in Provident Mutual's pension services business. This division sells pension management services both directly and through brokers who also represent many other financial services companies. In 1992 Provident audited channel functions and flows throughout the channel, and developed a plan to help move a sales prospect toward the buying stage. Provident then approached selected brokers and offered to share the targeted customer analysis tool it had developed. Provident salespeople and brokers worked together as a sales team, contacting mutually selected prospects. In just 90 days, they closed $2 million in new business, and by the end of the year they had increased sales by 47% over the previous year, even while the rest of the industry showed flat or declining sales numbers.[69] Without a willingness to share complex, detailed information, this channel might, at best, have shown no sales increases and at worst, might have demonstrated significant domain conflict as independent brokers allocated sales time to accounts other than those of Provident Mutual.

An open information-sharing approach can pay off handsomely for both the party sharing the information and for the information recipient. In the wake of dissatisfaction with General Motors' supplier relationships, these suppliers are turning to the other big U.S. automakers for greater shares of their business. Chrysler positions itself as a partner to its components suppliers, and seeks to decrease systemwide costs. Its partnering stance led one castings supplier to actually recommend replacing its own (metal) intake manifolds with plastic ones, saving Chrysler $3 per car. This suggestion of course cost the supplier the business on the manifolds, because it did not make plastic parts. But Chrysler rewarded the supplier with new orders for suspension components in return.[70]

Armstrong World Industries, Inc., the tile maker, uses a *channel diplomat* approach to preventing and resolving channel conflict. It has centralized customer service for many of its distributors and retailers at its headquarters in Lancaster, Pennsylvania, assigning each of them a single contact person who is supposed to be fully versed in all of Armstrong's products and authorized to make adjustments of as much as $1,000 on the spot.[71] This shows the kind of concessionary behavior characteristic of information-intensive conflict management.

Joint membership in trade associations (e.g., the committee jointly founded by the Grocery Manufacturers of America (GMA) and the Food Marketing Institute that was responsible for developing the Universal Product Code) is another example of a problem-solving approach to conflict resolution. More recent efforts of this group include efforts to resolve conflict issues associated with ordering and billing, as well as furthering progress on the Efficient Consumer Response (ECR) efforts discussed in Chapters 2 and 9.[72]

Some channels use an *exchange of persons* as a conflict-management strategy.

This may involve a unilateral or bilateral trade of personnel for a specified period. For example, once a year, each of the top 60 executives of the franchisor Hardee's Food Systems, Inc., has to spend a week behind the counter of one of the company's restaurants.[73] Another example is the close connection between Wal-Mart and Procter & Gamble personnel. Although such exchanges require clear guidelines because of the possible disclosure of proprietary information, the participants take back to their home organizations a view of their job in an interorganizational context and a personal and professional involvement in the channel network, as well as added training. Participants in such programs also have the opportunity to meet with channel counterparts who have the same specific tasks, professions, and interests. These shared tasks form the basis of continuing relationships that are extraorganizational in content and interorganizational in commitment.

Finally, *co-optation*, a persuasion-oriented channel conflict-management strategy, is the process of absorbing new elements into the leadership or policy-determining structure of an organization as a means of averting threats to its stability or existence. Effective co-optation may bring about ready accessibility among channel members in that it requires the establishment of routine and reliable channels through which information, aid, and requests may be brought. For example, August Busch, chairman of Anheuser-Busch Cos., meets with a 15-member wholesaler panel four times a year to hear their complaints and suggestions.[74] And in the automobile industry, manufacturers are starting to involve dealers in more and more functions that formerly were carried out only by manufacturers. For example, Oldsmobile dealers sat on a committee to review the advertising agency contract the company had with Leo Burnett; and Mercedes includes seven dealer members on its marketing committee, which previews new models and offers marketing advice to the company. One advertising agency spokesperson responsible for the GM Saturn account says, "You can't fully eliminate conflict and disagreement. But if you work together you can resolve it in a way that everybody buys into it."[75]

Co-optation thus permits the sharing of responsibility so that a variety of channel members may become identified with and committed to the programs developed for a particular product or service. However, as with any information-intensive conflict-resolution method, co-optation carries the risk of having one's perspective or decision-making process changed. It places an "outsider" in a position to participate in analyzing an existing situation, to suggest alternatives, and to take part in the deliberation of consequences.

The best working relationships will take into account a number of these steps, not just one. For instance, 3M, a company noted for its marketing skills, uses 11 different ways of staying in close contact with and managing conflict in its office products distribution system: (1) association involvement, (2) a dealer advisory council, (3) a program called Business Planning Partners, (4) fieldwork, (5) personal letters, (6) a market needs conference, (7) a branch coordinators' conference, (8) a national office study, (9) market needs research, (10) individual distributor conferences, and (11) informal minicouncils.[76]

INFORMATION-PROTECTING STRATEGIES   Here, common goals are not expected by either party to the conflict-resolution process. The scope and nature of disagreements are viewed as fixed, and there is a zero-sum orientation (that is, if you win, I lose). The process may be characterized by nonconcessionary or inflexible behaviors, such as threats or promises. Relevant third parties who might be viewed as potential allies may be brought into the dispute via processes like mediation or arbitration.

Mediation is the process whereby a third party attempts to secure settlement of a dispute by persuading the parties either to continue their negotiations or to consider procedural or substantive recommendations that the mediator may make. The mediator typically has a fresh view of the situation, and may perceive opportunities that "insiders" cannot. Solutions might be given acceptability simply by being suggested by the mediator. Effective mediation succeeds in clarifying facts and issues, in keeping parties in contact with each other, in exploring possible bases of agreement, in encouraging parties to agree to specific proposals, and in supervising the implementation of agreements.[77] For example, mediation by a former Businessland executive was instrumental in resolving an extremely dysfunctional conflict between Businessland, at one time the largest company-owned chain of personal computer stores, and Compaq Computer Corp., one of its largest suppliers.[78]

The Centre for Dispute Resolution (CEDR) was launched in 1990, backed by the Confederation of British Industry. It uses a variety of techniques, including mediation, to resolve channel and other business conflicts.[79] Since its launch, CEDR has handled about 360 cases, worth approximately £1.5 billion, with a 90 to 95% success rate.[80] And 11 large franchisors (Pizza Hut, McDonald's, Burger King, Dunkin' Donuts, Hardee's, Holiday Inn Worldwide, Jiffy Lube International, Southland Corp., Wendy's, Kentucky Fried Chicken, and Taco Bell) launched a mediation program in February 1993 to prevent disputes with franchisees from progressing to the litigation stage. The franchisors have signed a pledge that they will seek mediation before going to court to settle disputes. Franchisees have not been asked to sign the pledges, but they see it as a positive sign that disputes may be settled amicably so that the franchise relationship is preserved.[81]

Mediation can also encourage channel members to increase their communication with each other regarding their objectives and goals. In fact, it is possible for a mediator to combine channel members' often conflicting utility functions to arrive at an appropriate group (or channel) utility function. This function, which also can take into account the power of the individual channel members, can be used to predict outcomes in bargaining situations.[82]

An alternative to mediation is *arbitration*. Arbitration can be compulsory or voluntary. Compulsory arbitration is a process wherein the parties are required by law to submit their dispute to a third party whose decision is final and binding. Voluntary arbitration is a process wherein parties voluntarily submit their dispute to a third party whose decision will be final and binding. An important development regarding arbitration was enacted under a 1979 Federal Trade Commission (FTC) order in the U.S. Airco, a producer of industrial gases, settled FTC antitrust charges by agreeing to permit its distributors to take disputes over purchases of certain Airco products to private arbitration.[83] Under the order, Airco agreed that, among other things, if it refused to sell any gas or welding product to a distribu-

TABLE 7-2 Predictions on the Choice of Conflict Resolution Methods

CONTEXTUAL CATEGORIES WITH SOME SAMPLE VARIABLES[a]	THEORETICALLY PREDICTED CHOICE OF CONFLICT RESOLUTION METHODS[b]	
	Under Symmetric Power Conditions	Under Asymmetric Power Conditions
Issue Characteristics:		
High precedent-setting potential	Info-Protecting	Info-Protecting
High stakes	Info-Intensive	Info-Protecting
High complexity	Info-Intensive	Info-Protecting
High functionality of conflict	Info-Intensive	Info-Intensive
Relationship Characteristics:		
High relationalism	Info-Intensive	Info-Intensive
High dependency (other party's)	Info-Intensive	Info-Protecting
High trust	Info-Intensive	Info-Protecting
High frequency of contact	Info-Intensive	Info-Intensive
Personality Characteristics:		
High autonomy-seeking	Info-Protecting	Info-Protecting
High self-esteem	Info-Intensive	Info-Intensive
High similarity	Info-Intensive	Info-Intensive
Environmental Characteristics:		
High munificence	Info-Intensive	Info-Intensive
High uncertainty	Info-Intensive	Info-Protecting
Structural Characteristics:		
High bureaucratization	Info-Protecting	Info-Protecting
High organizational integration	Info-Intensive	Info-Protecting

[a]All the characteristics refer to how they may apply to the party capable of selecting the conflict resolution methods (usually, the dominant party).
[b]"Info-Protecting" refers to an information-protecting conflict resolution strategy (called a "low-risk" strategy by Dant and Schul). "Info-Intensive" refers to an information-intensive conflict resolution strategy (called a "high-risk" strategy by Dant and Schul).
Source: Adapted from Rajiv P. Dant and Patrick L. Schul, "Conflict Resolution Processes in Contractual Channels of Distribution," *Journal of Marketing,* Vol. 56 (January 1992), p. 41.

tor, the distributor could demand arbitration to determine if Airco's action was in reprisal for the distributor's election to purchase from a supplier other than Airco. The order states that arbitration must be held in accordance with the Commercial Arbitration Rules of the American Arbitration Association unless otherwise agreed by the parties and that the decision of the arbitrators will be final and binding on both parties. The FTC's directive is far from unique: more and more companies are seeking dispute resolution in private courts because the public courts are jammed with a huge backlog of cases.[84]

WHEN TO USE WHICH STRATEGIES TO RESOLVE CONFLICT?   Dant and Schul relate the characteristics of channel members to the likelihood of observing a particular conflict resolution strategy in a set of hypotheses summarized in Table 7-2. Their hypotheses suggest that characteristics of the *issue over which there is conflict,* the *relationship,* the *personality of the more powerful channel member,* the *environment,* and the *structure of the relationship* all affect whether information-protecting or information-intensive strategies are best.

Dant and Schul test a subset of the hypotheses concerning the issues and the relationship, using the fast-food franchising industry as a sample, and find modest support for their theoretical predictions. They conclude that:

> [An information-protecting strategy] appears to be preferred for disputes having high precedent-setting potential, stakes, and complexity and when franchisees' dependence is high. Conversely, [information-intensive conflict resolution processes are] seemingly relegated to low risk issues entailing low precedent-setting potential, stakes, and complexity and when franchisee dependence is low. . . .
>
> . . . The use of third-party intervention . . . is usually preceded by considerable deterioration in the franchisee-franchisor relations. . . . Despite their power advantage, franchisors would do well to extend the use of integrative mechanisms to important issues. Though that approach means higher risks, the corresponding long-term payoffs . . . are also likely to be higher.[85]

The implication is clear: when at all possible, using information-intensive conflict resolution strategies is recommended, because they enhance the longevity of and coordinative attitude in the channel relationship.

Channel Power as a Conflict Management Tool

SCOPE AND SIGNIFICANCE OF THE USE OF POWER   The bases of power can be used to shift the marketing flows among institutions and agencies within the channel, thereby creating a more efficient and effective allocation of resources. The control achieved by some firms over selected decision variables or marketing efforts of others is a major factor in the level of performance obtained by the channel as a whole and by each of its members. It should, however, be noted that the scope of control does not have to be broad in order for success to be achieved. In fact, within most channels, because of the degree of specialization referred to earlier, the scope of any channel member's power over others may be limited to only a few of the marketing flows. For example, transportation agencies are likely to have little desire to influence promotional activities in the channel, and many consumer goods manufacturers prefer leaving decisions dealing with financing end-user purchases in the hands of retailers.

Having the power to evoke changes in marketing channels does not mean that a firm necessarily must use it in order to achieve its ends. In fact, although the use of certain power bases is sometimes destructive, the nonuse of others is also viewed negatively. Gaski and Nevin have found support for their observation that

> if sources of power are present but application is withheld, the consequences may be much different from, perhaps opposite, what they would be if the sources were actively exercised. For instance, the imposition of harsh sanctions on channel members (exercised coercive sources of power) seems certain to cause dissatisfaction and conflict, but the dormant presence of the potential to invoke such sanctions (unexercised coercive sources) could conceivably be regarded by franchisees or dealers as benevolent restraint. Likewise, the granting of beneficial assistance (exercised noncoercive

sources) should be favorably received, but withholding of such benefits (unexercised noncoercive sources) may not be.[86]

The fact that a channel member has power sources simply indicates that it has the *potential* for influence.[87] When it wants to change the behavior of another channel member, it will employ a variety of *influence strategies*—the means of communication used in the application of a firm's power. Frazier and Summers suggest that power resources can be converted into persuasive messages via:

- Threats

- Legalistic pleas

- Promises

- Requests

- Recommendations

- Information exchange.[88]

The medium is the message. For example, threats will obviously produce more conflict than will requests. In fact, the tone of a channel relationship is likely to be worse the more contingent is the promised (or threatened!) outcome on a specific channel member's actions and the more negatively that promise (or threat) is framed.[89]

There may not even be agreement on exactly how much power different channel members have. Table 7-3 shows the difference in opinion among players in the grocery industry about shifts in channel power. Clearly, the sentiment that power is shifting toward retailers is shared more by manufacturers than by retailers.[90]

Further, power tends to beget power. That is, if one party has more power than another and it employs the power to exploit (in a negative sense) the other's dependence, the weaker party will strive to develop some means of countervailing the stronger's advantage. In some cases, weaker agents have bonded themselves more closely to their customers in order to protect the transaction-specific investments they have made for their principals. Thus, they increase their customers' dependence on them (and vice versa) in order to safeguard the sunk assets they have accumulated on behalf of the principals for whom they work.[91] Another means of developing countervailing power, especially for small businesses like franchisees, has been the formation of associations and pursuit of collective bargaining with franchisors. Small suppliers can also take steps to reduce their dependence on single large customers; for example, Davis Electric Wallingford Corp., a small maker of wire, cable, and fiber-optic machinery, found that its sales to AT&T dropped from about $2 million to one-tenth that level in 1992. For a company with an annual sales volume of $8 to $10 million, this is a risk that is hard to manage. The company responded by investing more money in research to develop new products that appeal to small but growing customers, thus diversifying its customer base.[92]

▶ **TABLE 7-3** **Opinions of Power Shifts in the Grocery Channel**

Has Power Shifted?

	PERCENTAGE OF RESPONDENTS SAYING:	
CHANNEL MEMBER	There Has Been a Power Shift (%)	There Has Not Been a Power Shift (%)
Retail Chains	41	59
Wholesalers	21	79
Manufacturers	27	73

Which Way Has Power Shifted?

	PERCENTAGE OF RESPONDENTS SAYING:	
CHANNEL MEMBER	Power Has Shifted Toward Retailers (%)	Power Has Shifted Toward Manufacturers (%)
Retail Chains	72	28
Wholesalers	46	54
Manufacturers	86	14

Source: "Does ECR Spell a New Era?" *Progressive Grocer,* 61st Annual Report, April 1994, p. 24.

CONFLICT CONTROL VIA THE EXERTION OF POWER   Channel power is not only a lever to marshal resources for productive activity; its exertion can also be a means of resolving or controlling conflict. Different bases of channel power may be more or less useful in different conflict situations. Here, we give some representative examples to show the relationship between conflict sources and power bases.

For example, goal conflict can be effectively reduced by the exertion of reward power. When using an independent distributor to sell the company's product line, a manufacturer may offer push money or "spiffs" to the distributor's sales force (with the approval of the management of the distributor firm). This is any form of financial incentive tied to the sale of this company's product. Spiffs can be very helpful in inducing the distributor sales force to exert greater effort on the promoted products than on other firm's products also sold by the distributor. They may be particularly useful, for instance, when trying to generate early sales of a new product that is not well understood in the market and will, therefore, require significant sales force effort to succeed. Thus, reward power may help diminish the goal divergence between the manufacturer (who would like to increase profits on its own product line) and the distributor (whose objective is maximum profits across all its lines jointly, not just this manufacturer's line).

Similarly, domain conflict can be managed through the use of legitimate power. For example, the use of multiple sales agents in one market area can generate significant domain conflict, as all agents will be competing for sales across the same base of customers. The manufacturer's choice of distribution intensity is clearly a legitimate right, and therefore its decision about the number of outlets represents the exertion of its legitimate power. UMI, a seller of electronic library and reference materials, exercises its legitimate power by designating no more than two distributors each in selected overseas markets. It finds that exclusive distributors may not develop the market as aggressively as it would like (an example of goal conflict!), but appointing two distributors in the same market creates a competitive environment that nevertheless grows sales more than proportionately in these areas. It recognizes, however, that designating many distributors would be counterproductive, because their relevant domains would overlap too much and the distributors' incentive to sell for UMI would decrease.[93]

Perception-of-reality conflict resolution often requires the use of expert power through the development and use of specialized knowledge. In the example of Bayou Gasket & Hose discussed above, Bayou and PPG both had misgivings at the beginning of their alliance involving Vendor City. Bayou's concerns were that PPG would not order as much product as was expected from Bayou, thus making Bayou's decision to locate in Lake Charles, Louisiana, an unprofitable one. PPG was concerned that, after committing to rely on Bayou for most of its supply of gaskets and hoses, Bayou would not deliver sufficient quantity and quality. Only after investing in information about the relationship (in this case, by taking the risk of starting the relationship and finding out that both parties wanted it to work) could these perception-of-reality conflicts be resolved.

Leadership and Effective Channel Management

The key to effective channel management is to find executives within channel member organizations who take a broad, interorganizational perspective of distribution opportunities and problems. Unless this kind of leadership can be found—one that stresses the interdependency of the channel network and the need for relationship building—it is highly unlikely that a channel will be very successful or even that the channel will survive over time. Clearly, if all channel members share this vision of superordinate goals, the channel is approaching something like nirvana. However, this is an unlikely turn of events. In the absence of total agreement of attitudes among channel members, it becomes necessary for a channel "leader" to use one or more of the levers described above to effect outcomes in the channel that further the best interests of its members.

Clearly, the use of these levers implies that power may be imbalanced in the channel, potentially leading to channel conflict. Anderson and Weitz argue that power imbalance leads to a perception of decreased continuity in a channel relationship, suggesting that balanced power relationships imply greater stability.[94] Bucklin and Sengupta's findings from a study of co-marketing alliances echo these points, showing that alliances characterized by imbalances in either power or in the resources invested by the partners are less successful than more balanced alliances.[95] A 1991 study by McKinsey, the management consulting firm, addressed this issue in the context of joint ventures. The study concluded that 50/50 ownership, whenever possible, is preferable in order to ensure that both partners are fully committed. (Of the joint ventures studied, 56% succeeded when ownership was equally divided, compared with only a third of those with an uneven shareholding split.) The study went on to suggest, however, that even where ownership is equally divided, *one partner should be clearly responsible for ultimate management control.* The study found no instances of a successful joint venture where management control was shared evenly between the owners.[96] Similarly, Bleeke and Ernst studied cross-border alliances and found that (a) alliances between strong and weak companies rarely work; and alliances that evenly split financial ownership are more likely to succeed than those where one partner holds a majority interest. They find that "what matters is clear management control, not financial ownership."[97] These findings together suggest the need for balance (i.e., the inability of one channel member to consistently and universally dominate another channel member), yet with leadership (i.e., the ability to chart a course for the channel and use levers such as power, conflict management policies, or contract design to make the channel hew to that course).

Finally, lest channel members become complacent after making the supreme effort of designing and implementing channel management systems as we have discussed above, we need to remind them to continually monitor the performance and satisfaction levels of all channel members throughout the course of the channel relationship. Communication between channel members is a critical element in maintaining a healthy relationship—or at least in identifying emerging sources of conflict before they begin to hamper overall channel performance. A periodic channel audit, not only of the mechanisms by which channel flows are performed, but also of the perceived sources of power, conflict, and control in the channel can help all channel members keep themselves informed of how their channel partners believe the relationship to be progressing. This kind of free flow of information is one of the most powerful means of preventing and solving channel conflicts (particularly perception-of-reality conflict).

▶ SUMMARY AND CONCLUSIONS

The link between designing a customer-driven distribution system (as we focused on in Chapters 5 and 6) and managing that optimal channel design, the topic of this chapter, is close and immediate. Once the optimal channel design is defined, it cannot produce benefits for all channel members unless and until it is managed effectively. Each channel member must be motivated to exert its best efforts to further the main goals of the entire channel, or else the channel will not merit the name "superorganization."

Once the optimal customer-driven channel system has been designed, it is necessary to amass the relevant channel resources to produce the target markets' desired service outputs. Because distinct channel members typically do not have coincident goals and objectives from the outset, effective channel management requires the use and development of channel power, the development of channel commitment and trust, and the design of appropriate contracts to produce coordinated behavior.

Despite the best efforts of channel members, however, channel conflict persists in ongoing distribution channel relations. Channel conflict can arise from divergent goals of channel members, from disagreements over the domain of action or responsibility in the channel, or from differing perceptions of reality. If not dealt with, conflict can become pathological: that is, it can destroy a channel relationship entirely.

Fortunately, several mechanisms for dealing with channel conflict exist. High-risk strategies, such as the use of channel diplomats, joint membership in trade associations, the exchange of personnel, or cooptation promise the best chance of a coordinated outcome, but can carry significant amounts of risk because they involve significant information exchanges. Lower-risk strategies, such as mediation and arbitration, involve less information exchange and hence less of a risk of loss of proprietary knowledge, but suggest an overall less-cooperative attitude toward channel relations. Finally, power itself is frequently used as a conflict control mechanism, although the results of many investigations suggest that balanced, rather than imbalanced, power relationships in channels tend to be the longest-lasting and most satisfying to the participants.

The ultimate goal in channel management is the creation and adoption of the main goals by all channel members. If the channel can move toward this ideal, it is closer to satisfying its target customers' demands for service outputs, and this in turn helps the channel to maximize the size of its total profit pie. It is up to the channel members themselves to find those ways that make the coordinative solution to channel management also the most profitable one. Creative and effective channel leadership is, therefore, a critical element in this process.

DISCUSSION QUESTIONS

1. Why would you be unlikely to observe naturally occurring coordinated channels?

2. Some manufacturers use exclusive distributors (i.e., distributors who promise not to carry any directly competitive products), whereas other manufacturers do not seek exclusivity from their distributors. Using the concepts of inherent characteristics, come to a conclusion about which type of distributor will tend to get higher payments from its manufacturer (holding all other factors constant) and defend your answer.

3. When Apple Computer entered the Czech marketplace in the early 1990s, it chose to license an agent who was given exclusive rights to develop the Czech market for five years. At the end of five years, Apple had the right of first refusal to buy out the agent and turn the channel into a wholly owned Apple sales office. Alternatively, Apple could extend the agent's contract or the agent could seek to sell the rights to the Apple business to another entrepreneur. Describe which parties hold decision management rights and which hold decision-control rights, as well as who bears organizational risk. Make a prediction about the outcome.

4. "All conflict in channel relations is undesirable." Critically evaluate this statement.

5. Wherehouse Entertainment Inc., a 339-store retailer based in Torrance, California, recently began selling used compact disks (CDs) in its stores alongside new ones. Immediate responses by music companies included withdrawal of cooperative advertising support by Sony, Warner Music, Capitol-EMI, and MCA. They argue that it may be legal to resell a used CD, but doing so cuts into the profits from new CDs and deprives artists of royalties. Garth Brooks, the best-selling artist of 1992, has refused to release his CDs to stores selling used disks. Another retail chain that sells used CDs

retorts that the major record label companies should look to their owned distribution channels first as culprits, and stop selling CDs at cut-rate prices through record clubs offering deep-discount promotions. Categorize the emergence of channel conflict that this move by Wherehouse has produced, and make some suggestions about how to control or manage the conflicts.

6. What is the relationship between coercive and reward power? What about between coercive power and expert, referent, or legitimate power? Give three examples to illustrate your arguments.

7. Toy maker "Step 2" refuses to sell its products through Wal-Mart because it claims it loses all control over the huge discounts at which retailers like Wal-Mart sell its products. Some smaller retailers are starting to flock to Step 2 products because, as one retailer said, "If you have a different product, you don't have to worry about matching a price of $59.95 and not making any margin." Describe what sources of channel power have been exercised in this example by Wal-Mart and by Step 2, and use this insight to explain why smaller retailers are happy to carry Step 2's products.

8. Digital Equipment Corporation management was rudely surprised by third-quarter fiscal 1994 sales and financial results. They found that sales costs were rising rapidly and discounting was eating into profit margins. DEC's salespeople were discounting product prices deeply to increase their sales volumes and bonus compensation. DEC salespeople had long been paid with a compensation plan that all but ignored incentive components, and it was widely agreed that the DEC salesperson was not a risk-taker. In fact, industry analysts maintained that the lack of a commission pay structure drove away the best salespeople. Comment on this conclusion, based on the discussion above of contract design.

9. "Gray marketing" refers to the practice of shipping branded, authentic product into a foreign market through unauthorized distribution channels. For example, Minolta cameras used to be manufactured in Japan, shipped to authorized resellers in Hong Kong, and then reshipped by these authorized resellers to unauthorized dealers in Europe and the United States. The authorized resellers were believed to have done this because they could get very low per-unit transfer prices if they bought large quantities at a time from the manufacturer; but these large quantities left them with overstocks, which were most easily depleted by diverting them to third markets. Describe what sources of conflict arise from gray marketing, and suggest methods of action that would curb the gray market. Comment on the manufacturer's incentives to curb gray market activity.

10. How are the concepts of channel commitment and trust related to the concept of channel coordination?

ENDNOTES

[1]See William J. Baumol, John C. Panzar, and Robert D. Willig, *Contestable Markets and the Theory of Industry Structure* (New York: Harcourt, Brace, Jovanovich, 1988), p. 170.

[2]John Schopler, "Social Power," in Leonard Berkowitz (ed.), *Advances in Experimental Social Psychology*, Vol. 2 (New York: Academic Press, 1965), p. 187. See also Robert A. Dahl, *Modern Political Analysis* (Englewood Cliffs, NJ: Prentice-Hall, 1964), p. 40; and Kjell Gronhaug, "Power in Organizational Buying," *Human Relations*, Vol. 32 (1979), pp. 159–180.

[3]See Janet E. Keith, Donald W. Jackson, and Lawrence A. Crosby, "Effects of Alternative Types of Influence Strategies Under Different Channel Dependence Structures," *Journal of Marketing*, Vol. 54 (July 1990), pp. 30–41.

[4]Adel I. El-Ansary and Louis W. Stern, "Power Measurement in the Distribution Channel," *Journal of Marketing Research,* Vol. 9 (February 1972), p. 47.

[5]Richard M. Emerson, "Power-Dependence Relations," *American Sociological Review,* Vol. 27 (February 1962), pp. 32–33.

[6]See Peter R. Dickson, "Distributor Portfolio Analysis and the Channel Dependence Matrix: New Techniques for Understanding and Managing the Channel," *Journal of Marketing,* Vol. 47 (Summer 1983), p. 41.

[7]For example, in a major study of wholesaler–manufacturer relationships, Bagozzi and Phillips found that supplier (manufacturer) control is a function of supplier substitutability, control of critical resources by the supplier, and the magnitude of the resources exchanged. Richard P. Bagozzi and Lynn W. Phillips, "Representing and Testing Organizational Theories: A Holistic Construal," *Administrative Science Quarterly,* Vol. 27 (September 1982), p. 484.

[8]See John F. Gaski, "The Theory of Power and Conflict in Channels of Distribution," *Journal of Marketing,* Vol. 48 (Summer 1984), p. 23. See also James R. Brown, Robert F. Lusch, and Darrel D. Muehling, "Conflict and Power-Dependence Relations in Retailer-Supplier Channels," *Journal of Retailing,* Vol. 59 (Winter 1983), p. 72.

[9]These concepts are central to strategic contingency theory and resource dependence theory. For the former, see D. J. Hickson et al., "A Strategic Contingencies Theory of Intraorganizational Power," *Administrative Science Quarterly,* Vol. 16 (June 1971), pp. 216–229; for the latter, see Jeffrey Pfeffer and Gerald R. Salancik, *The External Control of Organizations: A Resource Dependence Perspective* (New York: Harper & Row, 1978).

[10]Dexter Hutchins, "Having a Hard Time with Just-in-Time," *Fortune,* June 9, 1986, p. 64. Copyright 1986 Time, Inc. All rights reserved.

[11]Dana Milbank, "Consumer-Goods Makers, Growing Wary of Big Chains, Try to Forge Small Links," *Wall Street Journal,* June 24, 1991, p. B1. Some companies cited in the article include Goodyear, General Electric, Quaker State, and Kodak.

[12]Our discussion of the bases of power draws on John R. P. French and Bertram Raven, "The Bases of Social Power," in Dorwin Cartwright (ed.), *Studies in Social Power* (Ann Arbor: University of Michigan Press, 1959), pp. 150–167.

[13]Jonathan Dahl, "Travel Agents' Fare Share Soars as Airlines Log Losses," *Wall Street Journal,* February 23, 1993, p. B1. Subsequent reductions in the commissions in the mid-1990s could imply that the rewards had exceeded the airlines' ability to pay the travel agents.

[14]For complete reviews of the academic literature in this area, see Anne T. Coughlan, "Salesforce Compensation: A Review of MS/OR Advances," in *Handbooks in Operations Research and Management Science: Marketing* (vol. 5), Gary L. Lilien and Jehoshua Eliashberg, eds., (Amsterdam: North-Holland, 1993); and Anne T. Coughlan and Subrata K. Sen, "Salesforce Compensation: Theory and Managerial Implications," *Marketing Science,* Vol. 8 (Fall 1989), pp. 324–342. Empirical evidence on sales force compensation in the United States is given in Anne T. Coughlan and Chakravarthi Narasimhan, "An Empirical Analysis of Salesforce Compensation Plans," *Journal of Business,* Vol. 65 (January 1992), pp. 93–122. Another reference is Churchill, Ford, and Walker, *Salesforce Management* (Homewood, IL: Richard D. Irwin, Inc., 1981).

[15]See, for example, Neil M. Ford, Orville C. Walker, and Gilbert A. Churchill, Jr., "Differences in the Attractiveness of Alternative Rewards Among Industrial Salespeople: Additional Evidence," Report No. 81-107 (Cambridge, MA: Marketing Science Institute), December 1981; Gilbert A. Churchill, Jr., Neil M. Ford, and Orville C. Walker, Jr., "Personal Characteristics of Salespeople and the Attractiveness of Alternative Rewards," *Journal of Busi-*

ness Research, Vol. 7 (June 1979), pp. 25–50; Gilbert A. Churchill, Jr., Neil M. Ford, Steven W. Hartley, and Orville C. Walker, Jr., "The Determinants of Salesperson Performance: A Meta-Analysis," *Journal of Marketing Research,* Vol. 22 (May 1985), pp. 103–118; and Thomas N. Ingram and Danny N. Bellenger, "Personal and Organizational Variables: Their Relative Effect on Reward Valences of Industrial Salespeople," *Journal of Marketing Research,* Vol. 20 (May 1983), pp. 198–205.

[16]Frank Lynn & Associates, *Client Communique,* Vol. 5 (December 1993), pp. 2–3.

[17]See Robin Cooper and Robert S. Kaplan, "Measure Costs Right: Make the Right Decisions," *Harvard Business Review,* September-October 1988, pp. 96–103.

[18] William M. Bulkeley, "Lotus to Raise Price of 1-2-3 and End Discounters' Edge," *Wall Street Journal,* November 28, 1988, p. B1.

[19]David A. Baldwin, "The Power of Positive Sanctions," *World Politics,* Vol. 24 (October 1971), pp. 19–38; John F. Gaski and John R. Nevin, "The Differential Effects of Exercised and Unexercised Power Sources in a Marketing Channel," *Journal of Marketing Research,* Vol. 22 (May 1985), pp. 130–142.

[20]See Kevin Done, "VW Steps Up the Pressure on Suppliers," *Financial Times,* March 4, 1993, p. 16; Douglas Lavin, "Lopez, Chief of Purchasing, Is Leaving GM," *Wall Street Journal,* March 12, 1993, p. A3; Kevin Kelly, Zachary Schiller, and James B. Treece, "Cut Costs or Else," *Business Week,* March 22, 1993, pp. 28–29; Oscar Suris, "GM Tries to Heal Supplier Relations While Sticking to Cost-Cutting Goal," *Wall Street Journal,* August 9, 1993, p. B5; Kevin Kelly and Kathleen Kerwin, "There's Another Side to the Lopez Saga," *Business Week,* August 23, 1993, p. 26; and Greg Gardner, "Low Marks," *Chicago Tribune,* September 5, 1993, Section 17, p. 7.

[21]Doron P. Levin, "Honda's Ugly Little Secret," *New York Times,* May 2, 1993, Section 3, p. 1.

[22]Ann Hughy, " 'Gray Market' in Camera Imports Starts to Undercut Official Dealers," *The Wall Street Journal,* April 1, 1982, p. 23. See also Larry S. Lowe and Kevin McCrohan, "Gray Markets in the United States," *The Journal of Consumer Marketing,* Vol. 5 (Winter 1988), pp. 45–51; Wayne Lilley, "The Graying of the Marketplace," *Canadian Business* (August 1985), pp. 46–54.

[23]For a description of some of the systems put in place by McKesson and others, see Russell Johnson and Paul R. Lawrence, "Beyond Vertical Integration—The Rise of the Value-Adding Partnership," *Harvard Business Review* (July–August 1988), pp. 94–101.

[24]Peter Jerram, "Changing Channels: New Models for CD Distribution," *New Media,* (June 1994), pp. 48–55.

[25]Bill Saporito, "Is Wal-Mart Unstoppable?" *Fortune,* May 6, 1991, p. 58.

[26]See Erin Anderson, "The Salesperson as Outside Agent or Employee: A Transaction Cost Analysis," *Marketing Science,* Vol. 4 (Summer 1985), p. 238.

[27]See Paul Merrion, "Tougher Pact Riles Big Mac Owners," *Crain's Chicago Business,* September 17, 1979, p. 33.

[28]See James G. March and Herbert A. Simon, *Organizations* (New York: John Wiley and Sons, Inc., 1958), p. 165. The implementation of uncertainty-absorbing techniques could also be viewed more broadly as the use of *information power* rather than the enhancement of *expert power.* Informational influence or persuasion is involved when A provides information not previously available to B or when A points out contingencies of which B had not been aware. B may do what he might not otherwise have done, because with the new information he may view the specific action suggested by A to be in his own best interest, aside from

any consideration for A or possible rewards and punishments that A might mete out. Thus, information power is based on the acceptance by B of the logic of A's arguments rather than on A's perceived expertise. See Bertram H. Raven and Arie W. Kruglanski, "Conflict and Power," in Paul Swingle (ed.), *The Structure of Conflict* (New York: Academic Press, 1970), p. 73.

[29]International Data Corporation, *Reseller Requirements Analysis: An In-depth Look at VARs' Priorities, Expectations, and Vendor Preferences* (Framingham, MA.: International Data Corporation, 1989), p. 4.

[30]John R. P. French and Bertram Raven, "The Bases of Social Power," in Dorwin Cartwright (ed.), *Studies in Social Power* (Ann Arbor: University of Michigan Press, 1959), p. 161.

[31]"How Leonard Lauder Is Making his Mom Proud," *Business Week,* September 4, 1989, p. 69.

[32]See "OshKosh B'Gosh May Be Risking Its Upscale Image," *Business Week,* July 15, 1991, p. 140; and G. Pascal Zachary, "Apple Will Sell Low-End PCs Via Discounter," *The Wall Street Journal,* May 23, 1991, p. B1.

[33]Patricia Sellers, "Keeping the Buyers You Already Have," *Fortune,* (Autumn/Winter 1993), pp. 56–58.

[34]Jeremy Schlosberg, "Hewlett- Packard: Can Bigger Be Better?" *VARBusiness,* March 1990, p. 56.

[35]F. Robert Dwyer, Paul H. Schurr, and Sejo Oh, "Developing Buyer-Seller Relationships," *Journal of Marketing,* Vol. 51 (April 1987), p. 18.

[36]Nirmalya Kumar, Lisa K. Scheer, and Jan-Benedict E. M. Steenkamp, "The Effects of Perceived Interdependence on Dealer Attitudes," *Journal of Marketing Research,* August 1995.

[37]Erin Anderson and Barton Weitz, "Determinants of Continuity in Conventional Industrial Channel Dyads," *Marketing Science,* Vol. 8 (Fall 1989), p. 315.

[38]See J. Rempel, J. Holmes, and M. Zanna, "Trust in Close Relationships," *Journal of Personality and Social Psychology,* Vol. 49 (1985), pp. 95–112.

[39]See James C. Anderson and James A. Narus, "A Model of Distributor Firm and Manufacturer Firm Working Partnerships," *Journal of Marketing,* Vol. 54 (January 1990), p. 48. Also see Louis C. Young and Ian F. Wilkinson, "The Role of Trust and Cooperation in Marketing Channels: A Preliminary Study," *European Journal of Marketing,* Vol. 23 (1989), pp. 109–122.

[40]See Richard Waters, "Drugs Industry Seeks Prescription for Growth," *Financial Times,* May 11, 1994, p. 20; and Elyse Tanouye, "Owning Medco, Merck Takes Drug Marketing The Next Logical Step," *Wall Street Journal,* May 31, 1994, p. A1.

[41]Representative references in the literature dealing with these constructs includes Nirmalya Kumar, Jonathan D. Hibbard, and Louis W. Stern, "The Nature and Consequences of Marketing Channel Intermediary Commitment," *Marketing Science Institute Working Paper* No. 94-115, September 1994; James C. Anderson and James A. Narus, "A Model of Distributor Firm and Manufacturer Firm Working Partnerships," *Journal of Marketing,* Vol. 54 (January 1990), pp. 42–58; Robert M. Morgan and Shelby D. Hunt, "The Commitment-Trust Theory of Relationship Marketing," *Journal of Marketing,* Vol. 58 (July 1994), pp. 20–38; and Nirmalya Kumar, Lisa K. Scheer, and Jan-Benedict E. M. Steenkamp, "The Effects of Supplier Fairness on Vulnerable Resellers," *Journal of Marketing Research,* Vol. 32, No. 1 (February 1995), pp. 54–65.

[42]Jan B. Heide, "Interorganizational Governance in Marketing Channels," *Journal of Marketing,* Vol. 58 (January 1994), pp. 71–85. This quote comes from page 74.

[43]*Ibid.*, p. 74.

[44]The Economics literature has long known of this concept. As early as 1981, Klein and Leffler wrote their fundamental article, "The Role of Market Forces in Assuring Contractual Performance" (*Journal of Political Economy*, Vol. 89, pp. 615–641), which introduced the idea of self-enforcing agreements. A self-enforcing agreement is a contractual device that causes the parties involved to *want* to uphold the agreement after the contract is struck; in transaction cost analysis terms, it minimizes the potential for postcontractual opportunistic behavior.

[45]See Jack Keough and Christine Forbes, "Welcome to Vendor City," *Industrial Distributor* (May 15, 1991), pp. 32–36. Also see Gregory S. Carpenter and Anne T. Coughlan, "Alliances with Opportunism: Sustainable Distribution-Partnership Strategies with Transaction Costs," working paper, Kellogg Graduate School of Management, January 1994.

[46]See Louis W. Stern and J. L. Heskett, "Conflict Management in Interorganization Relations: A Conceptual Framework," in Louis W. Stern (ed.), *Distribution Channels: Behavioral Dimensions* (Boston, MA: Houghton Mifflin Co., 1969), pp. 288–305; Larry J. Rosenberg and Louis W. Stern, "Conflict Measurement in the Distribution Channel," *Journal of Marketing Research*, Vol. 8 (November 1971), pp. 437–442; Michael Etgar, "Sources and Types of Intrachannel Conflict," *Journal of Retailing*, Vol. 55 (Spring 1979), pp. 61–78; Ernest R. Cadotte and Louis W. Stern, "A Process Model of Dyadic Interorganizational Relations in Marketing Channels," in Jagdish N. Sheth (ed.), *Research in Marketing*, Vol. 2 (Greenwich, CT: JAI Press, 1979); and Torger Reve and Louis W. Stern, "Interorganzational Relations in Marketing Channels," *Academy of Management Review*, Vol. 4 (July 1979), pp. 405–416.

[47]Allan J. Magrath and Kenneth G. Hardy, "A Strategic Framework for Diagnosing Manufacturer-Reseller Conflict," Marketing Science Institute Report No. 88-101 (Cambridge, MA.: Marketing Science Institute, 1988), p. 2. See also James R. Brown and Ralph L. Day, "Measures of Manifest Conflict in Distribution Channels," *Journal of Marketing Research*, Vol. 18 (August 1981), pp. 263–274.

[48]Jeffrey A. Tannenbaum, "Once Red-Hot PIP Faces Legal Assault by Franchisees," *Wall Street Journal*, April 8, 1993, p. B2.

[49]Oliver E. Williamson, *Markets and Hierarchies: Analysis and Antitrust Implications* (New York: The Free Press, 1975), p. 6.

[50]Mark Bergen, Shantanu Dutta, and Orville C. Walker, Jr., "Agency Relationships in Marketing: A Review of the Implications and Applications of Agency and Related Theories," *Journal of Marketing*, Vol. 56, (no. 3, July 1992), p. 2. The citation from Arrow is Kenneth J. Arrow, "The Economics of Agency," in *Principals and Agents: The Structure of Business*, J. Pratt and R. Zeckhauser, eds., Boston: Harvard Business School Press, 1985, pp. 37–51.

[51]Kyle Pope, "Dealers Accuse Compaq of Jilting Them," *Wall Street Journal*, April 7, 1993, p. B1.

[52]Bergen, Dutta, and Walker, *op. cit.*, p. 2.

[53]Erle Norton, "Last of the U.S. Tire Makers Ride Out Foreign Invasion," *Wall Street Journal*, February 4, 1993, p. B4.

[54]See Louis W. Stern, "Antitrust Implications of a Sociological Interpretation of Competition, Conflict, and Cooperation in the Marketplace," *Antitrust Bulletin*, Vol. 16 (Fall 1971), pp. 509–530.

[55]Tim Clark, "Marketing Alliances Starting to Pay Off," *Business Marketing*, May 1993, p. 46.

[56]Patrick J. Kaufmann and V. Kasturi Rangan, "A Model for Managing System Conflict During Franchise Expansion," *Journal of Retailing*, Vol. 66 (Summer 1990), p. 155.

[57]Yumiko Ono, "Contacts by Mail Change Industry's Look," *Wall Street Journal*, October 11, 1994, p. B1.

[58]Christina Duff, "Nation's Retailers Ask Vendors to Help Share Expenses," *Wall Street Journal*, August 4, 1993, p. B4.

[59]Timothy L. O'Brien, "Unjustified Returns Plague Electronics Makers," *Wall Street Journal*, September 26, 1994, p. B1.

[60]Robert M. Morgan and Shelby D. Hunt, "The Commitment-Trust Theory of Relationship Marketing," *Journal of Marketing*, Vol. 58 (July 1994), p. 25. See also Erin Anderson and Barton Weitz, "Determinants of Continuity in Conventional Industrial Channel Dyads," *Marketing Science*, Vol. 8 (Fall 1989), pp. 310–323; James C. Anderson and James A. Narus, "A Model of Distributor Firm and Manufacturer Firm Working Partnerships," *Journal of Marketing*, Vol. 54 (January 1990), pp. 43–58; and Christine Moorman, Rohit Deshpandé, and Gerald Zaltman, "Factors Affecting Trust in Market Research Relationships," *Journal of Marketing*, Vol. 57 (January 1993), pp. 81–101.

[61]Kyle Pope, "Dealers Accuse Compaq of Jilting Them," *Wall Street Journal*, April 7, 1993, p. B1.

[62]K. W. Thomas and W. H. Schmidt, "A Survey of Managerial Interests with Respect to Conflict," *Academy of Management Journal*, Vol. 19 (June 1976), pp. 315–318.

[63]James C. Anderson and James A. Narus, "A Model of Distributor Firm and Manufacturer Firm Working Partnerships," *Journal of Marketing*, Vol. 54 (January 1990), p. 45. Morgan and Hunt posit the same mechanism relating trust to functional conflict [Robert M. Morgan and Shelby D. Hunt, "The Commitment-Trust Theory of Relationship Marketing," *Journal of Marketing*, Vol. 58 (July 1994), p. 26].

[64]Kenneth E. Boulding, "The Economics of Human Conflict," in Elton B. McNeil (ed.), *The Nature of Human Conflict* (Englewood Cliffs, NJ: Prentice-Hall, Inc., 1965), pp. 174–175. See also William P. Dommermuth, "Profiting from Distribution Conflicts," *Business Horizons* (December 1976), pp. 4–13; and Lewis A. Coser, *The Functions of Social Conflict* (Glencoe, IL: The Free Press, 1956).

[65]George John, "An Empirical Investigation of Some Antecedents of Opportunism in Marketing Channels," *Journal of Marketing Research*, Vol. 21 (August 1984), p. 287.

[66]John Griffiths, "Nissan Sacks UK Importer and Plans New Network," *Financial Times*, December 28, 1990, p. 1; Kevin Done, "Nissan Gets Back in the Driving Seat," *Financial Times*, December 31, 1990, p. 10; Kevin Done, "Dealers Angry Over Nissan Decision," *Financial Times*, January 25, 1991, p. 7; and John Griffiths, "Nissan UK Loses Battle to Return Franchise," *Financial Times*, August 1, 1991, p. 12.

[67]The weight of power is a specification of how much A influences B. When the *weight* of A's power over B is at its maximum, it may be referred to as *control*. At this point, A can predict with certainty that B will respond in the desired manner.

[68]Rajiv P. Dant and Patrick L. Schul, "Conflict Resolution Processes in Contractual Channels of Distribution," *Journal of Marketing*, Vol. 56 (January 1992), pp. 38–54; and James G. March and Herbert A. Simon, *Organizations* (New York: John Wiley & Sons, Inc., 1958). Dant and Schul use the terms "high-risk" and "low-risk" to denote what we call "information-intensive" and "information-protecting," respectively.

[69]Marty Jacknis and Steve Kratz, "The Channel Empowerment Solution," *Sales and Marketing Management,* March 1993, pp. 48–49.

[70]Kevin Kelly, Zachary Schiller, and James B. Treece, "Cut Costs or Else," *Business Week,* March 22, 1993, p. 29.

[71]Vindu P. Goel, "Armstrong Sharpens Its Focus in Shadow of Belzbergs," *The Wall Street Journal,* November 27, 1989, p. A5.

[72]See Louis W. Stern and Patrick J. Kaufmann, "Electronic Data Interchange in Selected Consumer Goods Industries," in Robert D. Buzzell (ed.), *Marketing in an Electronic Age* (Boston: Harvard Business School Press, 1985), pp. 52–73.

[73]"Hardee's: The Bigger It Grows, the Hungrier It Gets," *Business Week,* May 4, 1987, p. 106.

[74]"Even August Busch Can Only Handle So Much Beer," *Business Week,* September 25, 1989, p. 187.

[75]Mary Connelly, "Auto Dealers Flex their Muscles," *Advertising Age,* March 22, 1993.

[76]Presentation by J. P. Wilkins, marketing director, Office Products, 3M Company, St. Paul, MN, 1984.

[77]For a review of various "alternative dispute resolution" approaches, see Todd B. Carver and Albert A Vondra, "Alternative Dispute Resolution; Why It Doesn't Work and Why It Does," *Harvard Business Review,* Vol. 72 (May–June 1994), pp. 120–130.

[78]See G. Pascal Zachary and Andy Zipser, "Businessland is Compaq's Land Yet Once Again," *The Wall Street Journal,* March 8, 1990, p. B1; and G. Pascal Zachary, "Businessland Founder Struggles to Pull Firm Out of a Deep Slide," *The Wall Street Journal,* March 18, 1991, p. A1.

[79]Simon Carne, "Alternative Way to Solve Disputes," *Financial Times,* March 21, 1991, p. 14.

[80]Diana Bentley, "Mediation Is Quicker and Cheaper," *Financial Times,* January 25, 1994, p. 15. In another study by the Center for Public Resources (a nonprofit group providing mediators and arbitrators), 406 companies tracked since 1990 have saved more than $150 million in legal fees and expert witness costs by using alternatives to litigation. More than $5 billion was at stake in the cases. See Ellen John Pollock, "Mediation Firms Alter the Legal Landscape," *Wall Street Journal,* March 22, 1993, p. B1.

[81]See Rhonda Richards, "Businesses Vie for More Control," *USA Today,* January 5, 1993, pp. 1B, 2B; Ellen Joan Pollock, "Food Concerns Opt to Mediate, Not Litigate," *Wall Street Journal,* February 11, 1993, p. B1; Jeffrey A. Tannenbaum, "New Head of Franchiser Group Stresses Self-Regulation," *Wall Street Journal,* March 11, 1993, p. B2; and Michele Galen, Laurel Touby, Lori Bongiorno, and Wendy Zellner, "Franchise Fracas," *Business Week,* March 22, 1993, pp. 68–73.

[82]Jehoshua Eliashberg, Stephen A. LaTour, Arvind Rangaswamy, and Louis W. Stern, "Assessing the Predictive Accuracy of Two Utility-Based Theories in a Marketing Channel Negotiation Context," *Journal of Marketing Research,* Vol. 23 (May 1986), p. 102.

[83]"Airco Agrees to Settle Disputes with Distributors Through Arbitration," *FTC News Summary,* April 13, 1979, p. 3.

[84]See "Center Helps Firms Avoid Litigating Circumstances," *Chicago Tribune,* January 12, 1986, Section 7, p. 7; Richard Koenig, "More Firms Turn to Private Courts to Avoid Expensive Legal Fights," *The Wall Street Journal,* January 4, 1984, p. 23; and G. Christian Hill, "California Is Allowing Its Wealthy Litigants to Hire Private Jurists," *The Wall Street Journal,* August 6, 1980, p. 1.

[85]Rajiv P. Dant and Patrick L. Schul, "Conflict Resolution Processes in Contractual Channels of Distribution," *Journal of Marketing*, Vol. 56 (January 1992), p. 50.

[86]John F. Gaski and John R. Nevin, "The Differential Effects of Exercised and Unexercised Power Sources in a Marketing Channel," *Journal of Marketing Research*, Vol. 22 (May 1985), p. 132.

[87]Gary L. Frazier, "Interorganizational Exchange Behavior in Marketing Channels: A Broadened Perspective," *Journal of Marketing*, Vol. 47 (Fall 1983), p. 71.

[88]Gary L. Frazier and John O. Summers, "Perceptions of Interfirm Power and Its Use Within a Franchise Channel of Distribution," *Journal of Marketing Research*, Vol. 23 (May 1986), p. 172.

[89]See Lisa K. Scheer, *The Effect of Influence on Channel Climate: An Examination of Influence Type and Outcomes*, Northwestern University Ph.D. dissertation, Evanston, IL., June 1990.

[90]See, for example, Paul R. Messinger and Chakravarthi Narasimhan, "Has Power Shifted in the Grocery Channel?" Working Paper, Washington University, forthcoming in *Marketing Science*, Vol. 14, No. 2 (Spring 1995); and Kusum L. Ailawadi, Norm Borin, and Paul W. Farris, "Channel Power and Performance: A Cross-Industry Analysis," Working Paper, Dartmouth College, June 1994. They argue that profitability changes do not favor an argument that retailers' power has increased.

[91]Jan B. Heide and George John, "The Role of Dependence Balancing in Safeguarding Transaction-Specific Assets in Conventional Channels," *Journal of Marketing*, Vol. 52 (January 1988), pp. 20–35.

[92]Michael Selz, "Some Suppliers Rethink Their Reliance on Big Business," *Wall Street Journal*, March 29, 1993, p. B2.

[93]Conversation with Paul Tucci, Director of International Sales and Marketing, UMI International, January 1995.

[94]Erin Anderson and Barton Weitz, "Determinants of Continuity in Conventional Industrial Channel Dyads," *Marketing Science*, Vol. 8 (Fall 1989), pp. 310–323.

[95]Louis P. Bucklin and Sanjit Sengupta, "Organizing Successful Co-Marketing Alliances," *Journal of Marketing*, Vol. 57 (April 1993), pp. 32–46. The authors also find that alliances are more successful when the business environment is turbulent, implying that they provide a lower-risk way to gain access to products or technology than using the risk-laden marketplace.

[96]Guy de Jonquieres, "Equal Partnerships Stand a Better Chance of Success," *Financial Times*, May 15, 1991, p. 11.

[97]Joel Bleeke and David Ernst, "The Way to Win in Cross-Border Alliances," *Harvard Business Review*, Vol. 69 (November–December 1991), pp. 127–128.

APPENDIX

AEROQUIP CORPORATION'S FUNCTIONAL DISCOUNT PROGRAM (PRELIMINARY)

WHAT IS FUNCTIONAL DISCOUNT PRICING?

In order to generate rational, equitable, and motivational marketing channel compensation systems, a basic rule of thumb that should guide the process is as follows: *compensation in distribution should be given on the basis of the degree of each channel member's participation in the marketing flows.*

SO WHAT DOES THAT MEAN?

Distributors should be compensated for performing marketing functions which otherwise would be performed by Aeroquip.

HOW DOES THE SYSTEM WORK?

The Distribution channel will be segmented into three groups. Each group is asked to perform different marketing functions. Aeroquip will compensate distributors for performing additional marketing functions through an increased discount.

WHAT ARE THE THREE DISTRIBUTION GROUPS CALLED?

The three Distribution groups are:

Premier Distributor	(PR)
Authorized Distributor	(AU)
Affiliate Distributor	(AF)

WHAT PRICING AND DISCOUNTS ARE RELATED TO THE DISTRIBUTION GROUPS?

- Premier Distributor

    a. Base discount = 80.5% off list

Source: Aeroquip Corporation Internal documents. Published by permission of Aeroquip Corporation.

Distribution Group Features

ACTIVITIES OR SERVICES	PR	AU	AF
Base Requirements:			
Facility and hours to meet market demand	✓	✓	✓
Good credit standing with Aeroquip	✓	✓	
Minimum of one outside salesperson/approved branch	✓	✓	
Functional Criteria:			
Inventory to serve market need	✓	✓	
Approved inventory management system	✓		
Complete hose assembly shop	✓		
Basic hose assembly shop		✓	
Crimp capability			✓
Will call counter and retail display area	✓		
Certification of people dealing with =A products	✓	✓	
Certification of Aeroquip Specialist	✓		
Certification of hose assembler	✓		
Certification of hose shop	✓		
SalesMate	✓		
EDI ordering and invoicing	✓		
Reporting of user sales	✓		
Market planning	✓		
Aeroquip Support Services:			
Promotional allowance of 0.75%/last year's sales	✓		
Promotional allowance of 0.50%/last year's sales		✓	
Direct interface with Regional Mgr	✓		
Telemarketing contact from Aeroquip		✓	
Sales and support from Aeroquip Premier			✓
Market analysis and sales leads	✓		
Meet comp. pricing support	✓		
Optional Functional Adders:			
Redistribution discount	✓		
Product mix discount	✓		

b.   Optional discounts available to Premiers

Redistribution = added 1.0% off list on all Aeroquip products sold to approved Affiliate Distributors

Product mix = added 0.5% off list on all Aeroquip products purchased so long as only Aeroquip adapters, couplings, Thermoplastic hose & fittings and Teflon hose & fittings are purchased, stocked, and marketed

■   Authorized Distributor

Base discount = 79.0% off list

■ Affiliate Distributor

Suggested price = 76.9% off list

CAN YOU GIVE AN EXAMPLE OF HOW THIS PRICING WOULD WORK?

Assuming an item's list price was $1.00, the relationship of the three groups would be as follows:

		Price
Premier base	→	$0.195
Premier base plus redistribution discount	→	$0.185
Premier base plus redistribution and product mix discount	→	$0.180
Authorized base	→	$0.210
Affiliate suggested	→	$0.231

Note: This would mean that a Premier Distributor could sell to an approved Affiliate at the suggested price and, with both discounts, would make 2.1% gross margin. The selling price must be at or below the suggested Affiliate price for the Premier Distributor to receive the redistribution discount.

WHAT IS MEANT BY AN "APPROVED" AFFILIATE?

Each of the Distributor groups will have a signed agreement to establish them. In the case of the Affiliate, while their direct contact will be the Premier, they will also have a relationship to Aeroquip. Affiliates will be set up based on market need and with the approval of the Aeroquip Regional Manager.

AEROQUIP'S DISTRIBUTOR GUIDING PRINCIPLES

Division of Labor

"Aeroquip and its channel partners recognize there are responsibilities that are uniquely those of Aeroquip, those of Distributors and those that are shared."

Learning Oriented

"Aeroquip seeks to partner with organizations that share its commitment to creativity, innovation and fact-based analysis and decision-making."

Market Driven

"For each segment we choose to enter, we will be the best at understanding and meeting end-user needs. We will be the #1 supplier in each geographic market we target."

System Perspective

"Aeroquip and its channel partners view and manage our businesses as part of an integrated system. Our objective is to eliminate non-value added activities in the system, optimize total system inventory required to execute market and segment actions, decrease cycle time, minimize variability, increase throughput, and demonstrate continuous improvement by subscribing to Aeroquip's AQ+ program."

Trusting and Information Sharing

"Total system excellence based on an open sharing of information and a high level of trust between participants."

Shared Risks and Rewards

"Aeroquip and its channel partners recognize and commit to an equitable sharing of risks and rewards."

8/ MARKETING CHANNEL POLICIES *and* POTENTIAL LEGAL CONSTRAINTS

◀◀◀◀◀◀

*T*here are a number of policies that channel managers can use to administer distribution systems. However, because each and every policy used in managing marketing channels restrains or redirects the activities of the various members of channels, there is always the possibility that, at one time or another, the affected parties are going to react negatively to the restrictions imposed. In the United States, negative reactions often bring lawsuits because of the litigious nature of the society. The policies discussed in this chapter are, for the most part, in common use, but all have been challenged as potential violations of federal or state antitrust laws.

The purpose of this chapter is twofold. First and foremost, it catalogues a variety of policies that are available for managing channels and explains the reasons why they might be adopted. Second, it concurrently lays out when and how such policies might run afoul of the federal antitrust laws. Although there is growing interest on the part of state attorneys general in antitrust issues, the focus here is solely on matters of concern to the federal government of the U.S. (Foreign readers who may have limited interest in U.S. law are, nevertheless, urged to note the channel policies explained here in order to gain a better understanding of the breadth of managerial alternatives available in directing channel members.)

The policies addressed below are as follows:

- market coverage policies

- customer coverage policies

- pricing policies

- product line policies

- selection and termination policies

- ownership policies

Although it would be more consistent with the focus of this text to start the discussion with ownership, selection, and termination policies, the channel design and management issues surrounding these policies have previously been covered in

EXHIBIT **8-1** / **Principal Laws Affecting the Interorganization Management of Marketing Channels**

Act	Key Provisions ◀ ◀ ◀
Sherman Antitrust Act, 1890	1. Prohibits contracts or combinations in restraint of interstate and foreign commerce. 2. Makes monopoly or attempt at monopoly a crime in interstate or foreign commerce.
Clayton Antitrust Act, 1914	Where competition is substantially lessened it prohibits: 1. Price discrimination in sales or leasing 2. Exclusive dealing 3. Tying contracts 4. Interlocking directorates among competitors 5. Intercorporate stockholding
Celler–Kefauver Act, 1950	Prohibits purchase of assets of another firm if competition is lessened.
FTC Act, 1914	1. Prohibits unfair trade practices injurious to competition or a competitor. 2. Sets up FTC to determine unfairness.
Robinson–Patman Act, 1936	1. Discriminatory prices are prohibited if they reduce competition at any point in the channel. 2. Discriminatory prices can be given in good faith to meet competition. 3. Brokerage allowances are allowed only if earned by an independent broker. 4. Sellers must give all services and promotional allowances to all buyers equally if the buyers are in competition. Alternatives must be offered. 5. Buyers are prohibited from knowingly inducing price discrimination. 6. Price discrimination can be legal if it results from real cost differences in serving different customers. 7. Prohibits agreement with competitors to charge unreasonably low prices to destroy competition.
FTC Trade Practice Rules	1. Enforced by FTC. Define unfair competition for individual industries. These practices are prohibited by FTC. 2. Define rules of sound practice. These rules are not enforced by the FTC, but are recommended.

some detail in Chapters 5, 6, and 7. Therefore, we begin this chapter by addressing policies having to do with market coverage, product, and price decisions before returning to ownership, selection, and termination.

The principal federal antitrust laws affecting the setting of these policies are listed in Exhibit 8-1.

▶ MARKET COVERAGE POLICIES

One of the key elements of channel management is deciding how many sales outlets should be established in a given geographic area and what kind of participation in the marketing flows should be required from each of the outlets so that the needs of existing and potential customers may be adequately served. To a large extent, the issue of market coverage is one of market presence. Strong market presence is found in situations where all major customer segments are addressed and where products are consistently offered to buyers at the time a purchase decision is made.[1] Combined with "hit rate" (a company's ability to win a high percentage of the sales opportunities it sees), it is one of the critical elements determining a company's market share.[2]

Three basic coverage policies appear to be available: (1) *intensive distribution*, whereby a product or brand is placed in as many outlets as possible, (2) *selective distribution*, whereby a product or brand is placed in a more limited number of outlets in a defined geographic area, and (3) *exclusive distribution*, whereby a product or brand is placed in the hands of only one outlet in a specific area. These choices are applicable to both vertically integrated and nonvertically integrated systems, although clearly the capital required to establish a wholly owned channel characterized by intensive distribution might be staggering. Generally, however, discussion of these policies is most directly applicable to channels comprising independently owned institutions and agencies.

Intensive distribution appears to be a rational strategy for goods that people wish to purchase frequently and with minimum effort; examples are tobacco products, soft drinks, soap, newspapers, chewing gum, gasoline, candy bars, and aspirin among consumer goods, and maintenance, repair, and operating items (e.g., lubricants, drill bits, and light bulbs) among industrial goods. Selective distribution can be used for goods that buyers seek out and can range from almost intensive to almost exclusive; examples are certain brands of television sets (e.g., Zenith, Sony), mattresses (e.g., Simmons), cosmetics (e.g., Elizabeth Arden, Estee Lauder), industrial supplies (e.g., Norton abrasives), electrical equipment (e.g., Square D circuit breakers), and clothing (e.g., Arrow shirts). Exclusive distribution is used to bring about a greater partnership between seller and reseller and is commonly found in the marketing channels for commercial air-conditioning equipment, some brands of apparel, high-priced household and office furniture, and construction and farm machinery. Channel structure also tends to interact with the degree of market exposure. For example, using numerous wholesale intermediaries (i.e., "long" channel structures) often permits greater market decentralization and thus intensive distribution, whereas the opposite tends to hold for shorter, more direct channels.

Pitfalls of Intensive Distribution

It could be argued that the more intensive a product's distribution, the greater the sales that product will achieve in the short run. Thus, if Pioneer, a producer of high-quality stereophonic components, decided to disband its present system of selective distribution in favor of a more intensive arrangement, one could predict with certainty that its sales would increase in the short run. But, as Pioneer expanded the number of its outlets to include drugstores, supermarkets, discount stores, and other outlets, adverse consequences would be highly likely over the long term. First, because some of the new outlets would undoubtedly begin to use the Pioneer brand as a loss leader to attract traffic, retail prices on Pioneer components would begin to drop, and valued outlets such as audio specialty stores might have second thoughts about selling a product on which profit margins were becoming slimmer and slimmer.

Second, service would deteriorate. Drugstores, supermarkets, and discount stores might not be willing to install after-sale service facilities, and repair work under warranty arrangements with consumers would have to be assumed by those stores with such facilities or by the manufacturer. Often, warranty business is not the most lucrative element of a service department's repair work, and leading stores offering such service would become increasingly disaffected at having to handle problems with equipment sold by other concerns. When General Electric decided to adopt more intensive distribution for its small electrical ("traffic") appliances some years ago, it found that it could not obtain adequate service from its expanded retail network. The company had to institute a nationwide, company-owned chain of service centers in order to solve this significant marketing problem. Eventually, it sold off its entire traffic appliance business to Black & Decker. To some extent, the widespread availability of consumer electronics in superstores and discounters, such as Circuit City, Best Buy, and Wal-Mart, is a major reason why these retailers offer virtually limitless return policies to customers. Rather than investing in repair facilities, they merely ship the returned merchandise (defective or not) back to the manufacturers for credit against future purchases.[3]

Third, it is likely that, because of its intensive distribution strategy, Pioneer would find itself assuming greater participation in a number of the marketing flows. Thus, promotion by the company would probably have to be increased, because dealers who once were willing to promote the product (through advertising and especially through in-store personal selling and display) might find their margins reduced to the point where such efforts were no longer affordable, and turn instead to other brands of stereo equipment that they might have in stock. Discount stores not providing services to end-users would take "free rides" on the services provided by more service-oriented dealers, further discouraging the latter from pushing the brand. In addition, more of the burden of holding inventory would undoubtedly have to be assumed by Pioneer as more outlets were added. In fact, it is possible to conceive of Pioneer's having to sell stereo equipment on a consignment basis in order to secure distribution in some outlets.[4]

Problems not unlike the Pioneer example befell makers of personal computers in the late 1980s. What happened was that companies like IBM, Apple, and Zenith Data Systems had expanded their networks of dealers to such an extent that there was too much competition among them for the slackening demand they were facing. In order to reduce inventories, the dealers would sell their excess stock of PCs to unauthorized dealers, like no-frills discounters such as 47th Street Photo in New York, thereby fostering the growth of the gray market for PCs. Margins declined as prices dropped, and dealers stopped providing service outputs required by many end-users. IBM, Apple, and Zenith made big cuts in the number of deal-

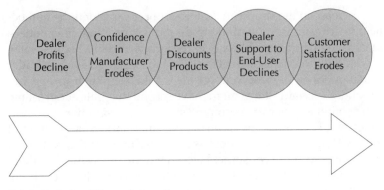

FIGURE 8-1   Effects of saturation.
Source: Richard E. Koon, Director of Retail Sales, IBM Corporation, presentation at the Marketing Science Institute/Duke University Conference on "Managing Marketing Channel Relationships" held at Duke University, Durham, NC, September 13–14,1984.

ers, especially among those who were permitted to carry new, highly advanced, higher-margin products. As a result, many dealers became more specialized, dropping some manufacturers' products so that they could concentrate on a few main lines and focus on fewer types of customers.[5]

Clearly, the type of distribution coverage employed interacts with the product itself (e.g., notice that the Pioneer and computer examples involve shopping or specialty goods, not convenience items) and with other elements of the marketing mix. Gaining sales volume in the short run without an eye to long-run consequences is a dangerous goal for numerous companies. Uncontrolled distribution is likely to bring with it some of the serious problems depicted in Figure 8-1. Richard Hamilton, former chairman and CEO of Hartmarx Corporation, a major clothing manufacturer, once observed that "you can take 50 years to build a brand and you can ruin it in three through careless distribution."[6] On the other hand, intensive distribution in the context of a well-developed marketing program for meeting the needs of both distributors and end-users is a logical and appropriate approach for tens of thousands of products.

In selecting a market coverage policy, it is best to consider the relationship between store and product types. Bucklin has combined the traditional threefold classification of consumer goods (convenience, shopping, and specialty goods) with a threefold classification of outlets according to patronage motives (convenience, shopping, and specialty stores) in order to facilitate decision making in this area.[7] As can be seen in Exhibit 8-2, knowledge of consumer behavior is again the key to determining distribution intensity.

Tradeoffs in Selecting a Market Coverage Policy

The selection of a market coverage policy involves a consideration of relevant tradeoffs. As indicated, channel members who decide to adopt an intensive policy generally relinquish a significant amount of control over the marketing of their products within the channel. The only way they can reestablish control in these cases is

EXHIBIT **8-2** / **Selection of Suitable Coverage Based on the Relationship Between Type of Product and Type of Store**

CLASSIFICATION	CONSUMER BEHAVIOR	MOST LIKELY FORM OF DISTRIBUTION
Convenience store/ convenience good	The consumer prefers to buy the most readily available brand of product at the most accessible store.	Intensive
Convenience store/ shopping good	The consumer selects his purchase from among the assortment carried by the most accessible store.	Intensive
Convenience store/ specialty good	The consumer purchases his favorite brand from the most accessible store carrying the item in stock.	Selective/exclusive
Shopping store/ convenience good	The consumer is indifferent to the brand of product he buys but shops different stores to secure better retail service and/or retail price.	Intensive
Shopping store/ shopping good	The consumer makes comparisons among both retail-controlled factors and factors associated with the product (brand).	Selective/exclusive
Shopping store/ specialty good	The consumer has a strong preference as to product brand but shops a number of stores to secure the best retail service and/or price for this brand.	Selective/exclusive
Specialty store/ convenience good	The consumer prefers to trade at a specific store but is indifferent to the brand of product purchased.	Selective/exclusive
Specialty store/ shopping good	The consumer prefers to trade at a certain store but is uncertain as to which product he wishes to buy and examines the store's assortment for the best purchase.	Selective/exclusive
Specialty store/ specialty good	The consumer has both a preference for a particular store and for a specific brand.	Selective/exclusive

Source: Louis P. Bucklin, "Retail Strategy and the Classification of Consumer Goods." *Journal of Marketing,* Vol. 23 (January 1963), pp. 50–55. The table itself was developed by and appears in Burton Marcus et al., *Modern Marketing* (New York: McGraw-Hill, Inc., 1975), p. 550. Reprinted with permission of McGraw-Hill, Inc.

to assume greater participation in each of the marketing flows. For example, O. M. Scott & Sons Company, a prominent manufacturer of lawn products, decided to adopt a less selective distribution policy because it wanted to obtain more exposure for its product line among the large percentage of medium- to upper-income homeowning families who, according to a marketing research study, were not users of lawn fertilizers.[8]

In order to obtain the proper merchandising support throughout its expanded reseller base, Scott found it necessary to develop special detailed programs for each retail account. Monthly sales plans were formulated by Scott account executives in terms of the retailers' requirements, and promotional plans were defined for each store. Many of these programs involved more than 50 pages of plans developed for an individual account. As a result of this programmed merchandising, retail store executives rarely had to make a decision that was not covered in detail in the individual account prospectus. Scott's programs were first instituted in department stores and subsequently were developed for supermarkets and other types of mass merchandisers. Therefore, not only did Scott assume the investment burden involved in formulating marketing plans for each channel member, but it was also able, through its store-by-store programmed merchandising efforts, to retain many of the policies it had adopted when its distribution was more selective (display guidelines, advertising incentives, and the like). Scott relied heavily on its expert power base in the marketing of lawn products, as well as the promise of significant profits, to convince resellers to participate in programs they would not otherwise have adopted.[9]

On the other hand, as channel members move toward exclusive distribution, role expectations become more sharply delineated. Specific agreements are possible with respect to degrees of participation in the marketing flows. But each of these agreements demands careful attention to rights and obligations. For an exclusive distribution policy, the bargaining points (and relevant tradeoffs) generally concern the following:

1. *Products Covered.* The specific items in the line that are to be handled by the exclusive wholesaler or retailer must be clearly delineated. For example, there may be certain products, especially those of a highly technical nature, that a supplier will wish to sell through its own specially trained sales force. Other products will be made available for sale through exclusive distributors. To avoid future conflict over the division of product line responsibilities, a clear understanding must be forged among the channel members as to the domains of each with regard to the items in the line. In the cases where an item has been assigned to a distributor, any sales of that item by the supplier in the distribution's territory should be credited to the distributor.

2. *Classes or Types of Customers.* Agreement over who is responsible for various types of customers must be arrived at to prevent future dysfunctional conflict. Thus, as in the case of products covered, the supplier may wish to retain the right to sell directly to specific classes of customers, such as the military, or to very large commercial accounts (e.g., General Motors). Any sales to customers allocated to distributors or dealers must be credited to the latter if domains are not to be violated. The expectations of who is to serve whom must be clearly understood and/or resolved at the outset.

3. *Territory Covered.* Clearly, this is another crucial element in establishing relevant domains. In many cases, agreement on territorial boundaries can prevent future jurisdictional disputes among the distributors handling the supplier's products.

4. *Inventories.* The questions to be resolved here are who is going to bear the burden of holding and owning inventories and how much inventory is to be held, and where. In situations of fluctuating price levels, these questions become particularly acute. Suppliers may have to enter into price guarantees or may have to consign merchandise when economic conditions are turbulent.

5. *Installation and Repair Services.* This bargaining issue is obviously relevant for durable goods in both the industrial and consumer goods sectors. Here, questions about handling warranties are crucial, and the rights and obligations of suppliers and distributors must be clearly specified. Distributors may be asked to commit resources to the training of service personnel, and suppliers may have to assure distributors that troubleshooters will be on call for situations that are beyond the distributors' service capabilities. Considerable conflict between channel intermediaries and manufacturers has appeared in the automobile, home appliance, electronics, and capital equipment industries due to inadequate specification of installation and repair roles.

6. *Prices.* Under exclusive distribution policies, the supplier is likely to agree to some form of price or margin guarantee in times of declining market prices. The distributor may agree to maintain "reasonable margins" in its prices to end-users, but, as discussed later in this chapter, legal constraints prohibit any collusion on this matter between the supplier and its distributors.

7. *Sales Quotas.* The establishment of unrealistic sales quotas has brought about considerable friction in channel relations. In agreeing to an exclusive distribution arrangement, the parties involved should arrive at a consensus on the way in which the quotas are to be calculated. They should also agree on the rewards to be received or the punishments to be levied for performance above or below the quotas arrived at.

8. *Advertising and Sales Promotional Obligations.* Responsibilities for the development of catalogs, sales aids, display work, local advertising and promotion, etc., must be specified in the agreement. The basis for calculating cooperative advertising allowances should be spelled out in detail so that each party realizes its obligation to the other.

9. *Exclusive Dealing.* In some situations, suppliers prefer that their distributors handle no products that will compete directly with their own. Exclusive "dealing" (which is explained later in this chapter) is product oriented, whereas exclusive "distribution" is geography oriented. Sometimes, but not always, they are coupled. Exclusive dealing may be especially appropriate if customers value distributor expertise so much that they are willing to trade-off broad brand selection to get it. If this is the case, then these suppliers will often be called on to give added promotional support to their distributors to ensure that the latter will be able to achieve a satisfactory sales volume in the product category affected.

10. *Duration, Provision for Renewal, and Termination.* If exclusive distribution is desired, then it is important that the specifics of each of the previous nine points be agreed on in writing. The contract established should, however, allow the parties enough flexibility to meet extraneous events and contingencies when they arise. In addition, it is important for the parties to agree on the length of time that the agreement is to be in effect and on renewal provisions. Especially important, given the legal implications involved, are specifics regarding when and how the arrangement can be terminated by either of the parties.

The preceding list is not exhaustive; it serves merely to indicate the detail required in formulating a market coverage policy as one moves toward the exclusive end of the spectrum. New entrants to an industry must often offer established channel intermediaries exclusive territories in order to entice them to distribute new products or brands with uncertain demand. And if there are too many competitors in any given geography, none of them will be able to operate at a scale required for efficient operations.

For examples of specific distributor agreements, see Appendixes 8A, 8B, and 8C. The agreements reproduced there were developed by the marketing department of the Industrial Products Group of Aeroquip Corporation, a major manufacturer of hoses and fittings. Aeroquip has a tiered distribution system comprised of premier, authorized, and affiliated distributors, each of which assumes a different role in Aeroquip's marketing channel.

Antitrust Concerns

Implicit in the term "market coverage" are issues concerned with geography or territory. The more a policy moves away from intensive, the fewer resellers of a particular brand there will be in any given area. Selective and exclusive coverage policies have been called, by antitrust enforcement agencies, "territorial restrictions," because they are used by suppliers to limit the number of resellers in a defined territory. Territorial assignments are, in reality, rewards or spatial allocations given by suppliers adopting selective or exclusive market coverage policies in return for distributors' promises to cultivate the geography they have been given.

The objective of a supplier instituting territorial and, as we shall see, a number of other kinds of so-called "vertical restraints" is to limit the extent of *intrabrand* competition. A critical issue that has evolved in antitrust cases is whether such policies, while severely restricting *intrabrand* competition, are actually promoting, or at least not substantially lessening, *interbrand* competition. Intrabrand competition is defined as competition among wholesalers or retailers of the same brand (e.g., Coca-Cola, Chevrolet, or Apple). Interbrand competition is defined as competition among all the suppliers of different brands of the same generic product (e.g., brands of soft drinks, automobiles, or personal computers). The rationale behind restricting intrabrand competition is that by protecting resellers of its brand from competition among themselves, a supplier will supposedly improve their effectiveness against resellers of other brands. From an interorganization management perspective, the attempt to dampen *intra*brand competition in order to strengthen *inter*brand competition makes a lot of sense. A manufacturer would often rather have the channel members handling its brand compete with those of other brands than to slug it out among themselves.

In the language of antitrust enforcement, territorial restrictions range from absolute confinement of reseller sales, which is intended to completely foreclose or eliminate intrabrand competition, to "lesser" territorial restrictions, designed to inhibit such competition. These lesser restrictions include areas of primary responsibility, profit pass-over arrangements, and location causes.

Absolute confinement involves a promise by a channel member that it will not sell outside its assigned territory. Often combined with such a promise is a pledge by the supplier not to sell to anyone else in that territory. When absolute confinement is combined with an exclusive distributorship, the territory can be considered "airtight." On the other hand, an *area of primary responsibility* requires the channel member to use its best efforts to maintain effective distribution of the supplier's goods in the territory specifically assigned to it. Failure to meet performance targets may result in termination, but the channel member is free to sell outside its area, and other wholesalers or retailers may sell in its territory.

Profit pass-over arrangements require that a channel member who sells to a customer located outside its assigned territory compensate the distributor in whose territory the customer is located. Such compensation is ostensibly to reimburse the distributor for its efforts to stimulate demand in its territory and for the cost of providing services on which the channel member might have capitalized. Finally, a *location clause* specifies the site of a channel member's place of business. Such clauses are used to "space" resellers in a given territory so that each has a "natural" market comprising those customers who are closest to the reseller's location. However, the reseller may sell to any customer walking through its door. Furthermore, the customers located closest to it may decide to purchase at more distant locations.

Any attempt to confine wholesalers' or retailers' selling activities to one area may be viewed as either a restraint of trade or as an unfair method of competition and therefore may be challenged under the Sherman Act or Section 5 of the FTC Act. The dominant antitrust perspective relative to territorial restrictions (market coverage policies) was established on June 23, 1977, when the Supreme Court handed down a decision in the *Sylvania* case.[10] Because of the significance of the *Sylvania* case, it is important to devote some time to understanding it.

Prior to 1962, Sylvania, a manufacturer of television sets, sold its sets through both independent and company-owned distributors to a large number of independent retailers. RCA dominated the market at the time, holding 60 to 70% of national sales, with Zenith and Magnavox as major rivals. Sylvania had only 1 to 2% of the market. In 1962, Sylvania decided to abandon efforts at saturation distribution and chose instead to phase out its wholesalers and sell directly to a smaller group of franchised retailers. Sylvania retained sole discretion to determine how many retailers would operate in any geographic area, and, in fact, at least two retailers were franchised in every metropolitan center of more than 100,000 people. Dealers were free to sell anywhere and to any class of customers, but agreed to operate only from locations approved by Sylvania.

Continental TV was one of Sylvania's most successful retailers in northern California. After a series of disagreements arising from Sylvania's authorizing a new outlet near one of Continental's best locations, Continental opened a new outlet in Sacramento, although its earlier request for approval for that location had been denied. Sylvania then terminated Continental's franchise. Continental brought a lawsuit against Sylvania. The Court sided with Sylvania, which had argued that the use of its territorial allocation policy permitted its marketing channels to compete more successfully against those established by its large competitors.

In its decision, the Court favored the promotion of *inter*brand competition even if *intra*brand competition were restricted. It indicated that territorial restrictions encourage interbrand competition by allowing the manufacturer to achieve certain efficiencies in the distribution of its products. And, in a footnote, the Court recognized that the imposition of such restrictions is consistent with increased societal demands that manufacturers directly assume responsibility for the safety and quality of their products. As a result of the Court's decision, territorial restrictions, when challenged, are to be evaluated under a "rule of reason" doctrine in which proof must be established that the restrictions substantially lessen interbrand competition. Furthermore, the burden is on the plaintiff to prove that the restraints are unreasonable. (For definitions of the various legal rules applied in vertical restraint antitrust cases, see Exhibit 8-3.)

EXHIBIT 8-3 / Legal Rules Used in Antitrust Enforcement

Per se illegality:	The marketing policy is automatically unlawful regardless of the reasons for the practice and without extended inquiry into its effects. It is only necessary for the complainant to prove the occurence of conduct.
Modified rule of reason:	The marketing policy is automatically unlawful if evidence of the existence and use of significant market power is found.

Exhibit 8-3 (continued)

Exhibit 8-3 (continued)

Rule of reason:	Before a decision is made about the legality of a marketing policy, it is necessary to undertake a broad inquiry into the nature, purpose, and effect of the policy. This requires an examination of the facts peculiar to the contested policy, its history, the reasons why it was implemented, and its competitive significance. Assessment is made as to whether the policy has substantially lessened interbrand competition.
Per se legality:	The marketing policy is presumed legal.

Although the use of territorial restrictions in the U.S. is widespread and, for the most part, legal, this is not true elsewhere in the world. For example, the Treaty of Rome, which established the European Economic Community (EC), holds to the premise that all agreements, vertical (i.e., between channel members on different levels of distribution) or horizontal (i.e., among competitors), are distortions of free trade. The EC competition rules essentially require manufacturers to supply goods to whoever wants to sell them. The only way in which manufacturers may employ policies like selective distribution is for them to secure "exemption" from the rules from the EC headquarters in Brussels. If the exemption does not exist, any policy that impedes "open distribution" is a potential breach of European commercial law.[11] Three industries in which exemptions have been granted are cars, consumer electronics, and perfume. In the case of cars and electronics, selective distribution is permitted on the grounds that the products are complex and need after-sales service. For perfume, the justification is that the products are luxury goods, which depend for their appeal on an aura of exclusivity maintained by high price, large investments in marketing, and a sophisticated sales environment. All of these exemptions have come under fire by consumer groups and discounters seeking supply.[12]

▶ **CUSTOMER COVERAGE POLICIES**

Suppliers may wish to set policies regarding to whom wholesalers or retailers may resell their goods and services. For a variety of reasons, suppliers may wish to reserve certain customers as "house accounts." These reasons include the desire to maintain close relationships with highly valuable accounts, the requirements of accounts for technical assistance, the efficiency associated with serving accounts on a direct basis, the expected profits on the sale, the need for price concessions to win certain accounts, and, in the case of some retailers, like Home Depot and Wal-Mart, the insistence of accounts to be sold on a direct basis. In other cases, suppliers may set customer coverage policies that have the goal of assuring that their goods and services will be sold by intermediaries capable of providing specific service outputs to their customers. This way, suppliers can be confident that their products are handled only by competent resellers.

Such policies have been used by a large number of manufacturers in their attempts to prevent the emergence of "gray markets," which appear when their brands are sold by unauthorized resellers. Clauses in contracts written by manufacturers often stipulate that authorized dealers are prohibited from selling their brands to anyone but bona fide end-users. Authorized dealers are often tempted to sell off their excess inventories to unauthorized dealers, such as 47th Street Photo, Kmart, Syms, and other discounters. The situation is particularly acute with regard to the importing of brand-name goods by companies that don't have the approval of the owners of U.S. trademarks for those goods.

In addition, suppliers might wish to allocate different accounts to different intermediaries. As Areeda and Kaplow point out:

> A cosmetics manufacturer . . . might permit one wholesaler to sell only to drugstores and permit a different wholesaler to sell only to beauty salons . . . It might do so for any one of three reasons or for all of them: to limit (intrabrand) competition or to facilitate price discrimination . . . or to achieve efficient specialization. The exploitation of different distribution outlets may call for different techniques of promotion, servicing, and payment.[13]

Customer coverage policies could also be used for safety reasons; certain specialized dealers may be willing to screen potential customers and/or provide information required in a product's use (e.g., herbicides).

Posner has pointed out an economic rationale underlying the use of such restrictions:

> There may be a class of customers who, because of size, sophistication, or special needs, do not require dealer services. The manufacturer may be in a better position than any dealer to provide these customers with whatever presale services they do require. If so, the manufacturer who allows his dealers to compete with him for such an account is inviting them to take a free ride on his services. He provides the services at a cost that he hopes to recoup in the price charged these customers; the dealers then offer the customers a lower price, which they can do since they do not incur any services expense with respect to these customers.[14]

Indeed, many of the reasons for adopting customer coverage policies are the same as those for the adoption of market coverage policies. For this reason, the antitrust concerns are handled similarly, as discussed in the following text.

Antitrust Concerns

The antitrust enforcement agencies and the courts refer to customer coverage policies as "customer" or "resale restrictions." Policies of this type become illegal when it can be shown that their effects tend to reduce competition substantially. At present, however, there are no clear guidelines that determine just how far suppliers may go in dictating to wholesalers or retailers the classes and kinds of customers to whom they may resell the suppliers' products or brands. The reason for this confusion is due primarily to the fact that the Supreme Court in its decision in the *Sylvania* case[15] did not distinguish between customer (resale) restrictions and territorial restrictions. The former are basically exercises of coercive power (e.g., prohibitions on distributors reselling to discount houses) whereas the latter are basically exercises of reward power (e.g., the granting of a monopoly on the sale of a brand within a defined territory).

Despite their different characters, territorial and resale restrictions are treated identically under the law. Both are viewed as restraints of trade and, therefore, are directly challengeable under the Sherman Act. But, given the *Sylvania* decision, their legality is to be judged under a rule-of-reason approach. That is, they will be considered *legal* if they have not substantially lessened interbrand competition.

Although the presence of gray markets is not necessarily an antitrust concern, it may be useful for channel managers to note that, in 1988, the Supreme Court upheld a Customs Service regulation *permitting* gray market imports. Gray markets are specifically permitted when the U.S. trademark is owned by a U.S. company with its own manufacturing facility abroad or when the U.S. trademark owner has established a subsidiary or affiliate abroad that is under the U.S. company's "common control."[16] Duracell batteries fit this description, for example, because they are manufactured abroad in plants owned by Duracell as well as in plants under Duracell's control. Gray market importers in the U.S. generally obtain their goods from foreign distributors who buy the products overseas.[17]

▶ PRICING POLICIES

There are many ways in which prices and price levels can be influenced throughout marketing channels. In fact, we have just finished discussing two of them—market coverage and customer coverage. Because these policies are both aimed at reducing or restraining the amount of intrabrand competition, the *indirect* effect of the reduction is, in theory, supposed to be an increase in the price of the brand from what it would have been in the absence of the policies. If the price is at a "reasonable" level, this means gross margins available to resellers may be sufficient to pay for the provision of service outputs desired by end-users (as assessed by the supplier setting the policy). In other words, restrictions on *intra*brand competition are, indirectly, supposed to result in higher prices and, thus, higher gross margins. Obviously, price competition induced by *inter*brand competitors can upset the entire apple cart.

Two policies are described here that have a *direct* effect on price—price maintenance and price discrimination. We separate the discussion of the two because their motivation, implementation, and antitrust concerns are very different.

Price Maintenance

Price maintenance in marketing channels is the specification by suppliers, typically manufacturers, of the prices below or above which other channel members, typically wholesalers and retailers, may not *resell* their products. Because of this, the policy is frequently called "resale price maintenance (RPM)." Some of the managerial reasons the policy is enacted are given below. (Note the similarity to the rationale for market and customer coverage policies given earlier.)

1.   Shoppers can gain information and services at full-price dealers and then purchase through price discounters. By not offering the same level of presale and postsale ser-

vices as full price dealers, such as extensive product information and demonstrations, and postsale installation, maintenance, and repair, discounters can "free ride" on the services offered elsewhere. Full-service dealers will then reduce services, leading to a reduction in demand, to the detriment of all parties. Resale price maintenance prevents discounting, reducing the extent of rival dealer free riding on services.

2. With local monopoly power, dealers will raise price above competitive levels, contrary to the interest of manufacturers and consumers. (A common example of this problem is in newspaper distribution.) Through the use of maximum resale price maintenance, price is maintained at a competitive level.

3. Manufacturers must gain entry to dealers faced with limited shelf and floor space. For many goods, dealer networks compatible with a product's quality and image are required. Manufacturers purchase such access through higher markups, advertising and brand name drawing power, advertising allowances to dealers, and other expenditures in competition with rival brands. Resale price maintenance provides a means for new manufacturers to gain dealer access by assuring dealers a given retail markup.[18]

In addition, if they can earn a "reasonable" retail markup, channel intermediaries may engage in quality certification for end-users so that the normal risks associated with purchasing a good or service are minimized.

Other business reasons for price maintenance include: (1) achieving channel members' goodwill, (2) buttressing the price-quality image of a brand by preventing its use as a loss-leader, (3) providing quality signals via sale through elite retail stores who would otherwise avoid a brand sold to discounters, (4) encouraging channel members to push the brand versus others they might carry, (5) supporting a broad network of specialty stores that otherwise would not survive discount competition, and (6) assuring widespread and immediate availability of a brand.[19] Finally, because price maintenance supposedly assures positive profits, termination (causing the loss of the positive profits) would be very costly to the channel members receiving them. Such powerful incentives (called, by economists, "quasirents") are likely to discourage price maintainers from becoming price discounters.[20]

ANTITRUST CONCERNS   Despite all of these reasons, which support channel managers' implementing an RPM policy, price maintenance is viewed by the courts as having pernicious effects, and it makes no difference whether maximum[21] or minimum prices are set. However, RPM can only be condemned as a per se violation of Section 1 of the Sherman Act if there is evidence of a qualifying agreement among two or more firms to impose the policy. This point was emphasized in 1984 in *Monsanto Company v. Spray-Rite Service Corporation.*[22] Spray-Rite (now-defunct) sued Monsanto after Monsanto cut off Spray-Rite's distributorship of herbicides in northern Illinois in 1968. Spray-Rite claimed that Monsanto did this because Spray-Rite would not join in an effort to fix prices at which herbicides were sold. Spray-Rite alleged a conspiracy between Monsanto and some of its distributors to set resale prices. The court found in Spray-Rite's favor, but made it clear that the presence of concerted action between Monsanto and its distributors was critical to its per se ruling. In fact, the court explicitly stated that "a manufacturer . . . generally has a right to deal, or refuse to deal, with whomever it likes, as long as it does so independently." Citing the *Colgate* doctrine (discussed later in this chapter), the court went on to say that "the manufacturer can announce its resale prices in advance and refuse to deal with those who fail to comply." In other words, manufacturers may stipulate resale prices to their distributors as long as the stipulations are made on a one-to-one (unilateral) basis. Where concerted, conspiratorial action is found, a per se illegal ruling can be expected.

Reliance on the *Colgate* doctrine was the main reason why in 1983 Russell Stover, a major manufacturer of boxed chocolates, was not found guilty of unlawfully fixing retail candy prices. Russell Stover had announced in advance that it would refuse to deal with retailers who resold below the prices designated on lists, invoices, and order forms and the boxed candy itself. Stover wouldn't sell initially to stores that it believed would sell its products at less than designated prices, and it stopped dealing with established retailers who actually did so.[23]

The *Monsanto* decision may be viewed as a chink in the armor of the per se illegality status of resale price maintenance. The problem that *Monsanto* has created is how the term "agreement" ought to be defined and what evidence is sufficient to support a jury verdict that there was a price-fixing conspiracy. The Supreme Court said that evidence must be presented both that the distributor communicated its acquiescence regarding the manufacturer's resale pricing policy and that the acquiescence was sought by the manufacturer. It added that the mere fact that other distributors complained about a price cutter prior to termination wasn't sufficient to support a finding of agreement.

In a useful summary of the status of resale price maintenance as a result of the *Monsanto* decision, Sheffet and Scammon suggest that manufacturers might take the following steps if they want to legally control resale prices:

1. Act unilaterally, that is, statements and actions should come only from the manufacturer.
2. Avoid coercion, that is, don't use annually renewable contracts conditioned on dealer adherence to manufacturer's specified resale price.
3. Vertically integrate, that is, form a corporate vertical marketing system.
4. Avoid known discounters, that is, establish screening and performance criteria difficult for discounters to meet.
5. Announce resale price policy upfront, that is, the policy should be established when arrangements are first made with channel members and should specify that the manufacturer will refuse to deal with any dealer not willing to adhere to the announced terms.[24]

When examining resale price maintenance cases, the courts following in the wake of the *Monsanto* decision are sure to ask three basic questions: (1) Was there a conspiracy or combination to fix prices? (2) Was there a written agreement confirming the conditions of this conspiracy or combination? (3) Was coercion used to enforce the agreement?[25]

The chink in the per se armor has grown even larger since the *Monsanto* decision. In 1988, the Supreme Court ruled 6–2 that a manufacturer's agreement with one dealer to stop supplying a price-cutting dealer would not necessarily violate the Sherman Act.[26] The plaintiff, Business Electronics, was the exclusive retailer of Sharp calculators in Houston from 1968 to 1972. During that period, Sharp became dissatisfied with Business Electronics' policy of selling calculators at prices lower than those suggested by Sharp. In 1972 Sharp appointed Hartwell's Office World as a second retailer of its calculators in Houston. Subsequently, Hartwell told Sharp that it would quit distributing its products unless Sharp ended its relationship with Business Electronics, and, in 1973, Sharp terminated Business Electronics' dealership. Business Electronics then sued Sharp. The Supreme Court upheld an appeals court ruling that the agreement to terminate Business Electronics was not a per se violation of antitrust law. It stated that such an agreement would be illegal per se only if it had been part of an agreement by the manufacturer and one or more retailers to *fix prices at some level.* There was no proof in the case of such a *specific* price-fixing agreement between Sharp and Hartwell. Writing for the Court, Justice Antonin Scalia observed that it is sometimes legitimate and competitively useful for manufacturers to curb price competition among their dealers, and he referred to the "free rider" problem mentioned earlier as a reason for manufacturers' actions. Thus, if there is no specific agreement as to price between the complaining dealers and the manufacturer, the reasonableness of an agreement to terminate will be determined by the rule of reason, that is, by balancing the anticompetitive intrabrand effects against any pro-competitive interbrand effects.[27]

The *Monsanto* and *Business Electronics* decisions appear to have stimulated a number of manufacturers of upscale consumer goods, such as Prince Manufacturing Inc. (makers of Prince tennis racquets) and Specialized Bicycle Components (makers of mountain bikes), to use unilaterally implemented resale price maintenance as one of their major distribution policies.[28] In fact, it is claimed that resale prices are now being set for certain brands of televisions, sneakers, cameras, china, furniture, cosmetics, golf clubs, VCRs, women's sportswear, men's suits, stereos, toys, ceiling fans, watches, appliances, skis, cookware, perfume, chocolates, luggage, and video games, among others.[29] Some of the arguments being raised in opposition to the increasing price maintenance activity are:

- Fixed resale prices do not ensure that retailers will use their larger gross margins to provide service; they may simply pocket the extra money.

- Although interbrand competition may be fostered, vertical price fixing inhibits competition between stores carrying the same brand.

- If a manufacturer deems service to be essential, it can be required of all retailers through dealership contracts.

- Higher prices deny goods to consumers with less money.[30]

These misgivings represent, to a large extent, the beliefs of a large number of the members of Congress. Given Congress' feelings and the fact that the courts still hold that RPM is per se illegal, the antitrust enforcement agencies have continued to pursue RPM cases. Over the past decade, for example, the Federal Trade Commission brought cases against Reebok International Ltd. and its Rockport Co. subsidiary, Keds Corporation, Kreepy Krauly, and Nintendo, all of which were settled with consent orders.[31] And the Antitrust Division of the U.S. Department of Justice has declared that it is, once again, going to challenge RPM, even though the last vertical restraint case it filed was in 1980.[32] Evidence of its interest is the fact that, late in 1994, it began an antitrust investigation into the way automotive dealers set car prices and whether an industrywide move toward "no-haggle" sales is illegal vertical price-fixing. For example, the Saturn division of General Motors promotes one-price selling, and Oldsmobile advertises already discounted retail prices. At issue in the investigation are the subtle (and sometimes not-so-subtle) ways in which manufacturers pressure retailers to adopt minimum prices.[33]

The Supreme Court noted in *Business Electronics,* however, that the per se prohibitions on resale price maintenance do not apply "to restrictions on price to be charged by one who is in reality an agent of, not a buyer from, the manufacturer."[34] Here, the Court was quoting from *U.S. v. General Electric Co.*[35] where it was stated that

> The owner of an article . . . is not violating the common law, or the Anti-Trust Law, by seeking to dispose of his article directly to the consumer and fixing the price by which his agents transfer the title from him directly to the consumer.[36]

In the words of a lower court in a more recent case,

> . . . where the manufacturer bears the financial risks of transactions with the customers and continues to retain "title, dominion and control over its goods," then it is likely that the distributor is merely an agent for the manufacturer.[37]

Price Discrimination

When a seller offers or grants one buyer a lower price than another buyer on the exact same product, the seller is discriminating between the buyers by giving one of them a monetary reward. In actuality, discriminating among buyers, whether via prices, service outputs, or product features, makes abundant sense. From a managerial perspective, it would be foolish not to approach buyers typified by high-demand elasticities differently from those with low-demand elasticities. At the core of well conceived market segmentation schemes are discriminatory tactics, because segments are supposed to be solicited dissimilarly. In fact, optimal profits can only be achieved if sellers discriminate among buyers.

Costs, price sensitivity, and/or competition usually vary significantly across market segments. When this happens, Nagle and Holden argue that "a pricing strategy based on a single price for all sales is an imperfect compromise."[38] They suggest, instead, "segmented pricing" (i.e., price discrimination).

> With segmented pricing, management minimizes the need to compromise. Customers who are relatively price insensitive, costly to serve, or poorly served by competitors can be charged more than those who are relative price sensitive, less costly to serve, or well-served by competitors. Both sales and profitability improve.[39]

Although there are an infinite number of ways channel members can discriminate among their customers and suppliers, the focus here is mainly on price.

The major price policies that are enacted by channel managers tend to revolve around reductions from list price, promotional allowances and services, and functional discounts. The rationale for each of these is straightforward—the object is to increase demand, fight off competitors, reward customers, and/or compensate channel partners for services rendered. It is assumed that readers of this text are familiar with most of these basic strategic motivations, and, therefore, explanation of them here is unnecessary.[40]

ANTITRUST CONCERNS   There are times when price discrimination is illegal. These times are specified in the Robinson-Patman Act. However, trying to explain and understand the Robinson-Patman Act is like trying to learn Sanskrit; it induces two Excedrin headaches, at a minimum. We will make the discussion of it as short and simple as possible, leaving the intricacies to people with masochistic tendencies.

Price Discrimination by Sellers. When sellers offer different prices to different buyers, the most directly relevant part of the Robinson-Patman Act is Section 2(a), which states:

> It shall be unlawful for any person engaged in commerce, . . . either directly or indirectly, to discriminate in price between different purchasers of commodities of like grade and quality, where either or any of the purchases involved in such discrimination are in commerce, where such commodities are sold for use, consumption, or resale within [any area] under the jurisdiction of the United States, and where the effect of such discrimination may be to substantially lessen competition or tend to create a monopoly in any line of commerce, or to injure, destroy or prevent competition with any person who either grants or knowingly receives the benefit of such discrimination, or with customers of either of them.

Every phrase in the section has meaning and has been debated thoroughly, sometimes in book-long treatises. At the risk of oversimplification, a few of the more significant phrases can be interpreted as follows:

1. "like grade and quality"—Where products are of different materials or workmanship level, they are not ordinarily considered to be of "like grade and quality," but where differences are small and do not affect the basic use of the goods, then selling at price differentials has been attacked. For example, there have been challenges to price differences involving private label versus branded goods where the product was identical in both instances (i.e., evaporated milk made by Borden).[41]

2. "substantially lessen competition"—This factor is a critical issue in all antitrust cases (including those filed under Section 2(a) of the Robinson Patman Act), which are tried under the rule of reason doctrine. It has become increasingly difficult for plaintiffs to prove, because there is an important difference between injury to competitors and injury to competition. A loss of sales by one firm and their gain by another is the essence of competition, and the object of each competitor is to outsell rivals. Evidence of intent to destroy a competitor, however, may indicate an injury to competition.

Price discrimination between customers who are not competing is not illegal. This means it is perfectly legal for retailers to charge consumers different prices for identical goods and services (e.g., airline tickets, automobiles)—consumers are not "in competition" with one another. Also, if one retailer does business only on the east coast and another does business only on the west coast, a vendor may charge them different prices as long as they don't compete for the same end-users.

Price discrimination that injures any of three levels of competition may end up being prohibited by the Robinson-Patman Act.

1. *Primary Level.* Competition between two sellers may be injured when one of them gives discriminatory prices to some customers.

2. *Secondary Level.* Competition between two customers of a seller may be affected if the seller differentiates between them in price. In effect the seller is aiding one customer and harming the other in their mutual competition, and this is sufficient to cause substantial lessening of competition.

3. *Tertiary Level.* If a manufacturer discriminates in prices between two wholesalers such that the customers of one wholesaler are favored over those of the other, the competition is being injured by the price discrimination.

Perhaps one of the most important Robinson-Patman Act cases in decades was decided in 1993. It involved a primary level discrimination in which Liggett & Myers, formerly the Brooke Group, charged Brown & Williamson (B&W) with predatory pricing.[42] In 1980 Liggett, which had a 2.3% market share, introduced a generic, unadvertised cigarette that sold for 30% less than the general price. Eventually, B&W entered with a generic packaged in an identical box to Liggett's and began to undercut Liggett's price. B&W had a market share of around 12% at the time. During the 18-month price war that ensued, B&W allegedly cut its prices substantially below average variable cost. Liggett could not sustain the below-cost pricing, and the price of generic cigarettes rose.

Liggett sued under the Robinson-Patman Act, because B&W's predatory price cuts were implemented via promotional discounts that were given to different distributors in varying degrees—hence, the price discrimination. Although there are many aspects of this case that make for interesting reading and analysis from a marketing-management perspective, the most important is the decision itself. The Court's decision rested on its assessment of whether B&W could earn back, via monopoly pricing, the costs of its predatory actions after Liggett was quieted. The Court argued that, in addition to showing below cost prices, the plaintiff (Liggett) must also demonstrate "that the competitor had a reasonable prospect . . . of recouping its investment in below-cost prices."[43] As the Court noted, "Recoupment is the ultimate object of an unlawful predatory scheme; it is the means by which a predator profits from predation."[44] Through an analysis of competition in the cigarette industry, the Court came to the conclusion that B&W, despite the fact that it had quieted Liggett, didn't have the power to quiet R.J. Reynolds, Philip Morris, and the rest of its competitors and, therefore, would not be able to retrieve its investment. It found in favor of B&W, stating that, without recoupment, predatory pricing produces lower aggregate prices in the market, and consumer welfare is enhanced. A federal court in Texas followed the same line of reasoning shortly after the *Brooke Group* decision when it cleared American Airlines of predatory pricing against Northwest and Continental Airlines.[45]

Defenses to Price Discrimination Charges. Price discrimination, unlike resale price maintenance, is not a per se violation of the antitrust laws. There are three potential escape routes, beyond the fact that the discrimination may have an insignificant impact on competition. Discrimination may be justified through proof that (1) it was carried out to dispose of perishable or obsolete goods, or under a closeout or bankruptcy sale; (2) it merely made due allowance for differences in "the cost of manufacture, sale, or delivery resulting from the differing methods or quantities" in which the commodity was sold or delivered; or (3) it was effected "in good faith to meet an equally low price of a competitor." The first defense poses few problems, but the second and third have made grown persons cry.

Cost Justification Defense. As Scherer and Ross point out:

> Companies attempting to sustain a Robinson-Patman Act cost justification defense have seldom been successful because of the stringent standards set by the Federal Trade Commission, that is, requiring detailed documentation of full (not marginal) costs and causing the defense to fail if less than 100 percent of the price differential is shown to result from cost differences.[46]

The burden of proof is on the seller. For example, quantity discounts are permitted under Section 2(a) to the extent that they are justified by cost savings. The Supreme Court has, however, ruled that quantity discounts must reflect cost savings in deliveries made to one place at one time. This places limitations on the use of cumulative quantity discounts. In 1988 the Federal Trade Commission charged six of the nation's largest book publishers with illegally discriminating against independent bookstores by selling books at lower prices to major bookstore chains, such as Waldenbooks, B. Dalton, and Crown Books. The FTC said the publishers treated orders placed by the chains as a single order, even if the books were separately packed, itemized, and shipped to individual chain outlets. As a result, the chain stores were able to pay lower prices than independent bookstores "that receive shipments as large or larger than shipments to individual chain outlets."[47]

Pricing policies in the health care industry have attracted considerable litigious attention over the past decade. Late in 1994, 1,346 independent pharmacies in 15 states sued the largest drug manufacturers and mail order distributors, charging them with price discrimination. Early in 1994, four major grocery chains (Kroger, Albertson's, Safeway, and Vons) filed a suit in Cincinnati federal court charging 16 pharmaceutical firms and a mail-order prescription company with discriminatory and "pernicious" pricing. The suit claims the firms' pricing policies favor institutional pharmacies, health-maintenance organizations, and mail-order prescription ("pharmacy benefit management") companies with lower prices, while charging supermarket chains more. And late in 1993, similar charges were levied by 20 chain and independent drugstores in yet another suit.[48] All of these lawsuits, including the one involving the book publishers, were still pending at the time this text was printed.

Good Faith Defense. The good faith defense (which is found in Section 2(b) of the act) has proven as difficult to apply as the cost justification defense, but is even more confusing and complex (if that is possible). The defense is valid even if there is substantial injury to competition, but the burden of proving good faith falls on the defendant.[49]

1. The price being met must be lawful and not a price produced by collusion. A seller does not have to prove the price that it is meeting is lawful, but it must make some effort to find out if it is.

2. The price being met must really exist,[50] and the price must be met and not undercut. Price reductions on a "premium" product to the level of "standard" products can be a form of illegal price discrimination. If the public is willing to pay a higher price for the "premium" product, the equal prices may be considered beating and not meeting competition.

3. The competition being met must be at the primary level. Granting a discriminatory price to some customers to enable them to meet their own competition is not protected.[51]

According to a 1983 Supreme Court ruling, the good faith defense is applicable to gaining new customers as well as retaining old ones.[52] But firms practicing discrimination are only permitted to match rival prices exactly; they cannot undercut or "beat" them.[53]

Because of the difficulty encountered by companies in trying to apply the cost justification and good faith defenses and the likelihood that, in certain instances, the Robinson-Patman Act merely protects competitors from competition, numerous questions have been raised over the years about the act's ultimate value and equity. For example, Scherer and Ross complete their analysis of the act with the following delicately phrased understatement: "What is certain is that, despite efforts by the federal courts to make sense of the Robinson-Patman Act's complexities, legislative reform merits support."[54]

Price Discrimination by Buyers. When a seller discriminates in its pricing between two competing channel members, such an action can be viewed as an attempt to exercise reward power relative to the channel member receiving the lower price. When one of the channel members uses its power to force a discriminatory price from the seller, however, then such an action may be viewed as coercion by the buyer.

Section 2(f) of the Robinson-Patman Act makes it unlawful for a person in commerce knowingly to induce or receive a discrimination in price. To violate this section, buyers must be reasonably aware of the illegality of the prices they have received. This section prevents large, powerful channel members from compelling sellers to give them discriminatory lower prices. It is often enforced by means of Section 5 of the Federal Trade Commission Act on the grounds that this use of coercive power is an unfair method of competition.

It is also illegal for buyers to coerce favors from suppliers in the form of special promotional allowances and services. This stipulation is a potential weapon available to question the frantic activity in the grocery trade involving slotting allowances, trade deals, failure fees, and the variety of practices discussed in Chapter 2.[55] Although some large manufacturers, such as P&G and Kraft-General Foods, refuse to pay slotting allowances, smaller manufacturers are told to ante up or risk being frozen out of retail outlets. For example, to introduce their canned pie filling to half the country, Curtice-Burns had to make payments of $1 million up-front to retailers. Similarly, Shoprite Foods required an $86,000 slotting allowance to stock $172,000 worth of Old Capitol microwave popcorn.[56]

In an insightful analysis, Cannon and Bloom consider the possibility of whether slotting allowances might be declared illegal under the Robinson-Patman Act.[57] They look at a number of different charges that might be leveled against slotting allowances, including those involving buyer-induced price discrimination. With regard to a buyer's actions, they argue that the plaintiff (in this case, a small manufacturer) would have to prove that the buyer not only received illegal concessions, but also had good reason to believe that the allowances granted were illegal.[58] Also, the plaintiff may have difficulty proving that allowances were induced by the buyer as opposed to being offered by the plaintiff. Cannon and Bloom conclude that:

> Although Congress enacted Robinson-Patman to curtail the influence of powerful buyers, the enforcement of the law against *buyers* has proven difficult. The problem facing a plaintiff is the difficulty in providing the high standards of evidence the court requires. The difficulty of establishing this standard of evidence has resulted in relatively few suits brought under this law. Private plaintiffs are unlikely to have a great deal of success pursuing slotting allowance violations at this level.[59]

In addition, large buyers (such as A&P) have been known to set up dummy brokerage firms as part of their businesses in order to obtain a brokerage allowance from sellers, which in effect permits them to receive lower prices than their competitors. This form of coercive power is deemed illegal under Section 2(c) of the Robinson-Patman Act, which makes it unlawful to pay brokerage fees or discounts or to accept them except for services rendered in connection with sales or purchases. It also prohibits brokerage fees or discounts paid to any broker who is not independent of both buyer and seller.

The reality is, however, that, as is the case with slotting allowances, buyer-induced price discrimination is extremely difficult to prove and, therefore, seems to be widely practiced. For example, in 1991, Coca-Cola allegedly lost a major contract to Pepsi-Cola to provide soda-fountain service to Marriott Corp. after Coke refused to lend Marriott $50 million to $100 million at less than existing interest rates. Marriott is a hotel and food-service chain that provides food services for its own 600 hotels and about 2,300 restaurants and kitchens at schools, businesses, hospitals, and other institutions. Apparently, Pepsi was willing to lend Marriott the money. The Marriott business meant about $2 million in annual profit to Coke.[60]

Promotional Allowances and Services. In order to entice channel members to advertise, display, promote, or demonstrate their wares, suppliers use all sorts of monetary inducements. The doling out of these rewards is circumscribed by Sections 2(d) and 2(e) of the Robinson-Patman Act, which prohibit a seller from granting advertising allowances, offering other types of promotional assistance, or providing services, display facilities, or equipment to any buyer unless similar allowances and assistance are made available to all purchasers. Section 2(d) applies to *payments* by a seller to a buyer for the performance of promotional services; Section 2(e) applies to the actual *provision* of such services (e.g., display racks or signs). Because buyers differ in size of physical establishment and volume of sales, allowances obviously cannot be made available to all customers on the same absolute basis. Therefore, the law stipulates that the allowances be made available to buyers on "proportionately equal terms."

The prohibitions of these sections of the Robinson-Patman Act are absolute and are not dependent on injury to competition. Although meeting competition is a defense, cost justification of the discrimination is not. In other words, if, aside from meeting competition, it can be shown that discriminatory allowances exist and that the firms being discriminated against are in competition with each other, the violation is deemed to be illegal per se. However, for firms to be "in competition," they must be in sufficient geographical proximity to compete for the same customer groups. If, for example, retailers are involved, only those retailers in a limited market territory need be included when granting allowances. On the other hand, the market might be construed as national if mail-order companies are involved. In the latter situation, a manufacturer (or wholesaler) would have to grant allowances or services to all mail-order companies if they were to grant them to one. In addition, a time dimension is important in defining the domain of the allowance. For example, if advertising allowances are granted one month, they do not have to be granted to another buyer five months later. Otherwise, the initial allowance would determine all future allowances.[61]

Certain stipulations have been made regarding adherence to Sections 2(d) and 2(e).[62] Among them are the following:

1. Allowances may be made only for services actually rendered, and they must not substantially exceed the cost of these services to the buyer or their value to the seller.

2. The seller must design a promotional program in such a way that all competing buyers can realistically implement it.

3. The seller should take action designed to inform all competing customers of the existence and essential features of the promotional program in ample time for them to take full advantage of it.

4. If a program is not functionally available to (i.e., suitable for and usable by) some of the seller's competing customers, the seller must make certain that suitable alternatives are offered to such customers.

5. The seller should provide its customers with sufficient information to permit a clear understanding of the exact terms of the offer, including all alternatives, and the conditions on which payment will be made or services furnished.

The FTC has stipulated that when promotional allowances or merchandising services are provided, they should be furnished in accordance with a written plan that meets the listed requirements.[63] And, in the case of sellers who market their products directly to retailers as well as sell through wholesalers, it has been mandated that any promotional allowance offered to the retailers must also be offered, on a proportionately equal basis, to the wholesalers. The wholesalers would then be expected to pass along the allowance to their retail customers, who are in competition with the direct-buying retailers.[64]

In a 1990 revision of the *Guides for Advertising Allowances and other Merchandising Payments and Services,* the FTC recognized two ways of measuring proportional equality.

One way is based on the customer's cost—for example, placing newspaper advertisements in connection with the resale of products for which advertising allowances are provided. The other way is based on the seller's cost. For example, offering an equal amount of allowances or services per unit of sales, a traditional means of providing such allowances, satisfies the proportional equality requirement. For example, if a seller offers a promotional allowance of $1 per case to all competing customers, such an offer would be permissible under the revised Guides.[65]

In addition, the FTC reiterated its previous position that a company which grants a discriminatory promotional allowance may argue that the allowance was given in "good faith" to meet the promotional program of a competitor.

Functional Discounts. In Chapter 7, when channel compensation principles were initially discussed, something called the equity principle was introduced. That principle involves the use of reward power in granting discounts to individual channel members based on the functions (or marketing flows) they perform as they divide distribution labor. In theory, functional discounts should be allotted to each channel member on the basis of the degree of its participation in the marketing flows (e.g., physical possession, ownership, promotion, etc.) associated with making a product or service available to end-users. Indeed, the gross margins earned by channel members should reflect the value they add to the process of achieving availability. And, as pointed out in Chapter 7, functional discounts (or reward structures comparable to them) can be critical factors in assuring that the work of marketing channels is accomplished. For an example of a functional discount program, the reader should refer to Appendix A in Chapter 7.

In reality, the legality of functional discounts (which are a form of price discrimination) is something that has been shrouded in controversy and confusion for decades. One of the major reasons for the confusion is the fact that, historically, the discounts were primarily based on the level of distribution (e.g., wholesale vs. retail) in which a recipient resided and not strictly on the functions the company performed. For this reason, they are frequently called "trade" as opposed to "functional" discounts. Way back when, marketing channels were more straightforward than they are currently, and, therefore, trade discounts made some sense. When independent wholesalers sold to numerous, relatively small retail outlets, each level in the channel was distinct and could be rewarded differently (e.g., the wholesaler got a larger price discount from the manufacturer than the retailer). In addition, each level in the channel dealt with a specific class of customer (e.g., the wholesaler sold only to retailers, and retailers only to consumers). Wholesalers and retailers normally performed different functions in different markets and, thus, did not compete against each other.

Now, however, the commercial world is much more complex. Distinctions in distribution systems have blurred as wholesalers have formed voluntary chains and as retailers have vertically integrated backwards, assuming numerous wholesaling functions. Kmart, a major discount store chain, performs many of its own wholesaling operations. It receives in large lots from manufacturers, breaks bulk, assorts merchandise, and reships merchandise from its warehouses to its retail stores. However, it is generally classified as a "retailer" and, therefore, is supposedly entitled only to the functional (trade) discounts given to retailers. (It can, of course, avail itself of whatever quantity discounts are offered by its suppliers.)

The dilemma is as follows. If Kmart cannot receive a wholesaler's functional discount when it does, in fact, perform wholesaling functions, then it is being discriminated against. But if Kmart were to be given both a wholesaler's and a retailer's trade discount, then independent wholesalers who resell to independent retailers would argue that their customers (small retailers) are not able to compete with Kmart on an equal footing. And, to add to the mess, if Kmart did not receive the wholesale discount and a wholesaler decided to open up a warehouse club (like Price Club or Sam's) to sell to small business and to consumers (using the wholesale discount to cut prices below those at Kmart), what do you think Kmart would do? Scream bloody murder!!![66]

The problem underlying this whole controversy is one of classification. Because of it, the Food Marketing Institute (whose members are primarily supermarket chains), the Grocery Manufacturers of America, the National Association of Chain Drug Stores, and a number of other wholesale and retail trade associations issued the following statement in 1989:

> In the pricing and promotion of products, manufacturers should not make distinctions among competing distributor customers within the same market area based on "class of trade" or types of format. If a manufacturer develops prices, terms, promotions, deals, or packs designed to meet the marketing needs or desires of a particular class of trade or distributor format, the manufacturer should inform all competing distributor customers within the same market area, regardless of class of trade, of their availability and should grant these distributors an equal opportunity to qualify for these offerings.

Clearly, the concerns surrounding functional discounts only occur when suppliers are engaged in dual distribution, that is, they have multiple routes to the market and discriminate in price, via functional discounts, among the various routes. As Spriggs and Nevin observe, operating as a dual distributor offers several potential competitive advantages to the firm.

> It can enable a seller to reach previously untapped markets or adapt its product offerings to new market segments or buyer groups. . . . Dual distribution also can reduce overall transaction costs. If a wholesaler is too dependent on its retailers, dual distribution can help offset this dependence. Manufacturers also can encourage their existing wholesalers to become dual distributors to reach new markets because the total transaction costs are lower for the manufacturer than if it would have to manage exchange relationships with the additional wholesalers or retailers to reach the new customers and markets.[67]

Functional discounts are not specifically referred to in the Robinson-Patman Act, but, via a number of court decisions, it has been established that the stipulations of the act (including the defenses mentioned above) apply to them. (It should come as no surprise, then, that understanding what's going on requires a joint doctorate in legal studies and headache remedies.) Sparing the reader a recanting of all the debate in the court decisions dealing with these discounts, we will attempt to make the situation as clear as possible as quickly as possible. Our work has been made somewhat more easy due to a 1990 Supreme Court decision—*Texaco Inc. v. Ricky Hasbrouck, dba Rick's Texaco, et. al.*[68]

In *Hasbrouck,* Texaco had sold gasoline directly to a number of independent retailers in Spokane, Washington at its "retail tank wagon" prices, while it granted more substantial discounts to two distributors. Those two distributors sold the gasoline to service stations that the distributors owned and operated, passing on nearly all of the discount from Texaco. The distributor-controlled retailers thereby were able to sell well below the price charged by the independent retailers with which they competed. Between 1972 and 1981, the stations supplied by the two wholesaler-distributors increased sales dramatically, whereas sales at the competing independents declined.

Texaco argued that its discriminatory pricing was justified by cost savings, by a good faith attempt to meet competition, and as lawful functional discounts. The Ninth Circuit Court of Appeals and the Supreme Court did not accept Texaco's arguments in defense of its actions, even though they validated the use of the cost-based and good faith defenses in lawsuits challenging functional discounts.

The Supreme Court's affirmation of the cost justification defense is very significant for channel management, because this means that functional discounts are no longer merely tied to classification schemes. The Court stated that:

> In general, a supplier's functional discount is said to be a discount given to a purchaser based on the purchaser's role in the supplier's distributive system, reflecting, at least in a generalized sense, the services performed by the purchaser for the supplier.[69]
>
> . . . a legitimate functional discount constituting a reasonable reimbursement for a purchaser's actual marketing functions does not violate Section 2(a). . . .[70]

This case leaves the door open to manufacturers to use functional discounts to compensate channel members for their participation in specific marketing flows. Furthermore, it also suggests that functional discounts bearing a *reasonable* relationship to the supplier's savings or the channel member's costs are legal, refuting the need for *precise measurement.* There is still a problem about which cost-base to use, the supplier's or the reseller's. In the latter case, setting discounts based on the reseller's costs may grant different discounts to competing resellers and possibly larger discounts to less efficient buyers, a strange outcome indeed. In the former case, the discounts based on the seller's savings would not necessarily be adequate or fair compensation to the reseller for performing the function.[71] The sentiment seems to be in favor of using seller's savings, although both approaches have imperfections.

▶ **PRODUCT LINE POLICIES**

For a wide variety of logical reasons, channel managers may wish to restrict the breadth or depth of the product lines that their channel partners sell. Here, we look at the rationale for three policies—exclusive dealing, tying, and full-line forcing— as well as the antitrust concerns surrounding them.

Exclusive Dealing

Exclusive dealing is the requirement by a seller or lessor that its channel intermediaries sell or lease only its products or brands, or at least no products or brands in direct competition with the seller's products. If intermediaries do not comply, the seller may invoke negative sanctions by refusing to deal with them. Such arrangements clearly reduce the freedom of choice of the intermediaries (resellers). Some of the managerial benefits of exclusive dealing are listed below.

- Resellers become more dependent on the supplier, enabling the supplier to secure exclusive benefit of the reseller's energies. If the supplier has devoted considerable effort to develop a brand image, it may fear that the resellers will use the brand as a loss leader and that suppliers of other, directly competing brands stocked by the reseller will "free ride" off of the demand stimulated by the supplier's heavily promoted, well-known brand. The supplier may be concerned about free riding with regard to other services as well, such as the use of specialized display cases, the provision of technical training or financing, and assistance in the operations of the business.

- Competitors are foreclosed from selling through valuable resellers.

- With a long-term exclusive relationship, sales forecasting may be easier, permitting the supplier to achieve more precise and efficient production and logistics.

- Resellers may obtain more stable prices and may gain more regular and frequent deliveries of the supplier's products.

- Transactions between resellers and the supplier may be fewer in number and larger in volume.

- Resellers and the supplier may be able to reduce administrative costs.

- Both resellers and the supplier may be able to secure specialized assets and long-term financing from each other.

- Resellers generally receive added promotional and other support as well as avoid the added inventory costs that go with carrying multiple brands.[72]

Early in 1995, Goodyear decided to offer its independent dealers exclusive tire models that aren't to be sold through other retail outlets, such as Sears, Wal-Mart, and Discount Tire Co. of Arizona. Many of the new tire lines are comparable, if not identical, to Goodyear's existing lines. They are being sold, however, under different names to help the dealers compete with mass merchandisers who, due to quantity purchasing, have been able to undercut the dealers' prices.[73]

Requirements contracts are variants of exclusive dealing. Under requirements contracts, buyers agree to purchase all or a part of their requirements of a product from one seller, usually for a specified period and price. Such arrangements clearly reduce the freedom of choice of the buyer, but guarantee the buyer a source of supply at a known cost oftentimes over a very long period of time (e.g., 10 years).

ANTITRUST CONCERNS   Exclusive dealing lessens *interbrand* competition directly, because competing brands available from other suppliers are excluded from outlets. Exclusive dealing and requirements contracts are circumscribed mainly by Section 3 of the Clayton Act, which stipulates that

> it shall be unlawful for any person . . . to lease or make a sale or contract for sale of goods, wares, merchandise, machinery, supplies or other commodities, whether patented or unpatented, . . . on the condition, agreement, or understanding that the lessee or purchaser thereof shall not use or deal in the goods, . . . of a competitor or competitors of the lessor or seller, where the effect of such lease, sale, or contract for sale or such condition, agreement or understanding may be to substantially lessen competition or tend to create a monopoly in any line of commerce.

However, these policies may also violate Section 1 of the Sherman Act and Section 5 of the Federal Trade Commission (FTC) Act. Under the Sherman Act, various types of exclusive contracts may be deemed unlawful restraints of trade when a dominant firm is involved and when the contracts go so far beyond reasonable business needs as to have the necessary effect, or disclose a clear intention, of suppressing competition.[74] Under the FTC Act, the Federal Trade Commission has the power to stop such trade restraints at the outset without proof that they amount to an outright violation of Section 3 of the Clayton Act or other provisions of the antitrust laws. In other words, the FTC, using Section 5, has broad powers to declare "unfair" those practices that conflict with the basic policies of the Sherman Act and the Clayton Act, even though such practices may not constitute a violation of those laws.

A case decided in 1961 established the modern guidelines for assessing exclusive dealing policies from an antitrust perspective. The case, *Tampa Electric Co. v. Nashville Coal Co. et. al.,*[75] involved a contract between Nashville Coal and Tampa Electric, a Florida public utility producing electricity, covering Tampa's expected requirements of coal (i.e., not less than 500,000 tons per year) for a period of 20 years. Before any coal was delivered, Nashville declined to perform the contract on the ground that it was illegal under the antitrust laws because it amounted to an exclusive dealing arrangement, which foreclosed other suppliers from serving Tampa Electric. (In actuality, the price of coal had jumped, making the arrangement less profitable for the coal company.) Tampa brought suit, arguing that the contract was both valid and enforceable.

To be illegal, the court explained, such arrangements must have a tendency to work a substantial, not merely remote, lessening of competition in the relevant competitive market. Justice Clark, speaking for the majority, indicated that "substantiality" was to be determined by taking into account the following factors:

- the relative strength of the parties involved;

- the proportionate volume of commerce involved in relation to the total volume of commerce in the relevant market area;

- the probable immediate and future effects that preemption of that share of the market might have on effective competition within it.

The district court and the court of appeals had accepted the argument that the contract foreclosed a substantial share of the market, because Tampa's requirements equaled the total volume of coal purchased in the state of Florida before the contract's inception. The Supreme Court, in an interesting piece of economic reasoning, defined the relevant market as the *supply* market in an eight-state area, noting that mines in that coal-producing region were eager to sell more coal in Florida. When the market was defined as the entire multistate Appalachian coal region, the foreclosure amounted to less than 1% of the tonnage produced each year. The Court concluded that given the nature of the market (i.e., the needs of a utility for a stable supply at reasonable prices over a long period as well as the level of concentration), the small percentage of foreclosure did not actually or potentially cause a substantial reduction of competition, nor did it tend toward a monopoly.

The decision in this case indicates that the type of goods or merchandise, the geographic area of effective competition, and the substantiality of the competition foreclosed must all be assessed in determining illegality or legality. It also indicates that exclusive dealing arrangements or requirements contracts that are negotiated by sellers possessing a very small share of the relevant market have a good chance of standing up in court.[76] The critical issue may involve the definition of the relevant market; firms with large shares may still be circumscribed. And, when shares are sufficiently high (e.g., 30 to 40%), the so-called "modified" rule of reason standard established in *Tampa Electric* requires courts to examine the following factors:

- the duration of the contracts;

- the likelihood of collusion in the industry and the degree to which other firms in the market also employ exclusive dealing;

- the height of entry barriers;

- the nature of the distribution system and distribution alternatives remaining available after exclusive dealing is taken into account; and

- other obvious anti- or pro-competitive effects, such as the prevention of free-riding and the encouragement of the reseller to promote the supplier's product more heavily.[77]

Even though the *Tampa Electric* case was decided almost 40 years ago, legal battles surrounding exclusive dealing are very much alive. For example, in 1987, Ben & Jerry's Homemade Inc. filed a complaint in U.S. District Court in Boston accusing Häagen-Dazs (owned by Pillsbury) of violating a 1985 out-of-court settlement in which Häagen-Dazs agreed that it wouldn't coerce distributors into exclusive dealing arrangements. After the 1985 settlement, Häagen-Dazs established a supposedly noncoercive policy stipulating that it would sell ice cream only through distributors who did not sell competing products. According to Häagen-Dazs' vice president of sales, the company was merely trying to set policies similar to those that govern distribution relationships in many other food and drink categories. "Pepsi doesn't allow its bottlers to carry Coke. You really want to have someone who's going to give their best efforts to your product."[78] Ben & Jerry's suit hinged on whether Häagen-Dazs' influence on distributors could be considered "coercion" rather than uniform application of an announced policy.

Before readers shed too many tears for little ole Ben & Jerry, they should be informed that, in 1993, the company was accused of blocking its largest distributors from carrying Mattus', a low fat ice cream produced by a firm that originally built—and later sold—the Häagen-Dazs brand. Ben & Jerry said that its distributors voluntarily agreed not to carry other "superpremium" brands in exchange for exclusive territories.[79] Clearly, the capitalist spirit is alive and well, even in Vermont!

Exclusive dealing is a key element of some manufacturers' distribution strategies. For example, in April 1991, a Sun Microsystems Inc. directive prohibited Sun's authorized value-added resellers (VARS) in the U.S. from selling clones (machines that mimic Sun's), except lap-top machines which Sun doesn't make.[80] And when, in 1991, Groupe Schneider, a large French electrical equipment manufacturer, purchased Square D Co., considerable concern was raised by smaller competitors that Schneider would ask its independent U.S. distributors to exclusively deal with it, a policy it had already attempted to institute in Europe. The acquisition of Square D made Schneider the world's largest manufacturer of low voltage electrical-distribution equipment, such as circuit-breakers.[81]

Exclusive dealing has even reached college campuses. In 1992 Pennsylvania State University signed a $14 million, 10-year contract with Pepsi-Cola that made Pepsi the official beverage of the university. Pepsi was given exclusive rights to stock its products in all soda vending machines, supply all soda fountains, advertise exclusively on the giant scoreboard at the 94,000-seat Beaver Stadium, fill the soda cups at the stadium, and plaster its slogans all over the 21 campuses of the university.[82]

Channel intermediaries who are terminated because they violate the exclusive dealing policies of their suppliers by selling directly competitive products or brands are likely to have a difficult time claiming anticompetitive effects due to the termination. The reason is simple—by violating the suppliers' policies by taking on additional brands, the intermediaries actually increased interbrand competition, even though they were terminated for doing so in the process.[83]

Tying

Tying exists when a seller, having a product or service that buyers want (the *tying product*), refuses to sell it unless a second (*tied*) product or service is also purchased, or at least is not purchased from anyone other than the seller of the tying product. Thus, a manufacturer of motion picture projectors (the tying product) might insist that only its film (the tied product) be used with the projectors, or a manufacturer of shoe machinery (the tying product) might insist that lessees of the machinery purchase service contracts (tied service) from it for the proper maintenance of the machinery.

Many of the business reasons for using tying policies are similar to those for using exclusive dealing. That is because both policies are similar—their immediate aim is to lock in the purchase of a specific brand made by a supplier and lock out the purchase of directly competing brands. Additional reasons for tying, beyond those that apply from the discussion of exclusive dealing, are:

1. Transferring the market demand already established for the tying product (e.g., can closing machines) to the tied product (e.g., cans).

2. Using the tied product (paper) to meter usage of the tying product (copying machines).

3. Using a low-margin tying product (razors) to sell a high-margin tied product (blades).

4. Achieving cost savings via package sales, for example, the costs of supplying and servicing channel members might be lower the greater the number of products there are included in the "package."

5. Assuring the successful operation of the tying product (an automobile) by obliging dealers to purchase tied products (repair parts) from the supplier.[84]

ANTITRUST CONCERNS   A tying agreement in effect forecloses competing sellers from the opportunity of selling the tied commodity or service to the purchaser. Indeed, like exclusive dealing policies, the critical issue in the condemnation of tying is the foreclosing of interbrand competition from a marketplace. But tying contracts are viewed much more negatively by the courts than exclusive dealing arrangements or requirements contracts. For example, in distinguishing between a requirements contract and a tying contract in the *Standard Stations* case, Justice Frankfurter stated that tying arrangements "serve hardly any purpose beyond the suppression of competition.[85] Like exclusive dealing, tying is circumscribed by the Sherman Act, the Clayton Act, and the FTC Act. Given the overwhelmingly negative attitude of the courts toward tying, it is little wonder that its use would rarely be approved.

Certain types of tying contracts are, however, legal. The courts have ruled that if two products are made to be used jointly and one will not function properly without the other, a tying agreement is within the law. (Shoes are sold in pairs, and automobiles are sold with tires.) In other cases, if a company's goodwill depends on proper operation of equipment, a service contract may be tied to the sale or lease of the machine.[86] The practicality of alternatives to the tying arrangement appears to be crucial. If a firm will suffer injury unless it can protect its product, and there is no feasible alternative, the courts go along with tying agreements. Despite these exceptions, the general rule is that tying agreements are inherently anticompetitive and thus illegal per se.

Serious legal questions regarding tying agreements have been raised relative to the franchising of restaurants and other eating places, motels, and movie theaters, among others. As detailed in Chapter 6, an individual or group of individuals (franchisees) are usually permitted to set up outlets of a national chain in return for a capital investment and a periodic fee to the parent company (the franchisor). In some cases, the parent company also requires the franchise holders to buy various supplies, such as meat, baked goods, and paper cups in the case of restaurants, either from the corporation or an approved supplier. In franchising, the tying product is the franchise itself and the tied products are the supplies that the franchisee must purchase to operate his business. Companies with such requirements have argued that they are necessary in order to maintain the quality of their services and reputation. However, critics of such agreements assert that franchisors often require franchisees to purchase supplies and raw materials at prices far above those of the competitive market. The potential for a conflict of interest on the part of the franchisors is high.

In franchising, the primary tying "product" is the trademark itself (e.g., "McDonald's," "Budget" Rent-A-Car, "Sheraton" Hotels). Therefore, tying agreements that link the trademark to supplies have been sustained by the courts only when franchisors have been able to prove that their trademarks are inseparable from their supplies and that the tied product (the supplies) are, in fact, essential to the maintenance of quality control. For example, in a lawsuit involving Baskin-Robbins, a chain of franchised ice cream stores, certain franchisees contended the Baskin-Robbins ice cream products were unlawfully tied to the sale of the Baskin-Robbins trademark.[87] However, the tie-in claim was disallowed because the franchisees did not establish that the trademark was a product separate from the ice cream; in tying cases, two distinct products must be involved in order for tying to be present.

The decision in the *Baskin-Robbins* case is similar to that in a lawsuit against Carvel (a soft ice cream franchise), where the court concluded that Carvel's ingredient supply restrictions were justified by the need for quality control connected with the problem of ingredient secrecy.[88] In addition, in a lawsuit involving Dunkin' Donuts, the court stated that such tying agreements may be justified not only when the franchisor is attempting to maintain product quality, but also when it is attempting to enter a new market or industry *or* to preserve its market identity.[89]

In a decision involving the Chock Full O'Nuts Corporation, it was held that the franchisor "successfully proved its affirmative defense (to tying charges) of maintaining quality control with regard to its coffee and baked goods."[90] On the other hand, Chock Full O'Nuts was unsuccessful in defending its tying practices with respect to a number of other products (e.g., french fries, soft drink syrups, napkins, and glasses). The latter finding paralleled that in an antitrust case involving Chicken Delight.[91] The parent company's contract requiring Chicken Delight franchisees to purchase paper items, cookers, fryers, and mix preparations from the franchisor was declared to be a tying contract in violation of Section 1 of the Sherman Act. Chicken Delight failed to convince the court that its system should be considered a single product. The paper products were viewed as illegally tied to the franchise because they were easily reproducible. The issue of cookers, fryers, and spice items was less clear-cut, and the court left it to a jury to decide whether they were justifiably tied on the basis of quality control of the finished product. The jury eventually determined that quality control could have been effected by means other than a tie-in and thus rejected the franchisor's claims.

One special form of tying policy is called *full-line forcing*. Here a seller's leverage with a tying product is used to force a buyer to purchase its whole line of goods. This policy is illegal if the buyer is prevented from handling competitors' products. In the case of a farm machinery manufacturer, a court held that the practice was within the law, but implied that full-line forcing that caused the exclusion of competitors from this part of the market might be illegal if a substantial share of business was affected.[92] Block booking imposed by motion picture distributors and producers on independent theater owners can also be viewed as full-line forcing or tying. This practice compels theaters to take many pictures they do not want in order to obtain the ones they do. Independent producers have consequently been unable to rent their films to theaters whose programs were thus crowded with the products of the major firms. Similar arrangements have been found in the sale of motion picture "packages" to television. Such practices have typically been held to be illegal, especially when copyrighted films have been used as tying mechanisms.[93]

Other instances of prohibition of full-line forcing have occurred. For example, E&J Gallo Winery, the largest seller of wine in the United States, consented to a Federal Trade Commission order prohibiting it from, among other things, requiring its wholesalers to distribute any Gallo wines in order to obtain other kinds.[94] And Union Carbide Corporation agreed to a consent order prohibiting the company from requiring its dealers to purchase from it their total requirements of six industrial gases (acetylene, argon, helium, hydrogen, nitrogen, and oxygen) and from making the purchase of the six gases a prerequisite for dealers buying other gases or welding products.[95]

Even though tying has been labeled as "per se illegal," courts have sought answers to a number of critical questions before condemning these policies. For example, it is necessary to determine when conditions of economic power exist. In theory, where no leverage exists in a product, there can be no tying arrangement by coercion; the buyer can always go elsewhere to purchase. Thus, plaintiffs must prove more than the existence of a tie. As Sullivan points out, they must also show that the tying product is successfully differentiated and that the commerce affected by the tie is not *de minimus*.[96] The presumption against tying arrangements is, therefore, not quite as strong as the per se rule against horizontal price-fixing conspiracies.

Evidence of this comes from a 1984 Supreme court case involving hospital services.[97] In *Jefferson Parish,* anesthesiologist Edwin G. Hyde, who had been denied admission to the staff of East Jefferson Hospital, sued the governance board of the hospital because the hospital had an exclusive contract with a firm of anesthesiologists requiring that all anesthesiological services for the hospital's patients be performed by that firm. The Supreme Court agreed with the district court that the relevant geographic market was Jefferson Parish (i.e., metropolitan New Orleans) and not the neighborhood immediately surrounding East Jefferson Hospital. The Court reasoned that "Seventy percent of the patients residing in Jefferson Parish enter hospitals other than East Jefferson . . . Thus, East Jefferson's 'dominance' over persons residing in Jefferson Parish is far from overwhelming." The Court further explained that "the fact that the exclusive contract requires purchase of two services that would otherwise be purchased separately does not make the contract illegal. Only if patients are forced to purchase the contracting firm's services as a result of the hospital's market power would the arrangement have anticompetitive consequences." East Jefferson's market power was not significant enough to make the contract illegal.

The most important dictum in the *Jefferson Parish* decision was the following sentence, which provides the foundation on which other tying cases are to be analyzed:

The essential characteristic of an invalid tying arrangement lies in the seller's exploitation of its control over the tying product to force the buyer into the purchase of a tied product that the buyer either did not want at all, or might have preferred to purchase elsewhere on different terms.[98]

The issues on which courts are most likely to focus are whether (1) there are two distinct products; (2) the seller has required the buyer to purchase the tied product in order to obtain the tying product; (3) the seller has sufficient market power to force a tie-in; (4) the tying arrangement affects a substantial amount of commerce in the market for the tied product; and (5) whether the tie is necessary to fulfill a legitimate business purpose. However, as Scherer and Ross observe, these "structural" per se criteria are not likely to be satisfied for sellers with relatively small market shares, especially when the tying product is unpatented.[99]

The criteria are more likely to be satisfied in situations typified by the FTC's 1991 investigation of Sandoz Pharmaceuticals Corp. which was accused of violating antitrust laws by requiring buyers of Clozaril, a drug for schizophrenia, to also purchase a weekly blood test from a company under contract with Sandoz.[100] Sandoz's dominant position relative to the specific drug category under investigation was, at the time, obvious. The company agreed to settle the charges by promising not to require Clorazil purchasers to buy the blood monitoring service from Sandoz or anyone designated by Sandoz.[101] In Europe, reactions similar to those in the Sandoz situation are evident. For example, in 1994, Tetra Pak, the Swedish packaging group, lost its appeal to the Court of First Instance. The Court found, among other things, that customer contracts that tied Tetra Pak machine users to using Tetra Pak cartons were not objectively justified and were intended to strengthen the company's dominant position in such packaging by reinforcing its customers' economic dependence on it.[102]

One of the most remarkable and significant cases involving tying was decided by the U.S. Supreme Court on June 8, 1992. At that time, the Court ruled that Eastman Kodak Company would have to stand trial on a tying claim brought against it by 18 independent service organizations.[103] The case arose out of Kodak's efforts to keep to itself the business of servicing Kodak-brand copiers. Kodak had refused to sell replacement parts to independent service organizations (ISOs) that wanted to service Kodak copiers. The ISOs alleged that Kodak's conduct amounted to an illegal monopolization of the business of servicing Kodak-brand copiers and an illegal tying of the sale of servicing copiers to the sale of replacement parts.

To succeed on the tying claim, the ISOs had to prove that Kodak had "appreciable market power" in the business of selling replacement parts for Kodak-brand copiers. To succeed on the monopolization claim, the ISOs had to prove that Kodak had "monopoly power" in the sale of the replacement parts. Kodak argued that sales of its copiers represented, at most, 23% of the sale of copiers for all manufacturers, and the Supreme Court agreed that the 23% share did not amount to appreciable power in the copier sales business. But (and here's the rub) the Court found that Kodak controlled nearly 100% of the market for its replacement parts—which are not interchangeable with the parts of other manufacturer's machines—and between 80 and 95% of the service market. The Court reasoned that the relevant market for antitrust purposes is determined by the choices available to Kodak equipment owners who must use Kodak parts. Thus, Kodak's motion for summary judgment (i.e., it wanted the Supreme Court to dismiss the case because of its lack of market power in the copier market) was rejected by a 6 to 3 vote, and the case was sent back to the Federal District Court in San Francisco for trial.

▶ SELECTION AND TERMINATION POLICIES

A central theme throughout this text is that organizations must devote a great deal of time, attention, effort, and monetary resources to the design and management of their distribution systems. In order to achieve success with their marketing channels, channel managers must set up selection criteria with regard to potential channel partners and must monitor the performance of anyone admitted to the distribution system. Even with intensive distribution systems, selection procedures are necessary, because it is unlikely that every conceivable outlet will be given the opportunity to sell every intensively distributed product. (Most gas stations aren't asked to sell paper clips, for example.) Anytime anyone establishes selection criteria, there is an extremely high likelihood that there will be someone who doesn't make the cut-off, no matter how low the standards for admission are set. Therefore, refusing to deal with certain channel members is a key element of channel policy. The same rationale applies to performance criteria, which means that another key element of channel policy is termination.

Antitrust Concerns

Sellers can select their own distributors according to their own criteria and judgment. They may also announce in advance the circumstances under which they would refuse to sell to certain intermediaries. These two commercial "freedoms" were granted in *U.S. v. Colgate & Co.* in 1919 and are referred to as the *Colgate doctrine.*[104] The doctrine was formally recognized by Congress in Section 2(a) of the Robinson-Patman Act, which reads that "nothing herein contained shall prevent persons engaged in selling goods, wares, or merchandise in commerce from selecting their own customers in *bona fide* transactions and not in restraint of trade." Implicit in a seller's general right to select its preferred distribution system is the right to deal with certain channel members on a limited basis. General Motors, for example, is not obligated to sell Chevrolets to a Buick dealer.

The *Colgate* doctrine contains two explicit exceptions. First, the decision not to deal must be "independent" or unilateral (i.e., it can't be part of a conspiracy). Second, the refusal must occur in the absence of any purpose to create or maintain a monopoly. If a unilateral refusal to deal is ever illegal, it is when the refusal is undertaken by a monopolist, or by someone who hopes by the refusal to become one.[105]

Clearly, refusal to deal is a major "punishment" underlying a channel member's coercive power. After a number of court decisions dealing with the right of refusal to deal, the "right" has been narrowly confined. Suppliers may formally cut off dealers for valid business reasons, such as failure to pay or poor performance in sales or service. But where the suppliers have set up restrictive, regulated, or pro-grammed distribution systems and there are complaints that the dealers who are being cut off have somehow stepped out of line with the edicts of the programmed system, it becomes increasingly difficult to use the right to refuse to deal as a de-fense in treble-damage actions brought against the suppliers by the dealers. As Scammon and Sheffet point out, the courts generally ask two important questions in determining whether a refusal to deal violates the law:

1. Was the decision to delete certain channel members a unilateral decision on the part of the manufacturer?
2. Was there a legitimate business reason for change in channel membership?[106]

There continue to be lots of cases brought under Sections 1 and 2 of the Sher-man Act involving decisions by suppliers or franchisors to terminate an existing dealer, to substitute a "new" for an "old" dealer, or to vertically integrate. Al-though it appears the original selection of distributors or dealers for a new prod-uct poses no legal problems, it is increasingly clear that the termination of existing distributors and dealers can cause difficulties, even in the absence of group boy-cotts or conspiracies. As Neale and Goyder observe,

> once a manufacturer has selected a dealer he will be unable subsequently, without risking a treble-damage action, to drop him merely because he refuses to comply with the manufacturer's policy in any particular respect, unless that policy is one which in all circumstances does not constitute a violation of the antitrust laws.[107]

Thus, when exclusive dealing, customer or territorial restrictions, or other types of vertical restraints have been applied by a suppler within its distribution network and when a dealer is cut off from that network, the dealer may take the supplier to court, charging that the refusal to deal was based on the supplier's desire to main-tain an unlawful practice.

The orientation toward litigation in these cases has been furthered by partic-ularistic legislation, such as the Automobile Dealers Franchise Act of 1956, which entitles a car dealer to sue any car manufacturer who fails to act in good faith in connection with the termination, cancellation, or nonrenewal of the dealer's fran-chise. It is open to the manufacturer, however, to produce evidence that the dealer has not acted in good faith and that its own action was thereby justified. In nearly all the cases to date, this defense has been successful.[108] Nevertheless, an enormous amount of law suits are filed every year by franchisees who claim to be wrongly terminated by franchisors. Most of these cases are fought over contract and prop-erty rights; few of them involve antitrust.

▶ OWNERSHIP POLICIES

The make versus buy (vertical integration) question is another central concern in this text. The rationale for and against vertical integration by ownership (as contrasted by sociological or "soft" integration through interorganization management) has been explicitly discussed in Chapters 5 and 6. Here, then, we deal only with the antitrust concerns surrounding vertical integration. Frequently, the decision to vertically integrate puts a company in competition with independent channel intermediaries who are already carrying or being asked to carry the company's brands. We have already argued that most suppliers, for example, will have a number of different channels so that the needs of various market segments can be addressed. One of those channels is, in most cases, a direct channel comprised of salespeople employed by the company. As was pointed out in the discussion of functional discounts, when a firm uses multiple channels, it is said to be engaged in so-called "dual distribution." Clearly, dual distribution is the rule rather than the exception.

Antitrust Concerns

Vertical integration may come about through forward integration by a producer, backward integration by a retailer, or integration in either direction by a wholesaler or a logistics firm, such as a common carrier. Integration may be brought about by the creation of a new business function by existing firms (internal expansion) or by acquisition of the stock or the assets of other firms (mergers).

The two methods of creating integration are fundamentally different in their relationship to the law. Internal expansion is regulated by Section 2 of the Sherman Act, which prohibits monopoly or attempts to monopolize any part of the interstate or foreign commerce of the United States. External expansion is regulated by Section 7 of the Clayton Act and its amendment, the Celler-Kefauver Act, which prohibits the purchase of stock or assets of other firms if the effects may be to substantially lessen competition or tend to create a monopoly in any line of commerce in any part of the country.[109] Internal expansion is given favored treatment under the law. The theory seems to be that internal expansion expands investment and production and, thus, increases competition, whereas growth by merger removes an entity from the market.

Integration, whether by merger or internal expansion, may result in the lowering of costs and make possible more effective interorganizational management of the channel. It may also be a means of avoiding many of the legal problems previously discussed, because an integrated firm is free to control prices and allocate products to its integrated outlets without conflict with the laws governing restrictive distribution policies.

VERTICAL INTEGRATION BY MERGER   The danger, from an antitrust perspective, posed by vertical mergers is the same as that posed by many of the policies already discussed in this chapter—the possibility that vertical integration will foreclose competitors by limiting their access to sources of supply or to customers. Thus, prior to the purchase of McCaw Cellular by AT&T in 1994, the U.S. Justice Department focused attention on the fact that AT&T makes equipment, such as radio towers, that some of McCaw's competitors, including several regional Bell operating companies, use in their cellular-phone operations. Officials were concerned that the merger would give AT&T an incentive to charge McCaw's competitors more while providing poor service.[110] And, when, in 1993, Merck, the world's largest drug company, bought Medco Containment Services, the largest distributor of discount prescription medicines in the U.S., for $6.6 billion, competitors raised antitrust concerns about foreclosure from Medco. Indeed, when, in 1994, Eli Lilly, another major pharmaceutical manufacturer, indicated that it wanted to purchase PCS Health Systems, another enormous managed care drug distributor, for $4 billion, it agreed to restrictions imposed by the Federal Trade Commission preventing Lilly from unfairly pushing sales of its own brands through PCS or gaining information about prices at which competing drugs sell.[111] In a statement announcing its decision to reexamine the Merck/Medco merger and another one involving SmithKline Beecham (SKB) and Diversified Pharmaceutical Services (DPS), the FTC said "We remain concerned about the overall competitive impact of vertical integration by drug companies into the pharmacy benefits management market."[112] Although all of these mergers (including AT&T–McCaw) were eventually approved, the questions that were raised indicate that, from time to time, vertical mergers will draw the attention of the antitrust enforcement agencies.

The most significant vertical merger case over the last 45 years was decided in 1962 when the merger of the Brown Shoe Company and the G. R. Kinney Company, the largest independent chain of shoe stores, was declared illegal by the Supreme Court because it was believed that the merger would foreclose other manufacturers from selling through Kinney.[113] However, the truth of the matter is that, since the 1970s, the government has, by and large, refrained from challenging vertical mergers. The interest shown by the Federal Trade Commission in the Lilly–PCS, Merck–Medco, and SKB–DPS mergers is surprising, given that little concern has been voiced about other major vertical acquisitions for such a long period of time. In fact, some observers believe that the only way the Lilly–PCS or Merck–Medco mergers could threaten competition is if the combined companies so dominate the market that they are able to keep other companies from getting their drugs to consumers. But, they point out, the drug industry is fragmented enough to prevent that. No drug company, including Merck, has more than 10% of the U.S. prescription pharmaceutical business, and Medco distributes to 10 to 20% of prescription drug users.[114] Even so, in a consent injunction, Merck agreed to restrictions similar to those imposed on Eli Lilly.[115]

In its 1982 *Merger Guidelines*, the Justice Department announced that it would challenge vertical mergers only when they facilitated collusion or significantly raised barriers to new entry.[116] As a practical matter, the government will rarely intervene in vertical mergers. And, as Hovenkamp observes, "Prevailing judicial opinion now seems to be that vertical mergers should be condemned only in the most extreme circumstances."[117] Nevertheless, this should not be intepreted to mean that the issue is dead and gone. In addition to the drug mergers mentioned above, the Federal Trade Commission became active when, in 1994, TCI and Comcast, the largest and third-largest cable-TV companies in the U.S., agreed to form a joint venture to take ownership of QVC, one of two cable-shopping ventures that, at the time, controlled 98% of sales made via TV. The other was Home Shopping Network, which was 79% controlled by TCI. The vertical issue investigated by the Federal Trade Commission was whether existing and potential competitors to QVC and Home Shopping Network would have trouble getting on cable, because TCI and Comcast together controlled access to about 30% of cable-wired homes.[118] The merger was finally approved because the relevant market was defined as all of retailing, not just home shopping via television.

Vertical mergers also have attracted attention abroad. For example, in 1990, Grand Metropolitan, the United Kingdom food, beverage, and retailing conglomerate, and Elders IXL, the Australian brewer, agreed to a $5 billion pubs-for-breweries swap. Grand Met was to transfer its four breweries and the Ruddles, Watneys, Truman, and Webster's beer brands to Courage, owned by Elder, whereas Courage was to combine its 4,900 pubs with GrandMet's 3,570. A major challenge to the merger arose when the UK's Monopolies and Mergers Commission issued a 500-page report concluding that UK's large breweries were operating a "complex monopoly"—a series of practices that restrict competition. These were said to be centered on the long-established tied-house system, which ensures that most of Britain's 80,000 pubs stock the products of only one supplier—the company that owns them.[119] The merger was allowed, but only after the British government put into effect "guest beer orders" allowing pubs to stock beers from suppliers other than the ones that own them.[120]

VERTICAL INTEGRATION BY INTERNAL EXPANSION This form of integration is limited only by the laws preventing monopoly or attempts to monopolize. A firm is ordinarily free to set up its own supply, distribution, and/or retailing system unless this would overconcentrate the market for its product.[121] Section 7 of the Clayton Act specifically permits a firm to set up subsidiary corporations to carry on business or extensions thereof if competition is not substantially reduced.

DUAL DISTRIBUTION The term *dual distribution* describes a wide variety of marketing arrangements by which a manufacturer or a wholesaler reaches its final markets by employing two or more different types of channels for the same basic product. However, the dual arrangement whereby manufacturers market their products through competing vertically integrated and independently owned outlets on either the wholesale or retail level often creates controversy. This practice is customary in many lines of trade, such as the automotive passenger tire, personal computer, paint, and petroleum industries. Dual distribution also takes place when a manufacturer sells similar products under different brand names for distribution through different channels. This latter kind of dual distribution comes about because of market segmentation, or because of sales to distributors under private labels.

In all dual distribution situations, conflict among channel members is likely to be relatively high. But serious legal questions arise mainly in two situations: (1) when price "squeezing" is suspected or (2) when horizontal combinations or conspiracies are possible among competitors. The first situation brings about issues comparable to those found when examining the legality of and difficulties associated with the use of functional discounts. The second relates to potential restraints of trade arrived at in concert by vertically integrated firms and their customers.

Price Squeezes. A seller operating at only one market level in competition with a powerful vertically integrated firm might be subject to a price squeeze at its particular level. For example, a manufacturer of fabricated aluminum might be under pressure from price increases by its raw material (ingot) supplier. If the supplier were also a fabricator, it could take its gain from the price increase (which represents higher costs to the customer-competitor) and use all or a portion of the increased returns for marketing activities at the fabricating level. This was exactly the scenario in the Alcoa case.[122] A number of lower court decisions have declared unlawful an integrated supplier's attempt to eliminate a customer as a competitor by undercutting the customer's prices and placing the customer in a price squeeze.[123]

The same kind of competitive inequality arises from the granting of functional discounts when different functional categories may be represented by buyers who, at least in part of their trade, are in competition with each other. As was the situation in the previously mentioned *Hasbrouck* case, oil jobbers, for example, sometimes sell at retail, and they may use their functional discounts received as jobbers to advantage in competition with retailers. Such pricing raises the possibility of Robinson-Patman Act as well as Sherman Act violations.

When a supplier to an independent retailer also competes with the retailer by owning its own outlets, the possibility of a price squeeze exists if the integrated supplier is more aggressive in setting retail prices at its own outlets than it is in setting wholesale prices to the independent. Such a possibility was no doubt behind the passage of a law in Maryland (upheld by the U.S. Supreme Court in 1978) that prohibits oil producers or refiners from directly operating gasoline outlets.[124] The law, which permits oil companies to own retail stations as long as they do not use their own employees or agents to run them, also forbids discrimination among dealers in the supply and price of gasoline. It is analogous to legislation proposed in numerous other states designed to halt the trend of oil companies opening their own cut-rate, gasoline-only stations in competition with dealer-operated stations.

Horizontal Combinations or Conspiracies. In dual distribution situations, the distinction between purely vertical restraints and horizontal restraints may be critical in determining the legality of a marketing activity. Section 1 of the Sherman Act is not violated by the purely unilateral action of a supplier; there must be at least one additional party present whom the court may find combined or conspired with the supplier. As Bondurant has documented, the courts have not found it difficult to identify a host of potential conspirators.[125] Indeed, Bondurant has carefully cataloged a number of lower court decisions in this area, showing that when a supplier or a franchisor has integrated forward to the level of some of its customers, the following activities may be challenged and prohibited or circumscribed, depending on the specific situation:

1. Establishing territorial boundaries between the supplier and its customer/competitors;
2. Publishing lists of suggested resale prices;
3. Preventing or impeding price competition on the part of customer/competitors via such actions as raising prices to or withdrawing discounts from them;
4. Reserving certain national accounts and/or preventing customer/competitors from competing for such accounts.[126]

And in one case, the court of appeals reversed a district court and held that where a manufacturer has dominant or monopoly power over a given product, it must *preserve* the independent distributor of its products.[127] According to the court of appeals, the public benefits by being able to buy from a distributor who may handle competing products. Dominant manufacturers may replace distributors, but they may not enter into competition with them and destroy them.

In sum, each challenge to dual distribution is generally appraised in terms of its special circumstance. However, as Bondurant warns,

> the existence of direct competition between the supplier and its customers inevitably requires that the supplier's business decisions that affect the ability of its customers to compete be subjected to close antitrust scrutiny to determine the real motivation for the supplier's action.[128]

The question of intent will be crucial. The decision may rest on the issues raised in the *Sylvania* case discussed earlier in this chapter. There, a balancing of the effects of a marketing policy on *intra*brand and *inter*brand competition was mandated by the Supreme Court in situations involving vertical restraints.

▶ SUMMARY AND CONCLUSIONS

The setting of channel policies is at the center of distribution strategy. Policies are rules to guide the functioning of channels. They are the means by which, in the absence of outright ownership, channel managers can achieve effective integration, coordination, and role performance throughout the channel. However, whenever policies are set, there is the potential for conflict, because, for the most part, policies tend to be exclusionary, elitist, and/or restrictive. That is, policies are used to focus or redirect efforts of channel members and to assure that behavior within channels is not random. These limits on behavior have evoked a series of antitrust concerns.

This chapter has dealt, first and foremost, with policies and, secondarily, with antitrust. The large amount of space devoted to antitrust issues is necessary because these issues are complex and cannot be explained quickly or easily. And given the living nature of the issues, as pointed out repeatedly throughout the chapter, it is best not to review them quickly or in an off-hand manner, even though the major attention should be placed on the managerial rationale for adopting the specific channel policies.

Six different, but frequently interrelated, channel policy areas have been addressed in this chapter. They deal with market and customer coverage, pricing, product lines, selection and termination, and ownership. Regarding market coverage, the major focus is on the geographic spacing of channel members. It is in this policy area where attention is given to intensive versus selective versus exclusive distribution. The more intensive distribution becomes, the greater the sales a company can expect in the short run. However, the trade-off is that, over time, channel members are going to be less and less willing to provide costly service outputs because of the price competition that is likely to ensue from the presence of many intrabrand competitors in the same territory. This fact impels suppliers to consider selective and exclusive distribution policies, thereby dampening the amount of intrabrand competition. The legality of these policies is, following the *Sylvania* case, determined under a rule of reason doctrine.

Marketing managers may also wish to assure that only the "right" channel members service specific kinds of customers. They may want company-employed salespeople to call on technically sophisticated heavy users and distributor salespeople to call on other kinds of accounts. Or they may want authorized dealers to sell the company's brand to end-users and to prevent them from acting like master distributors, making sales to other, unauthorized dealers. These and other customer coverage policies like them are often called, by antitrust enforcement agencies, customer or resale restrictions. They are governed by the same line of reasoning applied to market coverage policies.

Both market and customer coverage policies have an indirect effect on prices. Direct effects are achieved via price setting procedures. Although there are a host of pricing policies that can be adopted in marketing channels, two of particular interest here are price maintenance and price discrimination. The former deals with the setting of specific resale prices throughout a marketing channel. The latter deals with setting different prices to different buyers. Resale price maintenance is per se illegal if there is some form of conspiracy or combination of channel members involved in setting or policing the policy. Otherwise, it can be adopted unilaterally. Price discrimination is at the heart of market segmentation strategies, but can run afoul of the law if it substantially lessens competition. It covers such significant activities as the granting of promotional allowances and services and the offering of quantity and functional discounts.

The product line policies addressed in this chapter—exclusive dealing, tying, and full-line forcing—are all adopted with the aim of gaining the undivided attention of channel members on suppliers' products. They restrict interbrand competition directly, whereas market and customer coverage policies restrict intrabrand competition. Because of this potential for foreclosing competitors, there is sometimes more concern shown about them by antitrust agencies than about the coverage policies. Exlusive dealing is the requirement by a supplier that its distributor sell or lease only its products or at least no products in direct competition with the supplier's products. Tying is the requirement that customers purchase other products in order to obtain a product they desire. Full-line forcing is a variant of tying, which covers a supplier's full line, for example, to obtain one item, the buyer must buy the entire line of items.

Finally, the vertical integration question is addressed by ownership policies. If the decision has been made to "make" (own one's own distribution system or source of supply) rather than to "buy" (deal with independently owned channel intermediaries or suppliers), then the choice remaining is either acquisition (or merger) versus internal expansion. Internal expansion seems to pose very little problem from an antitrust perspective. Until recently, the same was true for vertical mergers, but all of a sudden, in the wake of acquisition and merger activity in the pharmaceutical and entertainment distribution channels, the issue has been brought back to life. In any case, when vertical integration takes place and the company continues to employ other, nonintegrated channels as well, conflicts often arise with regard to "dual distribution." Because having multiple channels is more common than not, these types of conflicts are very important for managers to deal with, even though, for the most part, they do not often create antitrust problems for the vast majority of firms.

It should be noted that, relative to legal concerns, this chapter has addressed only federal antitrust law. The states have become much more active in the antitrust arena, and therefore marketing executives would make a serious mistake to ignore the vast outpouring of legislation and court case precedents regulating distribution practices in each of the states in which the products of their companies are sold.

DISCUSSION QUESTIONS

1. Debate the pros and cons of the following policies for the products listed below. (Forget about the antitrust issues; just ask yourself whether you would adopt them from a managerial point of view.)

Policies	Products/Brands
Exclusive distribution	Ping-brand golf clubs
Price maintenance	General Electric washing machines
Tying	DeWalt power tools
Exclusive dealing	Copeland compressors
Price discrimination	Wrigley chewing gum
	Mead notepads
	Liz Claiborne skirts

2. Which is preferable—intrabrand or interbrand competition? Can there be one without the other? Where do you stand on the issue of intrabrand competition: is it necessary in order for there to be viable general competition from a macro perspective? Discuss these questions in the context of resale restrictions and the granting of exclusive territories.

3. Which of the policies discussed in this chapter are governed by the following legal rules and why: (1) rule of reason, (2) per se illegal, (3) modified rule of reason, and (4) per se legal?

4. Do you believe that the Robinson-Patman Act should be stricken from the laws of this country? Debate the pros and cons of this question and come out with a position on it.

5. The president of an automobile accessory manufacturing business wants to purchase a chain of automotive retail stores. What managerial questions might you raise about the decision? What legal issues might this raise?

6. Discuss the similarities and differences between a tying contract and the business practice of reciprocity. Do the practices, on balance, appear to be significantly different?

7. Name five uses of coercive power that would be legal in interorganization management. Name five uses of reward power that would be legal.

8. From a strictly managerial perspective, what are the differences between market coverage and customer coverage policies? Do they accomplish the same or different ends

in the same or different ways? If different, why do you think they were coupled together in the *Sylvania* case by the Supreme Court justices? Was this a mistake?

9.   Which conflict management strategies suggested in Chapter 7 might be questionable from a legal perspective? Why?

ENDNOTES

[1]Frank Lynn & Associates, Inc., *Client Communique* (Chicago: Frank Lynn & Associates, Inc., October 1994), p. 2.

[2]*Ibid*. Another critical variable is the percentage of product that the market buys, which is offered by the focal company, that is, "product line coverage."

[3]Timothy L. O'Brien, "Unjustified Returns Plague Electronics Makers," *Wall Street Journal,* September 26, 1994, p. B1.

[4]Although the Pioneer example was contrived for illustrative purposes, it is not far from the truth. See *U.S. Pioneer Electronics Corporation,* Harvard Business School, ICH 9-579-079 (Boston: Harvard Business School, 1978; revised 1980). Also see Timothy O'Brien, "Unjustified Returns Plague Electronics Makers," *Wall Street Journal,* September 26, 1994, p. B1.

[5]David C. Rudd, "Zenith Data to Cut Dealerships," *Chicago Tribune,* Section 3, November 14, 1989, p. 3; Paul B. Carroll, "IBM Is Becoming More Dealer Friendly," *Wall Street Journal,* May 8, 1987, p. 6; Al Senia, "Inacomp Gets 'IBM-only'," *Computer Reseller News,* June 19, 1989, p. 1.

[6]Quoted in Steve Weiner, "Caught in a Cross Fire, Brand-Apparel Makers Design Their Defenses," *Wall Street Journal,* January 24, 1984, p. 12.

[7]Louis P. Bucklin, "Retail Strategy and the Classification of Consumer Goods," *Journal of Marketing,* Vol. 23 (January 1963), pp. 50–55.

[8]Ronald D. Michman and Stanley D. Sibley, *Marketing Channels and Strategies,* 2nd ed. (Columbus, OH: Grid Publishing, 1980), pp. 321–332.

[9]Programmed merchandising is discussed in Chapter 6.

[10]*Continental T. V., Inc. v. GTE Sylvania Inc.,* 433 U.S. 36 (1977).

[11]David Thunder, "Key Considerations in European Distribution," *Client Communique,* Vol. 3 (April 1991), p. 1.

[12]See John Griffiths, "Commission Plans Will Loosen Carmakers' Grip on Dealers," *The Financial Times,* October 6, 1994, p.6; "Carved Up," *The Economist,* October 31, 1992, p. 73; Guy de Jonquieres, "Electric Suppliers Blames for EC Price Variations," August 3, 1992, p.1; Robert Rice, "Whiff of Controversy Hangs in the Air," *The Financial Times,* November 16, 1993, p. 10; and Emma Tucker and Haig Simonian, "Brussels Plans to Give More Freedom to Car Dealers," *The Financial Times,* May 26, 1995, p. 1.

[13]Phillip Areeda and Louis Kaplow, *Antitrust Analysis: Problems, Text, Cases,* 4th ed. (Boston: Little, Brown and Company, 1988), p. 659

[14]Richard A. Posner, *Antitrust Law: An Economic Perspective* (Chicago: University of Chicago Press, 1976), p. 162.

[15]*Continental T.V., Inc. v. GTE Sylvania, Inc.,* 433 U.S. 36 (1977).

[16]*K Mart Corporation v. Cartier, Inc.,* 56 LW 4480 (1988).

[17]*Ibid.* Also, see Stephen Wermiel, "Justices Uphold Customs Rules on Gray Market," *Wall Street Journal,* June 1, 1988, p. 2; and "A Red-Letter Day for Gray Marketeers," *Business Week,* June 13, 1988, p. 30.

[18]These and other reasons can be found in Stanley I. Ornstein, "Exclusive Dealing and Antitrust," *The Antitrust Bulletin* (Spring 1989), pp. 71–74.

[19]See Areeda and Kaplow, *op. cit.,* pp. 630–635.

[20]See Paul H. Rubin, *Managing Business Transactions* (New York: The Free Press, 1990), pp. 126–127.

[21]For a court ruling on the setting of maximum prices, see *Albrecht v. Herald Co.,* 390 U.S. 145 (1968).

[22]*Monsanto Co. v. Spray-Rite Service Corp,* 104 U.S. 1464 (1984).

[23]*Russell Stover Candies, Inc. v. Federal Trade Commission,* 718 F. 2d 256 (1983).

[24]Mary Jane Sheffet and Debra L. Scammon, "Resale Price Maintenance: Is It Safe to Suggest Retail Prices?" *Journal of Marketing,* Vol. 49 (Fall 1985), pp. 89–90.

[25]*Ibid.,* p. 89.

[26]*Business Electronics Corp. v. Sharp Electronics Corp.,* 99 S.Ct. 808 (1988).

[27]Patrick J. Kaufmann, "Dealer Termination Agreements and Resale Price Maintenance: Implications of the *Business Electronics* Case and the Proposed Amendment to the Sherman Act," *Journal of Retailing,* Vol. 64 (Summer 1988), p. 120.

[28]Paul M. Barrett, "Anti-Discount Policies of Manufacturers Are Penalizing Certain Cut-Price Stores," *Wall Street Journal,* February 27, 1991, p. B1.

[29]Michael Arndt, "Consumers Pay More as Price-Fixing Spreads," *Chicago Tribune,* Section 7, August 18, 1991, p. 5.

[30]*Ibid.*

[31]*Keds Corp.,* FTC File No. 931-0067 (issued for public comment September 27, 1993); *Kreepy Krauly, U.S.A., Inc.,* C-3354 (final order issued December 20, 1991); and *Nintendo America, Inc.,* C-3350 (final order issued November 14, 1991). See, also, Viveca Novak and Joseph Pereira, "Reebok and FTC Settle Price-Fixing Charges," *Wall Street Journal,* May 5, 1995, p. B1.

[32]Viveca Novak, "Nasdaq Investigation Showcases New Moxie at Justice Department," *Wall Street Journal,* October 20, 1994, p. A1; and Joe Davidson, "U.S. to Begin Challenging Price-Fixing Involving Manufacturers, Distributors," *Wall Street Journal,* August 11, 1993, p. A3.

[33]Douglas Lavin, "U.S. Launches Antitrust Probe of Auto Dealers," *Wall Street Journal,* October 11, 1994, p. A3.

[34]*Business Electronics Corp.,* 485 U.S. at 733.

[35]272 U.S. 476, 486–488 (1926).

[36]*Ibid.*

[37]*Ryko Manufacturing Co. v. Eden Services,* 823 F.2d 1215 at 1223 (8th Cir. 1987).

[38]Thomas T. Nagle and Reed K. Holden, *The Strategy and Tactics of Pricing,* 2nd ed. (Englewood Cliffs, NJ: Prentice-Hall, 1995), p. 210.

[39]*Ibid.*

[40]If this assumption is wrong, the reader is encouraged to study Philip Kotler, *Marketing Management,* 8th ed. (Englewood Cliffs, NJ: Prentice Hall, 1994), pp. 487–523.

[41]*U.S. v. Borden Co.,* 383 U.S. 637 (1966).

[42]*Brooke Group Ltd. v. Brown & Williamson Tobacco Corp.,* U.S. 114 S.Ct. 13 (1993).

[43]*Ibid.* at 2588.

[44]*Ibid.*

[45]See Bridget O'Brian, "Verdict Clears AMR on Illegal Pricing Charges," *Wall Street Journal*, August 11, 1993, p. A3.

[46]F. M. Scherer and David Ross, *Industrial Market Structure and Economic Performance*, 3rd ed. (Boston, MA: Houghton Mifflin Co., 1990), p. 514.

[47]*FTC News Notes*, Vol. 89 (December 26, 1988), p. 1.

[48]Anita Sharpe, "Pharmacies Sue Drug Manufacturers and Distributors Over Pricing Policies," *Wall Street Journal*, October 18, 1994, p. B9; Dave Kansas, "Four Grocery Chains Sue 16 Drug Firms, Mail-Order Concern in Pricing Debate," *Wall Street Journal*, March 7, 1994, p. B5; and Steven Morris, "Independent Phamacies Face Bitter Pill," *Chicago Tribune*, Business Section, November 6, 1994, p. 1.

[49]See *Fall City Industries, Inc. v. Vanco Beverage, Inc.*, 460 U.S. 428 (1983).

[50]*Standard Oil Co. v. FTC*, 340 U.S. 231 (1951).

[51]*Federal Trade Commission v. Sun Oil Co.*, 371 U.S. 505 (1963).

[52]*Fall City Industries v. Vanco Beverage*, 460 U.S. 428, 446 (1983).

[53]*Ibid.*

[54]Scherer and Ross, *op. cit.*, p. 516.

[55]See, for example, "FTC Centers Its Sights on Slotting Allowances," *Advertising Age*, July 4, 1988, p. 1.

[56]Richard Gibson, "Supermarkets Demand Food Firms' Payments Just to Get on the Shelf," *Wall Street Journal*, November 1, 1988, p. 1.

[57]Joseph P. Cannon and Paul N. Bloom, "Are Slotting Allowances Legal Under the Antitrust Laws?" *Journal of Public Policy and Marketing*, Vol. 10 (Spring 1991), pp. 167–186.

[58]*Ibid.*, p. 179.

[59]*Ibid.*

[60]Martha Brannigan, "Coke is Victim of Hardball on Soft Drinks," *Wall Street Journal*, March 15, 1991, p. B1.

[61]See *Atlantic Trading Corp. v. FTC*, 258 F.2d 375 (2d Cir. 1958).

[62]Federal Trade Commission, *Guides for Advertising Allowances and Other Merchandising Payments and Services*, 16 C.F.R. part 240 (1983).

[63]*Ibid.*, 240.6.

[64]*FTC v. Fred Meyer Company, Inc.*, 390 U.S. 341 (1968).

[65]"Federal Trade Commission Adopts Changes in Robinson-Patman Act Guides," *FTC News*, August 7, 1990, pp. 1–2.

[66]For specific screams, see Fred Pfaff, "The Club Store Ruckus," *Food and Beverage Marketing*, May 1, 1989, p. 53.

[67]Mark T. Spriggs and John R. Nevin, "The Legal Status of Trade and Functional Price Discounts," *Journal of Public Policy & Marketing*, Vol. 13 (Spring 1994), p. 63.

[68]496 U.S. 492 (1990).

[69]496 U.S. 492 at 492 (1990).

[70]496 U.S. 492 at 493 (1990).

[71]For an excellent discussion of this problem, see Spriggs and Nevin, *op.cit.*, pp. 69–70.

[72]See Stanley I. Ornstein, "Exclusive Dealing and Antitrust," *The Antitrust Bulletin* (Spring 1989), pp. 71–79; and Areeda and Kaplow, *op.cit.*, pp. 773–776.

[73]Raju Narisetti, "Goodyear Plans to Offer Dealers Exclusive Lines," *Wall Street Journal*, January 23, 1995, p. A4.

[74]A. D. Neale and D. G. Goyder, *The Antitrust Laws of the U.S.A.*, 3rd ed. (New York: Cambridge University Press, 1980), p. 266.

[75]365 U.S. 320 (1961).

[76]Scherer and Ross, *op. cit.*, p. 563.

[77]Herbert Hovenkamp, *Federal Antitrust Policy* (St. Paul, MN: West Publishing Company 1994), p. 390.

[78]"Is Häagen-Dazs Trying to Freeze Out Ben & Jerry's?" *Business Week,* December 7, 1987, p. 65.

[79]Suein L. Hwang, "While Many Competitors See Sales Melt, Ben & Jerry's Scoops Out Solid Growth," *Wall Street Journal,* May 5, 1993, p. B1.

[80]Stephen Kreider Yoder, "Sun's Anti-Clone Decree Sparks Anger, Charges of Hypocrisy on 'Open Systems'," *The Wall Street Journal,* April 29, 1991, p. B4.

[81]Charles Storch and Bill Barnhart, "Successful Suitor Calls on Square D," *Chicago Tribune,* Section 3, May 14, 1991, p. 5.

[82]Anthony DePalma, "Penn State Got the Exclusive $14 Million, 10-Year Deal with Pepsi! Uh Hugh!" *The New York Times,* Educational Section, June 10, 1992, p. B8.

[83]*Power Draulics-Nielsen, Inc. v. Libby-Owens-Ford Co.,* 1987-1 Trade Cases (CCH), paragraph 67,558 (S.D.N.Y. 1987).

[84]See Areeda and Kaplow, *op.cit.,* 705–710.

[85]*Standard Oil Company of California v. U.S.,* 337 U.S. 293 (1949) at 305.

[86]*U.S. v. Jerrold Electronics Corp.,* 187 F. Supp. 545 (1960), affirmed *per curian* at 363 U.S. 567 (1961).

[87]*Norman E. Krehl, et al. v. Baskin-Robbins Ice Cream Company, et al.,* 42 F. 2d 115 (8th Cir. 1982).

[88]*Susser v. Carvel Corp.,* 332 F.2d 505 (2nd Cir. 1964).

[89]*Unger v. Dunkin' Donuts of America, Inc.,* 531 F.2d 1211 (3d. Cir. 1976).

[90]*In re Chock Full O'Nuts Corp. Inc.,* 3 Trade Reg. Rep. 20, 441 (Oct. 1973).

[91]*Siegel v. Chicken Delight, Inc.,* 448 F.2d 43 (9th Cir. 1971), *cert. denied,* 405 U.S. 95 (1972).

[92]*U.S. v. J. I. Case Co.,* 101 F. Supp. 856 (1951).

[93]*U.S. v. Paramount Pictures,* 334 U.S. 131 (1948); *U.S. v. Loew's Inc.,* 371 U.S. 45 (1962).

[94]"Consent Agreement Cites E&J Gallo Winery," *FTC News Summary* (May 21, 1976), p. 1. See also "Gallo Winery Consents to FTC Rule Covering Wholesaler Dealings," *Wall Street Journal,* May 20, 1976, p. 15.

[95]"Union Carbide Settles Complaint by FTC on Industrial-Gas Sales; Airco to Fight," *Wall Street Journal,* May 20, 1977, p. 8.

[96]Sullivan, *op. cit.,* p. 439.

[97]*Jefferson Parish Hospital District No. 2 v. Hyde,* 104 LW 1551 (1984). See also Robert E. Taylor and Stephen Wermiel, "High Court Eases Antitrust Restrictions on Accords Linking Sales of Goods, Services," *Wall Street Journal,* March 28, 1984, p. 6.

[98]*Jefferson Parish Hospital District No. 2 v. Hyde,* 466 U.S. 12 (1984).

[99]Scherer and Ross, *op. cit.,* p. 568.

[100]See Paul M. Barrett, "FTC's Hard Line on Price Fixing May Foster Discounts," *Wall Street Journal,* January 11, 1991, p. B1.

[101]*FTC News Notes,* Vol. 91 (June 17, 1991), p. 1; Paul M. Barrett, "Sandoz Settles FTC Charges Over Clorazil," June 21, 1991, p. B3.

[102]"Tetra Pak Appeal," *The Financial Times,* October 18, 1994, p. 10.

[103]*Eastman Kodak Co. v. Image Technical Service Inc.,* U.S. 112 S.Ct. 2072 (1992).

[104]*U.S. v. Colgate & Co.,* 250 U.S. 300 (1919).

[105]See Hovenkamp, *op.cit.* p. 263.

[106]Debra L. Scammon and Mary Jane Sheffet, "Legal Issues in Channels Modification Decisions: The Question of Refusals to Deal," *Journal of Public Policy & Marketing,* Vol. 5 (1986), p. 82.

[107]Neale and Goyder, *op. cit.,* p. 282.

[108]*Ibid.,* p. 282.

[109]Under the wording of Section 7 of the Clayton Act, it is unnecessary to prove that the restraint involved has actually restrained competition. It is enough that it "may" tend to substantially lessen competition.

[110]Edward Felsenthal and Joe Davidson, "Two Big Deals Spur Concerns About Antitrust," *Wall Street Journal,* December 9, 1993, p. B1.

[111]Thomas M. Burton, "Eli Lilly Agrees to Restrictions on Buying PCS," *Wall Street Journal,* October 26, 1994, p. A3.

[112]Viveca Novak and Elyse Tanouye, "FTC Restudies 2 Acquisitions by Drug Firms," *Wall Street Journal,* November 15, 1994, p. A16.

[113]*Brown Shoe Co. v. U.S.,* 370 U.S. 294, Vertical Aspects, 370 U.S. 323 (1962).

[114]Edward Felsenthal, "Antitrust Woes Aren't Seen for Merck," *Wall Street Journal,* July 30, 1993, p. B5.

[115]"Merck Agrees to Order Restricting Medco on Prices, Drug Lists," *Wall Street Journal,* March 1, 1995, p. B3.

[116]U.S. Department of Justice, *Merger Guidelines* (Washington, DC: June 14, 1982), pp. 22–26.

[117]Hovenkamp, *op. cit.,* p. 346.

[118]Viveka Novak, "TCI-Comcast Agreement to Buy QVC May Face an FTC Antitrust Challenge," *Wall Street Journal,* September 15, 1994, p. B3.

[119]Tom Maddocks, "Brewers Play the Tie-Break," *Business,* August 1990, p. 76; Philip Rawstorne, "A Change of Pace to Restructuring," *Financial Times,* September 19, 1990, p. 17; and Philip Rawstorne, "GrandMet Backed on $2.6bn Deal," *Financial Times,* November 21, 1990, p. 34.

[120]Philip Rawstorne, "Reduced Importance of the Brewer's Tie," *Financial Times,* February 25, 1991, p. 20.

[121]*Federal Trade Commission v. Consolidated Foods Corp.,* 380 U.S. 592 (1965).

[122]*U.S. v. Aluminum Co. of America,* 148 F. 2d 416 (2nd Cir. 1945).

[123]See, for example, *Columbia, Metal Culvert Co., Inc. v. Kaiser Aluminum & Chemical Corp.,* 579 F. 2d 20 (3rd Cir. 1978); *Coleman Motor Co. v. Chrysler Corp.,* 525 F. 2d 1338 (3d Cir. 1975); and *Industrial Building Materials, Inc. v. Inter-Chemical Corp.* 437 F. 2d 1336 (9th Cir. 1970).

[124]See Carol H. Falk, "Justices Uphold Bar to Oil Firms' Retail Outlets," *Wall Street Journal,* June 15, 1978, p.3; and "The Oil Majors Retreat from the Gasoline Pump," *Business Week* (August 7, 1978), pp. 50–51.

[125]Emmett J. Bondurant, "Antitrust Considerations in the Selection and Modification of Distribution Systems," *Antitrust Law Journal,* Vol. 49, no. 2 (1981), p. 778n.

[126]*Ibid.,* pp. 779–783.

[127]*Industrial Building Materials v. Inter-chemical Corp.,* 437 F.2d 1136 (9th Cir. 1970).

[128]Bondurant, *op. cit.,* p. 783.

APPENDIX

AEROQUIP CORPORATION
PREMIER DISTRIBUTOR AGREEMENT
(PRELIMINARY VERSION)

◀◀◀◀◀◀◀◀◀◀

AEROQUIP CORPORATION
1695 Indian Wood Circle
Maumee, Ohio 43537

PREMIER DISTRIBUTOR AGREEMENT

Date:_____, 19_____

AEROQUIP CORPORATION ("Aeroquip"), appoints

_____
(name of business organization)
located at _____ ("Premier Distributor)
(address)

as Aeroquip's non-exclusive distributor to purchase for resale the Products listed on attached Exhibit A. In consideration of such appointment and of the covenants and conditions contained in this Agreement, and intending to be legally bound, Premier Distributor and Aeroquip agree as follows:

1. PRODUCTS. So long as this Agreement remains in effect Premier Distributor shall have the right to purchase and resell the Aeroquip products listed on Exhibit A (the "Products"). Aeroquip reserves the right at its sole option, on not less than thirty (30) days prior written notice to Premier Distributor, to add products to or delete products from the Products listed on Exhibit A.

2. TERRITORY. The territory [and market segment] described in attached Exhibit B shall be Premier Distributor's area of primary responsibility ("Territory"). This agreement is non-exclusive, and Aeroquip reserves the right to establish additional distribution within the Territory or to redefine the Territory if in Aeroquip's sole discretion such additional distribution or redefinition is desirable to secure adequate market coverage for Aeroquip's Products within the Territory.

In the event that Premier Distributor has one or more branch facilities, any such facility which has not entered into a Premier Distributor Agreement or an Authorized Distributor Agreement with Aeroquip may, with the approval of Aeroquip's Regional Manager, be designated an "approved branch." Premier Distributor shall be responsible for stocking each of its "approved branches" with Aeroquip

Products. [Distributor agrees not to supply any such branch facility with Aeroquip Products unless such branch has been designated an "approved branch" in accordance with this paragraph.]

3. CERTAIN COVENANTS. So long as this Agreement remains in effect, Aeroquip and Premier Distributor shall use their best efforts to effect superior sales growth and profitability for Aeroquip Products in Premier Distributor's Territory in accordance with the Aeroquip Premier Distributor Philosophy and Division of Labor attached as Exhibit C, as such Exhibit may be amended from time to time. If at any time while this Agreement is in effect Aeroquip believes that Premier Distributor is not meeting its commitments as an Aeroquip Premier Distributor in accordance with the Premier Distributor Philosophy and Division of Labor, Aeroquip shall so notify Premier Distributor in writing, and Premier Distributor and Aeroquip shall within a period of ninety (90) days from the date of such notice develop a mutually agreeable plan to cure Premier Distributor's failure to meet its commitments as set out in Exhibit C. If at the end of such ninety (90) day period Aeroquip and Premier Distributor have not agreed on a plan, or if at any time after agreement on a plan in Aeroquip's reasonable judgment Premier Distributor continues to fail to meet its commitments as an Aeroquip Premier Distributor, Aeroquip may terminate this Premier Distributor Agreement in accordance with the provisions of section 11.

4. EXCLUSIVE DEALING POLICY. Aeroquip believes that a Premier Distributor who agrees to use its best efforts to sell the Aeroquip Products covered by this Agreement cannot fulfill this obligation if at the same time Premier Distributor is promoting and selling rubber hydraulic hose and fittings products manufactured by other firms which compete with Aeroquip's Products. Therefore, Aeroquip has a policy of dealing only with distributors which do not carry competing products. If at any time while this Agreement is in effect Premier Distributor distributes or represents as agent products which compete with the Aeroquip rubber hydraulic hose and fittings covered by this Agreement, then, notwithstanding any other provision of this Agreement to the contrary, Aeroquip may in its sole discretion terminate this Agreement upon at least three (3) days prior written notice to Premier Distributor.

5. TERMS OF SALE. The terms and conditions of sale applicable to sales of Aeroquip Products covered by this Agreement shall be Aeroquip's standard terms and conditions of sale in effect on the date of this Agreement and as they may thereafter be amended from time to time.

6. PRICING. So long as this Agreement remains in effect Premier Distributor shall be entitled to receive Aeroquip's Premier Distributor pricing for the Aeroquip Products and services covered by this Agreement. Such prices are subject to change from time to time without notice. Aeroquip may furnish Premier Distributor with suggested resale prices for the Aeroquip Products covered by this Agreement. In addition to Premier Distributor pricing, Premier Distributor shall be entitled to receive the following functional discounts when and to the extent that Premier Distributor performs either or both of the following functions:

Function	Functional Discount
Redistribution: To be eligible for this discount, Premier Distributor must sell Products to approved Aeroquip Affiliate Distributors in accordance with procedures from time to time established in Aeroquip's Distributor Manual. Premier Distributor shall at all times bear the credit risk of non-payment by the Affiliate Distributor.	The discount off list price specified in Exhibit C, applicable to the purchase by Premier Distributor of Products for resale to approved Affiliate Distributors.
Product Mix: To be eligible for this discount, Premier Distributor must purchase and stock only Aeroquip brand adapters, quick disconnect couplings, Thermoplastic hose and fittings and Teflon hose and fittings as offered in Aeroquip's current catalog.	The discount off list price specified in Exhibit C, applicable to the purchase by Premier Distributor of all Aeroquip Products for the following year.

7. PAYMENT. Premier Distributor will pay for all products which it purchases from Aeroquip pursuant to this Agreement in accordance with Aeroquip's standard payment terms then in effect.

8. WARRANTY.

(a) Aeroquip Corporation warrants, for a period of one (1) year from the date of original delivery, that its products are free from defects in material and workmanship. Aeroquip's obligation under this warranty is limited to repair or replacement at its factory of any product or component part thereof which shall be returned to Aeroquip, transportation charges prepaid, and which, following examination, Aeroquip determines in its sole discretion to be defective in material or workmanship. This is Aeroquip's sole warranty. AEROQUIP MAKES NO OTHER WARRANTY, EXPRESS OR IMPLIED, WITH RESPECT TO ITS PRODUCTS, AND ALL OTHER WARRANTIES, INCLUDING WITHOUT LIMITATION THE IMPLIED WARRANTIES OF MERCHANTABILITY AND FITNESS FOR A PARTICULAR PURPOSE, ARE EXPRESSLY EXCLUDED. Aeroquip neither assumes nor authorizes any person to assume for it any other obligation in connection with the sale of Aeroquip products. Aeroquip's warranty shall not apply to any product or component thereof which has been repaired or altered outside of Aeroquip's factory in any manner so as, in Aeroquip's sole judgment, to affect its serviceability, to any product which has been subject to misuse, negligence or accident, or to Aeroquip products which have been installed or used in a manner contrary to Aeroquip's printed instructions. Under no circumstances shall Aeroquip be liable for incidental or consequential damages arising from or in connection with the sale, use or repair of any Aeroquip product.

(b) Premier Distributor is authorized to extend Aeroquip's standard warranty set forth in subparagraph 8(a) to Premier Distributor's customers. Premier Distributor will assume sole responsibility and liability for any warranties or representations made by Premier Distributor or by its agents and customers which are different from or in addition to Aeroquip's standard warranty. Premier Distributor shall assume and indemnify Aeroquip against any and all liability arising from assembly or installation of Aeroquip products by Premier Distributor into assembled or finished products.

9. DIRECT SALES. Aeroquip reserves the right to make direct sales of Products to customers in Premier Distributor's Territory who request that Aeroquip sell directly to them and to whom Aeroquip is willing to sell directly, and no commission or other compensation will be payable to Premier Distributor for such sales. In the event that Aeroquip makes any direct sales to such customers with the assistance of Premier Distributor, Aeroquip may, in its sole discretion, pay Premier Distributor compensation for such sales in accordance with Aeroquip's then current practice. In the event that more than one distributor makes a material contribution to the receipt of an order for a direct sale by Aeroquip of Products, Aeroquip may allocate the compensation on such sale between or among such distributors in such manner and in such amounts as Aeroquip in its sole discretion may determine.

10. NATIONAL AGREEMENTS. From time to time Aeroquip may enter into National Agreements with customers requiring local stocking, including stocking at Premier Distributor's warehouse or warehouses. In such cases Aeroquip may arrange for payment of compensation to Premier Distributor in such manner and in such amounts as Aeroquip in its sole discretion may determine.

11. TERM AND TERMINATION. This Agreement shall continue in effect for one (1) year from the date of this Agreement and thereafter until terminated by either party upon not less than thirty (30) days prior written notice to the other party or upon such lesser notice as may be specified in any other provision of this Agreement. In addition to any other right of termination granted to either party in any other section of this Agreement, either party may immediately terminate this Agreement upon written notice to the other party in the event that:

(a) the other party (i) does not pay, or admits in writing its inability to pay, its debts generally as they become due, (ii) institutes or has instituted against it any proceeding in bankruptcy or any other insolvency or reorganization proceeding and such proceeding is not dismissed within sixty (60) days from the date of such institution, (iii) becomes insolvent or makes an assignment for the benefit of its creditors or becomes subject to any arrangement pursuant to any bankruptcy or equivalent law of any country, or (iv) if a receiver is appointed for its business or it discontinues its business; or

(b) the other party attempts to assign this Agreement without the prior written consent of the terminating party, or there is a substantial change in the ownership, management or control of the other party.

12. EFFECT OF TERMINATION. In the event notice of termination is given by either party under any provision of this Agreement:

(a) During the period between the date notice of termination is given and the effective date of such termination Aeroquip may take all steps which in its sole discretion are reasonably necessary to insure the continuity of distribution of Aeroquip's Products in Premier Distributor's Territory, including the appointment of a replacement distributor in such Territory.

(b) Upon termination of this Agreement for any reason, Premier Distributor may return for credit all unused Aeroquip Products in Premier Distributor's stock on the effective date of termination which Premier Distributor elects to sell back to Aeroquip, provided that such Products are of the then current design, are undamaged and have not been altered in any way, at such prices and in accordance with such terms and condition as may be specified in Aeroquip's standard product return policy then in effect.]

(c) Aeroquip and distributor each release and discharge the other, its employees and affiliates, from all claims for loss or damage arising or allegedly arising by reason of such termination, except for claims arising from a breach of the express terms of this Agreement.

13. CONFIDENTIALITY. Premier Distributor shall provide Aeroquip with a monthly report of so-called "point of sale" information, containing such information and in such form as Aeroquip shall reasonably require. Such information be and remain the property of Distributor, and upon termination of this Agreement Aeroquip shall return all original hard copies, if any, of such information to Premier Distributor. Aeroquip may use such information as it sees fit to aid in the distribution, marketing, sales, promotion or manufacture of its Products, but Aeroquip will not use any such information to the detriment of Premier Distributor and will not disclose such information to an unrelated third party without the consent of Premier Distributor. Aeroquip's obligation in the preceding sentence shall survive termination of this Agreement for any reason.

14. DISCLAIMER OF AGENCY. While Aeroquip and Premier Distributor are by this Agreement allied together to pursue mutual goals, Aeroquip and Premier Distributor are pursuing their independent self interests with respect to their activities undertaken pursuant to this Agreement. Aeroquip and Premier Distributor are independent contractors, and nothing contained in this Agreement shall make Aeroquip or Premier Distributor the agent or partner of the other party.

15. AMENDMENT. No amendment, supplement, modification or waiver of this Agreement shall be binding unless executed in writing by the party to be bound thereby.

16. NO WAIVER. The failure of either party at any time to require performance by the other party of any obligation provided for in this Agreement shall in no way affect the full right to require such performance at any time thereafter, nor shall the waiver by a party of a breach of any provision of this Agreement by the other party constitute a waiver of any succeeding breach of the same or any other such provision nor constitute a waiver of the obligation itself.

17. NOTICES. All notices or other communications which are required or permitted under this agreement shall be in writing and shall be deemed to be sufficiently given if by registered or certified mail, postage prepaid, and addressed to the party at the address first above written. Either party may, by written notice given hereunder, designate any different address to which subsequent notices or other communications shall be sent.

18. APPLICABLE LAW. This Agreement shall be governed by and construed and enforced in accordance with the laws of the State of Ohio.

19. INTEGRATION. This Agreement, together with its Exhibits and Aeroquip's Distributor Manual, Premier Distributor price lists and terms and conditions of sale, which are incorporated into this Agreement by reference, contain the entire understanding of the parties with respect to the transactions

contemplated. As such, they supersede all prior negotiations, commitments and writings, including but not limited to any prior distribution agreement in effect between the parties.

IN WITNESS WHEREOF, the parties have signed this Agreement as of the date first above written.

AEROQUIP CORPORATION

by_____

PREMIER DISTRIBUTOR

by_____

EXHIBIT A: PRODUCTS COVERED BY THE AGREEMENT

All Aeroquip Industrial Americas Group, Industrial Connectors Division products

EXHIBIT B: TERRITORY

Territory
[Market Segment]

EXHIBIT C: AEROQUIP PREMIER DISTRIBUTOR PHILOSOPHY AND DIVISION OF LABOR

Aeroquip's Commitment to the Premier Distributor. In addition to Premier Distributor pricing and functional discounts which Aeroquip makes available to Premier Distributor:

- Market Analysis. Aeroquip will share market analysis data with the Premier Distributor and provide it with sales leads in its marketing area that result from Aeroquip's promotional activities.

- Field Support. Aeroquip will ensure that its Regional Managers create an annual schedule of calls as part of an account support plan. This schedule will be tied closely to the creation, implementation and monitoring of the Premier Distributor's market plan.

- Inventory Planning. Aeroquip will create a team to analyze the inventory needs of the Premier Distributor. Goals for this analysis will include establishing inventory guidelines and reporting procedures that will help to increase the throughput efficiency of the distribution channel and reduce the inventory level.

- Advertising Allowance. Aeroquip will grant Premier Distributor advertising co-op support equal in value to 0.75% of Premier Distributor's sales of Aeroquip Products during the prior calendar year. This advertising allowance can be used by the Premier Distributor for a variety of Aeroquip sales promotion activities as approved by the Aeroquip Regional Manager or advertising manager. This would include approved promotions in support of Premier Distributor's Affiliate Distributors.

Premier Distributor's Commitment to Aeroquip. Acknowledging the value of Aeroquip Premier Distributor pricing and the availability to Premier Distributor of certain functional discounts:

■ Order Handling. Premier Distributor will maintain staffed and equipped office, warehouse and shipping facilities to continuously serve customers during normal business hours.

■ Account Status. Premier Distributor will maintain its account with Aeroquip in good standing as required by Aeroquip's credit manager.

■ Outside Sales. Premier Distributor will maintain an outside sales force with at least one Aeroquip-certified outside salesperson selling Aeroquip products.

■ Inventory Management. Premier Distributor will maintain an inventory level in Premier Distributor's Territory adequate to meet the market need as determined by Aeroquip market analysis. The Premier Distributor will utilize a computer based inventory management system which has been reviewed and approved by Aeroquip.

■ Complete Hose Assembly Shop. Premier Distributor will maintain at each branch a complete hose assembly shop that has the following or equivalent equipment and qualifications as verified by the Aeroquip Regional Manager:

  ■ Shop Aeroquip certified

  ■ One branch hose assembler Aeroquip certified

  ■ FT1340 or FT1360 crimp machine

  ■ FT1013 reusable machine

  ■ S1102 cut-off saw

  ■ FT1058 proof test stand

  ■ Hose cleaning equipment

■ Retail Capability. Premier Distributor will provide the capability for customers to have hose assemblies repaired while they wait. Premier Distributor will also provide a retail area not smaller than 8′ by 10′ in size where Aeroquip products and product advertising will be displayed.

■ Quality Certification—Training. Premier Distributor will insure that all personnel at each Premier Distributor branch involved with the sales or assembly of Aeroquip Products are trained and certified through successful completion of an Aeroquip on-site, local or Maumee Fluid Conveying Products School and are recertified via testing every three years.

■ Quality Certification—Product Specialist. Premier Distributor will have on staff a person to support Premier Distributor's Aeroquip sales and who meets the following capabilities and qualifications:

  ■ make Aeroquip product presentations at key accounts and for internal personnel

  ■ perform field equipment surveys to determine potential Aeroquip product applications and to make installation recommendations and/or do installation work as necessary

- setup, training and field support for Affiliate Distributors including assembly equipment having passed the Aeroquip equipment school

- trained in the use of SalesMate

- has passed Aeroquip product specialist certification test

- End-User Linkage—Point of Sale Information. Premier Distributor will establish with Aeroquip the capability to electronically communicate to Aeroquip market/user sales information by branch, including the following information with respect to user sales:

    - Aeroquip part number sold

    - Quantity sold

    - User name and address

    - SIC code (if available)

- End-User Linkage—EDI. Premier Distributor will link to Aeroquip via EDI for ordering and market data transfer. All but emergency orders must be placed via EDI.

- Market Coverage—Planning. Premier Distributor will work with the Aeroquip Regional Manager to complete a market plan to capture the available market potential as determined by Aeroquip analysis. The market plan will detail target accounts, account sales potential and the plan for reaching the goals. Goals for achieving market coverage may include adding salespeople, opening a satellite store, operating a mobile assembly van or such other activities upon which Premier Distributor and the Aeroquip Regional Manager may agree.

- Market Coverage—Performance Reporting. Premier Distributor will meet quarterly with the Aeroquip Regional Manager to review the Premier Distributor's sales performance compared to plan. This information will be transmitted to Aeroquip electronically and combined with user sales data to determine market penetration. Premier Distributor will also either periodically survey their customers for customer satisfaction or permit Aeroquip to conduct such surveys; in either case Aeroquip and Premier Distributor will share the results.

FUNCTIONAL DISCOUNTS

Redistribution Discount: [   ]%
Product Mix Discount: [   ]%

APPENDIX

AEROQUIP CORPORATION
AUTHORIZED DISTRIBUTOR AGREEMENT
(PRELIMINARY VERSION)

◄◄◄◄◄◄◄◄

AEROQUIP CORPORATION
1695 Indian Wood Circle
Maumee, Ohio 43537

AUTHORIZED DISTRIBUTOR AGREEMENT

Date:_____, 19_____

AEROQUIP CORPORATION ("Aeroquip"), appoints

_____
(name of business organization)

located at _____ ("Authorized Distributor")

(address)

as Aeroquip's non-exclusive distributor to purchase for resale the Products listed on attached Exhibit A. In consideration of such appointment and of the covenants and conditions contained in this Agreement, and intending to be legally bound, Authorized Distributor and Aeroquip agree as follows:

1. PRODUCTS. So long as this Agreement remains in effect Authorized Distributor shall have the right to purchase and resell the Aeroquip products listed on Exhibit A (the "Products"). Aeroquip reserves the right at its sole option, on not less than thirty (30) days prior written notice to Authorized Distributor, to add products to or delete products from the Products listed on Exhibit A.

2. TERRITORY. The territory [and market segment] described in attached Exhibit B shall be Authorized Distributor's area of primary responsibility ("Territory"). This agreement is non-exclusive, and Aeroquip reserves the right to establish additional distribution within the Territory or to redefine the Territory if in Aeroquip's sole discretion such additional distribution or redefinition is desirable to secure adequate market coverage for Aeroquip's Products within the Territory.

3. CERTAIN COVENANTS. So long as this Agreement remains in effect, Aeroquip and Authorized Distributor shall use their best efforts to effect superior sales growth and profitability for Aeroquip Products in Authorized Distributor's Territory in accordance with the Aeroquip Authorized Distributor Philosophy and Division of Labor attached as Exhibit C, as such Exhibit may be amended from time to time. If at any time while this Agreement is in effect Aeroquip believes that Authorized Distributor is not meeting its commitments as an Aeroquip Authorized Distributor in accordance with the Authorized Distributor Philosophy and Division of Labor, Aeroquip shall so notify Authorized Distributor in writing, and Authorized Distributor and Aeroquip shall within a period of ninety (90) days from the date of such notice develop a mutually agreeable plan to cure Authorized Distributor's failure to meet its commitments as set out in Exhibit C. If at the end of such ninety (90) day period Aeroquip and Authorized Distributor have not agreed on a plan, or if at any time after agreement on a plan in Aeroquip's reasonable judgment Authorized Distributor continues to fail to meet its commitments as an Aeroquip Authorized Distributor, Aeroquip may terminate this Authorized Distributor Agreement in accordance with the provisions of section 11.

4. EXCLUSIVE DEALING POLICY. Aeroquip believes that an Authorized Distributor who agrees to use its best efforts to sell the Aeroquip Products covered by this Agreement cannot fulfill this obligation if at the same time Authorized Distributor is promoting and selling rubber hydraulic hose and fittings products manufactured by other firms which compete with Aeroquip's Products. Therefore, Aeroquip has a policy of dealing only with distributors which do not carry competing products. If at any time while this Agreement is in effect Authorized Distributor distributes or represents as agent prod-

393 ▶

ucts which compete with the Aeroquip rubber hydraulic hose and fittings covered by this Agreement, then, notwithstanding any other provision of this Agreement to the contrary, Aeroquip may in its sole discretion terminate this Agreement upon at least three (3) days prior written notice to Authorized Distributor.

5. TERMS OF SALE. The terms and conditions of sale applicable to sales of Aeroquip Products covered by this Agreement shall be Aeroquip's standard terms and conditions of sale in effect on the date of this Agreement and as they may thereafter be amended from time to time.

6. PRICING. So long as this Agreement remains in effect Authorized Distributor shall be entitled to receive Aeroquip's Authorized Distributor pricing for the Aeroquip Products and services covered by this Agreement. Such prices are subject to change from time to time without notice. Aeroquip may furnish Authorized Distributor with suggested resale prices for the Aeroquip Products covered by this Agreement.

7. PAYMENT. Authorized Distributor will pay for all products which it purchases from Aeroquip pursuant to this Agreement in accordance with Aeroquip's standard payment terms then in effect.

8. WARRANTY.

(a) Aeroquip Corporation warrants, for a period of one (1) year from the date of original delivery, that its products are free from defects in material and workmanship. Aeroquip's obligation under this warranty is limited to repair or replacement at its factory of any product or component part thereof which shall be returned to Aeroquip, transportation charges prepaid, and which, following examination, Aeroquip determines in its sole discretion to be defective in material or workmanship. This is Aeroquip's sole warranty. AEROQUIP MAKES NO OTHER WARRANTY, EXPRESS OR IMPLIED, WITH RESPECT TO ITS PRODUCTS, AND ALL OTHER WARRANTIES, INCLUDING WITHOUT LIMITATION THE IMPLIED WARRANTIES OF MERCHANTABILITY AND FITNESS FOR A PARTICULAR PURPOSE, ARE EXPRESSLY EXCLUDED. Aeroquip neither assumes nor authorizes any person to assume for it any other obligation in connection with the sale of Aeroquip products. Aeroquip's warranty shall not apply to any product or component thereof which has been repaired or altered outside of Aeroquip's factory in any manner so as, in Aeroquip's sole judgment, to affect its serviceability, to any product which has been subject to misuse, negligence or accident, or to Aeroquip products which have been installed or used in a manner contrary to Aeroquip's printed instructions. Under no circumstances shall Aeroquip be liable for incidental or consequential damages arising from or in connection with the sale, use or repair of any Aeroquip product.

(b) Authorized Distributor is authorized to extend Aeroquip's standard warranty to Authorized Distributor's customers. Authorized Distributor will assume sole responsibility and liability for any warranties or representations made by Authorized Distributor or by its agents and customers which are different from or in addition to Aeroquip's standard warranty. Authorized Distributor shall assume and indemnify Aeroquip against any and all liability arising from assembly or installation of Aeroquip products by Authorized Distributor into assembled or finished products.

9. DIRECT SALES. Aeroquip reserves the right to make direct sales of Products to customers in Authorized Distributor's Territory who request that Aeroquip sell directly to them and to whom Aeroquip is willing to sell directly, and no commission or other compensation will be payable to Authorized Distributor for such sales. In the event that Aeroquip makes any direct sales to such customers with the assistance of Authorized Distributor, Aeroquip may, in its sole discretion, pay Authorized Distributor compensation for such sales in accordance with Aeroquip's then current practice. In the event that more than one distributor makes a material contribution to the receipt of an order for a direct sale by Aeroquip of Products, Aeroquip may allocate the compensation on such sale between or among such distributors in such manner and in such amounts as Aeroquip in its sole discretion may determine.

10. NATIONAL AGREEMENTS. From time to time Aeroquip may enter into National Agreements with customers requiring local stocking, including stocking at Authorized Distributor's warehouse or warehouses. In such cases Aeroquip may arrange for payment of compensation to Authorized Distributor in such manner and in such amounts as Aeroquip in its sole discretion may determine.

11. TERM AND TERMINATION. This Agreement shall continue in effect for one (1) year from the date of this Agreement and thereafter until terminated by either party upon not less than thirty (30) days prior written notice to the other party or upon such lesser notice as may be specified in any other provision of this Agreement. In addition to any other right of termination granted to either party in any other section of this Agreement, either party may immediately terminate this Agreement upon written notice to the other party in the event that:

(a) the other party (i) does not pay, or admits in writing its inability to pay, its debts generally as they become due, (ii) institutes or has instituted against it any proceeding in bankruptcy or any other insolvency or reorganization proceeding and such proceeding is not dismissed within sixty (60) days from the date of such institution, (iii) becomes insolvent or makes an assignment for the benefit of its creditors or becomes subject to any arrangement pursuant to any bankruptcy or equivalent law of any country, or (iv) if a receiver is appointed for its business or it discontinues its business; or

(b) the other party attempts to assign this Agreement without the prior written consent of the terminating party, or there is a substantial change in the ownership, management or control of the other party.

12. EFFECT OF TERMINATION. In the event notice of termination is given by either party under any provision of this Agreement:

(a) During the period between the date notice of termination is given and the effective date of such termination Aeroquip may take all steps which in its sole discretion are reasonably necessary to insure the continuity of distribution of Aeroquip's Products in Authorized Distributor's Territory, including the appointment of a replacement distributor in such Territory.

(b) Upon termination of this Agreement for any reason, Authorized Distributor may return for credit all unused Aeroquip Products in Authorized Distributor's stock on the effective date of termination which Authorized Distributor elects to sell back to Aeroquip, provided that such Products are of the then current design, are undamaged and have not been altered in any way, at such prices and in accordance with such terms and condition as may be specified in Aeroquip's standard product return policy then in effect.]

(c) Aeroquip and distributor each release and discharge the other, its employees and affiliates, from all claims for loss or damage arising or allegedly arising by reason of such termination, except for claims arising from a breach of the express terms of this Agreement.

13. DISCLAIMER OF AGENCY. While Aeroquip and Authorized Distributor are by this Agreement allied together to pursue mutual goals, Aeroquip and Authorized Distributor are pursuing their independent self interests with respect to their activities undertaken pursuant to this Agreement. Aeroquip and Authorized Distributor are independent contractors, and nothing contained in this Agreement shall make Aeroquip or Authorized Distributor the agent or partner of the other party.

14. AMENDMENT. No amendment, supplement, modification or waiver of this Agreement shall be binding unless executed in writing by the party to be bound thereby.

15. NO WAIVER. The failure of either party at any time to require performance by the other party of any obligation provided for in this Agreement shall in no way affect the full right to require such performance at any time thereafter, nor shall the waiver by a party of a breach of any provision of this Agreement by the other party constitute a waiver of any succeeding breach of the same or any other such provision nor constitute a waiver of the obligation itself.

16. NOTICES. All notices or other communications which are required or permitted under this agreement shall be in writing and shall be deemed to be sufficiently given if by registered or certified mail, postage prepaid, and addressed to the party at the address first above written. Either party may, by written notice given hereunder, designate any different address to which subsequent notices or other communications shall be sent.

17. APPLICABLE LAW. This Agreement shall be governed by and construed and enforced in accordance with the laws of the State of Ohio.

18. INTEGRATION. This Agreement, together with its Exhibits and Aeroquip's [Distributor Policy], Authorized Distributor price lists and terms and conditions of sale, which are incorporated into

this Agreement by reference, contain the entire understanding of the parties with respect to the transactions contemplated. As such, they supersede all prior negotiations, commitments and writings, including but not limited to any prior distribution agreement in effect between the parties.

IN WITNESS WHEREOF, the parties have signed this Agreement as of the date first above written.

AEROQUIP CORPORATION

by_____

AUTHORIZED DISTRIBUTOR

by_____

EXHIBIT A: PRODUCTS COVERED BY THE AGREEMENT

All Aeroquip Industrial Americas Group, Industrial Connectors Division products

EXHIBIT B: TERRITORY

Territory
[Market Segment]

EXHIBIT C: AEROQUIP AUTHORIZED DISTRIBUTOR PHILOSOPHY AND DIVISION OF LABOR

Aeroquip's Commitment to the Authorized Distributor. In addition to Authorized Distributor pricing which Aeroquip makes available to Authorized Distributor:

■ Market Analysis. Aeroquip will share market analysis data with the Authorized Distributor and provide it with sales leads in its marketing area when there is no Premier Distributor in Authorized Distributor's Territory.

■ Field Support. Aeroquip will support the Authorized Distributor with telemarketing. The Aeroquip Regional Manager will also make periodic phone contact and sales calls on an as-needed basis.

■ Advertising Allowance. Aeroquip will grant Authorized Distributor advertising co-op support equal in value to 0.50% of Authorized Distributor's sales of Aeroquip Products during the prior calendar year. This advertising allowance can be used by the Authorized Distributor for a variety of Aeroquip sales promotion activities as approved by the Aeroquip Regional Manager or advertising manager.

Authorized Distributor's Commitment to Aeroquip. Acknowledging the value of Aeroquip Authorized Distributor pricing:

■ Order Handling. Authorized Distributor will maintain staffed and equipped office, warehouse and shipping facilities to continuously serve customers during normal business hours.

■ Account Status. Authorized Distributor will maintain its account with Aeroquip in good standing as required by Aeroquip's credit manager.

■ Outside Sales. Authorized Distributor will maintain an outside sales force with at least one Aeroquip-certified outside salesperson selling Aeroquip products.

■ Inventory Management. Authorized Distributor will maintain an inventory level in Authorized Distributor's Territory adequate to meet the market need as determined by Aeroquip market analysis.

■ Basic Hose Assembly Shop. Authorized Distributor will maintain at each branch a basic hose assembly shop that has the following or equivalent equipment as verified by the Aeroquip Regional Manager:

    ■ FT1380 crimp machine

    ■ S1104 cut-off saw

■ Quality Certification—Training. Authorized Distributor will insure that at least one person at each Authorized Distributor branch involved with the sales or assembly of Aeroquip Products is trained and certified through successful completion of an Aeroquip on-site, local or Maumee Fluid Conveying Products School and is recertified via testing every five years.

APPENDIX

AEROQUIP CORPORATION
AFFILIATE DISTRIBUTOR AGREEMENT
(PRELIMINARY VERSION)

◀◀◀◀◀◀◀◀

AEROQUIP CORPORATION
1695 Indian Wood Circle
Maumee, Ohio 43537

AFFILIATE DISTRIBUTOR AGREEMENT

Date:_____, 19_____

AEROQUIP CORPORATION ("Aeroquip"), appoints

_____
(name of business organization)

located at _____ ("Affiliate Distributor")
(address)

as Aeroquip's non-exclusive industrial products distributor to purchase for resale the products listed on attached Exhibit A. In consideration of such appointment and of the covenants and conditions contained in this Agreement, and intending to be legally bound, Affiliate Distributor agrees with Aeroquip as follows:

1. PRODUCTS. The products covered by this Agreement are the Aeroquip products listed on Exhibit A (the "Products"). Aeroquip reserves the right at its sole option, on not less than thirty (30) days prior written notice to Affiliate Distributor, to add products to or delete products from the Products listed on Exhibit A.

2. TERRITORY. This agreement is non-exclusive, and Aeroquip reserves the right at all times to establish and maintain additional industrial products distribution in Affiliate Distributor's market area.

3. TERMS OF SALE. Affiliate Distributor will purchase Aeroquip's Products from an authorized Aeroquip Premier Distributor on such terms and conditions (including price) upon which Affiliate Distributor and such Premier Distributor may agree. Aeroquip may from time to time publish suggested resale prices applicable to sales of Products by its Premier Distributors to its Affiliate Distributors, or by its Affiliate Distributors to their customers.

4. USE OF AEROQUIP NAME AND TRADEMARKS. So long as this Agreement remains in effect, Affiliate Distributor is authorized and licensed (a) to hold itself out and to represent itself as an authorized Aeroquip distributor, (b) to use the Aeroquip name and trademarks (including appropriate signage) in connection with Affiliate Distributor's sale or solicitation for sale of the Aeroquip Products covered by this Agreement, and (c) to receive from Aeroquip such sales support, product applications support and staff training which Aeroquip makes generally available to its Affiliate Distributors. All rights and licenses granted to Affiliate Distributor pursuant to this Agreement or granted to Affiliate Distributor while this Agreement is in effect shall immediately terminate upon expiration or termination of this Agreement for any reason.

5. AFFILIATE DISTRIBUTOR'S OBLIGATIONS. So long as this Agreement remains in effect, Affiliate Distributor agrees (a) to use its best efforts to sell the Aeroquip Products covered by this Agreement, (b) to establish and maintain satisfactory sales and service coverage, including warranty service for Affiliate Distributor's customers, for Aeroquip's Products in Affiliate Distributor's normal trading area, (c) to maintain an inventory of Aeroquip's Products sufficient to satisfy the requirements of Affiliate Distributor's customers for such Products, (d) to maintain an acceptable credit status with every

Premier Distributor with whom Affiliate Distributor does business, and (e) to cause its employees to be trained in the proper use and application of the Aeroquip Products.

6. DISTRIBUTION POLICY. Aeroquip believes that an Affiliate Distributor who agrees to use its best efforts to sell Aeroquip Products cannot fulfill this obligation if at the same time Affiliate Distributor is promoting and selling rubber hydraulic hose and fittings products manufactured by other firms which compete with Aeroquip's Products. Therefore, Aeroquip has a policy of allowing its name and trademarks to be used only by Affiliate Distributors which do not carry certain competing products. If at any time while this Agreement is in effect Affiliate Distributor distributes or represents as agent products which compete with the Aeroquip rubber hydraulic hose and fittings covered by this Agreement, then, notwithstanding any other provision of this Agreement to the contrary, Aeroquip may in its sole discretion terminate this Agreement upon not less than three (3) days prior written notice to Affiliate Distributor.

7. WARRANTY. The warranty applicable to all Aeroquip Products covered by this Agreement shall be Aeroquip's standard product warranty attached as Exhibit B. Affiliate Distributor will assume sole responsibility and liability for any warranties or representations made by Affiliate Distributor, its agents or employees which are different from or in addition to Aeroquip's warranty as set forth above. Affiliate Distributor will indemnify Aeroquip and its employees and affiliates against, and hold them harmless of and from, any and all loss, liability, cost or expense (including reasonable attorneys fees) which Aeroquip or its employees may at any time suffer or incur on account of warranties or representations (express or implied) made by Affiliate Distributor, its agents or employees, which warranties or representations are different from or in addition to Aeroquip's standard warranty or which in any way increase the liability of Aeroquip or its employees or affiliates over that expressly assumed by Aeroquip in its warranty attached as Exhibit B.

8. TERM. This Agreement shall continue in effect for one (1) year from the date of this Agreement and from year to year thereafter until terminated by either party upon not less than thirty (30) days prior written notice to the other party. In the event of termination of this Agreement, Aeroquip and distributor each release and discharge the other, its employees and agents, from all claims for loss or damage arising or allegedly arising by reason of such termination, including any obligation to repurchase Affiliate Distributor's unsold inventory of Aeroquip Products, but excluding claims arising from a breach of the express terms of this Agreement.

9. ASSIGNMENT. This Agreement may not be assigned by either party without the prior written consent of the other party. In the event of a substantial change in the ownership, management or control of a party, then, notwithstanding any other provision of this Agreement to the contrary, this Agreement may be terminated by the other party on not less than three (3) days prior written notice.

10. DISCLAIMER OF AGENCY. While Aeroquip and Affiliate Distributor are by this Agreement allied together to pursue mutual goals, Aeroquip and Affiliate Distributor are pursuing their independent self interests with respect to their activities undertaken pursuant to this Agreement. Aeroquip and Affiliate Distributor are independent contractors, and nothing contained in this Agreement shall make Aeroquip or Affiliate Distributor the agent or partner of the other party.

11. AMENDMENT. No amendment, supplement, modification or waiver of this Agreement shall be binding unless executed in writing by the party to be bound thereby.

12. NO WAIVER. The failure of either party at any time to require performance by the other party of any obligation provided for in this Agreement shall in no way affect the full right to require such performance at any time thereafter, nor shall the waiver by a party of a breach of any provision of this Agreement by the other party constitute a waiver of any succeeding breach of the same or any other such provision nor constitute a waiver of the obligation itself.

13. NOTICES. All notices or other communications which are required or permitted under this agreement shall be in writing and shall be deemed to be sufficiently given if sent by registered or certified mail, postage prepaid, and addressed to the party at the address first above written. Either party may, by written notice given hereunder, designate a different address to which subsequent notices or other communications shall be sent.

14. APPLICABLE LAW. This Agreement shall be governed by and construed and enforced in accordance with the laws of the State of Ohio.

15. INTEGRATION. This Agreement, together with its Exhibits, which are incorporated into this

Agreement by reference, contain the entire understanding of the parties with respect to the transactions contemplated. As such, they supersede all prior negotiations, commitments and writings.

IN WITNESS WHEREOF, the parties have signed this Agreement as of the date first above written.

AEROQUIP CORPORATION

by_____

AFFILIATE DISTRIBUTOR

by_____

EXHIBIT A: PRODUCTS COVERED BY THE AGREEMENT

All Aeroquip Industrial Americas Group, Industrial Connectors Division products offered through an Aeroquip Premier Distributor

EXHIBIT B: AEROQUIP'S STANDARD WARRANTY

Aeroquip warrants, for a period of one (1) year from the date of original delivery, that its Products are free from defects in material and workmanship. Aeroquip's obligation under this warranty is limited to repair or replacement at its factory of any product or component part thereof which shall be returned to Aeroquip, transportation charges prepaid, and which, following examination, Aeroquip determines in its sole discretion to be defective in material or workmanship. This is Aeroquip's sole warranty. AEROQUIP MAKES NO OTHER WARRANTY, EXPRESS OR IMPLIED, WITH RESPECT TO ITS PRODUCTS, AND ALL OTHER WARRANTIES, INCLUDING WITHOUT LIMITATION THE IMPLIED WARRANTIES OF MERCHANTABILITY AND FITNESS FOR A PARTICULAR PURPOSE, ARE EXPRESSLY EXCLUDED. Aeroquip neither assumes nor authorizes any person to assume for it any other obligation in connection with the sale of Aeroquip Products. Aeroquip's warranty shall not apply to any product or component thereof which has been repaired or altered outside of Aeroquip's factory in any manner so as, in Aeroquip's sole judgment, to affect its serviceability, to any product which has been subject to misuse, negligence or accident, or to Aeroquip Products which have been installed or used in a manner contrary to Aeroquip's printed instructions. Under no circumstances shall Aeroquip be liable for incidental or consequential damages arising from or in connection with the sale, use or repair of any Aeroquip product.

INFORMATION
SYSTEMS
and CHANNEL
MANAGEMENT

◀◀◀◀◀◀◀

*T*he collection, creation, management, and communication of information are critical to the efficiency and effectiveness of any marketing channel. In today's marketplace, new information technologies are revolutionizing the way distribution is organized and coordinated as well as reducing the cost of performing marketing flows and generating service outputs. Many terms have sprung up to describe these technological sources and uses of information; for example, "electronic data interchange," or EDI, is defined as "the exchange of information across organizational boundaries using Information Technology."[1] Another term, "interorganizational systems," refers to "all information systems that span corporate boundaries."[2] Bundles of technologies such as telecommunications linkages, electronic scanning, bar coding, database management, and multimedia offerings are generally involved in the application of information technology (or IT) in a channel. These electronic and database technologies highlight the growing importance of communication and information dissemination *among* organizations in a channel, rather than just *within* any given organization.

Experts differ over the benefits the huge IT investments create. At least one study argues that IT investments are paying off, claiming a return on investment in information systems of 54% for manufacturing and 68% for all businesses surveyed. Further, the gains appear to come not just from cost reduction, but also from revenue enhancement.[3] Another study, however, emphasizes the difference between the ability to *generate* data through technological advances and the ability to *use* the data: "The history of IT can be characterized as the overestimation of what can be accomplished immediately and the underestimation of long term consequences."[4] Given the huge investments being made and the debate over their productivity, it is important to understand how information technology can be used to enhance performance in the channel.

The impact of information systems on distribution channels can be far-reaching. They can "redefine market boundaries, alter the fundamental rules and basis of competition, redefine business scope, and provide a new set of competitive weapons."[5] Just as importantly, they change the emphasis in interorganizational relations from *separation* to *unification*. A channel member can be so closely allied with its upstream supplier or downstream customer that the very lines separating the organizations appear to blur. Physical distances become irrelevant in the face of electronic means of communication and information exchange. The very way in which channel members think about their relationships may change:

> Whereas traditional physical-based commodities (which are appropriable, scarce, and have decreasing returns to use) lead to concerns with boundaries, ownership, and allocation, *information* (which is nonappropriable, nonscarce, and has increasing returns to use) *results in the breaking down of boundaries and leads to issues of access, sharing, and creating opportunities for use.*[6]

Thus, information technology investments have an impact not only on the costs of running a channel, but also on the coordination of the channel.

This chapter examines how information systems affect all aspects of channel management. We first discuss the elements of a channel information system. We then investigate the significance of information system investment on the provision of service outputs to consumers, the cost of performing channel flows, and the level of power, conflict, and coordination in the channel. Changes in the roles that manufacturers, wholesalers, and retailers play because of new information technologies are also discussed. It is important to recognize that without a sound basis for communication and coordination in the channel, even large investments in information technology cannot solve interorganizational problems. But increasingly, *without* those investments in information systems, a channel cannot hope to remain competitive in today's market.

▶ ELEMENTS OF CHANNEL INFORMATION SYSTEMS

A channel information system must include not only the information itself, but a mechanism to preserve, collect, and interpret the information usefully. We highlight below the two major components of a channel information system: (a) the hardware and networks that make up the technological housing of the information system and (b) the database of information itself.

Hardware and Networks for Channel Information Systems

Hardware and networks refer to the computer systems, software, and associated technologies that permit information to be relayed among channel members electronically. We can differentiate among networks/hardware used (1) in business-to-business channel applications; (2) in retailing; (3) by both businesses and consumers (so-called "on-line computer services"); and (4) by consumers (so-called "interactive multimedia"). Some of these technologies are the bases for new, entirely electronic channels of distribution. Although these electronic channels only augment existing channel forms today, they could in some instances replace current forms in the future.

BUSINESS-TO-BUSINESS APPLICATIONS   Within a given distribution channel, dedicated electronic technologies are used to facilitate communication among channel members. In the apparel industry, for example, support for "Quick Response" (QR) programs means that fabric makers, apparel designers, and retailers must all be able to share information about product designs, orders, payment, and the like with little or no delay. Several technologies facilitate the implementation of a QR program:

- EDI helps turn paper-based documents into electronic ones, such as purchase orders, packing slips, and invoices. This increases accuracy and reduces labor formerly spent in reentering relevant data.

- Shipping container marking (SCM) involves labeling shipping containers with bar codes that uniquely identify each carton shipped, as well as its vendor, order number, and destination store. This permits a retailer to send a container directly to the sales floor without opening and sorting its contents.

- Bar-coding is also used at the point of sale (POS) to improve inventory control and minimize errors in pricing or promotional markdowns.[7]

In the hospital supply industry, the proliferation of many proprietary (and thus incompatible) EDI systems meant that hospitals initially had to use different computers or terminals for each vendor. The industry has been working on establishing networks based on a common data-communications standard for hospitals and suppliers to process orders, make electronic payments, and disseminate price and product information in order to reduce channel costs. Four of the largest hospital suppliers—Baxter International Inc., Eastman Kodak Co., Boise Cascade Corp., and Bergen Brunswig Corp.—were the initial sponsors of this initiative. The standardized electronic ordering system runs on desktop computers, using software originally developed by TSI International Software Ltd. Significant savings on both the hospitals' and suppliers' parts have been forecast: currently, a large hospital incurs between $30 and $40 of overhead when placing an order, whereas a supplier spends $24 to $28 to process that order. Costs could fall as low as $12 per order for hospitals and just 32 cents for suppliers with the new system, assuming wide acceptance of the common standards.[8]

Appendix 9A shows how one manufacturer of industrial hoses and fittings, Aeroquip Corporation, communicated the benefits of EDI to its distributors. The document emphasizes that EDI not only decreases the manufacturer's costs, but also decreases other channel members' costs while simultaneously increasing customer service.

Where standard land-based networks are difficult to install, satellite networks are being established. Volkswagen Europe uses a private satellite network (called a "very small aperture terminal," or VSAT, network) to link dealers to headquarters. VSAT's first use has been in Eastern Germany, where the standard telecommunications infrastructure is poor. The VSAT network handles everything from data communications to credit-card verification and in-store music. The company plans eventually to link all of its European dealers via the network. VSAT networks are already well-established, with more than 100,000 terminals in use worldwide.[9]

RETAILING APPLICATIONS   Retailers routinely use computer-based networks and hardware to enhance communications between stores and headquarters. Major chain retailers, such as Sainsbury and Marks & Spencers in the U.K., have invested in large-scale "fixed-link" networks to connect branch stores to a central computer at headquarters. In medium- to small-scale grocery businesses, telephone lines and networking software connect store computers. In all of these cases, point-of-sale data is collected at the store level and shipped to a computer at the retailer's headquarters either on a daily basis or, increasingly, more frequently throughout the day. Data are used to minimize stockouts, as well as to perform accounting functions or download price lists.[10] Computer systems have also been linked to electronic shelf-labeling systems, providing completely accurate pricing between shelf and checkout and generating labor savings as shelf price changes are no longer done manually. Vons' supermarkets have added such systems to their stores in California, at a cost of about $125,000 for 15,000 labels per store. The cost is particularly justified in stockkeeping units, such as dry grocery, dairy, and frozen food products, where repricing is frequent and labeling items is difficult.[11]

Some large retailers handle these functions by satellite: A&P grocery stores spent $10 million to install satellite earth stations at its stores. The system permits virtually instantaneous check clearance, pipes music to all the stores, and reprograms prices on checkout scanners instantly in all stores. Other retailers using similar satellite communications facilities include Wal-Mart, Kmart, Thrifty drugstores, Pathmark grocery stores, and Super Valu Stores.[12]

An entirely electronic grocery shopping service called Peapod is even available to shoppers of Jewel food stores in the Chicago area and Safeway stores in San Francisco.[13] With a personal computer and modem, shoppers can access the Peapod system and roam the aisles of a supermarket, as if one were actually traveling through the store. Or they can look for items by categories. Within a category, products and brands can be listed in many ways, including alphabetically or in unit price order. The system can maintain a list of frequently purchased items that shoppers need not key in every time they shop, to save on shopping time and on inadvertent omission of key items. All current shelf prices, including special sale prices, are posted on the system, and sales are flagged to shoppers. Coupons can be used, and once the shopping "trip" is over, home delivery is scheduled for as early as a few hours later. Peapod deals with consumer concerns about produce, meat quality, and freshness by employing a person whose sole job is to pick produce and by allowing detailed directions on the computerized shopping list (e.g., 8 bananas—2 green, 4 yellow, 2 overripe, not to exceed 4.5 pounds). The service is financially viable not only due to delivery fees paid by subscribing shoppers, but also due to the value of the Peapod database to grocery product manufacturers. Unlike other databases, the Peapod system gives an insight into the prevalence of out-of-stocks, because the consumers ask for their preferred items and sizes—but do not get those products that are out of stock. Also valuable are data on what substitute brands or sizes the consumer is willing to take; the system permits directions about allowable substitutions, generating data on closest substitutes to a shopper's most-preferred brand.

With all of these technologies available to retailers, many of them at significant initial adoption cost, how can a retailer decide which to use? Smart Store 2000, part of Andersen Consulting, is an R&D center opened in 1989 that forms a liaison between retailers and the suppliers of state-of-the-art retailing information technology. Advanced technologies, like automated checkout lanes that let customers ring up their own groceries or touch-screen computerized cash registers, are on display. Retailers can use the facility to investigate these technologies before adopting them formally. Hardware and software vendors value the direct access to retail management that Smart Store provides; over 80 vendors display more than 150 innovative technologies there.[14]

ON-LINE COMPUTER SERVICES   On-line computer services, along with interactive multimedia technologies (see below), form the infrastructure for the "information superhighway" that is beginning to link consumers with each other and with suppliers of goods and services. There is one largely noncommercial network, Internet, to which an estimated 20 million people have access. In addition, several commercial on-line services, among them Prodigy, CompuServe, America Online, GEnie, and Delphi, serve almost 5 million subscribers. Table 9-1 and Exhibit 9-1 summarize the size and offerings of these on-line network suppliers.

An individual can access these networks with a personal computer, modem, and account. Once on the network, individuals can "talk" electronically with one another via electronic mail, or e-mail. In addition, they can get information from electronic "bulletin boards" on a multitude of topics, including airline schedules and fares, weather, and the like. Products, such as airline tickets, books, and movies, can be purchased directly over the commercial networks. DEC corporation has even used the Internet to let potential business customers test the capabilities of two new high-performance computers by allowing customers to run their own software on the machines remotely. Over 2,500 potential customers logged on in a six-month period.

The ability both to communicate with and to sell to consumers is limited only by the diffusion of computer technology into consumers' homes. In 1994, only 13% of U.S. homes had a modem-equipped personal computer; only 50% of these buyers eventually connected with an on-line service, and most of these dropped their subscription when they got their first bill. Thus, although the promise of on-line computer services is great, their adoption has been limited to the computer-literate segment of consumers.[15]

INTERACTIVE MULTIMEDIA   Interactive multimedia (IM) for consumer use refers to electronic technology that shares the characteristics of television, telephone, and computer and brings information, shopping opportunities, and multimedia programming to consumers. IM involves the transformation of information (textual, graphic, and video) into computer language, so that it can move down a single communications channel (such as a telephone or fiber-optics line, or coaxial cable) to a modified television set or personal computer. It is also distinguished from stan-

▌**TABLE 9-1** **On-Line Computer Network Services**

CHARACTERISTICS	PRODIGY	COMPU-SERVE	AMERICA ONLINE	GEnie	DELPHI
# Subscribers	Over 2,000,000	1,500,000	500,000	400,000	80,000
Cost/month (5 hrs. online time)	$14.95	$33.00	$9.95	$24.00	$14.00
Selected Basic Services					
Electronic mail on Internet	Poor	Good	Good	Good	Good
Financial information	Excellent	Poor	Excellent	Good	Good
News wires	Excellent	Excellent	Excellent	Poor	Poor
On-line shopping	Excellent	Excellent	Excellent	Excellent	Excellent
Reference information	Excellent	Excellent	Excellent	Excellent	Excellent
Sports information	Excellent	Good	Good	Good	Good
Stock quotes	Excellent	Good	Excellent	Poor	Good
Travel services	Excellent	Excellent	Excellent	Excellent	Excellent
Selected Extra Services					
Bulletin boards	Excellent	Excellent	Excellent	Excellent	Good
Database search	Poor	Excellent	Poor	Excellent	Excellent
Health information	Good	Excellent	Good	Good	Excellent
Movie reviews	Good	Good	Good	Good	Good
On-line banking	Excellent	Excellent	N/A	N/A	N/A
Product support	Poor	Excellent	Poor	Excellent	Poor
Shareware	Poor	Excellent	Excellent	Excellent	Good
Ticket ordering	N/A	N/A	Good	N/A	N/A

Source: James Coates, "From On-Line Hangout to Data Superhighway," *Chicago Tribune,* January 16, 1994, Section 7, p. 1. © Copyrighted Chicago Tribune Company. All rights reserved. Used with permission.

dard video or audio reception by the information recipient's ability to respond to the information, for example, by buying a product or casting a vote.

Both the technology and the market for interactive multimedia are still developing. For example, it is not clear whether telephone, cable television, computer, or some combination of the three types of companies will provide the core technology for effecting an IM exchange. Mergers among members of these three industries are evidence that a combination of technologies may be necessary to make IM a commercial reality.

All of these industries stand to gain from a presence in the IM market. Telecommunications companies like AT&T and MCI are looking to IM to generate better margins from their networks—moving from "POTS" to "PANS" ("Plain Old Telephone Services" to "Pretty Awesome New Stuff"). Meanwhile, computer companies have an incentive to encourage customers to buy more powerful computers as their prices fall over time.

Time Warner Cable, the second-largest cable company in the U.S., ran a test in autumn 1994 of multimedia services in Orlando, Florida. Four thousand homes

EXHIBIT 9-1 / The Internet

WHAT IS THE INTERNET?

◄ ◄ ◄

The Internet is a loosely configured set of computer networks around the world. Twenty-five thousand corporate, educational, and research computers are part of the Internet. The Internet has no central computer. Instead, your messages contain an address code that lets any computer on the Internet forward your message to its destination.

HOW MANY PEOPLE HAVE ACCESS TO THE INTERNET?

More than 20 million people now have access to the Internet, including those on purely commercial on-line services that provide Internet access.

HOW DOES THE INTERNET DIFFER FROM PURELY COMMERCIAL ON-LINE SERVICES?

- It is a web of computers, not one central one.

- It does contain some purely noncommercial components, such as the National Science Foundation Network.

- It has no central manager; the Internet Society is a volunteer organization in Reston, VA with 2,000 individual and 84 corporate members that oversee the development of new communications protocols.

- Many commercial on-line services provide access to the Internet as an option; the reverse is not true.

WHAT CAN YOU DO ON THE INTERNET?

- Electronic mail

- Tap into remote computers (e.g., Nasdaq, Federal Reserve, Library of Congress)

- Use the World Wide Web to search for useful data across many computer sites

- Access "virtual shops"

- Access information provided by corporate users (e.g., product information or financial data from companies such as Apple Computer, Bell Atlantic, IBM, Schlumberger, and Silicon Graphics)

Source: Rick Tetzeli, "The Internet and Your Business," *Fortune*, March 7, 1994, pp. 86–96 © 1994 Time Inc. All rights reserved. Similar information is available from many sources, including William L. Goffe, "Computer Network Resources for Economists," *Journal of Economic Perspectives*, Vol. 8 (no. 3, Summer 1994), pp. 97–119; Jeffrey K. MacKie-Mason and Hal Varian, "Economic FAQs About the Internet," *Journal of Economic Perspectives*, Vol. 8 (no. 3, Summer 1994), pp. 75–96; and the citations therein.

were wired for the trial, and subscribers were able to order and watch videos delivered over their telephone lines, as well as do interactive shopping. If interactive shopping fulfills the promise that some industry watchers predict, it could replace the catalog marketing channel and account for as much as 5 to 10% of America's total retail sales over the next 10 years.

Meanwhile, Prodigy also tested a TV cable-based version of its computer on-line service, called Prodigy TV, in autumn 1994. The limitation to consumer adoption of this technology has been the initial cost of "souped-up" cable converter boxes, as powerful as a personal computer, but costing about $3,000. Prodigy TV would permit the television viewer to keep a television program on the screen while checking the weather, news, or sports, or even while shopping. The ultimate goal is the complete linking of television and computer-based on-line services.

Finally, alliances are springing up to provide interactive television services. Oracle, a software company, has teamed up with Bell Atlantic and several suppliers, such as Apple Computer and the *Washington Post*, to adopt a common software and media server (the source of video, audio, graphic, and textual information). Through a multimedia "set-top box" sitting on top of a household's television, the system can send feature-length films and provide access to shopping and information services. Oracle has also joined with US West, another of the Baby Bell companies, to provide interactive television services to its phone subscribers and to cable customers as well.[16]

Databases for Channel Information Systems

The database is the information that is stored on, and accessed from, a computer network. To be useful, this information must be converted into knowledge that can be used to make channels both more efficient and more effective. In this section, we discuss how databases are generated and their impact on customer service, and then discuss some retail and pharmaceutical-industry examples of database use.

DATABASE GENERATION   Figure 9-1 shows how databases can be generated at different levels of a distribution channel that uses "efficient consumer response" (or ECR) techniques. As can be seen, data are gathered from all levels of the channel. Data gathered at one level of the channel are used to improve management at other levels of the channel (e.g., scanner data gathered at the retail level are used upstream at the customer-distribution center level to improve inventory information and ordering processes). This interchange of information across different channel members highlights the importance of channel communication and coordination for more effective channel activity.

One type of database, the geographic information system (or GIS), uses computerized mapping techniques to visually summarize and present demographic and competitive data. Super Valu, the supermarket wholesaler, uses mapping software to help it pick sites. Western Auto, a Sears Roebuck subsidiary, uses it to match a store's inventory to local demographic profiles (with an improvement in break-even time from 18 months to 6 months on average). Cigna Insurance Company salespeople use a GIS to answer insurance brokers' questions about the number of Cigna-affiliated doctors in a certain radius of a client's employee base.[17]

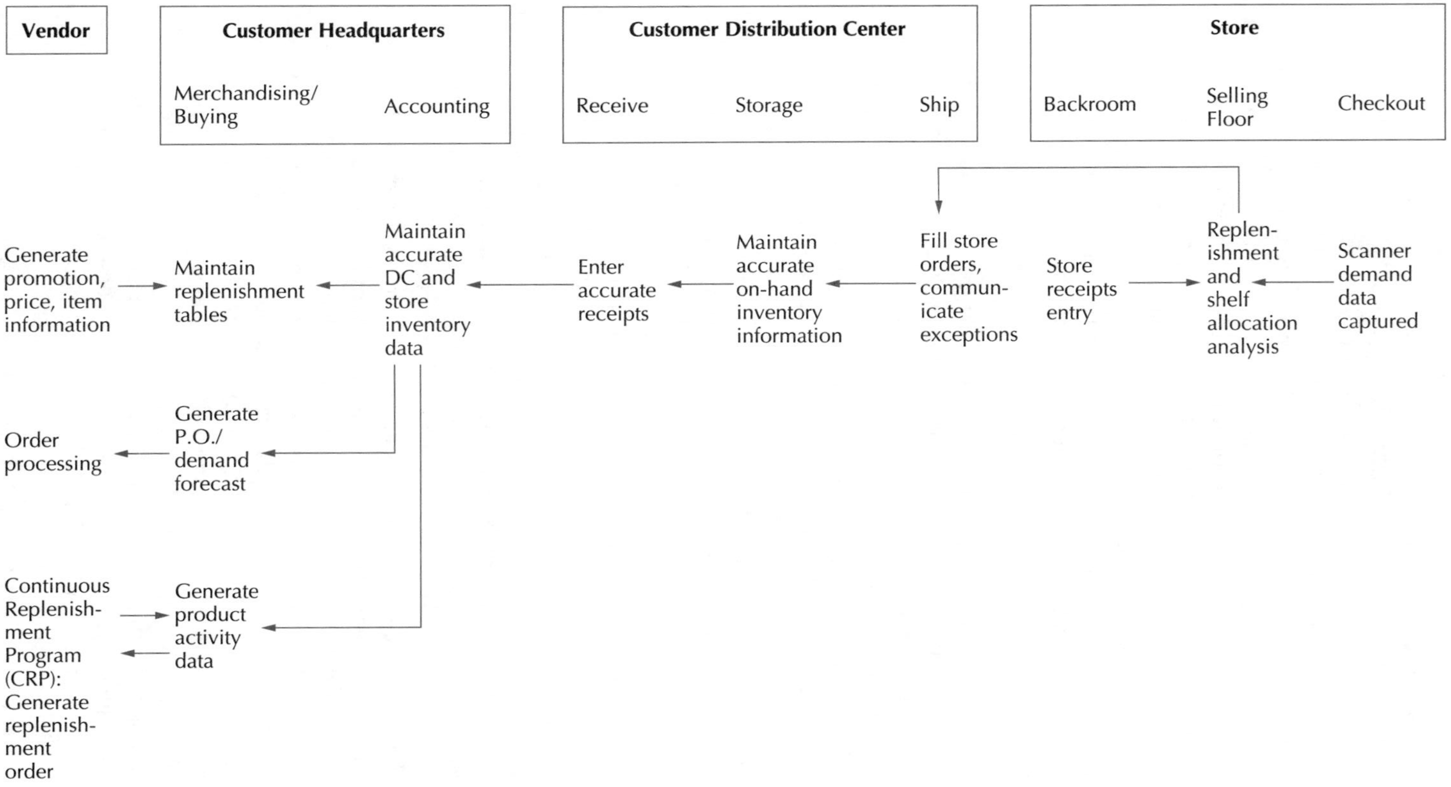

Vendor

Customer Headquarters
Merchandising/Buying | Accounting

Customer Distribution Center
Receive | Storage | Ship

Store
Backroom | Selling Floor | Checkout

Generate promotion, price, item information → Maintain replenishment tables

Maintain accurate DC and store inventory data

Order processing → Generate P.O./demand forecast

Continuous Replenishment Program (CRP): Generate replenishment order → Generate product activity data

Enter accurate receipts → Maintain accurate on-hand inventory information → Fill store orders, communicate exceptions

Store receipts entry → Replenishment and shelf allocation analysis → Scanner demand data captured

FIGURE 9-1 **Database components of an ECR system.**
Source: Adapted from "A User's Guide to Efficient Consumer Response," *Grocery Marketing,* August 1993, p. 14.

DATABASES AND CUSTOMER SERVICE   A database can also be used to improve customer service. For example, Whirlpool discovered leaks in one of its new washing-machine models; because it had a database of all purchases of Whirlpool appliances, it was able to contact the consumers who had bought the faulty model and repair it quickly. Whirlpool uses this information not only to keep its consumers happy, but also to lower its spare-parts inventories. It can further drive harder bargains with upstream components suppliers with the knowledge of what components move most quickly and are delivered most reliably. Otis Elevator Company has centralized customer service through its OtisLine service center, which handles 1.2 million calls a year, half of which are for unscheduled repairs. By tracking all these calls, Otis engineers can identify even subtle patterns of service problems, using this information to redesign either maintenance procedures or even the elevators themselves.[18]

RETAIL DATABASE USE   Retailers, particularly grocery and department store retailers, have been the biggest users of databases to improve channel-strategy execution. These databases center around consumer behavior patterns: their buying habits, responses to promotions, and the like. To implement ECR in the grocery chain, data suppliers like Information Resources, Inc. (IRI) and A.C. Nielsen offer data from a census of all stores in an area, not just a sampling of stores. Nielsen announced in April 1994 that it would take a minority ownership position in Efficient Market Services Inc. (EMS), the first research company to collect daily sales data in an entire retail chain. By the end of 1994, Nielsen and EMS put their ECR data collection system into more than 2,600 stores in 25 major markets in the U.S. All major U.S. markets, with more than 5,000 store systems, were to have been included by 1996. IRI announced in February 1994 that it would move from a weekly sample data-collection system to a weekly census system called InfoScan Census. These data systems give packaged goods manufacturers the ability to see how much of their product is selling on a weekly or daily basis, and in which specific stores in a trading area turnover is highest. Although retailers have used such data in the past to pressure manufacturers, now manufacturers can use these data to pressure retailers for better performance of their products at retail.[19]

External data suppliers are not a retailer's only source of data, however. Frito-Lay's delivery salespeople help build the company's retail database by using hand-held computers to track sales and stocking data, which are instantly sent back to headquarters. The company can use the data to convince retailers to improve their shelf space allocations or to counteract the forays of competitors.[20]

A number of retailers offer discounts with the use of magnetic stripe "membership" cards that let them better track customer sales. Staples, an office-goods retailer, uses this strategy to build a database that tells it how successful particular promotions are; whether a customer has moved or started patronizing a new Staples store; and what makes customers shop elsewhere. It based its decision to add a delivery service on an analysis of its database showing that the lack of deliveries was causing customer defections to competitors.[21]

Another database system, ShopperTrak, is used to count the number of consumers entering and leaving a store. It can provide information on peak traffic flows and, along with point-of-sale data, on "conversion rates"—what proportion of consumers entering a store actually end up buying merchandise. This information can distinguish between a store that appears to be well-patronized but has relatively low sales per shopper, and another higher conversion-rate store that may have fewer shoppers, but a greater proportion of buyers out of the total shopping pool. One store in New Jersey used this system to experiment with higher staff-to-customer ratios, trying ratios from 5:1 to 9:1. It discovered that the optimum was 7:1. Such data can help a store generate greater sales while simultaneously controlling costs. With a purchase price of about $4,000 per system, the software can pay for itself in as little as a year's time. These systems are especially valuable in creating loyalty; it is estimated to cost three to five times as much to attract a new customer as it costs to retain an existing customer.[22]

PHARMACEUTICAL DATABASE USE   The use of databases to improve targeted selling even extends to the ethical drug industry today. The $6.6 billion purchase of Medco by Merck in November 1993 has given the pharmaceutical firm unprecedented access to patient drug-use data as well as physician-prescribing data. As mentioned in Chapter 8, Medco is a mail-order drug company that manages pharmaceutical health plans for employers and independent health plans. In the process, it collects information on the prescription drug use of 33 million people in the U.S. Merck–Medco can use its information about the ethical drug use of a corporate client's employees to encourage those patients and their physicians to switch to a Merck-brand drug. Physicians participating in a health plan often must choose drugs from an approved list, called a "formulary," and Medco (which manages pharmaceutical benefits for 1,500 health plans), creates formularies for about 750 of these plans.[23]

▶ IMPACT OF INFORMATION SYSTEMS ON THE DELIVERY OF SERVICE OUTPUTS

> Simply stated, Quick Response is a strategy for tying apparel and textile retailing operations to apparel and textile manufacturing operations, in order to provide the flexibility needed to quickly respond to shifting markets. The strategy . . . [is] aimed at capitalizing on domestic manufacturers' strongest competitive advantage—proximity to domestic markets—by providing more suitable products, higher customer service levels, and shorter lead times than those offered by lower-priced foreign competitors. . . . Manufacturers and retailers ensure that they have the right product available to the consumer in the right place and at the right time.[24]

This example from the apparel industry illustrates how crucially important it is to offer every targeted customer segment its optimum service-output levels. Given high labor costs in the United States, the use of information technology to improve service-output levels could be critical to the survival of many American firms in the apparel industry as well as in other industries. It is thus important to understand how the development of channel information systems has affected the provision of these service outputs. Although information technology tends to have little impact on the generic service output of lot size, it has greatly affected the provision of spatial convenience, waiting/delivery time, and product variety to consumers. Although other service outputs can characterize channel relations in particular industries, such as information or postsale service, we concentrate here on the latter three generic service outputs in order to illustrate specific impacts.

SPATIAL CONVENIENCE   Spatial convenience used to mean locating retail stores close to a consumer's home or using salespeople to call directly on a business-to-businesss buyer. But instead of the buyer going to the seller, today's electronic technologies make it more cost-effective for the seller to come to the buyer. Home shopping continues to gain in popularity because of consumers' poverty of time. EDI prevents the need for business-to-business buyers to call their suppliers to reorder; instead, the reorder is done automatically when stocks drop below a critical level. Mail-order drugs make it easier for an elderly and less-mobile patient to get medication when needed.[25]

Paradoxically, it need not cost the channel more to provide this greater level of spatial convenience: for example, mail-order or electronic shopping channels do not need to pay rent for valuable storefront space, nor do they need to redecorate their stores frequently. Personnel needs drop when a retail outlet is not operated: maintaining an employee salesforce costs over $200 per sales call in consumer, industrial, and service firms.[26] The avoidance of these costs can and often does compensate for the cost of running an electronic network.

WAITING/DELIVERY TIME   Waiting and delivery times also shorten as information technology pervades the distribution channel. In one quick visit to the Dutch PTT (Post, Telephone, and Telegraph) office, Dutch telephone customers can get new telephone numbers, contracts, and the precise times their phones will be connected within the next two days. It used to take two weeks to set up a phone connection, but the goal is to make the connections instantaneous. PTT can improve delivery time in this way because it has channeled information from its mainframe computers down to individual terminals in the sales offices. Sales personnel can amass all the information they need quickly, instead of needing to gather information from several computerized sources, as was previously the case.[27]

A government has even used information technologies to improve delivery times through the distribution channel. The port of Singapore has instituted the TradeNet system, a nationwide EDI network linking manufacturers, shipping agents, freight forwarders, traders and government agencies. A user can send an electronic document to the relevant government agencies and have it returned within 30 minutes. This speed gives participating channel members an edge over competitors who do not use the TradeNet system, who may wait two or three days for written approvals from various government departments. The result has been an estimated S$1 billion savings to the Singaporean trading community.[28] In fact, Singapore runs the most efficient port in the world.

ASSORTMENT AND VARIETY   Channel information systems also help retailers provide a variety of products that better fit their consumers' demands for variety. As explained in Chapter 2, 7-Eleven Japan is able to turn over 70% of its stock per year because it can very quickly determine what sells to shoppers and what does not. By keeping an electronic eye on store stocks, retailers also avoid out-of-stocks, which can represent significant lost sales. And most catalog marketers use their tremendous database expertise to pretest what products are included in their catalogs, as well as to periodically delete slow-moving products from them. Thus, they have a very precise notion of what assortments catalog shoppers want to see, because they keep track of sales patterns so closely.[29]

Information technology can of course have a simultaneous impact on several service outputs at once (see Exhibit 9-2). And for a consumer used to a "high-touch" approach, the "high-tech" approach afforded by electronic interfaces can be daunting. These new channels sometimes force consumers to perform more functions than they previously did (e.g., using an ATM machine instead of having a face-to-face encounter with a bank teller)—a process called disintermediation.[30] Key to making disintermediation palatable to consumers is to make consumer self-service easier and more fun; new technologies like voice recognition will help increase consumers' willingness to serve themselves. From the service providers' point of view, the use of information technologies makes it more and more difficult to separate elements of customer service; marketing, selling, after-sales service, and invoicing are all tied together via one information system. Indeed, this is precisely the goal in many companies' reengineering efforts. This, in turn, means that the way in which channel flows are performed is changing—the topic of discussion in the next section.

▶EXHIBIT **9-2** / Service Output Changes in Hospital Supplies, Apparel, and Office Supplies

◀ ◀ ◀

BAXTER INTERNATIONAL AND VALUELINK

This $9 billion per year hospital-products company responded to its customers' complaints that they were spending too much money just storing and distributing supplies within the hospital. Baxter's response was to create ValueLink, a service that lets hospitals pass back to Baxter the inventory management function inside the hospital. Baxter receives daily electronic information in its warehouses on how much inventory each ValueLink customer is using, so it has an accurate count on reorders. The system is set up to tell Baxter exactly where in the hospital all the supplies should go. One Houston, Texas, hospital estimates the savings to them from using ValueLink will reach $800,000 over the five-year life of their contract with Baxter.

Baxter gets a service fee of 3 to 6% on sales. Even more important, Baxter often becomes the hospital's sole supplies provider. This can greatly increase Baxter's revenue from each

Exhibit 9-2 (continued)

Exhibit 9-2 (continued)

customer. This system works because Baxter provides high levels of spatial convenience and product variety to its customers, while minimizing delivery times.

VF APPAREL COMPANY

While studying the retail apparel industry, VF found that many retailers are routinely out of stock on as many as 30% of the items they want to sell. VF uses its "market response system," or MRS, a computerized link between the company and the cash registers of its retailers, to record detailed information about what sells at which stores. VF uses the point-of-sale information it gathers to time more precisely the delivery of merchandise to a retailer, rather than letting it sit in its own warehouses. Delivery times are cut from several weeks to as little as seven days. This attention to quick delivery times and appropriate product variety pays off for VF: its earnings nearly doubled on a sales increase of 13% in 1991, to $161 million on sales of $2.9 billion.

PHOENIX DESIGNS INC.

A subsidiary of Herman Miller Inc., this office furniture supplier used to sell office furniture in the standard way: independent dealers' sales reps would visit a customer's office, where the rep would gather ideas, take them back to the company's designer, and go back and forth for about six weeks, ending with a proposal for the customer. This arrangement irritated customers and lost sales for Phoenix.

Now, salespeople use portable PCs and a proprietary software program called Z-Axis to generate their own designs and proposals, with a turnaround time of just five days. One dealer has made a sale every time it has used the system with a prospective client (70 times). Some small dealers have reported sales increases using the system of as much as 1,000%. The system cost about $1 million, and has generated a 27% increase in after-tax income. The benefits to Phoenix of drastically cutting waiting and delivery time, while preserving the custom nature of the variety offered, have proven to be great.

▶ IMPACT OF INFORMATION SYSTEMS ON CHANNEL FLOW PERFORMANCE

General Electric had historically sought to give dealers the best price and payment arrangements when they bought appliances in truckload lots, as well as following GE's floor plan for product display. In the late 1980s, however, the cost of holding large inventories of GE products hurt the company's independent dealers in the face of growing competition from low-price, multi-brand chain stores. In response, GE reinvented the way it distributed appliances. Direct Connect, GE's computerized logistics system, eliminates the need for retailer inventories. Dealers can place orders for next-day delivery at any time. They get GE's best price, regardless of order size, as well as attractive financing and priority delivery scheduling. The dealers promise in return to sell nine major GE product categories, to generate at least 50 per cent of their sales from GE products, and to pay GE monthly through electronic funds transfer. The dealers benefit because they no longer pay inventory holding costs, yet are still able to respond quickly to consumers. GE has increased its dealer business significantly, while decreasing its distribution and marketing costs by 12 per cent.[31]

How have GE, and other companies in every type of business, used channel information systems to improve the execution of channel flows and functions? This

TABLE 9-2 Channel Flow Changes with Information Technology

FLOW	CHANGES DUE TO USE OF CHANNEL INFORMATION SYSTEMS
Physical Possession	• Just-in-time deliveries reduce physical possession flow throughout channel • Inventory no longer held at retail store • Cross-docking minimizes retailer warehousing • Some retailers take on shipping
Ownership	• Retailer ownership flow decreases (for custom orders, retailer bears no ownership flow) • Distributors/manufacturers also reduce flow performance via POS data shared by retailer
Promotion	• Instant coupon generation at grocery check-out • More finely targeted promotions using linked demographic and purchase-data databases
Negotiation	• Automation-induced decreases in paperwork let purchasing departments spend more time negotiating good deals • Retailers and manufacturers use POS data to justify price and terms demands—tighter link to performance
Financing	• Lowered need for financing due to lessened physical possession and ownership flows
Risking	• POS data generates better forecasts, reducing inventory risk • Greater postponement possible with quick response technologies, reducing speculative inventories
Ordering	• Automated reordering means no human involvement
Payment	• Electronic payment systems automate payment processes, minimize paperwork • Increased use of electronic funds transfer

example, described in Chapter 6 as an "administered vertical marketing system," highlights how implementing a computerized logistics system can affect many flows simultaneously, from physical possession and ownership to financing, risking, ordering, and payment. Channel information systems can even change the *order* in which channel functions are performed. Electronic order transmission, for example, triggers a supplier's fulfillment process earlier, whereas quick response lets retailers stock inventory later than they normally would.

Effective use of a channel information system produces lower total-channel operating costs *while maintaining or even increasing the level of end-user service outputs*. The counterbalancing of lower costs and higher end-user satisfaction is important to recognize; without the latter, channel performance would suffer if channel managers sought cost minimization for its own sake. Below, we profile how information technologies have affected the performance of each of the eight major channel flows. Table 9-2 summarizes the primary changes.

Inventory-Related Flows

The majority of channel information-system impacts have been felt in channel flows involving the creation, movement, and holding of inventory. Thus, these improvements simultaneously affect *physical possession, ownership, financing,* and *ordering.* In the text that follows, effects on the costs of performing these channel flows are described, and then the ways in which inventory replenishment has changed are discussed. Examples from various industries illustrate the implementation of these new inventory-handling systems.

IMPACT ON CHANNEL COSTS   One very noticeable effect on these flows is simply that the extent of their performance (and hence their costs) has decreased throughout the whole channel. "Just in time," "efficient consumer response," "EDI," and "quick response" all refer to sets of technologies and methods that reduce the time any product spends winding its way through the distribution channel to the end-user. The less time a product spends in the channel, the lower the overall costs of physical possession and ownership are likely to be. Because total inventories throughout the system decline, so do the costs of financing them. One estimate of the necessary investment in a quick response program is $100,000 for a small-sized firm; but the estimated break-even time is just one year, with an increase in retailers' return on assets of 7–12%, an increase in manufacturers' return on assets of 6–13%, and a 20–40% increase in retail sales. Industrywide, inefficiencies in the apparel distribution pipeline are estimated at $25 billion; industry analysts predict that the widespread adoption of quick response could cut these inefficiencies by half.[32]

POS DATA AND INVENTORY REPLENISHMENT   The costs of ordering and inventory replenishment fall through effective use of point-of-sale data. As each item is sold, the information is captured on the retailer's POS system, permitting instant updating of its inventory position. The remaining inventory level is then compared with a "model stock" level, typically set to cover expected demand 95% of the time. Replenishment orders can then be issued in one of three ways: (1) the retailer gives the supplier a blanket authorization to ship orders without buyer review of individual orders; (2) the supplier prepares an order and sends it to the buyer as a recommended replenishment order, with the buyer reviewing and authorizing the order; or (3) the retailer prepares replenishment orders and transmits them to the supplier via EDI. Cost declines derive from a lessening of the physical-possession flow, as product is supplied more quickly to retailers and hence their safety stocks of inventory can fall. (See Table 9-3 for effects of quick response technologies on response times in the apparel industry.)

For instance, Haggar Apparel Co., the menswear maker, uses a quick-response system called H.O.T. (for Haggar Order Transmission), which includes vendor marking of merchandise, EDI data transmission, automated electronic reordering, stock management, and replenishment. Over 500 retail stores downstream, and textile suppliers like Milliken upstream, are linked together through the system. Milliken reduced its minimum order sizes from 5,000 or 10,000 yards to just 1,000, and can now deliver orders in less than two weeks. Haggar has reduced its manufacturing cycle time from 14 days to 7. Quick-response systems also generate greater turnover rates for inventory; at Vanity Fair Mills, for example, model stocks for retailers are designed to generate an annual turnover rate of four times, about twice as high as before the adoption of their flow-replenishment system.[33] Du Pont Co. has also eliminated purchase orders in this way with about 5% of its suppliers who are

TABLE 9-3   Response Time from Fabric at Mill to Product in Store (in Working Days)

SYSTEM	STORE ORDER ENTERED	FABRIC ACQUIRED; APPAREL PRODUCTION PLANNED	GARMENT CUT	GARMENT SEWN	GARMENT RECEIVED; DISPLAYED AT STORE	TOTAL
"Very Quick" Response System	1	4	1	1	2	10 days (2 weeks)
"Quick" Response System	1	7	2	15	5	30 days (6 weeks)
Traditional "Average" System	8	32	7	20	58	125 days (25 weeks)

Note: The "Very Quick" system assumes a fully implemented Quick Response system, which may be an unrealistic goal at present. The "Quick" system response times, however, are possible with current technologies. The "Average" system summarizes typical response times under current conditions in the apparel industry. Current response times in this table assume that the garment design is completed and the fabric is in stock at the textile mill. If this is not true, total planning and production time routinely tops one year.

Source: Robert M. Frazier, "Quick Response in Soft Lines," *Discount Merchandiser,* January 1986, pp. 42, 44. Cited in Janice H. Hammond and Maura G. Kelly, "Quick Response in the Apparel Industry," Harvard Business School No. 9-690-038, April 1991, p. 15.

linked electronically with Du Pont's internal inventory system. When Du Pont is running short on an item, they deliver replacement stocks automatically.[34]

INVENTORY FLOW CHANGES IN THE GROCERY INDUSTRY   In the grocery industry, standard ordering practices had come to be dictated by manufacturers' promotional programs, which meant holding sometimes large inventories of trade-promoted products in retailer warehouses. But with new systems based on quick response, grocers are instead ordering based on what they forecast consumers will buy. Catalina Information Resources (CIR) is a joint venture between Information Resources Inc. and Catalina Marketing Corporation, building a national network of point-of-sale grocery data from 7,000 stores nationwide. Overnight, CIR generates individual store data on product movement; these data can be linked to stock positions and promotional activities. Better monitoring of out-of-stocks means that what might in the past have been interpreted as a problem with the effectiveness of a promotion can now be identified as resulting from poor stocking practices.[35]

Grocery retailers have also lowered their investment in physical-possession flows. For example, ICA Retailers in Sweden uses *cross-docking,* a process whereby distributors no longer deliver goods to the retail stores. Instead, they deliver directly to the retailer's receiving dock, with lots already divided up for each store. The merchandise never enters the warehouse, but instead is immediately loaded onto trucks for delivery to the stores.

ICA's cross-docking function is backed up by a state-of-the-art communications network that integrates and links its 2,700 individual stores with its distribution and marketing operations. An individual storeowner can enter daily product needs into a hand-held computer, and his orders are combined and rationalized with other retailers' orders to maximize the savings from large-scale ordering. ICA has shut down half of its 22 regional distribution centers and one of its three central warehouses as a result. In addition to the remaining two central warehouses, ICA runs two cross-docking facilities and will open a third. It may seem that the cross-docking function adds a layer to the distribution channel (see Figure 9-2), but the correspondingly smaller number of distribution centers needed and the lower prices ICA can negotiate with its suppliers more than make up the cost difference.[36]

Kao Corporation, Japan's biggest soap and cosmetics company, has used channel information systems to maximize the channel's flexibility. The company and its wholly owned wholesalers use a highly sophisticated system to deliver products within 24 hours to any of 280,000 stores, each of whose average order is for only seven items. One information system links sales, shipping, production, purchasing, accounting, research and development (R&D), marketing, retailers' cash registers, and salesmen's hand-held computers. This unification of information means that brand managers can see daily sales, stock, and production figures together. The company uses a test-marketing process called the Echo System, with focus groups and consumer feedback along with POS data from 216 retailers to gather quick information on new product launches. Because of Kao's command over market information, they are less dependent than other firms on sales forecasts and buffer inventories. Although the company made 564 household products in 1992, an increase of 66 over 1987, average inventory as a percentage of sales dropped to 8.6% from 9.2%. The company recognizes that flexibility is the result of a combination of relevant information and the ability to exploit that information throughout the whole channel.[37]

INVENTORY FLOW CHANGES IN THE HEALTH CARE INDUSTRY   In the health care industry, electronic linkages have existed between drug distributors and their retail customers since the mid-1970s. For some time now, retail druggists have been able to place an order simply by running a laser scanner over a bar-coded shelf label.

But even more, warehouse fulfillment processes in the industry have been refined. Previously, the manual filling of orders meant the possibility of errors. Now, a 12-ounce machine, designed in 1991 by McKesson in conjunction with Electronic Data Systems and worn on the order-filler's forearm, is a combination computer, laser scanner, and two-way radio in one. It receives an order via radio from the warehouse's central computer. A small screen on the machine displays the whereabouts of the desired items in the warehouse and plans an efficient route through the warehouse to pick the order. As the order filler chooses an item off the warehouse shelf, he points at the bar-coded shelf label and shoots a laser beam that scans the label and confirms the product choice. When the order is complete, the machine sends a radio signal back to the warehouse's main computer to update inventories and invoice the retail customer. Adoption of this technology has

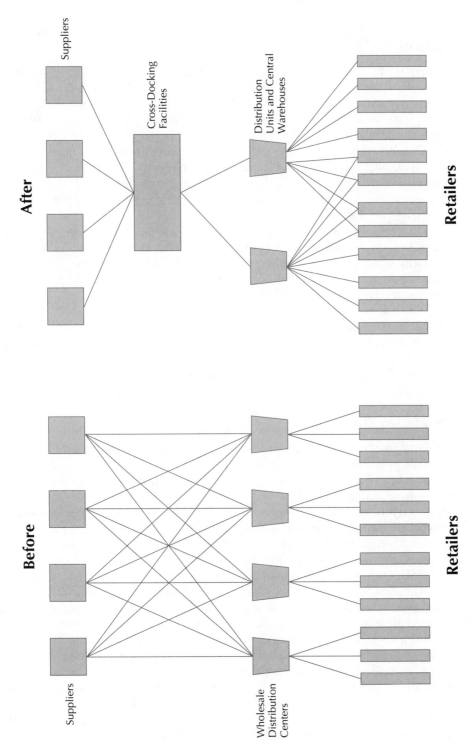

FIGURE 9-2 Cross-Docking at ICA.
Source: Hugh Carnegy, "Changes in Store at the Grocery," *Financial Times*, July 8, 1994, p. 10.

resulted in a 70% decline in order-filling errors and increases in order-fillers' productivity.[38]

INVENTORY FLOW CHANGES IN AIRLINES AND AUTOS   The airline industry uses its computer reservation systems (CRS) not only to check departure times and issue tickets, but also to manage the inventory of seats on any given flight. Almost 30 different fares are available on a Boeing 747 transatlantic flight. Airline pricing managers constantly seek the right balance between higher air fares and empty seats. The CRS lets them change fares daily—or even more frequently if necessary—and even leads airlines to switch jets to new routes if demand increases. American Airlines claims that one extra passenger on every flight would add $114 million to revenues and close to that amount in profits. Hence, precise inventory management of airline seats has a sizeable payoff.[39]

In 1994 J. D. Power & Associates launched a national computer network that provides daily reports to automobile dealers as well as manufacturers about what cars, with what options, are selling where, and for how much money. The database compiles 60 pieces of information on every transaction, and includes statistically meaningful samples by brand and region. The system even reveals per-vehicle profit, to inform sellers whether vehicles are selling because they are "hot" or simply because they are being sold at a discount or even a loss. Interest rates on car loans, the residential locations of buyers, and the relative profitability of leases versus vehicle sales are also included in the database. The goal is to help the auto channel reduce overall inventories even while improving selection in any given regional area.[40]

Promotion Flow

The combination of demographic and purchase data into one integrated database creates a powerful tool to improve the effectiveness of promotional efforts in the channel. Direct-mail marketers have for many years used these databases to decide to whom to send catalogs; how frequently to send them; which catalogs to send to which buyers; and how to organize merchandise on catalog pages. Today, electronically based promotional techniques are moving to other channels with great success. These promotional efforts would not be possible without information technologies, and the data to go with them, that permit channel members to identify and reach ever-more finely tuned segments of end-users.

Catalina Marketing sells its services to retailers who connect the company's computer to the supermarket's scanners. On the basis of what consumers buy, the Catalina system issues coupons at the checkout counter. These can be designed to get shoppers to try brands different from those currently purchased or to try related products. Thus, a Lean Cuisine buyer might get a coupon for a free sixth frozen dinner with the purchase of five others. Further, if a manufacturer issues coupons to buyers of competitors' products, Catalina generates data on how many of each competitor's products were sold—a good measure of relative brand strength. The manufacturer gets even more information from discovering the relative proportion of rival A's customers who switch to its brand because of the coupon, compared to the proportion of rival B's customers who switch. Switchers can then be issued further coupons to induce them to reuse the new brand. The net outcome of "electronic marketing" is a finely targeted way to promote through the grocery distribution channel.[41]

In a related promotional strategy, Vons Supermarkets in California offers a VonsClub card that gives automatic discounts on selected items in the grocery store. Shoppers simply give their cards to checkout clerks and instantly get electronic discounts on promoted items. Manufacturers pay Vons an 8-cent handling fee for each electronic coupon. (By contrast, paper coupons' handling fees must be split with a coupon clearinghouse.) Vons also uses the data it collects about Vons-Club shoppers to cluster them into 200 segments to whom targeted promotions are mailed. Packaged-goods manufacturers select the segments they wish to target and pay Vons to send laser-printed discount coupons to them. For example, Mc-Cormick & Co. sends coupons for its Cake Mate cake decorations only to those who have previously bought cake mixes. Beech-Nut identifies every VonsClub member who had purchased a baby product in the previous eight weeks, and can issue differentially higher-value coupons to Gerber customers than to Beech-Nut customers to induce switching.[42]

Manufacturers can also promote and sell their products through interactive multimedia-based kiosks. Zanussi, a white-goods producer (i.e., stoves, ovens, refrigerators, dishwashers, etc.) in Europe, has increased sales and brand awareness by installing interactive point-of-sale kiosks in 600 appliance stores in Great Britain. A Danish real estate agency has increased its market share from 15 to 23% by installing a point-of-sale kiosk in its outlets. And Sears Roebuck in the United States plans to cut thousands of staff and replace them with interactive multimedia ordering kiosks.[43] Many manufacturers also use interactive kiosks as promotional tools at trade shows. And at Heathrow Airport, an interactive shopping service called Galleria 21 offers touch-screen shopping and one-week delivery almost anywhere in the world for products by Bally of Switzerland, Waterford Crystal, and Burberry, among others.

The major impact of these new promotional tools is not to fully supplant more traditional promotional techniques, but to offer more finely targeted ways to reach a company's highest-potential customers or to increase awareness among potential customers.

Negotiation Flow

Intrachannel-member negotiations have also changed as a result of the adoption and use of various information technologies. Because of the automation of many purchasing functions, less manual attention needs to be paid to purchasing paperwork. More time can be spent on looking for good terms and conditions, and negotiating them with prospective suppliers. International Network Services (INS), Europe's biggest supplier of EDI services, estimates that the proportion of time purchasing departments spend on creating and pushing through paperwork has been cut from 80% to 20%—and that 20% is spent mainly on exceptions to the usual purchasing rules. The newly freed-up time can be spent negotiating better deals with suppliers.[44]

Another change in negotiation patterns arising from the use of information systems is the ability of both manufacturers and retailers to use hard-performance data to negotiate contracts. Such tools as direct product profitability (discussed in Chapter 10) let retailers judge which products should or should not remain on their shelves; it is up to manufacturers to prove to retailers that their products deserve retail shelf space. Conversely, the emerging ability of manufacturers to compare different retailers' performance selling their products gives them the information they need to negotiate merchandising and placement terms. As always, the best products for the target market will tend to get the best placement and generate the best sales; but instead of these decisions being made qualitatively, information systems permit them to be negotiated quantitatively.

Risking Flow

The adoption of uniform universal price codes (UPC) bar codes for merchandise, along with the use of EDI technologies, has given manufacturers and retailers a powerful tool to decrease production risk. Big retailers like J.C. Penney provide suppliers with up-to-date sales and inventory information so that they can better plan their production runs. Penney's system even turns out six-month forecasts for manufacturers like Levi Strauss to help them plan further in advance.[45] With such forecasting ability, it is less likely that manufacturers or retailers will be "stuck" with inventory that cannot sell at the end of a season.

Sport Obermeyer, a maker of ski wear, has used information technology and statistical methods to improve its production decisions and reduce the risks of either out-of-stocks or markdowns. In the mid-1980s the company found that its supply chain was lengthening, a critical problem in a fashion industry where forecasts are difficult and uncertain. It took steps to shorten delays in production by computerizing order-processing and computation of raw-materials requirements. It began early acquisition and storage of raw materials with long lead times. It started the "Early Write" program to encourage retailers to place orders for skiwear early, building participation to 20% of Sport Obermeyer's total sales.

But even with these steps, stockouts and markdowns were on the increase. The company began to use the forecasts of its "buying committee," a group of managers from various functional areas in the company, to estimate future demand. By taking independent forecasts from each member of the committee, the company discovered a positive relationship between the variance of their forecasts and the accuracy of the mean forecast in predicting future sales (that is, the greater was the variance in the committee members' forecasts, the less accurate the mean forecast was). It could then use this information to *differentially* speculate on the inventory of only those styles whose forecasts had a low variance—that is, of those styles for which the mean was a good predictor of future sales. By selectively speculating and selectively postponing its inventory decisions, Sport Obermeyer could reduce costs by about 2% of sales. Because profits in this industry average only 3% of sales, this represented a very significant profitability increase.[46]

Electronic technologies can also decrease financial risk in the channel. A satellite-linked used-car auction network called Aucnet is used by over 3,000 dealers in

Japan. The dealers buy and sell 3,500 used cars per week, which constitutes some 5% of the country's used-car sales. Data on the cars, including still photographic images, are sent to dealers' personal computers via satellite. Bidders use joysticks to register their bids with a central host computer. The system lets dealers trade cars while sitting in their offices instead of physically bringing the cars to a designated area to sell. The potential seller minimizes the risk of losing the money invested in bringing the car to the central auction location if the car does not actually sell. Sellers also get the benefit of keeping the cars on their lots until buyers actually appear. Aucnet managers minimize participants' risk of buying a "lemon" by rigorously inspecting and evaluating each used car using an established standard.[47]

One last interesting implication of the adoption of EDI technologies to better manage the channel has to do with those channel members who do not choose to adopt these technologies. For example, retailers like Wal-Mart who use EDI to force their suppliers to deliver inventory at specified times and in specified quantities essentially move inventory risk up the channel. This risk is not decreased in toto in the channel unless *all* channel members invest in the technology and adopt quick-response techniques to minimize work-in-process throughout the channel. For manufacturers to share in the risk reductions, however, retailers must share data and information systems with them to permit them to plan and execute their production runs efficiently. Without this sort of channel cooperation, zero suboptimization (see Chapter 4) throughout the channel is impossible.

Payment Flow

Finally, the channel cost of payment flows is also falling, thanks to the adoption of electronic payment and ordering systems. Because payments to a supplier can be made electronically with an EDI system, less paperwork is generated and personnel costs fall. Electronic funds transfers can even be automated, so that payment occurs when a shipment is received without any human intervention at all. More indirectly, routinizing payments makes it possible to bill customers less frequently (e.g., monthly instead of with each transaction), generating economies of scale in the payment process.

In the U.S., more than 35 million invoices were paid electronically in 1993, a 59% increase over 1992. Chevron U.S.A., for example, targeted its large vendors for an automated payments system and now makes more than 5,800 electronic payments monthly to its suppliers, almost 14% of the checks it once wrote. Electronic payments still make up less than 1% of all checks corporations write annually, but the number is on the increase. Companies save about 75 cents each time they do not write and process a check through their payment systems. Electronic payments confer the added advantage of knowing exactly when payment will be made, which increases the firm's flexibility in managing its cash reserves. Even the U.S. federal government makes electronic payments, in excess of $300 billion per year, to its suppliers.[48]

Although overall channel costs decrease with the use of electronic payment systems, the biggest losers may be the banks: nonbank payment houses are taking away much of their business. For example, a group of health-insurance companies have used Eli Lilly's PCS Inc. unit to set up an electronic information network to automate the processing of medical claims for payment. The ultimate goal is the automatic filing of claims against patients' health insurance when patients present their medical credit cards to cashiers at the doctors' offices or hospitals, rather than the current system of paper forms and manual keying in of charges. Were such a system to be adopted throughout the entire U.S. health care system, estimates of savings run as high as $20 billion per year.[49]

▶ IMPACT OF INFORMATION SYSTEMS ON CHANNEL POWER, CONFLICT, COORDINATION, AND COOPERATION

The development and use of information systems in distribution channels has significantly changed the way channel members interact with each other, while opening up opportunities for great gains in channel productivity. In this section we examine the changes in power endowments and uses among channel members, conflict issues arising from the use of channel information systems, and opportunities these systems provide for increased channel coordination and cooperation.

Impact of Channel Information Systems on the Possession and Use of Power

Many industry experts agree that the adoption of channel information systems, such as POS and EDI systems in the grocery and apparel industries, has shifted power away from manufacturers and toward retailers who directly serve the customer.[50] Retailers have a natural advantage in the use of marketing database information, because they can directly measure consumer response to products, promotions, and other marketing mix elements. The possession of this information naturally confers expert power on them, which is used not only to choose among different brands of products to stock in their stores, but also to develop and market their own-label brands (further reinforcing their power vis-à-vis upstream suppliers). For example, J. Sainsbury, the British retailer, keeps its scanner data research private and uses it to promote its own brands. And in turn, its brand image has given it referent power in its dealings with private-label suppliers.

Thus, it is not surprising that retailers have been in the forefront in the adoption of electronic technology to support channel information systems and have used their increased power to influence the actions of upstream suppliers. To make a quick response system work, the retailer needs its suppliers to adopt EDI technology so that orders can be electronically sent and quickly filled, invoice payment can be automated, and inventory holding can be minimized. Suppliers are not always anxious to adopt a technology they see as adding cost to their operations but no tangible short-term benefits. The retailer must use reward or coercive power to induce vendors to adopt the new methods. For example, Sears Roebuck first tried a low-key approach to encourage its suppliers to adopt EDI technology, working with Andersen Consulting to help with training and software adoption. But fewer than half of Sears' vendors signed on. It turned from this reward power approach to a coercive one, imposing strict deadlines for EDI adoption by the end of 1992.[51] Tesco, the British grocery retailer and a very early adopter of EDI, has also been accused of threatening to cut off suppliers who do not adopt its technology. Tesco management argues that its approach is not "bullying," but rather driving the business toward the future with up-to-date technologies.[52]

Although the adoption of channel information systems technologies may decrease total channel costs, the reluctance of suppliers to use them implies either that they are less educated in their benefits or that retailers are pocketing a disproportionately large portion of the net channel benefits for themselves. This possibility raises the question of what channel conflicts can arise from the adoption and spread of channel information-systems technology. We turn next to this question.

Channel Conflict Issues and Channel Information Systems

The major types of conflict that can arise between channel members as a result of use of channel information systems are goal conflict and perception-of-reality conflict. Although domain conflict could potentially arise as a result of the adoption of channel information systems, it has not been as widely observed as the first two kinds of conflict. The reluctance of retailers' suppliers to adopt EDI technology described above suggests the possibility of goal conflict. These suppliers believe the benefits of using the EDI system would not outweigh its expense: in short, they think it would decrease their profitability. For example, when instituting a continuous replenishment system, suppliers must wait until inventory held in the channel pipeline sells off before they can expect their first orders under the new system. They must also ship in small lots more frequently. All of these are negative consequences of changing over to an EDI system.

In a slightly different vein, Apollo Travel Services dropped Southwest Airlines from its Apollo airline-reservations system in May 1994, arguing that Southwest did not pay the booking fees of about $2.50 per ticket that other airlines routinely pay to be listed in the systems. This had not previously been a problem when Southwest (like other small carriers) was too small to be a major competitor. With Southwest's success, however, the airline alleged that Apollo (of which United Airlines and USAir are owners) purposely dropped them from the reservations system to inhibit their ability to compete. However, other airline reservations systems at the same time stopped listing Southwest as well, citing cost factors and the inequity of listing and ticketing Southwest flights at no cost when other competitors pay booking fees for the privilege. Southwest's goal is clearly to minimize cost, and the cost of joining all the major U.S. systems is estimated at $100 to $125 million, a figure that would wipe out its profits.[53] But other airlines and reservations systems also wish to maximize profit, and writing Southwest tickets at zero cost is inconsistent with that goal. Southwest must decide whether it can provide adequate service output levels to its consumers without participating in the computerized reservations systems.

Also significant is the potential for differing perceptions of reality when channel members start to use channel information systems. The results of a poll of grocery retailers, wholesalers, and manufacturers[54] on the benefits and effects of effi-

TABLE 9-4 **Perceptions of the Benefits of ECR in the Grocery Industry**

WHO WILL BENEFIT FROM ECR?

(Table shows percentage of respondents saying ECR will help the sector in question "a lot.")

BENEFICIARIES	CHAIN EXECUTIVE RESPONDENTS (%)	WHOLESALER EXECUTIVE RESPONDENTS (%)	MANUFACTURER RESPONDENTS (%)	AVERAGE (%)
Manufacturers	44	63	33	47
Chains	34	44	51	43
Wholesalers	22	15	20	19
Consumers	21	14	24	20
Brokers	11	6	9	9
Independents	3	6	9	6

Table can be read as follows: 44% of chain executives; 63% of wholesaler executives; and 33% of manufacturers said that manufacturers would benefit from ECR.

TRACKING THE POWER SHIFT

(Table shows percentage of respondents saying there was a power shift, and of those responding "Yes," which way power shifted.)

PERCENTAGE SAYING:	POWER SHIFT		WHICH WAY?	
	No (%)	Yes (%)	Toward Retailers (%)	Toward Manufacturers (%)
Chains	41	59	72	28
Manufacturers	27	73	86	14

Source: "Does ECR Spell a New Era?" *Progressive Grocer*, April 1994, pp. 22–25.

cient consumer response technologies are shown in Table 9-4. It is interesting that every class of channel member surveyed believed that its own level would experience the *least* (even though still positive in an absolute sense) benefits from ECR! It appears that a "grass is always greener on the other side of the fence" mentality prevails when it comes to evaluating the benefits of information technology adoption. Also evident from the results is a large discrepancy between manufacturers' and retailers' perceptions of power shifts from one level to the other: 73% of manufacturers, compared to only 59% of retailers, believe power is shifting. Of these, 72% of retail grocery-chain managers, but fully 86% of manufacturers, believe that power is shifting toward retailers.

Vlosky and Wilson[55] formalize these concerns in a model of the impact of information systems adoption on buyer–seller relationships in a channel. They study the adoption of the UPC bar-coding system in the wood products industry. Figures 9-3(a) and 9-3(b) summarize their view of the potential disruption in channel relationships. As Figure 9-3(a) shows, relationship disruption is a time-dependent phe-

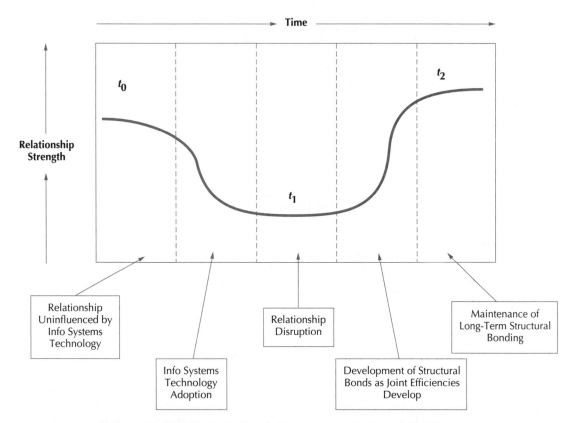

FIGURE 9-3A **Channel information technology influence on buyer–seller relationships.**
Source: Richard P. Vlosky and David T. Wilson, "Technology Adoption in Channels: Short-Term Pain and Long-Term Gain," Presentation at Second Research Conference on Relationship Marketing, June 12, 1994.

nomenon, reaching its maximum shortly after the information system is adopted and eventually improving with the development of structural bonds between the channel members and the maintenance of those bonds over the long term. Figure 9-3(b) shows exactly how the relationship is disrupted in the first place: through the creation of various gaps between desired and actual relationship satisfaction. Gaps are created through factors that lead to perception-of-reality conflicts (e.g., unmet expectations of support and value creation) and are mitigated through the building and maintenance of trust and stability in power-dependence relations. In their empirical investigation, they find support for the existence of short-term relationship disequilibrium as a result of adoption of a channel information system, due to differences in buyer–supplier perceptions of (a) interdependence between channel members; (b) value to the other partner of the information system; and (c) the potential for conflict as a result of information system adoption.

Channel conflicts are likely to arise whenever a significant channel investment is to be made that will benefit parties other than the one making the expenditure. This is certainly true of the adoption of channel information systems. If the current

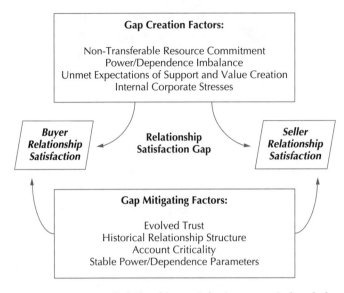

Gap Creation Factors:

Non-Transferable Resource Commitment
Power/Dependence Imbalance
Unmet Expectations of Support and Value Creation
Internal Corporate Stresses

| *Buyer Relationship Satisfaction* | Relationship Satisfaction Gap | *Seller Relationship Satisfaction* |

Gap Mitigating Factors:

Evolved Trust
Historical Relationship Structure
Account Criticality
Stable Power/Dependence Parameters

FIGURE 9-3B Relationship satisfaction gap induced by adoption of channel information technology.
Source: Richard P. Vlosky and David T. Wilson, "Technology Adoption in Channels: Short-Term Pain and Long-Term Gain," Presentation at Second Research Conference on Relationship Marketing, June 12, 1994.

beliefs about the benefits of such systems are true, these conflicts are a transitory phenomenon that will be resolved as the long-term benefits to all parties are revealed. Competitive pressures will also force channel members to adopt new technologies to preserve their position in the channel, as we already see in the refusal of Wal-Mart to deal with any supplier who does not use EDI technology. One of the solutions to potential channel conflicts is to work toward channel coordination and to adopt superordinate goals through the use of information technology. We discuss this possibility below.

Channel Information Systems: Opportunities for Channel Coordination and Cooperation

The adoption of channel information systems, like any fundamental change in channel management tools, shakes up the channel system and opens up opportunities for better coordination among its members. However, the full benefits a channel information system has to offer can *only* be enjoyed if the channel members involved cooperate with each other in the best interests of the whole channel, instead of pursuing their own narrow interests. This is so because the full exploitation of the benefits of information technology requires the sharing of the information acquired to help all channel members minimize the costs of providing adequate service output levels to the targeted segments of consumers. Fortunately, we now see many instances where the adoption of a channel information system itself heightens channel members' awareness that the pursuit of superordinate goals, not individual ones, will maximize the benefits of the system. We illustrate these points with some examples here.

Grocery manufacturers and retailers are moving from the mere desire to control and analyze large databases to the realization that cooperation enhances the productivity of that information. Although retailers may have increased their power relative to manufacturers (as detailed in Chapter 2) due to their superior access to point-of-sale data, manufacturers press for greater data interchange to improve the efficiency of the manufacturing-level operations as well. An Andersen Consulting study argues that the challenge of the 1990s will be to go beyond the adoption of EDI technologies, to attack inefficiencies at the manufacturing end through greater information exchange from the retail end of the channel. The study emphasizes the need for transparency and trust between channel partners for such an interchange to work: retailers need to trust sensitive sales data to manufacturers, and manufacturers must commit to tight delivery times for retailers and open up their operations to retailer scrutiny in return.[56] In the U.S., retailers like Kmart already see the benefits of sharing POS data with suppliers; for example, when West Bend began an EDI partnership with Kmart, the retailer shared two years' worth of prior sales data so that West Bend could more accurately plan its production levels. West Bend's management was more willing to adapt to Kmart's business methods when it was given the ammunition to meet the retailer's demands more efficiently.[57]

Baxter Healthcare's ValueLink program also requires close coordination between the hospital supply distributor and its hospital customers if the benefits of "stockless distribution" are to work. Under the ValueLink program, Baxter promises to deliver all of a hospital's supplies on a just-in-time basis, in ready-to-use packages, to each department in the hospital. This system obviates the need for a hospital supplies management area or personnel. Underlying the system's success is the notion that total system efficiency increases when the distributor takes on inventory and distribution functions in return for purchase commitments and data sharing on the part of the customer. A sophisticated database of all prior purchases can be used to forecast future hospital needs with great precision, reducing the need for large inventories of supplies and decreasing systemwide costs.

But the system implies ever-increasing levels of interdependence between Baxter and its hospital customer, as on the one hand the customer commits to Baxter as its prime (or even sole) source of supply, while on the other hand, Baxter commits to a 100% fill rate (no out-of-stocks!) and customized daily deliveries to all hospital departments. The cement that holds the partners to this level of coordination is the financial benefits it generates: for example, Presbyterian Hospital of Dallas, Texas garnered a one-time savings of $2.5 million, and expects annual savings of $650,000 over the lifetime of its five-year contract with Baxter, whereas Baxter will get $75 million in sales over the same period from the hospital.[58]

Glazer hypothesizes that more information-intensive firms are more likely to have as one of their strategic objectives maximizing the number of transactions with the same, loyal customers through sales of an ever-more diverse set of products.[59] He also hypothesizes that such firms are more likely to be involved in strategic alliances, to maximize the use of information and knowledge created in these organizations. Apparel industry firms have acted consistently with these hypotheses by creating several voluntary organizations involving members from different channel levels. One such organization is TALC, the Textile and Apparel Linkage Council. The group has set its main goals by establishing standards for width/length measurement, identification of fabric defects, and EDI data transmission, among other issues. The ultimate goal of all these organizations is to facilitate the adoption of quick-reponse technologies at all levels of the industry, therefore generating common benefits for all channel members.[60]

In some cases, the adoption of superordinate goals is more likely because the adoption of channel information systems erects exit barriers from the channel relationship. Not only may the one-time costs of adoption be significant, but switching costs are increased when channel partners invest in learning each other's operations and information systems. A source firm may thus seek an EDI relationship with a target firm in its channel not only for the sake of the efficiencies it may generate, but also because it serves to tie the target firm more closely to the source firm and makes it more likely that the target firm will see a junction between its own and the source firm's interests.[61] In the U.S., Procter & Gamble even recruits new sales managers by telling them that their job success will be measured on their ability to generate profits for both P&G and its retail customers. One P&G vice president managing the company's relationship with Wal-Mart said: "Historically, it was a question of how do I transfer as much of my cost as possible to the retailers and they were asking the same about us. No one understood how much their moves were costing others."[62]

▶ IMPACT OF CHANNEL INFORMATION SYSTEMS ON CHANNEL ROLE PERFORMANCE

Channel information systems have changed the way all channel members perform their jobs. Not only have they improved productivity at all levels, but they have permitted channel functions and flows to be allocated to the organization best suited to perform them, rather than in the organization that benefits most directly from them. Below we examine changes in the roles played by manufacturers, retailers, and wholesalers.

Changing Roles of Manufacturers

Before the widespread use of electronic channel information systems, manufacturers typically specialized in strictly manufacturing functions. It was more cost-efficient to spin off distribution functions to independent distributors, whose activities included the efficient handling and delivery of inventory and invoicing and payment functions with buyers. But powerful databases now permit manufacturers to predict demand more accurately, thus lessening the need for an extra channel member to hold safety stocks of inventory. EDI technologies make it easy for manufacturers to take back the ordering and payment functions formerly spun off to distributors.

Manufacturers can also assume some functions historically allocated to retailers. If retailers are willing to share point-of-sale data with their vendors, manufacturers can combine this with other marketing intelligence information to deliver inventory with very short lead times. Lee Apparel Co., the maker of denim and knit clothing, has taken this process one step further and actually manages the Lee clothes departments at several J.C. Penney stores. By controlling the flow of product through the entire channel, Lee plans on cutting production-cycle time by 40%, inventories by 30%, and production costs by 20%. The benefit to Penney's is reduced out-of-stocks and better merchandise management.[63]

Within the manufacturing firm, sales force roles have also changed due to advances in the use of channel information systems. One effect has been the strengthening of internal linkages between the sales force and other areas of the firm, such as marketing and engineering. Goodyear's field-sales representatives now use an account management and sales information system that instantly informs them of the current state of a customer's billing, orders, or delivery. The system links the reps to a central database and electronic mail system that is shared by other divisions of the company, so that the sales force shares access to data with marketing support people. Reps can use marketing support, for example, to help them design promotions or discounts for a dealer planning a grand-opening sale without the time delay of communicating by telephone or memos. Another firm, Polymer Technology Corp., uses an automated sales system to link together its sales, telemarketing, marketing, and customer service functions. Sales reps in the field use laptop computers to access the same central database used by the other marketing people back at headquarters.[64]

Channel information systems also improve sales force productivity and aid in internal cost control. There are about 8 million salespeople in the U.S., and with the average sales call costing more than $200, there is a strong incentive to improve the chances of those sales calls producing actual sales. The U.S. sales force automation market was about $1 billion in 1993 and is forecast to reach $2.7 billion in annual sales by 1997. Some of the applications of sales force automation systems include:[65]

- A new information network at John Deere's Power Systems division gives salespeople quick access to customer data that is used to prepare for a sales call.

- At the drug company, Dendrite International Inc., a database is used to help sales reps determine the highest-potential doctors to call on with information on a new product.

- Perkin-Elmer Corporation has created a "virtual office" for its sales force, giving its 200-plus North American salespeople powerful laptop computers and greater access to information.

- Hindustan Lever, India's largest consumer-goods company and an affiliate of Unilever, uses a computerized mapping system to plan supplies to rural areas and to plan sales routes more effectively. "Stockists," self-employed wholesalers who usually work exclusively for Hindustan Lever, visit outlets weekly in urban areas and fortnightly in rural areas, carrying goods by van, scooter, or even elephant. They file hand-written sales reports that are fed into the company's computer. The information gives head office managers information about local, rural markets that would otherwise be impossible to track and use.[66]

Salesforce automation systems can also be used to improve incentives for better salesforce performance. IBM gives its salespeople a new information system that reveals the margins on various products the company sells—previously a closely guarded secret in the company. This information lets the salespeople prioritize their efforts to maximize profits for the company, not just sales. IBM reinforced this incentive by tying 60% of 1994 salesforce pay to profits and the remaining 40% to customer satisfaction. This is a drastic change from 1993, when 20% of pay was tied to profits, and 1992, when the figure was just 6%. The strong dependence of total pay to profitability is only workable when salespeople themselves understand how their performance will map into pay, so the use of the new information system is key in implementing the incentive shift.[67]

Changing Roles of Retailers

New retail roles emerging as a result of more advanced channel information systems include mass customization, taking on payment functions previously fulfilled by middlemen, and collapsing the buying function through the use of EDI linkages directly to suppliers. The first trend, mass customization, is epitomized by the "apparel on demand" industry springing up in the U.S. It links domestic retailers with domestic manufacturers and gives consumers the ability to buy custom clothing at less than designer prices. The concept could save as much as 30% in total channel costs by reducing the need for inventory or markdowns. In 1994 Sung Park launched such a business, called Custom Clothing Technology Corp. (CCTC), which offers customized women's jeans priced at $48 and deliverable in less than two weeks. The operation is a virtual company, operating out of Park's home in Boston. Customers are electronically measured and select their preferred style of jeans in a store contracting for CCTC's just-in-time service. The jeans are cut in Vermont, sewn in Texas, and shipped directly to the customer. This trend makes the standard retailer more of an order-taker than an inventory-stocker and location to shop for goods.[68]

Retailers' use of electronic databases also permits them to take on payment functions previously filled by middlemen. Detroit-based Frank's Nursery & Crafts stores use a satellite system to link them directly with Visa USA Inc. Credit card charges are now authorized in just seven seconds, down from 45 seconds with standard phone connections to a credit-reporting agency. Savings on agency fees were so great that they paid for the $4 million satellite system.[69]

Some retail functions simply disappear with the use of electronic information systems. One Massachusetts retailer, Designs Inc., sells clothes made only by Levi Strauss & Co. They have no formal buying department at all; instead, a team of six people led by the retailer's president handles all the buying (in contrast to the buying departments of department stores, which can have hundreds of people). Design's cash registers are connected to Levi directly through the LeviLink automated inventory system, so routine inventory needs are met automatically with no human intervention. Levi ships directly to Designs stores, so that there is no need for warehouses or distribution centers. Designs even benefits from Levi's advertising, because its stores sell only Levi clothes.[70]

Changing Roles of Wholesalers

Given the changes occurring at the manufacturing and retailing levels due to the adoption and ever-increasing sophistication of channel information systems, the pressing question seems to be: what will the role of the wholesaler be in the future? As discussed in Chapter 3, standard wholesaling functions are being squeezed from both below and above in the channel. Various nonwholesalers are taking on traditional wholesaling roles in different channel situations. In the travel industry, for example, travel agents have historically been the intermediary through whom most travelers bought airline tickets. Travel agents still sell about 80% of the airline tickets written in the United States, but it is becoming easier and easier for corporate buyers to book their own reservations over the phone or through on-line computer services. Airlines are, of course, pleased to cut down on the commissions paid to the agents. An Arthur D. Little study predicts that by the year 2000, interactive airline ticketing systems could supplant 20 to 30% of agency sales. In this climate, it is up to the wholesalers to make themselves indispensable. They are using innovative techniques to do this, and in some cases even creating new channel members in the process.[71]

Singapore's TradeNet EDI network was described above, and constitutes the use of an electronic channel information system to increase the desirability of using Singapore as a port of call in the international distribution of goods. The country has linked the TradeNet system with analogous systems in the United States and in the port of Rotterdam in the Netherlands. Singapore's status as an EDI leader has created a new channel role for it: as consultant to other countries wishing to connect to global electronic trade networks.[72] Thus, a channel intermediary's investment in the most advanced information technologies can confer a competitive advantage on it and preserve its role as a viable wholesaler in the distribution channel.

New channel members are even arising to augment traditional distributor functions as EDI and other electronically based channel information systems penetrate distribution channels. For example, the firm Management Technology Inc. (MTI) sets up EDI systems for distributors interested in reducing their billing cycle times and increasing their inventory turns. One distributor credits the MTI system with saving it 20% on costs. After selling the original software into a distributor firm, MTI can then sell follow-up maintenance and updates worth as much as 40% of the original software purchase price.[73]

EDI service providers are springing up elsewhere as well. International Network Services of Great Britain is the biggest U.K.-based EDI services provider. Its customers include 78 of the top 100 U.K. companies, nine of the top ten retailers, the ten largest pharmaceutical companies, 17 of the top 20 nonlife insurers, 10 regional health authorities, and 4 clearing banks. Client companies use these services because they can direct electronic mail to the right recipient and also are capable of translating data between different computers or message standards.[74] And in the

U.S., companies like Vendor Logistics Services of Itasca, Illinois, supply bar-coding for small-to-medium size manufacturers who are required to use bar codes for sales into the electronic networks of large retailers like Kmart. The use of these bar codes for virtually all the stockkeeping units at a Kmart means the elimination of much of the warehousing and other logistical expenses that used to plague the retailer. And the small manufacturer spends less money using an outside firm like Vendor Logistics Services than it would bringing into its factories bar-coding technology on its own.[75]

Although standard wholesalers' functions and roles are being assailed on all sides in the channel, it seems clear that there are still many opportunities for the state-of-the-art wholesaler to prosper in today's advanced channel management environment. The aggressive use of IT tools, sometimes provided by new outside suppliers, is necessary to ensure the wholesaler's position in the channel. Manufacturers' and retailers' increased focus on and use of outsourcing (discussed in detail in Chapter 6) will continue to provide wholesalers with the opportunity to add significant value in the channel through their abilities to consolidate and routinize functions otherwise performed by each manufacturer or retailer separately.

▶ SUMMARY AND CONCLUSIONS

Advances in information technology in distribution have changed the entire landscape of channel management over the past decade. The new technologies themselves are fascinating and account for expenditures in the hundreds of millions of dollars annually. But what these technologies do to the management and coordination of the channel is absolutely fundamental: they cause channel members to look to one another in a synergistic way rather than in a competitive way. They change the nature of the channel game from zero-sum to positive-sum: the more data sharing and joint technology development channel members engage in, the greater the benefits to all will be:

> The adoption of an EDI linkage . . . is significantly different from the adoption of an innovative internal technology. EDI produces changes in the exchange relationship between the participating firms that have implications for both the internal economy and polity of the channel. The establishment of a sophisticated computer linkage between firms reflects a significant commitment to the relationship. Discrete transactions are subsumed in the creation of a long-term, complex relational exchange. Such linkage requires attention not only to the efficiency effects of the technology, but also to the effect it will have on the business relationship between the parties.[76]

Although the full advantages of EDI technologies have yet to be enjoyed, the trend is clearly in the direction of ever-increasing usefulness. Fortunately, with the greater use of electronic information technologies, the consumer is typically a winner as well, as the drop in systemwide costs is generally accompanied by an actual increase (or at worst, maintenance) of the quality of service outputs. The major potential losers are those channel members who do not adopt channel information sys-

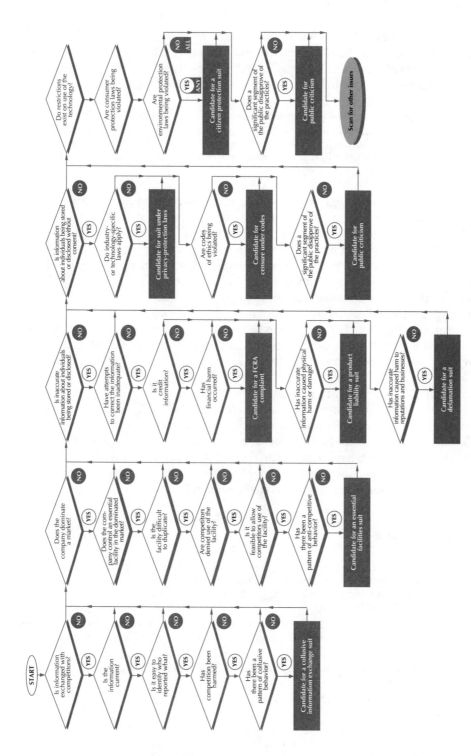

FIGURE 9-4 Question sequence for identifying legal and societal problems resulting from using information technologies.

Source: Paul N. Bloom, George R. Milne, and Robert Adler, "Avoiding Misuse of New Information Technologies: Legal and Societal Considerations," *Journal of Marketing*, Vol. 58 (January 1994), p. 106.

tems and thus fall behind the technology curve set in their industry. These firms will find it increasingly hard to compete and ultimately may be forced out of business as the use of electronic systems for everything from inventory management to invoicing becomes the norm, rather than a competitive edge.

> As with many technological innovations, the primary purpose for implementation of EDI may quickly become the status quo, with lasting competitive effects being derived from more subtle processes. The expected cost savings that have provided the impetus needed to spur EDI development will be duplicated throughout the competitive environment.[77]

It should be mentioned that there are some legal concerns with the unfettered spread of electronic information technologies in our distribution channels. Bloom et al.[78] profile various problems that can arise, including participating in collusive information exchanges, storing or transmitting inaccurate or harmful information, and violating consumers' privacy. Because the legality of some practices is still not firmly established one way or another, the authors provide a detailed checklist of questions that can be answered to highlight possible trouble areas facing the channel using EDI technology, consumer demographic and purchase data, and the like, reproduced in Figure 9-4. It remains to be seen whether any of these practices will be deemed illegal by the courts of the U.S., although there are already significant privacy concerns in other countries that make the sale and use of mailing lists problematic.

Finally, it is important to point out that the acquisition and implementation of channel information systems is not a panacea in and of itself. These systems must be used efficiently, with maximal data sharing among different channel members, to optimize their value in the channel. The term "garbage in, garbage out" is particularly appropriate here: these systems do not divest channel members of the responsibility for cooperating with one another and, indeed, bring the cooperative imperative to the forefront of channel management issues.

DISCUSSION QUESTIONS

1. Are electronic channel information systems a means of better organizing existing channel information or of actually improving and expanding the information available to channel members for making decisions? Is there a downside to increasing information flows? If so, what is it?

2. Why have retailers been quicker to implement electronic channel information systems than have channel members further upstream in the channel? Use grocery retailers as an example.

3. What does the concept of an electronic marketing channel mean? How is it different from a standard marketing channel?

4. Why is channel coordination so important to maximizing the benefits from today's channel information systems?

5. Are electronic channel information systems likely to increase or decrease the frequency of verbal communication between channel members? What bearing does the frequency of communication have on the level of channel coordination?

6. In April 1994, a consortium of 20 Silicon Valley companies, backed by $12 million in public monies, launched CommerceNet, a computer network designed both to increase the speed at which purchasing and payment occur and to serve as a testing ground for new ways of trading across Internet and other networks. One application will be a members-only computer store on the network. Eventually, members will be able to offer their own goods for sale over the network. Comment on the implications of CommerceNet for traditional channel management, as well as for competition in the computer industry.

7. It has been predicted that EDI systems would increase channel members' commitment to their interorganizational relationship, because they would require extended contact at various levels of both (or many) channel organizations involved. Do you agree or disagree? Apply a real example to illustrate your answer.

8. Give an example of a commercial situation where information technology has changed channel structure, functions, and/or relationships. Explain exactly which channel flows have been affected and why.

9. It is often stated that "information is power." What has to happen to information before it becomes "powerful"?

10. Use a specific retailing example to describe what power shifts have occurred between manufacturers and retailers in the recent past as a direct result of changes in the way IT is used in channel management. Given what you know about information technology investments by the parties, what would you predict for future power positions of these players?

ENDNOTES

[1]Chris Holland, Geoff Lockett, and Ian Blackman, "Planning for Electronic Data Interchange," *Strategic Management Journal*, Vol. 13 (1992), p. 539.

[2]Christopher Koch, (ed.), "The Power of Interorganizational Systems," *Indications*, Vol. 11 (no. 1, 1994), p. 1.

[3]*Ibid.*

[4]P. A. Strassman, *Information Payoff, The Transformation of Work in the Electronic Age* (New York: The Free Press, 1985).

[5]James E. Short and N. Venkatraman, "Beyond Business Process Redesign: Redefining Baxter's Business Network," *Sloan Management Review*, Fall 1992, p. 8.

[6]Rashi Glazer, "Marketing in an Information-Intensive Environment: Strategic Implications of Knowledge as an Asset," *Journal of Marketing*, Vol. 55 (October 1991), p. 7. See also "Who's Winning the Information Revolution," *Fortune*, November 30, 1992, p. 110.

[7]Janice H. Hammond and Maura G. Kelly, "Quick Response in the Apparel Industry," Harvard Business School No. 9-690-038, April 1991, p. 6.

[8]Ron Winslow, "Four Hospital Suppliers Will Launch Common Electronic Ordering System," *Wall Street Journal*, April 12, 1994, p. B8.

[9]Raymond Snoddy, "Satellite Network for VW Dealers," *Financial Times*, November 29, 1993, p. 17.

[10]Philip Manchester, "Microchip Marketing," *Financial Times*, November 20, 1990, section 4, p. VI.

[11]Gail Roberts, "26 Vons Stores to Get Electronic Shelf Labels," *Supermarket News*, October 18, 1993, pp. 1, 10.

[12]Sofia McFarland, "Supermarket Chains Turn to Satellites to Address Problems," *Wall Street Journal*, June 5, 1992, p. A5D.

[13]See for example Louise Kehoe, "On-Line for a Speedy Sale," *Financial Times*, June 23, 1994, p. 18; and Barbara Marsh, "Peapod's On-Line Grocery Service Checks Out Success," *Wall Street Journal*, June 30, 1994, p. B2.

[14]Nancy Ryan, "Ideas Ring Up Future Supermarkets," *Chicago Tribune*, May 16, 1991, section 3, p. 1.

[15]See "A Hitch-Hiker's Guide," *Economist*, December 25, 1993–January 7, 1994, pp. 35–38; James Coates, "From On-Line Hangout to Data Superhighway," *Chicago Tribune*, January 16, 1994, section 7, pp. 1, 6; "On-Ramps to the Info Superhighway," *Business Week*, February 7, 1994, pp. 108–109; Rick Tetzeli, "The Internet and Your Business," *Fortune*, March 7, 1994, pp. 86–96; and Amy Dunkin, "Ready to Cruise the Internet?" *Business Week*, March 28, 1994, pp. 180–181.

[16]See Jon Van, "Many Alternate Routes to Information Superhighway," *Chicago Tribune*, September 27, 1993, section 4, p. 3; "On-Ramps to the Info Superhighway," *Business Week*, February 7, 1994, p. 109; "The Oracle Speaks," *Economist*, February 19, 1994, pp. 72–73; Alan Cane, "A Whirlwind of Innovation," *Financial Times*, March 23, 1994, p. 2; Neil Buckley, "Reality Catches up with Vision," *Financial Times*, July 22, 1994, p. 10; and "The Interactive Bazaar Opens," *Economist*, August 20, 1994, pp. 49–51.

[17]Rick Tetzeli, "Mapping for Dollars," *Fortune*, October 18, 1993, pp. 91–96.

[18]John W. Verity, "The Gold Mine of Data in Customer Service," *Business Week*, March 21, 1994, pp. 113–114.

[19]Cyndee Miller, "New Battleground Looms for IRI and Nielsen," *Marketing News*, Vol. 28, (April 25, 1994), pp. 1, 3, 10.

[20]Diana Kunde, "Computer Use Stacks the Chips in Frito-Lay's Favor," *Chicago Tribune*, August 9, 1990, section 7, p. 10A.

[21]Victoria Griffith, "Smart Selling to Big Spenders," *Financial Times*, July 1, 1994, p. 16.

[22]See William M. Bulkeley, "Marketers Mine Their Corporate Databases," *Wall Street Journal*, June 14, 1993, p. B6; and Della Bradshaw, "The Science of Shopping," *Financial Times*, October 8, 1993, p. 16.

[23]See Chapter 8 for more discussion on the Merck–Medco relationship and similar ones in other pharmaceutical firms. Also, see Joan O'C. Hamilton and Catherine L. Harris, "For Drug Distributors, Information is the Rx for Survival," *Business Week*, October 14, 1985, p. 116; Ron Winslow and Hilary Stout, "Insurers Select McKesson Unit To Speed Claims," *Wall Street Journal*, July 22, 1992, p. B1; "Mail-Order Pharmacies Mushroom," *Marketing News*, January 18, 1993, p. 3; Elyse Tanouye, "Merck Will Exploit Medco's Database," *Wall Street Journal*, August 4, 1993, p. B1; Russell Mitchell and Joseph Weber, "And the Next Juicy Plum May Be . . . McKesson?" *Business Week*, February 28, 1994, p. 36; and "Days of Revolution," *Economist*, July 2, 1994, pp. 64–65.

[24]J. Hammond and M. Kelly, *Op. cit.*, p. 3.

[25]See, for example, Karen Lowry Miller, "Listening to Shoppers' Voices," *Business Week*, Reinventing America 1992 issue, p. 69; Howard Gleckman et al., "The Technology Payoff," *Business Week*, June 14, 1993, p. 60; and E. Tanouye, *Op. cit.*, p. B1.

[26]See the annual June editions of *Sales and Marketing Management*.

[27]Andrew Fisher, "Speed Is of the Essence," *Financial Times*, August 3, 1993, p. 7.

[28]Larry Donovan, "Wired for Trade in Singapore," *Financial Times*, July 20, 1993, p. 7.

[29]See Sheila Jones, "A Short Life on the Shelf," *Financial Times*, January 28, 1992, p. 26; and Matt Nannery, "Keeping the 'C' in ECR," *Supermarket News*, November 15, 1993.

[30]Faye Rice, "The New Rules of Superlative Service," *Fortune*, Autumn/Winter 1993, p. 51.

[31]C. Koch, (ed.), *Op cit.*, p. 6.

[32]Robert D. Buzzell and Gwen Ortmeyer, "Channel Partnerships: A New Approach to Streamlining Distribution," Marketing Science Institute Report No. 94-104, 1994.

[33]J. Hammond and M. Kelly, *Op. cit.*

[34]Howard Gleckman et al., "The Technology Payoff," *Business Week*, June 14, 1993, pp. 58–59.

[35]Howard Schlossberg, "Info Network Promotes Better Manufacturer–Retailer Logistics," *Marketing News*, January 3, 1994, p. 26.

[36]See Michael J. McCarthy, "Supermarkets Reorganize Distribution To Help Fight K, Wal and Other Marts," *Wall Street Journal*, January 19, 1993, p. B5; and Hugh Carnegy, "Changes in Store at the Grocery," *Financial Times*, July 8, 1994, p. 10.

[37]Thomas A. Stewart, "Brace for Japan's Hot New Strategy," *Fortune*, September 21, 1992, p. 68.

[38]Myron Magnet, "Who's Winning the Information Revolution," *Fortune*, November 30, 1992, p. 111.

[39]See Daniel Green, "Airline Ticket Shops Bridge the Atlantic," *Financial Times*, March 9, 1992, p. 15; Paul Betts, "Biggest Airline Reservations Systems Merge," *Financial Times*, February 2, 1993, p. 17; and Bridget O'Brian, "Giant Reservations System to Dump Southwest," *Wall Street Journal*, April 22, 1994, p. B1.

[40]James Bennet, "A Way for Car Dealers to Squeeze Out the Lemons," *New York Times*, March 6, 1994, business section, p. 11.

[41]M. Magnet, *Op. cit.*, p. 112.

[42]Larry Armstrong, "Coupon Clippers, Save Your Scissors," *Business Week*, June 20, 1994, pp. 164-166. Parenthetically, we would expect that if *all* retailers introduced their own proprietary couponing and database systems, manufacturers might find it prohibitively hard to use the mountains of data coming out of incompatible systems. There is thus an important role for companies like IRI or A.C. Nielsen to play, because they can compile data from many supermarkets or many cities for a manufacturer's use.

[43]Peter Lloyd, "Expectations Are High," *Financial Times*, September 21, 1993, section 3, p.VII.

[44]John Kavanagh, "Start of a World Free from Paper," *Financial Times*, June 23, 1992, special section, p. 6.

[45]M. Magnet, *Op. cit.*, p. 112.

[46]Marshall L. Fisher, Janice H. Hammond, Walter R. Obermeyer, and Ananth Raman, "Making Supply Meet Demand in an Uncertain World," *Harvard Business Review*, May–June 1994, pp. 83–93.

[47]Emiko Terazono, "Satellite Sales," *Financial Times*, July 15, 1994, p. 10.

[48]Fred R. Bleakley, "Electronic Payments Now Supplant Checks At More Large Firms," *Wall Street Journal*, April 13, 1994, pp. A1, A9.

[49]R. Winslow and H. Stout, *Op cit.*, p. B1.

[50]See, for example, Jonathan R. Copulsky and Michael J. Wolf, "Relationship Marketing: Positioning for the Future," *Booz Allen & Hamilton Outlook*, August 1991, pp. 39–46; Guy de Jonquieres, "Retailers Plan for Last-Minute Rush," *Financial Times*, December 24, 1991, p. 15; R. Glazer, *Op cit.*, pp. 1–19; and Jim Bessen, "Riding the Marketing Information Wave," *Harvard Business Review*, September–October 1993, pp. 150–160.

[51]Jon Van, "Retail and Apparel Trades Tailor New Technology, Systems," *Chicago Tribune*, March 16, 1992, section 4, pp. 1, 5.

[52]John Kavanagh, "Supermarket Pioneer," *Financial Times*, "Software at Work" special section, Spring 1993, p. 15.

[53]B. O'Brian, *Op cit.*, p. B1.

[54]"Does ECR Spell a New Era?" *Progressive Grocer*, April 1994, pp. 22–25.

[55]Richard P. Vlosky and David T. Wilson, "Technology Adoption in Channels: Short-Term Pain and Long-Term Gain," presentation at Second Research Conference on Relationship Marketing, June 12, 1994.

[56]John Thornhill, "High-Tech Future for Food Retailers," *Financial Times*, May 18, 1992, p. 3.

[57]Anne T. Coughlan, Kent Grayson, and Jonathan Hibbard, "West Bend Case," Kellogg Graduate School of Management, 1992.

[58]J. Short and N. Venkatraman, *Op cit.*, pp. 7–21.

[59]R. Glazer, *Op cit.*, pp. 1–19.

[60]J. Hammond and M. Kelly, *Op cit.*

[61]Ramon O'Callaghan, Patrick J. Kaufmann, and Benn R. Konsynski, "Adoption Correlates and Share Effects of Electronic Data Interchange Systems in Marketing Channels," *Journal of Marketing*, Vol. 56 (April 1992), pp. 45–56.

[62]Barnaby J. Feder, "Moving the Pampers Faster Cuts Everyone's Costs," *New York Times*, July 14, 1991, section F, p. 5.

[63]J. Van, *Op cit.*, pp. 1, 5; and John Schmeltzer, "Retailers Shrink to Fit Tight Market," *Chicago Tribune*, October 18, 1992, section 7, pp. 1, 12.

[64]Edmund O. Lawler, "Reaping Multiple Benefits," *Business Marketing*, May 1993, pp. 60–61.

[65]John W. Verity, "Taking a Laptop on a Call," *Business Week*, October 25, 1993, pp. 124–125.

[66]Stefan Wagstyl, "Mapping Out Sales to India," *Financial Times*, December 16, 1993, p. 11.

[67]Ira Sager, "IBM Leans on its Sales Force," *Business Week*, February 7, 1994, p. 110.

[68]Martha E. Mangelsdorf, (ed.), "State of the Art: Quick-Response Apparel," *Inc.*, November 1993, p. 35.

[69]David Woodruff, "High Tech Keeps a Retailer from Wilting," *Business Week*, June 14, 1993, p. 64.

[70]Richard S. Teitelbaum, "Designs Inc.," *Fortune*, Vol. 127, Issue 3 (Feb. 8, 1993), p. 127.

[71]Zachary Schiller and Wendy Zellner, "Making the Middleman an Endangered Species," *Business Week*, June 6, 1994, pp. 114–115.

[72]L. Donovan, *Op cit.*, p. 7.

[73]Jerry Lazar, "Wholesale Effort: An Inventory System Boosts a Company's Efficiency," *Varbusiness*, Vol. 7, no. 16 (November 1992), pp. 133–134.

[74]Paul Taylor, "Towards a World Without Paper," *Financial Times*, October 13, 1992, section 3, p. 4.

[75]James Coates, "Going Digital Not Optional: Big Stores Dragging Little Suppliers into the Electronic Age," *Chicago Tribune*, May 30, 1994, section 4, pp. 1, 2.

[76]R. O'Callaghan, P. J. Kaufmann, and B. R. Konsynski, *Op cit.*, p. 45.

[77]*Ibid.*, p. 53.

[78]Paul N. Bloom, George R. Milne, and Robert Adler, "Avoiding Misuse of New Information Technologies: Legal and Societal Considerations," *Journal of Marketing*, Vol. 58 (January 1994), pp. 98–110.

APPENDIX

9A /

EDI AT AEROQUIP CORPORATION (PRELIMINARY VERSION)

◀◀◀◀◀◀◀◀◀

WHAT IS ELECTRONIC DATA INTERCHANGE (EDI)?

Electronic Data Interchange (EDI) is the exchange of business data electronically between business partners, using computer-readable standard formats to permit data to be transferred without having to rekey the data from one application to another. EDI is not FAX or E-MAIL.

WHY IS EDI IMPORTANT?

EDI allows businesses to effectively manage and reduce the costs associated with manual processing of paperwork within their organization while significantly improving processing time for greater customer service.

Historically, companies or institutions conduct business using paper-based documents that represent two structures:

> **Non-Formatted:** letters, memos, etc.
> **Formatted:** purchase orders, invoices, etc.

Source: Aeroquip Corporation internal documents. Published by permission of Aeroquip Corporation.

The processing and handling of these manual business documents represent exposure to:

- Lost time

- Increased inventory levels

- Rekeying errors

- Reduced customer service

- High clerical costs

WHAT ARE THE ADVANTAGES OF BEING ON EDI FOR ORDERING AND INVOICING?

While EDI is not for emergency orders, a fully integrated EDI system does provide real benefits for stock orders such as:

- Computer-to-computer data transmission

- Same-day order entry

- Next-day order acknowledgment and shipment information

- Reduced part number errors and next day acknowledgment if any should occur

Electronic invoicing with immediate transmission of the invoice:

- Elimination of mail delays

- More time for reconciliation of shipments

- More time to take advantage of prompt payment terms

BENEFITS OF EDI

- Reduced business transaction cycle time

- Reduced costs of manual processing and filing

- Reduced inventory investment

- Reduced purchasing lead time

- Reduced error rates

- Reduced postal costs

- Increased customer service

- Increased accuracy and elimination of lost documents

- Increased sales

- Increased inventory turns

- Increased profitability

- Improved partnerships

WHY USE EDI?

- Cost savings

- Improved information processing

- Improved customer service

- Competitive advantage

EDI = Less Cost + Greater Customer Service

HOW DOES EDI WORK?
EDI COMPONENTS

For EDI to work, each business partner must have:

A. **Hardware:** moderately sized personal computer to a large mainframe, and a modem for communications. A printer is optional.

B. **Communications Software:** to transmit EDI data. PC communication software is typically contained within the EDI translation software. Mainframe communication software is usually a separate piece.

C. **EDI Translation Software:** that generates and interprets EDI formatted data. EDI software is available for the mainframe and PC. The PC software can be a front-end processor to format the data into an application readable format or a stand-alone application. The following list contains several PC translation packages available today.

Company Name	Software Name	Initial Expense	Annual Maint. Fee
Geis	EDI*PC	$1,395	0
Harbinger	Intouch Plus	$2,740 (w/mailbx)	$640
Supply Tech	STX	$2,495	$660
IBM	Quick EDI Plus	$1,795	$980

and many others . . .

All fees are approximations.

We recommend that distributors contact these vendors of translation software to find the software that will meet their needs.

D.   **Value Added Network (VAN):** a service for storing electronic information. Aeroquip is currently using three different networks: GEISCO, EDI*NET (MCI), and Harbinger. We will not be providing a direct connection into our systems. If you are using a VAN other than the three mentioned, you will need to contact your VAN to determine how your company can use that VAN's services to communicate to one of Aeroquip's VANs.

EDI*NET and GEISCO provide interconnection services with the following VAN's:

Agridata

AT&T

Compuserve EDI Service

REDINET (Control DATA Corp.)

GEISCO (General Electric Information Services)

Harbinger

Advantis (IBM)

Klienschmidt

Railinc

Sears Technology Services

Ordernet (Sterling Software)

Transettlements

Union Pacific

Userbase

Western Union

Others . . .

EDI charges will be handled as follows:

■   Those using GEISCO, EDI*NET, or Harbinger

Charges will be split between Aeroquip and the trading partner. The sender of data is responsible for charges incurred in sending data and the receiver is responsible for charges incurred in receiving data.

■   Those on other VANs

Aeroquip is responsible for charges incurred on GEISCO, EDI*NET, and Harbinger. The trading partner is responsible for charges incurred on their VAN.

PUTTING IT ALL TOGETHER

Once each trading partner has set up the hardware, software, and network connections, EDI data can be transmitted. The following example shows the process of company A sending a document to company B:

Company A
Business documents are translated into industrial standard electronic formats by an EDI translator. The data is placed into a computer "mailbox" (on a VAN) by use of a computer modem via a phone line. The VAN transfers the data to company B's mailbox.

Company B
Company B pulls the business documents from its mailbox, by use of their computer modem dialed through a phone line by the computer. The data pulled from the mailbox is translated into business documents by an EDI translator. The data can then be viewed, printed, or passed into company B's internal application for processing (desired approach).

WHY ARE EDI STANDARDS NEEDED?

Businesses have been communicating from computer to computer for years using a variety of private formats. These private formats made open intercompany communications frustrating and difficult to achieve. A need for a single standard format was evident for exchanging business information.

The American National Standards Institute (ANSI) developed EDI standards for common business transactions. EDI standards outline the areas of:

- Mandatory/Optional Information

- Sequencing

- Meaning of the information

- Transmittal of documents

These standards have provided an unambiguous language that could be used and understood by all trading partners.

AEROQUIP DISTRIBUTOR SERVICES PACKAGE
EDI DOCUMENTS (ANSI X.12 STANDARDS)

Documents currently traded with distributors:

- Purchase Order (850)

- Purchase Order Acknowledgement (855)

- Invoice (810)

- Functional Acknowledgement (997)

Documents to be traded in the future with distributors:

- Advanced Ship Notice (856)

- Request for Quotation (840)

- Response to Request for Quote (843)

- Purchase Order Change (860)

- Purchase Order Change Acknowledgement (865)

10 / ASSESSING MARKETING CHANNEL PERFORMANCE

◀◀◀◀◀◀◀

*I*n corporate governance circles, it is fashionable to talk about the "stakeholders" of the corporation. This means not just shareholders, but other parties interested in the health and performance of the organization. Governments, consumers, and employees can be considered stakeholders in some situations.

In a marketing-channels context, the stakeholders are the channel members themselves as well as the customers or consumers they serve. Performance thus has both efficiency and effectiveness characteristics: it measures such things as total channel profitability as well as target segments' satisfaction with the level of service outputs supplied to them.

This chapter deals first with the issue of overall financial performance of a corporate entity, such as a manufacturer, distributor, or retailer. Two tools, the strategic profit model and economic value analysis, help channel members to appraise the health and viability of current or prospective channel partners, as well as permitting channel members to examine the sources of problems in financial performance. The chapter next investigates what contributions each channel member makes to overall channel performance. Activity-based costing (ABC), direct product profit (DPP), and efficient consumer response (ECR) are the relevant "alphabet soup" concepts to assess sources of cost and profitability at a flow-by-flow level. Ultimately, recognizing that channel profitability is a direct function of the satisfaction levels of target market segments, the notion of auditing service quality in the channel is discussed briefly. Throughout, it will be seen that improving channel performance (and thus profitability) requires an unrelenting focus on the basic elements of channel activity: the flows and functions performed by channel members that not only add cost to the channel, but are at the heart of its value generation.

▶ FACETS OF CHANNEL PERFORMANCE

Total channel performance is a multidimensional construct. It encompasses both financial performance measures of channel members and measures of contributions to society of the channel. Further, financial performance measures may themselves be the result of underlying performance on various channel tasks and duties. In this

447 ▶

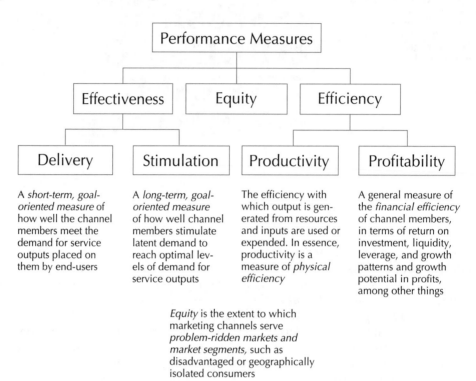

FIGURE 10-1   Performance measures in marketing channels.

section we discuss the societal measures of performance and underlying factors that may lead to strong financial performance in a channel. This discussion sets the stage for our later discussion of financial performance measures.

Gauging the Societal Contributions of Distribution

A broad perspective on channel performance appropriately takes account of three elements: effectiveness, equity, and efficiency. Figure 10-1 shows how these "3E's" contribute to overall channel performance at a macro level. Effectiveness is defined as the worldwide ability of channels to deliver the service outputs required by end-users as cost effectively as possible. No recent studies of cross-country effectiveness have been conducted, but it is safe to say that the industrialized parts of the world do a better job of meeting service output demands than do other regional players, simply due to the superior infrastructure and political stability existing in the more industrialized countries.

Equity is the degree to which every member of a country has the same opportunity to use, and ability to access, the marketing channels existing in that country. Under such a definition, the level of equity is fairly poor in worldwide distribution. Even in the United States, the poor suffer severe discrimination. A detailed report, issued by New York City's Department of Consumer Affairs in 1991, showed that prices are highest in impoverished inner-city neighborhoods, where shoppers pay significantly more but get inferior food and poor service.[1] According to the report, far fewer supermarkets do business in poor areas, and those that exist there are smaller and poorly stocked, compared with stores in middle-class areas.

Efficiency refers to how cost effectively a society's resources are being used to accomplish specific outcomes. Because these specific outcomes are generally the provision of service outputs to target consumer segments, efficiency and effectiveness are intimately tied together. In the industrialized world, real progress has been made at increasing efficiency, mainly as the result of improvements in information technology (IT), which have permitted all of the benefits discussed in detail in Chapter 9. Even with this progress, however, distribution remains a heavily labor-intensive activity, and although gains have been made, the distributive trades throughout the world are, on average, far behind manufacturing in terms of output per work hour. In less-modern societies, wholesaling and retailing are even more labor intensive than in the industrialized nations. If the gains in these nations could be exported to the nonindustrialized parts of the globe, the world's standard of living would rise significantly.

The Multidimensional Nature of Channel Member Performance from a Micro Viewpoint

What are the factors that jointly produce good performance in a channel member? Although some studies have suggested ad hoc performance measures, one study focusing on determining a reliable barometer for performance found that seven facets contribute to perceptions of strong performance of one channel member by another.[2] This study examined a supplier's perception of the performance of a reseller in its channel, using data from two different supplier companies. One supplier was a major vehicle leasing company with a network of over 5,000 dealers throughout the United States and Canada. The other was a division of a *Fortune* 500 corporation, selling through about 1,000 resellers. The seven facets of reseller performance, along with detailed questions designed to measure each facet, are reproduced in Exhibit 10-1.

EXHIBIT 10-1 / Questionnaire for Measuring Channel Member Performance[a]

SALES PERFORMANCE ◀ ◀ ◀

1. Over the past year, the dealer has been successful in generating high (rental revenues/sales volume)[b] for (the supplier),[c] given the level of competition and economic growth in his market area.

2. Compared to competing dealers in the (district/territory), this dealer has achieved a high level of market penetration for (the supplier).

3. Last year, the revenues that this dealer generated from (the supplier) was higher than what other competing dealers within the same (neighborhood/territory) generated.

Exhibit 10-1 (continued)

Exhibit 10-1 (continued)

FINANCIAL PERFORMANCE

1. (The supplier)'s cost of servicing the dealer is reasonable, given the amount of business that the dealer generates for the (supplier).

2. The dealer's demands for support (some examples) have resulted in inadequate profits for (the supplier).

3. (The supplier) made inadequate profits from this dealer over the past year because of the amount of time, effort, and energy that (the supplier) had to devote to assisting him.

RESELLER COMPETENCE

1. The dealer has the required business skills necessary to run a successful (kind of business the supplier is in) business.

2. The dealer (has amassed/demonstrates) a great deal of knowledge about the features and attributes of (the supplier)'s products and services.

3. The dealer and his personnel have poor knowledge of competitors' products and services.

RESELLER COMPLIANCE

1. In the past (the supplier) has often had trouble getting the dealer to participate in its (some program important to the supplier) program.

2. The dealer almost always conforms to (the supplier)'s accepted procedures.

3. The dealer has frequently violated (stipulations/terms and conditions) contained in his (contract/agreement) with (the supplier).

RESELLER ADAPTATION

1. The dealer senses long-term trends in his market area and frequently adjusts his selling practices.

2. The dealer is very innovative in his marketing of (the supplier)'s products and services in his (neighborhood/territory).

3. The dealer makes an effort to meet competitive changes in his (neighborhood/territory).

RESELLER GROWTH

1. The dealer will either continue to be or will soon become a major source of revenue for (the supplier).

2. Over the next year, (the supplier) expects its revenue generated from this dealer to grow faster than that from other competing (of the supplier) dealers within the same (district/territory).

3. In the past (the supplier)'s (business with the dealer/market share through the dealer) has grown steadily.

CUSTOMER SATISFACTION

1. (The supplier) has (frequently) received complaints from customers regarding this dealer.
2. The dealer goes out of his way to make his customers happy.
3. The dealer provides (customers/end-users) with good assistance in the solution of any problems involving (the supplier)'s products and services.

[a]All items measured using 7-point Likert-type scales.

[b]Alternative phrasing, depending on the supplier's business and organization, for example, U-Haul vs. Digital Equipment Company.

[c]The name of the supplier would appear here, for example, Motorola, Nabisco.

Source: Nirmalya Kumar, Louis W. Stern, and Ravi S. Achrol, "Assessing Reseller Performance From the Perspective of the Supplier," *Journal of Marketing Research*, Vol. 29 (May 1992), pp. 251–252.

The researchers found that the questions did a good job of representing the seven facets of performance. Moreover, the seven performance facets themselves were found to be distinct measures of the supplier's perception of reseller performance. So, for example, reseller competence, reseller compliance, reseller adaptation, and reseller growth were all found to be distinct reseller characteristics that each contributed positively to performance perceptions by suppliers. The list is indicative of the factors one channel member weighs when assessing the performance of another.

These insights provide guidelines to consider when building an overall picture of channel member performance. They suggest underlying factors that may well correlate with overall financial performance measures at the level of the channel member or the overall channel. We discuss some methods of measuring these financial performance levels next.

▶ AGGREGATE MEASURES OF CHANNEL MEMBER FINANCIAL PERFORMANCE

The Strategic Profit Model

No single measure of performance fully reflects the financial well-being of a firm. The financial performance of wholesalers and retailers is multidimensional, requiring an examination of (1) profitability, or return on investment, (2) liquidity, or the ability of the firm to meet its financial liabilities within a time frame, (3) capital structure, or leverage ratio, (4) growth pattern of sales and profits, and (5) growth potential of sales and profits. However, return on investment is accepted as an aggregate performance measure in the retail and wholesale trades. The strategic profit model (SPM) has been developed by managerial accountants to evaluate and diagnose profitability problems such as those that confront retailers and wholesalers. The SPM is portrayed in Figure 10-2.

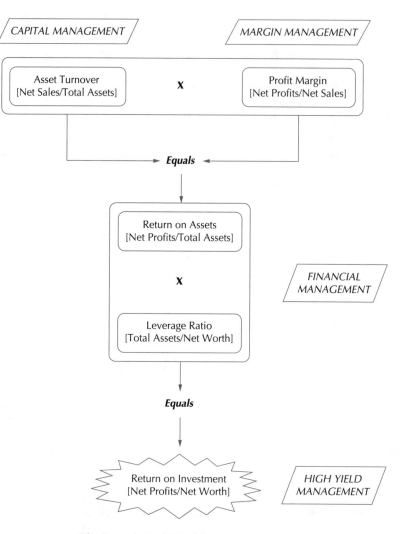

FIGURE 10-2   The Strategic Profit Model.

The SPM involves multiplying a company's profit margin by its rate of asset turnover and its leverage ratio to derive its rate of return on net worth. Exhibit 10-2 defines the relevant financial terms used in the SPM. Let us look briefly at each of the components of the model.

NET PROFITS AFTER TAX/NET SALES (PROFIT MARGIN)   The relationship of reported net profit after tax to sales indicates management's ability to recover the cost of merchandise or services, the expenses of operating the business (including depreciation), and the cost of borrowed funds from revenues generated during a given period, as well as its adeptness in leaving a margin of reasonable compensation to the owners for providing their capital at a risk. The ratio of net profit to sales essentially expresses the cost/price effectiveness of the operation.

EXHIBIT **10-2 / Definition of Terms
in the Strategic Profit Model**

THE INCOME STATEMENT ◀ ◀ ◀

The terms below appear on a firm's income statement, the document reporting a company's
financial performance (typically on an annual basis).

Net Sales = Gross Sales – Customer Returns – Customer Allowances
Gross Margin = Net Sales – Cost Of Goods Sold (COGS)
Net Profit after Tax = Gross Margin – Total Expenses – Taxes

THE BALANCE SHEET

The terms below appear on a firm's balance sheet, which describes the company's financial
situation at a point in time.

Total Assets = economic resources controlled by the firm, such as accounts receivable,
inventory, and cash.
Total Liabilities = all debts that must be repaid by the company at some time in the future.
Current liabilities must be repaid within one year, whereas *long-term
liabilities* have a repayment period of greater than one year. Liabilities
include accounts payable and notes payable.
Net Worth = Total Assets – Total Liabilities
That is, the net worth of the company is defined to be what is left over after
subtracting total liabilities from total assets. Common stock and retained
earnings are two types of net worth.

THE STRATEGIC PROFIT MODEL

Using these definitions, we can derive the key elements of the Strategic Profit Model (SPM)
as follows:

Profit Margin = Net Profit after Tax ÷ Net Sales
Asset Turnover = Net Sales ÷ Total Assets
Return on Assets = Profit Margin × Asset Turnover
= Net Profit after Tax ÷ Total Assets
Leverage Ratio = Total Assets ÷ Net Worth
Return on Investment, or Return on Net Worth = Return on Assets × Leverage Ratio
= Profit Margin × Asset Turnover
× Leverage Ratio
= Net Profit after Tax ÷ Net Worth

In Exhibit 10-2, one can see that gross margin and total expenses (consisting
of operating expenses and interest expenses) are the key elements in deriving profit
margins. Bates has argued that:

Of all the factors that affect retail profits, gross margin . . . is probably the most important. The exact impact of gross margin depends largely on the cost structure of the
firm.[3]

He points out that the operating challenge for retailers is to generate higher gross margins without diminishing price competitiveness:

> The key is to look beyond price and think more directly about gross margin planning. There are numerous ways to enhance gross margin.

- More effective purchasing, especially via consolidation of suppliers

- Mark-down control

- Shrinkage reduction, especially via proper measurement and control

- Merchandise mix, emphasis on higher margin items via display procedures, product adjacencies, and suggestion selling

- Price adjustments, especially via increases on non-price sensitive items.[4]

And, in a study of 18 supermarket chains, Livingstone and Tigert demonstrate that "the *spread* between the gross margin ratio and the operating expense ratio is a critical element in determining return on investment. Clearly, operating profit drives return on investment for supermarkets."[5] [Remember that return on investment (ROI) is equal to profit margin times asset turnover times leverage ratio.] Their results, therefore, show that of the three factors, profit margin is the primary driver of ROI among supermarkets. They point out that asset turnover is usually rapid for supermarkets; this accounts for the relatively small impact in ROI made by improvements in turnover in their simulation.[6]

A major dilemma for most service industries such as retailing and wholesaling is the fact that companies end up adding personnel due to the increasing complexity and quality of service. Clearly, this factor explains why their operating ratios are difficult to reduce. This also explains why the distributive trades have frequently lagged behind manufacturers in measured productivity growth. The exception seems to be financial services, which have been automated at a rapid rate.[7]

NET SALES/TOTAL ASSETS (ASSET TURNOVER) Although the net profit margin shows how well the firm performs given a particular level of sales, it does not show how well the firm uses the resources, or assets, at its command. The amount of net profit may be entirely satisfactory from the point of view of the firm's sales volume; however, sales volume may be insufficient in relation to capacity—the amount of capital invested in assets used in obtaining sales. The ratio of net sales to total assets is a measure of the effectiveness of management's employment of capital and may show whether there is a tendency toward overinvestment in assets, especially in inventory and receivables in the case of wholesalers and retailers. This ratio (sometimes referred to as the *turnover ratio*) provides a clue as to the size of asset commitment required for a given level of sales or, conversely, the sales dollars generated for each dollar of investment.[8]

NET PROFITS AFTER TAX/TOTAL ASSETS (RETURN ON ASSETS)   Neither the net profit margin (net profits after tax/net sales) nor the turnover ratio (net sales/total assets) by itself provides an adequate measure of operating efficiency. The net profit margin ignores the utilization of assets, whereas the turnover ratio ignores profitability on sales. The return on assets ratio (ROA), or earning power, resolves these shortcomings. As pointed out by Van Horne, an improvement in the earning power of a firm will result if there is an increase in turnover on existing assets, an increase in the net profit margin, or both.[9] The interrelation of these ratios is shown in the SPM (Figure 10-2). Two firms with different asset turnovers and net profit margins may have the same earning power. For example, if wholesaler A has an asset turnover of 4:1 and a net profit margin of 3% and wholesaler B has an asset turnover of 1.5:1 and a net profit margin of 8%, both have the same earning power—12%—despite their vast differences in operating modes. Thus, earning power can be improved by increasing sales revenue through higher prices (and probably lower volume) or higher volume (probably at lower prices). This may increase both profit margin and turnover. Costs can be reduced to the point where they do not affect quality, and profit margin can be widened through improved control. The amount of capital employed can be reduced by increasing the turnover of inventory and accounts receivable, and by using fixed assets more efficiently.

TOTAL ASSETS/NET WORTH (LEVERAGE RATIO)   The ratio of total assets to net worth indicates how reliant a firm is on borrowed funds for both short- and long-term purposes. Net worth is what remains after the firm's liabilities are subtracted from the firm's assets. In a publicly traded firm, common stock and retained earnings are two types of net worth. The firm can thus raise money in two ways: by issuing stock (thus reducing leverage) or by issuing debt (thus raising leverage).

The lower the leverage ratio, therefore, the more the firm is being financially supported by owners' equity as opposed to debt capital. Although a low ratio indicates a high degree of solvency as well as a desire by management to rely on ownership or equity capital for financing purposes, it also indicates that management is probably highly conservative and risk-averse. Debt capital requires fixed interest payments on specific dates and eventual repayment, as well as the threat of legal action by creditors if payments are overdue. On the other hand, dividends on ownership capital are paid at the discretion of the directors, and there is no provision for repayment of capital to stockholders.

Equity capital is, however, typically more costly than debt capital. Thus, by retaining an excessive amount of ownership capital relative to debt capital, the company may be foregoing opportunities to trade on its equity (so-called *leveraging operations*) by refusing to borrow funds at relatively low interest rates and using these funds to earn greater rates of returns. Consequently, aggressive management will often rely heavily on debt capital, because if there is a difference between these two rates on a large investment base, management can increase earnings per share without having to increase the number of common shares outstanding.

NET PROFITS/NET WORTH (RETURN ON INVESTMENT, OR RETURN ON NET WORTH)   The main interest of the owners of an enterprise will be the returns achieved by management effort on their share of the invested funds. An effective measure of the return on owners' investment (ROI) is the relationship of net profit to net worth. This ratio reflects the extent to which the objective of realizing a satisfactory net income is being achieved. A low ratio of net profits to net worth may indicate that the business is not very successful because of several possible reasons: inefficient and ineffective production, distribution, financial, or general management; unfavorable general business conditions; or overinvestment in assets. A high ratio may be a result of efficient management throughout the company's organization, favorable general business conditions, and trading on the firm's equity (effective leveraging).

As McCammon and his colleagues have explained, the SPM has four important managerial purposes:

1.   The model specifies that a firm's principal financial objective is to earn an adequate or target rate of return on net worth.

2.   The model identifies the three "profit paths" available to an enterprise. That is, a firm with an inadequate rate of return on net worth can improve its performance by accelerating its rate of asset turnover, by increasing its profit margin, or by leveraging its operations more highly, assuming future cash flows are sufficient to cover additional borrowing costs.

3.   The model dramatizes the principal areas of decision making within the firm, namely, capital management, margin management, and financial management. Furthermore, firms interrelating their capital, margin, and financial plans may be described effectively as engaged in the practice of high-yield management.

4.   The model provides a useful perspective for appraising the financial strategies used by different organizations to achieve target rates of return on net worth.[10]

Shown in Tables 10-1a and 10-1b and 10-2a and 10-2b are the SPM data on leading U.S. and non-U.S. retailers and wholesaling/trading companies (remember, however, that there are millions of retailers and hundreds of thousands of wholesalers, as pointed out in Chapters 2 and 3 above). The tables show that retailers tend to have a higher ROI than wholesalers, although this pattern is shaped largely by the much lower ROIs in the huge Japanese trading companies than in non-Japanese trading companies or wholesalers. It is also clear from these tables that a company can achieve a given ROI in various ways. For example, Wal-Mart's ROI of 23.92% is quite similar to Gap's ROI of 25.66%. However, Wal-Mart achieved its ROI performance with a much lower return on assets (driven by a much lower profit margin) than Gap, whereas Gap is much less highly leveraged than Wal-Mart. Similarly, contrasting Bergen Brunswig and SHV Holdings among wholesalers, one sees that although both have very similar leverage ratios, Bergen Brunswig has a higher asset turnover, whereas SHV has the higher profit margin. These examples illustrate that fundamentally, it is the interaction among the three elements of the SPM (higher merchandise turnover, higher profit margins, and higher leverage of existing assets) that jointly determines the overall financial performance of a channel member.

TABLE 10-1A Leading U.S. Retailers: Strategic Profit Model Variables[a]

COMPANY	NET SALES ($MM)	FISCAL YEAR-END	ASSET TURNOVER	PROFIT MARGIN	RETURN ON ASSETS	LEVERAGE RATIO	ROI
Grocery							
Albertson's, Inc.	$11,283.7	2/3/94	3.62	3.0%	10.9%	2.25	24.5%
American Stores	$18,763.4	1/29/94	2.74	1.3%	3.6%	4.17	15.0%
Weis Markets, Inc.	$ 1,441.1	12/25/93	1.79	5.1%	9.1%	1.13	10.3%
General Merchandise							
Dayton Hudson	$19,233.0	1/29/94	1.82	2.0%	3.6%	4.04	14.4%
Dollar General Corporation	$ 1,133.0	1/31/94	3.18	4.3%	13.6%	1.66	22.6%
Wal-Mart Stores, Inc.	$67,344.6	1/31/94	2.87	3.5%	9.9%	2.41	23.9%
Apparel							
Gap, Inc.	$ 3,295.7	1/29/94	2.10	7.8%	16.5%	1.56	25.7%
The Limited, Inc.	$ 7,245.1	1/29/94	1.82	5.4%	9.8%	1.69	16.6%
Department Stores							
Dillard Department Stores, Inc.	$ 5,130.6	1/29/94	1.20	3.1%	3.7%	2.18	8.1%
Nordstrom, Inc.	$ 3,590.0	1/31/94	1.70	3.9%	6.6%	1.91	12.7%
J.C. Penney Company, Inc.	$19,578.0	1/29/94	1.39	4.8%	6.7%	2.81	18.7%
Specialty Stores							
Avon Products, Inc.	$ 4,007.6	12/31/93	2.17	3.3%	7.2%	5.91	42.3%
Bed Bath & Beyond	$ 305.8	2/27/94	3.09	7.2%	22.1%	1.50	33.2%
Best Buy Co., Inc.	$ 3,006.5	2/26/94	4.32	1.4%	5.9%	2.82	16.7%
Circuit City Stores, Inc.	$ 4,130.4	2/28/94	2.93	3.2%	9.4%	2.19	20.6%
Duty Free International	$ 376.4	1/31/94	1.17	7.3%	8.5%	1.46	12.5%
Lands' End, Inc.	$ 733.6	1/29/94	3.54	4.6%	16.2%	1.56	25.2%
Office Depot Inc.	$ 2,579.5	12/25/93	2.23	2.5%	5.5%	2.47	13.5%
Sportmart Inc.	$ 338.4	1/30/94	2.45	2.3%	5.7%	2.24	12.8%
The Home Depot	$ 9,238.8	1/30/94	2.14	5.0%	10.6%	1.69	17.9%
Toys "R" Us, Inc.	$ 7,946.1	1/29/94	1.39	6.1%	8.4%	1.90	16.0%

[a]SPM variable definitions are as in Exhibit 10-2.

Source: Company Annual Reports and Distribution Research Program, The University of Oklahoma.

TABLE 10-1B The Largest Non-U.S. Retailing Companies: Strategic Profit Model Variables

COMPANY	NET SALES ($MM)	FISCAL YEAR-END	ASSET TURNOVER[b]	PROFIT MARGIN[b]	RETURN ON ASSETS[b]	LEVERAGE RATIO[a,b]	ROI[b]
Ito-Yokado (Japan)	$26,488.0	2/28/94	1.75	2.0%	3.6%	2.32	8.3%
Daiei (Japan)	$24,369.3	2/28/94	1.57	0.2%	0.3%	14.00	4.5%
Carrefour (France)	$21,750.6	12/31/93	5.56	2.4%	13.6%	1.94	26.4%
Jusco (Japan)	$16,130.1	2/28/94	1.43	1.6%	2.3%	4.95	11.3%
Promodes (France)	$15,997.6	12/31/93	2.66	0.8%	2.1%	7.59	15.7%
J. Sainsbury (G. Britain)	$15,919.4	3/31/94	1.95	1.3%	2.6%	1.82	4.7%
Koninklijke Ahold (Netherlands)	$14,587.9	12/31/93	9.16	1.3%	11.6%	1.48	17.1%
Nichii (Japan)	$13,033.9	2/28/94	1.00	-0.7%	-0.7%	6.41	-4.3%
Tesco (G. Britain)	$12,914.7	2/28/94	1.75	3.5%	6.1%	1.81	11.0%
Seiyu (Japan)	$11,990.3	2/28/94	0.78	0.6%	0.4%	13.31	5.8%
Kaufhof (Germany)	$11,558.2	12/31/93	2.91	1.0%	2.9%	5.07	14.5%

[a]Leverage ratio is calculated as the ratio of total assets to stockholders' equity as reported in *Fortune*. Their definition of stockholders' equity is the sum of capital stock, paid-in capital, and retained earnings at the company's year-end.
[b]Calculations of asset turnover, profit margin, return on assets, leverage ratio, and ROI follow the definitions in Exhibit 10-2.

Source: Data on sales, profits, assets, and stockholders' equity from Rajv Rao, "The Year of Mixed Results: The World's Largest Service Corporations," *Fortune*, August 22, 1994, p. 189. © 1994 Time Inc. All rights reserved.

TABLE 10-2A Leading U.S. Wholesalers: Strategic Profit Model Variables[a]

COMPANY (INDUSTRY)	NET SALES ($MM)	FISCAL YEAR-END	ASSET TURNOVER	PROFIT MARGIN	RETURN ON ASSETS	LEVERAGE RATIO	ROI
Arrow Electronics Inc. (electronics)	$ 2,535.6	12/31/93	2.57	3.2%	8.3%	2.44	20.2%
Bergen Brunswig Corp. (drugs)	$ 7,483.8	9/30/94	3.97	0.8%	3.0%	4.28	12.8%
Genuine Parts Company (automotives)	$ 4,384.3	12/31/93	2.45	5.9%	14.4%	1.30	18.7%
Handleman Company (entertainment)	$ 1,066.6	4/30/94	1.64	2.6%	4.3%	2.21	9.4%
Lawson Products, Inc. (industrial)	$ 195.7	12/31/93	1.19	9.3%	11.0%	1.22	13.5%
Loblaw Companies Ltd. (grocery)	$ 9,356.1	1/1/94	3.59	1.0%	3.6%	2.64	9.5%
Pioneer-Standard Electronics, Inc. (electronics)	$ 580.8	3/31/94	2.96	3.4%	10.0%	2.10	21.1%
Super Valu Inc. (grocery)	$15,936.9	2/26/94	3.93	1.2%	4.6%	3.36	15.4%
Sysco Corporation (food service)	$10,942.5	7/2/94	4.10	2.0%	8.1%	2.25	18.2%
W.W. Grainger, Inc. (industrial)	$ 2,628.4	12/31/93	1.96	5.7%	11.1%	1.43	15.9%

[a]SPM variable definitions are as in Exhibit 10-2.

Source: Company Annual Reports and Distribution Research Program, The University of Oklahoma.

TABLE 10-2B The Largest Non-U.S. Wholesaling/Trading Companies: Strategic Profit Model Variables

COMPANY	NET SALES ($MM)	FISCAL YEAR-END	ASSET TURNOVER[b]	PROFIT MARGIN[b]	RETURN ON ASSETS[b]	LEVERAGE RATIO[a,b]	ROI[b]
Mitsui (Japan)	$163,453.2	3/31/94	2.26	0.1%	0.2%	12.79	2.5%
Mitsubishi (Japan)	$160,109.4	3/31/94	1.88	0.1%	0.2%	12.50	2.5%
Sumitomo (Japan)	$157,551.2	3/31/94	3.22	0.0%	0.1%	7.10	1.0%
Itochu (Japan)	$155,161.8	3/31/94	2.46	-0.1%	-0.2%	13.86	-2.9%
Marubeni (Japan)	$144,502.6	3/31/94	2.04	0.0%	0.1%	16.09	1.2%
Nissho Iwai (Japan)	$ 95,462.9	3/31/94	2.08	0.1%	0.2%	19.47	4.2%
Tomen (Japan)	$ 64,631.2	3/31/94	2.96	0.0%	0.1%	19.25	1.3%
Nichimen (Japan)	$ 53,482.7	3/31/94	2.48	0.1%	0.2%	15.06	2.5%
Kanematsu (Japan)	$ 52,746.7	3/31/94	3.20	-0.1%	-0.4%	17.54	-6.4%
Veba Group (Germany)	$ 37,064.5	12/31/93	1.16	1.4%	0.2%	3.68	5.8%
Toyota Tsusho (Japan)	$ 15,756.6	3/31/94	2.17	0.1%	0.3%	5.64	1.6%
Franz Haniel (Germany)	$ 14,771.0	12/31/93	2.53	0.6%	1.5%	6.92	10.5%
Hyundai (S. Korea)	$ 13,738.7	12/31/93	35.44	0.1%	1.8%	4.39	7.7%
Kawasho (Japan)	$ 13,302.5	3/31/94	1.72	0.1%	0.1%	17.01	2.1%
Sinochem (PRC)	$ 13,241.0	N/A	0.31	0.7%	0.2%	N/A	N/A
SHV Holdings (Netherlands Antilles)	$ 11,897.2	12/31/93	1.83	0.2%	2.8%	4.23	11.6%

[a]Leverage ratio is calculated as the ratio of total assets to stockholders' equity as reported in *Fortune*. Their definition of stockholders' equity is the sum of capital stock, paid-in capital, and retained earnings at the company's year-end.
[b]Calculations of asset turnover, profit margin, return on assets, leverage ratio, and ROI follow the definitions in Exhibit 10-2.

Source: Data on sales, profits, assets, and stockholders' equity are from Rajv Rao, "The Year of Mixed Results: The World's Largest Service Corporations," *Fortune*, August 22, 1994, p. 189. © 1994 Time Inc. All rights reserved.

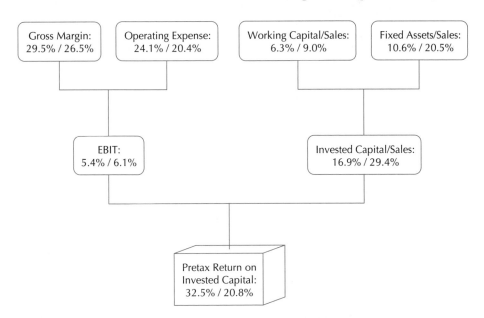

FIGURE 10-3 Economic performance, Circuit City versus category killer composite, 1992.

The first number in each box describes Circuit City, whereas the second number in each box describes the category killer composite. Thus, pretax return on invested capital in 1992 was 32.5% for Circuit City, and 20.8% for the category killer composite.

EBIT means Earnings Before Interest and Taxes and is equal to Gross Margin minus Operating Expense. Invested Capital/Sales is equal to Working Capital/Sales plus Fixed Assets/Sales. Pretax Return on Invested Capital is equal to EBIT divided by Invested Capital/Sales.

Source: "The Retail World and Its Implications," J. L. Kellogg Graduate School of Management Business Discussion, McKinsey & Company, Inc., April 1994.

Even within a retailing category, performance can differ significantly from retailer to retailer. Consider the following example, depicted in Figure 10-3. Comparing Circuit City with its category killer fellows, one can see that its pretax return on invested capital (similar to the SPM's return on assets) is much greater than the category killer average. Even though Circuit City's earnings are lower than the average for this type of retailer, its amount of invested capital (of both the fixed-assets type and the working capital or inventory type) is so much lower than the average that its return on capital exceeds the average by over 10 percentage points. That is, Circuit City makes lower earnings in some absolute sense, but makes those earnings from much lower capital stocks than do other category killers. It is thus more efficient in its usage of capital than its competitors.

One can also compare an average warehouse club store with an average non-warehouse grocery store (see Figure 10-4). Here, note that earnings are essentially equal between the two grocery retailers. They end up being equal because the warehouse store beats the nonwarehouse grocery store on operating expense, whereas the nonwarehouse grocery store does better on gross margin grounds. But because the warehouse store makes those earnings off of a much lower capital base, its pretax return on invested capital is 39% versus the nonwarehouse grocery

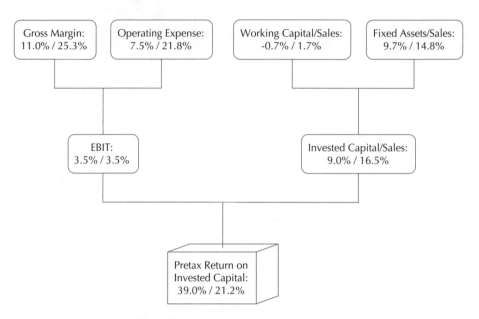

FIGURE 10-4 Economic performance, warehouse club versus nonwarehouse store, 1992.

The first number in each box describes a prototypical warehouse club store, whereas the second number in each box describes the prototypical nonwarehouse grocery store. Thus, pretax return on invested capital in 1992 was 39.0% for the warehouse club, and 21.2% for the nonwarehouse grocery store.

EBIT means Earnings Before Interest and Taxes and is equal to Gross Margin minus Operating Expense. Invested Capital/Sales is equal to Working Capital/Sales plus Fixed Assets/Sales. Pretax Return on Invested Capital is equal to EBIT divided by Invested Capital/Sales.

Source: "The Retail World and Its Implications," J.L. Kellogg Graduate School of Management Business Discussion, McKinsey & Company, Inc., April 1994.

store's return of just over 21%. The main driver of increased efficiency in the warehouse store is the lower fixed asset base, consisting of the value of the building, fixtures, and equipment. Unlike average grocery stores, the warehouse club store does not have a distribution center, a prime contributor to fixed assets. Rather it gets product directly from manufacturers via consolidators (themselves set in place by the manufacturers). The "performance winners" can thus succeed through a combination of superior sales productivity and system cost efficiencies.[11]

Finally, McKinsey has also compared performance of a large supermarket with that of a supercenter.[12] The typical new supercenter has about 170,000 square feet of store space and generates average annual revenues of $52 million. These stores sell a full range of grocery items, including general merchandise and perishables. Their higher returns as compared to a large supermarket stem from a low cost structure, which more than compensates for their higher working-capital-to-sales ratio (see Figure 10-5 for comparative performance data). Exhibit 10-3 further shows that, although the productivity of the perishables side of the business is extremely poor, excellent returns from the general merchandise area, along with healthy returns from elsewhere in the supercenter, combine to create a superior return overall. This type of analysis not only helps the channel manager evaluate the

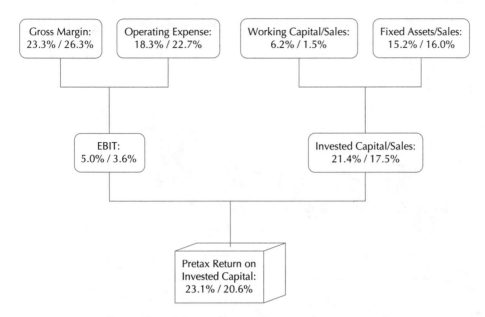

FIGURE 10-5   Economic performance, supercenter versus large supermarket.

The first number in each box describes a prototypical supercenter, while the second number in each box describes the prototypical large supermarket. Thus, pretax return on invested capital was 23.1% for the supercenter, and 20.6% for the large supermarket.

EBIT means Earnings Before Interest and Taxes and is equal to Gross Margin minus Operating Expense. Invested Capital/Sales is equal to Working Capital/Sales plus Fixed Assets/Sales. Pretax Return on Invested Capital is equal to EBIT divided by Invested Capital/Sales.

Source: McKinsey & Company, "Supercenters and the Future," a speech to the Grocery Industry, Food Marketing Institute, Midwinter Executive Conference, Orlando, FL, January 15–18, 1995.

relative profitability of one channel form over another, but on a more "micro" level, what departments or lines drive productivity of a particular channel form.

Economic Value Analysis

Beyond the variables on which the SPM focuses, a tool called *economic value analysis* emphasizes the importance of the *total cost of capital*.[13] Specifically, economic value (or EV) is defined as:

$$EV = \text{after-tax operating profit} - \text{total annual cost of capital}$$

Managers have begun to focus on EV because performance tools like the SPM do not account for the cost of using capital. The capital used by a company can be debt (that is, borrowed money) or equity (e.g., common stock). The cost of debt capital is well-defined: it is the interest paid on the debt, less any tax deductions for interest payments. But the cost of equity capital is not so well-defined. Here, the economic concept of *opportunity cost* comes into play. The opportunity cost of a firm's equity capital is the return an equity investor could have gotten by investing his or her money in another set of companies with a similar risk profile. Then a company's

EXHIBIT 10-3 / Supercenter Financial Returns by Category (in percentage)

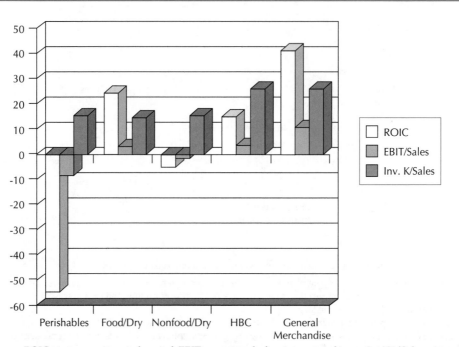

ROIC = return on invested capital; EBIT = earnings before interest and taxes; Inv. K/Sales = invested capital/sales. Categories represented in exhibit are, respectively: perishables; dry grocery—food; dry grocery—nonfood; HBC; and general merchandise.
Source: McKinsey & Company, "Supercenters and the Future," a speech to the Grocery Industry, Food Marketing Institute, Midwinter Executive Conference, Orlando, FL, January 15–18, 1995.

total cost of capital is an appropriately weighted average of the cost of its debt capital and its equity capital.

The total cost of capital is, of course, the weighted average cost of capital times the amount of capital employed by the company. This raises the question of how much capital is in fact used by a channel member. Capital consists of equipment, real estate, and working capital (inventories, cash, and receivables). But proponents of EVA urge that even nontraditional expenditures be classified as capital investments, if they are expected to generate a return over a period of years to come. For example, classical accounting practice dictates that salesforce training costs be treated as an expense (that is, these costs are accounted for entirely in the year they are incurred), but an EVA approach advocates treating them as an investment. If a $1,000,000 training program can be expected to bear fruit over, say, a five-year period, then it should be treated the same way as a five-year investment of $1,000,000 in electronic-data interchange (EDI) hardware and software for ordering and payments. Thus, *all* sources of capital must be added up to come up with the true total capital stock being used by the firm.

Once total capital costs are estimated, EV is straightforward to calculate as the difference between operating profit after tax and total capital costs. Thus, EV measures the profit made by the company over and above that which could be earned in an analogous set of investments. It is a measure of the real economic value added of the enterprise. In publicly held firms, it tends to correlate closely with the firm's stock price, because it measures performance in much the way an equity investor would measure it for investment purposes. It helps managers of any type of firm— manufacturing, distribution, or retailing—discipline their use of capital in the generation of profits. In contrast, a focus on ROI alone (which does not factor in the cost of the capital used to generate returns) can lead companies to overinvest in capital and thus to lower their efficiency in production or distribution.

EVA has produced surprising results for some firms. The freight company CSX runs a very capital-intensive business, using thousands of railcars, containers, and locomotives. It adopted EVA as a measure of performance in 1988 and discovered that its CSX Intermodal business, in which freight is moved from trains to trucks or ships, had an EVA of –$70 million! That is, Intermodal actually lost $70 million in 1988 after accounting for all the costs of capital. By using EVA to streamline its distribution business, CSX increased its freight volume by 25% by 1993, but dropped the number of containers and trailers used from 18,000 to 14,000. This was done by lowering the idle time per container car, so that the capital employed was generating revenue more of the time. CSX was also able to reduce its locomotive fleet from 150 to 100, because it discovered its freight was arriving earlier at its destinations than it could be unloaded. By running a train with three locomotives instead of four, at a slower speed, CSX was able to reach its destinations on time but at a much lower cost of capital used. These changes contributed to a significant improvement in CSX's EVA, to +$10 million in 1992. CSX's stock price also responded, increasing from $28 in 1988 to $75 in 1993.[14] The gains to any channel business characterized by high capital costs, such as CSX, of adopting an EVA focus can thus be significant.

An EVA focus was also responsible for Quaker Oats' abandoning of tradeloading practices in 1992. Prior to that time, performance at Quaker was measured by quarterly earnings (which ignores the cost of capital). To make quarterly earnings targets, managers offered big discounts to the retail trade to stock up on Quaker products. This in turn generated cyclical sales patterns, with relatively low sales at the beginning of each quarter and a huge increase in sales at the end of every quarter. Total inventory holding costs increased, and extra warehousing space was needed to hold the (temporarily) high inventories. Once managers started to be compensated on the basis of "controllable earnings" (which subtracts from earnings the cost of holding both raw materials and finished goods), end-of-quarter trade-loading came to an end. The company's stock price temporarily fell, but later rebounded. Quaker closed five of its 15 warehouses, saving $6 million per year in salaries and capital costs.[15] Using EVA can thus change not only a company's effective use of capital stocks, but can also change its policies throughout the channel. Clearly, in Quaker's case, the exertion of reward power (through the use of controllable earnings as a basis for management compensation) was also critical for the success of the EVA approach.

Variants on EVA have been suggested as approaches for looking at distribution costing issues. For example, Levy and Van Breda have observed that

> The question of who should perform marketing functions and at what level can be measured with traditional accounting/financial measures. Specifically, the financing, risking, and payment functions are related to gross margin, quantity discounts, and transportation expenses. The possession/ownership functions can be measured through inventory carrying costs. The promotion function is partially measurable through advertising and personal selling expense. The ordering function is directly measurable. The profitability derived from participation in the combination of these functions provides each channel member with a basis for the final function, negotiation.[16]

They propose a residual income (RI) paradigm to measure the relative profitability of various channel function configurations.[17]

> Residual income is the excess of net earnings over the cost of capital. The combination of channel functions yielding the highest RI will be optimal from a financial perspective when . . .

$$RI = GM + QD - PICC - FICC - TE - SE - OE$$

where

RI   = residual income
GM   = gross margin
QD   = quantity discounts on purchases
PICC = physical inventory carrying costs
FICC = financial inventory carrying costs
TE   = transportation expenses
SE   = service expenses
OE   = ordering expenses.

In a simulation, Levy and Van Breda show that residual income is directly affected by changes in lead time, lead-time variation, suppliers' service level, invoice cost, quantity discount breaks, the discount percentage component in the financial terms of sale policy, and interest rates.

One drawback to the use of EVA is its potential for encouraging managers to minimize capital investments. Thus, the company must assess over what time period the capital stock will be productive, and not avoid capital investments just because they diminish current-year EV. An integration of EVA tools with the company's overall strategic plan is thus crucial.[18] For example, Baxter Healthcare, a leading manufacturer and distributor of hospital supplies, offers the ValueLink stockless distribution program to hospitals. The program is a variation on the "just-in-time" inventory methodology that is used in modern manufacturing. The ValueLink program virtually eliminates the need for a hospital to warehouse products; Baxter manages the inventory, delivering supplies when needed (frequency varies with point of use needs) and in the exact quantities needed. The supplies are delivered to the point of use in the hospital in a ready-to-use form. This enables hospitals to trim down their own supply operations by reducing departmental safety stock levels, while also reducing the costs to store and distribute supplies. The hospital benefits in other areas of operational efficiency as well. Space utilization (that is, con-

version of warehouse space to an outpatient clinic), streamlined purchasing procedures, staffing levels, and others—all can be reevaluated to allocate resources to provide more and better patient care. This increases the hospital's EV, a good result.

Like many "just-in-time" programs, ValueLink is not well-suited for every
hospital customer. A strong trust between supplier and customer must exist for this
type of partnership to be successful. For example, the hospital increases its dependence on Baxter as its warehouse is converted to revenue-generating space. On the
other hand, Baxter increases its commitment to the hospital through the distribution investments necessary to ensure the supplies will be in the right place at the
right time. Baxter's strategic imperative in selling the ValueLink program is not only
to emphasize the profit-making opportunities and the cost-saving generation, but
also to show its continued incentive for long-term partnerships with its hospital customers.[19] (ValueLink is a trademark of Baxter Healthcare.)

EVA, along with the strategic profit model, provides insights into the ways
in which channel member companies can maximize their overall economic efficiency. One channel member can use these tools to appraise the abilities of another
potential channel partner as well, or to suggest ways to improve the joint efficiency
and effectiveness of the channel. Along with this more "macro" emphasis, however,
it is also necessary to measure the "true" costs of performance of each channel activity in assessing overall channel performance. The next section speaks to this issue.

▶ **EVALUATING CHANNEL MEMBERS' CONTRIBUTIONS
TO CHANNEL PERFORMANCE**

The SPM and EVA are useful tools for identifying not only the overall financial
strength of a company, but also potential avenues to increase channel productivity and performance. However, these tools may provide too aggregate a focus to
help in the allocation of specific functions and flows to various channel members.
On a more "micro" level, two financial tools—activity-based costing and direct
product profit—have proven useful in assessing what specific functions cost and
what profitability is generated as a result.

Activity-Based Costing

Activity-based costing, or ABC, refers to a method of allocating costs to products
via the activities necessary to produce those products.[20] The concept was first introduced by Robin Cooper and Robert Kaplan in 1988,[21] and has since then been
applied in many manufacturing, distribution, and service firms. ABC builds on the
basic concept that *all costs attributable to a product should be accounted for*. This includes
logistics, production, service, technology, marketing, sales, administrative, and information resources costs. On a product level, once these costs are fully accounted
for, management has a much better idea of what products are truly more costly than
others to produce. The insights derived may overturn management preconceptions
and cause the company to abandon products or product lines totally, or to shift production away from some products and toward others.

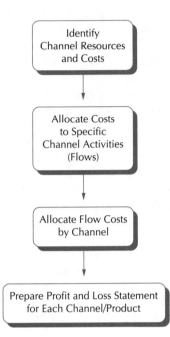

FIGURE 10-6
The activity-based costing process in distribution channels.

The applicability of this concept to the distribution channel context is immediate. For *product*, we can read *channel* or even *product × channel*. That is, one can use ABC to compare the productivity of one channel form against another, or to compare the productivity of selling one product versus another through a particular channel in question.

The key to understanding ABC is the progression depicted in Figure 10-6. To understand the profitability of selling product X through channel Y, it is necessary to identify the resources used and the total costs of using them. Typically, these costs are initially expressed in familiar accounting categories. Next, however, these costs must be allocated to the performance of specific channel functions and flows (e.g., instead of knowing the total cost of salaries, those costs need to be divided into the salary costs of doing physical possession, promotion, and other flows). The total flow costs are then allocated to specific channels, so that the promotional flow costs through the retail channel are known, for example. Finally, with these data, a profit and loss statement by channel (and by product or even customer, if data have been broken up that way) can be constructed. This permits the firm to judge the relative profitability of different channel efforts.

The benefits of using ABC can be summarized as follows:

1. ABC provides superior information for decision making, by:
   a. Separating winners from losers, whether at the customer, product, or channel level;

TABLE 10-3 Harrison Manufacturing Company Profit and Loss Statement (in thousands of dollars)

Sales		$35,000
Cost of Goods Sold		20,000
Gross Margin		15,000
Expenses:		
Salaries	$3,000	
Advertising	2,500	
Trucking	500	
Rent	3,500	
Insurance	1,400	
Supplies	1,000	
Total Expenses		11,900
Net Profit		3,100

     b. Indicating which customers to chase, via a customer-level ABC analysis; and

     c. Redirecting capital investment to less costly processes or flows.

2. ABC drives a company to undertake strategic improvements, whether they be:

     a. Implementing a just-in-time (JIT) distribution and delivery system;

     b. Improving product design; or

     c. Closing the quality gap between one's own channel offering and those of the competition.[22]

This process can be applied at the level of a specific company inside a channel, or more generally, at a channel-wide level. Consider a hypothetical example at the company level, concerning the Harrison Manufacturing Company, a producer of plastic towel racks, dish drains, soap dishes, and other kitchen and bathroom accessories. Table 10-3 shows Harrison's profit and loss statement, with costs presented in the usual accounting categories. Consistent with the first box of Figure 10-6, we need to identify the channel resources used to sell Harrison's products, and assign costs to them. Suppose that the company's channel costs are limited to those resources associated with the marketing flows of physical possession (storage and delivery); promotion (personal selling, advertising, sales promotion, and publicity); and ordering and payment (billing and collecting). Then, consistent with the second box of Figure 10-6, we need to show how each of the natural expense items shown in Table 10-3 was incurred through Harrison's participation in each of the flows. The breakdown is presented in Table 10-4. For example, it was determined that most of the salaries went to sales agents and the rest went to an advertising manager, a sales promotion manager, a traffic manager, and an accountant, along with various support personnel in each area.

This simplistic example belies the difficulty of splitting natural expenses into functional cost groups. Generally, careful study is required, along with considerable research, before the costs can be allocated appropriately. An example of the various means by which natural expense categories may be assigned to various functional categories is provided in Exhibit 10-4. Also, note that it has been assumed that all the natural expenses listed in Table 10-3 were directly allocable to the func-

TABLE 10-4 **Functional (Flow) Expense Breakdown (in thousands of dollars)**

| NATURAL EXPENSES | TOTAL | PHYSICAL POSSESSION | | PROMOTION | | | ORDERING AND PAYMENT |
		Storage	Delivery	Personal Selling	Advertising	Sales Promotion	Billing and Collection
Salaries	$ 3,000	$ 150	$ 100	$2,000	$ 500	$ 200	$ 50
Advertising	2,500				1,500	1,000	
Trucking	500		500				
Rent	3,500	2,500	50	500	200	100	150
Insurance	1,400	1,000	350				50
Supplies	1,000		500	100	150	150	100
Total	$11,900	$3,650	$1,500	$2,600	$2,350	$1,450	$350

EXHIBIT **10-4 / Classification of Natural Expense Items into Functional (Flow) Cost Groups**

▶ ▶ ▶

Expense Items	Means by Which Natural Expense Items Are Assigned to Functional Cost Groups	Functional Cost Groups to Which Natural Expense Items Are Assigned
Sales salaries and expense	Time study	Order routine and promotion
Truck expense	Direct (to cost group)	Handling (or delivery)
Truck wages	Direct (to cost group)	Handling (or delivery)
Truck depreciation	Direct (to cost group)	Handling (or delivery)
Outside trucking	Direct (to cost group)	Handling (or delivery)
Warehouse wages	Time study (or direct to cost group)	Handling, storage, and investment
Office wages	Time study (or direct to cost group)	Order routine, reimbursement, or other functions
Executive salaries	Managerial estimate	All functional groups
Rent	Space measurement	All functional groups
Storage (outside)	Direct (to cost group)	Storage
Warehouse repairs	Managerial estimate	Storage and handling
Warehouse supplies	Managerial estimate	Storage and handling
Insurance:		
Property & equipment	Managerial estimate	All functional groups
Inventory	Direct (to cost group)	Investment
Personnel	Wages	All functional groups
Office expense	Direct (to cost groups and managerial estimate)	Order routine, reimbursement, promotion, or other functions
Utilities	Some direct (to cost groups), others via space measurement	All functional groups
Professional services	Managerial estimate	Functions benefitted
Taxes, inventory	Direct (to cost group)	Investment
Social Security	Add to wages	All functional groups
Bad debts	Direct (to cost group)	Reimbursement

tional (flow) groupings. Clearly, this may be an oversimplification, because many of the expenses incurred by a firm do not relate directly to the performance of marketing functions.

The third step in Figure 10-6 requires that Harrison allocate flow costs to the various channels used to distribute its product line. Some of the bases available for allocating selected costs associated with various functional categories to different channel or customer groupings are shown in Exhibit 10-5.

The Harrison Manufacturing Company sells directly to department stores, discount houses, and supermarket chains. Using allocation bases similar to those shown in Exhibit 10-5 and applying the results to the Harrison example yield the data in Table 10-5. For example, inspection of the Harrison shipping records showed that the company shipped 500,000 cases of product to department stores, 1,000,000 cases to discount houses, and 800,000 cases to supermarket chains. The total of 2,300,000 cases were shipped for a total cost of $1,500,000 (taken from Table 10-4), or an average cost per case of $0.65. Similarly, it costs Harrison $3.65 per cubic foot of warehouse space to store the merchandise it sells, $236.00 for every sales call made to each of the stores in the various retail chains, and $35.00 for billing and collecting per order. The advertising and sales promotion figures (1.57x and 1.45x) reflect the multipliers that must be applied to each advertising and sales promotion dollar expended by Harrison in each channel. These multipliers permit inclusion of the cost of the support (personnel, rent, and supplies) that has to be given to each of these functional areas.

The final step in applying ABC to distribution channel profitability is the preparation of a profit and loss statement for each channel. In Table 10-6, the cost of goods sold has been allocated to each channel in proportion to the revenues that the channel delivers to Harrison. The expense figures are derived from the information in Table 10-5. Although it is clear from Harrison's distribution cost analy-

---

EXHIBIT **10-5** / **Selected Bases of Manufacturer's Allocation of Functional (Flow) Cost Groups to Channels or Customer Groupings**

Functional Cost Groups	Bases of Allocation to Channels or Customer Groupings
Storage of finished goods	Floor space occupied
Order assembly (handling)	Number of invoice lines
Packing and shipping	Weight or number of shipping units
Transportation	Weight or number of shipping units
Selling	Number of sales calls
Advertising	Cost of space, etc., of specific customer advertising
Sales promotion	Cost of promotions
Order entry	Number of orders
Billing	Number of invoice lines
Credit extension	Average amount outstanding
Accounts receivable	Number of invoices posted

TABLE 10-5 Allocating Functional Group Costs to Marketing Channels

ALLOCATION BASES	PHYSICAL POSSESSION		PROMOTION			ORDERING AND PAYMENT
	Storage (floor space occupied in own warehouse, thousands cu. ft.)	Delivery (number of shipping units, thousands cases)	Personal Selling (number of sales calls, thousands)	Advertising (cost of advertising space, $ thousands)	Sales Promotion (cost of promotions, $ thousands)	Billing and Collection (number of orders, thousands)
Channel Types:						
Department stores	200	500	1	$ 150	$ 100	1
Discount houses	450	1,000	4	700	400	5
Supermarket chains	350	800	6	650	500	4
Total	1,000	2,300	11	$1,500	$1,000	10
Functional group cost ($ thousands)	$3,650	$1,500	$2,600	$2,350	$1,450	$350
Average Cost	$ 3.65	$ 0.65	$ 236.00	1.57x	1.45x	$ 35.00

TABLE 10-6 Profit and Loss Statement for Harrison's Channels (in thousands of dollars)

	DEPARTMENT STORES	DISCOUNT HOUSES	SUPERMARKET CHAINS	TOTAL
Sales	$7,500	$15,500	$12,000	$35,000
Cost of goods sold	4,400	8,800	6,800	20,000
Gross Margin	3,100	6,700	5,200	15,000
Expenses				
Storage ($3.65 per cu. ft.)	730	1,643	1,277	3,650
Delivery ($0.65 per case)	325	650	525	1,500
Personal selling ($236 per call)	236	946	1,416	2,600
Advertising (1.57 ·)	235	1,095	1,020	2,350
Sales promotion (1.45 ·)	145	580	725	1,450
Billing and collecting ($35 per order)	35	175	140	350
Total Expenses:	1,706	5,089	5,103	11,900
Net profit (or loss)	1,394	1,611	97	3,100
Profit-to-sales ratio (%)	18.6%	10.4%	0.8%	8.9%

Note: Apparent addition errors are due to rounding.

sis that all channels are returning a net profit (in reality, a contribution to profit, as not all cost figures have been included in this hypothetical example), the return from serving supermarket chains is very low relative to the return from the other two channels. In addition, the return from the department store channel is surprisingly high: this channel simply uses fewer of Harrison's channel flow resources than do the other two channels. Thus, from a policy perspective, Harrison might use this ABC analysis to justify increasing its business to department stores and/or deemphasizing sales to supermarket chains.

Before a decision is made to emphasize or deemphasize a particular channel in response to an ABC analysis like the one above, however, management should answer the following kinds of questions:

- To what extent do buyers buy on the basis of the type of retail outlet versus the brand? Would they seek out the brand in those channels that are to be emphasized?

- What are the future market trends regarding the importance of these channels?

- Have marketing efforts and policies directed at the channels been optimal?

For example, such a decision would have to be reviewed in light of the possibility that smaller production runs and a reduced scale of production with the same amount of fixed costs would increase the unit manufacturing costs. In addition, a forecast of just what will happen to sales volume over a certain period is needed in order to assess the possible change in distribution policy. It is also necessary to estimate the decrease in total expense that would result from the action.

Besides the decision-making dilemma, there is also the issue of what costs to focus on in an activity-based costing exercise. O'Guin argues that all costs, both fixed and variable, should be included in an ABC analysis:

> ABC debunks the myth of fixed costs. Using today's cost accounting systems, accountants assume many costs are fixed because they do not understand how to control these costs. However, costs are only fixed over a given time horizon. Over the long term all costs are variable—if one understands what creates the cost. . . . ABC allows one to identify the policies, systems, or processes that trigger activity, thereby creating cost. ABC, by ferreting out what really drives costs, allows us to attack and reduce the so-called fixed costs such as sales force expense, engineering, planning, and depreciation.[23]

Even if only direct and traceable costs are allocated and examined in an ABC analysis, as is done in the example above, however, insights into appropriate channel management can still be gleaned. This type of approach gives the channel manager information on the contribution-to-profit figure, if not the net profit figure.

Activity-based costing has been widely used in different channel situations. The following examples profile a few of its applications:[24]

- Cooper and Kaplan describe a building supplies company that distributed its products through six channels. Across all its products, the company had an average gross margin of 35%. Marketing costs for the six channels averaged 16.4% of sales, with general and administrative expenses averaging another 8.5%. The company therefore applied a flat 25% of sales charge against every channel's revenue to account for SG&A expenses. One channel, called OEM (original equipment manufacturer), was a prime target for elimination, because of its low 2% operating margin and 4% return on investment. But the OEM channel in fact used virtually no resources in several major selling categories: advertising, catalog, sales promotion, and warranty. In the remaining selling categories, the OEM channel used proportionately fewer resources per sales dollar than the other major channels. The OEM business also required far less investment in working capital—accounts receivable and inventory—than the other channels. ABC uncovered this discrepancy and helped the firm reallocate SG&A costs more equitably across the channels. The result was a revised cost allocation, leading to a revised operating margin of 9% and a revised return on investment of 30%, comparable to that of the other channels used by the firm.[25]

- Bellcore is the centralized organization supporting the seven regional telephone holding companies after the breakup of the Bell system in 1984. Rule-of-thumb cost allocations caused internal "service centers" at Bellcore (word-processing, graphics, technical publications, and secretarial services functions) to bear an unfairly high cost. This caused them to charge uncompetitively high prices for their services, which in turn led to engineers and scientists either typing their own papers or hiring outside services to do the work. A "death spiral" ensued, with the service centers needing to raise prices more and more to cover their high cost base. The internal transfer cost of typing rose at one point to $50 per page! An application of ABC to the system reallocated costs appropriately to the relevant departments of Bellcore, resulting in more realistic (i.e., lower) cost allocations to the service centers and their return to viability and high usage.[26]

■ General Electric Medical Systems manufactures imaging machines used in hospitals and clinics. The company's field engineers formerly carried about 200 pounds' worth of service manuals on every service call. Several trips to and from the car per service call, often supplemented by phone calls back to the office to check procedures, were not uncommon. Technicians estimated that 15% of their time was taken up in such activities. The solution proposed was to give every field engineer a laptop computer with CD-ROM readers that could carry relevant materials directly to the customer's site, a seemingly very expensive proposition. But an ABC analysis supported the decision, and the result was a 9% productivity increase, equivalent to a $25 million increase in profits. This improvement does not account for the potential gains from field engineers' increased ability to send information back to headquarters to improve service performance and initial product design.[27]

Has ABC improved management practice? The evidence is mixed. Anecdotes like those above suggest the high potential for improved performance that ABC offers. But not all executives agree that ABC is a panacea. In one study, only 8% of executives surveyed believed that their ABC efforts paid off in terms of profitability or continuous improvement of production or distribution processes. But rather than condemn ABC across the board as an accounting and strategic tool, the study's researchers found some common pitfalls to be avoided in implementing ABC, among them:[28]

■ Failing to perform adequate litmus tests (i.e., ABC may not be right for every company or every channel, particularly if traceable costs such as labor costs are a high percentage of total costs. In this case, standard cost analyses perform as well as ABC and are considerably easier to implement.)

■ Failing to understand the strategic nature of the business.

■ Failing to obtain top management support for ABC.

■ Failing to clearly define goals and objectives.

■ Failing to form cross-functional teams.

■ Failing to train the team members.

■ Relying exclusively on complex software and external consultants.

■ Failing to empower team members.

■ Focusing on changing culture versus behavior.

■ Focusing on short-term breakthroughs versus long-term continuous improvements.

ABC cannot replace management's strategic decision making; it is, however, a potent tool for improving the quality of that decision making by accurately and fully representing the costs of running a channel targeted at a specific segment of customers.

Direct Product Profit

Another approach to assessing channel member performance is "Direct Product Profit" (DPP). DPP focuses on the financial performance of individual items or stockkeeping units (SKUs) from the perspective of "downstream" channel members looking "up" the channel at specific vendors.

The concept of DPP was developed in the early 1960s by McKinsey and Company for General Foods Corporation.[29] DPP creates an individual profit and loss statement for each product carried. The system measures product performance by:

- adjusting gross margin for each item to reflect deals, allowances, forward-buy income, cash discounts, etc.

- identifying and measuring costs that are directly attributable to that product (e.g., labor, space, inventory, transportation).[30]

The method requires detailed accounting data, preferably generated through an analysis like activity-based costing. It took the explosion of computerization and modern-day scanning systems to make it a reality.[31]

DPP information provides wholesalers and retailers with more accurate measures of the contribution of a product to their profit than do the traditional measures of value—gross margin, gross profits, and gross profit per unit of space. DPP focuses only on direct costs that are affected by the operating or merchandising practices associated with each product, however. Other expenses that are essentially fixed (e.g., indirect labor, headquarters overhead, etc.) are excluded. An illustration for two different dry grocery products is provided in Table 10-7. It shows that the "true" contributions of two different items can vary substantially. It also shows that gross margin can be a misleading indicator of actual performance. Indeed, as Willard Bishop, a food-industry consultant, points out, "there is oftentimes very little correlation between gross margin and direct product profit."[32] Some of the options available to manufacturers who seek to improve the DPP contribution of their items are listed in Exhibit 10-6.

DPP strikes a practical balance between net profit, which is relatively meaningless for individual products, and gross profit, which ignores direct operating cost and cash discounts. A *Progressive Grocer* study reported in the *CPDA News* agrees:

> In fact, if done well, Direct Product Profit could represent a quantum improvement over gross-margin measurements and stand traditional thinking on its head by disclosing to retailers that products with a high gross margin may actually contribute less to the bottom line than those with a lower margin.[33]

TABLE 10-7 Direct Product Profit Example

The following illustration for two different dry grocery products highlights the key elements of DPP:

	ITEM A (%)	ITEM B (%)
Sales Revenues	100.0	100.0
– Cost of goods	79.5	76.5
Gross margin	20.5	23.5
+ Cash payment discounts	1.6	0.0
+ Deals/allowances	2.0	1.2
+ Forward-buy profits (net)	1.3	0.0
+ Backhaul revenues	0.8	0.0
Adjusted gross margin	26.2	24.7
Warehouse costs		
– Labor	1.1	1.6
– Space	1.0	1.2
Transportation costs		
– Labor/equipment	1.2	1.5
Store costs		
– Stocking labor	2.6	2.9
– Checkout labor	1.7	1.9
– Space (energy, occupancy)	2.2	2.7
Headquarters costs		
– Inventory carrying	0.7	0.4
Total direct product costs	10.5	12.2
Direct Product Profit:	15.7	12.5

Source: "Insight Report: Direct Product Profitability in Perspective," *Competitive Edge* (a publication of Willard Bishop Consulting, Ltd.), Vol. 5 (September 1984), p. 2.

The slim earnings generated by food distributors pose a mandate to boost productivity and reduce cost. DPP methodology forces distributors to learn about the cost behavior of warehouse and storage functions in considerable detail—receiving, moving to storage, paperwork, selecting, checking, loading, and space cost. For small items, shelving and checkout costs must be closely examined; for large items, conserving shelf space is a must.[34] Knowledge of DPP can be especially helpful in improving space management.

The Food Marketing Institute (FMI) has embraced the DPP concept and is coordinating industry efforts to develop a unified DPP model. In 1985 a unified dry-grocery-goods model was released by FMI, and this model has since become the standard of the industry.[35] Since then, FMI has released DPP models for magazines, meats, produce, and bakery products. Such efforts are based on a strong belief that DPP data can be used to foster more and better cooperation between distributors and manufacturers. First, knowledge of DPP can help to identify high-cost products or activities that are susceptible to improvement through manufacturer–distributor joint action, including package size, case size, case and package design, and/or delivery methods. Second, DPP data can help distributors and manufacturers improve distributor profitability by supplementing research-based data on product movements and shelf facings to develop store shelving plans, testing

▶ **E**XHIBIT **10-6** / **Manufacturers' Options to Improve the DPP**
Contribution of Their Items

▶ ▶ ▶

- Consolidation of retail product size

- Streamlining package configurations

- Better utilization of case cube

- Backhaul (customer pickup) programs

- Drop shipments to stores

- Product line reductions

- Case-pack modularity

- Consolidated shipping programs

- Customized "mixed" pallet ordering

- Smaller case packs (for slow movers)

- Prebuilt display modules

store display methods and locations, and conducting product category profit studies. Finally, understanding DPP can materially affect a manufacturer's sales strategies and programs. By learning more about distributors' costs and how they behave, manufacturers should be able to shape their deals to win greater trade acceptance.[36]

DPP is not without its critics, however. The primary application of DPP that has been reported is to add/drop decisions.[37] But, as Borin and Farris point out, the only DPP figures available for *new* items would be projections subject to the optimism of the manufacturers.[38] Furthermore, when Farris, Olver, and DeKluyver surveyed buyers on the decision criteria used to drop particular SKUs, they found that DPP was rarely used, even by those buyers with DPP systems in place. Movement, gross margin, and even "service from supplier" dominated DPP considerations.[39] Borin and Farris also point out problems in using DPP for pricing and space allocation decisions.[40] For example, they note that if DPP is used as the sole criterion for allocating shelf space and too little space is allocated, stockouts will occur, and even if short-term category sales and profits do not suffer, long-term category sales may. In addition, if a customer is lost to another retailer, the loss is far greater than the lost revenues from a single category would predict. Similarly, if promotion of an item increases sales in other categories, DPP will not reflect these benefits.[41]

Reports on the use of DPP vary greatly.[42] When low usage rates are reported, they may reflect a poor understanding of DPP, the time and effort to implement DPP, and/or a feeling that the manager can achieve the same results with present systems.[43] It is also clear that it takes a great deal of time and expense to collect and input the data required by DPP systems. Given these problems, Borin and Faris constructed a "Merchandising Attractiveness Index" (MAI), based on a linear regression of gross margin, dollar sales, unit sales, and shelf area occupied, measures that were more readily available to distributors. They found that their index yielded predicted values of DPP that were virtually identical to DPP in the nine dry-grocery categories they studied. They conclude that "MAI may be a far less expensive way to implement the basic concept of DPP."[44]

In addition to DPP and the measures incorporated in MAI, distributors rely on such tools as:

- **space management systems** that analyze sales and inventory, by item, and recommend changes in shelf-space utilization and product positioning (e.g., Apollo, SpaceMan, SpaceMAX, Accuspace, and HOPE);

- **promotional analysis** that evaluates responsiveness of a product, product category, or a product subcategory to the various promotional variables of price, advertising, and display [e.g., Information Resources Inc.'s (IRI) "Category Promotion Report"];

- **price analysis** that assesses the general price level of a product, product category, or product subcategory versus the market (e.g., IRI's "Category Pricing Report").[45]

Efficient Consumer Response (ECR)

As discussed earlier in this text, Efficient Consumer Response refers to a family of practices that are designed to improve the efficiency of delivery, stocking, and replenishment of inventory in a distribution channel. The notion behind ECR is that the availability of inventory at the point of purchase, say a retail store, should be matched as closely as possible to the time at which the product will be bought— rather than holding "safety stocks" of inventory on the chance that product will be demanded, or on the other hand, stocking out because of underforecasts of demand. Interest in ECR has been greatest in consumer-goods industries, such as the grocery industry and the apparel industry.[46] However, it came initially out of the automobile industry's focus on just-in-time delivery practices.

The ECR Performance Measures Operating Committee, co-sponsored by several grocery manufacturers' associations, wholesalers, and retailers' organizations, has reported on the performance improvements that could be expected from implementation of ECR practices throughout the food industry.[47] They emphasize that implementation of improved processes for handling, shipping, storing, merchandising, and replenishing inventory must pervade the whole distribution channel. If only a subset of the channel members use electronic data interchange technologies to keep track of stock levels and expedite ordering, for example, the extent to which ordering lags can be lessened is limited. They therefore consider "value chain analysis," or the analysis of efficiency throughout the entire channel, as the realm within which a channel should implement ECR techniques.[48]

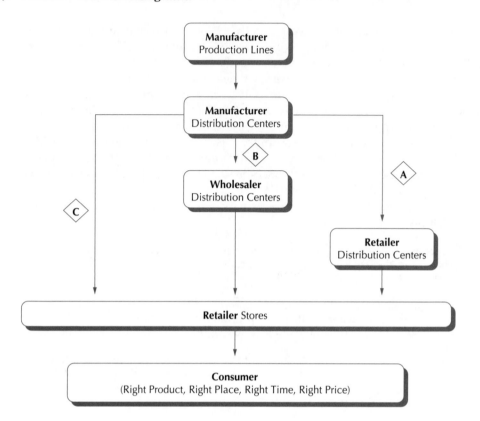

FIGURE 10-7 **Product distribution channels in the U.S. grocery industry.**

Product Distribution Channel Types:

A. Self-Distributing Retailer.
B. Wholesaler-Supplied System.
C. Manufacturer Direct Store Delivery (DSD).

Source: Joint Industry Project on Efficient Consumer Response, "Applying Value Chain Analysis to the Grocery Industry," 1994, p. 1. Reprinted with permission of the Grocery Manufacturers of America, Inc.

The study gives detailed analyses of the major distribution channel forms in the grocery industry, including self-distributing retailers, wholesaler-supplied systems, and manufacturer-direct-store delivery (DSD) systems. The distinctions among these channel forms are detailed in Figure 10-7. The Grocery Industry Activity Model, reproduced in Exhibit 10-7, shows the mapping from more general business processes (introduce products, merchandise products, promote products, and replenish products) to the specific activities constituting those processes. The study goes on to identify which channel members are involved in which activities, by channel type, and to offer ideas for reallocating functions and creating incentives for improvements in channel performance.

The study found that although operating costs in grocery chains totalled $307

EXHIBIT 10-7 / Grocery Industry Activity Model

BUSINESS PROCESS	PRIMARY ACTIVITY
Introduce Products	Conduct basic research Develop new products
Merchandise products	Manage product catagories Manage store operations Serve consumers
Promote products	Manage consumer advertising Mange store advertising Manage consumer promotions Manage in-store promotions Manage costumer deals
Replenish products	Manage store orders Manage customer orders Procure materials Produce products Store and stage products Deliver products Manage invoices

Source: Joint Industry Project on Efficient Consumer Response, "Applying Value Chain Analysis to the Grocery Industry," 1994, p. II-3. Reprinted with permission of the Grocery Manufacturers of America, Inc.

billion, or 81.6% of total sales of $376 billion in the United States, ECR-related cost reductions throughout the industry could promise as much as $24 billion of operating cost reductions and $6 billion of financial savings. Table 10-8 summarizes operating costs by trading partner in standard grocery channels, whereas Table 10-9 shows operating cost reductions that could be experienced under full ECR implementation throughout the industry. Savings range from about 3% for suppliers up to as much as 12% for self-distributing retailers. The study suggests detailed ways to measure the activities engaged in by each grocery channel member, so that (a) benchmarking of current cost levels can be done, and (b) ideas for cost reduction through ECR can be identified and acted on.

▶ THE RESULT OF CHANNEL PERFORMANCE: AUDITING SERVICE QUALITY

The primary task of marketing channels is the delivery of desired service outputs to target customer or consumer segments. It is thus critical to assess the quality of these delivered services. Parasuraman, Zeithaml, and Berry originally proposed that the determinants of service quality, especially for banks, telecommunications companies, repair firms, and other organizations involved in service business, are those listed in Exhibit 10-8.[49] Their later research indicated that five determinants are central, because they are able to capture facets of all of the 10 originally conceptualized dimensions. The five determinants are:

Tangibles: Appearance of physical facilities, equipment, personnel, and communication materials;

Reliability: Ability to perform the promised service dependably and accurately;

Responsiveness: Willingness to help customers and provide prompt service;

Assurance: Knowledge and courtesy of employees and their ability to convey trust and confidence;

Empathy: Caring, individualized attention the firm provides its customers.[50]

They have developed a questionnaire to measure service quality that focuses on these determinants.[51]

▶ **TABLE 10-8** **Total Grocery Industry–**
Operating Costs by Trading Partner

ECR TRADING PARTNER	COSTS BY DISTRIBUTION CHANNEL ($MM)			TOTAL BASELINE COSTS ($MM)
	Self-Distributing Retailer	Wholesaler-Supplied System	Direct Store Delivery (DSD)	
Retailers	$ 31,310	$25,636	$21,062	$ 78,008
Wholesalers		6,240		6,240
Manufacturers	51,279	37,570	35,975	124,824
Suppliers	38,962	28,546	26,209	93,717
Brokers	2,360	1,730	177	4,267
Totals:	$123,911	$99,722	$83,423	$307,056

ECR TRADING PARTNER	COSTS BY DISTRIBUTION CHANNEL (% OF SALES)			TOTAL BASELINE COSTS (% OF SALES)
	Self-Distributing Retailer	Wholesaler-Supplied System	Direct Store Delivery (DSD)	
Retailers	8.3	6.8	5.6	20.7
Wholesalers		1.7		1.7
Manufacturers	13.6	10.0	9.6	33.2
Suppliers	10.4	7.5	7.0	24.9
Brokers	0.5	0.5	0.1	1.1
Totals:	32.8	26.5	22.3	81.6

Source: Joint Industry Project on Efficient Consumer Response, "Applying Value Chain Analysis to the Grocery Industry," 1994, p. 4. Reprinted with permission of the Grocery Manufacturers of America, Inc.

TABLE 10-9 **Total Grocery Industry—Operating Cost Reduction by Trading Partner (all figures in $ million)**

ECR TRADING PARTNER	REDUCTIONS BY DISTRIBUTION CHANNEL ($MM)			TOTAL BASELINE REDUCTIONS ($MM)
	Self-Distributing Retailer	Wholesaler-Supplied System	Direct Store Delivery (DSD)	
Retailers	$3,791	$3,009	$2,174	$ 8,974
Wholesalers		703		703
Manufacturers	4,611	3,604	2,770	10,985
Suppliers	1,401	1,023	804	3,228
Brokers	127	99	8	234
Totals:	$9,930	$8,438	$5,756	$24,124

Source: Joint Industry Project on Efficient Consumer Response, "Applying Value Chain Analysis to the Grocery Industry," 1994, p. 5. Reprinted with permission of the Grocery Manufacturers of America, Inc.

EXHIBIT 10-8 / Determinants of Service Quality

RELIABILITY involves consistency of performance and dependability. It means that the firm performs the service right the first time. It also means that the firm honors its promises. Specifically, it involves:

- accuracy in billing;
- keeping records correctly;
- performing the service at the designated time.

RESPONSIVENESS concerns the willingness or readiness of employees to provide service. It involves:

- knowledge and skill of the contact personnel;
- knowledge and skill of operational support personnel;
- research capability of the organization, for example, securities brokerage firm.

ACCESS involves approachability and ease of contact. It means:

- the service is easily accessible by telephone (lines are not busy and they don't put you on hold);
- waiting time to receive service (e.g., at a bank) is not extensive;
- convenient hours of operation;
- convenient location of service facility.

Exhibit 10-8 (continued)

Exhibit 10-8 (continued)

COURTESY involves politeness, respect, consideration, and friendliness of contact personnel (including receptionists, telephone operators, etc.). It includes:

- consideration for the consumer's property (e.g., no muddy shoes on the carpet);

- clean and neat appearance of public contact personnel.

COMMUNICATION means keeping customers informed in language they can understand and listening to them. It may mean that the company has to adjust its language for different consumers—increasing the level of sophistication with a well-educated customer and speaking simply and plainly with a novice. It involves:

- explaining the service itself;

- explaining how much the service will cost;

- explaining the trade-offs between service and cost;

- assuring the consumer that a problem will be handled.

CREDIBILITY means trustworthiness, believability, honesty. It involves having the customer's best interests at heart. Contributing to credibility are:

- company name;

- company reputation;

- personal characteristics of the contact personnel;

- the degree of hard sell involved in interactions with the customer.

SECURITY is the freedom from danger, risk, or doubt. It involves:

- physical safety (Will I get mugged at the automatic teller machine?);

- financial security (Does the company know where my stock certificate is?);

- confidentiality (Are my dealings with the company private?).

UNDERSTANDING/KNOWING THE CUSTOMER involves making the effort to understand the customer's needs. It involves:

- learning the customer's specific requirements;

- providing individualized attention;

- recognizing the regular customer.

TANGIBLES include the physical evidence of the service:

- physical facilities;

- appearance of personnel;

- tools or equipment used to provide the service;

- physical representations of the service, such as a plastic credit card or a bank statement;

- other customers in the service facility.

Source: A. Parasuraman, Valarie A. Zeithaml, and Leonard L. Berry, "A Conceptual Model of Service Quality and Its Implications for Future Research," *Journal of Marketing*, Vol. 49 (Fall 1985), p. 47.

► SUMMARY AND CONCLUSIONS

Assessing channel performance is a complicated, detail-oriented, and time-consuming matter. The number of pieces of information required can be astounding: consider the list of performance criteria suggested to resellers and vendors of computer hardware, software, and peripherals outlined in Exhibit 10-9. Although the list might vary from industry to industry, it is likely to be as long and as detailed as that in the computer industry for the careful channel manager.

Channel performance can be measured along different dimensions and at different levels. Because performance is a multidimensional construct, it is important to recognize what good performance means for channel effectiveness, channel equity, and channel efficiency. At a micro, within-channel level, research has identified seven behavioral dimensions found to correlate with perceptions of performance of a reseller by a supplier. This suggests the possibility that a rich array of performance dimensions may characterize any relationship between channel members.

Performance measurement at a more aggregate level can also be useful. At the level of the company or channel member as a whole, the Strategic Profit Model provides insights into the elements leading to high return on investment. Economic value analysis supplements the ROI focus of the SPM by measuring performance as the difference between net profit and the full costs of capital, appropriately measured. These tools, aggregate as they are, are well-suited to an assessment of the overall health of a prospective or current channel partner, and can also help in the diagnosis of channel management problems.

At the level of channel flow performance, activity-based costing is a tool to plot out the mapping among resources, activities, and products or channels. It explicitly allows for individual channel flow cost accounting, and maintains the importance of allocating all costs to the level of focus (be it product, channel, or product x channel). ABC is useful in assessing sources of profitability in the grocery industry, where direct product profit has been applied to measure the profitability of stockkeeping units in the grocery store. A poor DPP showing has been responsible for many a product's loss of shelf space!

These more micro-level analyses point to the crucial importance of measuring costs accurately in the channel. Along with ABC, efficient consumer response (ECR) techniques are used in industries like groceries and apparel to cut significant costs from the channel without compromising on service levels. In the final analysis, however, customer or consumer satisfaction is the bottom-line goal; any profitability a channel accrues stems fundamentally from the target market's happiness with the channel's product-plus-service-output offering. Empirical measurement of service quality is now a possibility that, paired with these efficiency-oriented approaches, can add the critical element of effectiveness to overall channel performance.

EXHIBIT **10-9 / Performance Criteria in the Computer Industry for Resellers and Vendors**

RESELLER PERFORMANCE ASSESSMENT ◀ ◀ ◀

Three categories of measures are encouraged when measuring the performance of a computer hardware, software, or peripherals reseller: (1) revenue, (2) expense, and (3) productivity.

Revenue Measures

- Top line revenue

- Blend of revenue in units among hardware, software, peripherals

- Product vs. service revenue blend

- Revenue sources (installed base vs. noninstalled base)

- Margin (in dollars or percentage)

- Realized margin

- Before tax profit

- Revenue per person

- Margin dollars per person

- Profit per person

Expense Measures

■ Expense Ratios:
Marketing (in dollars or percentage)
Sales (in dollars or percentage)
Administration (in dollars or percentage)
R&D (in dollars or percentage)
Service and support (in dollars or percentage)

■ Activity Data:
Direct mail (quantity)
Telemarketing (quantity)
Seminars (quantity / number per seminar / prospects per seminar)
Prospects (quantity)
Demonstrations (quantity / number of prospects)
Sales (quantity / average size)

■ Cost/Activity Data:
Cost per direct mail piece
Cost per telemarketing call
Cost per seminar
Cost per seminar attendee
Prospects per attendee
Cost per prospect
Cost per demonstration
Sales per demonstration
Cost per sale
Cost per revenue dollar
Cost per gross margin dollar

Productivity Measures

■ Revenue per square foot

■ Margin dollars per square foot

■ Revenue per FTE (full-time equivalent employee)

■ Margin dollars per FTE

■ Revenue dollars per expense dollar

■ Margin dollars per expense dollar

■ Revenue dollars per inventory investment (at cost)

■ Margin dollars per inventory investment (at cost)   Exhibit 10-9 (continued)

Exhibit 10-9 (continued)

- Service charge-out rate divided by direct labor cost

- Service staff percentage utilization

- Revenue per salesperson

- Margin dollars per salesperson

- Average sale

- Average account size

- Revenue blend by account

- Transactions per day

- Transaction size (dollars, gross profit dollars, item)

- Transaction cost (dollars, hours)

VENDOR PERFORMANCE ASSESSMENT

Some key questions for resellers to ask when considering carrying a vendor's line include:

- Vendor Strategy:
  How committed is the vendor's senior management to the product and the indirect channel to sell the product?
  Does vendor management have a clear idea of the markets and niches that they want their product(s) sold into?
  How do indirect channels, and the indirect channel strategy, fit into the vendor's total business strategy? Does the head of the Channels Program report to V.P. Sales or is there a V.P. Channels?
  What recruiting strategy does the vendor plan to use to build their channel? Is the vendor selective, or are they signing up "anyone who can fog a mirror"?
  How selective is the vendor when it comes to signing up channel partners? Are there going to be any barriers to entry erected?

- Vendor Management Ability:
  Is the vendor making money? Do they have the cash to make the required investment in getting a channels program operating properly?
  Does the indirect channel have its own Profit and Loss Statement or are the results of the channel mixed up with the results of the direct salesforce?
  How well does the vendor appear to understand the needs of the channel for both a business and a product proposition?
  Do the vendor's channel programs reflect the apparent understanding?
  What types of skills do the vendors' channel development and channel management personnel have?

- Vendor Track Record:
  Does the vendor have a history of revising margins downward just as channel partners begin to make money in a territory or a vertical market?
  Does the vendor have a history of taking territories direct when a channel partner is beginning to make good money in the market?
  Do channel personnel and channel programs change often?
  Does the vendor have a habit of recruiting new channel partners without giving existing channel partners an oportunity to increase their commitment to the vendor?
  Do channel conflict (direct vs. indirect) issues get resolved fairly or are conflicts always resolved in favor of the direct sales force?

- Vendor Business Proposition: Can a reseller make money with this vendor?

Source: Bruce R. Stuart, *Reseller Management Handbook,* 4th Edition (Vancouver, Canada: CHANNEL-CORP Management Consultants Inc., 1994), Chapters 36 and 39.

DISCUSSION QUESTIONS

1. Explain how capital, margin, and financial management are interrelated. What are the hurdles to the practice of high-yield management within marketing channels?

2. Describe in qualitative terms what you perceive to be the strategic profit models (or the strategies for achieving high return on investment) for such firms as Neiman-Marcus (a department store catering to middle-class and above consumers), A&P, Levitz (a furniture warehouse-showroom chain), Graybar Electric (a wholesaler of major appliances), and McKesson (a drug wholesaling firm).

3. What does economic value analysis have to say to a wholesaler/distributor being pressured to adopt just-in-time delivery systems by some of its downstream customers?

4. From an activity-based costing perspective, what is a "resource"? What is an "activity"? How do these terms translate into the channel context?

5. Is it important to account for all costs in a distribution-oriented activity-based costing analysis? Can you still learn something if you have not accounted for all costs? If so, what?

6. Debate the pros and cons of using direct product profit estimates from the perspective of a grocery chain, like Safeway.

7. Debate the pros and cons of using direct product profit estimates from the perspective of a packaged-goods manufacturer, like Procter & Gamble.

8. Why is the word "consumer" a part of the term ECR?

9. Why is it important that ECR practices be adopted by all channel members for the ECR concept to be successful in controlling channel costs?

10. Give an example of a channel situation where significant reductions in channel flow costs, arising out of one of the analytic bases discussed in this chapter, both reduced total channel costs and maintained or raised consumer service quality.

ENDNOTES

[1]Alix M. Freedman, "The Poor Pay More for Food in New York, Survey Finds," The *Wall Street Journal*, April 15, 1991, p. B1.

[2]Nirmalya Kumar, Louis W. Stern, and Ravi S. Achrol, "Assessing Reseller Performance From the Perspective of the Supplier," *Journal of Marketing Research*, Vol. 29 (May 1992), pp. 238–253.

[3]Albert D. Bates, "Pricing for Profit," *Arthur Andersen Retailing Issues Letter*, Vol. 2, No. 8 (Center for Retailing Studies, Texas A&M University, September 1990), p. 2.

[4]*Ibid.*, pp. 2, 3.

[5]J. L. Livingstone and D. J. Tigert, "Financial Analysis of Business Strategy," Babson College Working Paper, Wellesley, 1987, p. 4. Note that the gross margin ratio is defined as the gross margin divided by net sales, whereas the operating expense ratio is defined as operating expenses divided by net sales.

[6]*Ibid.*, p. 5.

[7]For an excellent discussion of these issues, see John Gapper, "The High Price of Customer Contact," *Financial Times*, April 4, 1990, p. 16.

[8]It should be noted that, although simple to calculate, the overall asset turnover is a crude measure at best, because the balance sheets of most well-established companies contain a variety of assets recorded at widely different cost levels of past periods.

[9]James C. Van Horne, *Financial Management and Policy*, 7th ed. (Englewood Cliffs, NJ: Prentice-Hall, 1986), pp. 781–782.

[10]Robert F. Lusch, Deborah S. Coykendall, James M. Kenderine, and Bert C. McCammon, Jr., *Wholesaling in Transition* (Norman, OK: University of Oklahoma Distribution Research Program, 1989), pp. 15, 17.

[11]"The Retail World and Its Implications," presentation at the J. L. Kellogg Graduate School of Management by McKinsey & Company, Inc., April 1994.

[12]McKinsey & Company, "Supercenters and the Future," a speech to the Grocery Industry, Mid-Winter Conference of the Food Marketing Institute, Orlando, FL, January 15–18, 1995.

[13]Economic value has been written about in several business publications. Some of these include Shawn Tully, "The Real Key to Creating Wealth," *Fortune*, September 20, 1993, pp. 38–50, © 1993 Time Inc. All rights reserved; Terence P. Paré, "GE Monkeys with Its Money Machine," *Fortune*, February 21, 1994, pp. 81–82; and Michael Z. Rabin, Uta Werner, and James M. McTaggart, "Beyond Performance Measurement: The Use and Misuse of Economic Profit," *Commentary*, a Marakon Associates publication (August 1994). The discussion in this section builds on these sources.

[14]S. Tully, *Op. cit.*, pp. 39–40.

[15]*Ibid.*, pp. 49–50.

[16]Michael Levy and Michael Van Breda, "A Financial Perspective on the Shift of Marketing Functions," *Journal of Retailing*, Vol. 60 (Winter 1984), pp. 28–29.

[17]*Ibid.*, pp. 26, 29. See also Michael Levy and Charles A. Ingene, "Residual Income Analysis: A Method of Inventory Investment Allocation and Evaluation," *Journal of Marketing*, Vol. 48 (Summer 1984), pp. 93–104.

[18]M. Rabin, U. Werner, J. McTaggart, *Op. cit.*, p. 25.

[19]Presentation by Armando Bombino, "Baxter Healthcare," at J. L. Kellogg Graduate School of Management, Northwestern University, February 1995.

[20]For an excellent overview of activity-based costing, see Michael C. O'Guin, *The Complete Guide to Activity-Based Costing* (Englewood Cliffs, NJ: Prentice-Hall, 1991), especially chapters 2 and 3.

[21]Robin Cooper and Robert S. Kaplan, "Measure Costs Right: Make the Right Decisions," *Harvard Business Review*, Vol. 66 (no. 5, September–October 1988), pp. 96–103.

[22]M. O'Guin, *Op. cit.*, pp. 60–69.

[23]*Ibid.*, p. 32.

[24]A rather extensive, but comprehensive, example of ABC applied to distribution channel analysis for a medical bed manufacturer is found in M. O'Guin, *Ibid.*, Chapter 7.

[25]R. Cooper and R. Kaplan, *Op. cit.*, pp. 100–101.

[26]Edward J. Kovac and Henry P. Troy, "Getting Transfer Prices Right: What Bellcore Did," *Harvard Business Review*, Vol. 67 (no. 5, September–October 1989), pp. 148–154.

[27]Terence P. Paré, "A New Tool for Managing Costs," *Fortune*, June 14, 1993, p. 129.

[28]Bala Balachandran, "Strategic Activity Based Accounting," *Business Week Executive Briefing Service*, Vol. 5 (1994), p. 22. The author cites on this page the following paper: Nandu N. Thondavadi and Bala V. Balachandran, "What Is Going Wrong with Activity Based Costing?" Northwestern University Working Paper, November 1993.

[29]*The Economics of Food Distributors*, McKinsey General Foods Study (New York: General Foods Corporation, 1963).

[30]"Insight Report: Direct Product Profitability in Perspective," *Competitive Edge* (a publication of Willard Bishop Consulting Economists, Ltd.), Vol. 5 (September 1984), p. 1.

[31]*CPDA News* (December 1985–June 1986), pp. 14–15.

[32]"Insight Report: Direct Product Profitability in Perspective," p. 2.

[33]*CPDA News, op. cit.*

[34]*The Economics of Food Distributors, Op cit.*, pp. 37–38.

[35]Food Marketing Institute, *Direct Product Profit Manual* (Washington, D.C.: Food Marketing Institute, 1986.)

[36]*The Economics of Food Distributors, op. cit.*, pp. 34–35.

[37]Touche Ross International, *Third Annual Direct Product Profitability and Space Management Industry Progress Survey Results*, March 1988.

[38]Norm Borin and Paul Farris, "An Empirical Comparison of Direct Profit and Existing Measures of SKU Productivity," *Journal of Retailing*, Vol. 66 (Fall 1990), p. 300.

[39]Paul Farris, James Olver, and Cornelius DeKluyver, "The Relationship Between Distribution and Market Share," *Marketing Science*, Vol. 8 (Spring 1989), pp. 107–128.

[40]Borin and Faris, *op. cit.*, pp. 300–302.

[41]*Ibid.*, pp. 301–302.

[42]Widespread use is reported by Touche Ross International, *op. cit.* and limited use is reported by Farris, Olver, and DeKluyver, *op. cit.*, 107–128.

[43]Borin and Faris, *op. cit.*, p. 302. See, also, Priscilla Donegan, "DPP is Still Growing," *Progressive Grocer*, December 1988, pp. 39–45.

[44]Borin and Faris, *op. cit.*, p. 297.

[45]Willard R. Bishop, Jr., "Category Management: An Emerging Approach to the Grocery Business," presented at the FMI Conference on Merchandising and Technology, January 24, 1989, p. 13.

[46]For an overview of the application of ECR techniques to the apparel industry, see Janice H. Hammond and Maura G. Kelly, *"Quick Response in the Apparel Industry,"* Harvard Business School Publication No. 9-690-038, 1991. The principles of its application there are quite similar to those in the grocery industry, and we therefore concentrate in the discussion following on the grocery industry context.

[47]Joint Industry Project on Efficient Consumer Response, "Applying Value Chain Analysis to the Grocery Industry," 1994.

[48]*Ibid.*, p. 6.

[49]See A. Parasuraman, Valarie A. Zeithaml, and Leonard L. Berry, "A Conceptual Model of Service Quality and Its Implications for Future Research," *Journal of Marketing*, Vol. 49 (Fall 1985), pp. 41–50.

[50]Valarie A. Zeithaml, A. Parasuraman, and Leonard L. Berry, *Delivering Service Quality* (New York: The Free Press, 1990), p. 26.

[51]*Ibid.*, pp. 181–186.

11 / INTERNATIONAL MARKETING CHANNELS ◀◀◀◀◀◀

*E*xcept for the smallest marketers of goods and services, it is doubtful that any commercial institution can avoid contact with the international marketplace in one form or another, even if such avoidance were somewhat desirable. The opportunities to be gained from trading with foreign companies, serving foreign consumers, or offering assortments of merchandise selected from the world's production are simply too great to pass by.

Involvement in the international marketplace is not a trivial extension of marketing and channel management in the home country, however. The international distribution channel can be viewed as having three environmental components, only one of which exists when marketing inside one's own country: the home-country environment, the host-country environment, and the transnational environment (which can encompass region-wide organizations such as the European Community [EC], the North American Free Trade Association [NAFTA], the Asian Free Trade Association [AFTA], the South American trading bloc [MERCOSUR], the General Agreement on Tariffs and Trade [GATT], and the like). All three environments affect both the *feasible* sets of channel arrangements and the *desirable* channel structure and management policies in international marketing. Exhibit 11-1 outlines important factors in the host country that directly influence channel structure.

Exhibit 11-1 / Host Country Factors Influencing International Channel Design and Management

1. *The actors*: profile of consumers (population characteristics) and profile of decision mak- ◀ ◀ ◀
   ers (executives in private and public sectors).
2. *The resources*:
   GNP and its distribution
   Technology
   Stock of capital goods.

Exhibit 11-1 (continued) **493** ▶

Exhibit 11-1 (continued)

3. *Environmental conditions*:
   Geography and typography
   Urbanization
   Ethnographic diversity
   Racial homogeneity and identification
   Religious homogeneity and identification
   Linguistic homogeneity
   Political stability.

4. *Executive behavior*:
   In the government and public sector:
       Imposition of price controls
       Price subsidies
       Control of promotion practices
       Consumer protection laws
       Environmental protection laws
   In the private sector:
       R&D expenditures
       Promotional budgets
       Physical distribution expenditures
       Price discount structure.

Source: Adel I. El-Ansary and Marilyn L. Liebrenz, "Comparative Marketing Systems Analysis: Revisited," in Erdener Kaynak and Ronald Savitt, eds., *Comparative Marketing System*, p. 37. Reprinted with permission of Greenwood Publishing Group, Inc., Westport, CT. Copyright © 1984 by Praeger Publishers.

Beyond this, international channel management frequently involves *multinational* management issues, such as the issue of how uniformly a channel strategy can be applied across many countries or market regions. One can thus view international channel management as differing from domestic channel management in the extent of environmental differences present in the former, which often serve as constraints on the way channels are designed.

Consider just two of the more pressing governmental and regional developments facing international channel managers in recent history: NAFTA and GATT. The passage of NAFTA in 1994 marked the beginning of even greater openness among the markets of Canada, the United States, and Mexico. By September 1994, just six months after the signing of the agreement, almost half of the 1,000 U.S. respondents to a KPMG Peat Marwick survey said that they either had completed or were developing a market entry strategy for the Mexican market. Interestingly, the most common response to the question of what NAFTA's effects would be was that it would increase the respondent firms' ability to penetrate the rest of Latin America.[1] Clearly, the effects of this limited regional agreement ripple outward to the marketing decisions made in adjoining countries. But despite this optimism about the Latin American region, even the passage of NAFTA has not made the border transparent. Some U.S. marketers report difficulties dealing with a Mexican government overrun with bureaucracy. As mentioned in Chapter 2, Wal-Mart's Supercenter in Mexico City was forced to close for 24 hours in mid-1994 because government inspectors found its products lacked proper labeling. Radio Shack de Mexico, a joint venture between Tandy and the Mexican retailer Grupo Gigante, opened in Mexico in 1992, but has faced many border-crossing and tariff problems, and slowed its plans for store expansion as a result.[2] Reconciling the contradictory messages implied by the passage of a major regional trade agreement, on the one hand, *and* the persistence of local authorities in protecting local interests, on the other, is clearly a significant challenge.

Changes in the rules governing international trade pervade more than just regional trading blocs, however. The General Agreement on Tariffs and Trade successfully concluded the Uruguay Round of talks in December 1993, with the promise of reductions in worldwide trade barriers that some experts estimate will lead to an annual increase of $270 billion to the $30 trillion world economy by the year 2002.[3] A summary of the key results of the latest round of GATT negotiations is shown in Exhibit 11-2: it provides for lowering tariffs and nontariff barriers in wide classes of trade, from agricultural products to services. This has profound implications for both firms selling (or planning to sell) overseas and those staying at home. The overseas marketer is likely to see lower entry barriers to foreign market selling, whereas the competitor who stays at home is conversely likely to see more competition from foreign entry. The bottom line is that no firm can escape the increasing level of competition implied by changes in the international rules of the trading game.

Beyond changes like these in the legal and governmental environment, different countries and regions simply have different norms for doing business and different underlying market conditions that can cast difficulties in the path of the would-be international marketer. Although it is impossible to deal with each country separately (the number of countries in the world is greater than 170, and sometimes seems to be growing by the week!), some relevant examples will suffice to show the peculiarities of individual markets. Additional highlights can be found in the discussion of developments in international retailing in Chapter 2.

WESTERN EUROPE   A focus on retailing is instructive to see the impact of changing industry structure, changing government regulation, and international profit opportunities on channel behavior. Rigid regulatory environments protected European retailers in the past, creating havens for small, lower-profit, higher-priced competitors. However, these traditional outlets are being threatened today by a combination of increased price sensitivity and decreased brand loyalty of consumers, on the one hand, and transnational market entry, on the other.[4]

Some of the entrants taking advantage of the identified profit opportunities are U.S.-based. For example, Price/Costco Inc., the biggest U.S. warehouse club company, opened an outlet outside London in 1994. J. Sainsbury, Britain's largest supermarket chain (and its most profitable), tried to challenge Price/Costco's legal status as a wholesaler in British courts, arguing that Price/Costco should compete

EXHIBIT 11-2 / Outline of Provisions of December 1993 GATT Agreement

SECTION OF AGREEMENT OR INDUSTRY CONCERNED	GATT PROVISIONS	MAIN IMPACT
General Industrial Tariffs	Cut by rich countries by more than one-third. Over 40% of imports enter duty-free. Key traders scrap duties for pharmaceuticals, construction equipment, medical equipment, steel, beer, furniture, farm equipment, spirits, wood, paper and toys.	Easier access to world markets for exporters of industrial goods. Lower prices for consumers. Higher-paying jobs through promotion of competitive industries.
Agriculture	Subsidies and import barriers cut over six years. Domestic farm supports reduced by 20%, affecting U.S. sugar, citrus fruit, peanuts, among others. Subsidized exports cut by 36% in value and 21% in volume. All import barriers converted to tariffs and cut 36%. Japan's and South Korea's closed rice markets gradually open. Tariffs on tropical products cut by over 40%.	Lower food prices for consumers in previously protected countries. Better market opportunities for efficient producers. Special treatment for developing countries.
Services	Freer trade in financial, legal, and accounting services comes under international trading rules for the first time. Further talks on telecommunications and financial services planned. Specific terms of market access still to be worked out, particularly with developing countries.	Boost for trade in services, worth $900 billion annually in crossborder trade in 1993 and another $3 trillion in business of foreign subsidiaries. Further liberalization to be negotiated.
Intellectual Property	Extensive agreement on patents, copyright, performers' rights, trademarks, geographical indications (wine, cheese, etc.), industrial designs, microchip layout designs, trade secrets. International standards of protection, and requirements for effective enforcement. Extra time for developing countries to put rules in place.	Boost for foreign investment and technology transfer. But poor countries with weak patent protection fear higher prices for drugs and seeds. Many developing nations have a decade to phase in patent protection for drugs. France refuses to liberalize market access for U.S. entertainment industry.
Textiles and Clothing	Quotas in effect under the Multi-Fiber Arrangement (MFA) since 1974 for importation of textiles and clothing are progressively dismantled over 10 years, and tariffs reduced. Developing countries reduce trade barriers. Normal GATT rules apply at the end of 10 years.	Developing countries able to sell more textiles and clothing abroad. Reduced prices for consumers worldwide because of fairer textiles and clothing trade (worth $248 billion in 1992).
Antidumping	Previous rules allowing antidumping duties to be levied to combat dumping (exports priced below domestic prices) made more clear. Permitted duties lapse after 5 years. Rules promulgated covering the circumvention of antidumping duties by relocating production.	More difficult to use antidumping duties for trade harassment. Harder to dodge duties by relocating.
Subsidies	Previously, subsidized exports could be met with countervailing duties. Change: definition of which subsidies are legal and which are not: some prohibited, some nonactionable (e.g. research or regional development). Others are actionable if they harm competitors. More leeway for developing countries. Further talks on civil aircraft subsidies.	Tighter curbs on subsidy use, especially for exports. More difficult to use antisubsidy actions for trade harassment.

SECTION OF AGREEMENT OR INDUSTRY CONCERNED	GATT PROVISIONS	MAIN IMPACT
Safeguards (actions to protect domestic industry from sudden import surges that threaten serious injury, e.g., via "voluntary" export restraints)	Rules for conduct of investigations laid down. Measures not to exceed four years, must be progressively liberalized over their lifetime.	Lower prices for consumers and importers. Better access to markets for efficient producers. Increased pressure on inefficient producers to improve performance.
Technical Barriers (product regulations, standards, used by governments to ensure product safety for consumers and the environment)	Better rules to ensure that technical norms, testing, and certification procedures do not prevent trade. Rules deal with animal and plant health and safety measures.	Reduction in costs of complying with different standards and regulations. Environmental and consumer groups fear that higher standards than international norms may be discouraged.
Government Procurement	Enlarged coverage in separate accord to include services, public works, procurement by regional and local governments and public utilities. Separate telecommunications negotiations in 1994.	Value of procurement contracts subjected to open international bidding could rise from $32 billion in 1990 to over $1 trillion.
World Trade Organization	GATT becomes permanent world trade body covering goods, services, and intellectual property rights with a common disputes procedure.	Boost to the status of international trading rules, and more effective advocacy and policing of the open trading system.
Dispute Settlement	Rules to increase automaticity and reduce delays in adoption and implementation of reports. Provision for binding arbitration and appeals. Single disputes procedure for all trade areas.	Harder to block panel judgments. Speedier and more automatic procedures to enhance World Trade Organization's authority in settling disputes. Restraint of U.S. unilateral action by inclusion of virtually all trade in the multilateral system.

Source: Adapted primarily from "GATT: The Deal Is Done," *Financial Times,* December 16, 1993, p. 4, with some supporting points from Louis S. Richman, "What's Next After GATT's Victory?" *Fortune,* January 10, 1994, p. 66.

under the more stringent regulations governing retailers in Britain. It lost this legal battle, and was forced to drop prices on 300 basic food items to counter Price/Costco's offering.[5] Other U.S.-based entrants to the European market include Toys "R" Us, with stores in several countries; Staples, the office supply retailer, operating eight German warehouse stores with a local partner, MAXI-Papier; Kmart, which purchased 13 department stores in the Czech Republic and Slovakia; and T.J.

Maxx, the clothing discounter. The belief is that these retailers can actually be *more* profitable in Europe than in the U.S., because their competition in Europe is still full-margin retailers.[6]

Transnational entries via acquisition or expansion have also occurred between European retailers in different countries. For example, Tesco of the U.K. bought the 92-store Catteau supermarket chain in France in December 1992. Kingfisher retailing group of the U.K. bought Darty, the French electrical retailer, in early 1993. Ahold of the Netherlands, Aldi and Tengelmann of Germany, and the French Promodès and Carrefour all accrue more than 30% of their sales outside their home countries.[7]

These events signal potentially large profit opportunities from transnational retail expansion. On the flip side, local regulations still constrain retail operations differentially in different European markets. Portugal limited the establishment of new hypermarkets in 1993 in an effort to protect small shopkeepers. The move was viewed as necessary because hypermarkets increased their share of Portuguese retail sales from 5.4% in 1987 (one year after the first hypermarket opened) to 31% in 1992, with a total of only 31 store sites.[8] On a different dimension, the British "Resale Prices Act of 1976" prevents a manufacturer from setting minimum resale prices for his products (except in the book and pharmaceutical industries) and has forced many manufacturers to sell to discounters even when they believe doing so will tarnish the reputation of their products.[9]

Germany has been the home of several laws inhibiting retail activity. The *Zugabeverordnung* makes it illegal to offer free gifts in connection with the exchange of goods in Germany, and the *Rabattgesetz* prohibits offering products on sale except at predesignated sales periods in the year. The *Ladenschutzgesetz* further restricts the hours that German shops may remain open per week. Despite some modifications in the first two German laws, American Express was still forced in 1993 to halt advertising of a promotion involving an offer of bonus points redeemable for air travel and hotel accommodations for each Deutsche mark spent with an American Express card. German competition authorities argued that the action violated the *Zugabeverordnung*, because it involved offering another good (airline miles or hotel credits) along with sales of American Express card services. American Express unsuccessfully took its case to the European Court, an EC-wide legal venue, which ruled that restrictions on a foreign company's right to trade in a host country are not harmful as long as domestic companies must operate under the same laws.[10] These examples highlight the importance of first recognizing market and profit opportunities, such as those in European retailing, and second being able to work under discrepancies among different local legal practices.

RUSSIA AND FORMER SOVIET BLOC COUNTRIES   Given their history under Soviet rule, these countries are still learning how to compete in a capitalistic marketplace. Further, the lack of a consistent quality of distribution infrastructure hampers foreign companies' efforts to enter and establish distribution in the same manner as in the West: for example, Warsaw's road system and overall economic level is much more highly developed than elsewhere in Poland. This suggests the need for not just a national, but really a regional, focus on distribution strategy within a country.

One study of the Czech and Slovak Republics, Hungary, and Poland found that household spending on food, drink, and tobacco is 70% of total income in Poland and 50% in Hungary, whereas it averages only 19% of total income across EC member countries. Further, as much as 25% of grocery expenditures is estimated to go to black-market products. Although Russians and Eastern Europeans exhibit high awareness of Western brands, they also show low brand loyalty. This has made it difficult for Western packaged-goods manufacturers to hold customers for repeat purchases. However, various promotional efforts have been highly successful, such as a contest run by a Western European coffee company in the Czech Republic offering a chance to win a car: this promotion drew entries from almost one-third of the whole country's population![11] The lack of brand loyalty could be due at least in part to the following common attitude toward provision of service outputs along with products in Poland:

> Polish businesspeople are absolutely obsessed with product as a marketing variable, leftover baggage from the old regime. Many firms believe their products should be sold based on their own merit without any support by sales or advertising. The concept of a total product as the sum of everything about it (packaging, service, etc.) was novel.[12]

This lack of sophistication in distribution channel management is also evident in Russia. AT&T discovered that direct mail was an alien concept there in 1993, when its 4,000-piece mailing to promote business telephone systems was held up in the Russian post office because it looked highly suspicious. AT&T's advertising agency had to step in to clear up the confusion with Russian postal officials. Creative steps also had to be used to develop an appropriate mailing list, as phone directories and mailing lists are not available to the Russian public. The entire approach had to be much more basic than AT&T's business promotions in the U.S.[13]

Russian governmental constraints, inexperience in managing a market-based economic system, and a thriving black market all make it extremely difficult to compete there. One report notes:

> The distance Russia has to go to develop a modern market economy is highlighted when one considers the common features that underlie the many different "brands" of capitalism around the world.
>
> One is a competitive price system; a second is a system of agreed-upon "rules of the game." The latter extend from general values . . . to specific laws and regulation. They also include norms—for instance, a dispute over a contract should not be settled by murder but by a court. And a market system is embedded in a legal, cultural, and institutional context that supports its workings.
>
> By these criteria, Russia has a long way to go on the road to a mature market system. . . . A body of rules and laws is yet to be written. Even lawyers are in short supply and good independent judges are even more scarce. The concept of property, fundamental to a market system, is far from worked out.[14]

One foreign firm facing these market constraints in 1994 was Trinity, the General Motors dealership in Moscow. It had to pay duties and value-added taxes totalling 166% of a car's value, so that a Chevrolet Caprice that sold for $24,000 in the U.S. would sell in Moscow for $58,000. And Russian law gave buyers broad rights to claim defects at any time during a product's warranty period. The dealer then had just 20 days to replace the car entirely, after which it was fined 1% of the car's retail price for every day it was late! This was a tough standard to live up to, since it took Trinity about 30 days to ship a car from the U.S. to Moscow. Trinity planned to decrease warranty coverage from one year to just a few months to minimize its liability. Meanwhile, Trinity management estimated that in 1994, 80% of the cars imported into Moscow came not via authorized channels, but via black or gray markets where duties are not paid (although bribes are)—making it impossible to grow sales aggressively.[15]

Despite these limitations, foreign companies continue to enter Russia. Over 90 foreign retailers had entered the Russian market by 1995, including 24 from Germany, 14 from France, 10 from the U.S., and 8 each from Finland, Italy, and the U.K. They compete with Russia's 350,000 shops, 95% of which have privatized, and about 75,000 street kiosks. They are encouraged by the lower degree of competition implied by the amount of retail space per capita in Russia (only one-third that in western European countries), combined with increasing incomes per capita and an awareness of foreign products.[16] Foreign entrants cope with the market's constraints by adjusting their expectations (McDonald's management admitted in 1993 that they had no idea when they would recoup their initial $50 million investment in Russia, but nevertheless went ahead with expansion in a number of outlets)[17] or by partnering with local firms who can help them negotiate the Russian market (as did Cincinnati, Ohio-based Vision Express, which partnered with local businesspeople to open stores both in Russia and in the Baltic states). Dean Butler, head of Vision Express, believed that "only a partner native to the system can figure out how to get gasoline, negotiate with customs officials and maneuver through the bureaucracy."[18]

JAPAN   Constraints specific to the Japanese market, as well as recent changes in those constraints, characterize channel management in Japan. Local as well as foreign competitors have to run a gauntlet of regulations to open a superstore, for example. The Large-Scale Retail Store Law, long a barrier to the entry of large stores into established retail areas, has been relaxed in recent years but still poses hurdles: it can delay a store's opening, reduce the store's planned size, force early store closings (by 7:00 p.m., for example), and restrict the number of days per year that stores can be open. Separate government licenses are required to sell fish, meat, bread, dairy products, ethical drugs, and more; over 40 laws must be obeyed to open a store.[19]

Some foreign entrants to the Japanese market find they must change the way they manage their channels because of industry practice or local economic conditions more than overt governmental regulation. Citibank has been expanding its branch network in Japan, and has found particular difficulty in offering broad automatic teller machine (ATM) services. Japanese city banks jointly own the Bancs network, with 27,000 cash machines around the country. But Citibank was offered access to the network only if it would bear half the total costs of building the network. It declined the offer, instead setting up 40 on-site ATM's and 20 off-site ones. Real estate costs made it too expensive to duplicate the expanse of the Bancs network, so instead, Citibank has tried a strategy of exceeding the service levels of the competition. It became the only bank to offer 24-hour ATM service.[20] Thus, it has tried to trade off the spatial convenience of its ATM service (fewer outlets) for lower waiting times (round-the-clock access).

Sometimes a partner with local expertise is necessary to get through the informal channel entry barriers in Japan. International Game Technology (IGT), a U.S. slot-machine maker, set out to sell its machines in Japan in 1989, after noticing that its three largest competitors in Nevada were Japanese. The Japanese market offered an immense opportunity, as the country has about two-thirds of the world's total slot machines—about 800,000. The difficulties IGT encountered arose out of the close-knit Japanese industry, characterized by mutual understandings among local competitors. For example, the company could not get a copy of the specifications for slot machines in Japan, because government regulators did not have openly available specifications. Only members of *Nichidenkyo*, the industry trade association, were told of the machine specifications. When the company tried to join *Nichidenkyo*, it discovered that any new member must be recommended by three current members, and have three years of manufacturing experience in Japan—a virtual Catch-22. Japanese spokespeople maintained that the rules were designed not to keep out foreign competition, but to screen out Japanese companies tied to organized crime. IGT eventually hired Jun Okawa, a former MITI bureaucrat, to help it penetrate the market, and simultaneously asked its local U.S. government representatives for help. After four years and numerous product redesigns, IGT was finally ready to export its first machine to the Japanese market in 1993. Downstream in the channel, pachinko parlor operators may be more than ready for slot-machine competition: one operator noted that with the former tightknit set of Japanese producers, "Every time the price of one machine went up, the price of all the machines went up by the same amount."[21]

Some constraints shaping channel and entry strategy in the Japanese market are shifting, however. Japanese consumers have become better-traveled and more savvy about good value and bargain-hunting. Recession in the early 1990s helped increase Japanese consumers' price sensitivity. As a result, discount retailers have found improving market opportunities, in categories as diverse as clothing, furniture, and consumer electronics. From 15 to 30% of discounters' wares are imported, compared with less than 5% at standard department stores, implying a significant opportunity for foreign manufacturers seeking retail outlets.[22]

Further, Japanese manufacturers are starting to abandon the system of "multiple price fixing," where prices (and hence gross profit margins) were dictated all the way through the distribution channel, resulting in retail price maintenance as well. In April 1994, Ajinomoto abandoned this system in its restaurant-products lines (and was in the process of doing so for its consumer lines) in favor of a simpler one setting a single price for the first-tier wholesaler and letting the market clear the remainder of the channel.[23]

Many retailers are themselves refusing to maintain manufacturers' suggested retail prices; a survey done by Japan's Fair Trade Commission reported that between 1989 and 1994, the percentage of toy retailers setting suggested retail prices dropped from 70 to 30%. More than 80% of retailers surveyed said that the advances made by Toys "R" Us were the cause of the change in their pricing policies. Such changes on both the manufacturer and retailer sides signal a shift in leverage toward retailers, particularly large ones, just as has been the trend in both Europe and the U.S.[24] Even high-end manufacturers like Shiseido, the cosmetics and skin-care products company, have moved away from expensive items toward a focus on increased volume, in response to the dual influence of increased consumer price sensitivity and the rise of discount retailers. Experts estimate that their chain of 25,000 franchised chain stores could shrink by half over the next 20 years, and that the number of Shiseido-employed beauty consultants in department stores could be decreased as well.[25]

CHINA Many manufacturers and retailers eye the People's Republic of China (PRC) with enthusiasm, given its 1.2 billion population. Attention often focuses on cities like Guangzhou, the capital of Guangdong province, whose 6 million relatively wealthy (by Chinese standards) inhabitants can find everything from Pizza Hut to Louis Vuitton handbags in their city. However, it is critically important to remember that not all of China's 1.2 billion inhabitants are high-potential consumers of even the most mundane (by developed-market standards) consumer goods. The average urban household income in 1994 was 355 yuan ($42) a month, whereas rural households averaged less than 1,000 yuan *annually*. Inflation of as much as 30% in some cities leaves real income stagnant for many. And the market is immensely diverse. Even if a company can identify the most wealthy Chinese, the complexity and government control of the distribution system make it difficult to reach them.[26]

A 1994 McKinsey study estimated that about 100 million Chinese had incomes of at least $1,000 annually, thus falling into the "economically active" population. A DRI/McGraw-Hill manager identified three main parts of China's consumer market:

- Imported luxury goods, such as high-price spirits, designer watches, and certain cosmetics, could find a market of 5 million people. This would represent the richest 1% of those living in urban areas, but only the top 0.2% of those in the countryside.

- Imported "middle-class" products, such as jeans and cheap training shoes, could sell to around 20 million people: the top 2.5% in cities and the top 1% in rural areas.

- Locally made "middle-class" goods, such as cheap electrical appliances, would have a potential market of 65 million people: the top 10% in urban areas and the top 4% in rural areas. This would also include most "fast-moving consumer goods" (FMCG), such as detergents and packaged foods."[27]

There is general agreement that the distribution channel is key to any company's success in China. The Chinese distribution network is still largely government-owned, and foreign firms are often forbidden to set up their own distribution networks (exceptions include companies like Avon, with its network of 40,000 direct-selling "Avon ladies" in southern and eastern China).[28] Logistics and physical distribution can be a nightmare: one company reportedly resorted to using the People's Liberation Army as a distribution mechanism after discovering that only one-third of its shipments were reaching their market destinations intact![29] Shipments from Shanghai to Beijing (a distance of just 1,000 kilometers) can take as long as three weeks, and effective cross-country distribution could be several years away. And labor shortages, particularly of managerial staff, constrain the growth of many companies' Chinese marketing efforts.

Added to this is the fact that the retail market is highly fragmented: FMCG stores in Beijing, Shanghai, and Guangzhou together account for less than 1% of the country's 13 million stores. All but 4 million Chinese stores are in small towns and villages. And for still-obscure reasons, stores in different cities stock wildly different arrays of products. Such differences could reflect regional taste differences or simply distribution inefficiencies; if the latter, there could be significant opportunities for improving product assortment and variety for the Chinese consumer.

Despite these problems, and the associated political and economic risks of distributing in China, many companies have chosen to enter the market. Japanese investment in China in the March–September 1993 period jumped by 58% over year-earlier figures, whereas Japanese investment in the U.S. dropped by 20% comparing the same periods. Japanese retailers Yaohan and Daiei both announced significant investment plans in China, Yaohan planning $500 million in investment and Daiei planning its first Chinese supermarket with an investment of over $30 million.[30] Among global consumer packaged-goods manufacturers, Unilever has planned to invest $100 million per year over the 1994–1999 period, with a goal of increasing Chinese sales from $200 million in 1994 to $1.5 billion by the year 2000. Nestlé has plans to grow sales from its 1994 level of SFr 200 million to SFr 1 billion in a few years. And Procter & Gamble has also planned a significant presence in China. One businessman summed up the risk-return tradeoff in this market by saying: "If you wait until the risks in China are lower, then you will simply be too late."[31]

OTHER ASIAN MARKETS No two Asian countries have followed the same development paths, so current conditions vary tremendously from country to country. In a 1993 study entitled "The East Asian Miracle," the World Bank pointed out that the top eight East Asian economies (Hong Kong, Indonesia, Japan, Malaysia, Singapore, South Korea, Taiwan, and Thailand) grew at an average annual rate of 5.5%, which was more than twice as fast as other East Asian countries and three times as fast as Latin America. Their share of world exports of manufactures jumped from 9% in 1965 to 21% in 1990. All of them allocated a relatively high share of the Gross Domestic Products, GDP, to basic primary and secondary education, critical for building a skilled labor force. And most emphasized export promotion and an outward-looking commercial focus. But the eight countries all followed different policies regarding protectionism, export promotion, regulation, and the like: Hong Kong has been the most free-market oriented, whereas Japan and South Korea have been the most interventionist in their policies.[32] One immediate implication is that foreigners seeking to build distribution channels and a marketing presence throughout Asia must treat each country separately, being aware of inter-country differences not just in size and GDP per capita, but also in infrastructure, government control, and cultural fundamentals.

From these insights and examples, some immediate conclusions emerge. First, although the framework for channel analysis described in this book applies equally well within a single country or across country borders, there are undoubtedly issues that need to be raised when considering international expansion that simply do not face the domestic marketer. We can characterize these issues as constraints that shape the channel structure and ongoing management decisions the company makes. Second, there are some channel management issues that tend to arise seldom, if ever, in domestic marketing, but rather more frequently in international marketing. These issues need to be confronted if a successful domestic marketer is to extend its success overseas. Third, a relevant question to ask is (a) whether and (b) how extensively a company can globalize its domestic distribution strategy? That is, how much of a successful channel formula in one market can be extended and copied to foreign markets?

To speak to these issues, we first discuss the formation of international distribution channels and modes of entry to foreign markets (the international analog to the domestic question of choice of institutional form of the channel). Following is a discussion of effectiveness issues in the international channel, including understanding transnational differences in demands for service outputs and their implications for the optimal split of channel functions and flows in foreign markets. A focus on coordinating the international channel follows, concentrating on the key channel management issue of international gray marketing. Finally, the question of degree of globalization of the transnational channel system is discussed.

▶ INTERNATIONAL CHANNEL FORMATION AND MODES OF ENTRY

When forming an overseas channel, three key questions must be answered:

1. What *modes of entry* can be used?
2. What *factors* affect the *optimal* entry mode?
3. *Who* is the right channel partner?

This section deals with each of these questions in turn.

Alternative Modes of Entry

A company's mode of entry is its method of getting its product(s) to the foreign market. Different modes vary in their cost, risk, and productivity. One study of U.S. companies' entry modes showed the range of choices (see Table 11-1).

Just over half of the firms chose exporting of one form or another, a relatively low-investment option. Of those that chose a higher-investment option, the favorite was ownership from start-up, in some sense the opposite pole from exporting in terms of investment and ongoing involvement in the foreign channel.

More formally, Root describes foreign market entry as being of two fundamental types: exporting, or some other entry mode involving the transfer of the entrant's technological, capital, or human skills to the foreign country. He lists several alternatives within these two broad forms (see Exhibit 11-3).

TABLE 11-1   **Entry Strategies of U.S. Companies in Foreign Markets**

ENTRY MODE	PERCENTAGE OF RESPONDENTS
Export	51
Licensing	7
Joint Venture	11
Ownership via Start-up	20
Ownership via Acquisition	11

Source: Strategic Management Group Inc., *Export to Win* (Philadelphia, PA: Software, 1989). Quoted in Warren J. Keegan, *Global Marketing Management* (Upper Saddle River, NJ: Prentice-Hall, 1995), p. 350.

EXHIBIT **11-3** / **Options for Foreign Market Entry**

Export Entry Modes   ◄ ◄ ◄

Indirect
Direct agent/distributor
Direct branch/subsidiary

Resource-Transferring Modes: Contractual Entry Modes

Licensing
Franchising
Technical agreements
Service contracts
Management contracts
Construction/turnkey contracts
Contract manufacture
Countertrade arrangements

Resource-Transferring Modes: Investment Entry Modes

Sole venture: new establishment
Sole venture: acquisition
Joint venture: new establishment/acquisition

Source: Reprinted with permission of Lexington Books, an imprint of Simon & Schuster Inc., from Franklin R. Root, *Entry Strategies for International Markets*, Revised and Expanded, p. 26. Copyright © 1994 by Lexington Books.

Export entry modes, the simplest form of expansion, are distinguished by the fact that the company's product is manufactured outside the target country. Exportation can be achieved directly, through the use of distributors or agents in the target market (the "direct agent/distributor" path), or by establishing overseas marketing subsidiaries (the "direct branch/subsidiary" path). In contrast, indirect exporting involves the use of domestic middlemen, such as trading companies, domestic export management companies, or piggybacking.[33] Small companies that do not have the resources to set up their own sales offices or subsidiaries may rely on an export management company (EMC) to build their international sales. The EMC is an international specialist that functions as the exclusive export department for several allied but noncompeting manufacturers. An EMC usually solicits business in the name of the manufacturer and may even use the manufacturer's letterhead. Although EMC's are independent intermediaries, they *are* the manufacturing firm as far as the potential overseas buyer is concerned. They operate under contract and are compensated by salary, commission, or retainer plus commission. There are between 2,000 and 2,500 EMCs operating in the U.S., accounting for as much as 10% of U.S. exports. Examples include Dreyfus & Associates Ltd., which handles export functions for eight tool manufacturers and had sales of $2.5 million in 1992, and International Projects Inc., a Toledo, Ohio, company that handles the products of 16 makers of pleasure boats, hospital supplies, air conditioner-repair equipment and stationery, with 1992 sales of $8 million.[34]

Through piggybacking, a manufacturer (the "carrier") uses its foreign distribution facilities to sell another company's (the "rider's") products alongside its own. The rider retains control over its products' total marketing strategy, including pricing and advertising. Successful piggybacking typically means selling complementary (rather than substitutable) product lines, to maximize both sales synergies and the incentive for the carrier to promote the rider's products. Piggybacking provides a low-risk, easy way for a rider to begin export marketing operations; it helps broaden the product lines of the carrier; and it generates economies of scale due to fuller utilization of the carrier's distribution system.[35] Examples of piggybacking include the following:

▪ Pepsi agreed to bottle and distribute Cadbury Schweppes brands, including Schweppes and Canada Dry, in Hungary, Poland, the Czech Republic, and Slovakia, in early 1993. Meanwhile, Cadbury Schweppes still bottles Pepsi products in southern Spain and France, while Pepsi distributes Cadbury Schweppes products in parts of the U.S.[36]

▪ Giordano Ltd., a Hong Kong clothing retailer, and J.C. Penney agreed to sell their clothing through the Aoyama Trading Co. discount chain in Japan in 1994.[37]

▪ Crisoba Productos Consumidor, a Mexican company owned by Scott Paper and Mexican investors, distributes Glad Bags for First Brands and tampons for Tambrands. Clorox manufactures bleach in Mexico, but uses Colgate-Palmolive's distribution channel to sell it there.[38]

- On July 1, 1991, Shop America introduced catalogs through 7-Eleven (Japan) Company's 4,000 stores in Japan. The venture used a computer system allowing 7-Eleven clerks to send orders directly to Shop America's New York home office.

- Kauai Kookie Kompany of Hawaii sells its cookies through Japanese travel agencies. The cookies are featured in catalogs along with other *omiyage*, or gifts, from Hawaii. The Japanese traveler can purchase the cookies on returning from Hawaii, avoiding having to carry them home.[39]

The advantage of exportation to foreign markets is that it involves minimal investment; thus, the risk of failure will not usually affect the overall activities of the firm. The disadvantage of relying mainly on exporters, however, is the ensuing loss of control over many aspects of the marketing of the firm's products in foreign markets.

Contractual entry modes involve nonequity associations between or among firms in the home and target markets, and produce the transfer of technology or skills. For example, licensing is a contractual mode of entry whereby a domestic company forges a contractual agreement with a foreign company to manufacture and/or sell the domestic firm's products abroad with the understanding that a certain percentage of the profits will accrue to each of the parties. The "home" company generally is expected to furnish technical assistance to the foreign firm. The main advantages of this route are the low investment required by the home company and the assurance that at least some form of purposive marketing strategy will be adopted for the firm's products. As with exportation, however, there may be little real control over the licensee's operation. It is even possible that the licensee will eventually acquire the technical expertise of the home firm, possibly developing into a competitor of the licensor. Thus, channel power in such situations may rapidly shift to the foreign licensee. On the other hand, some companies use licensing to help make their products the market standards. Apple Computer Company licensed the software for its Newton personal digital assistant to Sharp and Matsushita, among other companies, when it introduced the Newton in the fall of 1993. Its hope was that licensing would speed the creation of related products that would in turn increase Newton's sales.[40]

Investment entry modes imply some degree of ownership of production or distribution facilities by the entering firm in the target country. In a joint venture, two or more firms share the investment and risk of the expansionary effort. Common problems that need to be ironed out in a successful joint venture include harmonizing different accounting and control systems or management approaches and coming to an agreement about sales of the joint venture product in third markets where the partners may be competitors. The fact of mutual investment, however, differentiates the joint venture from the above entry modes and implies fewer problems of control. Examples of joint ventures for distribution include:

- A 75% British Telecommunications PLC, 25% MCI Communications Inc. joint venture called Concert is just one of several multinational joint ventures aiming to compete for the communications business of the world's multinational corporations. Concert launched its first jointly developed products worldwide in 1994, and markets its services by claiming that they are better at providing common worldwide service norms. The Concert JV signed on Nippon Information & Communication Corp. of Japan, itself a 50-50 joint venture between NTT and IBM, as its local distributor for jointly developed "virtual private network services" in 1994.[41]

- German film manufacturer Agfa formed a joint venture with Daiei of Japan to sell its film through Daiei stores at discount prices. The film does not bear the Agfa name, although it does say "Made in Germany." Fuji Photo Film had dominated the Japanese market with 75% market share, with most of the rest of the market going to Konica and Kodak Japan Ltd. Meanwhile Agfa has a 36% market share in Europe, but less than 1% in Japan before its joint venture with Daiei. Since the formation of the JV, Agfa's share has risen to 3% of the Japanese market, and its costs of selling are lower because it sells very large shipments to just one reliable customer.[42]

- Burger King formed a joint venture with Seibu Railway (which runs not only a railway but also a baseball park, theme parks, and ski resorts) to form Burger King outlets in Japan. Seibu supplied the real estate and operated the outlets, whereas Burger King contributed know-how and appliances. The arrangement was a 50-50 profit-sharing venture. Seibu planned to open up to 300 outlets over a few years in its railway stations and leisure facilities.[43]

- Unilever has formed eight joint ventures in China since the mid-1980s to produce and sell everything from skin creams to ice cream. It has taken a bigger and bigger equity stake in each successive joint venture; the maximum is an 85% stake in its Beijing ice-cream factory. But distribution and infrastructural problems prevent Unilever from taking 100% ownership; for example, distribution systems in China are product-specfic, so Unilever cannot distribute soap through its toothpaste distributor.[44]

- McDonald's formed a 50-50 joint venture with Den Fujita in Japan in 1971 to develop the McDonald's franchise there. Fujita's contributions were to handle the bureaucratic hurdles of expanding a business in Japan and to find good real estate on which to develop the restaurants. More recently, Mr. Fujita has signed similar joint venture deals with Blockbuster Video and Toys "R" Us. He plans to open McDonald's restaurants inside the Toys "R" Us stores to capitalize on the synergies between them.[45]

Another major investment route to expansion overseas is through creation of a sole venture, either through new establishment or acquisition. The outcome of 100% equity ownership is the same in either case. The company that uses this entry mode must commit to learning the mores and nuances of each foreign market it enters. New establishment of a wholly owned channel typically takes longer than acquisition, which produces instant access to the market. Risk is greater with complete equity ownership, because greater capital expenditure and management time is involved. In addition, there is always the risk of expropriation or nationalization, particularly in politically unstable countries. Advantages, however, include greater control and enhanced competitiveness in the target market. These benefits are clearly worth the investment in many cases: U.S. direct investment abroad was projected to be more than $500 billion in 1995.[46] Some examples of foreign ventures created through acquisition include:

- Gehe, a large German pharmaceutical distributor, announced a takeover offer for Office Commercial Pharmaceutique, France's largest ethical drugs wholesaler in 1993. Gehe earned half its money from wholesaling, 25% from drug manufacture, and the balance from mail-order activities. The two companies already had an alliance with AAH, a U.K. wholesaler.[47]

- J. Sainsbury, the U.K.'s biggest food retailer, bought 50% of the voting shares of Giant Food, a Washington, D.C.-based supermarket group, in 1994. Combined with its 1987 purchase of Shaw's, a New England grocer, this acquisition made Sainsbury the eleventh largest grocery chain in the U.S.[48]

- Rewe, a large German food retailer, bought a 26% stake in Budgens, a small U.K. grocery chain, in 1993. Rewe operated over 1,400 discount grocery outlets in Germany, as well as supermarkets and hypermarkets. Rewe was just one of many European retailers attracted to U.K. food retailing by its high margins. As a result, discount stores are the fastest-growing portion of the U.K. grocery market.[49]

Finally, much has been said about *strategic alliances* (not only in distribution circles, but also in manufacturing, research and development [R&D], and the like). We do not treat strategic alliances as a separate entry mode here because a strategic alliance can be any one of a number of the previously mentioned options. It may or may not involve equity investment by the alliance partners; thus, although joint ventures classify as strategic alliances, they are not the only ones. A strategic alliance is that subset of channel arrangements involving more than an arms'-length relationship, but less than total equity ownership, where the partners seek mutual gain by contributing complementary skills and inputs to create market opportunities and profits that neither could have done by itself. Alliances like the partnership formed by J. Sainsbury of the U.K., Esselunga of Italy, Delhaize of Belgium, and Docks de France in 1994 (described in Chapter 2) exemplify arrangements involving shared expertise and cooperation in buying and marketing without any cross-equity sharing.[50]

Alliances have been shown to be more likely to succeed when the partners are equals than otherwise. A spirit of teamwork, rather than a strict 50-50 split, appears to be the critical factor here. However, a McKinsey study suggests that even in alliances with equal equity ownership shares for each partner, success rates are greater when one partner has sole authority to *run* the alliance; joint decision making tends to be less successful. The partner with deeper knowledge or expertise is typically the one with operating control. This finding on operating control does not lessen the importance of building a solid relationship in an alliance, however. David Ernst and Joel Bleeke of McKinsey argue that U.S. firms fall short on this dimension in alliances, and they argue that a collaborative attitude is likely to contribute to greater alliance success than a noncooperative attitude.[51]

Factors Affecting the Optimal Entry Mode

A whole host of factors, both internal and external to the entrant firm, affects the best choice of mode of entry in the foreign market. This very complex decision is depicted in Figure 11-1. The figure shows that the mode of entry directly affects all

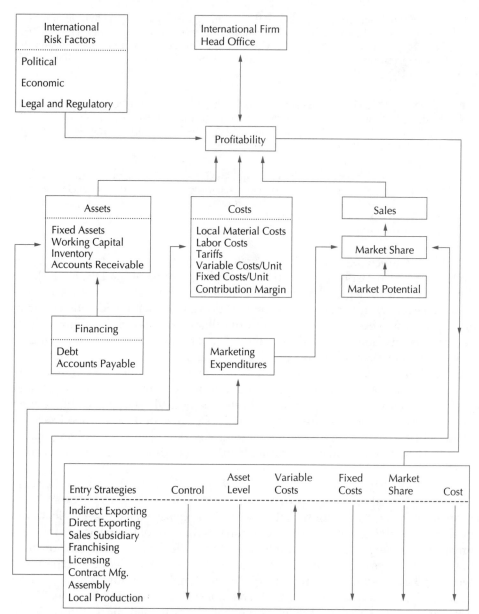

Direction of Arrow Indicates Increase or Decrease in That Factor.

FIGURE 11-1 **Factors affecting market entry decisions.**
Source: Jean-Pierre Jeannet and H. David Hennessey, *Global Marketing Strategies,* Third Edition, p. 318. Copyright © 1995 by Houghton Mifflin Company. Used with permission.

elements contributing to the entrant's profitability in the foreign market, as do external factors involving international risk. But *how* do each of these factors affect optimal entry mode? Root provides some guidelines for external and internal factors, reported in Table 11-2.

▐ TABLE 11-2 External and Internal Factors Influencing the Entry Mode Decision

A. External Factors (Foreign Country)

	GENERALLY FAVORS				
FACTORS	Indirect and Agent/ Distributor Exporting	Licensing	Branch/ Subsidiary Exporting	Equity Investment/ Production	Service Contracts
Low sales potential	X	X			
High sales potential			X	X	
Atomistic competition	X		X		
Oligopolistic competition				X	
Poor marketing infrastructure			X		
Good marketing infrastructure	X				
Low production cost				X	
High production cost	X		X		
Restrictive import policies		X		X	X
Liberal import policies	X		X		
Restrictive investment policies	X	X	X		X
Liberal investment policies				X	
Small geographical distance	X		X		
Great geographical distance		X		X	X
Dynamic economy				X	
Stagnant economy	X	X			X
Restrictive exchange controls	X	X			X
Liberal exchange controls				X	
Exchange rate depreciation				X	
Exchange rate appreciation	X		X		
Small cultural distance			X	X	
Great cultural distance	X	X			X
Low political risk			X	X	
High political risk	X	X			X

B. External Factors (Home Country)

	GENERALLY FAVORS				
FACTORS	Indirect and Agent/ Distributor Exporting	Licensing	Branch/ Subsidiary Exporting	Equity Investment/ Production	Service Contracts
Large market				X	
Small market	X		X		
Atomistic competition	X		X		
Oligopolistic competition				X	
Low production cost	X		X		
High production cost		X		X	X
Strong export promotion	X		X		
Restrictions on investment abroad	X	X			X

Table 11-2 (continued)

C. Internal Factors

	GENERALLY FAVORS				
FACTORS	Indirect and Agent/ Distributor Exporting	Licensing	Branch/ Subsidiary Exporting	Equity Investment/ Production	Service Contracts
Differentiated products	x		x		
Standard products				x	
Service-intensive products			x	x	
Service products		x		x	x
Technology-intensive products		x			
Low product adaptation	x				
High product adaptation		x	x	x	
Limited resources	x	x			
Substantial resources			x	x	
Low commitment	x	x			x
High commitment			x	x	

Source: Reprinted with permission of Lexington Books, an imprint of Simon & Schuster Inc., from Franklin R. Root, *Entry Strategies for International Markets*, Revised and Expanded, pp. 36–38. Copyright © 1994 by Lexington Books.

The right entry mode to choose is then a function of these factors and their impacts on profitability, market share, and other output measures the firm may value.[52] Table 11-3 provides a template for evaluating alternative entry modes. A manager would use it by rating each entry option (one per row of the table) using qualitative ranking or quantitative data available for the market in question. Next, importance weights for the criteria (the columns of the table) must be allocated, as a high ranking on one criterion may not sway entry choice if that criterion is not itself important for the firm's overall decision. An overall rating for each entry mode can then be calculated using a "weight times rating" formulation to calculate a weighted average. Even though strict financial or numerical measures may not be available for all cells in the table, Root argues that "Even a crude use of an entry strategy matrix holds the promise of better entry decisions. . . . What is demanded is . . . systematic comparisons of alternative modes."[53]

Choosing the Right Channel Partner Overseas

Once a firm has decided on the appropriate channel entry mode, it must still identify and recruit the right partners to fill channel roles. In overseas market entry, this is often a difficult task. Good distributors, for example, may simply not be available or if they are, may be difficult to find. Sources of information about potential partners are summarized in Exhibit 11-4.

When candidate channel partners have been identified, the entrant must use

TABLE 11-3 Comparison Matrix for Entry Modes

CRITERIA

MODES	Investment	Sales	Costs	Profit Contribution	Market Share	Reversibility	Control	Risk	Other
Indirect Export									
Agent/ Distributor Export									
Branch/ Subsidiary Export									
Licensing									
Franchising									
Other Contractual Agreements									
Investment: New Establishment									
Investment Acquisition									
Joint Venture									
Mixed									

Source: Reprinted with permission of Lexington Books, an imprint of Simon & Schuster Inc., from Franklin R. Root, *Entry Strategies for International Markets*, Revised and Expanded, p. 185. Copyright © 1994 by Lexington Books.

EXHIBIT 11-4 / Information Sources for Locating Foreign Channel Partners

▶ ▶ ▶

1. *U.S. Department of Commerce.* The Agent Distributor Service is a customized service of the Department of Commerce, which locates distributors and agents interested in a certain product line. Also, the department's Export Marketing Service can be used to locate distribution partners.

2. *Banks.* If the firm's bank has foreign branches, they may be happy to help locate distributors.

3. *Directories.* Country directories of distributors or specialized directories, such as those listing computer distributors, can be helpful.

4. *Trade shows.* Exhibiting at an international trade show or just attending will expose managers to a large number of distributors and their salespeople.

5. *Competitor's distribution partners.* Sometimes a competitor's distributor may be interested in switching product lines.

6. *Consultants.* Some international marketing consultants specialize in locating distributors.

7. *Associations.* There are associations of international intermediaries or country associations of intermediaries. For example, Japan has numerous industry associations.

8. *Foreign consulates.* Most countries have a commercial attaché at their embassies or a separate consulate, both of which are helpful in locating agents/distributors in their country.

Source: Jean-Pierre Jeannet and H. David Hennessey, *Global Marketing Strategies*, Third Edition, pp. 402–403. Copyright © 1995 by Houghton Mifflin Company. Used with permission.

some decision criteria to winnow the list down to the best choice. Exhibit 11-5 summarizes important factors that systematically affect the choice of channel partner overseas.

More specifically, a company may deal with many different types of intermediaries in international marketing. Table 11-4 lists the primary functions performed by the major kinds of domestic middlemen selling to foreign markets. Domestic middlemen are located in the producer's home country and provide marketing services from the domestic base. There are two basic types of independent wholesale marketing intermediaries: *agents* and *merchants*. The main difference between the two is that the merchant takes title to the products to be sold, whereas the agent does not.[54] One can contrast the description of an export management company (EMC) above with that of a manufacturer's export agent (MEA) below.[55]

> **Manufacturer's Export Agent:** an independent businessperson who usually does not operate under the manufacturer's name. An MEA may represent manufacturers of related and noncompeting products, may operate either on an exclusive or nonexclusive basis, and is compensated through commissions. The agent also works under contract, but it is short term, and the agent does not offer as many services as an EMC.

Unlike domestic agents, domestic *merchants* are independent businesses that bear the majority of trading risks and take title to the products they handle. They

EXHIBIT 11-5 / Factors Influencing the Choice of Overseas Channel Partners

◀ ◀ ◀

1. *Cost*

    Initial costs, maintenance costs, and logistics costs are the three categories of channel costs. Initial costs are the costs of locating and setting up the channel; maintenance costs include ongoing costs of the sales organization, advertising, and profits to intermediaries. Logistics costs include costs of transportation, storage, bulk-breaking, and customs paperwork. One study found that of five different channels, a consumer-goods firm selling directly to a distributor in a country was the most profitable. The least profitable was exporting directly to retailers in a country.

2. *Capital Requirement*

    Capital costs include inventory costs, cost of goods in transit, accounts receivable, and inventories on consignment. These costs are offset by cash-flow patterns from each channel alternative: for example, an import distributor often pays for goods when they are received, before they are sold downstream in the foreign country channel. The establishment of a direct sales channel thus often requires the greatest capital investment, whereas using distributors often reduces the investment required.

3. *Product and Product Line*

    The nature of the product or line sold affects channel selection. Products that are perishable or have short shelf lives must be sold through shorter channels. Technical products often require either direct sales or highly technical channel partners, whereas nontechnical products can move through longer channels to more diverse and numerous final retail destinations. A broader product line may be more attractive to a distributor or a dealer than is a single item, whereas narrow product lines may need to be sold through an agent.

4. *Control*

    A direct salesforce offers the greatest degree of control over price, promotion, amount of sales effort, and type of retail outlet. In contrast, longer channels often result in much lower levels of control; the manufacturer may not even know who is buying its products in the foreign market. Manufacturers can compensate for lower levels of control in indirect distribution channels, however, by increasing their local presence in the foreign market through less costly means, such as joint sales calls by the international sales manager with distributor salespeople.

5. *Coverage*

    The geographic market coverage that a manufacturer desires may be easy to achieve in urban areas in overseas markets, but more difficult in rural or less-developed areas. Channel members may be chosen for their specific abilities to reach more remote geographic areas. Coverage also includes the concept of full representation for all lines a company wishes to sell within a given market. In many instances, a company may prefer to use only one major type of distribution, but to achieve coverage, it may have to use multiple channels.

6. *Synergy*

    The choice of channel partners can be influenced by the complementary skills that enhance the total channel system's productivity. For example, a potential distributor partner may have local market knowledge, whereas the manufacturer may contribute product and technical expertise.

Source: Jean-Pierre Jeannet and H. David Hennessey, *Global Marketing Strategies*, Third Edition pp. 399–402. Copyright © 1995 by Houghton Mifflin Company.

▶**T**ABLE 11-4 **Characteristics of Domestic Middlemen Serving Overseas Markets**

	AGENT				
TYPE OF DUTIES	EMC	MEA	Broker	Buying Offices	Selling Groups
Take title	No	No	No	No	No
Take possession	Yes	Yes	No	Yes	Yes
Continuing relationship	Yes	Yes	No	Yes	Yes
Share of foreign output	All	All	Any	Small	All
Degree of control by principal	Fair	Fair	Nil	Nil	Good
Price authority	Advisory	Advisory	Yes (at market level)	Yes (to buy)	Advisory
Represent buyer or seller	Seller	Seller	Either	Buyer	Seller
Number of principals	Few–Many	Few–Many	Many	Small	Few
Arrange shipping	Yes	Yes	Not usually	Yes	Yes
Type of goods	Manufactured goods and commodities	Staples and commodities	Staples and commodities	Staples and commodities	Complementary to their own lines
Breadth of line	Specialty–wide	All types of staples	All types of staples	Retail goods	Narrow
Handle competitive lines	No	No	Yes	Yes—uses many sources	No
Extent of promotion and selling effort	Good	Good	One shot	N.A.	Good
Extend credit to principal	Occasionally	Occasionally	Seldom	Seldom	Seldom
Market information	Fair	Fair	Price and market conditions	For principal not for manufacturer	Good

N.A. = Not available.

Source: Philip Cateora, *International Marketing*, 7th ed. (Homewood, IL: Richard D. Irwin, 1990), p. 607. Copyright © 1990 by Richard D Irwin. Reprinted by permission.

also prefer to make a profit from the products they sell rather than to receive a fee.[56] Merchant middlemen provide a variety of import and export wholesaling functions that involve purchasing for their own accounts and selling in other countries. One kind of domestic merchant, the *export merchant*, can be described as follows:[57]

> **Export Merchant:** a merchant who seeks out needs in foreign markets and buys directly from the manufacturer according to their specifications, taking title to the goods. Export merchants have overseas contacts through which the goods are sold under the export merchant's name either to wholesalers or retailers. They assume all the risks,

| | MERCHANT | | | |
Norazi	Export Merchant	Export Jobber	Importers and Trading Companies	Complementary Marketers
Yes	Yes	Yes	Yes	Yes
Yes	Yes	No	Yes	Yes
No	No	Yes	Yes	Yes
Small	Any	Small	Any	Most
Nil	None	None	Nil	Fair
Yes	Yes	Yes	No	Some
Both	Self	Self	Self	Self
Several per transaction	Many sources	Many sources	Many sources	One per product
Yes	Yes	Yes	Yes	Yes
Contraband	Manufactured goods	Bulky and raw materials	Manufactured goods	Complementary to line
N.A.	Broad	Broad	Broad	Narrow
Yes	Yes	Yes	Yes	No
Nil	Nil	Nil	Good	Good
No	Occasionally	Seldom	Seldom	Seldom
No	Nil	Nil	Fair	Good

and their compensation consists of a markup percentage that is based on market conditions. In general, an export merchant resembles a domestic wholesaler.

Rather than dealing with the home-country agents or merchant middlemen, a manufacturer may choose to deal directly with the middlemen located in foreign markets. Table 11-5 summarizes the primary functions of foreign-based middlemen. One example of direct distribution through an agent is the *export broker*:[58]

Export Broker: brings the foreign buyer and the U.S. seller together. Brokers work on commission, do not take title to or possession of the goods, and assume no financial responsibility relative to the export transaction. They are used most often in the export of commodities.

TABLE 11-5 Characteristics of Middlemen in Foreign Countries

TYPE OF DUTIES	AGENT					MERCHANT		
	Broker	Manufacturers Representative	Managing Agent	Comprador	Distributor	Dealer	Import Jobber	Wholesaler and Retailer
Take title	No	No	No	No	Yes	Yes	Yes	Yes
Take possession	No	Seldom	Seldom	Yes	Yes	Yes	Yes	Yes
Continuing relationship	No	Often	With buyer, not seller	Yes	Yes	Yes	No	Usually not
Share of foreign output	Small	All or part for one area	N.A.	All one area	All, for certain countries	Assignment area	Small	Very small
Degree of control by principal	Low	Fair	None	Fair	High	High	Low	Nil
Price authority	Nil	Nil	Nil	Partial	Partial	Partial	Full	Full
Represent buyer or seller	Either	Seller	Buyer	Seller	Seller	Seller	Self	Self
Number of principals	Many	Few	Many	Few	Small	Few major	Many	Many
Arrange shipping	No	No	No	No	No	No	No	No
Type of goods	Commodity and food	Manufactured goods	All types manufactured goods	Manufactured goods	Manufactured goods	Manufactured goods	Manufactured goods	Manufactured consumer goods
Breadth of line	Broad	Allied lines	Broad	Varies	Narrow to broad	Narrow	Narrow to broad	Narrow to broad
Handle competitive lines	Yes	No	Yes	No	No	No	Yes	Yes
Extent of promotion and selling effort	Nil	Fair	Nil	Fair	Fair	Good	Nil	Nil usually
Extend credit to principal	No	No	No	Sometimes	Sometimes	No	No	No
Market information	Nil	Good	Nil	Good	Fair	Good	Nil	Nil

N.A. = Not available.

Source: Philip Cateora, *International Marketing*, 7th ed. (Homewood, IL: Richard D. Irwin, 1990), p. 610. Copyright © 1990 by Richard D. Irwin. Reprinted by permission.

Foreign merchant intermediaries render services that are similar to those of a domestic wholesaler. Among the most important merchant middlemen in international commerce are the trading companies. The origin, functions, and scope of operations of trading companies are discussed in Exhibit 11-6. Although the functions of various agent and merchant middlemen generally follow the description of U.S. middlemen found in Chapter 3, it should be emphasized that in foreign commerce there seem to be very few "pure" types.

Ｅxhibit **1 1 -6 / Trading Companies**

HISTORY   ◀ ◀ ◀

In 1498, the opening of the sea route from Europe to India via the Cape of Good Hope created new trade opportunities for European merchants. Soon, the monarchs of Europe chartered these traders and gave them exclusive proprietorship in specific areas and protection by the naval forces in exchange for export taxes. As a result, the East India company of the Netherlands was formed in 1602, closely followed by the British East India Company and the French East India Company.

Soon after establishing a strong foothold on the colonial territories of South and Southeast Asia, the European traders traveled east and reached Japan. Eventually, the European trading companies dominated the Japanese import market as a result of their superior vessels, trading experience, and the unfair treaties the European empires had forced the Japanese to accept.

Later, to reduce their dependence on the European traders, the Japanese government provided incentives to Japanese merchants to start their own trading companies. Thus, Mitsui Bussan, Mitsubishi Trading Company, C. Itoh (later split into C. Itoh and Marubeni), and Suzuki Shoten (later called Nissho) were established. These trading companies, and a few others that were created later, have since developed into huge trading organizations with globally integrated activities. They are today's *sogoshosha*, loosely translated as general trading company (GTC).

FUNCTIONS

The primary functions of trading companies located within a given country include accumulation, transportation, and distribution of goods imported from other countries. To supplement these activities, other services are frequently offered as well. For example, U.S. trading companies offer a wide array of services including providing their clients with international market research, consulting, marketing, insurance, product research and design, trade documentation, legal assistance, and facilities for merchandise handling and wholesaling. Moreover, they often finance imports and exports of goods, and either finance or directly invest in distributors and retailers. However, the first function of trading companies is as intermediaries, not only facilitating trade in a variety of products to all parts of the world, but also actively looking for and developing new sources of demand; they specialize in the buying and selling of goods rather than the production of goods.

DEVELOPMENT IN OTHER COUNTRIES

In the early 1970s the consistent growth of the *sogoshosha* during the worldwide recession attracted the attention of many other countries' governments. The United States, Brazil, Korea, Taiwan, Thailand, the Philippines, and Turkey started to develop their own GTC systems modeled after the *sogoshosha*. Bank of America, Citicorp, General Electric, General Motors, and Sears are among the large American firms that have formed export trading companies. For the most part, GTCs have been very successful. For example, the Japanese trading companies account for half of their countries' imports and buy $15 billion annually in U.S. goods for export to Japan. Although the increased willingness of Japanese companies to deal face to face with suppliers and customers threatens the *sogoshoshas'* reason for existence, these trading companies are transforming themselves over time to move into underlying businesses, such as energy and communications and away from pure commodity handling functions.

Source: Dong-Sung Cho, *The General Trading Company Concept and Strategy* (Lexington, MA: D.C. Heath and Company, 1987), pp. 1–8; Vern Terpstra, *International Dimensions of Marketing*, 2nd ed. (Boston: PWS Kent Publishing Company, 1988), p. 110; Erik Wiklund, *International Marketing* (New York: R. R. Donnelley, 1986), pp. 28–30; and "Sprightly Dinosaurs?" *The Economist*, February 11, 1995, pp. 55–57.

International distribution through intermediaries always necessitates compromise. The compromise involves the loss of control over foreign marketing operations in exchange for relatively low-cost representation. An advantage of using intermediaries is that they provide local market knowledge and contacts. As with all middlemen, effectiveness depends on the careful selection of middlemen and how well a manufacturer can optimize distributor performance through a mutually satisfying relationship.[59]

▶ INTERNATIONAL CHANNEL EFFECTIVENESS ISSUES

As described in Chapter 5, designing an effective channel involves understanding different segments' demands for service outputs for the products to be sold, and assigning channel flows and functions to create those service outputs. It thus requires both a demand-side and a production-side point of view. In overseas markets, meeting service output demands may mean totally different things than in the home market; and designing an effective channel to deliver those service outputs efficiently may require that the channel manager deal with all sorts of issues that do not shape domestic channel decisions. We discuss each of these sets of issues in this section.

Meeting Service Output Demands in the International Channel

As the discussion of channel planning in Chapter 5 suggests, the heart of distribution channel success lies in identifying and meeting target consumer or customer segments' demands for service outputs. As the examples below demonstrate, firms try to find overseas market opportunities where service ouptut demands match those in the home country's target market; and, in situations where no match is possible, the goal is to shift the mix of service outputs supplied to fit market-specific needs.

The key service output demands of the Hong Kong shopper are for *spatial convenience* (because of the difficulty of carrying purchases home on public transportation) and *small lot sizes* (because of the generally small apartments), combined with intense price sensitivity. The opening of Value Clubs, a warehouse club concept owned by Wal-Mart, in Hong Kong in late 1994, therefore might seem only a marginally good fit. The Value Club concept clearly appealed to the price-conscious shopper, but failed to provide the other service outputs the Hong Kong shopper demands. But Wal-Mart reputedly viewed Hong Kong as a market research laboratory to learn how to please the Chinese consumer, in preparation for later market entry into the People's Republic of China. Wal-Mart's Asian partner was Ek Chor Distribution System, a subsidiary of C.P. Pokphand, which has extensive investments in China.[60]

In catalog selling, on the other hand, U.S. retailers have by and large waited until the early 1990s to make significant forays overseas. The reason for increased interest has been an evolution in service output demands, particularly in Japan and in western Europe, to parallel more closely the U.S. catalog consumer's demands for *high spatial convenience,* combined with an increased ability to deliver *low waiting and delivery times.* Two-worker families are increasingly common in these foreign markets, creating that "poverty of time" that is crucial for the success of mail-order channels. Among the actors are Eddie Bauer entering Germany, L.L. Bean and Lands' End targeting Japan, and J. Crew moving into France. Eddie Bauer management sees growth depending on specialty catalogs' ability to market the catalog itself as a brand that can have common appeal across national boundaries. Success will also depend on the ability to reproduce U.S. marketing and logistics abilities overseas, so that the delivery of the key service outputs consumers expect will be guaranteed.[61]

Maintaining the appropriate *assortment and variety* is also critical in foreign market success. For example, Pizza Hut International was given permission to create a wholly owned subsidiary in India in 1994, with plans to establish a chain of pizza restaurants over the next seven years. PepsiCo, the owner of Pizza Hut, decided to build its largest restaurant in the world in New Delhi, a 600-seat store combining Pizza Hut and Kentucky Fried Chicken under one roof. This broad assortment decision was prompted by market research indicating that the Indian family preferred multicuisine restaurants to more narrow-line ones. Further, other fast-food franchisors entering India (such as McDonald's and Burger King) needed to consider altering their classic assortment emphasizing beef and pork in cultures like India's, where religious rules prohibit eating these foods.[62]

Sometimes, however, foreign market entrants can offer the same assortment and variety across many markets, thus saving money on costly market-specific offerings. Kraft Europe has moved toward more of an emphasis on common offerings across markets, after a see-saw strategy first emphasizing uniform product and marketing strategies across Europe in the early 1980s, and then changing to a decentralized structure with few or no commonalities across markets. Kraft has set up eight European "core teams" covering the company's principal product categories and main marketing functions. The teams have made agreements to rationalize specifications and packaging on 1,000 Kraft product lines sold in more than one country. Some of these products used to come in more than 50 versions, not because of true inter-market demand differences, but simply because of a lack of inter-market coordination.[63]

Finally, *customer service* demand differences across markets, or changes over time within one market, can affect the success of a foreign market entry. Recessions in the early 1990s in Japan and in Western Europe made many consumers there willing to trade off lower overall service levels for lower prices. This has been a major factor in the rise of discounters in both markets. Discount grocers in Great Britain, for example, use bare-bones store fittings or even sell out of cardboard boxes. They combine this with limited *assortments* and *spatially inconvenient* (but low-rent) sites to be able to offer lower prices to their customers. The forecast of market share increases for such stores in Great Britain was from 9% in 1993 to 14–15% by 1996.[64] The trend toward less customer service is echoed in Japan, where in 1993 stores began to charge for delivering parcels and to cut back on elaborate wrapping for consumers. This was in stark contrast to trends in the previous decade, when Japanese department stores were so successful that they could afford luxurious appointments like marble floors and in-store museums.[65]

Conversely, some marketers have expanded into foreign areas where customer service norms are far below those at home.[66] Kmart's purchase of 13 stores in the previously state-owned Prior retail chain in the former Czechoslovakia (now the Czech Republic and Slovakia) brought with it the need to update not only the furnishings and merchandise in the stores, but also the overall service level offered to consumers. All the Czech stores are multistory, ill-lit, and lack parking facilities. Store clerks had no concept of customer service; accustomed to leaning on sales counters, they had to be trained to go out on the sales floor. They were required to wear name tags identifying them as clerks and saying "I'm here for you." But management discovered that the clerks were actually hiding in nooks and crannies of the stores to avoid having to help customers. The offending nooks and crannies have since been removed.[67] Clearly, if and when Kmart can introduce a level of customer service even approximating what is the norm in its U.S. stores, it can be perceived as a service leader in this type of market.

Thus, meeting (or beating!) local service output demands in foreign markets is a task requiring the entering firm both to know demand and then to redesign its channel offering to match the market. How companies have allocated the performance of channel flows to meet these varying service output demands is the focus of the next section.

Channel Flow Performance in International Channels

Designing an effective channel in overseas markets parallels the task of doing so in the home market. But in some situations, the organization and performance of specific channel flows must change. Consider the specifics of organizing flows in Poland, profiled in Exhibit 11-7. It quickly becomes clear that flows from physical possession all the way through to payment must be observed and monitored in the overseas marketing channel; simply extrapolating from the home-country experience will not work.

▶ ▶ ▶ **EXHIBIT 11-7 / Getting the Job Done: Channel Flows for Consumer Goods in Poland**

Western consumer-goods companies operating in Poland find that effective distribution is one of the most important elements of successful market penetration. Some companies are taking a combination of approaches to distribution, seeking the most cost-effective solutions in a market where economic conditions vary considerably from region to region.

Prior to 1989, Poland had only a handful of retailers. The hard-currency retailer Pewex, the Centrum department stores, and the Ruch news kiosks imported most Western goods, and handled their own distribution. Today, there are tens of thousands of retail outlets throughout the country, most of them single family-run shops. Wholesale warehouses also exist in Poland's largest cities. However, most operate by simply waiting for retailers to pick up supplies on a cash basis.

Western consumer-goods companies and the distribution firms that serve them are taking a more aggressive approach. Their salespeople are actively promoting brands with retailers and extending credit to steady customers.

Thomas Keller, managing director of Brands International, a Warsaw-based packaged foods and personal-care items distributor, says that Western firms come seeking help in building retailers' brand awareness. "We believe in helping consumer companies develop a consumer franchise for brands and hold onto it," Mr. Keller states. "We go directly to the retailer, we fight for shelf space, we track each sale and client."

Western consumer-goods and distribution companies say they are following a number of procedures in order to get their goods out to the largest possible number of stores. These include the following:

Ensuring regional coverage through a network of regional warehouses. For example, Brands International, with a staff of 135, operates 38 small warehouses through Poland, each of which is equipped with a 4.9-ton delivery vehicle. The company serves 18,000 retailers directly as well as a few dozen wholesalers, who in turn serve an estimated 15,000 more small retailers.

Use of a network of salespeople to deliver to retailers, promote new products, take orders, and collect payments from previous deliveries. Poland's inadequate infrastructure means that extra flexibility is required. Companies must be willing to sell to shopkeepers who continue to come to the supplier's warehouse to obtain goods. Further, phone service is poor and many new shops lack phones, so the order-taking process can be difficult. Small package-delivery services are limited as well, although this was expected to improve in the near future.

Extension of credit and other financial incentives to reliable retailers. All of the companies that *Business Eastern Europe* spoke to said they extended credit to retailers and wholesalers. Most did so after initial regular deliveries on a cash basis, or on the basis of a credit check conducted by company sales representatives. Although companies say that supplier credit entails some risk, default rates have in fact been comparable to those in Western countries. One way to limit risk has been through more frequent deliveries of smaller lot sizes.

Use of traditional wholesalers to fill in the "black holes" in the retail system. These "black holes" are the extremely small sellers, such as street merchants. Companies can structure pricing policies so as to encourage wholesalers to serve retailers not already covered by the company or the distributor's own delivery system.

Source: Tom Lavell, "Establishing Effective Distribution," *Business Eastern Europe*, August 16, 1993, pp. 7–8. © The Economist Intelligence Unit. Reproduced by permission of The Economist Intelligence Unit.

In this section, we first discuss how physical possession and ownership flows are managed in international channels by discussing physical distribution and sourcing. Specific examples of alterations in other channel flows are then discussed. For example, one peculiarly international phenomenon, *countertrade*, is a special way of organizing the *payment* flow in international channels. Throughout, the reader will see how unique market and cultural situations lead a firm to organize flows differently overseas than would be done in the home market.

INTERNATIONAL PHYSICAL DISTRIBUTION   International physical distribution channels are more complex in the world marketplace than in domestic markets. When all factors have been considered, international physical distribution is usually more expensive than it is in a domestic situation. Increased shipping distances, documentation costs, the larger inventory levels required, longer order-cycle times, tariffs, and other factors, such as underdeveloped marketing and distribution channels, combine to increase the cost of international distribution. Logistics costs usually range as follows:

- 8 to 10% of the delivered price for trade within a continent (e.g., Europe, North America);

- 20 to 30% of the delivered price for trade between continents (e.g., Europe to South America);

- 30 to 35% for shipments requiring movement between and within continents.[68]

For example, the Campbell Soup Company found its physical distribution costs in the United Kingdom were 30% higher than in the United States. Extra costs were incurred because soup was purchased in small quantities—English grocers typically purchase 24-can cases of *assorted* soups. In the U.S., typical purchases are made in 48-can cases of *one* soup purchased by dozens, hundreds, or carloads. The purchase habits in Europe forced the company to use an extra wholesale level in its channel to facilitate handling small orders. Purchase frequency patterns also ran up billing and order costs; both U.K. retailers and wholesalers buy two or three times as often as their U.S. counterparts. Sales-call costs became virtually prohibitive. These and other distribution cost factors not only caused Campbell to change its price patterns, but also forced a complete restructuring of the channel system.[69]

In addition to the high cost of international physical distribution, the international marketer is faced with a number of other problems, among them the following:

- Shipping rates and charges may vary. Although water-carrier conference members are not allowed to vary rates, a shipper may obtain lower rates from nonconference carriers, that is, carriers who are not members of a rate-setting cartel. However, the shipper should be prepared to pay penalties on any conference-carrying shipping it might do in the same geographic area. Also, water shipping rates are determined on the basis of weight and measurement. The cubic displacement of a shipment must be carefully watched. In the trucking industry, annual road taxes vary by country: a heavy truck in France pays about Ffr 375 in tax, whereas one in Germany or Great Britain pays about 80 times as much![70]

- The liability for loss and damage in international shipping is less than in domestic shipping. This means an additional burden on the shipper to provide adequate insurance coverage and extra protective packaging.

- The physical distribution manager has to deal with a vast number of legal requirements and regulations imposed by governments of countries with which the company deals.

- Containerization is a logical solution used by international shippers to offset expensive packaging costs and loss because of damage and pilferage. However, containerization adds its own costs, including extra loading fees and container rental fees.

- The diversion of goods from the authorized channel of international distribution results in the development of a controversial channel, called the *gray market,* which is discussed later in this chapter.

The European single market has had a dramatic effect on multinational distribution operations in Europe, resulting in a need for greater geographical coverage. As a result of the single market, the distribution industry is altering its role from that of traditional transport operator to that of manager of a varied range of supply chain activities: forwarding, consolidation, warehouse management, picking and packing, transportation, and electronic data interchange. The trend toward farming out logistics to outside firms, popular in the early 1990s, seems to have peaked. Some manufacturers have taken logistics flows back in-house, aided by ever-improving information technology helping them to manage inventory movement and storage.[71] Those remaining with third-party logistics providers are in many cases seeking tighter partnerships to guarantee high-quality service. Third-party suppliers are responding by extending across Europe themselves, either on their own (e.g., U.K. companies Transport Development Group and Exel Logistics) or through logistics alliances that let them promise pan-European service to a customer (e.g. Parceline, whose logistics services are provided through an alliance with three major partners).[72]

Another European issue is increasing road congestion, leading to possible environmental damage. The EC forecasts that the volume of freight on EC roads will reach 16.5 billion tons by the year 2010, nearly double its 1989 level. Various suggestions have been made to deal with this trend. One is to allow heavier trucks on long-distance routes, which would mean fewer trips and a smaller total number of vehicles (although each one would be bigger). Connected to this have been efforts to increase trucks' carrying capacity and to use lighter materials in their manufacture. Others suggest constraining truck traffic to nighttime hours, particularly around city centers, where congestion during the daytime is the worst. Yet another alternative is to switch more freight to rail and away from truck transportation, and to this end, the development of a European high-speed rail freight network is underway. Finally, the 1994 opening of the Channel Tunnel linking England and France means that U.K. companies can transport freight into mainland Europe via rail.[73]

In the Far East, physical distribution arrangements range from the sublime to the ridiculous. The Port Authority of Singapore, one of the world's busiest container ports, has automated every step of its processes, including clearing customs and the movement of containers from a freight forwarding agent to a ship. A vessel arrives at and departs from the port every three minutes on average. At any one time, 700 ships are in port. The port can turn around a ship carrying 1,000 TEU's (twenty-foot equivalent units, the standard container measure) in less than 12 hours, faster than any other regional port.[74] At the other end of the physical distribution spectrum, China is viewed as lacking even basic wholesaling and distribution systems. Yaohan, the Japanese retailing group, announced plans to set up a large computerized distribution center of its own in Beijing in 1993, to be completed by 1995. Its hope was to improve on the two- to three-month lag time to replace a product that was sold from a store shelf![75] This primitive physical distribution infrastructure also plagues U.S. beer makers seeking to penetrate the fragmented Chinese beer market. It is so hard to ship beer across provincial borders that even the largest brand in the market, Chinese Tsingtao beer, has only a 2% market share.[76]

INTERNATIONAL PROMOTIONAL FLOWS   An independent intermediary such as an export management company (EMC) may be responsible for promotional efforts including exhibitions at foreign trade fairs, promotional product brochure translation and production, and trade advertising for foreign markets. Williamson and Bello argue that the manufacturing firm pays for these promotional services in one way or another, the most common methods being a direct payment via a price reduction on the product to be exported, or an indirect payment given through straight wholesale pricing combined with exclusive distribution rights given to the EMC on the manufacturer's product in a given market or markets. Their research, using data from U.S. EMCs, indicates that there is no "free lunch": if a manufacturer wants its EMC to engage in nonprice promotional activities like those above, it must (and does) give direct payments tied to the performance of those duties.[77] In short, the "Equity Principle" of Chapter 7 is at work in promotional flows overseas as well as elsewhere throughout a channel.

INTERNATIONAL NEGOTIATION FLOWS   Negotiation with buyers in international channels can be extraordinarily complicated. The firm's customers may themselves be multinational firms, in which case the lack of a coordinated negotiation policy across national boundaries strains the buyer–seller relationship considerably. No buyer likes to find out that its German office paid more for a product than its French office! This has profound implications for the way in which the seller's channel and sales efforts are organized: for example, the concept of "national account managers" becomes insufficient to deal with the level at which the buyer–seller negotiation actually takes place.

In some markets, however, the tables are turned, and it is the sellers themselves who would like to initiate coordinated negotiation efforts. One of the most visible situations is found in the European pharmaceutical industry. Western Europe's market for health care is still largely government run, and each country's government sets prices it is willing to pay for specific ethical drugs. Because these prices can be significantly different in the various countries, an incentive for diversion or gray marketing arises. One technique pharmaceutical firms are now using to combat these practices is to negotiate pan-European prices for certain new drugs, thus removing the incentive for cross-border movement of product.

INTERNATIONAL FINANCING FLOWS   Financing functions in international channels can be quite different than those in one's home country, due to differences in infrastructural development, inflation, and macroeconomic conditions, and the multinational nature of returns to distribution effort. Two examples illustrate how these factors operate:

- Brazilian inflation has been among the world's highest for many years. Inflation topped 20% a month for 15 months during 1992–1993, and was in four figures annually for many years. When inflation is 1.25% *per day*, and interest rates are even higher, credit control and cash management take on paramount importance. The financial director of BAT Industries' Brazilian subsidiary said: "Our main challenge is to ensure that money earned from sales all round the country reaches headquarters in Rio as rapidly as possible in order to invest it. An hour lost can be an opportunity gone." The company gives stockists only three to five days to pay, minimizing their financing flow performance. Companies seek to collect receivables quickly, but to delay payments to suppliers, so as to earn profits by investing the money in the interim. Such activities mean that marketing is finance-driven rather than consumer-driven.[78]

- The U.S. film industry has been forced to think in a more sophisticated way about the returns to developing a feature-length film. Video distribution (as opposed to first-run movie showings) has come to account for roughly half of all movie revenue. Although the U.S. market is almost saturated, video and pay-TV are comparatively underdeveloped markets in Europe. This means that financing of a film is much more complex: a film that is successful at the movie-theatre box office will likely make good money in the video market, but that revenue is relatively slow in coming in, particularly if cross-border revenues are factored in. A banker deciding what pictures to finance must thus forecast not only international box-office revenues, but also worldwide video revenues.[79]

INTERNATIONAL ORDERING AND PAYMENT FLOWS AND COUNTERTRADE Differences between domestic and transnational channel transactions from an ordering and payment perspective are best represented by the practice of countertrade. There is a great deal of ambiguity surrounding the definition of countertrade and its various forms in the government and business arenas. Countertrade is sometimes used synonymously with barter.[80] However, the term encompasses more than just bartering. Countertrade actually describes six types of transactions: (1) barter, (2) clearing arrangements, (3) switch trading, (4) buy-back, (5) counterpurchase, and (6) offset. All of these transactions have one characteristic in common: a seller provides a buyer with goods or services and, in exchange, promises to receive goods or services from the buyer. There are important differences between the different forms of countertrade, however.[8]

- *Barter.* Pure barter is the direct exchange of products under a single contract and, in the simplest case, without the use of money. Difficulties in determining and agreeing on the relative value of traded goods has hampered the interest in bartering. No letters of credit are used in this arrangement.[82]

- *Clearing Arrangement.* A clearing arrangement is a form of barter in which a large number of exchanges are consolidated in a single contract to purchase a specified value of goods and services. Each country sets up an account that is debited whenever one country imports from another. At the end of a time period, imbalances are cleared through hard currency payments or the transfer of merchandise. A clearing arrangement introduces the concept of credit to the barter arrangement.[83]

- *Switch Trading.* Rather than using a bilateral trade agreement, switch trading involves a triangular agreement. When goods from the buying country are not easily usable or salable, it may be necessary to bring in a third party to dispose of the merchandise. For a large discount, the third party pays hard currency for the unwanted goods.[84]

- *Buy-back.* In terms of dollar value, buy-back is the fastest growing form of countertrade. Under this arrangement, the exporting company builds a plant in the buyer country, provides technology and equipment, and agrees to purchase a certain percentage of the plant's output over a given number of years.[85]

- *Counterpurchase.* In these transactions, the exporter agrees to buy unrelated goods from a shopping list set up by the importer sometime over the next few months to few years. Often, items that do not otherwise have a ready market are included on the list.[86]

- *Offset.* This term is usually used to describe compensatory practices in military trade, but it also applies to large civilian procurements. The seller agrees to sell a product at a set price to a buyer and receives payment in cash. As a condition of purchase, however, the seller must agree to reciprocal concessions (such as purchasing goods from the buyer in a specified time period) to the buyer.[87]

Countertrade is a common and growing practice. The gradual reduction of trade barriers in the former Soviet Union and the People's Republic of China has spurred countertrade.[88] Another reason for its growth is that many countries simply do not have enough foreign exchange to pay for everything they would like to import. This is especially true for less-developed countries (LDCs) and Eastern Bloc nations. Moreover, many countries resort to countertrade because, for various reasons, they are unable to sell many of their products on the world market.[89] Finally, in situations in which the transaction costs of using the market are high, but the government prohibits (for whatever reason) vertical integration, Hennart argues for a transaction-cost rationale for countertrade of the buy-back and counterpurchase types.[90] In these situations, buy-backs or counterpurchases can serve as a bond preventing opportunistic behavior by the seller after the contract has been struck.[91] Some examples of countertrade include:

- *ICI and Davy Powergas*, two British firms who sold a methanol plant to the Soviets for $250 million and agreed to buy back 20% of the production of the plant from 1981–1990 for around $350 million.[92]

- *PepsiCo*, which has engineered a series of spectacular countertrades with the old Soviet Union, trading vodka in the West for soft-drink concentrate over there.[93]

- In Egypt, a major Swiss company, *Aluswiss*, which exports alumina to its newly constructed plant and takes back a portion of the finished aluminum as payment for its investment.[94]

Countertrade arrangements of one kind or another account for around 25% of world trade. The percentage is even higher for East–West commerce. In the future, countertrade will probably become an even more significant component of global trade. However, most U.S. companies have not readily adapted to this growing practice, insisting instead upon cash deals. Japanese and European firms have more readily accepted countertrade and, consequently, have won many sales away from U.S. companies.[95] During the late 1980s and early 1990s, however, several large U.S. companies developed specialized countertrading capabilities.[96] They include the Cyrus Eaton Company, Occidental Petroleum, Coca-Cola, Avon, Colt Industries, Grumman International, Boeing, McDonnell Douglas, Dupont, Dow Chemical, Cyanamid, Raytheon, Motorola, Xerox, Kodak, Chrysler, Burroughs, and IBM.[97]

Nevertheless, the U.S. is still far behind other nations in adopting countertrading policies. For example, Japan, South Korea, Australia, Canada, and all European nations have offset policies, whereas the United States does not. Additionally, even when the best prepared U.S. company has a major deal in the works, it must turn to a foreign trading company to market the products that are accepted in the countertrade. For example, in its recent $100 million sale of radar equipment to Jordan in exchange for phosphate, Westinghouse relied on the Japanese trading giant Mitsubishi to sell the mineral through its network.[98]

► COORDINATING THE INTERNATIONAL CHANNEL

Making the efficient (albeit constrained) channel design work well depends on what sources of power can be brought to bear on foreign channel partners. The most distinctive power sources, and changes in channel power, in overseas markets tend to be of the legitimate and expertise variety. As in domestic channel relationships, foreign channel partners tend to seek balance in their power relationships, and when this balance is disrupted, the channel structure may destabilize, harming the entering firm's ability to market effectively. Not only are there distinctive power issues in international channels; there are also conflict situations specific to overseas marketing, two of which we focus on being ethics differences (creating goal conflict) and gray marketing (creating goal and domain conflict). The bottom line is that coordination in overseas channels is often more challenging than in single-market channels, because of differences in power bases between channel members and different cultural bases for behavior. These make it very difficult to build superordinate goals in, and hence to coordinate, the channel.

Power Bases in International Channels

Potential differences in the way power is both perceived and used are exemplified in a 1993 study of power perceptions in U.S.–Japanese channel relationships.[99] Using a sample of Japanese firms importing U.S.-made consumer goods, the authors find that U.S. partners view power sources along a "mediated/nonmediated" dichotomy, where mediated power sources include reward, coercion, and legal legitimate power, and nonmediated sources include referent, expert, traditional legitimate, and information power. But Japanese firms view power along a "paternalistic" dichotomy, with authoritative power sources (including coercion, referent, and both legal and traditional legitimate power) and nurturing power sources (including reward, expert, and information power). The authors point out that these differences in classification can result in the sending of mixed messages—in effect, creating perception-of-reality conflicts between the partners. Further, although the Japanese do respond in kind to the exercise of specific power sources by their U.S. partners, consistent with the precepts of reciprocal action theory, the response process is complicated by their different perception of power types:

> If a U.S. supplier exercises a nonaggressive form of power that is interpreted as aggressive by the Japanese, they will respond in kind with aggressive actions. To the U.S. firm, this response seems to violate the normal rules of business, yet it is entirely consistent with both Japanese and U.S. practices of responding in kind to the use of power.[100]

Learning about and understanding these perceptual classifications of power may be crucial to preserving an attitude of trust and coordination in the cross-cultural channel relationship.

Beyond the perceptual issues in power relationships in channels, there have been many examples of the use, creation, endowment, or loss of *legitimate* power in transnational channels. Some examples include:

- On January 1, 1994, the U.K. and Ireland joined the rest of the European Community in applying more detailed rules governing the relationships between principals and agents. Among other changes, a terminated agent could demand commissions on sales made after termination, if its efforts were responsible for the later sales. And if an agent was terminated without violating contract terms, it could now sue for payment, the value depending on what commissions he or she would have made had he or she retained the position. These and other changes heralded a significant increase in agents' power, endowed by purely legal means.[101]

- The U.K.'s Monopolies and Mergers Commission (MMC) supported a "complex monopoly" of perfume manufacturers in a judgment in November 1993 against a discount drugstore, Superdrug. Superdrug had alleged that perfume houses were unfairly refusing to supply it, with the intent of maintaining high prices and making monopoly profits. The MMC ruling was viewed as consistent with the European Community's attitude toward perfume makers, which specifies that selective distribution in perfumes is permissible when (1) manufacturers can assess a store's staff prior to deciding whether to supply it; (2) the standards applied to select or reject candidate retailers are nondiscriminatory, including no permitted discrimination based on the retailer's pricing policy; (3) a retailer is required to participate in promotional activities for the manufacturer and to carry a minimum stock level; and (4) a retailer is allowed to resell to other retail outlets. These criteria stemmed from cases involving Yves Saint Laurent and Givenchy, and were designed to support a strong brand image for these products in the market. Challenges to the ruling were continuing by other retailers seeking access to the products for discount selling.[102]

- The Japanese beer industry has for a long time been intensely concentrated, with 98% of all sales accounted for by the top four brewers. The big four, Kirin, Asahi, Sapporo, and Suntory, were protected by the Ministry of Finance, which controls brewing permits and required any new entrant to commit to brewing at least 2 million liters of beer a year—a significant entry barrier to a de novo entrant. Suntory was the only new entrant in the last 15 years. But with the increasing liberalization of the Japanese economy, the minimum production requirements have decreased to 60,000 liters a year. Small brewers are springing up all over Japan, with 150 members in a new Small Brewers' Association. Combined with (or perhaps even spurred on by) this decrease in the big four's legitimate power, retailers are also attacking the brewers' pricing policies, rebelling against the system of retail price maintenance that has persisted for years. The Ministry of Finance has started permitting any store of at least 10,000 square meters (107,600 square feet) to get a liquor license immediately, thus spurring on the price competition at retail and further weakening the brewers' muscle.[103]

- Small retailers in Japan have historically had a great deal of clout in retail policy. The Large-Scale Retail Store Law was designed to protect their interests, and required any retailer opening a new store of more than 5,000 square meters to gain the approval of the other local retailers before opening its outlet. This routinely meant delays of up to 10 years in new store openings. But in the past several years, many events have combined to weaken the power of the small retailer, much of which was in fact legislated to begin with. One of the outcomes of the Strategic Impediments Initiative (SII) talks between the U.S. and Japan was to relax the conditions in the Large-Scale Retail Store Law, so that maximum delays would be no more than 18 months to get approval for new store establishment. And the fall of the Liberal Democratic Party (LDP) from power in 1993, after 38 years in office, meant that small retailers' ties to government and their influence over government policy has been weakened ever since.[104] This represents an opportunity for both indigenous discount retailers and non-Japanese entrants to increase their presence and leverage in the Japanese retailing system.

Perhaps the most interesting general insight from these examples is that legal-based legitimate power can be granted or withdrawn rather abruptly. It is not a "natural" form of power; it is endowed on the channel member by the government. As such, it may cripple the indigenous firm as much as it helps it: either by making the indigenous firm less competitive in the outside market, or by hurting that firm when the protective legal constraints are lifted.

The use of *expert* power, on the other hand, can cement the channel captain's leadership of the channel in international markets. Consider this example:

Holiday Inn, the franchised hotel chain, has more than 1,700 hotel locations worldwide, about 100 of which are owned (the rest are franchised). The U.K. brewer Bass bought Holiday Inn in 1990, with a major priority being restoring the luster of the brand name. Managers would report stories like that of "the couple, travelling through the U.S. some years ago, who entered a Holiday Inn and left minutes later, appalled by the squalor," along with diametrically opposed stories like the one of the American woman who arrived in Beijing, saw a Holiday Inn, and wept with relief. Such inconsistency was rightly perceived to be very harmful to the overall brand image. The goal was not to *maximize* service, but rather to promise and deliver on *good, consistent* service. Holiday Inn management used its expertise power to increase inspection frequency from once per year to twice per year. Seventy-five locations were stripped of their franchises in 1991, and 30 more were "fired" in 1992. Management expected to do the same to another 75 outlets in 1993. They replaced central training in Atlanta with a more decentralized model, where trainers called "Roads Scholars" would travel to the hotels themselves to perform the training. These uses of expertise power clearly have a flavor of coercion and reward to them as well: franchisees who do not "toe the line" will be taken out of the chain, leaving a more solid, consistently good quality set of outlets from which all can benefit in the future. Holiday Inn sees this as particularly crucial in a time of increasing international travel, because all large hotel groups encourage their U.S. customers to use their hotels when they travel to new locations.[105]

Balancing Power in International Channel Relationships

Some interesting insights concerning balancing power in channel relationships can be gleaned from looking at selected international examples. Those reported below show how (a) changes in leverage at one level of the channel can spur significant structural changes at another level of the channel, in an effort to rebalance power; (b) conversely, when a previously existing balance is upset, the newly disadvantaged channel members are likely to react to protect their interests; and (c) coordinative, trusting, balanced channel relationships can also be more efficient and profitable than those exhibiting less coordination. Consider each principle in turn.

- *Changes in leverage can ripple down or up through a channel*: One of the reasons cited for intensified pressures to integrate retailing transnationally in Europe is the increasingly multinational nature of the suppliers selling to the retailers. For example, U.K. retailer Kingfisher's acquisition of French electrical goods retailer Darty in 1993 was not only to give Darty the capital to fuel European expansion, but was also due to a desire to increase its bargaining power vis-à-vis pan-European giants (themselves the result of mergers) like Philips-Whirlpool and Bosch-Siemens.[106]

- *Upsetting the balance of power causes strong repercussions*: The plastics industry in Japan embraced just-in-time (JIT) delivery strategies with a vengeance. The system offered rewards to both sides: buyers of plastics were guaranteed low stockkeeping costs and minimal amounts of cash tied up in inventory, while suppliers enjoyed high prices and profits as well as loyal customer bases. But total demand for ethylene, the basic material used to make plastics, dropped by 8% between 1993 and 1994, and other raw material prices followed suit. Given falling demand and prices, buyers' ability to offer rewards to sellers diminished, and suppliers' costs of delivering in a JIT fashion began to be viewed as simply too high. But for some time, individual suppliers were unable to end JIT. Finally, the petrochemicals industry association, the suppliers' trade group, decided that all members would simultaneously end the practice in March 1994. Had the buyers' demand remained strong, the high cost of supporting JIT deliveries probably would not have been enough to cause sellers to revolt against the system.[107]

- *Coordination can increase profits and decrease channel costs*: Japanese *keiretsu*, or industrial groupings, are sets of loosely affiliated companies that have many cross-shareholding and directorship ties. They also commonly do business together, and a *keiretsu* typically encompasses the full range of buyers and sellers in a complete supply chain (or many industries' worth of supply chains). Although the *keiretsu* have been attacked as anticompetitive, a somewhat different, but also plausible, view holds that they perform very important coordinative and joint risk-sharing functions. For example, the *keiretsu* bank might lend a *keiretsu* member money for an industrial project at a lower rate than the manufacturing firm could get outside. But this lower rate not only imposes lower financing costs on the manufacturing firm, it might also be cost-minimizing from a channel-wide perspective, as the bank can more closely monitor and guide the borrower's performance than would be possible in an arms'-length relationship. Although these principles have been widely described in a Japanese industrial context, they apply in other markets as well.[108]

Ethics, Corruption, and Bribery in International Channels: Sources of Goal Conflict

One of the hard facts of international marketing and selling is that it is very difficult to sell in some markets, or to some segments of buyers, without "greasing some palms." This has proven to be a problem in areas like China, Eastern Europe, and the countries of the former Soviet Union, partly due to the fact that capitalism is a young concept in these markets. Many foreign executives stationed in Russia must hire bodyguards to protect them from the Russian Mafia, and may have to make (sometimes thinly disguised) payments to mob-related organizations to stay in business. Practices like commercial bribery are against the law for U.S. firms, even when operating overseas, so this becomes more than an exercise in optimal budgeting and use of rewards in the foreign channel! Rooting out corruption inside organizations (especially those Eastern European businesses acquired by outsiders) is difficult, because old habits run deep. One Western food and beverage manufacturer has simply tried to finesse the problem by hiring only young employees straight out of universities. Its philosophy is that "it is better to have someone weak on experience than someone who has been polluted ethically."[109]

Gray Marketing: A Source of Goal and Domain Conflict

The *gray market* involves the selling of trademarked products through channels of distribution that are not authorized by the trademark holder. It can involve unauthorized distribution of goods either *within* a market, which occurs when manufacturer-authorized channel members sell trademarked goods to unauthorized channel members who then distribute them to consumers within the same market, or it can take place *across* markets, which occurs when goods intended for one country are diverted into an unauthorized distribution network that imports them into another country. Unauthorized distribution across markets develops in international settings; hence, *international gray markets*, sometimes called "parallel importing," are formed. Our focus is mainly on parallel importing. Some recent examples of gray marketing include the following:

- As the above-mentioned discussion on negotiation flows indicates, there is a flourishing gray market trade in ethical drugs in Europe. It has been produced by the requirement that goods move freely within the European Community, combined with government-mandated prices that vary from country to country. The French government-controlled prices of ethical drugs, for example, are about half the levels of those in the U.K. The situation is of course worsened by fluctuations in exchange rates. The short-run benefit of lower prices to consumers is counterbalanced by a long-term threat of lessened incentives for pharmaceutical research and development. One London-based drug importer estimated that 120 of the products it imports are concurrently parallel imported in the U.K., out of about 3,000 products on the market. And six of the world's seven top drugs were gray marketed in the EC in 1993 alone. Estimates are that as much as 30% of Zantac, Glaxo's highly successful anti-ulcer drug, are reimported into the U.K. after manufacture there and exportation to an outside market, although at an aggregate level, only about 2% of the EC's total prescription sales are gray

▼ TABLE 11-6   **Major Parallel Importers in Japan**

IMPORTERS	PAID-UP CAPITAL IN ¥ MILLION	EMPLOYEES	ANNUAL SALES IN ¥ MILLION
Sundries/Watches			
Chelsea International	20	35	2,975[a]
Oiso Sangyo	80	300	14,445[b]
Rapid Japan	16	12	755[b]
Sansho	5	30	2,500[a]
Sunarrow	30	25	2,770[a]
Tanaka Trading	15	9	920[a]
Wako	20	5	770[b]
Watanabe	20	11	600[a]
Will	10	11	501[a]
Alcoholic Beverages			
Itoman & Co.	145	1,411	447,777[b]
I.W.A. Japan	7	30	4,983[a]
Megane Drug	99	370	7,800[a]
Seiyu	7,643	11,374	866,307[c]
Seiwa Trading	50	12	5,012[a]
Shigematsu & Co.	50	41	6,121[b]
Toa Shoji	50	110	26,419[a]
Toko Trading	8	10	1,482[b]
Yamaya	50	35	3,221[a]
Soft Drinks			
Nishimoto Trading	45	68	13,189[b]
Pacific Trading	72	80	16,774[a]
Perry Liquor Sales	10	53	1,530[b]
Ryukyu Shoji	16	14	1,005[b]
Processed Foods			
Kyodo Food Products	4	7	2,320[a]
Suzusho	48	40	5,845[b]
Automobiles			
CAT Japan	30	20	3,962[a]
Elite Sports	10	20	1,234[b]
International Tsusho	30	13	458[b]
Jiron Automobile	9	12	1,080[a]
Lincoln Motors	20	20	2,059[a]
Nissho Iwai	42,471	5,430	10,138,974[c]
Sunauto	60	7	2,046[a]
Tomita Auto Kyoto	120	31	4,360[b]

[a] = 1986 sales data
[b] = 1987 sales data
[c] = 1988 sales data

Source: "Japan: Strong Yen, Rising Imports Are Changing Importing Methods and the Distribution System," *East Asian Executive Reports* (Vol. 11, no. 5, May 1989), p. 17; cited in Jack G. Kaikati, "Don't Crack the Japanese Distribution System—Just Circumvent It," *The Columbia Journal of World Business*, Summer 1993, p. 43. Reprinted by permission of JAI Press Inc., Greenwich, Connecticut.

marketed. The Netherlands and Germany are two other European countries where high maintained prices produce an incentive for the gray market. Pharmaceutical companies are fighting back by negotiating (sometimes with difficulty) common EC-wide prices for new drugs, such as for Glaxo's migraine headache remedy Imigran.[110]

■ Toshio Miyaji, owner of the Japanese discount chain Jonan Denki, took over half of his store's work force on a short European trip over the New Year's holiday. In a three-night trip including Paris and Amsterdam, the employees had the responsibility for shopping designer store sales at Chanel, Louis Vuitton, and the like. Each person bought 50 bargain items and carried them back to Japan, where they were put on sale in Jonan Denki's Japanese stores. Despite the trip cost of ¥390,000 (about $3600 at then-prevailing exchange rates) per person, the company claimed profits of ¥600,000 from the venture, not to mention indirect benefits of increased publicity for the flashy retailer.[111]

Far from being a secret, parallel importers are well-known in their markets. Table 11-6 lists major parallel importers in Japan, indicating not only the variety of goods that tend to lend themselves to gray marketing, but also the array of suppliers of gray market goods and their annual sales volumes.

The diversion of the product at some point in the distribution channel to unsanctioned intermediaries initiates the gray market. The individuals arranging this flow are known as *diverters*. Three common routes for the passage of gray market goods, shown from a U.S. point of view, are depicted in Figures 11-2a through 11-2c.

A product's potential for gray market activity is enhanced when: (1) exchange rates fluctuate; (2) gray market products can get a "free ride" on money spent by conventional distributors on advertising, displays, and servicing products; (3) prices of goods sold in one country are higher than those in another country; and (4) there is sufficient product quantity to supply gray marketers, for example, when quantity discounts create incentives for overbuying in the authorized channel.

The advantages of the gray market are that the manufacturer enjoys increased sales in the short run as a result of the expanded sales in the gray market, and the consumer enjoys lower prices and greater access to products. However, the negative aspects of the gray market are pervasive. The manufacturer loses control of the distribution system, downstream channel members may be reluctant to carry and promote the product, and opportunities increase for the entry of black market products. The impact the gray market has on wholesalers and retailers is very obvious: diminished sales volume due to sales lost to gray marketers, increased price competition, diminished incentive to support manufacturers' products through advertising and after-purchase service support, and erosion of loyalty in the distribution system. These factors, in turn, negatively impact on the manufacturer's investment in the distribution system.

Some (but not all) gray market goods are not covered by the manufacturer's warranty. Many consumers do not realize that the manufacturer's warranty may not be valid until they have a problem with the product and seek warranty service. Another issue for consumers is the possibility of being excluded from product recalls and notices originating from the manufacturer. If the consumer does learn about the recall, authorized dealers may refuse to perform the needed repairs or service on the gray market good.

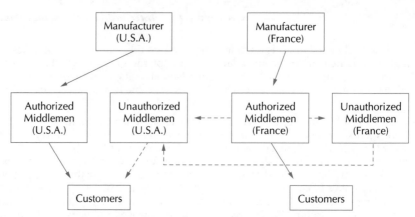

(a) Products made overseas by American firms

Here, a product may be made overseas by an American firm's subsidiary or joint venture. Somewhere in the authorized channel, marketing control is lost, and some of the product finds its way to the U.S. market where it competes with similar domestically produced products.

U.S. law does not protect the American firm in this circumstance. Although the American firm is the authorized trademark owner, it cannot stop unauthorized imports because control is lost legally once a product's title changes hands.

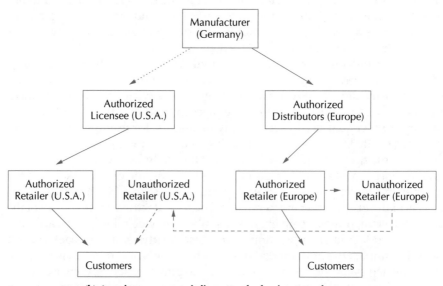

(b) American company is licensee of a foreign manufacturer

Here, a foreign manufacturer licenses an American company to be the exclusive importer of a product bearing a foreign name or trademark. The American company registers the foreigner's name, becoming the legal trademark owner in the U.S., and agrees to pay royalties. It then develops the market for the product.

Suppose a third-party trader or retailer in Europe purchases an allotment of the product, which was intended for the Spanish market, in Amsterdam. The trader ships the product to Philadelphia to clear customs and sell in the U.S. through the gray market. However, since 1930, the U.S. Bureau of Customs has used the 1930 Tariff Act to prevent goods from being brought into the U.S. by a foreign trader. The Bureau of Customs prevents the goods from clearing customs unless the American licensee agrees to their importation in writing. This puts an effective stop to this type of gray market trading.

FIGURE 11-2 Three routes for gray market goods.

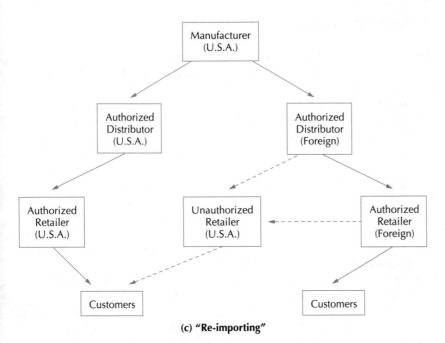

(c) "Re-importing"

Here, a manufacturer exports from its producing base, only to have the exports diverted back later to the home market. These "re-imports" are not true parallel imports, because there are no authorized imports with which they compete. However, they generate the same level of concern among the company's authorized middlemen. Re-imports may never pass through any foreign marketing channels or even clear customs. They may simply sit at a port for a few days before being loaded onto a return carrier.

FIGURE 11-2   (continued)
Source: Robert E. Weigand, "Parallel Import Channels—Options for Preserving Territorial Integrity," *Columbia Journal of World Business,* Spring 1991, pp. 54–55. Reprinted by permission of JAI Press Inc., Greenwich, Connecticut.

A solid line indicates authorized merchandise; a dashed line indicates unauthorized merchandise; and a dotted line indicates a license arrangement.

It is important to recognize that gray market goods are by and large not illegal. For example, the Japanese Fair Trade Commission declared in 1972 that it was illegal to prevent or hinder parallel imports. Japanese courts have also ruled that parallel imports do not infringe on the trademark rights of sole agents.[112] In the U.S., gray market goods satisfying the conditions in Figure 11-2b have been found in the courts to be illegal, unless the American licensee or trademark holder agrees to their importation in writing. However, there is no legal protection against gray market product entering via channels like those in Figures 11-2a or 11-2c. Gray market products are genuine branded goods, and should be distinguished from black market products, which are counterfeit versions of true branded goods (the classic "Rolex in Hong Kong" phenomenon). Gray market goods carry legitimate trademarks; the only difference between gray market products and authorized products is their method of distribution.[113]

▶ CAN INTERNATIONAL CHANNELS BE "GLOBAL"?

How should a company organize its channel operations across multiple countries? The stages of development of a transnational corporation have been divided into domestic, international, multinational, global, and transnational, in increasing stages of evolution.[114] These approaches emphasize progression in the management structure, attitudes, and climate of the corporation as well as in its marketing mix strategies. More advanced stages correspond to increasingly boundary-blind organizations, and the transnational corporation has been described as the "stateless firm."

For our purposes, it is important to focus on one key issue in globalization: can a channel manager in the company's home country devise a channel strategy that is *common* across markets (what one would call a global channel strategy), or is the strategy better *localized* to each market's specific conditions?[115] If some elements must be customized by market, which ones are they, and how can this be done in as cost-effective a manner as possible?

A fully global (that is, undifferentiated) approach to international marketing and channel management is virtually impossible, because of (a) consumer heterogeneity across world markets; (b) differences in macroeconomic, regulatory, and environmental conditions; (c) economic limits to the benefits of globalization; and (d) differences across markets in the behaviors of channel partners. The following examples illustrate these four contributors to the limit on globalization of channels:

- *Consumer heterogeneity across world markets*:
  —Local content appears to be critical in growing the European market for on-line computer services. An assortment of new competition entered the field in 1995, including Europe Online SA, Olivetti, and Apple Computer's "eWorld." Compuserve subscribers doubled in the 1994 year in Europe, to 200,000. Players have discovered that just providing a way to plug into U.S.-based services has little appeal to Europeans—their demands for assortment and variety are different. They want local content—information that is relevant to them, particularly given the higher connect-time cost in Europe than in the U.S. for these services. To meet these market-specific needs, Apple hired a talent scout in London to find local services to put on-line, and Europe Online plans on offering European publications like the *Financial Times* and France's *Elle* magazine.[116]
  —Swedish furniture seller IKEA's entry into Warsaw, Poland tested the retailer's formula for selling furniture the mass-market, high-volume way. Management tried to keep the stores the same as IKEA stores in the West, but found that local consumers were more price-conscious, willing to take on do-it-yourself projects, and simply lower-income. To keep retailing costs lower and pass on the savings to Polish consumers, IKEA's Warsaw store is bare-bones on the customer service dimension. One advantage IKEA had was that it already sourced 15% of its furniture in Eastern Europe, and therefore knew the distribution system there. However, it estimated it would need at least 60% local production to meet the pricing needs of its target consumers. It has been forced to take financial stakes in some suppliers, given the threat of market foreclosure due to recent German acquisitions of many Polish furniture factories. Low Polish incomes have meant that consumers buy products in different ways than in the West: for example, many buy dishes or silverware one piece at a time. This means that IKEA has had to be careful not to update the product line nearly as often as they would do in the West.[117]

■ *Differences in macroeconomic, regulatory, and environmental conditions*:
—UPS, the package delivery company, has found varying conditions in overseas markets that alter its business methods. Legal constraints on physical distribution like truck restrictions on weekends and holidays, or night curfews at airports, hamper delivery efforts. UPS has to deal with nine different value-added taxes in the 12 EU nations alone, each in a different currency and all charged on international transport. To circumvent the labor laws, UPS modified its U.S. practice of using employee drivers; in Europe it hired self-employed drivers. And Germans were shocked to see brown shirts as required uniforms, given the history of World War II.[118]
—The level of market saturation (and hence the intensity of competition) facing a retailer entering various foreign markets varies all over the world. Retail competition is stiff in Belgium, for both food and apparel sellers. The Canadian market has warehouse clubs and category killers gaining share. Hypermarket chains are well-established in France and in Germany. But Italy is underserved by large specialty chains. The rise of discounters in Japan has been documented previously. Mexico's retail market has only recently started facing competition from larger retail chains. And Spain is less saturated as a retail market than the rest of Europe.[119] These variations need to be taken into account when planning a new market entry, as a strategy that works well in one market may fail in another—not because the strategy is inherently faulty, but because the competitive environment is different.

■ *Economic limits to the benefits of globalization*:
One of the strongest rationales for globalizing the firm's marketing and distribution strategy is economies of scale and scope. The argument is that the average cost of carrying out the marketing strategy falls when total cost is spread across more markets, given the largely fixed-cost nature of many marketing and distribution functions. This logic led many firms to create regional or even pan-European warehouses, requiring common products and labeling across all European countries. However, requirements to customize labeling by country, as well as congestion in transportation routes throughout the EC, have diminished the benefits of centralizing logistics functions. Thus, the benefits of economies of scale have been tempered by the continued need for market-by-market flexibility. As a result, many firms have hired third-party distributors rather than build their own capital-intensive centralized warehouses.[120]

■ *Differences across markets in the behaviors of channel partners*:
Wal-Mart has been unable to fully replicate its U.S. strategy in its Mexican stores. Although there are multiple reasons for this, one is the difference in channel relations and practices in the two countries. Wal-Mart is still not big enough in Mexico to wield the bargaining power with local suppliers that it has in the U.S. In addition, suppliers there are used to shipping directly to individual stores, not to retailer warehouses.[121]

It is interesting and important to point out that although *products* or *brands* can often be standardized across markets (consider the success of the Disney Store: when an outlet opened in Hong Kong in December 1994, there were so many shoppers trying to crowd into the store that there was almost a riot!),[122] the complexity of distribution channel management makes it impossible in most situations to have a completely nondifferentiated approach to various world markets.

The implication of this insight is not to throw up one's hands and abandon all efforts at cost control through standardization. Rather, it is useful to standardize those functions and flows that can be efficiently and effectively standardized, and to customize those that must be market-specific. Opportunities for standardization may exist in a subset of all world markets even if they are not completely globally available, and if so, they can be exploited. For example, U.S.-based mass merchandise retailers have successfully entered the Canadian market, offering lower prices and better customer service than their Canadian counterparts. They can succeed at this strategy because the Canadian consumer is so similar to the U.S. consumer. The same extrapolation of retail format might not work nearly as well in a country with a lower disposable income and poorer infrastructure than Canada's.[123] Similarly, the lowering of border restrictions in the European Community has permitted Whirlpool to harmonize and simplify its production and sales organization throughout Europe. The number of sales offices has dropped from 17 to 4. Thirty warehouses have become just 16, with an ultimate goal of having only 5 or 6. Parts and components are sourced globally, and the company shares technology across national borders.[124] These situations exemplify what can be called a "glocal" attitude: acting globally wherever possible, but being always ready to take a local point of view to meet the market's needs.[125] One author, advising U.S. retailers about opportunities overseas, said it this way:

> It would be a mistake to assume that globalization is as easy as opening the box and recreating concepts already tested in the U.S. The trick is to take advantage of the world's fascination with Western habits, while understanding that each market has its own unique cultural and economic environment.[126]

Prahalad and Hamel argue that the successful global competitors are able to distinguish between managing *core competencies* and managing *business units*. The company that does the latter is doomed to failure, because it will not have built for itself a solid foundation on which to compete. They state:

> In the long run, competitiveness derives from an ability to build, at lower cost and more speedily than competitors, the core competencies that spawn unanticipated products. The real sources of advantage are to be found in management's ability to consolidate corporatewide technologies and production skills into competencies that empower individual businesses to adapt quickly to changing opportunities.[127]

This suggests that the answer to the question posed in the title of this section is "Yes—and no." The "yes" part of the answer revolves around the recognition of the importance of preserving and reaping the benefits of the company's strategic abilities in the channel and the world market. Is the company excellent at logistics? Incredibly responsive to and perceptive about changing consumer demands? Able to manage finicky channel partnerships? Whatever the firm's core channel management skill in the home market that imparts superior performance, that skill should be exploited in overseas ventures. But the "no" part of the answer is that despite the global need to exploit the firm's core competence when managing international channels, it must not forget to be sensitive to the unavoidable differences between markets and to adjust the channel strategy accordingly.

SUMMARY AND CONCLUSIONS

Designing and managing the international marketing channel involves the same general process of analysis as is necessary in a domestic channel situation: one must be aware of variations in the target market segments' demands for service outputs, design and allocate channel flows to meet those needs, and seek to coordinate the channel on an ongoing, day-by-day basis, using power creatively to manage the emerging system. However, the many examples mentioned in this chapter exhibit how the domestic channel creation and management process may have to be re-defined or modified for foreign markets or for multinational channel management. In particular, it is helpful to think of the international channel-management process as being a *constrained subset* of the domestic channel-management process, with the constraints being those imposed by environmental factors (government regula-tion, local competition differences, and the like), demand factors (variations in val-uation of service outputs across markets), and cost factors (differences between mar-kets in implementation cost of specific channel strategies). Specific examples of the marketing channel environment in various important markets bolster this view.

How a firm chooses to establish its channels overseas is called the *mode of entry* decision. A wide array of modes of entry are available to the would-be in-ternational channel manager, varying by cost, control, risk, and market potential. The right choice for mode of entry is a complex function of many predictive fac-tors pertaining to the firm, its products, and the market it wishes to enter. Once an entry mode has been chosen, the entering firm still faces the sometimes daunt-ing task of finding the actual channel partners to fill projected roles in the inter-national channel.

Efficiency issues in managing international channels concern both the meet-ing of target consumers' and customers' service output demands, and specifying roles to be played by each channel member in the international channel. Service out-put demands vary widely across different markets even for the same product, de-pending on consumers' ability to shop in a fashion similar to that in the home mar-ket. These variations immediately imply alterations in the performance of channel flows across national borders. It is a rare company that has exactly the same split of flow performance in all of its international channels.

Coordination of foreign marketing channels means dealing with some actions that are rarely found in the home market. The widespread practice of gray mar-keting epitomizes these challenges. Differences in cultural norms of doing business are also common problems in managing conflict in the international channel.

The process of building and managing a multinational distribution system would be made much easier if the company could simply clone its distribution chan-nel across national boundaries. But true globalization is a fantasy in distribution channel management. The best the internationally minded firm can hope for is a "glocal" focus, combining the cost benefits of globalization where possible with the superior responsiveness of local market flexibility.

One final caution is in order. Some firms believe that international expansion is just too complicated, or that they do not need to consider it because the home market is "big enough." Even companies in this situation need to be sensitive to and aware of the principles and concepts introduced in this chapter, because *competition the world over is becoming more and more international*. Even if this company never expands its distribution channel network overseas, it will almost surely face global competition, because foreign competitors will enter its home market. It behooves the smart competitor to foresee and plan for this situation.

DISCUSSION QUESTIONS

1. Would a company seeking to enter a foreign market choose to use piggybacking as an entry mode if it could sign on an independent distributor instead? Why or why not?

2. Explain why many companies choose to first enter a foreign market through nonequity ownership modes (such as exporting), and then later on change their channel structure in the overseas market to some form of equity investment (a joint venture or total vertical integration)? Is this likely to be a wise channel strategy? (Draw on the discussion in Chapters 6 and 7 for your answer.)

3. Explain why the "category killer" retail format has been so successful in western Europe in many product categories but *not* in grocery products. Appeal to variations in service output demands of target consumer segments in your answer.

4. What are the different implications for channel management strategy of entering a foreign market where target customers expect *equal or greater* levels of service outputs, versus a market where target customers have become accustomed to *lower* levels of service outputs? Give examples to defend your answer.

5. Describe ways in which the macroeconomic environment in a foreign country can shape the way a channel performs the financing flow. Comment on the implications for other aspects of channel flow performance.

6. Give three examples of market situations in which different forms of countertrade would be attractive. Show why each example demands a different "flavor" of countertrade.

7. What is the relationship between inter-country cultural differences and the likelihood of perception of reality conflict in channels? Goal conflict? Domain conflict?

8. What underlying conditions most favor the emergence of a gray market? What products are most likely to be gray marketed? Why?

9. What is the closest example you can think of to a truly "global" channel? How close does it come to complete commonality of strategy across country markets?

ENDNOTES

[1] Cyndee Miller, "U.S. Marketers Set Sights South of Mexico," *Marketing News*, October 10, 1994, p. 9.

[2] Geri Smith, "NAFTA: A Green Light for Red Tape," *Business Week*, July 25, 1994, p. 48.

[3] Bob Davis, "From 'Fast Track' to French Films, Making Sense of World Trade Talks," *Wall Street Journal*, December 13, 1993, p. A16.

[4]Guy de Jonquieres, "British Retailers Warned of Threat to their Profits," *Financial Times*, June 28, 1993, p. 14.

[5]Carla Rapoport, "The New U.S. Push Into Europe," *Fortune*, January 10, 1994, p. 73.

[6]*Ibid.*, p. 74.

[7]Neil Buckley and Ian Rodger, "Sticking to the Border," *Financial Times*, May 20, 1993, p. 9.

[8]Susanne Rindlisbacher, "Shops March to War," *Financial Times*, November 8, 1993, p. IV.

[9]William Bishop, "Defying the Discounters," *Financial Times*, February 25, 1993, p. 8. Bishop points out interestingly that the European Commission has always allowed selective distribution, itself often a roundabout means of effecting resale price maintenance.

[10]See, for example, "Swaddled," *The Economist*, July 24, 1993, p. 67, and David Waller, "Charged up over Competition Law," *Financial Times*, June 23, 1994, p. 16.

[11]Gary Mead, "Grocers' Guide to the East," *Financial Times*, July 15, 1993, p. 7.

[12]Michael Muth, "Marketing Still Inconsistent in Poland," *Marketing News*, January 2, 1995, p. 2.

[13]Sue Kapp, "AT&T Reaches Out To Russian Execs," *Business Marketing*, May 1993, p. 70.

[14]Daniel Yergin and Thane Gustafson, "Let's Get Down to Business, Comrade," *Financial Times*, July 9, 1994, Section II, pp. I, X.

[15]Adi Ignatius, "GM Dealer Hits Rough Road in Russia," *Wall Street Journal*, June 28, 1994, p. A15.

[16]Neil Buckley, "Consumers Know What they Want," *Financial Times*, April 10, 1995, p. III, Special Section on Russia.

[17]Leyla Boulton, "Big Macs Rake in the Roubles," *Financial Times*, June 2, 1993, p. 2.

[18]Valerie Reitman, "To Succeed in Russia, U.S. Retailer Employs Patience and Local Ally," *Wall Street Journal*, May 27, 1993, p. A1.

[19]James Sterngold, "Is Japan's Sam Walton Up to the Job? . . . No Shortage of Red Tape," *New York Times*, December 4, 1994, Section 3, pp. 1, 4.

[20]Paul Abrahams, "Keeping the Customer Satisfied 24 Hours a Day," *Financial Times*, April 8, 1994, p. 19.

[21]Jacob M. Schlesinger, "A Slot-Machine Maker Trying to Sell in Japan Hits Countless Barriers," *Wall Street Journal*, May 11, 1993, p. A1.

[22]See, for example, Larry Holyoke, "What? Everyday Bargains? This Can't Be Japan," *Business Week*, September 6, 1993, p. 41; and Larry Holyoke and William Glasgall, "A Bargain Basement Called Japan," *Business Week*, June 27, 1994, pp. 42–43.

[23]Charles Smith, "Opening Time," *Far Eastern Economic Review*, May 5, 1994, p. 66. See also Takeshi Matsuzaka, "Ajinomoto to Abandon Price-Setting," *The Nikkei Weekly*, February 7, 1994.

[24]William Dawkins, "Revolution in Toyland," *Financial Times*, April 8, 1994, p. 9.

[25]Jennifer Cody, "Shiseido Strives for a Whole New Look," *Wall Street Journal*, May 27, 1994, p. A5C.

[26]"How Not to Sell 1.2 Billion Tubes of Toothpaste," *The Economist*, December 3, 1994, p. 75.

²⁷*Ibid.*, pp. 75–76.

²⁸*Ibid.*, p. 76.

²⁹"Inscrutable or Just Hard to Find?" *The Economist*, April 29, 1995, pp. 72–73.

³⁰Jennifer Cody, "Big Japanese Retailers Rush to Set Up Operations in Asia's Developing Markets," *Wall Street Journal*, July 8, 1994, p. A4.

³¹Roderick Oram, "A Consuming Interest in China," *Financial Times*, September 28, 1994, p. 17.

³²See, for example, "A Survey of Asia: A Billion Consumers," *The Economist*, October 30, 1993, Special Section; "Economic Miracle or Myth?" *The Economist*, October 2, 1993, pp. 41–42; and "The Battle for Asia," *Fortune*, November 1, 1993, pp. 126–149.

³³Daniel C. Bello and Nicholas C. Williamson show that export management companies can themselves be differentiated by their economic structure: conventional, administrative, or contractual. The economic structure has implications for performance and flexibility in foreign market entry. See Daniel C. Bello and Nicholas C. Williamson, "Contractual Arrangement and Marketing Practices in the Indirect Export Channel," *Journal of International Business Studies*, (Summer 1985), pp. 65–82.

³⁴Michael Selz, "More Small Firms Are Turning to Trade Intermediaries," *Wall Street Journal*, February 2, 1993, p. B2.

³⁵See, for example, Gerald Albaum, Jesper Standskov, Edwin Duerr, and Laurence Dowd, *International Marketing* (New York: Addison-Wesley Publishing Company, 1989), pp. 170–172; Vern Terpstra, *International Dimensions of Marketing*, 2nd ed. (Boston: PWS Kent Publishing Company, 1988), p. 4; Warren J. Keegan, *Global Marketing Management*, 5th ed. (Englewood Cliffs, NJ: Prentice-Hall, 1995), p. 601; and Jean-Pierre Jeannet and H. David Hennessey, *Global Marketing Strategies*, 3rd ed. (Boston: Houghton Mifflin Company), pp. 408–409.

³⁶Guy de Jonquières, "Pepsi and Cadbury-Schweppes Agree East Europe Franchise Deal," *Financial Times*, January 29, 1993, p. 1.

³⁷Yumiko Ono, "Japanese Retailer Shows Low Prices Suit Salarymen Fine," *Wall Street Journal*, February 14, 1994, p. A8.

³⁸Laurence Hecht and Peter Morici, "Managing Risks in Mexico," *Harvard Business Review* (July–August 1993), p. 40.

³⁹The last two examples are from Jack G. Kaikati, "Don't Crack the Japanese Distribution System—Just Circumvent It," *The Columbia Journal of World Business* (Summer 1993), p. 41.

⁴⁰Warren J. Keegan, *Global Marketing Management*, 5th ed. (Englewood Cliffs, NJ: Prentice-Hall) p. 354.

⁴¹Richard L. Hudson, "BT and MCI Get Distributor in Japan, Launch Joint Products World-Wide," *Wall Street Journal*, July 8, 1994, p. B6.

⁴²Emiko Terazono, "Japan's Brands Feel the Pinch, Too," *Financial Times*, April 28, 1994, p. 9; and Hiroshi Fukunaga and Kyoko Chinone, "The Price Revolution (Here at Last!)," *Tokyo Business* (October 1994), p. 8.

⁴³Emiko Terazono, "A Whopping Venture," *Financial Times*, November 4, 1993, p. 8.

⁴⁴"Wait—and You'll Be Too Late," *Financial Times*, November 7, 1994, p. VI.

⁴⁵James Sterngold, "Den Fujita, Japan's Mr. Joint-Venture," *New York Times*, March 22, 1992, Section 3, p. 1.

⁴⁶Warren J. Keegan, *Global Marketing Management*, 5th ed. (Englewood Cliffs, NJ: Prentice-Hall, 1995), p. 357. Also see Sak Onkvisit and John J. Shaw, *International Marketing Analy-*

sis and Strategy (Columbus, OH: Charles E. Merrill Publishing Company, 1989), p. 389, and Stephen Young, James Hamill, Colin Wheeler, and J. Richard Davies, *International Market Entry and Development* (Englewood Cliffs, NJ: Prentice-Hall, 1989), p. 240.

[47]Christopher Parkes, "Gehe Deal to Create Leading European Drug Distributor," *Financial Times*, February 19, 1993, p. 16.

[48]Neil Buckley, "Retailers' Global Shopping Spree," *Financial Times*, October 12, 1994, p. 17.

[49]Andrew Bolger and Neil Buckley, "Rewe Buys 26% of Budgens," *Financial Times*, April 24–25, 1993, p. 8.

[50]See Neil Buckley, "Baked Beans across Europe," *Financial Times*, April 14, 1994, p. 9; Neil Buckley, "Sainsbury Joins European Alliance," *Financial Times*, April 7, 1994, p. 16; and "Links in the Food Chain," *EuroBusiness*, May 1994, p. 15.

[51]Stratford Sherman, "Are Strategic Alliances Working?" *Fortune*, September 21, 1992, pp. 77–78.

[52]See also Daniel C. Bello and Ritu Lohtia, "Export Channel Design: The Utilization of Foreign Distributors and Agents," Working Paper, Georgia State University, 1995, and Daniel C. Bello and Li Zhang, "The Quasi-Integrated Export Channel," Working Paper, Georgia State University, 1995. The former deals with the choice between two independent channels, a distributor or an agent, and argues that market diversity, the nature of specific assets, and production cost economies drive overseas channel choice. The latter argues that channel performance is affected by a firm's monitoring of the channel and by commitments to channel continuity.

[53]Franklin R. Root, *Entry Strategies for International Markets* (New York: Lexington Books, 1994), p. 184.

[54]Gerald Albaum, Jesper Standskov, Edwin Duerr, and Laurence Dowd, *International Marketing* (New York: Addison-Wesley Publishing Company, 1989), p. 159.

[55]The following examples are taken from G. Albaum, J. Standskov, E. Duerr, and L. Dowd, *op. cit.*, pp. 166–168; and S. Onkvisit and J. Shaw, *op. cit.*, pp. 507–513.

[56]S. Onkvisit and J. Shaw, *op. cit.*, p. 514.

[57]Subhash Jain, *Export Strategy* (Westport, CT: Greenwood Press, Inc., 1989), p. 164; and S. Onkvisit and J. Shaw, *op. cit.*, p. 515.

[58]S. Jain, *op. cit.*, p. 167.

[59]*Ibid.*, pp. 178–180.

[60]Neil Herndon, "Wal-Mart Goes to Hong Kong, Looks at China," *Marketing News*, November 21, 1994, p. 2.

[61]Gregory A. Patterson, "U.S. Catalogers Test International Waters," *Wall Street Journal*, April 19, 1994, p. B1.

[62]Shiraz Sidhva, "Pizza Hut Heads for New Delhi Middle Classes," *Financial Times*, January 12, 1994, p. 18.

[63]Guy de Jonquières, "Cross-border Kraftsmen," *Financial Times*, June 17, 1993, p. 7.

[64]Neil Buckley, "Decade of the Deep Discount," *Financial Times*, April 21, 1993, p. 22.

[65]Yumiko Ono, "Japanese Department Stores Fall From 1980's Heyday," *Wall Street Journal*, February 9, 1993, p. B4.

[66]See the similar example in Chapter 2 for more information on Kmart in Eastern Europe.

[67]See Neil King Jr., "Kmart's Czech Invasion Lurches Along," *Wall Street Journal*, June 8, 1993, p. A11, and David Rocks, "A New Retail Concept in Prague: No Scowling," *Chicago Tribune*, January 12, 1994, Section 1, p. 8.

[68]James Stock and Douglas Lambert, *Strategic Logistics Management* (Homewood, IL: Richard D. Irwin, 1987), p. 647.

[69]Philip Cateora, *International Marketing* (Homewood, IL: Richard D. Irwin, 1990), p. 540.

[70]"Rays of Hope and Prophecies of Doom," *EuroBusiness* (May 1994), p. 46.

[71]Phillip Hastings, "Mixed Pattern of Change," *Financial Times*, September 3, 1992, Section III, p. II.

[72]David Robinson, "Logistics Go with the Flow," *EuroBusiness* (November 1993), p. 94.

[73]See Charles Batchelor, "Volume Could Treble by 1996," *Financial Times*, May 6, 1994, Section 3, p. III; John Griffiths, "A Freer Flow of Goods," *Financial Times*, March 12, 1993, p. 9; and David Robinson, "Logistics Go with the Flow," *EuroBusiness* (November 1993), p. 94.

[74]Kieran Cooke, "Singapore Finds Quay to Success," *Financial Times*, January 13, 1994, p. 10.

[75]Emiko Terazono, "Beijing Distribution Centre for Yaohan," *Financial Times*, November 3, 1993, p. 8.

[76]Marj Charlier, "Injured in U.S. Beer Wars, Heileman Heads for China," *Wall Street Journal*, November 14, 1994, p. B1.

[77]Nicholas C. Williamson and Daniel C. Bello, "Product, Promotion and 'Free Market' Pricing in the Indirect Export Channel," *Journal of Global Marketing*, Vol. 6, no. 1 (1992), pp. 31–54.

[78]Christina Lamb, "A Rollercoaster Out of Control," *Financial Times*, February 22, 1993, p. 8.

[79]Tony Glover, "Four Weddings and a Film Industry," *EuroBusiness* (June 1994), pp. 30, 33.

[80]Christopher Korth, "An Overview of Countertrade," in Christopher Korth (ed.), *International Countertrade* (Westport, CT: Greenwood Press, 1987), p. 2.

[81]Jean-Francois Hennart, "Some Empirical Dimensions of Countertrade," *Journal of International Business Studies* (Second Quarter 1990), p. 244.

[82]Stephen Young, James Hamill, Colin Wheeler, and J. Richard Davies, *International Market Entry and Development* (Englewood Cliffs, NJ: Prentice-Hall, Inc., 1989), p. 244.

[83]Jean-Francois Hennart, "Some Empirical Dimensions of Countertrade," *Journal of International Business Studies* (Second Quarter 1990), p. 244.

[84]S. Onkvisit and J. Shaw, *op cit.*, p. 693.

[85]Costas Alexandrides and Barbara Bowers, *Countertrade Practices, Strategies, and Tactics* (New York: John Wiley and Sons, 1987), p. 7.

[86]Jean-Francois Hennart, "The Transaction-Cost Rationale for Countertrade," *Journal of Law, Economics, and Organization* Vol. 5, no. 1, (Spring 1989), p. 129.

[87]Costas Alexandrides and Barbara Bowers, *Countertrade Practices, Strategies, and Tactics* (New York: John Wiley and Sons, 1987), p. 7.

[88]Matt Schaffer, "Countertrade as an Export Strategy," *The Journal of Business Strategy* (May/June 1990), p. 36.

[89]Michael Kublin, "A Guide to Export Pricing," *Industrial Management* (May/June 1990), p. 32.

[90]See Chapter 6 for a discussion of transaction cost analysis. This theory would suggest that when the transaction costs of using the market are too high, firms optimally choose a "hierarchy" of some sort, the extreme form being vertical integration.

[91]Jean-Francois Hennart, "The Transaction-Cost Rationale for Countertrade," *Journal of Law, Economics, and Organization* Vol. 5, no. 1 (Spring 1989), pp. 127–153.

[92]Jean-Francois Hennart, "Some Empirical Dimensions of Countertrade," *Journal of International Business Studies* (Second Quarter 1990), p. 246.

[93]Matt Schaffer, "Countertrade as an Export Strategy," *The Journal of Business Strategy* (May/June 1990), p. 36.

[94]*Ibid.*

[95]*Ibid.*

[96]*Ibid.*

[97]Costas Alexandrides and Barbara Bowers, *Countertrade Practices, Strategies, and Tactics* (New York: Wiley, 1987), pp. 55–56.

[98]Schaffer, *op. cit.*, pp. 33–35.

[99]Jean L. Johnson, Tomoaki Sakano, Joseph A. Cote, and Naoto Onzo, "The Exercise of Interfirm Power and Its Repercussions in U.S.-Japanese Channel Relationships," *Journal of Marketing*, Vol. 57 (April 1993), pp. 1–10.

[100]Jean L. Johnson, Tomoaki Sakano, Joseph A. Cote, and Naoto Onzo, "The Exercise of Interfirm Power and Its Repercussions in U.S.-Japanese Channel Relationships," *Journal of Marketing*, Vol. 57 (April 1993), p. 8.

[101]Charles Batchelor, "New Rules for Old Agreements," *Financial Times*, July 27, 1993, p. 13.

[102]Robert Rice, "Whiff of Controversy Hangs in the Air," *Financial Times*, November 16, 1993, p. 10.

[103]"Only Here for the Biru," *The Economist*, May 14, 1994, pp. 69–71.

[104]William Dawkins, "Consumers' Champion in the Japanese High Street," *Financial Times*, February 22, 1994, p. 24.

[105]Michael Skapinker, "Brushing off the Welcome Mat," *Financial Times*, February 18, 1993, p. 13.

[106]See Maggie Urry and Alice Rawsthorn, "Retail Monarchs in Search of Global Empires," *Financial Times*, February 5, 1993, p. 13, and Neil Buckley and Alice Rawsthorn, "Takeover Creates Europe-wide Retailer," *Financial Times*, February 19, 1993, p. 15.

[107]Paul Abrahams, "Just in Time Now Just Too Much," *Financial Times*, March 30, 1994, p. 15.

[108]"Japanology, Inc.," *The Economist*, March 6, 1993, p. 15.

[109]E. S. Browning, "BSN Finds Eastern Europe Expansion Hard to Swallow," *Wall Street Journal*, January 5, 1993, p. B6.

[110]Paul Abrahams, "Single Market Puts Drugs on Roundabout," *Financial Times*, January 18, 1993, p. 2.

[111]"Shop Tactics in Tokyo," *The Economist*, February 5, 1994, p. 69.

[112]Jack G. Kaikati, "Don't Crack the Japanese Distribution System—Just Circumvent It," *Columbia Journal of World Business* (Summer 1993), p. 43.

[113]In addition to the specific references in this section, material was drawn from J. Barry Mason and Morris L. Mayer, *Modern Retailing Theory and Practice*, 5th Edition (Homewood, IL: Richard D. Irwin, 1990), p. 739; Louis P. Bucklin, *The Gray Market Threat to International Marketing Strategies*, Marketing Science Institute Working Paper, Cambridge, MA, 1990; Gary Cianci, "Skirmish Won, Gray Market War Continues," *Chain Store Age Executive* (August 1988), pp. 60–64; Larry Lowe and Kevin McCrohan, "Minimize the Impact of the Gray Market," *Journal of Business Strategy* (November–December 1989), pp. 47–50; and Dale Duhan and Mary Jane Sheffet, "Gray Markets and the Legal Status of Parallel Importation," *Journal of Marketing* (July 1988), pp. 75–82.

[114]See, for example, Warren J. Keegan, *Global Marketing Management* (Englewood Cliffs, NJ: Prentice-Hall, 1995), pp. 43–54, and Jean-Pierre Jeannet and H. David Hennessey, *Global Marketing Strategies* (Boston, Houghton Mifflin Company, 1995), pp. 3–6.

[115]Douglas J. Tigert, "Retailing Newsletter 1993-1" (Babson College, February 1993), pp. 3–4, talks about this dichotomy as taking a *global* versus an *international* point of view. The former means standardizing the company's marketing strategy virtually totally across markets, whereas the latter means customizing certain elements of the strategy to each local environment.

[116]Richard L. Hudson, "On-Line Firms Try to Win Europe's Modems and Minds," *Wall Street Journal*, January 13, 1995, p. B4.

[117]Stephen D. Moore, "Sweden's Ikea Forges Into Eastern Europe," *Wall Street Journal*, June 28, 1993, p. B5A.

[118]Dana Milbank, "Can Europe Deliver?" *Wall Street Journal*, September 30, 1994, p. R15.

[119]Cyndee Miller, "Overseas Expansion Hot, but Caution Urged," *Marketing News*, January 31, 1994, pp. 1, 11.

[120]Andrew Baxter, "Delivering the Goods," *Financial Times*, January 18, 1993, p. 6.

[121]Bob Ortega, "Wal-Mart Is Slowed By Problems of Price And Culture in Mexico," *Wall Street Journal*, July 29, 1994, p. A1, A5.

[122]Carla Rapoport and Justin Martin, "Retailers Go Global," *Fortune*, February 20, 1995, p. 106.

[123]"Barbarians at the Checkout," *The Economist*, September 17, 1994, pp. 75–76.

[124]Robert L. Rose, "Whirlpool Is Expanding in Europe Despite the Slump," *Wall Street Journal*, January 27, 1994, p. B4.

[125]In Frank Feather's book, *The Future Consumer* (Toronto: Warwick Publishing Co., 1993), p. 21, the author attributes the origin of the word "glocal" to Akio Morita, then president of Sony Corporation, and says that Morita first used this term in 1989. See also Christopher Lorenz, "The Transnational's Identity Crisis," *Financial Times*, March 19, 1993, p. 10, for a discussion of the balance between global integration and market responsiveness.

[126]Larry R. Katzen, "Retailing—The Global Mandate," *Arthur Andersen Retailing Issues Letter*, Vol. 5, no. 5 (September 1993), pp. 1–2.

[127]C.K. Prahalad and Gary Hamel, "The Core Competence of the Corporation," *Harvard Business Review*, Vol. 90, no. 3 (May–June 1990), p. 81.

NAME INDEX

General Electric, 202, 238, 253, 341, 414
General Electric, Direct Connect Program, 238–239
General Electric Credit Corporation, 240
General Electric Medical Systems, 475
General Foods Corporation, 296, 476
General Mills, 73
General Motors, 209, 233, 294, 316, 317
General Motors Acceptance Corporation, 11
General Nutrition Cos., 258, 261
GEnie, 82, 405
Genuine Parts, 126, 240, 295
GESCO, 43
Giant Food, 509
GIB, 85, 86
Gift market, as a third-party influencer format, 48
Gigante, 84
Giordano Ltd., 506
Glad Bags, 506
Glaxo Pharmaceuticals, 533, 535
Gleem, 72
Global, 49
GMROI (gross margin return on inventory), 53–54, 102
GMROL (gross margin per full-time equivalent employee), 53
Good faith defense, 357–358
Goodyear Tire & Rubber Company, 23, 253–254, 268, 287, 311, 364, 431
Grand Metropolitan, 227, 376
Graybar Electric, 124, 241
Gray markets/marketers, 294–295, 341, 348, 350, 525, 533–537
Great Lakes Terminal and Transport Company (GLT&T), 28–29
Great Plains Software, 298
Green marketing, reverse distribution and, 38–41
G.R. Kinney Company, 375
Grocery Industry Activity Model, 480
Grocery Manufacturers of America (GMA), 316, 362
Gross margin per full-time equivalent employee. *See* GMROL
Gross margin of profit, defined, 102
Gross margin return on inventory (GMROI), 53–54, 102
Gross margin return per full-time equivalent employee (GMROL), 53
Groupe Schneider, 367
Grumman International, 529
Grupo Gigante, 495
Gucci, 78

"Guerilla Marketing," 80
Guides for Advertising Allowances and other Merchandising Payments and Services, 360
Guinness' United Distillers, 227
GUM department store, 86

H

Häagen-Dazs ice cream, 366–367
Haggar Apparel Co., 176–177, 416
Hallmark/Ambassador Cards, 23, 24,242
Halston III, 70
Handy Andy, 60
Hanes, 205, 238
Hardee's Food Systems, Inc., 317, 318
Harley-Davidson, 170, 297
Harmonious relationships, 25–26
Harrison Manufacturing Company, 471–472
Hartmarx Corporation, 342
Hartwell's Office World, 353
Hasbrouck case, 363, 377
Hattori Seiko, 89
H.E.B. Grocery Company, 242
Hecht's, 63
Henri Bendel, 78
Herman Miller Inc., 187, 414
Hewlett-Packard, 170, 192, 202, 254, 298
Highland, 61
High-touch retailers, 60
Hilmer, Frederick G., 226
Hilton Hotels, 260
Hindustan Lever, 431–432
Hit rate, 340
Holiday Inn, 250, 262, 531
Holiday Inn Worldwide, 318
Home-base, 86
Home Depot Inc., 12, 50, 51, 56, 59–60, 61–62, 74, 83, 113, 348
Home party format, 47
Home Shopping Network, 49, 82, 375–376
Home shopping
  retailing potential of, 81–82
  television and satellite networks, 49
Honda Motor Company, 294
Honeywell, 170
HOPE (space management system), 479
Horizontal restraints, in pricing, 377
Hughes Aircraft Co., 12
Hybrid marketing, 267
Hypermarket channel format, 44
Hypermarket USA, 44